C000027044

1,000,000 Books
are available to read at

Forgotten Books

www.ForgottenBooks.com

Read online
Download PDF
Purchase in print

ISBN 978-1-5283-0430-6
PIBN 10932141

This book is a reproduction of an important historical work. Forgotten Books uses state-of-the-art technology to digitally reconstruct the work, preserving the original format whilst repairing imperfections present in the aged copy. In rare cases, an imperfection in the original, such as a blemish or missing page, may be replicated in our edition. We do, however, repair the vast majority of imperfections successfully; any imperfections that remain are intentionally left to preserve the state of such historical works.

Forgotten Books is a registered trademark of FB &c Ltd.
Copyright © 2018 FB &c Ltd.
FB &c Ltd, Dalton House, 60 Windsor Avenue, London, SW19 2RR.
Company number 08720141. Registered in England and Wales.

For support please visit www.forgottenbooks.com

1 MONTH OF FREE READING

at

www.ForgottenBooks.com

By purchasing this book you are eligible for one month membership to ForgottenBooks.com, giving you unlimited access to our entire collection of over 1,000,000 titles via our web site and mobile apps.

To claim your free month visit:

www.forgottenbooks.com/free932141

* Offer is valid for 45 days from date of purchase. Terms and conditions apply.

English
Français
Deutsche
Italiano
Español
Português

www.forgottenbooks.com

Mythology Photography **Fiction** Fishing Christianity **Art** Cooking Essays Buddhism Freemasonry Medicine **Biology** Music **Ancient Egypt** Evolution Carpentry Physics Dance Geology **Mathematics** Fitness Shakespeare **Folklore** Yoga Marketing **Confidence** Immortality Biographies Poetry **Psychology** Witchcraft Electronics Chemistry History **Law** Accounting **Philosophy** Anthropology Alchemy Drama Quantum Mechanics Atheism Sexual Health **Ancient History** **Entrepreneurship** Languages Sport Paleontology Needlework Islam **Metaphysics** Investment Archaeology Parenting Statistics Criminology **Motivational**

QUARTERLY JOURNAL

OF THE

ROYAL

METEOROLOGICAL SOCIETY.

EDITED BY

A COMMITTEE OF THE COUNCIL.

VOL. XXVI.—1900.

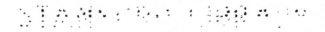

LONDON:
EDWARD STANFORD, 26 & 27 COCKSPUR STREET,
CHARING CROSS, S.W.
1900.

184561

STANFORD LIBRARY

CONTENTS.

PAGE

The Diurnal Variation of the Barometer in the British Isles. By RICHARD H. CURTIS, F.R.Met.Soc. (Six Illustrations) . . . 1

Hurricane at Sombrero, September 1899 25

A Short Note on Earth Temperature Observations. By G. J. SYMONS, F.R.S., Secretary. (Illustration) 27

Air Currents in Thunderstorms 32

Note of a Remarkable Dust Haze experienced at Teneriffe, Canary Islands, February 1898. By ROBERT H. SCOTT, D.Sc., F.R.S. 33

The Climatic Conditions necessary for the Propagation and Spread of Plague. By BALDWIN LATHAM, M.Inst.C.E., F.R.Met.Soc. (Plate I. and Twenty-one Illustrations) 37

Proceedings at the Ordinary Meeting, November 15, 1899 . . . 95

Proceedings at the Ordinary Meeting, December 20, 1899 . . . 95

Correspondence and Notes :—

Retirement of Dr. R. H. Scott, F.R.S., from the Meteorological Office 96

International Meteorological Congress, Paris, 1900 . . . 96

Solar Halos and Mock Suns, January 11, 1900 . . . 97

Recent Publications 99

A New Reduction of the Meteorological Observations at Greenwich. An Address delivered to the Royal Meteorological Society, January 17, 1900. By F. CAMPBELL BAYARD, LL.M., President. (Plates II.-VII.) 101

Atlas of Meteorology 112

Report on the Phenological Observations for 1899. By EDWARD MAWLEY, F.R.H.S., Secretary. (Plate VIII. and Two Illustrations) 113

Circulation of the Atmosphere in the Southern Hemisphere . . . 138

Results of Percolation Experiments at Rothamsted, September 1870 to August 1899. By ROBERT H. SCOTT, D.Sc., F.R.S. (Four Illustrations) 139

PAGE

Meteorology of Tropical Africa 151
Proceedings at the Ordinary Meeting, January 17, 1900 . . 152
Proceedings at the Annual General Meeting, January 17, 1900 . 152
Proceedings at the Ordinary Meeting, February 21, 1900 . . 154
Hurricanes and Birds 154
GEORGE JAMES SYMONS, F.R.S. (Portrait—Plate IX.) . . 155
Correspondence and Notes :—
Minimum Temperatures on Mountain Peaks . . . 162
Kite and Balloon Station near Berlin 163
Vertical Circulation of the Atmosphere . . . 163
Hurricanes of the Far East 165
Recent Publications 169
Royal Meteorological Society, Jubilee Celebration, April 3-4, 1900 . 173
Commemoration Meeting, April 3, 1900 174
Jubilee Address. Prepared by the late G. J. SYMONS, F.R.S., President 176
Jubilee Address (complementary to Mr. Symons'). By C. THEODORE WILLIAMS, M.D., F.R.C.P., President 181
Conversazione 188
Commemoration Dinner, April 4, 1900 192
List of PRESIDENTS, 1850-1900. (Plates X. and XI.) . . . 202
Report of the Council for the Year 1899 203
Balance-Sheet for the Year 1899 206
Inspection of Stations, 1899. By WILLIAM MARRIOTT, F.R.Met.Soc., Assistant-Secretary 210
Obituary Notices 214
Books, etc., purchased during the Year 1899 220
Donations received during the Year 1899 221
Reports of Observatories, etc. 231
The Circulation of Water in the North Atlantic 234
The Riviera in the last Century 234
Remarks on the Weather Conditions of the Steamship Track between Fiji and Hawii. By CAPT. M. W. CAMPBELL HEPWORTH, F.R.Met.Soc. (Plate XII.) 235
Climatology of the Sonnblick Group 241
Temperature of the Free Air 242
The Ether Sunshine Recorder. By W. H. DINES, B.A., F.R.Met.Soc. (Illustration) 243

PAGE

Comparison by means of Dots. By ALEX. B. MACDOWALL, M.A., F.R.Met.Soc. (Two Illustrations) 247

Proceedings at the Ordinary Meeting, March 21, 1900 . . 251

Correspondence and Notes :—

Kite Experiments at Blue Hill Meteorological Observatory . 252

Vertical Gradients of Temperature, Humidity, and Wind Direction 252

Tule Fog 253

Meteorological Charts of the Southern Ocean between the Cape of Good Hope and New Zealand 253

Recent Publications 255

The Wiltshire Whirlwind of October 1, 1899. By the late G. J. SYMONS, F.R.S. (Plate XIII.) 261

Memorial to the late Mr. G. J. SYMONS, F.R.S. . . . 272

Rainfall in the West and East of England in relation to Altitude above Sea-level. By WILLIAM MARRIOTT, F.R.Met.Soc. (Two Illustrations) 273

Description of Halliwell's Self-recording Rain Gauge. By JOSEPH BAXENDELL, F.R.Met.Soc. (Plate XIV.). . . . 281

Heavy Rainfall in Local Storms 286

Proceedings at the Ordinary Meeting, May 16, 1900 . 287

Proceedings at the Ordinary Meeting, June 20, 1900 . 287

Correspondence and Notes :—

The Climate and Diseases of Northern Brazil . . . 288

Radcliffe Observatory, Oxford. 291

The "Southern Cross" Expedition to the Antarctic, 1898-1900 292

The Geographical Distribution of Relative Humidity . 296

Rainfall of the Central Rhine Provinces . . . 297

The Climate of the Valley of the Joux (Jura) . . . 298

Recent Publications 299

Index 303

LIST OF PLATES.

PLATE

I. Tensional Difference Maximum and Minimum 6 inches Ground, and Maximum and Minimum Dew Point, Croydon.

II. Royal Observatory Greenwich—
Frequency of Barometer Readings, 1848-98.

III. Do.—Frequency of Maximum Temperatures, 1848-98.

IV. Do.—Frequency of Minimum Temperatures, 1848-98.

V. Do.—Frequency of Relative Humidity Values, 1848-98.

VI. Do.—Frequency of Amounts of Rainfall, 1848-98.

VII. Do.—Frequency of Wind Directions, 1848-98.

VIII. Map showing position of the Phenological Stations, 1899.

IX. George James Symons, F.R.S. (President 1880-1 and 1900).

X. Presidents of the Royal Meteorological Society, 1850-1877.

XI. Presidents of the Royal Meteorological Society, 1878-1900.

XII. Trade Winds of the Pacific Ocean between Fiji and Hawaii.

XIII. The Wiltshire Whirlwind of October 1, 1899.

XIV. Halliwell's Self-recording Rain Gauge.

ERRATA.

Page 85, Heading of Diagram, No. 18, *for* Colaba Observatory, Bombay, *read* Mortality, Bombay City.

,, 233, *For* "since 1859" *read* "since our records of rain commenced in 1859."

OXFORD LIBR.

② QUARTERLY JOURNAL

OF THE

ROYAL METEOROLOGICAL SOCIETY

VOL. XXVI.] JANUARY 1900 [No. 113.

THE DIURNAL VARIATION OF THE BAROMETER IN THE BRITISH ISLES.

BY RICHARD H. CURTIS, F.R.Met.Soc.

[Read November 15, 1899.]

THE Meteorological Council has recently published a set of mean values of barometrical pressure for four differently situated stations for each month of the year, obtained from hourly observations made over a period of twenty-five years.[1] These values will probably be useful to the Fellows in more than one branch of inquiry, and as the volume in which they are published may not always be readily available for reference, I have thought it would serve a useful purpose to epitomize them in the *Quarterly Journal*, in four brief tables, as hourly differences from the daily means, for each month and for the year.

The observations upon which the means are based were obtained from the records of barographs at the following four observatories maintained by the Meteorological Council, viz. Kew, Aberdeen. Falmouth, and Valencia, during the twenty-five years ending with 1895.

A detailed description of the barographs used was given in the *Report of the Meteorological Office* for the year 1867; but it may be repeated here that their record is obtained by means of photography, and without the intervention of any mechanical contrivance requiring to be operated by the mercury of the barometer. A beam of light from a lamp is caused to pass through the space between the top of the column of mercury and the top of the tube, and is focussed upon a sheet of photographic paper, carried upon a drum which is rotated by a clock. The resulting trace is, therefore, a continuous dark band of varying width,—becoming wider as the mercury falls and increases the space between its surface and the top of the tube, and narrower as it rises and the space becomes contracted. No scale of

[1] *Appendix to Hourly Means for the Year* 1895.

	Jan.	Feb.	Mar.	Apr.	May.	June	July	Aug.	Sept.	Oct.	Nov.
Daily Mean	ins. 29·7002	ins. 29·7645	ins. 29·7336	ins. 29·7974	ins. 29·8403	ins. 29·8466	ins. 29·7470	ins. 29·7350	ins. 29·7772	ins. 29·6956	ins. 29·6828
G.M.T.					Hourly	Differen	ce from	Daily M	eans.		
0 a.m.	+·0050	+·0044	+·0103	+·0022	+·0060	+·0072	+·0080	+·0068	+·0070	+·0028	+·0043
1 ,,	+·0002	+·0014	+·0060	−·0029	+·0011	+·0030	+·0032	+·0017	+·0034	−·0015	−·0007
2 ,,	−·0007	−·0007	+·0014	−·0068	−·0028	−·0011	−·0015	−·0022	−·0004	−·0060	−·0027
3 ,,	−·0038	−·0063	−·0062	−·0114	−·0072	−·0055	−·0066	−·0070	−·0063	−·0124	−·0069
4 ,,	−·0079	−·0097	−·0101	−·0143	−·0094	−·0060	−·0076	−·0098	−·0100	−·0146	−·0094
5 ,,	−·0122	−·0117	−·0117	−·0138	−·0084	−·0053	−·0071	−·0099	−·0113	−·0156	−·0104
6 ,,	−·0128	−·0116	−·0101	−·0083	−·0048	−·0024	−·0045	−·0066	−·0073	−·0133	−·0088
7 ,,	−·0108	−·0087	−·0068	−·0039	−·0023	+·0003	−·0019	−·0035	−·0035	−·0086	−·0057
8 ,,	−·0041	−·0022	−·0015	·0000	+·0006	+·0029	+·0005	+·0001	+·0010	−·0015	+·0017
9 ,,	+·0028	+·0017	+·0013	+·0023	+·0013	+·0026	+·0003	+·0017	+·0037	+.0016	+·0051
10 ,,	+·0083	+·0054	+·0043	+·0044	+·0017	+·0029	+·0006	+·0025	+·0046	+·0054	+·0092
11 ,,	+·0100	+·0082	+·0047	+·0044	+·0023	+·0028	+·0011	+·0029	+·0033	+·0064	+·0094
Noon.	+·0045	+·0060	+·0041	+·0039	+·0013	+·0017	+·0004	+·0021	+·0022	+·0047	+·0044
1 p.m.	−·0021	−·0006	−·0009	+·0023	·0000	−·0008	−·0006	+·0009	−·0009	+·0003	−·0010
2 ,,	−·0045	−·0048	−·0048	−·0001	−·0012	−·0015	−·0009	−·0003	−·0040	−·0014	−·0035
3 ,,	−·0054	−·0081	−·0087	−·0040	−·0040	−·0041	−·0027	−·0027	−·0072	−·0040	−·0058
4 ,,	−·0023	−·0065	−·0090	−·0049	−·0056	−·0063	−·0049	−·0049	−·0080	−·0031	−·0027
5 ,,	−·0007	−·0041	−·0073	−·0047	−·0068	−·0084	−·0062	−·0059	−·0069	+·0003	−·0009
6 ,,	+·0021	+·0025	−·0003	−·0006	−·0047	−·0065	−·0042	−·0040	−·0022	+·0072	+·0034
7 ,,	+·0037	+·0050	+·0046	+·0043	−·0007	−·0040	−·0014	·0000	+·0039	+·0088	+·0042
8 ,,	+·0069	+·0076	+·0083	+·0114	+·0055	+·0003	+·0033	+·0070	+·0095	+·0108	+·0047
9 ,,	+·0069	+·0077	+·0090	+·0121	+·0099	+·0062	+·0077	+·0091	+·0093	+·0104	+·0045
10 ,,	+·0071	+·0090	+·0095	+·0115	+·0113	+·0087	+·0099	+·0097	+·0091	+·0100	+·0042
11 ,,	+·0051	+·0076	+·0079	+·0100	+·0098	+·0077	+·0086	+·0083	+·0071	+·0073	+·0022
Midt.	+·0037	+·0078	+·0067	+·0077	+·0075	+·0057	+·0063	+·0055	+·0043	+·0057	+·0016

	Jan.	Feb.	Mar.	Apr.	May.	June	July	Aug.	Sept.	Oct.	Nov.	Dec.
ily	ins.	ins.	ins.	ins.	ins.	ins.	ins.	ins.	ins.	ins.	ins.	ins.
an.	29·7711	29·7761	29·7481	29·6796	29·7786	29·8040	29·7711	29·7637	29·7877	29·6990	29·7026	29·7593
M.T.					Hourly	Differen	ce from	Daily M	eans.			
a.m.	+·0042	+·0050	+·0077	+·0054	+·0042	+·0047	+·0047	+·0058	+·0059	+·0021	+·0059	+·0036
,,	−·0013	+·0003	+·0038	−·0002	−·0018	−·0023	−·0018	−·0006	+·0006	−·0021	−·0006	−·0034
,,	−·0024	−·0040	−·0015	−·0066	−·0082	−·0086	−·0089	−·0066	−·0052	−·0078	−·0035	−·0054
,,	−·0029	−·0097	−·0103	−·0119	−·0133	−·0147	−·0152	−·0123	−·0123	−·0153	−·0079	−·0063
,,	−·0073	−·0145	−·0145	−·0159	−·0170	−·0164	−·0173	−·0167	−·0165	−·0181	−·0122	−·0107
,,	−·0118	−·0146	−·0149	−·0168	−·0149	−·0147	−·0161	−·0168	−·0177	−·0178	−·0124	−·0145
,,	−·0124	−·0132	−·0122	−.0108	−·0088	−·0095	−·0110	−·0110	−·0124	−·0159	−·0116	−·0137
,,	−·0087	−·0099	−·0072	−·0056	−·0042	−·0049	−·0056	−·0054	−·0059	−·0101	−·0076	−·0102
,,	−·0004	−·0001	+·0003	−·0010	+·0015	+·0004	+·0003	+·0008	+·0019	+·0006	+·0033	−·0021
,,	+·0073	+·0054	+·0047	+·0024	+·0031	+·0019	+·0018	+·0037	+·0074	+·0056	+·0087	+·0059
,,	+·0146	+·0108	+·0090	+·0070	+·0057	+·0043	+·0045	+·0069	+·0119	+·0101	+·0137	+·0149
,,	+·0190	+·0167	+·0121	+·0092	+·0085	+·0071	+·0072	+·0080	+·0118	+·0116	+·0159	+·0161
on.	+·0089	+·0137	+·0105	+·0072	+·0074	+·0073	+·0075	+·0072	+·0100	+·0076	+·0062	+·0056
p.m.	−·0029	+·0046	+·0048	+·0058	+·0059	+·0064	+·0065	+·0062	+·0068	+·0011	−·0018	−·0045
,,	−·0100	−·0042	−·0030	+·0028	+·0040	+·0051	+·0052	+·0047	+·0024	−·0028	−·0084	−·0109
,,	−·0104	−·0089	−·0082	−·0032	·0000	+·0026	+·0033	+·0008	−·0027	−·0055	−·0106	−·0103
,,	−·0076	−·0090	−·0107	−·0055	−·0019	+·0004	+·0007	−·0016	−·0056	−·0052	−·0079	−·0061
,,	−·0051	−·0065	−·0100	−·0057	−·0042	−·0027	−·0019	−·0038	−·0060	−·0024	−·0048	−·0026
,,	−·0001	+·0006	−·0034	−·0037	−·0042	−·0025	−·0022	−·0044	−·0034	+·0053	+·0014	+·0025
,,	+·0027	+·0046	+·0020	−·0005	−·0020	−·0011	−·0004	−·0023	+·0005	+·0087	+·0038	+·0058
,,	+·0060	+·0062	+·0074	+·0083	+·0031	+·0020	+·0031	+·0051	+·0076	+·0111	+·0054	+·0093
,,	+·0061	+·0072	+·0091	+·0115	+·0107	+·0097	+·0100	+·0095	+·0080	+·0128	+·0071	+·0103
,,	+·0067	+·0084	+·0105	+·0115	+·0115	+·0119	+·0120	+·0100	+·0080	+·0128	+·0081	+·0112
,,	+·0045	+·0061	+·0082	+·0093	+·0088	+·0086	+·0092	+·0078	+·0051	+·0084	+·0056	+·0096
dt.	+·0021	+·0057	+·0057	+·0073	+·0056	+·0049	+·0057	+·0048	+·0007	+·0052	+·0045	+·0068

any kind is marked upon the trace except one of time, which is produced by causing the clock to cut off the light for four minutes every two hours. But practically the top of the tube affords a fixed datum point from which the width of the trace can be measured; and the value of this point, as well as the scale value of the trace, having been determined, readings can be obtained with considerable accuracy by means of a tabulating instrument, carrying a vernier and reading to thousandths of an inch. There is a special arrangement attached to the barometer, by means of which an automatic correction is applied to the trace, for the expansion of the mercury with temperature; but no correction is applied to the tabulated readings, as published, for the heights of the barometers above mean sea level.

A number of control readings of a standard barometer were made daily,—generally five each day,—and from the differences between these and the corresponding measurements of the trace, a daily residual correction was obtained, and applied to the latter in order to get rid of certain small but unavoidable errors, which were always liable to arise from such causes as sluggish action of the automatic temperature correction, or shrinkage of the paper during the washings involved in the photographic processes.

In addition, a rather elaborate system was adopted for checking the results, the details of which may be found in the *Reports of the Meteorological Office*;[1] but, as the final outcome of the whole, the data secured may fairly be regarded as being of excellent quality, from which thoroughly reliable, and strictly comparable, results can be obtained.

It is obvious that these mean values will make it possible to study more fully than one has hitherto been able to do the seasonal changes which occur in the march of the diurnal variation of pressure over the British Isles; and also that they afford data for studying the effect upon that phenomenon of the geographical position, and the physical surroundings, of the places of observation; and having necessarily had to make myself tolerably familiar with the values in the course of their preparation, I propose to call attention to a few of the more striking features of the oscillation which they appear to me to exhibit.

It is unfortunate for the purpose of any inquiry into the diurnal variation of barometrical pressure that the time employed at the observatories was in every case Greenwich mean time[2]; for if we start with the assumption that these diurnal oscillations, like those of temperature, and indeed of every kindred meteorological phenomenon, are directly dependent upon the earth's diurnal rotation, it becomes necessary to consider them at each place with reference to the meridian distance of the sun, or, in other words, to use the local apparent time of the station.

In the following discussion, therefore, the mean values as published by the Meteorological Council have been corrected:—(1) for the longitude of the place, and also, by the application of a mean monthly correction, for the equation of time; and (2) for the disturbing effect of the casual or non-periodic variations, the effect of which often is to produce different

[1] See *Reports* for the years ending March 1869, and 1890. Particulars as to the Observatories themselves will be found in the *Quarterly Weather Report* for 1870, *Hourly Readings* for 1885, and *Hourly Means* for 1891 and 1892.

[2] Mean time must necessarily be kept by the clocks, but this can be allowed for when measuring the barograms.

mean values for the two ends of the mean day. This last error has been got rid of by assuming that the disturbances giving rise to it were spread equally over the entire day, and applying to each hour a proportional part of half the difference between the two terminal values, in opposite directions in the a.m. and p.m. The noon value, upon which the diurnal curve is, as it were, pivoted, is left unaltered.

It is hardly necessary to observe that the principal features of a curve exhibiting the diurnal march of barometrical pressure are two minima and two maxima,—the first minimum occurring early in the morning and the second in the afternoon, whilst the first maximum falls in the forenoon and the second not far from ten o'clock in the evening. Between the tropics the oscillation may amount to as much as a tenth of an inch, but its mean amplitude decreases as the latitude increases, and the greatest amplitude, as exhibited by the mean values now under consideration, amounts to not much more than three-hundredths of an inch.

Notwithstanding this small mean range, however, the phenomenon may be distinctly observed on quiet days when the barometer is not disturbed by the non-periodic fluctuations already referred to, and under such conditions in summer the oscillation occasionally approaches a tenth of an inch. The non-periodic movements are generally so much larger than the regularly recurring tidal oscillations that the latter are as a rule entirely masked by them. But even in unquiet periods, when the casual fluctuations are dominant, the diurnal atmospheric tide will always manifest itself if the hourly observations of the barometer for a short period are meaned, although to get a true average view of the phenomenon it is of course necessary that the observations should extend over a considerable period, so as to eliminate accidental peculiarities, due to the influence of abnormal conditions of weather.

The whole phenomenon of the double oscillation recurs with each diurnal rotation of the earth, and is propagated from east to west, and therefore, in what follows, I have dealt with the four observatories in the order of their longitude, beginning with the most easterly.

It is not always possible to locate with absolute precision the critical epochs of any phase of the phenomenon, partly because to do so would require mean values at closer intervals than one hour, but also because in some instances the pressure remains near its highest or lowest value, with but very little change, for a considerable time, the curve formed when the values are exhibited graphically being in such cases very flat. In order to locate the phases as closely as possible I have therefore made a graphical interpolation between the mean hourly values, in each month, which gives the following as the main features of the change of epoch.

The Seasonal Change of Epoch of the Four Phases of the Phenomenon.

The First Minimum.—At each of the four observatories this phase of the daily oscillation occurs later in winter than in summer, there being a gradual shifting of the epoch earlier as the sun moves northwards, and a return in the opposite direction, towards noon, as its declination decreases again, but this movement is more marked at the eastern than at the western stations. In every case the earliest time of the occurrence of the phase is in June.

At *Kew*, which is both the most eastern and also the most continental of the four stations, the time of the phase varies from a few minutes after 5 a.m. in January to just before 3.30 a.m. in June; after which month it comes gradually back again to 5 a.m. in December.

At *Aberdeen* the change in time with the change of season is very similar to that observed at Kew, but as a rule the phase occurs about half an hour later than at Kew all through the year.

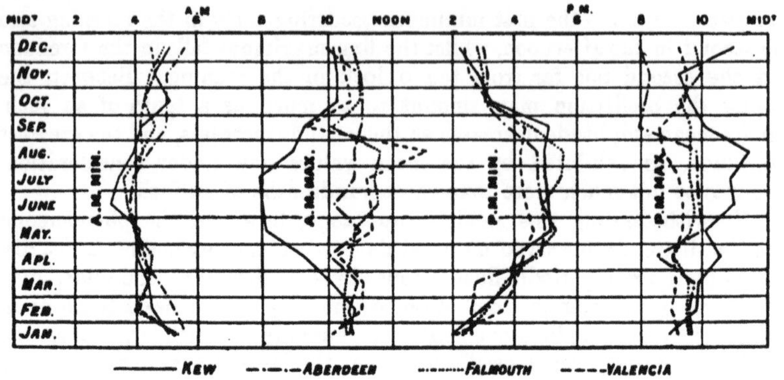

FIG. 1.—Change of Epoch of the Four Phases.

At *Falmouth* in December and January the phase occurs at about 5 a.m., but in February there is an abrupt change to 4 a.m., after which month until November the change of epoch is very slight, and covers only about half an hour.

At *Valencia* the time of occurrence throughout the year is almost the same as at Falmouth.

At the two eastern stations, therefore, there is a gradual shifting of the epoch, from winter to summer and back again, over an interval of about two hours; whilst at the two western stations the change from February to June is trifling, and the principal change of the year occurs in mid-winter.

The First Maximum.—The seasonal change of epoch exhibited at the four stations by this, the second, phase is far more varied than that observed in the case of the first phase.

At *Kew* the latest time of occurrence is 10.45 a.m. in February, after which it gradually falls earlier, till in May, June, and July, it occurs at 8 a.m. It then recedes again during the autumn to 10.30 a.m. in November and December, thus covering a range of epoch of nearly three hours.

At *Aberdeen* the changes from month to month are irregular and very slight. Speaking generally, the phase occurs at about 10.30 a.m., and the range of epoch is less than half an hour.

At *Falmouth* there is a decided tendency for the phase to occur later in summer than in winter. In January its time is about 10.30 a.m., but in June and July it falls three-quarters of an hour later, at 11.15 a.m.; after which it becomes earlier again and remains near 10.30 a.m. during the rest of the year.

At *Valencia* the changes of time are somewhat erratic, as at Aberdeen.

The phase occurs latest in summer, as at Falmouth, and slightly earlier in September than in any other month, as is also the case at Falmouth and Aberdeen. In August the epoch cannot be satisfactorily located, but omitting that month the times range from 11.30 a.m. in May, to a little before 10 a.m. in September.

The Second Minimum.—The change of epoch shown by this phase is at once the most marked, and the most uniform in character, at each of the four observatories. The change is, however, in the reverse direction to that shown by the first minimum, and becomes later as the season passes from winter to summer, and *vice versâ*.

At *Kew* the earliest time of occurrence of the phase is 2 p.m. in January, from which month it steadily becomes later until May, when it falls at 5 p.m. From May to August there is very little change, although the actual latest time is about 5.15 p.m. in July; after July it gradually falls earlier again until it is observed at 2.10 p.m. in December. The change is therefore fairly uniform throughout the year, and covers a range of about three and a quarter hours.

At *Aberdeen* only a small change of epoch occurs during the winter, from November to March. From March to April it goes back an hour and a half, and from thence to October the change is very similar to that exhibited at Kew, but the maxima generally occur a few minutes earlier than at the latter station. The range of epoch is from 2.45 p.m. in January, to 4.50 p.m. in May and June, and thus covers only about two hours.

At *Falmouth* the change of epoch is very similar to that observed at Kew, the chief difference being that the critical point of the phase is generally reached a few minutes later, and that the actual latest time, 5.25 p.m., is reached in August instead of in July. But the amplitude of the change—three and a quarter hours—is the same at both places, and at both there is exhibited the same small amount of change during the summer months.

At *Valencia*, from September to April, the epoch of the phase is almost identical with that observed at Falmouth; but from April to September it changes but little, and falls earlier than at Falmouth. The time varies from 2.10 p.m. in January to 4.50 p.m. in June, and therefore covers a range of nearly two and three-quarter hours from winter to summer.

The Second Maximum.—Kew is the only station at which this phase shows any approach to a regular seasonal change of epoch.

At *Kew* the phase occurs as early as 9 p.m. in January, after which it gradually becomes later, until in June it falls at 11 p.m. It then gets earlier again, and in December is observed at about 9.30 p.m., so that it covers a range of about two hours, the change occurring in a fairly uniform manner throughout the year.

At *Aberdeen* the critical point of the phase is not well defined in the winter months, but it probably occurs at about 8 p.m. in January and February, and then recedes to about 9.45 p.m. in May. From thence to August there is scarcely any change, but in September the phase abruptly shifts earlier again, to a little after 8 p.m.

At *Falmouth* the phase occurs at about 9.30 p.m. all the year through.

At *Valencia* also the change throughout the year is very slight, but the critical part of the phase is generally reached a few minutes earlier than at Falmouth, and its earliest occurrences are in August and September.

To sum up the above it may be said that Kew is the only one of the four observatories at which a uniformly progressive seasonal change of epoch is observable with each of the four phases of the double oscillation. Both of the morning phases become earlier with the approach of summer, and get later again as the year declines; whilst the two afternoon phases change their epoch in the reverse direction.

At the other three (Coast) stations the two minima alone show a change of a similar character, and it is only with the afternoon minimum that it is especially well marked. In the case of the two maxima the changes of epoch are slight, and they show no such regular progression as is exhibited at Kew.

The change of epoch from month to month will be easily followed by referring to the diagram, Fig. 1.

Seasonal Change of Amplitude of the Four Phases of the Phenomenon.

The different phases of the oscillation show at all the stations a remarkable seasonal change as regards their amplitude, and if these changes

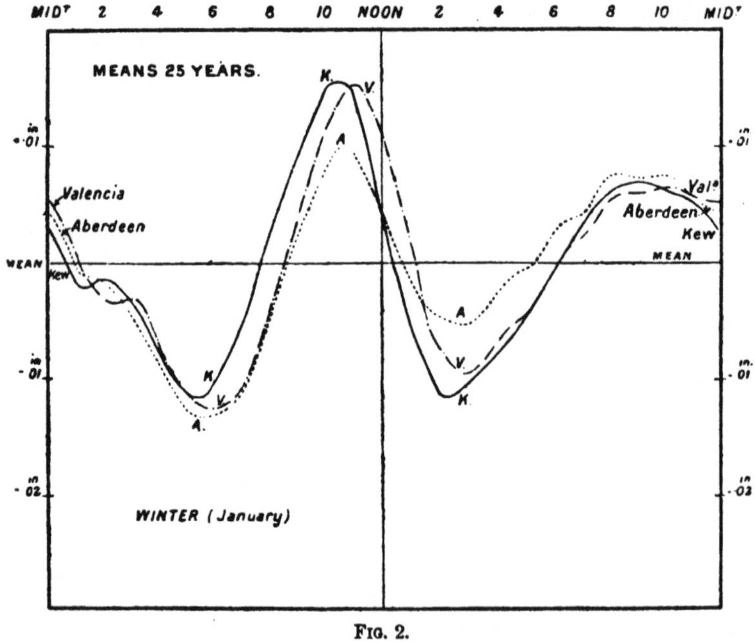

FIG. 2.

are compared with each other it is found that they are by no means alike at all the observatories. In every case, however, they exhibit a fairly uniform progression from winter to summer, and back again to winter, so that in describing the changes it will be sufficient to deal with a typical summer and winter month, it being understood that the change from one to the other is, upon the whole, a uniformly progressive one.

At *Kew*, in winter, the morning and afternoon minima are each about

·010 inch below the mean pressure for the day, whilst the first maximum rises about ·015 inch above it. This maximum is the chief feature of the oscillation. It is led up to from the first minimum by a steady increase of pressure lasting nearly five hours; remains near its highest point for about an hour; and is then followed by a decided fall, which brings along the second minimum in about three hours. The increase of pressure which follows the latter phase continues for seven hours, and the second maximum, when reached, gives way again very gradually before the decrease which leads once more to the morning minimum.

In the months of December and January this decrease is quite arrested for about an hour at 1 a.m., and indeed there occurs a slight rise forming the *third maximum*, observed only in winter, to which Rykatcheff first called attention in 1879.[1] The only trace of this phase of the oscillation shown in other months is a slight retardation of the rate of fall observable at the same hours in November and February.

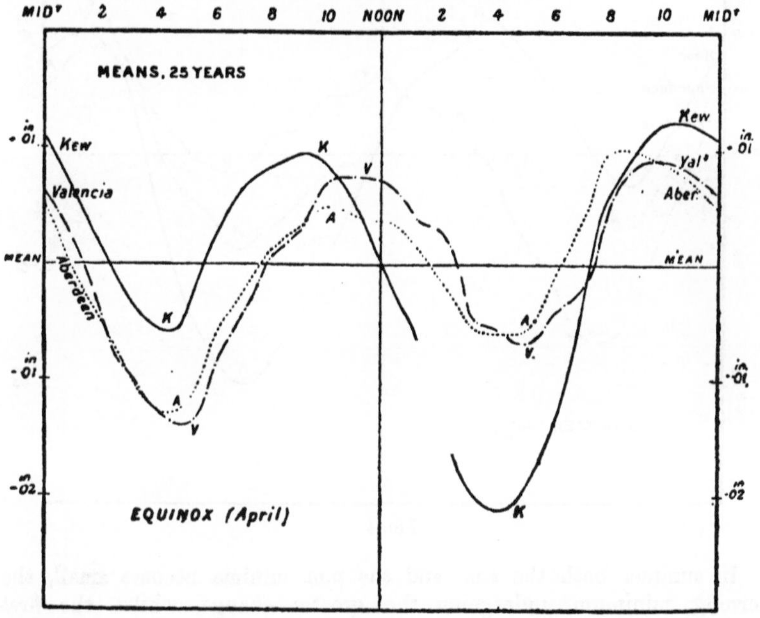

FIG. 3.

With the approach of spring and summer the amplitude of the morning oscillation becomes greatly diminished, whilst that of the afternoon becomes increased. In May and June the first minimum falls but slightly below the mean, whilst the first maximum rises to only about two-thirds of its winter amount. The fall which follows it, however, lasts longer than in winter, and leads to a deep second minimum, ·015 inch below the mean, which now forms the chief feature of the oscillation. This in its turn is quickly succeeded by a brisk rise, which lasts about six hours before the second maximum is reached, about ·010 inch above the mean,

[1] *La marche diurne du baromètre en Russie, et quelques remarques concernant ce phénomène en général*, par M. RYKATCHEFF, 1879.

and is then followed pretty promptly by the descent which leads again to the morning minimum.

At *Aberdeen* the seasonal change is different. In winter the two morning phases are the most prominent features of the oscillation, the minimum being about ·015 inch below and the maximum ·010 inch above the mean pressure for the day. The afternoon minimum and the second maximum are both much smaller than the corresponding morning phases, being respectively about ·005 inch below and ·007 inch above the mean; and it is noteworthy that the recovery of pressure which follows the afternoon minimum is somewhat unsteady. In December and January the "third maximum" between 1 a.m. and 2 a.m. is clearly indicated.

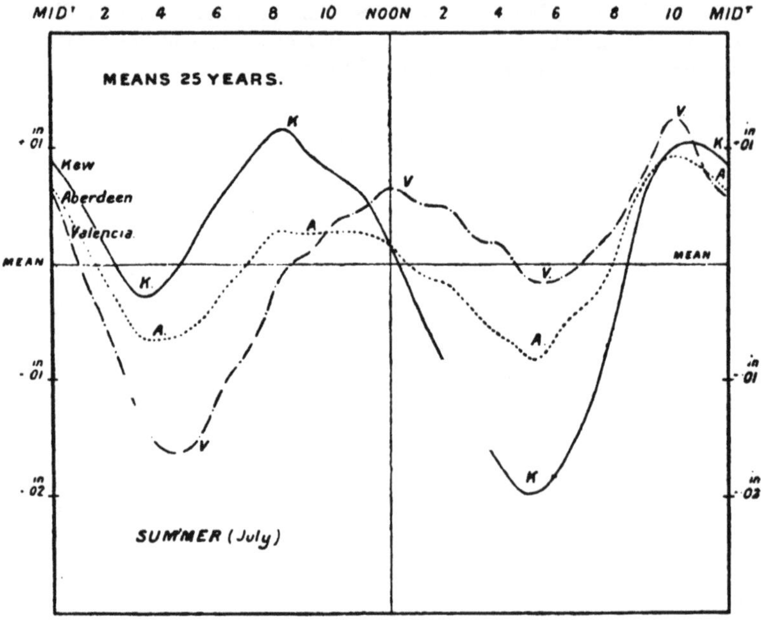

FIG. 4.

In summer both the a.m. and the p.m. minima become small, the morning minimum undergoing the greater change, whilst the first maximum becomes so small that it scarcely rises above the mean for the day, and the small oscillation it exhibits becomes spread over about thirteen hours. The second maximum, however, rises by a steady increase of pressure to about ·010 inch above the mean, and is now the most prominent phase of the four. The maximum range at this place, in summer, is only about one half of that observed at Kew in the same season.

At *Falmouth*, in winter, the most prominent phase of the oscillation is the first maximum, which rises sharply to nearly ·020 inch above the daily mean of pressure, and is at once followed by an equally brisk fall. The first minimum is about ·013 inch, and the second minimum rather less, below the mean, and they are separated by an interval of about nine hours. The increase of pressure which follows the afternoon minimum is less rapid and a little irregular, and the maximum when reached is only about ·008 inch above the mean. The fall leading to the morning minimum does not set in at once, and as at the other stations it is temporarily checked, in December and January, early in the morning.

With the approach of summer the morning minimum becomes a little deeper; but the first maximum decreases to half its winter height, and the second minimum only falls to about ·003 inch below the mean, the two minima being 13 hours apart. The rise which follows is, however, very brisk, and in four hours carries the oscillation to about ·012 inch above the mean, to the second maximum. The extreme range of the diurnal oscillation in summer is therefore nearly ·030 inch, which is slightly less than occurs in winter.

At *Valencia* the seasonal change is similar in character to that observed at Falmouth. In winter the amplitude of the oscillation amounts to about ·030 inch; and in December and January the small early maximum is indicated as at the other stations.

In summer the first maximum is much smaller than in winter and only exceeds the mean by ·005 inch, whilst the second minimum becomes merely a small dip of ·006 inch, and therefore only just falls below the mean, the interval between the two minima covering from 12 to 13 hours. The highest point is reached by the second maximum at about 9 p.m., and is about ·012 inch above the mean. The total range of the oscillation amounts to about ·030 inch.

To sum up the above: in winter the most salient feature of the phenomenon, at each of the stations, is the morning maximum, which separates the two minima of nearly equal depth by only about 9 hours. The evening maximum is relatively small, is less abruptly reached, and divides the afternoon minimum from that of the succeeding morning by about 15 hours.

The existence of the "third maximum" in January is also unmistakably indicated, and its persistence year by year at each of the stations shows it to be a true phase of the diurnal oscillation in mid-winter, and not a result of causes which are merely accidental in their action.

The change which takes place in the character of the oscillation as summer approaches is not the same at inland as at coast stations, nor is it the same on the east coast as on the west. At inland places, as represented by Kew, the morning minimum becomes much shallower than in winter; the afternoon minimum becomes much deeper, and the two maxima become of equal height; but the afternoon minimum is not reached till 14 hours after the morning one.

On the east coast, as represented by Aberdeen, both the minima become small, and the first maximum smaller still, whilst the second maximum, developing quickly, becomes the most prominent phase of the four.

On the west coast, as represented by Falmouth and Valencia, the morning minimum becomes much deeper, the first maximum and second minimum both much smaller, but the second maximum much higher; thus exactly reversing the change observed inland.

Influence of Temperature.

It may now be of interest to compare briefly these seasonal changes in epoch and character, observed in the diurnal barometric tide, with the corresponding changes shown in the diurnal march of temperature, at the same stations; and as all the data for such a comparison are given in the volume already referred to,[1] this can readily be done.

At *Kew* in the winter the mean change of temperature during the first eight hours of the day is very slight; the minimum is reached at about 8 a.m., after which hour the temperature rises till the maximum is reached at 2 p.m., when a fall sets in and continues until midnight. The mean range of the movement is from about 1°·5 below the mean for the day to 2°·5 above it, or about 4° in all. With the approach of spring and summer the time of the minimum falls earlier, and the decrease of temperature is continued beyond midnight into the early morning, the actual minimum becoming more sharply marked. From May to July the time of the minimum temperature is about 4 a.m., but in August it begins to fall later again, and by November it is back to 7 a.m. From June to September the maximum occurs at 3 p.m., which is only one hour later than its time in mid-winter; and the amplitude of the mean daily range in midsummer is about 14°.

At the other three stations the general features of the seasonal march of this element are very similar to those observed at Kew; but the daily range is always less, and the rise to the maximum is not only more gradual but it is less promptly followed by the succeeding fall, so that although the maximum is lower it is usually maintained for a longer period.

It is not easy to correlate the changes in the diurnal march of the two elements,—pressure and temperature—either as regards epoch or amplitude.

In the first place there does not appear to be any direct connection between the epoch of the critical portions of the pressure oscillations and those of temperature, and whilst, *e.g.*, the epoch of maximum temperature only varies about an hour throughout the year, that of the first maximum and second minimum of pressure,—the two phases of that oscillation which might be supposed to be most directly affected by the maximum of temperature, range, as we have seen, over several hours. Similarly, although both the minimum of temperature and the morning minimum of pressure become earlier as the summer approaches, the change is not equal in the two elements, and it is not possible to directly connect them as cause and effect; and further, it is only at Kew that anything approaching a regularly progressive change of epoch is observed in each of the four phases of the pressure oscillation.

In the next place, the change which occurs in the amplitude of the temperature oscillation from month to month, although varying in amount is yet similar in character at each of the four stations, whilst the changes which are observed in the pressure oscillation differ at the various places very materially. Thus with the increase in the amount and range of temperature at both places, we have at Kew a great

[1] *Hourly Means for the Year* 1895, Appendix.

decrease of the morning and a large increase of the afternoon barometric minima, whilst at Valencia we get just the reverse; and whilst at Kew the two maxima undergo but a slight change, at Valencia the morning maximum becomes much reduced and the evening maximum considerably increased.

The question then arises whether temperature reacts upon the pressure oscillation indirectly, through the agency of some other element; and one naturally turns first to the aqueous vapour of the atmosphere for an answer.

It is unfortunate in this connection that the series of long-period means of pressure and temperature which we are now using does not include data for determining the daily march of the hygrometric condition of the atmosphere; but there have been published mean values for the wet bulb for individual years for the period 1887-95, and these I combined, in the case of certain months, in order to get means for the nine years. From the mean hourly difference between the dry and wet bulb temperatures thus obtained I worked out the mean hourly values of humidity and of vapour tension, for the months of January, April, July, and October, which months I thought would represent sufficiently well the annual march of the phenomena; and by combining upon a single diagram for each month the curves of those elements with those of pressure and temperature, their intercomparison was rendered easy.

The result showed that in winter, at each of the four observatories, both the mean relative humidity and the mean tension of vapour remain almost unchanged from midnight till 8 a.m. or 9 a.m., the first change accompanying, or quickly following, the first rise of temperature. This, however, is not until two or three hours after the increase of pressure which follows the first minimum has begun, and when it is in full progress. At this season of the year both the humidity and the vapour tension show a very simple daily change, the former decreasing, and the latter increasing, with the rise of temperature, and *vice versâ*. But at no part of the day do these movements properly synchronise with that of the pressure curve, for beginning after the pressure has begun to increase they continue without change for some hours after the first maximum of pressure is passed; and indeed it is not until the second minimum is almost reached that the tension decreases again and the dampness of the air begins to increase, the new movement continuing until midnight, and therefore until after the second maximum has been reached and passed.

In April there is rather less uniformity in the occurrence of the phases of the hygrometric phenomena, and they cover a greater range than in midwinter, but upon the whole the remarks made respecting January apply to the spring month also.

In July the hygrometrical curves show larger and more important differences between the stations, and while at each place the relative humidity shows a fairly symmetrical decrease and increase, corresponding to the rise and fall of temperature, the march of vapour tension becomes more irregular. With the earlier rise of temperature the vapour tension also begins to increase early in the morning; but after continuing to do so during the first two or three hours following sunrise the rise generally ceases at about 7 a.m., and then for several hours it changes little and unsteadily. At Falmouth this condition lasts till the afternoon, when the tension very slowly decreases, the whole daily oscillation being but small. At Kew, after about noon, the check is followed by a second and steady increase of tension, which lasts till the evening, when a fall sets in and continues till next morning. At Aberdeen the first rise is rapid for a couple of hours; then a slight fall occurs, and is followed by a second rise, the whole oscillation being similar to that observed at Kew, but on a somewhat smaller scale. At Valencia the morning check is slighter, and the increase and decrease is more symmetrical throughout the day than is the case elsewhere.

In October also the hygrometrical phenomena vary somewhat at the four stations, but the curves are more symmetrical throughout the day, and upon the whole are more similar to each other than is the case in July.

But nowhere is it possible to trace from the curves any consistent and direct relation between the increase or decrease of vapour tension, or of humidity of the air, and the diurnal rise or fall of the barometer; for hygrometrical changes which began whilst a given movement of the barometer was in progress are found to continue unchanged till long after that movement has become reversed; and combinations which seem to hold good in certain cases are negatived in others. In short, both as regards their epoch and character, it seems impossible to synchronise directly the changes in these different elements, or to indicate precisely their relation to each other.

A rise in the mean temperature of the air is almost always accompanied by a diminution in its relative humidity, and at least during the colder part of the year by an increase in the tension of its vapour.

But this is the season of the year in which there is comparatively little difference in the barometric oscillation as it is observed at each of the four stations. In the warmer months the change in the tension of vapour with change of temperature does not follow so simple a progression, and while the air becomes warmer, and its relative dryness continues to increase, its elastic force ceases to do so and even becomes less.

Although it is not very obvious how these two conditions of the aqueous vapour are co-related as regards the effect they jointly produce upon the barometer, yet it is difficult to resist the conviction that in this irregularity in the diurnal march of its elastic force lies the explanation, to some extent at least, of the differences which are observed between the summer and winter diurnal oscillations of pressure, and perhaps of the differences observed in the summer oscillations at the different stations also. But we cannot fully understand this part of the problem until we know more of the temperature and hygrometric conditions of the upper air. The mass and weight of the atmosphere are altered by the addition of water vapour to its lower strata, and its tension is increased by the inertia of the air; but this is, in its turn, modified by convection currents set up as the temperature rises, and it is important to know how far the influence of such currents extends.

At any rate it is impossible to study the curves without feeling certain that in the simple diurnal oscillation of temperature lies the original source, the *primum mobile*, of the more complex daily barometric movement, and that its action is by no means always a direct one. That the final result may be brought about through the action of more than one secondary agent is quite possible, but that the aqueous vapour of the atmosphere is one of them hardly admits of doubt.

In order to further test this suggested effect of temperature I now tried to trace its action upon the barometer curve under more stringent conditions.

All the comparisons hitherto made were based upon mean results for long periods, in which it may fairly be expected that the effects of abnormal temperatures, or of range of temperature, have been smoothed out and cancelled by each other. I therefore now took for comparison shorter periods, in which these abnormal conditions existed, choosing in the first place similar months of high and low mean temperature, in order to see what effect, if any, such conditions produced upon the barometric oscillation.

The following summarises the results of this stage of the comparison :—

January. Temperature below the mean.—Little or no difference from what was observed under mean conditions was exhibited by the curves at either of the four observatories.

Temperature above the mean.—At Kew the morning minimum became a good deal deeper, whilst the afternoon minimum and the second maximum both became smaller.

At Aberdeen the oscillation changed its character completely. The first minimum was of normal depth, but it was followed by a small maximum, and that in its turn by a deep second minimum, instead of a shallow one, and then came a very high second maximum, the range from the afternoon minimum to the maximum amounting to ·04 inch.

At Falmouth and Valencia the changes were unimportant.

April. Temperature below the mean.—At Kew the first maximum became much decreased in height, but beyond this there was no important change.

At Aberdeen, Falmouth, and Valencia only a small departure from mean conditions was observed.

Temperature above the mean.—At Kew the first minimum became so small as scarcely to reach the mean for the day; but the first maximum was much increased, and was followed by a very deep second minimum, the fall amounting to ·05 inch. The second maximum was of normal height. At Aberdeen the oscillation approximated closely to that at Kew under similar conditions; but the range of pressure was less, although double what it is under normal conditions.

At Falmouth and Valencia the first maximum was somewhat increased, but the other phases showed little change.

July. Temperature below the mean.—At Kew the first minimum is deepened, while the second minimum and the second maximum both become very small, and the extreme range of the oscillation becomes reduced to ·02 inch.

At Aberdeen the first maximum becomes practically extinguished, the movement of pressure between the first and second minima being so small and irregular as to reduce the oscillation to one maximum at night, and one minimum in the day. At Falmouth and Valencia less change was observed than at the other stations, the principal being a slight deepening of the morning minimum.

Temperature above the mean.—At Kew the first minimum became very small, but the second very deep indeed, with two high maxima; the range from the first maximum to the second minimum exceeding ·04 inch. At Aberdeen the first maximum and the afternoon minimum are both more pronounced than with mean temperature conditions. At Falmouth the second minimum becomes deeper than with mean temperature conditions. At Valencia there is little difference from the mean.

It should be remarked that both at Valencia and Falmouth the mean and also the extreme temperatures vary within narrower limits than at the two eastern stations, and exceptional weather conditions are also, as a rule, less persistent.

Some mean results for July which were available for Armagh, a station about 35 miles inland from the eastern shore of the Irish Sea, gave results which were intermediate in character between Kew and Aberdeen. With warm conditions the curve approximated more to the Kew curve and with lower temperatures to that of Aberdeen.

But even a month is too long a period throughout which to ensure having similar conditions of temperature, and therefore I now tried to carry

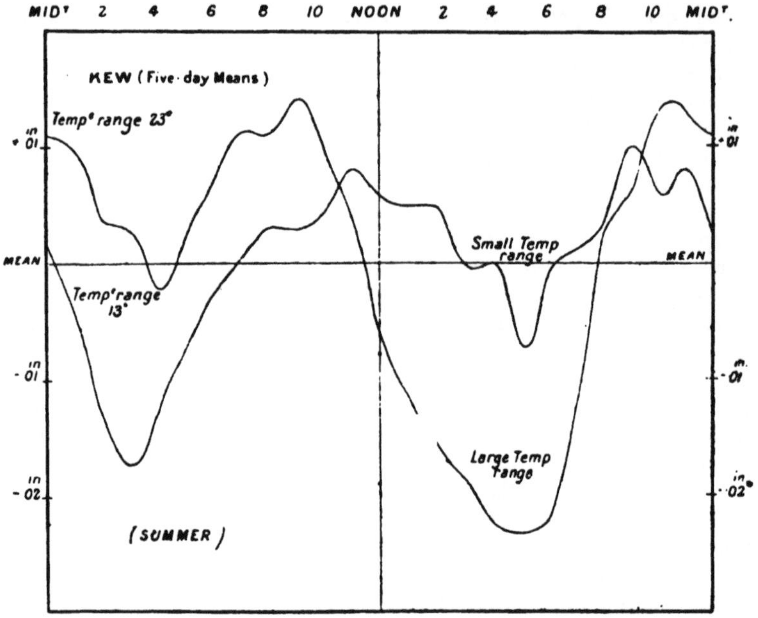

FIG. 5.

the comparison still further by using hourly means of pressure for the shorter period of five days, and also the hourly observations for some single days, so as to allow of such a condition being entirely fulfilled.

In this step a new difficulty arose—to find the required temperature conditions combined with barometric conditions sufficiently steady, and free from non-periodic oscillations, as to allow the true diurnal tide to show itself without distortion, the time being generally too brief for the non-periodic changes to cancel each other by the usual process of averaging.

The general result of this part of the work was to confirm the conclusions already arrived at from the monthly means; but not only did the character and range of the oscillations, due to high or low temperatures, now become more pronounced, but it also became apparent that the daily

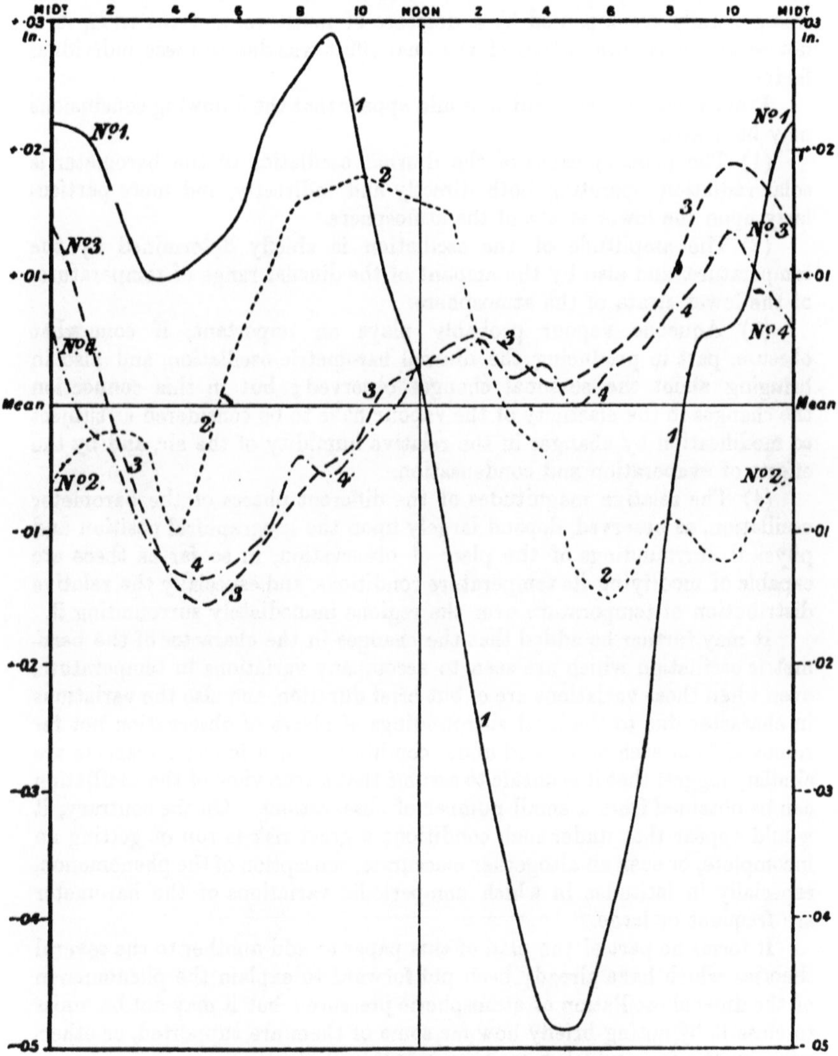

FIG. 6.

Nos. 1 and 2.—KEW curves for single days.
No. 1.—Mean temp. 60°. Range = 27°. No. 2.—Mean temp. 65°. Range = 9°.
Nos. 3 and 4.—VALENCIA curves for months.
No. 3.—July 1887, Mean temp. 62°. Range = 7°.
No. 4.—July 1879, Mean temp. 55°. Range = 5°.

range of temperature was an even more powerful factor than the actual amount of the temperature; whilst the state of the sky, as influencing both terrestrial and solar radiation, was seen to be another important factor.

Another result which seemed to be established was, that when the air was dry the morning minimum became smaller, and the afternoon minimum deeper; whilst an increase of moisture beyond the normal amount tended to produce an exactly opposite result. But since an increase of temperature was generally accompanied by a decrease of moisture, and *vice versâ*, it is not certain what proportion of the final effect was due to these individual factors.

From what has been said it would appear that the following conclusions may be drawn:—

(1) The primary cause of the diurnal oscillation of the barometer is solar radiation, operating both directly and indirectly, and more particularly upon the lower strata of the atmosphere.

(2) The amplitude of the oscillation is chiefly determined by the temperature, and also by the amount of the diurnal range of temperature, of the lower strata of the atmosphere.

(3) Aqueous vapour probably plays an important, if somewhat obscure, part in producing the diurnal barometric oscillation, and also in bringing about the seasonal changes observed; but in this connection the changes in the elasticity of the vapour have to be considered as subject to modification by changes in the relative humidity of the air, and by the effects of evaporation and condensation.

(4) The relative magnitudes of the different phases of the barometer oscillation, as observed, depend largely upon the geographical position and physical surroundings of the place of observation, in so far as these are capable of modifying its temperature conditions, and especially the relative distribution of temperature over the regions immediately surrounding it.

It may further be added that the changes in the character of the barometric oscillation which are seen to accompany variations in temperature, even when those variations are of but brief duration, and also the variations in character due to the local surroundings of places of observation not far removed from each other, and under conditions which in other respects are similar, suggest that it is unsafe to assume that a true view of the oscillation can be obtained from a small number of observations. On the contrary, it would appear that under such conditions a great risk is run of getting an incomplete, or even an altogether inaccurate, conception of the phenomenon, especially in latitudes in which non-periodic variations of the barometer are frequent or large.

It forms no part of the plan of this paper to add another to the several theories which have already been put forward to explain the phenomenon of the diurnal oscillation of atmospheric pressure; but it may not be amiss to close it by noting briefly how far some of them are supported, or otherwise, by the facts which have been mentioned above.

Perhaps these theories may be divided roughly into two classes, in the first of which the phenomenon is regarded as the combined result of two very different and independent agencies, one being temperature, whilst the other is obscure, but is probably some kind of gravitational undulation or wave. These are supposed to produce separate oscillations, having distinct periods, but more or less overlapping each other, the observed barometrical oscillation being the result of their combined action. In the second class the phenomenon is regarded as being entirely due to temperature, acting directly or indirectly, and either by increasing the tension of the air, where there is resistance to its expansion upon being warmed, or by setting up gravitational currents which affect the mass, and therefore the weight, of the atmosphere over the place of observation, the currents succeeding each other in a regular manner, and in such a way as to cause the sequence of barometer movements observed.

Of the first class, the theory that the movement of the barometer is primarily the result of a simple diurnal undulation, set up by the action of solar radiation upon the upper strata of the atmosphere, but modified near the earth's surface by other agencies, is difficult to reconcile with the little knowledge we possess as to the range of temperature in the upper atmosphere; and also with the facts brought out by the present inquiry, which show that the conditions of temperature near the surface of the earth are of themselves competent to bring about a complete transformation in the character of the pressure oscillation. We have seen, for example, that a change in the local conditions of temperature, confined to a single day, is sufficient to vary the amplitude of the oscillation, and also to give to it at one place quite a different character from that which a similar change would produce at another; and the magnitude of these effects is so great as to suggest that in these lower temperature conditions probably lies the real source of the entire phenomenon. The theory is based mainly upon the results obtained from the treatment of observations by Harmonic Analysis, and there would seem to be some danger of forcing such deductions, and of carrying them further than the method itself warrants. Rykatcheff remarks with reference to this point that it is important to remember that the formula employed is not deduced from the theory of the diurnal march of the barometer, but it is a series which may be employed to represent the march of any phenomenon having a periodical function; and he asserts that in certain cases it may give fictitious values, which will not truly represent the real phenomena of nature as they are revealed by observation.[1]

Amongst the other class of theories mention may be made of the emphasis which Dove places upon the part played by the elastic force of vapour, as distinct from the weight of the dry air, when both these elements are acted upon by changes of temperature, and by the rate and amount of the evaporation and condensation by which those changes are accompanied. Following a similar line, others have attributed the morning minimum almost entirely to loss of tension caused by the deposition of dew; and the maximum following it to an increase of tension caused by the inertia of the upper strata of the atmosphere when evaporation was in progress; whilst others again have looked upon the phenomenon as the result of the simple heating and cooling of the air, producing ascending and descending currents, and also accompanied by variations in elasticity due to inertia, but not depending to any marked degree upon the hygrometrical condition of the atmosphere.

Both Rykatcheff and Buchan have regarded the sequence of the phenomena as due mainly, but not exclusively, to alternating lateral —easterly and westerly—movements of masses of air, from and towards the place of observation, set up under the influence of solar radiation.

[1] *La Marche Diurne du Baromètre en Russie*, p. 78.

Movements in both directions may be proceeding simultaneously, but at different levels, and the critical epochs of change of the different phases are determined by the moment when the one begins to predominate over the other.

Rykatcheff has sought for a corroboration of his theory from anemometrical observations made at various places, but he has confined his explanation entirely to the movements of the atmosphere named, attaching but little importance to variations in tension due to the inertia of the air.

Buchan, on the other hand, has regarded the first two phases of the phenomenon as being due directly to temperature affecting the tension of the air, and the evening maximum as being caused by an increase of mass resulting from lateral currents; whilst the afternoon minimum he considers to be due to an ascending current of warm air; apparently he regards the vapour in the air only with reference to its capacity to absorb heat, and not from the same standpoint as Dove.

The greatest difficulty in the task of unravelling the cause of the phenomenon lies, without doubt, in the fact that so little is known of the conditions which obtain in the upper air. In this respect we have practically nothing to go upon but surmise. Mountain observatories help us but little, because they do not tell us what takes place in the *free air*. The mass of the mountain upon which they are placed, its effect in deflecting the currents of air which reach them, and also upon the temperature of the air surrounding them—not to mention other causes which affect the accuracy of the actual observations themselves,[1] are all factors which it is impossible to evaluate, but which doubtless influence considerably the diurnal pressure oscillation as it is observed at such stations.

At the same time almost every suggested explanation involves, to a greater or less extent, causes and effects which are supposed to originate, or to be continued, in regions much higher than the comparatively low levels at which mountain observatories are possible; and such causes are always hypothetical, if indeed in some instances they are not opposed to the ideas which the little knowledge we do possess would appear to warrant.

It is therefore only when we are dealing with actual observations near the earth's surface and with the deductions they clearly warrant, that we are upon really sure ground.

We have seen that whatever may be the *primum mobile* of the phenomenon, the temperature conditions near the earth's surface are all-powerful in its further development. These very probably act upon the barometer to some extent by varying the tension of the air, and of the aqueous vapour the air contains; but for a full explanation of the facts shown to exist there would also seem to be required some system of atmospheric currents, capable of affecting the mass of the atmosphere above the place of observation; and it is not difficult to understand how such currents should result from these same conditions of surface temperature.

[1] *E.g.*, see a paper by Dr. Buchan in the *Proc. Roy. Soc. Edin.*, vol. xviii., on "The Influence of high Winds on the Barometer at the Ben Nevis Observatory"; from which it appears that in strong winds the barometer reading may be from ·025 inch to ·150 inch too low, and is probably below the truth with nearly all winds.

For example, in summer, when the effects of insolation are greatest, and the differences in the march of the phenomenon as observed at different stations are most marked, we find at Aberdeen both the morning maximum and the afternoon minimum so much reduced as to be scarcely noticeable, whilst at Kew only the morning maximum is reduced, and that but little, whilst the afternoon minimum becomes greatly developed. Aberdeen is a coast station, with sea to the eastward and a hilly region to the westward, and whilst the range of temperature is small both at Aberdeen and in the hills, it is probably considerably less over the sea to the eastward. Under these conditions there could be but little increase of tension due to increase of temperature, and the temperature gradients would also be slight, so that no considerable currents of air would be set in motion, and therefore little change of mass would result from that cause; and generally one might expect the oscillation of pressure to be small, as it is. Kew, on the other hand, is, relatively to Aberdeen, a continental station, and the temperature gradients are far more considerable. Whilst, therefore, one might possibly expect a greater variation in tension due to increased range of temperature, it would also appear likely that more important temperature gradients would be set up, accounting for the deep afternoon minimum, which is seen to become deeper as the range of temperature becomes greater, and also for the rapid increase of pressure which succeeds it.

In Valencia, again, we have a coast station with the ocean to the westward, instead of to the eastward as in the case of Aberdeen, and the positions of the region (land) most likely to be influenced by insolation being therefore reversed, one might expect that the direction of any flow of air, due to temperature gradient, would be reversed in like manner. The character of the oscillation observed shows that this is probably the case, for in summer whilst there is a deep first minimum there is scarcely any second minimum at all, and the oscillation becomes little more than a single one in the 24 hours. Assuming the cause of the oscillation to be a change in the mass of superincumbent atmosphere, this would be explained as follows: The deep morning minimum is due to a westerly current from the warmer sea towards the land, cooled during the night by radiation; but as the land becomes heated by the sun this current ceases, and is succeeded by another from the land towards the sea, causing the first maximum. Owing, however, to the small change of temperature over the ocean there is but a slight temperature gradient in that direction so that the air does not flow away over the sea, and so bring about an afternoon minimum, but becomes piled up over the coast station, causing the high evening maximum which is observed, and which gives way in its turn when the land again cools enough to set up the westerly, landward current once more.

Buchan explains the morning maximum, generally, as being simply due to "the expansive force called into play by the increase of temperature," the barometer "continuing to rise, not because the mass of atmosphere overhead is increased, but because a higher temperature has increased the tension or pressure."[1] But this hypothesis does not quite meet the fact that in winter the increase of pressure begins, and gets into full swing,

[1] Article "Meteorology," *Encycl. Brit.*, ninth edition.

some hours before the time of sunrise, or of minimum temperature; which fact seems to be better met by Rykatcheff's view, that the increase of pressure is due to an increase of mass, caused by a current from the already warmed region to the east, which becomes stronger as the sun approaches the meridian of the place of observation. The afternoon minimum is explained by both Buchan and Rykatcheff as the result of a diminution of mass, due to gravitational currents flowing away from the place of observation, and set up by the approach of the maximum temperature; and, similarly, both regard the evening maximum as due to increase of mass, resulting from currents in the opposite direction.

This conclusion, however, would hardly lead us to expect that the morning minimum, which follows this accession of mass, is "due not to the removal of any of the mass of air overhead, as happens in the case of the afternoon minimum, but to a reduction of the tension or pressure of the air, consequent upon a reduction in the temperature through radiation," which is the view held by Dr. Buchan,[1] but which is not, I think, supported by the facts brought out in the present comparison.

The result of the comparison which I have made of the phenomena as observed at these four stations, and under different conditions, leads me to the conclusion that changes in the mass of the atmosphere, due to gravitational currents set up by changes of temperature conditions, are much more important factors in all the phases of the oscillation than are the changes in tension due to the inertia and viscosity of the air.

DISCUSSION.

The President (Mr. F. C. Bayard) said that the Fellows of the Society were much indebted to Mr. Curtis for his admirable paper. Several years ago he himself had gone into the matter, using results for five years from the seven observatories in connection with the Meteorological Office; and Mr. H. S. Eaton had also worked at this subject, using one year's figures only. In the present paper Mr. Curtis had given far more observations and much more knowledge. Ferrel, in his book, *A Popular Treatise on the Wind*, also gave a statement on this matter, but his conclusions are quite different from those arrived at by Mr. Curtis.

Mr. E. D. Archibald remarked that, although he had not been able to see the paper before the meeting, and only heard a portion of it, Mr. Curtis was to be congratulated on having had the courage and ability to tackle such a big problem. Most meteorologists were content to walk round it rather than attempt to plunge into it. He was glad to find that Mr. Curtis was inclined to accept Rykatcheff's hypothesis, by which the double diurnal oscillation is assumed to arise from motions across the meridians of the upper air, induced by the successive arrival of the sun over different points of the earth due to the terrestrial diurnal rotation. In order to test the existence of such motions, experiments with anemometers at high levels or on kites might be employed. In America, where they flew them two miles high, it might be possible to start such work. He agreed with Mr. Curtis that the employment of the harmonic analysis was sometimes misunderstood. The resolution of a complex diurnal curve into diurnal, semi-diurnal, etc., components did not necessarily imply that such components had a separate physical existence. They might or they might not. Comparison

[1] Article "Meteorology," *Encycl. Brit.*, ninth edition.

of many analyses from many places would prove this. In his own paper "On the Diurnal Variation of the Various Meteorological Elements at Calcutta" in the *Indian Meteorological Memoirs*, the results from a number of places in Northern India generally tended to show that the first or diurnal component, usually regarded as due to temperature, varied greatly according to locality; while the second or semi-diurnal component was nearly independent of locality, and was evidently due to general rather than local causes. Great caution had, however, to be observed in regard to treating such components as completely separate entities. For his own part, he did not think the results of such a method commensurate with the immense labour involved in its calculations. He considered the tropics, where local irregularities were a minimum, and the oscillation itself a maximum, more adapted to the study of the phenomenon than these latitudes. Mr. Curtis's diagrams, however, were distinctly valuable in showing the effect of season and humidity in causing special variations. In many points they resemble those which were exhibited by the Indian stations in different months and seasons, and the paper was a valuable contribution to the differential study of the problem.

Mr. W. H. Dines said the thanks of the Society were due to Mr. Curtis for the great trouble he had taken in working up such a large set of observations. The phenomena presented considerable difficulty, and it seemed as though no perfectly satisfactory explanation could be yet given. The daily oscillation could be explained easily enough; for the air on the sunny side of the globe must be warmer than that on the reverse side, and the twelve hours of daylight provided ample time for some of the warmed air to flow off above, and thus produce the afternoon minimum. The semi-diurnal oscillation seemed to be a sort of aerial tide produced by the heating effect of the sun. All free bodies had a certain definite period of oscillation; and a very small disturbing force, if applied in the right way, would set up in such bodies a large oscillation. He might mention a swing as an example. A heavy person might be set swinging by a piece of fine cotton that would break with the strain of a few ounces. It was only necessary to continue a series of slight pulls with the cotton, and to time the pulls so that they should exactly coincide with the period of oscillation of the swing. This principle was one of constant occurrence in natural phenomena; a certain anomaly in the moon's motion for a long time puzzled astronomers, but was at length found to be due to an extremely small disturbing force. The force was so very small, that it had been altogether neglected, but it chanced to coincide in period with a certain term in the harmonical expression of the moon's motion, and this produced an effect entirely out of proportion to its own intrinsic importance. Now Lord Kelvin had suggested that the natural period of oscillation of our atmosphere, taken as a whole, might be about twelve hours; and if so, it might explain the semi-diurnal oscillation. The difficulty was that the temperature variation had a period of twenty-four hours instead of twelve; but harmonic analysis showed that there was also a semi-diurnal term in the temperature variation; and it must be remembered that the harmonic analysis of curves could not invent terms that did not exist. The theory he had thus briefly sketched had been put forward by Dr. Hann of Vienna, a translation of whose paper by Dr. Scott was given in the *Quarterly Journal*, vol. xxv. p. 40. To him (Mr. Dines), this theory seemed to explain and fit in with the observed facts much better than any other; and Dr. Hann's paper was certainly well worth perusal, although for himself he would much have preferred the data to have been put in the form of curves, rather than to have been given as equations.

Mr. H. S. Wallis said that he had been interested in comparing the monthly means for twenty-five years for Kew given in the paper with the means for forty years recently published for Camden Square; and also with the means for a hundred years given by H. S. Eaton in his paper read before the Society in 1880.

He thought that any one who plotted the three sets of figures as a diagram would agree with him that neither the twenty-five years nor the forty years was long enough to give a true monthly mean, and would be doubtful whether even the hundred years was long enough.

Mr. G. J. SYMONS said that Mr. Glaisher had given in his *Diurnal Range Tables* corrections for the diurnal range of the barometer, based on two-hourly readings at Greenwich; and he (Mr. Symons) had plotted the Kew curve under Mr. Glaisher's, but found that they did not compare very well together, the Kew values in the morning being practically half those of Greenwich, and the afternoon minimum much more marked at Kew than at Greenwich, while the evening maximum is practically identical.

Mr. C. HARDING was pleased to notice the elimination of foreign matter in the paper, such as periodic and non-periodic changes. Mr. Glaisher had probably taken no such care, therefore it was not surprising that Mr. Curtis's figures did not agree well with his. Mr. Curtis had used local time, thus bringing everything to a standard and making them all comparable. The late Mr. Blanford had worked out the mean diurnal range of the barometer for India, extending the curves over the sea; and he, Mr. Harding, had re-worked the figures, but with a different result, due to no notice being taken of periodic changes. Some twenty-five to thirty years ago he had taken out the means in mid-Atlantic, near the equator, and had noticed the steady march of epochs and amplitudes; but his results were different from those of Mr. Curtis. He was glad Mr. Curtis had only used arithmetical means. He had himself acquired the knowledge of using the harmonic analysis, but believed that for years its use had only hampered the means, although good points were shown by the first and second co-efficients. Mr. Curtis had given the facts, which will allow the theories to step in afterwards.

Mr. R. INWARDS inquired if Mr. Curtis had extended his investigations to the readings obtained at high-level observatories, and thought that the records from the mountain stations in South America would be most suitable for this purpose.

Mr. R. H. CURTIS, in reply, said he did not think it safe to attach much importance to anemometer observations in connection with the phenomena of the barometrical oscillation. Supposing the phenomenon to be due to the translation of masses of air, the rate of movement would probably not be rapid, and it would most likely occur in the upper air; and in view of the not altogether satisfactory exposure of many anemometers, not to mention other difficulties peculiar to the instruments themselves, and which became important directly it was sought to compare their records *inter se*, he could not attach to their records so much weight as Rykatcheff had given to them. The suggestion of Mr. Archibald, as to anemometer experiments at high levels by means of kites, if it could be carried out, was much more promising. With reference to what had been said respecting the employment of the harmonic analysis in this investigation, he thought it most important to remember that that formula is not based upon the barometric oscillation, and that there are limitations to its use in that connection. It is too generally assumed that each component necessarily represents a distinct and separate cause. It may be the case, but it is doubtful; and meanwhile it would appear that a good deal of ingenuity is wasted in suggesting causes to fit them, which probably have no real existence. The converse of this is to doubt—as has more than once been done—whether such features of the phenomenon as the early maximum in winter are "true physical features," merely because there did not appear to be anything in the harmonic expression which corresponded to them; and this notwithstanding the fact that the mean values may exhibit the particular feature with perfect clearness and regularity. He had read Dr. Hann's paper more than once, but he could not resist the conviction that many of the conclusions stated in it had been based on quite inadequate data. In reply to Mr. Inwards, he said he had not used mountain observations in the present discussion. The remarks of Mr. Symons, and of Mr. Wallis, referred rather to the accuracy of the data given in the tables. From his knowledge of the instruments used, and of the manner in which the observations had been dealt with, he felt quite justified in characterising the values now given as excellent, and better than any which had previously been published. Possibly Mr. Wallis had overlooked the fact that the values given are not reduced to mean sea-level, although they are corrected for temperature. For his own part, he considered mean values of pressure derived from twenty-five years' observations sufficiently good for any practical purpose.

Hurricane at Sombrero, September 1899.—Capt. M. W. C. Hepworth, of the Meteorological Office, has communicated the following note :—

"On August 7 and September 8, 1899, hurricanes passed over the island of Sombrero, and from the report of the principal keeper at the lighthouse on that island the storm on September 8 appears to have been of exceptional violence. The observer, J. A. Richardson, sent to the Meteorological Office, in addition to the log kept by himself and his assistant A. L. Richardson, an excerpt from the journal of D. C. Richmond, the lighthouse-keeper at Phillipsburg on the island of St. Martin.

"Sombrero is in lat. 18° 36′ N. and long. 63° 28′ W., the position of St. Martin being lat. 18° 5′ N. and long. 63° 5′ W.; these islands therefore lie directly in the mean track of the West India hurricanes.

"At 2 a.m. on September 8 the pressure at Sombrero, by a mercurial barometer supplied by the Meteorological Office, was 30·0 ins., and was diminishing; the wind was North (true); the velocity of the wind, by a dial anemometer, was 13 miles an hour, the weather being cloudy, hazy, and 'dirty looking.'

"By noon the velocity of the wind had increased to 57 miles, and at 4.30 p.m. it had backed to North-west. By 5 p.m. the anemometer showed a rate of 60 miles, and at 5.30 p.m. a rate of 86 miles an hour. The wind was still North-west, and the barometer stood at 29·50 ins., having ceased to fall. After 5.30 p.m. the anemometer was put out of action by the loss of the cups; but, according to the report of the observer, the fury of the tempest was at its height between 7 p.m. and midnight.

"At St. Martin the aneroid barometer—errors not known—stood at 30·05 ins. at 6 a.m. on the 8th, and commenced to fall slowly; the recorded direction of the wind—whether true or magnetic does not appear—was then North-north-west in a moderate breeze, which does not seem to have increased materially until 2 p.m. The reading of the aneroid was then 29·85 ins., and pressure was still diminishing; the sea, however, during this time had become very rough and was breaking heavily on the sand-bar.

"Intermittent rain then commenced, the wind increased, becoming squally, and the sky overcast. A few flashes of lightning and a peal of thunder, accompanied by heavy rain, are recorded at 2.45 p.m. by this observer, who at 3.50 p.m. remarks: 'Wind still North-north-west, aneroid 29·70 ins.'; but at 3.55 p.m. he states: 'Wind now West by North, and blowing very hard during the squalls.'

"Pressure remained the same until after 4.30 p.m., but at 6.40 p.m. had diminished, the aneroid recording 29·65 ins., and dropping five hundredths during the squalls. The wind had veered to North-west, and had increased very considerably; but backed again in a squall at 7.28 p.m. from West, and at 7.35 p.m. was still from that point, 'blowing in severe squalls of long duration,' when the observer considers that the centre of the cyclone bore north, and was distant about 35 miles.

"By cross-bearings of the centre roughly estimated by means of the data supplied by the observer at this station and by the light-keeper at Sombrero at different times, in an attempt to trace its track while in the vicinity of these islands at the time in question, it appears to have been situated North-north-west (true), distant about 50 miles from the former island, and about 35 miles distant from the latter, bearing about North-west by West (true).

"I will now quote the Remarks Column of the Sombrero Register:—

"'The morning (of the 8th) opened with a very suspicious look, barometer falling. At 12 noon a most fearful cyclone, accompanied with a dreadful sea and heavy rain, swept over the islands, the worst one I have ever experienced for the past thirty years that I have been here. The sea covered more than two-thirds of the island, and ripped up nearly everything it struck. The anemometer cups blew off and went to pieces, not damaging the spindle. What time it happened I know not, for we were all at the top of the tower at 6.10 p.m.; but the strongest part of the cyclone was between 7 p.m. and midnight. The vibration of the tower was indescribable. A most fearful night.'

"After midnight the wind shifted to South-west and moderated somewhat, barometer rising rapidly, and at 6 a.m. on the 9th it had considerably abated, backing to South, and subsequently to South-south-east as a fresh to moderate breeze. At St. Martin the wind shifted at 7.45 p.m. on the 8th to South-west by West, and was blowing with great violence at that time. At 8 p.m. it was from South-west, and was still increasing, debris flying about and striking violently against the house. At 9.50 p.m. the aneroid indicated 29·50 ins., and soon afterwards commenced to rise.

"The strongest wind here appears to have been experienced between 9.30 and 11 p.m.

"The following note appears at the end of the manuscript received from the light-keeper at Phillipsburg:—

"'During this storm I also observed and noted the lowest fall (*sic*) of a Dutch barometer in my possession, which was 21 millimetres, its standard (? reading before the advent of the storm) was 763 millimetres, and at 9.30 p.m. it registered 742 millimetres.'"

A SHORT NOTE ON EARTH TEMPERATURE OBSERVATIONS.

By G. J. SYMONS, F.R.S., Secretary.

[Read November 15, 1899.]

During a hot week in July last I made a few extra readings with a pair of thermometers, of which the bulbs were 1 foot below the surface of the ground, with the view to ascertaining (1) the influence of slight shade, (2) the amount of daily range, and (3) the approximate curve of daily fluctuation.

I wish it to be understood that I had not time to undertake a complete investigation, and that I submit this note, not as settling any of these points, but solely with the view of calling attention to them.

The thermometers were not standard instruments, but, on testing them with my Kew Standard, I found that there was no error near the temperature concerned (60° to 70°) of 0°·2, therefore no correction has been applied. They were of the ordinary pattern, insulated, mounted on short wooden rods, and dropped into wrought-iron tubes with caps. One thermometer was sunk in a grass plot fully exposed to the sun, except late in the evening, this is regarded as the standard. The other was sunk in garden mould, north-west of some plants of rhubarb, and was, during most of the day, somewhat shaded by the leaves, but not surrounded by them.

Table I. gives the actual readings.

TABLE I.—Readings of Thermometers 1 Foot below Surface.

July	Exposed Thermometer.									Sheltered Thermometer.								
	7	8	9	10	11	12	13	14	15	7	8	9	10	11	12	13	14	15
	°	°	°	°	°	°	°	°	°	°	°	°	°	°	°			°
Midn.		68·1							68·9		65·5							67·1
1 a.m.																		
2 ,,																		
3 ,,																		
4 ,,																		
5 ,,																		
6 ,,																		
7 ,,																		
8 ,,																		
9 ,,	64·1	66·5	67·1	67·9	67·1	68·7	67·7	67·0	66·9	63·0	65·0	66·0	66·6	66·1	67·4	66·9	66·3	66·0
10 ,,		66·3					67·5	67·0	66·9		65·0					66·9	66·3	66·0
11 ,,		66·3				68·6		66·9	66·9		65·0				67·3		66·2	66·0
noon		66·4				68·8	67·5	67·0			65·0				67·3	66·9	66·2	
1 p.m.		66·6				68·7	67·6	67·1			65·1				67·4	66·9	66·2	
2 ,,		67·2			68·0	68·8	67·8	67·2			65·3			66·3	67·4	66·9	66·3	
3 ,,		67·1					68·0	67·4			65·4					67·0	66·4	
4 ,,					68·6	69·1	68·2	67·6						67·0	67·7	67·1	66·5	
5 ,,					68·9	69·1	68·4	67·8						67·1	67·9	67·2	66·7	
6 ,,																		
7 ,,	67·3									65·0								
8 ,,	67·5									65·2								
9 ,,	67·8	69·1			70·0		69·1	68·1		65·5	67·0			68·0		68·0	67·2	
10 ,,	68·0	69·3								65·5	67·0							
11 ,,	68·1	69·0			70·0	69·3	69·1			65·5	67·0			68·2	68·0	68·2		

Table II. gives the results of an attempt to deduce some inferences from them. In order to get rid of the influence of secular change, the entry under 9 a.m. is *not* the actual reading on each day, but the mean of the 9 a.m. readings on it and the subsequent one, and the amounts entered are the differences between the observed values and these means.

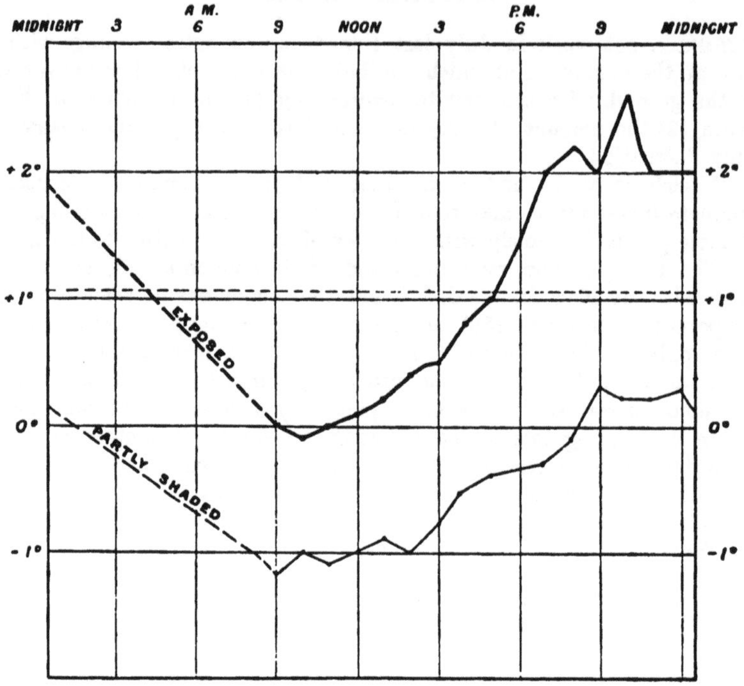

Approximate Curve of Temperature at 1 foot in Summer.

The mean differences for each hour, as given by this table, have been plotted on the diagram, and they seem to lead to the following conclusions :—

In hot summer weather, without rain, the temperature of a properly exposed 1-foot earth thermometer—

(1) is at its minimum about 10 a.m., and rises to its maximum about 10 p.m.

(2) the daily range is about 2°·5.

(3) the mean daily temperature line is crossed about 4 a.m. and about 5 p.m.

(4) the shadow of any adjacent leaves not merely halves the amount of the daily range, but reduces the temperature at all hours by from 1° to 1°·5.

With reference to (4), it would be interesting to know what occurs (*a*) under grass and (*b*) under bare soil.

From the foregoing it appears that 9 a.m. (the usual hour for reading earth thermometers) is very nearly the time of minimum. As in sunless winter weather there is probably no daily range, we may guess that its

TABLE II.—DIFFERENCES OF TEMPERATURES AT EACH HOUR FROM THE ADOPTED MEAN OF THE EXPOSED THERMOMETER AT 9 A.M.

EXPOSED THERMOMETER.

July . .	7	8	9	10	11	12	13	14	15	Mean
Adopted Mean for 9 a.m.	° 65·3	° 66·8	° 67·5	° 67·5	° 67·9	° 68·2	° 67·4	° 66·9	° 66·9	°
Midnight		+2·8							+1·1	+2·0
1 a.m.										
2 ,,										
3 ,,										
4 ,,										
5 ,,										
6 ,,										
7 ,,										
8 ,,										
9 ,,	−1·2	− ·3	−·4	+·4	− ·8	+ ·5	+ ·3	+ ·1	·0	− ·2
10 ,,		− ·5					+ ·1	+ ·	·0	− ·1
11 ,,		− ·5				+ ·4		·	·0	·0
Noon		− ·4				+ ·6	+ ·1	+ ·		+ ·1
1 p.m.		− ·2				+ ·5	+ ·2	+ ·		+ ·2
2 ,,		+ ·4			+ ·1	+ ·6	+ ·4	+ ·		+ ·4
3 ,,		+ ·3					+ ·6	+ ·		+ ·5
4 ,,					+ ·7	+ ·9	+ ·8	+ ·		+ ·8
5 ,,					+1·0	+ ·9	+1·0	+ ·		+1·0
6 ,,										
7 ,,	+2·0									+2·0
8 ,,	+2·2									+2·2
9 ,,	+2·5	+2·3			+2·1		+1·7	+1·2		+2·0
10 ,,	+2·7	+2·5								+2·6
11 ,,	+2·8	+2·2			+2·1	+1·1	+1·7			+2·0

SHELTERED THERMOMETER.

July . .	7	8	9	10	11	12	13	14	15	Mean
	°	°	°	°	°	°	°	°	°	°
Midnight		+·2							+·2	+·2
1 a.m.										
2 ,,										
3 ,,										
4 ,,										
5 ,,										
6 ,,										
7 ,,										
8 ,,										
9 ,,	−2·3	−1·8	−1·5	−·9	−1·8	−·8	−·5	−·6	−·9	−1·2
10 ,,		−1·8					−·5	−·6	−·9	−1·0
11 ,,		−1·8				−·9		−·7	−·9	−1·1
Noon		−1·8				−·9	−·5	−·7		−1·0
1 p.m.		−1·7				−·8	−·5	−·7		− ·9
2 ,,		−1·5			−1·6	−·8	−·5	−·6		−1·0
3 ,,		−1·4					−·4	−·5		− ·8
4 ,,					− ·9	−·5	−·3	−·4		− ·5
5 ,,					− ·8	−·3	−·2	−·2		− ·4
6 ,,										
7 ,,	− ·3									− ·3
8 ,,	− ·1									− ·1
9 ,,	+ ·2	+ ·2			+ ·1		+·6	+·3		+ ·3
10 ,,	+ ·2	+ ·2								+ ·2
11 ,,	+ ·2	+ ·2			+ ·3	−·2	+·8			+ ·3

average throughout the year is about 1°; if so, the means published are about half a degree below what they would be if based upon observations made hourly day and night.

I am conscious of the slender foundation upon which the above conclusions rest, but I do not remember seeing any determination of the daily temperature curve beneath the surface, and trust that this note may soon be supplanted by a better one.

P.S. Since writing the above note the author has found some records made towards the close of the great frost of 1895. As they tend to emphasise the importance of exposure, he briefly epitomizes the results. The thermometers were of the usual pattern, but each was in bare soil; one, north-east of buildings, had very little sun, and none after about 10 a.m., the other had practically all the sunshine that there was. The shaded one generally read about 1° lower, until rain set in, then both read alike. Later on, in April and May, when the north-east one had only the morning sun, and the other had it all day long, the latter exceeded the former by from 3° to 4°·5. This shows conclusively that, for strict comparison, the instruments must be fully exposed; and it also shows that we must not assume the subsoil temperature of a shaded street or court to be that shown by a thermometer at the same depth at a properly equipped meteorological station.

DISCUSSION.

The President (Mr. F. C. BAYARD) said the Society was indebted to Mr. Symons for his paper. There were many points of interest in it, some of which, however, had been solved by Mr. H. Mellish in his recent paper (*Quarterly Journal*, vol. xxv. p. 238).

Mr. E. MAWLEY said that Mr. Symons's short paper was very suggestive, and clearly indicated the importance of placing all earth thermometers in fully exposed positions if comparable results were to be obtained from them. The author inquired what occurs under grass and under bare soil? Now he (Mr. Mawley) happened to have in each of his percolation gauges an earth thermometer at the depth of 1 foot. The gauges in question, which are a yard square and a yard deep, contain the natural soil of the district, and have no vegetation growing on them. They are sunk in the ground nearly level with the surface of the same lawn, and have a similar exposure to the thermometer at 1 foot under grass. Taking the same 9 days in July last as the author had done, he found that at 9 a.m. the thermometer under the bare soil in the gauges read on an average 1°·3 higher than the one under grass. Consequently, had Mr. Symons' thermometers been either both under bare soil or under grass, the differences between the readings of the one exposed and that partly shaded would have come out even greater than shown in the diagram. A fortnight ago, at Mr. Bentley's suggestion, he had buried a Richard thermograph in the ground so that its bulb remained 1 foot beneath the surface and within a few feet of a 1-foot earth thermometer on the same lawn. For the past 13 days the mean daily range had been 1°·9, and the times of mean minimum and mean maximum 6 a.m. and 9 p.m. respectively. He had, however, reason to think that the tin box in which the thermograph was enclosed was larger than it should be, and that the few inches of air space above the thermograph caused the daily range to be greater than it otherwise would have been. He hoped to continue his experiments with the same instrument under more natural conditions, and to report to the Society at some future time the results he had obtained.

Mr. W. Marriott said that earth temperature observations formed an important item in the *Meteorological Record*, and in the number about to be published the tables of earth temperatures had been greatly extended. Great efforts were made to secure uniform observations; but apparently an idea had gone abroad that they were not so. In the *Hints to Meteorological Observers* directions were given for placing the instruments under grass; and at the inspection of the stations it was seen that these were complied with. Mr. Symons' instruments were not placed under similar conditions, one being under grass while the other was in bare soil. It would have been better for the comparison if two thermometers had been placed under grass and two in bare soil. It would also have been better if means had not been given in the tables, as for two hours they were based on only one observation, and this accounted for some of the irregularities in the curves. He (Mr. Marriott) had taken readings at Norwood of an earth thermometer at 1 foot both at 9 a.m. and 9 p.m. for over 21 years. The mean range of temperature from 9 a.m. to 9 p.m. for each month was as follows:—

Jan.	Feb.	Mar.	April.	May.	June.	July.	Aug.	Sept.	Oct.	Nov.	Dec.	Year.
0°·1	0°·3	0°·7	1°·1	1°·3	1°·3	1°·2	1°·1	0°·8	0°·4	0°·2	0°·1	0°·7

It would be an advantage to know how much grass should be put down to protect the thermometer, and whether the plot should be a few feet or 10, 20, or 30 feet square. At Greenwich the earth thermometers were under a wooden shelter or box, and were close to an asphalt path. It would be interesting to compare observations from instruments placed below long grass and short grass, also between grass thickly sown and lightly sown, and between thickly shaded and lightly shaded places. Mr. Marriott exhibited some lantern slides showing the exposure of the earth thermometers at several of the Society's stations.

Mr. B. Latham remarked that he also had buried a thermograph at 1 foot in the ground, but had registered a much greater range than Mr. Mawley; the range for one week in August being 5°. It was difficult to get good results, for although the instrument had been covered over with a plank, and over this an oil-cloth, the air filled up the empty space between the surface and the instrument. The thermograph showed that in August the highest temperature of the ground occurred about 6 p.m., and the lowest temperature about 8 a.m. For many years he had taken soil temperature observations, and had at work for over 20 years two registering thermometers which registered the maximum and minimum temperatures of the ground at 6 ins. in depth. On July 21 last a maximum temperature of 87°·1 was registered, and a minimum temperature of 72°·4, or a difference of 14°·7. It was an important thing to get earth temperature observations; but in his opinion it did not matter so much whether they were under grass or in bare soil, so long as the observations were regularly taken, and then they would be comparable from time to time.

Mr. E. D. Archibald remarked that the earth thermometer shaded by leaves, according to Mr. Symons, read 1° lower than that under open ground. This appeared to tally with Dr. Fernow's report on the results of thermometers suspended in the air in forests and those in the open.

It would be interesting to have more extended experiments undertaken in a similar way with earth thermometers.

It was possible that, apart from any immediate practical utility, such comparisons would throw fresh light on the as yet obscure physical problems in connection with the relative absorption of solar heat by the surface of the earth and the lowest layers of air. He thought Mr. Mawley's observations were of great value, and suggested that, in order to have closer comparisons at rapidly graduated depths, a shelf or row of shelves might be cut out of the ground, thermometers placed therein, and insulation and access afforded by a movable block of earth as a cover.

Dr. R. H. Scott said that at the forest observing stations in Germany, such as those started by Prof. Ebermayer in Bavaria and by Prof. Müttrich in North Germany, the system had been to establish pairs of stations, one in the forest and the other in adjacent cleared farm-land. At these stations comparative observations of, *inter alia*, earth temperature were systematically carried out, and the results regularly printed.

Mr. G. J. Symons, in reply, stated that he had attained his object in having placed upon record various remarks by the Fellows present. He had no intention of teaching anything, and was glad to find that continuous observations of underground temperature had been started, and that more would follow. Mr. Marriott's figures at Norwood agreed very closely with what the paper indicated as probable, but threw little light upon the form of the daily curve

---

Air Currents in Thunderstorms.—It is well known that in general a thundercloud is fed by currents of air flowing toward its centre with a gentle ascending gradient that becomes very steep within the cloud itself. But the descending rain, both by cooling the air through which it falls and by driving it downward, causes an outward wind near the ground and near the centre of the thunderstorm. On August 5, 1899, Mr. Wm. A. Eddy, of Bayonne, N.J., sent up a small hot-air balloon at 4.15 p.m. as a heavy thunderstorm was approaching. After ascending vertically for 100 feet it was caught in the current that swept it toward the centre of the storm, and at the same time it rose until it was fully 2000 feet above the earth and finally penetrated the cloud with falling rain. It was then driven downward and backward until it reached a point on the earth quite near its starting-point. Two other similar experiments with the same results had been made by Mr. Eddy on July 22 and 27.

This is an interesting method of studying the currents of air in the atmosphere. It may not be wholly new, but it is well worthy of frequent repetition.—*U.S. Monthly Weather Review.*

NOTE OF A REMARKABLE DUST HAZE EXPERIENCED AT TENERIFFE, CANARY ISLANDS, FEBRUARY 1898.

By ROBERT H. SCOTT, D.Sc., F.R.S.

[Read December 20, 1899.]

From February 16 to 19, 1898, there was a remarkable prevalence of fine dust in the air over the Canary Islands, and the following notes and observations of the phenomena, which were made by Mr. A. Samler Brown near Santa Cruz, Teneriffe, on the southern side of the island, at 25 feet above the sea, have been sent by him to the Meteorological Office.

Since, however, these observations are an interesting and fairly complete record of the phenomena connected with the dust haze over the Atlantic, as observed at a single station, it seems desirable to place them within the reach of meteorologists generally, and the following note has accordingly been prepared.

At the time in question the body of dust-laden air extended over a very large area. Thus, at 4 p.m. on February 17 the SS. *La Plata*, outward bound to Brazil, being in lat. 29° 43′ N., long. 15° 23′ W., reports: "Thick fog of fine sand, ship coated with fine light brown sand"; while at 8 a.m. on the same day, in approximately lat. 6° 8′ N., long. 13° 14′ W., the R.M.S. *Norman* reported "Hazy weather," and at 4 p.m. "Thick mist," both "haze" and "mist" being probably due to the presence of dust in the air. At 10 p.m., however, in about lat. 9° 22′ N., long. 15° 22′ W., there can be no question on the point, for the entry is made: "Air laden with fine dust." The consequent obscuration was so great that the lead was kept going all night.

How far the dust cloud extended across the Atlantic it is difficult to say, but at noon on the same day, in lat. 24° 58′ N., long. 24° 31′ W., the ship *Loch Torridon*, bound to Adelaide, reported "Hazy on horizon," which may very likely have been the western edge of the cloud.

For a distance, therefore, of some 1500 miles from north to south, with great extension to the westward, and probably also to the eastward, solid matter in a finely divided form was diffused through the atmosphere.

The haze during this period was exceptionally dense—so much so that a German steamer, the *Carl Woerman*, was two days and three nights on the voyage from Teneriffe to Las Palmas, a distance she usually covered in five hours; while the *Tintagel Castle* of the Donald Currie Line was delayed for thirty hours, and the *Roslin Castle*, homeward bound, had the dust so thick that for 900 miles the sun and stars were obscured and the ship was delayed two days.[1]

[1] Capt. Maloney of the *Briton* states that he entered the dust storm about 80 miles south of Madeira, and was in it for a distance of between 1800 and 1900 miles. He was without observations for a distance of about 2000 miles, because not only was the weather thick, but the red particles of sand were as fine and light as air—so fine that it was impossible to sweep them up on the ship. After being on the bridge for an hour and a half, the officers' clothing was perfectly red. The weather was thick, night and day, and there was no horizon, so that he had to go over 2000 miles on a dead reckoning. He did not emerge from the dust until getting between 400 and 500 miles south of Cape de Verde.

The course of the Cape boats is too well known to need description. For determining the north and south boundaries of the dust storm the details given by Capt. Maloney seem the most definite. It is also of interest to know that the dust was so very fine all along the

The preceding note has been drawn up by Mr. J. A. Curtis, F.R.Met.Soc.

Mr. Brown's memoranda are as follow :—

February 14.—Sky clear, but view obstructed by the usual haze attending a South wind. The South wind (Viento del Sur, or Levante) is invariably accompanied by this haze. At such times the Peak is visible from all parts of the island, but would not be represented on a sensitised plate, even from a comparatively short distance. Such haze may perhaps always be accompanied by dust. If so, the dust is not always perceptible.

February 15.—About mid-day there was a slight shower of rain, evidently arising from abnormal conditions which I did not take sufficient notice of to describe. During the afternoon the wind rose almost to a gale, and during the night the alternate hot gusts (which shook the house) and calms were almost terrifying. During the night the sky became obscured.

February 16.—Morning broke with a high white fog extending on all sides and obscuring the hills and sea. Objects at a greater distance than a mile could not be seen even indistinctly. As the day went on, the fog grew worse, until long before mid-day we could not see anything at all for a greater distance than 150 yards. Up till about 11 a.m. the sun could be seen like a white silver ball (or, according to the eyesight of others, of a greenish colour), but presently it disappeared altogether, and, except on one occasion for a few moments, we saw it no more for nearly two days.

In the afternoon the wind had fallen entirely, and the waves, which were accompanied by a considerable ground swell, rolled out of nothing, as it were, and burst upon the beach. The horizon at this time was very limited.

By the evening the descent of a fine dust became very noticeable—at first white, and then, when a certain quantity had accumulated, of a sandy red colour. Everything, inside the house and out, was covered; and, if a looking-glass were cleaned, you could write your name upon it in less than half-an-hour's time.

At 8.30 p.m. I collected some dust on a piece of clean paper covered with white of egg. The breeze at the time was slight, all traffic was suspended, and the only foreign substances which may have reached the paper were insects such as moths and gnats, and possibly some pollen from an Austrian pine. Many of the insects were of species not commonly found on the islands.

During the evening and night there was a strong smell as of a smoking lamp or burning candle grease. My wife and I, on separate occasions, and without reference to each other, went round the house to try and discover the cause.

The observations during the evening were :—

	Barometer. ins.	Dry-bulb. °	Wet-bulb. °	Rel. Hum. %
5.30 p.m.	30·09	66·0	55·0	48
7.30 p.m.	30·10	66·0	54·5	47
9 p.m.	30·10	66·0	51·5	39
10.15 p.m.	30·10	65·8	50·8	36

The minimum temperature during the night (16th-17th) was 61°.

February 17.—The morning broke with the fog thicker than the day before, and almost windless. The dust still appeared white, but was now thick enough to alter the appearance of the landscape still to be seen—trees, flowers, rocks, leaves, etc. appearing dull in colour, but not losing their hues entirely.

course kept. I was led to believe that it was much coarser nearer the African coast. Indeed, one captain told me that he threw it overboard by the shovelful, but a friend told me that in Bathurst, River Gambia, it was very fine.—A. S. Brown.

During part of the morning the fog cleared a little, and the sun could be seen. Later on it thickened again, but cleared by 10 p.m. enough to render a few stars visible.

The dust fell so straight that articles were stencilled out on the furniture; a comb, for instance, being reproduced as it would be by direct sunlight upon sensitised paper, with unblurred edges. If a looking-glass were cleaned and turned face upwards, in half-an-hour's time it was possible to collect, with one sweep of a piece of cotton wool, enough dust to show the colour, which was of a reddish yellow.

The number of moths about was so great that in Santa Cruz, at a place where the electric light fell on a white wall, the surface of the wall was speckled with them. Afterwards I found a mole-cricket in the garden, which it is practically certain was carried there by the storm. I also caught a large moth on the roof, which unfortunately I released. The fact that it made a sort of barking noise, audible at twenty yards' distance, may help to locate the centre of the storm area, if the species can be identified by this fact.

	Barometer. ins.	Dry-bulb. °	Wet-bulb. °	Rel. Hum. %
3 a.m.	...	63·0	49·0	38
8.15 a.m.	30·13	63·5	53·0	49
3 p.m.	30·08	69·0	63·0	68
4 p.m.	30·09	67·5	62·5	73
7 p.m.	30·11	65·0	61·5	81
9 p.m.	30·10	65·5	61·3	77
11.30 p.m.	30·11	63·0	58·3	74

Minimum temperature during the night (17th-18th), 59°·3.

February 18.—Morning brighter, dust still falling, but smell of burning less perceptible. About 10 a.m. the sun cast a shadow for the first time since the arrival of the fog. It then disappeared, but as clouds became partially visible it is probable that it was not hidden by the fog itself. After mid-day, however, the fog did thicken again, being much denser than when the stars were visible the night before. At 10 p.m. no stars could be seen.

	Barometer. ins.	Dry-bulb. °	Wet-bulb. °	Rel. Hum. %
9 a.m.	30·13	64·3	58·3	68
10 a.m.	30·13	66·8	59·3	62
4 p.m.	30·13	65·3	60·3	73
6.30 p.m.	30·10	64·5	58·5	68

Minimum temperature during night (18th-19th), 57°·5.

February 19.—Much clearer; hills three miles away visible, but still hazy. By mid-day the sun was shining brightly, and as the evening went on the fog entirely disappeared, the sky being partially clouded.

	Barometer. ins.	Dry-bulb. °	Wet-bulb. °	Rel. Hum. %
9 a.m.	30·15	65·5	53·3	44
Noon.	30·13	68·8	57·5	49
2.30 p.m.	30·13	68·3	58·0	51
9 p.m.	30·20	62·5	54·8	59

Minimum temperature during night (18th-20th), 58°. Maximum on 19th, 69°.

February 20.—The morning was quite clear, and the weather had become normal.

	Barometer. ins.	Dry-bulb. °	Wet-bulb. °	Rel. Hum. %
8 a.m.	30·17	64·0	54·5	53
10.30 a.m.	30·21	67·5	55·5	47
0.45 p.m.	30·18	68·0	57·3	50
5 p.m.	30·14	64·0	55·0	55
9.30 p.m.	30·20	62·0	54·3	59

At 9.30 p.m. a few drops of rain fell. Maximum temperature, 68°. Minimum during night (20th-21st), 54°·5.

February 21.—Morning bright and very clear. Sun very hot. Grand Canary, 50 miles distant, very clearly visible. Cumuli clouds.

	Barometer.	Dry-bulb.	Wet-bulb.	Rel. Hum.
	ins.	°	°	%
10.30 a.m.	30·17	65·8	54·5	48
2.45 p.m.	30·11	67·0	55·3	47

[NOTE.—I see that Mr. Perry of Puerto Orotava says that the sun was blue. Curiously enough, two observers in Madeira persist in declaring that it was red, as is the case in a London fog.

It may interest readers to know that the ss. *Flachat* was wrecked on Anaga Point, Teneriffe, the night before the fog (February 15-16), and that many of the survivors, who managed to clamber up the rocks, were lost in the mountains for some days. The death-like stillness and the uncanny state of the atmosphere during this period, following on the alarm of the wreck, was a most terrifying experience to these unfortunate people.—A. S. BROWN.]

Three specimens of the dust were collected by Mr. Brown, and accompany his original notes.

Mr. Alfred Perry, of Sitiò de Cullen, Puerto Orotava, has kept a Meteorological Register for many years, and the following extracts from his Reports will be of interest:—

METEOROLOGICAL OBSERVATIONS AT PUERTO OROTAVA, TENERIFFE, FEBRUARY 14-20, 1898.

64 FEET ABOVE MEAN SEA-LEVEL.

DAY.	Barometer at Mean Sea-Level.		Air Temperature.				Humidity.					
							Dep. of Wet.		Vapour Tension.		Percentage.	
	9 a.m.	9 p.m.	9 a.m.	9 p.m.	Min.	Max.	9 a.m.	9 p.m.	9 a.m.	9 p.m.	9 a.m.	9 p.m.
	ins.	ins.	°	°	°	°	°	°	in.	in.	%	%
14	30·23	30·19	63·6	59·0	57·2	67·7	3·0	2·2	·485	·430	83	87
15	30·16	30·05	60·0	63·3	57·3	67·3	4·8	2·0	·374	·512	72	88
16	29·96	30·01	66·0	63·0	58·9	68·8	12·2	3·9	·288	·446	44	78
17	30·09	30·08	63·0	60·3	57·3	65·0	3·4	3·5	·462	·413	80	80
18	30·10	30·09	63·7	60·8	58·0	67·4	4·0	2·5	·457	·452	77	85
19	30·09	30·15	62·5	60·3	55·4	69·6	5·3	4·0	·399	·399	70	77
20	30·16	30·14	64·8	59·1	53·2	70·0	6·1	4·2	·413	·376	68	75

DAY.	Wind Direction and Force.				Cloud Amount.		Rain.	REMARKS.
	9 a.m.		9 p.m.		9 a.m.	9 p.m.	9 a.m.	
							in.	
14	NE	2	S	1	8	3	·06	⊙° in night.
15	S	1	NE	5	10	10	...	⊙° in night and during day.
16	SE	6	Calm	0	10	10	...	Strong "South" weather.
17	Calm	0	Calm	0	10	10	...	See below.
18	S	1	Calm	0	10	10	·02	⊙° shower in night. ≡ not so thick.
19	S	1	NE	1	4	4	...	≡ cleared at noon.
20	NE	1	S	1	5	8	...	Great visibility.

17th.—A dust haze amounting to fog. Dust fell very heavily. It was a very fine brown dust. The sun was also a perfect blue ball.

THE CLIMATIC CONDITIONS NECESSARY FOR THE PROPAGATION AND SPREAD OF PLAGUE.

By BALDWIN LATHAM, M.Inst.C.E., M.Inst.M.E., F.G.S., F.S.S., F.R.Met.Soc., F.S.I., etc.

(Plate I.)

[Read December 20, 1899.]

THE outbreak of bubonic plague which occurred in Hong-Kong in 1894 and in India in 1896, its continuance in these places, and its spread to other localities, even into Europe, show how necessary it is that the climatic conditions necessary for the development and the abatement of the plague should be thoroughly examined.

Plague is a very ancient disease, and past experience shows that it is the most fatal of all epidemic diseases. For a period of probably over 1300 years, plague at times used to ravage this country. The last recorded indigenous deaths from plague in London occurred in the year 1697; and in the year 1704 plague as a cause of death was removed from the London bills of mortality. In the year 1720 the city of Marseilles was grievously afflicted with plague, and lost by that outbreak, it is stated, 60,000 of its inhabitants. Plague also affected Toulon, Aix, and Arles in 1720. It is calculated that one-third of the population in those places died, and that in the district of Provence, out of a population of 247,899, there were 87,659 who died of plague.[1] The plague, it is reported, left Europe in the year 1841, and has not been since recorded until its recent return to Oporto in the present year. Like cholera, enteric or typhoid fever, yellow fever, and some other diseases, it has been looked upon as a soil poison, or a poison which evidently undergoes preparation in the soil to fit it for its deadly course.

Dr. Pariset, a French doctor, expounded the view that plague was due to a soil poison generated from decomposing bodies in a soil periodically saturated with water; and Dr. Charles Creighton gives numerous examples of a similar state of things in his work *A History of Epidemics in Britain.*

It may be taken for granted that the bubonic plague is primarily due to a specific organism or microbe of infinitesimal size—so small that probably 250 millions of them would be required to cover a square inch of surface; and they are so light as to be easily carried by the air or vapour of water. The cause of plague being due to living organisms is clearly set out in the writings at the time of the Great Plague of London; for the *City Remembrancer* (which is said to be the notes of Dr. Gideon Harvey, His Majesty's Physician to the Tower, who lived in the time of the Great Plague, and was Physician in Ordinary to Charles II. in his exile) mentions [2]:—

[1] Bascome's *History of Epidemic Pestilences*, p. 122.
[2] *City Remembrancer*, vol. i. pp. 128-129.

"There is great reason to believe that most epidemical distempers mankind is subject to proceed from poisonous insects of that extraordinary smallness that they are not to be discovered by the naked eye; so light that they float in the air, and so are sucked into the stomach by the breath; such insects not being among us commonly, but only when they are brought to us from some remote place by the wind, or in goods hatched or nourished by some intemperance of the air, or from poisonous vapours rising from bogs, ponds, ditches, or some such unwholesome funds of stagnated water."

That plague is conveyed by human intercourse and in other ways, there can be no doubt; and there can also be little doubt that it is infectious and contagious, and that it is greatly influenced by pestilential emanations from polluted and water-logged soils. Dr. Rugoel is quoted, in a publication by the Government of India on the plague in India, to say of the plague, that a "fomite without pestilential atmosphere is insufficient for the production of the disease, which atmosphere approaches by slow, silent and imperceptible degrees, no human barrier being able to oppose its progress." [1]

Plague is produced by a combination of circumstances or conditions, the first being the presence of the germ, and the second the conditions necessary for its development and distribution. In districts in which the conditions for its development and conveyance are absent, the disease can make no headway. The conditions in which plague germs live and die appear to be local and controllable.

"The plague is reckoned an exotic disease, never bred in England, always imported, particularly from the Levant, the coasts of Africa, the lesser Egypt, etc., where it is familiar." [2]

In every country, the period of the year or the season has an influence in staying or in promoting and spreading the ravages of the disease. The contagious principle is exhaled in greater quantity and is more virulent under certain meteorological conditions which seem to be ascertainable.

The fact of simple contagion or infection will not explain the propagation of epidemics. This was clearly pointed out by the late Dr. Farr,[3] where he mentions that "the facilities of intercourse, and the frequency of contact with the sick, are not greater when the disease is increasing, or is at its height, than when it is stationary or declining."

Sydenham says: "The particular seasons of the year which favour particular complaints are carefully to be observed. I am ready to grant that many diseases are good for all seasons. On the other hand, there is an equal number that, through some mysterious instinct of nature, follow the seasons as truly as plants and birds of passage." [4]

Speaking of plague, the same author said:—

"If the changes and the seasons of the year had nothing to do with the character of the disease in question—if the pestilential virus, unmodified by atmospheric variations, were transmitted from man to man by a continuous series of propagations, it would of necessity follow that, from the very moment that the plague had found its way into some populous city, deaths would succeed deaths in one continuous and indefinite series, until at last no one would be left upon whom the murderous *miasma* might fasten itself. But it has been

[1] *Government of India—Plague in India*, 1896, 1897, R. Nathan, vol. ii. p. 76.
[2] *The City Remembrancer*, vol. i. pp. 32-33.
[3] *Second Annual Report of Registrar-General*, p. 94.
[4] *Works of Thomas Sydenham*, vol. i. pp. 14-15.

observed that the contrary to this has often taken place. The number of dead that in the single month of September amounted to some thousands, by the end of November diminished and was reduced to almost nothing."[1]

The conditions that lead to the rise and fall of the plague in any country in which it has established itself show such a marked periodicity that it cannot be accounted for on any supposition of infection or contagion; but while it is admitted that plague is due to a specific microbe, it cannot spread except under certain meteorological conditions associated with the conditions of the ground, which must be in such a state as to exhale what is necessary for the propagation and spread of this particular disease.

Certain conditions of the soil and the water in the soil are necessary for the development of plague and other diseases, such as a high degree of pollution combined with certain hygrometric conditions. Some authorities are of opinion that it is greatly augmented by a cadaverous poison[2] in the soil, due to the presence of dead bodies and to refuse from slaughter-houses. Plague, like most soil poisons, may be disseminated in various ways, by air, water, food, or by direct inoculation; but certain climatic conditions are necessary for its development and spread as an epidemic, as will be clearly shown. If any one of the conditions necessary for its development is absent, the disease cannot become epidemic or even spread to a great extent. In the supplement to the *Ninth Report of the Local Government Board*, quoting the paper of Surgeon-General Francis, it is stated that "the concurrent existence of these several epidemics seems to show that the general meteorological conditions were such as to call into action the operation of influences peculiar to each locality: malarious fevers in one, yellow fever in another, typhus in a third, and plague in a fourth."

Plague is undoubtedly a disease of the poor, and attacks most readily those living on a low diet. This was observed by the medical writers who lived in the time of the Great Plague of 1665; and Dr. Nath. Hodges, who wrote on the plague, points out that there is an affinity between the plague and the scurvy, a disease which is known to be greatly influenced by diet, as he says: "The affinity between a pestilence and a scurvy is not a slight and supposititious conjecture."[3]

It has been observed that plague will destroy a vast number of persons in a certain season, and at another time will only seize here and there a person and go no further. It will also be noted that the deaths from plague, remittent fever, and diseases of the respiratory system, other than phthisis, and phthisis itself, follow each other in parallel lines. The sanitary measures which have been carried out in places like Bombay, and which appear to have had no effect whatever on the three epidemics which have already occurred, will sooner or later, if persevered in, influence the result, as it takes years for the pure rain from heaven to wash the soil to the great depths to which it has been polluted in such cities. Unfortunately, throughout India, there have been no percolation experiments made, with the view of determining what proportion of the rain which falls really passes through the soil.

[1] *Works of Thomas Sydenham*, vol. i. pp. 100-101.
[2] *A History of Epidemics in Britain*, by Dr. Creighton, vol. i. p. 162.
[3] *Loimologia*, p. 80.

This is a point of the utmost importance to be observed in all countries, especially in those subject to malarial fevers and other epidemic diseases.[1]

The regular periodicity of plague is one of its marked features; that is, in a particular country, it usually rises to its height at a particular period of the year, and always at the same period in the same place; and in different countries the period when this maximum of the disease is reached differs considerably. This is a fact which appears to have been well known at the time of the Great Plague, for in the *City Remembrancer* it is stated that: "The plague annually visits some nations, but the time of its first appearance differs in proportion to their distance from the Equator; those who are most remote have it latest, and are most free, because the cold air, which abounds with nitre, will always check its fury; those nearer have it longer, because the heat and moisture continue many more months."[2] If it had been added that the elevation of a place, which affects its temperature, also influenced plague, it also would have been a correct statement to make, as the mean temperature of places diminishes as they recede northward or southward from the Equator, and also with the elevation above the sea-level; moreover, the temperature of the ground, which will be shown to be a most material agency in the propagation and diffusion of plague, is also governed by the geographical position of the place. It should be said, however, that the early writers on the plague had observed the fact that houses in valleys are much more liable to contagion than those situated upon eminences.[3]

The same author has also drawn attention to the immunity of foreigners in India to the attacks of the plague, for he says:—

> "It is a common observation, that famine is often succeeded by pestilence; and that this calamity generally begins among the poor, whose food is the worst. Indeed, it has hardly been ever known when the distemper did not begin among the poor."—"Surat, in the East Indies, is seldom free from plague, yet foreigners who trade there are in no danger. The inhabitants neither eat flesh nor drink wine, live very poorly, on herbs, rice, water, etc. This fare, with the heat of the climate, makes them liable to malignant distempers, from which those who feed well are more secure."[4]

This statement is exactly in accord with the modern experience in the recent outbreaks of plague in Hong-Kong and in India.

The marked periodicity of plague is so striking, and the evidence of this periodicity recurring regularly is so abundant, that the disease must be due to some specific cause which enables its incidence to rise and fall at regular times. When this country was subject to epidemics of plague, it usually arrived at its maximum destructive power about the months of August or September. In Bombay, the three epidemics which have occurred in the last three years show that the disease arrived at its maximum destructive power in the months of February or March. As an example, which can be multiplied to any extent, I may say that the first bill of mortality extant in this country is that for London for the year 1563, which will be found in Stowe's *Memoranda*,

[1] The author has repeatedly drawn the attention of engineers in India at the time of his inspections to the importance of having percolating gauges set up, but hitherto without success.

[2] *City Remembrancer*, vol. i. p. 82. [3] *Ibid.*, vol. i. p. 90. [4] *Ibid.*, vol. i. pp. 84-85.

published by the Camden Society. In that year the maximum number of deaths are reported to have taken place in the week ending October 1, when 1828 deaths occurred from plague. This time, having regard to the alteration in the Calendar, would now be represented by the middle of October. The average weekly mortalities were more in September than in October, namely 1351 in September, and 1165 in October. The following figures give the deaths from plague in London in this outbreak:—

		No. of Deaths.			No. of Deaths.
1563	June	22	1564	January	24
,,	July	112	,,	February	19
,,	August	596	,,	March	6
,,	September	1351	,,	April	4
,,	October	1165	,,	May	3
,,	November	363	,,	June	2
,,	December	184			

The next bills of mortality, which are extant, are in the Marquis of Salisbury's Library at Hatfield, and are for the years 1578 to 1582. From these it appears that in 1578, according to present reckoning, the disease was at its highest at the end of September; in 1579 at the end of August; in 1580 in the middle of June, but the attack was very slight in this particular year; in 1581 in the middle of September; and in 1582 in the middle of October. The details of these bills are given in Dr. Creighton's *History of Epidemics in Britain*.[1] A collection of the London bills of mortality, commencing with the year 1592, and containing bills for several of the epidemic years of plague, has been published, from which it will be seen that the incidence of the disease was the same in all the great outbreaks.[2]

In the *Health of Towns Commission Report*, vol. i. p. 262, the mortality from plague in seventeen parishes of York is given for the year 1604, and is as follows:—

	No. of Deaths.		No. of Deaths.
June	53	October	115
July	249	November	93
August	638	December	45
September	793		

It is shown that the sweating sickness of 1551 and the cholera of 1832 had nearly the same incidence in York as the plague of 1604.

In the Great Plague of London of 1665, the largest number of plague burials occurred about the beginning of September, according to our reckoning of time, when 7165 deaths are recorded in one week; but we know that these figures in the bills of mortality do not express the full force with which this disease visited London. The following figures give the average weekly deaths from plague in London for the year 1665:—

January	0	July	1032
February	¼	August	3809
March	0	September	6558
April	½	October	2875
May	9	November	862
June	148	December	244

The disease appears to have commenced in May, to have risen rapidly in June, July, and August, and subsided from October to the end of the year.

[1] *History of Epidemics in Britain*, vol. i. pp. 341-344.

[2] A collection of the yearly Bills of Mortality for London, published in 1759.

In Colchester, in 1665, the plague arrived at its maximum near the end of September, when the maximum deaths were about 143 per week, and declined to 29 per week in the following January, after which the disease again increased and reached its maximum of 153 per week in July 1666, and fell early in December to an average of 1 per week.

In Marseilles, in the great epidemic of 1720, it was reported in May that plague was rife in Palestine and Syria. Before the end of June ships had arrived from those countries at Marseilles, and several deaths had occurred amongst those connected with the shipping from those parts. It was not until July 9, however, that an indigenous case of plague was discovered in the city, from which time the pestilence spread with such great rapidity, that on August 23 it was stated that a thousand persons died per day, and that on the 28th of that month the plague had redoubled its ravages. From that time the plague began to decline; early in October it was reported that several persons in the hospitals had recovered from the plague—which appears to have been unusual in that outbreak—and by December there were no fresh plague cases.

In Bombay City, in the first epidemic, the largest number of plague deaths, 845, is reported to have occurred in the week ending Feb. 16, 1897.

In the second epidemic in 1898, the largest number of plague deaths occurred in the week ending March 8, when there were 1283 deaths.

In the third epidemic, the largest number of plague deaths occurred in the week ending March 21, 1899, when there were 1128 deaths.[1]

There was an increase in the general death-rate in deaths from remittent fever and deaths from respiratory diseases, other than phthisis; and in August, September, and October 1898 there was a similar recrudescence of disease. It will be hereafter seen that the climatic conditions accompanying these recurrences are the same as occur in the general outbreaks of the plague epidemics.

It should be noted that after the commencement of the plague there was a considerable exodus of the population from the city of Bombay, and this has lessened the mortality; for it was estimated that in February 1897 the population of the city did not exceed 450,000, whereas the population at the census of 1891 was 821,764. At the present time the population is very much over-estimated, thereby making the city apparently much healthier than it really is.

In the supplement to the *Ninth Report of the Local Government Board* there is an extract from Surgeon A. R. Lynch's journal for H.M.S. *Mosquito*, on the China Station, 1879, in which he says, referring to the plague endemic at Pakhoi: "The disease first makes its appearance in the month of May, and continues till September. It is *always* preceded by a similar epidemic among the lower animals, and the general opinion of the Chinese is, that it is due to some heavy earthy effluvia, which attacks animals inversely as their respiratory organs are elevated from the ground. Thus rats are first impregnated with the poison, then pigs, dogs, cattle, and ponies. This preliminary illness among the lower animals is so premonitory, that all who can afford to leave look on it as a warning for them to change their residence."[2]

[1] In 1900 the largest number of weekly plague deaths was 780, which occurred in the week ending 20th March.

[2] *Supplement to Ninth Report of Local Government Board*, p. 48.

The following table [1] will show the average weekly births and deaths in Bombay City from September 1896 to the present time:—

AVERAGE WEEKLY BIRTHS AND DEATHS, CITY OF BOMBAY.

Months.	Births.*	Total. Deaths.	Plague. Deaths.	Remittent Fever. Deaths.	Respiratory Diseases. Deaths.
1896					
September	327	649	18	157	91
October	291	682	77	164	102
November	269	689	64	134	112
December	326	1280	222	280	156
1897					
January	177	1707	400	406	252
February	76	1736†	721	341	203
March	78	1270	543	201	116
April	90	871	321	99	104
May	130	571	91	61	93
June	217	533	25	70	95
July	216	644	9	100	112
August	221	939	17	143	147
September	209	851	39	140	152
October	230	764	41	109	138
November	244	706	56	76	136
December	263	825	134	76	137
1898					
January	280	1409	559	61	228
February	214	2027	1095	81	245
March	146	2121†	1135	96	268
April	135	1285	556	74	192
May	139	687	139	68	130
June	180	494	35	61	94
July	198	529	56	53	100
August	222	718	114	58	128
September	254	826	155	76	138
October	251	883	186	72	140
November	243	625	55	65	127
December	270	727	97	83	144
1899					
January	228	1259	336	92	226
February	182	1894	759	132	288
March	176	2360†	1086	161	266
April	145	1629	633	107	178
May	152	975	247	83	134
June	146	563	56	46	107
July	180	542	57	41	83
August	213	653	74	55	99
September	226	667	90	66	96
October	248	780	100	93	131
November	229	869	102	96	160
December	280	1321	214	128	222

* The births before the plague made its appearance in Bombay averaged over 300 per week; during the year 1899 they averaged 196 per week, indicating a very much smaller population at the reproductive ages.

† The period of maximum deaths in the epidemic of 1899-1900 occurred in the week ending 27th February, when 2831 deaths were recorded.

[1] This table has been principally derived from the published statements recorded in the weekly issues of the *Times of India* and *Bombay Gazette*, as I have been unable to get the information from the local authorities of Bombay City, although I have made repeated application. The attention of Lieut.-Col. T. S. Weir, Medical Officer of Health of the City of Bombay, was drawn to the purport of this paper so long since as March 1898.

The death of the rats from the plague is one of the signs that they get their infection from the soil, as they have the greatest opportunity of getting directly the contagion, from their habit of life, burrowing as they do in the soil in the places afflicted with plague. It has been observed both in Hong-Kong, Bombay, and other places, that dead rats are invariably found before a general outbreak of plague, and in this respect the information they convey does not differ from that which has been known centuries ago with regard to the outbreak of plague in other places.

In the *Parliamentary Paper* for August 1894, it is stated that "in Dr. Sharp Deane's report on the health of Pakhoi I observe the following statement: 'The Chinese are of opinion that the bubonic plague emanates from the ground, and is favoured by a long continuance of dry weather, when the earth becomes porous and numerous fissures appear on the surface, facilitating the escape of whatever causes the disease.'"[1]

Skene, in his *Edinburgh Essay on Plague*, in 1568, gives as a sign of impending plague "the moles and serpents leaving their holes, as when the moudewart and serpent leavis the eird beand molestit be the vapore contenit within the bowells of the samin." He adds: "If the domesticall fowls become pestilential, it is ane signe of maist dangerous pest to follow."[2]

Thomas Lodge, who wrote upon the London plague of 1603, says: "And when as rats, moules, and other creatures (accustomed to live underground) forsake their holes and habitations, it is a token of corruption in the same, by reason that such sorts of creatures forsake their wonted places of aboade."[3]

Dr. Hodges, who lived in the time of the Great Plague of 1665, says: "That subterraneous animals such as moles, mice, serpents, conies, foxes, etc., as conscious of approaching mischief, leave their burrows and lie open in the air, which is also a certain sign of a pestilence at hand."[4]

Père Fenouil, missionary of Yünnan, says, "that not only human beings, but domestic animals and even rats are attacked by the pestilence," and that "the plague is really a pestilential emanation slowly rising in an equable stratum from the ground, and as it increases in depth all animals are, as it were, drowned in its poisonous flood.[5]

In the *City Remembrancer* it is stated that "Mr. Boyle attributes plague principally to the effluvia or exhalations from noxious minerals"[6]; and Sydenham says, with regard to epidemic diseases: "There are different conditions in different years. They originate neither in their heat nor in their cold, their wet or their drought; but they depend upon certain hidden and inexplicable changes within the bowels of the earth. By the effluvia from these the atmosphere becomes contaminate, and the bodies of men are predisposed and determined, as the case may be, to this or that complaint."[7]

1 *Parliamentary Paper*, C7545, Aug. 1894, p. 5.
2 *A History of Epidemics in Britain*, by Charles Creighton, M.A., M.D., vol. i. p. 173, footnote.
3 *A History of Epidemics in Britain*, by Charles Creighton, M.A., M.D., vol. i. p. 173.
4 *Loimologia*, p. 42.
5 *Parliamentary Paper on Plague*, 1879, C2262.
6 *City Remembrancer*, vol. i. p. 95.
7 *Works of Thomas Sydenham*, Sydenham Society, vol. i. pp. 33, 34.

The conditions which are conducive to the spread of plague are identical with those which give rise to the escape of malaria from the ground; and the ground itself exercises an enormous influence upon plague, as will be noted by the fact that in all the epidemics persons living on the ground floors suffer to a much greater extent than those who live in the higher stories of the houses; but not only so, but the rate of mortality appears to be greater amongst those living on the ground floors than it is with those living at an elevation above the ground.

Sir John Pringle, Bart., a former President of the Royal Society, observes exactly the same conditions with reference to the outbreaks of remittent fevers in the army in the Low Countries; and it is curious that it appears that malaria never rises from a water surface, for it does not begin to spread until the water disappears. So with plague; in the midst of wastes which are always water-logged so that the water is always present, plague, although imported, is not spread. This immunity from plague is also clearly shown by the escape from the disease of those living over water, both in the great epidemic of 1665 in London, and also more recently in Bombay.

Water is a germicide for the bacillus of plague and most other of the soil poisons. This is shown in the report on the plague of India, wherein it is stated that "it has been seen that under ordinary conditions the bacillus appears to die rapidly in water.[1]

It appears that the docks at Bombay were filled with ships during the time of the plague, which was extremely rife in the district in close proximity to them. Dr. Thomas Blaney says: "It is indeed a remarkable fact that while plague raged all over Mandvi district, the crews of the ships in the docks remained uninfected during both epidemics, while the distance between the shore residents and the ships was well within striking distance of infection. It may be mentioned that the crews of the ships in the docks were largely composed of Mahomedans and Portuguese, classes very susceptible to plague infection, and not wholly of Europeans or "immune persons."[2]

It has also been shown that on infected vessels having a most insanitary and dirty people on board two cases of plague occurred at sea after inspection before departure, but the disease did not spread. In no instance did the disease appear amongst those who remained on vessels, even in cases where persons had been removed and afterwards developed plague. "It would seem that the circumstances of a sea voyage are inimical to the plague microbe."[3]

In the Great Plague of London in 1665 "many merchants, ship-owners, and the like, locked themselves up and lived close shut up on ship-board supplied with provisions from Greenwich, Woolwich, and single farmhouses on the Kentish side. It was surprising to see several hundred sail of ships which lay in rows of two and two, and some places three such lines in the breadth of the Thames, from Ratcliff and Rotherhithe, as far as Gravesend, and some beyond, even in every place where they could ride with safety as to wind and weather. Nor was it heard

[1] *Government of India—The Plague in India*, 1896.97 R. Nathan, vol. i. p. 51.
[2] *The Times of India*, February 18, 1899, p. 153.
[3] *Government of India—The Plague in India*, 1896-97, R. Nathan, vol. iii. pp. 346, 347.

that the plague reached any of the ships below Deptford, though the people went frequently on shore to the country towns, villages, and farm-houses to buy fresh provisions. More than 10,000 people who attended ship affairs were sheltered here from the contagion."[1]

It is also stated, that in the time of the great epidemic of plague in London, "watermen and others whose occasions employed them much upon the river, and in the cold, suffered least in the late sickness."[2]

It is also noted with reference to the same epidemic, that "notwithstanding the violence of the plague in London and many other places, it never was on board the fleet; and yet there was a strong press in the river, and even in the streets, for seamen. A war with the Dutch was not very grateful to the people, the seamen went with reluctancy, and many complained of being dragged away by force; yet it proved a happy violence to many, who would probably have increased the general calamity, many of their families having fallen in the common and dreadful desolation."[3]

In 1748, during the campaign in Dutch Brabant, inundations had been made about the fortified towns, but on the preliminaries of peace being signed the water was drained off at the beginning of summer, the result being that sickness "raged at Breda and in the neighbouring villages." The States of Holland "gave orders to let in the water again, and to keep it up till winter, as a means of stopping the disease."[4]

It is also known that during the period of plague affecting Egypt that the rise of the Nile checked it. It is stated that at Cairo "the plague every year constantly preys upon the inhabitants, and is only stopped when the Nile, by overflowing, washes away this load of filth; the cold winds, which set in at the same time, lending their assistance by purifying the air."[5]

The experience also in China, where plague is more or less endemic, shows that the rainy season usually puts a stop to it. It is stated: "As a rule, the summer rains, by washing the streets, put an end to the plague for the year."[6]

It will be seen, from the experience extending over all the epidemics of plague, that plague itself is not propagated over a water surface, but the whole of the outbreaks occur over land areas.

It should be observed, with reference to the floors of the houses of the lower classes in India, who are the class most afflicted with plague, that these floors are the natural earth usually covered with a mixture of mud and cow dung. It has been calculated that the quantity of cow dung as applied to the floors of the houses in India is at the rate of about 1100 cwts. per acre per annum, while the usual rate of application for the cultivation of market gardens is about 120 cwts. per acre per annum.

"Among the reasons that Erasmus gives why the English were so subject to the plague is the following: Their floors are usually made of clay covered with rushes that grow in the fens, which are so slightly renewed now and then that the lower part remains sometimes for twenty

[1] *City Remembrancer*, vol. i. p. 363.
[2] *Loimologia*, "Essay on Causes of Pestilential Diseases," by John Quincy, M.D., p. 278.
[3] *City Remembrancer*, vol. i. p. 437.
[4] *Observations on the Diseases of the Army*, Sir John Pringle, Bart., p. 62.
[5] *City Remembrancer*, vol. i. p 87.
[6] *Parliamentary Paper* C7461, July 13, 1894, p. 14.

years together, and in it a collection of spittle, vomit, urine of dogs and men, scraps of fish, and other filthiness not to be named, hence upon change of weather a vapour is exhaled very pernicious to the human body; and salt fish is the common and favourite food of the poor."[1]

It has been observed in the recent plague epidemics in China that the inhabitants of houses with paved floors suffered considerably less from plague than those with earthen floors.[2]

Some persons at the present time attribute the cause of plague to the presence of rats, and that the bacillus of plague is indigenous to rats, and is communicated by rats to human beings. It has been already observed that in all epidemics rats, amongst other animals, have been shown from the remotest periods to have been subject to plague; and it is well known that the death of rats has preceded the outbreak of plague among human beings; but it appears that the attributing of plague epidemics to rats is mistaking the effect for the cause. That rats are subject to plague there cannot be a doubt, but that they themselves are the cause of plague is extremely doubtful; they may no doubt be made the means of spreading and implanting the bacillus in the soil, which appears necessary for the propagation of plague. On this Dr. M'Candless of Hoihow says: "Through the agency of infected rats or human beings, and even cats and pigs, the disease can become lodged in a house, in the ground or perhaps in a drain, and the poison continue active until the plague cultures run their course or die out."[3]

It will be noted with reference to the course which plague takes, that its marked periodicity would not appear to be due to any particular contagion, as has been already pointed out: that the contagion or transmission of disease by rats cannot account for the regular course of the plague rising and falling in each country attacked in the same period in every year, while the periods differ in different countries. This question of rats being the cause of plague has received investigation at the hands of Dr. Thomas Blaney[4] of Bombay, who has pointed out, first with reference to the shipping in the docks at Bombay, which were in direct communication with the particular neighbourhood which suffered considerably from plague, and where rats could pass from the ships to land just as easily at the plague time as in former periods, that there was no plague on board ship within the docks. Moreover, he has shown that in the first epidemic of the plague in 1896 and 1897 at Bombay most of the rats were killed off, but that did not prevent the subsequent epidemics which have occurred since that period. He then gives some remarkable statistics with reference to the supposed infection caused by rats, for which purpose he selects certain districts in the city of Bombay which are known as grain districts, where there exists every condition essential for the life and multiplication of rats in the various granaries; and for comparison he selects other districts in the city in which there

[1] *History of Market Harborough*, by W. Harrod, p. 60.

[2] It is essential that the floors of all houses in malarious countries should be impermeable, and that as little disturbance as possible of the soil should be made in epidemic periods.

[3] *China Imperial Maritime Customs Medical Reports*, for half-year March 31, 1896, p. 99.

[4] *Times of India*, February 18, 1899, p. 153.

are no large grain stores or likely to be any large number of rats, and compares the death-rate from plague in each of these districts:—

Rat Districts.	Plague Deaths.	Rate of Mortality per 1000.
Mandvi	834	8·95
Oomerkharry . . .	259	4·93
Dongre	267	8·80
Market	182	4·06
	Average . .	6·68

Non-Rat Districts.	Plague Deaths.	Rate of Mortality per 1000
Parel	603	20·98
Sion	469	23·46
Sewri	122	20·12
Mahim	666	35·99
	Average . .	25·14

It will be seen from the above figures that in the rat districts the average mortality from plague was 6·68 per 1000, while in the non-rat districts it was 25·14 per 1000; and therefore he concludes that rats are not an essential agent in the spread and maintenance of plague.

In the time of the Great Plague of London it appears that a dead set was made against animals, the same as has been since done in many epidemics arising from various diseases.

During the Great Plague of 1665 all cats and dogs in London were ordered to be killed, as they were esteemed capable of conveying the infection; and it is said that a prodigious number of these creatures were destroyed—forty thousand dogs and five times as many cats. All possible endeavours were used to destroy mice and rats,—multitudes of them were destroyed by ratsbane and other poisons,[1]—and yet we know that the plague pursued its even course just the same as it had done in other preceding plagues, having exactly the same marked periodicity as in former outbreaks.

Some facts may now be noted with regard to what has been observed in connection with the meteorological conditions attending the outbreak of plague and its sudden stoppage. One of the very marked circumstances is the fact that plague suddenly dies out when the temperature rises above a certain point. Referring to the outbreak of plague in Mesopotamia in 1873 and 1874, it is stated that "with the accession of the hot season in June the disease (as would appear to be customary with the plague in Mesopotamia, when it is prevalent there) rapidly declined and apparently died out, to reappear at the beginning of winter."[2] It is stated that with reference to the plague in Mesopotamia, the "plague broke out and reached its acme of intensity in the spring, and died out suddenly during the summer season when the *great heat* declared itself and the thermometer rose to 45° or 50° C. (113° to 122° F.). During the prevalence of plague the thermometer ranged between 5° and 30° C. (41° to 86° F.), and when it rose to 30° C. (86° F.) the disease had reached its maximum of intensity. As the temperature increased from

[1] *City Remembrancer*, vol. i. p. 313.

[2] *Parliamentary Paper*, *Plague*, C2262, 1879, p. 24.

30° to 45° C. (86° to 113° F.) the epidemic began to diminish, and as soon as the thermometer got up to 45° C. (113° F.) it ceased abruptly."[1]

It has been stated that "in Europe and Africa the plague is destroyed or suspended between 60° and 80°."[2]

Experiments which have been made with the plague bacillus show that it is killed by an exposure for fifteen minutes to a heat of 70° C. (158° F.)[3]

It is mentioned of the plague, that "it was equally fatal in Sind with its arid climate and extreme variations of heat and cold, in the moist and equable Konkan, which receives the full force of the monsoon torrents, and in the comparatively dry uplands of the Deccan. But in all these places the hottest part of the year succeeded completely, or for the time, in subjugating the epidemic."[4]

"In all plagues with which Aleppo has been visited in this century, the contagion is said to have regularly and constantly ceased in August and September, the hottest months of the year."[5]

It has also been noted that the outbreak of plague has occurred at a period of sudden fall of temperature: "Dr. Petresco is disposed to assign the great outburst of plague at Vetlianka during the week ending December 21st to a sudden fall of temperature, causing a relatively greater crowding of the families, in consequence of the more careful exclusion of fresh air from the living-room, and greater heating of the stoves."[6]

The same observation has been made with reference to the plague in India occurring in the cold season, as a rule driving the people more into their houses than at other periods. This, of course, would not hold good in the case when the plague was epidemic in England, as it usually occurred in the warmest periods of the year and gradually declined with the cold periods. The conditions which lead to the eruption of plague in India cannot be looked upon as merely incident to cold driving people within their habitations, but is due to causes which are brought into operation, first in stopping plague by an increase of temperature, and secondly in increasing plague by a sudden fall in temperature.

In order to reconcile the varied conditions under which plague breaks out in different countries, and how under certain conditions it is stayed in its progress, it is necessary to understand thoroughly the hygrometric conditions of the ground. In my address as President of this Society in January 1892, I particularly directed attention to some experiments which had been carried on for some years with regard to the hygrometric condition of the ground, especially on the subjects of condensation in and of evaporation from the ground. There cannot be a doubt that the conditions which ordinarily produce evaporation from water or land surfaces are identical with the conditions which produce exhalations from the ground, and that these exhalations consist largely of vapour of water carrying matters injurious to health with them.

The experiments to which I refer were made with an earth hygro-

[1] *Parliamentary Paper, Plague*, C2262, 1879, p. 51.
[2] *Supplement Ninth Report Local Government Board*, p. 83.
[3] *Government of India—The Plague in India*, 1896-97, R. Nathan, vol. i. p. 26.
[4] *Ibid.*, 1896-97, R. Nathan, vol. i. pp. 53, 54.
[5] *Philosophical Transactions*, vol. liii. p. 23.
[6] *Supplement Ninth Report Local Government Board*, p. 29.

meter consisting of cylinders filled with earth freely suspended in a perforated tube, within the earth, at depths of 1 foot and 2 feet below the surface. The general result showed that these earth cylinders in the day time, when the air was warmer than the earth, increased in weight, but at night time, when the temperature of the air fell below that of the earth, the cylinders lost weight; showing that when the air was warmer than the earth condensation took place, but that when the earth was warmer than the air evaporation took place. These experiments threw considerable light upon the influence of malaria, and explained some well-established facts known in reference to the influence of malaria, such as the circumstance that malarious countries can be traversed with impunity in the day time but are very fatal at night. The fact is that in all warm and malarious countries, especially in the day time, when the air is warmer than the ground, no exhalations take place from the ground, but at nightfall, when the ground is often very much warmer than the air, these exhalations, accompanied with the vapour of water, escape from the ground. A further investigation of this subject was of the greatest importance with a view to showing what connection there was between the hygrometric state of the ground and the spread of diseases which are generally known as soil poisons.

With this view, I have considered in what way any ordinary meteorological observer can carry on the observations necessary for determining the periods of the year when exhalations escape from the ground, and the quantity that then arises. It is necessary therefor that the temperature of the earth should be ascertained in every case; and it is desirable that these observations should be carried on to a considerable depth, as in all probability in the case of plague it would appear that the temperature of the ground at considerable depths, in warm countries, has a very marked effect upon the incidence of the plague. It should be here noted that there does not appear to be any marked connection between the temperature of the ground and plague, simply viewed as temperature; but it will be shortly seen that temperature exercises an enormous power in the elimination of vapour from the ground. It is essential also to determine the temperature of the dew-point; and with this view I had erected, previous to June 1898, a Stevenson thermometer-screen in which there are two maximum and two minimum thermometers, one of each being a wet-bulb thermometer. From these I have calculated the maximum and minimum dew-point every day. The maximum and minimum temperatures of the ground are also registered at 6 inches in depth, and the ground temperature is also taken daily at 2 feet 6 inches and at 5 feet in depth. Having got both the dew-point and the temperatures of the ground, in order to determine what evaporation or exhalation takes place, we must have recourse to what is known as Dalton's Law, $V - v$, where V represents the vapour tension due to the temperature of the ground or evaporating surface, v being the vapour tension due to the temperature of the dew-point. The greatest amount of evaporation or exhalation would therefore take place when we have the maximum temperature of the ground and the minimum dew-point; and at all times the exhalation takes place in proportion to the tensional difference between the ground temperature and the temperature of the dew-point.

The following table shows the results of the observations taken at my house at Croydon :—

Month.	Temperature.				Dew-Point.		Tensional Difference.				
	Mean Max. of Ground at 6 inches.	Mean Min. of Ground at 6 inches.	Mean Temp. of Ground at 30 inches.	Mean Temp. of Ground at 60 inches.	Mean Max. Dew-Point.	Mean Min. Dew-Point.	Max. Dew-Point & Max. Ground, 6 ins.	Min. Dew-Point & Max. Ground, 6 ins.	Min. Dew-Point & Min. Ground, 6 ins.	Min. Dew-Point and Ground, 30 ins.	Min. Dew-Point and Ground, 60 ins.
1898	°	°	°	°	°	°	in.	in.	in.	in.	in.
June	67·6	59·3	56·8	54·0	53·7	47·4	·262	·347	·177	·134	·090
July	70·8	62·3	61·4	58·1	55·8	49·2	·308	·403	·211	·194	·132
August	71·9	63·6	63·6	60·4	57·8	51·9	·303	·396	·202	·202	·140
September	67·0	57·4	61·9	60·4	55·0	47·6	·228	·331	·142	·224	·196
October	55·0	50·6	55·5	56·2	51·3	45·9	·055	·124	·060	·132	·144
November	46·4	40·9	50·5	52·5	45·4	38·6	·012	·082	·022	·133	·162
December	44·3	38·6	46·6	48·6	43·5	37·5	·009	·067	·009	·093	·118
1899											
January	41·4	34·9	43·6	45·6	40·8	34·8	·006	·059	·001	·082	·104
February	41·4	34·1	42·6	44·1	39·0	33·5	·023	·069	·004	·081	·097
March	41·4	33·8	41·6	43·1	38·0	29·6	·032	·097	·030	·099	·114
April	51·6	44·1	47·0	46·0	42·5	37·9	·110	·154	·061	·095	·083
May	60·2	49·9	52·2	50·1	46·5	39·5	·205	·280	·118	·149	·120
June	73·3	61·5	59·0	55·5	54·2	46·5	·399	·503	·229	·183	·124
July	77·9	66·7	64·0	59·8	57·5	53·0	·482	·552	·252	·193	·111
August	77·2	65·0	66·4	62·7	57·8	53·3	·455	·527	·210	·241	·163
September	63·9	53·0	61·5	60·7	52·4	46·5	·200	·277	·086	·229	·214
October	50·5	44·4	52·8	54·7	48·9	39·3	·021	·127	·053	·160	·188
November	47·5	42·5	50·2	51·7	46·0	40·2	·018	·080	·023	·115	·135
December	36·3	32·7	43·5	46·7	36·2	28·2	·000	·060	·032	·129	·165

The differences in vapour tension are measured in decimals of an inch of mercury ; and mercury is 13·59 times heavier than water at 32° F., and diminishes in weight $\frac{1}{5550}$ part for every degree F. the temperature is raised. The vapour tension is the actual pressure above a vacuum.

It will be observed from these observations that the tensional difference between the temperatures of the ground, and the minimum temperature of the dew-point, varies slightly from year to year ; but this is not more variable than were the outbreaks of plague, when plague was a visitant of this country. It will also be seen that these differences in vapour tension are in accord with the periods when plague was rife in this country, and that they rise and fall with the periods when plague was rife.

It should also be observed with reference to this subject, that the vapour tension should arrive at its maximum some period previous to that of the plague ; and in this respect it should be noted that it has been observed in India that "a certain time elapses before the infection gets a firm hold of the town or village, as indicated by the death-rate, after the first probable infection from without. It of course varies, and is by no means well defined, but it would appear to be at least a month." [1]

In the case of the city of Bombay a series of meteorological observations are given which have been kindly supplied to me by Mr. N. A. F. Moos

[1] *Report of Sanitary Commissioner Government of Bombay*, Surgeon Lieut.-Col. J. W. Clarkson, p. 91, 1897.

of Colaba Observatory, Bombay. The following table, showing the tensional differences, has been calculated from the observations:—

Month.	Tensional Difference.							
	Mean Dew-Point and 9 ins. Ground.	Min. Dew-Point and 9 ins. Ground.	Mean Dew-Point and 20 ins. Ground.	Min. Dew-Point and 20 ins. Ground.	Mean Dew-Point and 60 ins. Ground.	Min. Dew-Point and 60 ins. Ground.	Mean Dew-Point and 132 ins. Ground.	Min. Dew-Point and 132 ins. Ground.
1896	in.	in.	in.	in.	in.	in.	in.	in.
August . . .	·213	·318	·301	·406	·347	·452	·343	·448
September . .	·274	·440	·329	·495	·337	·503	·337	·503
October . . .	·305	·651	·347	·693	·317	·663	·293	·639
November . .	·376	·669	·464	·757	·464	·757	·421	·714
December . .	·407	·684	·514	·791	·567	·844	·533	·810
1897								
January . . .	·342	·653	·461	·772	·569	·880	·562	·873
February . .	·331	·577	·420	·666	·524	·770	·538	·784
March . . .	·298	·601	·358	·661	·422	·727	·432	·735
April . . .	·297	·666	·316	·685	·312	·681	·297	·666
May . . .	·332	·445	·364	·477	·324	·437	·259	·372
June . . .	·278	·426	·351	·499	·326	·474	·240	·388
July . . .	·232	·378	·336	·482	·360	·506	·293	·439
August . . .	·221	·329	·300	·408	·335	·443	·312	·420
September . .	·224	·322	·303	·401	·319	·417	·296	·394
October . . .	·283	·571	·359	·647	·374	·662	·336	·624
November . .	·394	·659	·513	·778	·555	·820	·513	·778
December . .	·389	·685	·513	·809	·598	·894	·575	·871
1898								
January . . .	·369	·631	·480	·742	·570	·832	·562	·824
February . .	·350	·776	·460	·886	·525	·951	·507	·933
March . . .	·354	·873	·430	·949	·445	·964	·411	·930
April . . .	·353	·637	·416	·700	·372	·656	·296	·580
May . . .	·414	·566	·486	·638	·406	·558	·291	·443
June . . .	·347	·479	·470	·602	·422	·554	·284	·416
July . . .	·289	·414	·421	·546	·425	·550	·323	·448
August . . .	·300	·410	·419	·529	·423	·533	·354	·464
September . .	·280	·429	·396	·545	·400	·549	·345	·494
October . . .	·348	·694	·433	·779	·388	·734	·333	·679
November . .	·428	·717	·543	·832	·526	·815	·451	·740
December . .	·412	·781	·550	·919	·578	·947	·520	·889
1899								
January . . .	·414	·706	·574	·866	·693	·985	·674	·966
February . .	·364	·659	·475	·770	·556	·851	·549	·844
March . . .	·357	·658	·434	·735	·442	·743	·415	·716
April . . .	·398	·620	·473	·695	·421	·643	·356	·578
May . . .	·413	·559	·488	·634	·417	·563	·318	·464
June . . .	·369	·565	·491	·687	·452	·648	·329	·525
July . . .	·345	·468	·455	·578	·455	·578	·361	·484
August . . .	·358	·496	·467	·605	·462	·600	·389	·527
September . .	·361	·456	·469	·564	·465	·560	·400	·495
October . . .	·365	·826	·442	·903	·430	·891	·361	·822
November . .	·413	·709	·549	·845	·570	·866	·505	·801
December . .	·434	·724	·567	·857	·637	·927	·589	·879

In this table the minimum dew-point is the extreme dew-point each month, and differs in that respect from the Croydon table, in which the minimum dew-point is the average of all the days of the month. The rise and fall of the tensional differences in this table will be found to agree in a remarkable manner with the rise and fall of the plague. The influence will be more clearly seen by reference to the diagrams.

It will be seen in Bombay that the tensional differences arrive at their maximum just before the maximum outbreak of plague, and that they then rapidly fall, and also that at greater depths of the ground there is a very marked parallelism between these outbreaks and the tensional differences.

I have also prepared a set of diagrams showing the various meteorological conditions and the incidence of plague, and have added to them a further set of diagrams which shows what would be the ordinary effects of evaporation or exhalation, taking into consideration the movement of the wind, which has a very material influence upon evaporation, and probably upon exhalation, and for this purpose I have used Dr. Pole's formula for Evaporation, which is as follows :—

$$E = \frac{T^2 - t^2}{A\ (100 - W)}$$

T Temperature of the ground.
t Temperature of dew-point.
W Wind, miles per hour.
A Coefficient. Taken for Bombay at 80.
E Evaporation or exhalation, depth per day in inches.

It will therefore be noted that, with reference to these observations, it is quite clear that if the temperature of the air does increase beyond the temperature of the ground, so that its dew-point is above the temperature of the ground, instead of evaporation taking place, condensation takes place, and to this increased high temperature may be entirely due the sudden stoppage of plague after a certain high temperature has been reached, which, by raising the temperature of the dew-point, stops all exhalation from the ground, and will cause condensation to take place instead of evaporation.[1] So also, where it has been observed that a sudden fall of temperature causes plague to arise. A fall of temperature means that the temperature of the dew-point must fall, and the tensional difference between a low dew-point and a high ground temperature would at once lead to exhalations escaping in large quantity from the ground, and so lead to the liberation of the plague bacillus from the ground, accompanied with the exhalations necessary for its development. Some years ago I made an inspection of the city of Bombay, and found that there had been a general increase in the deaths arising from diseases of the respiratory system other than phthisis, which I found was traceable to the blocking of the natural drainage outlets from the city, and the consequent stagnation in the movement of the underground waters. As these diseases follow, in parallel lines, the outbreak of plague, it would naturally follow that plague was affected by similar conditions. I also made an inquiry in the year 1890, and reported on the condition of the city of Poona, which has recently suffered so frightfully from the ravages of plague. The sanitary description of Poona will suffice to give a description of all the places in which plague has been more or less rife.

[1] If the air of a house infected with plague was warmed and saturated with vapour of water so as to equal or exceed the vapour tension due to the temperature of the ground, it would effectually prevent emanations from the ground, thus imitating the mode nature adopts in stopping such emanations.

Poona stands at a level of about 1800 feet above sea-level, has a mean temperature of about 78°; the temperature is highest in April or May, when it reaches 86°, it is lowest in January and December, when it falls to 72°, but readings as low as 44° have been recorded. The average velocity of the wind is about 242 miles per day; it is least in January, when it is about 132 miles, and greatest in July, when it is about 404 miles. The barometer is lowest in July and highest in December. There were no observations of ground temperature. The geological formation consists of basaltic rocks which in places crop out at the surface, and is overlaid with argillaceous alluvium known as "Moorum." Previous to the years 1874 and 1875 the health of Poona was said to be extremely good, but in that year a canal was opened for irrigation purposes, which has subsequently had a most deleterious influence on the health of the district. The population of Poona with its suburbs and cantonment in 1891 was 161,390.

There are about 1300[1] wells within the city, of which 500 were in daily use, in addition to which about 2½ million gallons of water were daily brought into the city. The subsoil water-level of the district has been raised, the ground has become saturated by injurious cultivations in and around the city. The consumption of water has been increased by the introduction of the canal water for domestic purposes, without any adequate means for its removal. The river, which had previously ensured the movement of the subsoil water and replenished the wells, was dammed at its natural outlet, causing stagnation of the subsoil water and an increase of fever in the canal-irrigated districts. It was also reported in the documents submitted to me, that an increase in mosquitoes and flies had occurred in the city, which had, previously to the introduction of the canal, been almost absent. There were six slaughter yards within the city without any proper drains, and there were sixty-four burial grounds also within the city. It was apparent that the ground was impregnated with filth of man and beast; and the consequence was that the health of the population was in a very bad state. The number of admissions to dispensaries and hospitals was enormous compared to the population of the city, some years numbering at least one-half of the total population of the place.

As a further evidence of the unhealthiness of the city of Poona, in 1898, out of every 1000 births, it is recorded that there were 574·65 deaths of children under one year of age.

A description of Hong-Kong which was given by Surgeon-Major Black, F.R.Met.Soc., some few years ago entirely accords with the description I gave of Poona.

The conditions producing disease in India are in entire accord with the experience in other places, as it has been stated that "in Dutch Brabant, where the people are more or less subject to intermitting fevers, in proportion to the distance of this water from the surface, so that, by looking into their wells, one may form a judgment of the comparative healthfulness of the several villages."[2]

Sir John Pringle also mentions: "There were two villages near Cyndhoven called Lind and Zelst, the one 10 and the other 14 feet above

[1] On the plans of Poona there were shown 1419 wells.

[2] *Observations on Diseases of the Army*, by Sir John Pringle, Bart., p. 62.

the surface of the water (an extraordinary height in that country), and it was observable how much better the soldiers kept their health in both those places than in any other of the 'cantonments.'"[1]

It may also be observed that in the city of Ahmedabad, which has had plague imported time after time into it, during the three epidemics that have occurred in India, it has never made any headway in that city, although a few indigenous cases have occurred. In this city the subsoil water level varies from 33 feet to 22 feet in depth below the surface, rising about 2 or 3 feet above these levels during the rains from July to October. In the city of Calcutta, into which plague has been imported, there is a large amount of subsoil water, and there is at times a movement of this subsoil water in the direction of the sewers amounting to something like nineteen million gallons a day.[2] This movement of the subsoil water has to some extent, no doubt, protected Calcutta.

It should also be borne in mind that the conditions which lead to emanations from the ground also control the emanations from the human body, and that these emanations are always looked upon as extremely infectious, as is recorded in the *City Remembrancer*, vol. i. p. 61. "Infectious irradiations flowing from bodies influenced with the pest, as they constantly issue out by transpiration, and more open passages, and diffuse their malignity accordingly."

The temperature of the human body may be raised in fever to 104°, the tension of the vapour at that temperature would be equal to 2·167 inches of mercury, so that with the dry atmosphere such as occurs in times when plague is most rife, the power to exhale vapours from the human body is enormously increased.[3]

The conditions under which plague is propagated and spread being known, means can and ought to be provided for its effectual prevention, and until these measures can be carried out, the only effectual remedy of combating the plague is to vacate the infected site.

I am indebted to the Right Hon. Lord George Hamilton and the Assistants at the India Office for copies of the Annual Reports of the Sanitary Commissioners of several provinces in India, to Mr. N. A. F. Moos of Colaba Observatory, Bombay, for meteorological observations, and to Mr. W. Marriott for preparing and exhibiting the slides of the diagrams.

The following Tables are appended giving observations at Bombay:—

1. Temperature of the Ground, Bombay Observatory, at a depth of 9 inches.
2. Do. do. do. 20 inches.
3. Do. do. do. 60 inches.
4. Do. do. do. 132 inches.
5. Mean Temperature of the Air, Bombay Observatory.

[1] *Observations on Diseases of the Army*, by Sir John Pringle, Bart., p. 63.

[2] The height of the tides govern the amount of the subsoil water at Calcutta, and the tides also render the subsoil water brackish. The experience of the year 1900, following a period of successive drought, has brought into action forces that have resulted in a very high death rate from plague taking place in Calcutta.

[3] It is a matter of some doubt if plague is really infectious, or whether the germs do not require to undergo some development in the ground before they become active; but in the interest of humanity, until more is known about the subject, it is desirable that plague should be treated as an infectious disease.

6. Minimum Temperature of the Air, Bombay Observatory. Least value of individual observations.
7. Vapour Tension due to the Temperature of the Ground in Bombay at a depth of 9 inches.
8. Do. do. do. 20 inches.
9. Do. do. do. 60 inches.
10. Do. do. do. 132 inches.
11. Mean Monthly Vapour Pressure, Bombay Observatory.
12. Minima Monthly Vapour Pressure, Bombay Observatory.
13. Barometric Pressure, Bombay Observatory.
14. Mean Velocity of the Wind, Bombay Observatory, in miles per hour.
15. Cloud, Bombay Observatory, Means of Estimates at 6, 10, 14, 16, and 22 hours daily, the whole sky reckoned as 10.
16. Rainfall, Bombay Observatory, Newman's Gauge 4½ feet above the ground.[1]
17. Deaths from all causes in Bombay, from the Reports of the Government Sanitary Commissioner of Bombay.
18. Deaths from Fever in Bombay, from the Reports of the Government Sanitary Commissioner of Bombay.

[1] The small amount of rainfall in India generally in the year 1899 promises to be the prelude to a more unhealthy season, as usually periods of drought and periods following droughts are generally very unhealthy, as they bring into action greater depths of the polluted subsoil.

TABLE I.—Temperature of the Ground, Bombay Observatory, at a Depth of 9 Inches.

Months.	1890.	1891.	1892.	1893.	1894.	1895.	1896.	1897.	1898.	1899.
January	77·7°	77·0°	78·2°	76·2°	77·9°	76·5°	78·6°	77·2°	77·7°	76·9°
February	78·9	76·3	79·5	75·0	78·7	76·8	77·9	76·9	78·4	78·8
March	81·0	79·3	80·7	78·6	80·9	80·6	80·7	79·0	81·5	82·2
April	83·5	82·3	85·5	83·1	83·7	83·0	84·9	83·1	85·1	85·3
May	85·2	84·8	86·9	84·9	85·8	85·4	86·8	85·7	87·6	87·3
June	83·9	86·8	84·8	83·8	85·1	85·3	85·6	85·7	86·9	86·6
July	82·3	83·4	83·9	82·5	83·0	83·4	83·4	83·7	84·9	85·7
August	81·1	82·6	81·7	81·8	82·6	82·2	81·7	82·9	84·3	85·4
September	81·3	81·9	80·7	81·6	81·3	81·5	82·8	82·9	83·7	85·1
October	81·9	82·8	82·4	82·0	82·0	82·8	84·6	83·1	85·6	86·0
November	80·8	81·6	80·1	81·3	80·2	82·4	83·1	80·8	84·4	83·4
December	78·8	79·3	78·2	79·3	78·4	79·2	80·6	78·4	82·0	81·3
Means	81·4	81·5	81·9	80·8	81·6	81·6	82·6	81·6	83·5	83·7

TABLE II.—Temperature of the Ground, Bombay Observatory, at a Depth of 20 Inches.

Months.	1890.	1891.	1892.	1893.	1894.	1895.	1896.	1897.	1898.	1899.
January	80°·3	80°·1	80°·9	79°·4	80°·2	79°·7	81°·3	80°·9	81°·1	81°·8
February	80·7	78·9	81·5	78·0	80·8	79·2	80·5	79·7	81·7	82·1
March	82·3	80·7	81·9	79·9	82·0	81·9	81·9	80·8	83·6	84·3
April	84·3	83·0	85·6	83·2	84·6	83·9	85·5	83·6	86·7	87·2
May	86·1	85·4	87·5	85·6	86·6	86·2	87·5	86·5	89·3	89·1
June	86·2	87·5	87·1	85·8	87·1	87·1	87·8	87·5	89·8	89·5
July	84·9	86·0	86·2	84·8	85·7	85·7	86·0	86·4	88·2	88·4
August	83·4	84·7	84·4	83·9	84·9	84·4	84·1	85·0	87·3	88·1
September	83·0	84·0	82·8	83·6	83·6	83·7	84·3	85·0	86·7	87·8
October	83·7	84·2	83·6	84·0	83·8	84·4	85·7	85·1	87·7	87·9
November	83·2	84·0	82·7	83·7	82·7	84·2	85·4	84·1	87·3	86·9
December	81·6	82·1	80·8	82·5	81·4	82·2	83·6	82·1	85·7	84·9
Means	83·3	83·4	83·7	82·9	83·6	83·5	84·5	83·9	86·3	86·5

TABLE III.—Temperature of the Ground, Bombay Observatory, at a Depth of 60 Inches.

Months.	1890.	1891.	1892.	1893.	1894.	1895.	1896.	1897.	1898.	1899.
January	82°·4	82°·6	83°·0	81°·8	83°·2	82°·5	83°·3	83°·9	83°·6	85°·0
February	82·3	81·6	82·7	80·9	82·6	81·6	82·6	82·7	83·5	84·3
March	82·7	81·6	82·8	80·9	82·8	82·1	82·4	82·6	84·0	84·5
April	83·9	82·7	84·4	82·3	84·1	83·3	84·2	83·5	85·6	85·9
May	85·3	84·4	86·1	84·5	85·5	85·1	86·0	85·5	87·4	87·4
June	86·3	86·1	87·0	85·6	86·6	86·6	87·4	86·9	88·7	88·6
July	85·9	86·8	86·8	85·3	86·5	86·4	86·7	87·0	88·3	88·4
August	84·6	85·5	85·6	84·6	85·5	85·4	85·3	85·9	87·4	88·0
September	83·8	84·7	84·2	84·3	84·6	84·7	84·5	85·4	86·8	87·7
October	83·7	84·5	83·4	84·3	84·3	84·5	84·9	85·5	86·6	87·6
November	83·9	84·5	83·4	84·3	84·1	84·5	85·4	85·2	86·9	87·4
December	83·5	83·9	82·6	84·2	83·5	84·0	85·0	84·4	86·4	86·7
Means	84·0	84·1	84·4	83·6	84·4	84·2	84·8	84·9	86·3	86·8

TABLE IV.—Temperature of the Ground, Bombay Observatory, at a Depth of 132 Inches.

Months.	1890.	1891.	1892.	1893.	1894.	1895.	1896.	1897.	1898.	1890.
January	82°·8	82°·6	83°·1	81°·8	82°·8	82°·6	83°·2	83°·7	83°·4	84°·5
February	82·4	82·1	82·7	81·4	82·5	82·0	82·6	83·1	83·0	84·1
March	82·4	81·9	82·7	81·2	82·4	82·0	82·4	82·9	83·1	83·8
April	82·8	82·1	83·2	81·5	82·8	82·4	83·1	83·1	83·6	84·2
May	83·5	82·9	84·0	82·3	83·5	83·2	83·8	83·8	84·5	84·9
June	84·2	84·0	84·8	83·2	84·2	84·1	84·7	84·7	85·3	85·6
July	84·6	84·7	85·3	84·0	85·0	84·7	85·3	85·3	85·8	86·1
August	84·4	85·0	85·2	84·0	84·9	84·7	85·2	85·3	85·7	86·2
September	83·9	84·6	84·2	83·7	84·3	84·5	84·5	84·8	85·4	86·1
October	83·5	84·3	83·2	83·6	84·0	84·2	84·3	84·5	85·2	85·9
November	83·4	83·8	82·6	83·4	83·5	83·9	84·3	84·1	85·0	85·8
December	83·0	83·6	82·4	83·3	83·2	83·5	84·1	83·8	84·9	85·5
Means	83·4	83·5	83·6	82·8	83·6	83·5	84·0	84·1	84·6	85·2

TABLE V.—Mean Temperature of the Air, Bombay Observatory.

Months.	1890.	1891.	1892.	1893.	1894.	1895.	1896.	1897.	1898.	1899.
	°	°	°	°	°	°	°	°	°	°
January	75·1	74·1	75·5	72·9	75·1	73·2	75·9	73·6	74·6	72·0
February	77·2	73·5	77·3	72·1	76·7	74·8	75·3	74·1	75·2	75·1
March	79·3	77·7	79·1	77·3	79·5	79·2	79·4	77·0	79·2	79·5
April	82·4	81·1	85·0	82·7	82·5	81·9	84·2	82·3	83·1	82·4
May	83·9	83·7	85·7	83·6	84·6	84·1	85·8	84·6	85·1	84·9
June	81·4	84·9	82·5	81·8	82·9	83·1	83·4	85·0	83·1	82·5
July	79·8	80·8	81·3	80·5	80·6	80·9	80·9	81·3	81·0	81·8
August	78·7	80·5	79·1	80·0	80·5	79·9	79·5	81·1	80·6	81·4
September	79·5	79·8	78·8	79·8	79·0	79·5	81·6	81·0	80·0	81·2
October	80·1	81·4	81·2	80·2	80·2	81·3	83·4	81·4	83·4	82·8
November	78·5	79·3	78·0	79·2	78·0	80·6	81·0	77·9	81·0	79·4
December	76·1	76·7	75·7	76·5	75·5	76·4	77·8	74·9	77·9	77·2
Means .	79·3	79·5	79·9	78·9	79·6	79·6	80·7	79·5	80·4	80·0

TABLE VI.—Minimum Temperature of the Air, Bombay Observatory. Least Value of Individual Observations.

Months.	1890.	1891.	1892.	1893.	1894.	1895.	1896.	1897.	1898.	1899.
	°	°	°	°	°	°	°	°	°	°
January	67·1	63·2	64·4	62·9	66·8	62·0	66·7	62·1	64·2	60·5
February	68·9	60·3	67·2	59·8	65·3	63·2	67·2	65·1	65·3	67·6
March	72·9	69·7	67·2	68·5	70·2	72·6	70·3	67·9	64·5	71·2
April	75·6	73·8	76·9	74·9	75·2	75·4	76·8	72·0	76·0	75·5
May	78·8	77·5	80·3	76·4	79·8	78·9	80·5	78·8	79·6	78·5
June	75·3	76·6	76·4	75·0	75·9	76·0	75·7	76·1	75·6	75·8
July	75·3	73·7	74·8	75·2	75·3	75·4	76·0	74·7	74·2	76·7
August	74·8	75·4	74·3	74·9	74·5	74·7	75·7	77·2	75·8	75·8
September	73·5	74·1	74·2	75·1	74·3	72·0	75·6	75·8	74·5	74·6
October	72·4	75·0	76·0	72·9	73·6	73·6	77·6	73·6	76·9	75·7
November	70·2	69·8	70·2	71·5	70·6	72·6	67·9	69·8	72·3	73·3
December	66·9	68·2	68·2	68·2	65·1	67·5	64·8	67·1	65·0	69·9
Means .	72·6	71·4	72·5	71·3	72·2	72·0	72·9	71·7	72·0	72·9

TABLE VII.—Vapour Tension due to the Temperature of the Ground at 9 Inches in Depth at Bombay.

Months.	1890.	1891.	1892.	1893.	1894.	1895.	1896.	1897.	1898.	1899.
	in.	in.	in.	in.	in.	in.	in.	in.	in.	in.
January	·949	·927	·965	·903	·955	·912	·977	·934	·949	·924
February	·987	·906	1·007	·868	·981	·921	·955	·924	·971	·984
March	1·057	1·000	1·047	·977	1·053	1·043	1·047	·990	1·074	1·099
April	1·146	1·103	1·222	1·131	1·154	1·128	1·200	1·131	1·207	1·215
May	1·211	1·196	1·278	1·200	1·234	1·219	1·274	1·230	1·307	1·295
June	1·161	1·274	1·196	1·157	1·207	1·215	1·226	1·230	1·278	1·266
July	1·103	1·142	1·161	1·110	1·128	1·142	1·142	1·154	1·200	1·230
August	1·060	1·114	1·081	1·084	1·114	1·099	1·081	1·124	1·176	1·219
September	1·067	1·088	1·047	1·077	1·067	1·074	1·121	1·124	1·154	1·207
October	1·088	1·121	1·106	1·092	1·092	1·121	1·188	1·131	1·226	1·242
November	1·050	1·077	1·026	1·067	1·030	1·106	1·131	1·050	1·180	1·142
December	·984	1·000	·965	1·000	·971	·997	1·043	·971	1·092	1·067
Means .	1·072	1·079	1·092	1·055	1·082	1·081	1·115	1·083	1·151	1·158

TABLE VIII.—VAPOUR TENSION DUE TO THE TEMPERATURE OF THE GROUND AT 20 INCHES IN DEPTH AT BOMBAY.

Months.	1890.	1891.	1892.	1893.	1894.	1895.	1896.	1897.	1898.	1899.
	in.	in.	in.	in.	in.	in.	in.	in.	in.	in.
January	1·033	1·026	1·053	1·003	1·030	1·013	1·067	1·053	1·060	1·084
February	1·047	·987	1·074	·958	1·050	·997	1·040	1·013	1·081	1·095
March	1·103	1·047	1·088	1·020	1·092	1·088	1·088	1·050	1·150	1·176
April	1·176	1·128	1·226	1·135	1·188	1·161	1·222	1·150	1·270	1·290
May	1·246	1·219	1·303	1·226	1·266	1·250	1·303	1·262	1·379	1·370
June	1·250	1·303	1·286	1·234	1·286	1·286	1·315	1·303	1·401	1·388
July	1·200	1·242	1·250	1·196	1·230	1·230	1·242	1·258	1·332	1·340
August	1·142	1·192	1·180	1·161	1·200	1·180	1·169	1·203	1·295	1·328
September	1·128	1·165	1·121	1·150	1·150	1·154	1·176	1·203	1·270	1·315
October	1·154	1·173	1·150	1·165	1·157	1·180	1·230	1·207	1·311	1·319
November	1·135	1·165	1·117	1·154	1·117	1·173	1·219	1·169	1·295	1·278
December	1·077	1·095	1·050	1·110	1·070	1·099	1·150	1·095	1·230	1·200
Means	1·141	1·145	1·158	1·126	1·153	1·151	1·185	1·164	1·256	1·265

TABLE IX.—VAPOUR TENSION DUE TO THE TEMPERATURE OF THE GROUND AT 60 INCHES IN DEPTH AT BOMBAY.

Months.	1890.	1891.	1892.	1893.	1894.	1895.	1896.	1897.	1898.	1899.
	in.	in.	in.	in.	in.	in.	in.	in.	in.	in.
January	1·106	1·114	1·128	1·084	1·135	1·110	1·139	1·161	1·150	1·203
February	1·103	1·077	1·117	1·053	1·114	1·077	1·114	1·117	1·146	1·176
March	1·117	1·077	1·121	1·053	1·121	1·095	1·106	1·114	1·165	1·184
April	1·161	1·117	1·180	1·103	1·169	1·139	1·173	1·146	1·226	1·238
May	1·215	1·180	1·246	1·184	1·222	1·207	1·242	1·222	1·299	1·299
June	1·254	1·246	1·282	1·226	1·266	1·266	1·299	1·278	1·353	1·349
July	1·238	1·274	1·274	1·215	1·262	1·258	1·270	1·282	1·336	1·340
August	1·188	1·222	1·226	1·188	1·222	1·219	1·215	1·238	1·299	1·323
September	1·157	1·192	1·173	1·176	1·188	1·192	1·184	1·219	1·274	1·311
October	1·154	1·184	1·142	1·176	1·176	1·184	1·200	1·222	1·266	1·307
November	1·161	1·184	1·142	1·176	1·169	1·184	1·219	1·211	1·278	1·299
December	1·146	1·161	1·114	1·173	1·146	1·165	1·203	1·180	1·258	1·270
Means	1·167	1·169	1·179	1·151	1·182	1·175	1·197	1·199	1·254	1·275

TABLE X.—VAPOUR TENSION DUE TO THE TEMPERATURE OF THE GROUND AT 132 INCHES IN DEPTH AT BOMBAY.

Months.	1890.	1891.	1892.	1893.	1894.	1895.	1896.	1897.	1898.	1899.
	in.	in.	in.	in.	in.	in.	in.	in.	in.	in.
January	1·121	1·114	1·131	1·084	1·121	1·114	1·135	1·154	1·142	1·184
February	1·106	1·095	1·117	1·070	1·110	1·092	1·114	1·131	1·128	1·169
March	1·106	1·088	1·117	1·064	1·106	1·092	1·106	1·124	1·131	1·157
April	1·121	1·095	1·135	1·074	1·121	1·106	1·131	1·131	1·150	1·173
May	1·146	1·124	1·165	1·103	1·146	1·135	1·157	1·157	1·184	1·200
June	1·173	1·165	1·196	1·135	1·173	1·169	1·192	1·192	1·215	1·226
July	1·188	1·192	1·215	1·165	1·203	1·192	1·215	1·215	1·234	1·246
August	1·180	1·203	1·211	1·165	1·200	1·192	1·211	1·215	1·230	1·250
September	1·161	1·188	1·173	1·154	1·176	1·184	1·184	1·196	1·219	1·246
October	1·146	1·176	1·135	1·150	1·165	1·173	1·176	1·184	1·211	1·238
November	1·142	1·157	1·114	1·142	1·146	1·161	1·176	1·169	1·203	1·234
December	1·128	1·150	1·106	1·139	1·135	1·146	1·169	1·157	1·200	1·222
Means	1·143	1·146	1·151	1·120	1·150	1·146	1·164	1·169	1·187	1·212

TABLE XI.—Mean Monthly Vapour Pressure, Bombay Observatory.

Months.	1890.	1891.	1892.	1893.	1894.	1895.	1896.	1897.	1898.	1899.
	in.	in.	in.	in.	in.	in.	in.	in.	in.	in.
January	·589	·568	·621	·560	·616	·580	·628	·592	·580	·510
February	·641	·557	·637	·548	·658	·608	·629	·593	·621	·620
March	·721	·648	·755	·684	·727	·738	·743	·692	·720	·742
April	·836	·810	·897	·807	·841	·818	·869	·834	·854	·817
May	·866	·873	·875	·871	·858	·861	·915	·898	·893	·882
June	·907	·919	·923	·899	·929	·923	·948	·952	·931	·897
July	·870	·904	·908	·875	·893	·889	·908	·922	·911	·885
August	·824	·873	·869	·855	·867	·863	·868	·903	·876	·861
September	·821	·862	·851	·839	·852	·851	·847	·900	·874	·846
October	·815	·814	·871	·799	·855	·831	·883	·848	·878	·877
November	·717	·662	·652	·748	·665	·754	·755	·656	·752	·729
December	·644	·589	·641	·620	·647	·596	·636	·582	·680	·633
Means	·771	·757	·792	·759	·784	·776	·802	·781	·798	·775

TABLE XII.—Minima Monthly Vapour Pressure, Bombay Observatory.

Months.	1890.	1891.	1892.	1893.	1894.	1895.	1896.	1897.	1898.	1899.
	in.	in.	in.	in.	in.	in.	in.	in.	in.	in.
January	·337	·327	·314	·314	·432	·351	·387	·281	·318	·218
February	·400	·206	·298	·253	·344	·333	·347	·347	·195	·325
March	·543	·402	·355	·424	·441	·505	·477	·389	·201	·441
April	·598	·547	·691	·561	·657	·503	·617	·465	·570	·595
May	·700	·715	·674	·749	·762	·696	·816	·785	·741	·736
June	·788	·817	·799	·782	·808	·792	·790	·804	·799	·701
July	·787	·704	·802	·759	·741	·811	·774	·776	·786	·762
August	·725	·773	·751	·760	·748	·733	·763	·795	·766	·723
September	·723	·734	·764	·720	·773	·719	·681	·802	·725	·751
October	·448	·589	·561	·513	·615	·526	·537	·560	·532	·416
November	·394	·426	·375	·380	·480	·492	·462	·391	·463	·433
December	·360	·347	·430	·402	·431	·353	·359	·286	·311	·343
Means	·567	·549	·568	·551	·603	·568	·584	·557	·534	·537

TABLE XIII.—Barometric Pressure, Bombay Observatory, 87 Feet above Sea-Level.

Months.	1890.	1891.	1892.	1893.	1894.	1895.	1896.	1897.	1898.	1899.
	ins.	ins.	ins.	ins.	ins.	ins.	ins.	ins.	ins.	ins.
January	29·910	29·952	29·929	29·907	29·928	29·930	29·945	29·946	29·961	29·950
February	29·911	29·939	29·863	29·938	29·920	29·926	29·944	29·904	29·868	29·894
March	29·841	29·866	29·811	29·866	29·855	29·840	29·848	29·865	29·843	29·857
April	29·788	29·835	29·761	29·791	29·787	29·803	29·776	29·821	29·779	29·799
May	29·754	29·766	29·754	29·755	29·784	29·782	29·796	29·774	29·759	29·760
June	29·632	29·734	29·657	29·648	29·636	29·654	29·618	29·664	29·649	29·660
July	29·666	29·653	29·608	29·687	29·658	29·689	29·665	29·629	29·628	29·732
August	29·756	29·749	29·693	29·728	29·694	29·704	29·736	29·672	29·744	29·759
September	29·785	29·792	29·740	29·775	29·758	29·799	29·821	29·759	29·759	29·847
October	29·857	29·859	29·797	29·826	29·806	29·820	29·878	29·840	29·810	29·847
November	29·920	29·898	29·897	29·899	29·933	29·933	29·865	29·897	29·856	29·936
December	29·947	29·960	29·968	29·958	29·945	29·936	29·953	29·951	29·916	29·954
Means	29·814	29·834	29·790	29·815	29·809	29·818	29·820	29·810	29·798	29·833

TABLE XIV.—MEAN VELOCITY OF THE WIND, BOMBAY OBSERVATORY, IN MILES PER HOUR.

Months.	1890.	1891.	1892.	1893.	1894.	1895.	1896.	1897.	1898.	1899.
January	9·7	10·2	8·9	10·2	9·3	9·7	8·5	9·5	9·3	9·5
February . . .	10·2	11·4	10·5	10·8	8·6	9·4	10·8	10·2	10·1	9·1
March	12·9	12·5	9·8	8·6	10·9	11·5	10·6	9·1	10·1	10·3
April	11·1	10·4	10·3	11·2	9·0	9·7	9·5	10·1	9·2	8·4
May	10·7	11·2	11·5	10·6	9·4	9·2	8·8	8·6	9·2	9·4
June	17·6	12·4	12·0	14·6	14·4	15·1	14·8	13·7	14·0	12·7
July	20·4	18·1	19·0	14·5	17·5	17·3	20·4	14·3	16·2	15·7
August . . .	16·2	16·0	13·0	14·3	13·9	14·8	14·9	15·1	15·4	11·1
September . . .	10·4	11·3	11·7	11·7	9·5	8·9	8·3	10·0	9·0	8·9
October . . .	9·0	9·6	7·6	7·7	9·5	9·0	7·7	8·5	7·6	6·8
November . . .	8·0	10·5	9·4	10·0	10·2	8·6	9·3	9·6	8·7	8·1
December . . .	9·4	11·0	8·2	9·1	8·7	9·5	9·9	10·1	9·6	7·7
Averages .	12·1	12·1	11·0	11·1	10·9	11·1	11·1	10·7	10·7	9·8

TABLE XV.—CLOUD, BOMBAY OBSERVATORY. MEANS OF ESTIMATES AT 6, 10, 14, 16, AND 22 HOURS DAILY. THE WHOLE SKY RECKONED AS 10.

Months.	1890.	1891.	1892.	1893.	1894.	1895.	1896.	1897.	1898.	1899.
January	0·4	0·2	0·8	0·7	0·3	0·9	0·2	2·0	0·0	0·4
February . . .	0·7	0·7	0·6	0·6	0·4	1·7	1·2	0·8	0·9	1·2
March	2·1	1·2	0·7	0·7	1·9	1·3	0·9	1·0	0·6	0·4
April	3·0	2·0	2·3	2·8	1·7	0·9	2·1	2·0	1·9	2·2
May	2·5	3·3	3·2	3·3	2·2	3·0	2·9	3·3	2·7	3·5
June	9·2	5·4	6·8	7·6	8·2	7·0	8·5	7·4	7·2	7·9
July	9·5	9·3	9·1	8·6	8·6	8·7	9·3	8·7	9·2	8·5
August . . .	8·9	9·0	9·2	8·8	8·9	8·6	8·8	8·7	8·6	6·9
September . . .	6·6	7·7	7·6	7·3	8·4	7·7	4·7	7·5	7·3	5·1
October . . .	2·5	2·2	4·6	1·6	5·5	4·2	1·1	3·7	2·0	2·2
November . . .	2·3	1·1	0·7	2·3	1·2	1·3	2·8	0·1	1·8	·5
December . . .	2·7	0·7	1·7	2·2	1·0	1·5	2·5	0·4	1·5	·9
Averages .	4·2	3·6	3·9	3·9	4·0	3·9	3·8	3·8	3·6	3·3

TABLE XVI.—RAINFALL, BOMBAY OBSERVATORY, NEWMAN'S GAUGE 4½ FEET ABOVE THE GROUND.

Months.	1890.	1891.	1892.	1893.	1894.	1895.	1896.	1897.	1898.	1899.
	ins.	ins.	ins.	ins.	ins.	ins.	ins.	ins.	ins.	ins.
January	...	...	...	...	0·22	...	...	0·01	...	...
February . . .	...	...	...	0·14	...	0·07	...	...	0·17	...
March	...	0·20	...	...	0·06	...	...	...	...	...
April	0·01	...	...	0·02	0·01	...	...	...	...	1·57
May	0·06	...	0·11	6·30	...	0·08	0·26	...	0·16	0·08
June	24·55	13·99	13·30	21·47	16·87	17·84	28·02	14·40	27·21	20·81
July	21·54	32·48	23·80	16·14	26·16	18·04	36·44	30·19	20·72	4·72
August . . .	10·61	6·94	36·56	13·55	8·40	15·97	20·77	13·82	5·28	5·23
September . . .	6·45	22·54	18·73	7·54	12·04	11·91	1·62	20·60	19·94	3·49
October . . .	0·58	1·04	1·89	0·45	3·08	3·62	0·01	2·51	0·48	...
November . . .	1·25	...	0·67	1·63	...	0·06	0·53	...	0·13	...
December . . .	0·13	...	...	...	0·01	...	...	...	...	...
Totals .	65·18	77·18	95·12	67·24	56·85	67·59	87·65	81·53	74·09	35·90
Rainy Days	116	100	114	124	124	109	102	108		

TABLE XVII.—Deaths from all Causes in Bombay. From Reports of the Sanitary Commissioner, Bombay.

Months.	1889.	1890.	1891.	1892.	1893.	1894.	1895.	1896.	1897.	1898.
January .	2064	1788	1749	2381	1779	2037	2119	2138	7462	6669
February .	1754	1641	1799	2294	1693	2277	2055	2224	6814	8146
March .	1982	2546	2089	2431	1838	2307	2182	2504	5305	9147
April .	2046	1710	2046	2560	2310	2416	2298	2528	3500	5076
May . .	2075	1527	1973	2322	2254	2506	2571	2392	2332	2773
June . .	1774	1327	1836	1787	1853	2175	2008	2001	2163	1977
July . .	2038	1531	1812	2191	1844	2579	1982	2257	2941	2267
August .	2045	1638	2118	2257	2141	2602	2032	2627	3883	3061
September	2027	1637	2151	2106	1834	2150	1811	2593	3448	3416
October .	1774	1663	2042	2032	1744	2087	1806	2831	3221	3472
November .	1692	1475	1766	1907	1659	1863	1774	2865	2822	2449
December .	1777	1748	2120	1910	1853	1909	2017	6090	3584	3164
Totals .	23,048	20,231	23,501	26,178	22,802	26,908	24,655	33,050	47,475	51,617

TABLE XVIII.—Deaths from Fever in Bombay. From Reports of the Sanitary Commissioner, Bombay.

Months.	1890.	1891.	1892.	1893.	1894.	1895.	1896.	1897	1898	1899
January . .	574	464	754	447	451	549	580	5699	3227	
February . .	485	503	788	410	571	503	596	7549	4869	
March . . .	999	658	688	440	558	572	615	5263	5452	
April . . .	563	565	885	724	538	562	802	2838	2509	
May . . .	549	612	742	828	614	755	694	902	863	
June . . .	437	538	516	513	469	586	504	522	425	
July . . .	521	502	671	404	574	475	507	540	517	
August . . .	505	619	597	450	542	516	624	653	836	
September . .	469	653	567	409	450	416	758	734	1075	
October . .	485	594	479	411	598	382	634	598	1053	
November . .	400	503	530	382	585	466	738	575	536	
December . .	481	612	493	393	467	557	1779	1014	853	
Totals .	6468	6823	7708	5811	6414	6339	8831	26,887[1]	22,215	

[1] 10,237 plague.

Description of Diagrams (pp. 68-88).

No. 1 (p. 68).—The strong line represents the weekly deaths from plague in the city of Bombay from time to time as they have been published. The dotted line indicates the average monthly temperature of the ground at the depth of 9 inches. It will be observed from this diagram that the temperature of the ground would appear to have no influence upon the increase of the plague, and that as a rule the temperature of the ground was lowest preceding the greatest mortality from plague; but it will be seen hereafter that the temperature of the ground has an enormous influence on the plague, not measured as temperature, but measured by its power to exhale vapours, and this is dependent upon its temperature but is controlled for the time being by the temperature of the dew-point of the air.

No. 2 (p. 69).—The strong line in this diagram represents the weekly deaths from plague in the city of Bombay. The dotted line indicates the average monthly temperature of the ground at the depth of 20 inches.

The remarks under No. 1 apply to this diagram and the two succeeding ones.

No. 3 (p. 70).—The strong line represents the weekly deaths from plague in the city of Bombay. The dotted line indicates the average monthly temperature of the ground at the depth of 60 inches. In this case it will be seen that the lowest temperature falls somewhere about the time of greatest intensity of the plague. The fluctuations of the temperature of the ground are less than at shallower depths.

No. 4 (p. 71).—The strong line represents the weekly deaths from plague in the city of Bombay. The dotted line indicates the average monthly temperature of the ground at the depth of 132 inches. In this case it will be seen that the lowest temperature falls somewhere about the time of greatest intensity of the plague. The fluctuations of the temperature of the ground are also less than at shallower depths, and the temperatures are very high at this depth.

No. 5 (p. 72).—The strong line shows the weekly deaths from plague in the city of Bombay, the upper line with dots upon it the mean temperature of the air, and the lower dash line the minimum temperature of the air. It will be noted in this diagram that plague begins to be rife when the temperature begins to fall, it gets to its height shortly after the period of lowest temperature, and begins to decline shortly after the temperature rises. It would appear from this diagram that there is a general conformity between temperature and plague: the most plague with the lowest temperature, and least plague with the highest temperature. These conditions show that with the lowest temperature we have also the lowest dew-point and the greatest difference between the temperature of the ground and the temperature of the dew-point.

No. 6 (p. 73).—The strong line in this diagram shows the weekly deaths from plague in the city of Bombay, and the dash line the amount of cloud. It will be seen from this diagram that plague is most rife when there is the least cloud. This is quite the contrary to what has been supposed to be the case, as it has been reported that cloudy weather appears to have increased the mortality from plague in Bombay.

No. 7 (p. 74).—The strong line represents the weekly deaths from plague in the city of Bombay, while the dash line indicates the monthly average height of the barometer. It will be observed in this case that, during outbreaks of plague, as a rule the barometer is falling, and the fall continues long after the plague has begun to subside. The fall of the barometer has a most material effect upon eliminating air and vapours from the ground. This is very clearly shown in this country in the case of the blowing wells of Northallerton, in which, whenever the barometer falls, a strong current of air sets out of these wells, whereas, when the barometer is rising, there is a strong current into the wells. In this case, however, the fall continues so long after the epidemic that it cannot be supposed that the barometric pressure has any material influence upon the rise and fall of plague, although when plague is most rife its influence favours the escape of air and vapours from the ground.

No. 8 (p. 75).—The strong line shows the weekly deaths from plague in the city of Bombay, while the dash line represents the monthly average velocity of the wind in miles per hour. It will be observed from this diagram that the wind may, and probably does, exercise some influence upon plague; that is, when there is the greatest wind to clear the air, there appears to be the least plague, and that, on the contrary, during the period the plague is epidemic the winds are sluggish and would allow any malarious influence to linger within the district subject to such outbreaks. In no case, however, does the least movement of the wind correspond with the highest rates of mortality.

No. 9 (p. 76).—The strong line indicates the weekly deaths from plague in the city of Bombay. The two dotted lines indicate the tensional difference, that is, the difference of the vapour tension due to the temperature of the ground at 9 inches in depth and the vapour tension due to the temperature of the dew-point; the upper line with dots upon it being the difference between the temperature of the ground and the minimum dew-point, while the lower dash line indicates the difference between the mean temperature of the ground and the mean dew-point, and it is by means of these differences in vapour tension that exhalations take place from the ground. It will now be seen that, during the period when plague is most rife, or preceding it, these tensional differences are greatest, and the power of exhaling vapours from the earth is also at its maximum, and that there is a regular rise and fall in these tensional differences about the period, or preceding the period, when plague is most rife. Of course, it should be noted that these are monthly differences of the vapour tension, while the deaths from plague are weekly, and therefore they are liable to error in not being able to show exactly the maximum and minimum periods when the differences occurred. With more observations as to vapour tension, I am convinced that a better result would be shown.

These remarks apply also to Nos. 10 and 11.

No. 10 (p. 77).—The strong line indicates the weekly deaths from plague in the city of Bombay. The two dotted lines indicate the tensional difference, that is, the difference of the vapour tension due to the temperature of the ground at 20 inches in depth and the vapour tension due to the temperature of the dew-point; the upper line with dots upon it being the difference between the temperature of the ground and the minimum dew-point, while the lower dash line indicates the difference between the mean temperature of the ground and the mean dew-point.

No. 11 (p. 78).—The strong line indicates the weekly deaths from plague in the city of Bombay. The two dotted lines indicate the tensional difference, that is, the difference of the vapour tension due to the temperature of the ground at 60 inches in depth and the vapour tension due to the temperature of the dew-point; the upper line with dots upon it being the difference between the temperature of the ground and the minimum dew-point, while the lower dash line indicates the difference between the mean temperature of the ground and the mean dew-point. It will be observed that when we come to the greater depths of the ground there is an intermediate fluctuation which agrees with the intermediate fluctuations which have occurred in the deaths from plague in Bombay, showing that the lines are getting very much more parallel with plague than they were at the shallower depths.

No. 12 (p. 79).—The strong line indicates the weekly deaths from plague in the city of Bombay, and the dotted line indicates the total weekly deaths in Bombay. The dash line and the line with dots upon it indicate the tensional difference, that is, the difference of the vapour tension due to the temperature of the ground at 132 inches in depth and the vapour tension due to the temperature of the dew-point; the line with dots upon it being the difference between the temperature of the ground and the minimum dew-point, while the dash line indicates the difference between the mean temperature of the ground and the mean dew-point. It will be observed that when we come to the greater depths of the ground there is an intermediate fluctuation which agrees with the intermediate fluctuations which have occurred in the general deaths and in the deaths from plague in Bombay, showing that the lines are getting very much more parallel with plague than they were at the shallower depths.

No. 13 (p. 80).—The strong line indicates the weekly deaths from plague in the city of Bombay. The dash line indicates the exhalation from the ground at a depth of 9 inches, calculated from the formula given in the paper, in which the influence of wind is taken into account. The temperatures both of the ground and of the dew-point are monthly records, while the plague is a weekly record, and are liable to error in not being able to show exactly the maximum and minimum periods when the extreme differences occurred. It will be seen that now there begins to be a considerable degree of parallelism between the exhalation as calculated and the outbreak of plague; that this influence commences about the time the plague begins to increase.

No. 14 (p. 81).—The strong line indicates the weekly deaths from plague in the city of Bombay. The dotted line indicates the exhalation from the ground at 20 inches in depth, calculated from the formula given in the paper, in which the influence of wind is taken into account. It will be seen from this diagram that there is an intermediate rise corresponding with the intermediate rises in the death-rate from plague in 1897, and a similar rise which corresponds with the increase in the general death-rate in 1898, which is shown on Diagram No. 17.

No. 15 (p. 82).—The strong line indicates the weekly deaths from plague in the city of Bombay. The dotted line indicates the exhalation from the ground for 60 inches in depth, calculated from the formula given in the paper, in which the influence of wind is taken into account. It will be seen from this diagram that there is an intermediate rise corresponding with the intermediate rises in the death-rate from plague in 1897, and a similar rise which corresponds with the increase in the general death-rate in 1898, which is shown on Diagram No. 17.

No. 16 (p. 83).—The strong line indicates the weekly deaths from plague in the city of Bombay. The dotted line indicates the total weekly deaths in Bombay. The dash line indicates the exhalation from the ground for 132 inches in depth, calculated from the formula given in the paper, in which the influence of wind is taken into account. It will be observed from this diagram that, in all probability, the temperature and exhalations from the greater depths of the soil have a most marked influence on the spread of plague, and that the lines showing exhalation are absolutely parallel with either the general causes of death or the deaths from plague which occurred in the city of Bombay during the three outbreaks of 1896, 1897-98, and 1898-99.

No. 17 (p. 84).—The strong line indicates the weekly deaths from plague in the city of Bombay, and the dotted line the total weekly deaths in Bombay. It will be seen that there were intermediate outbreaks of disease between July and November 1897 and 1898, which are extremely marked in the general death-rate, but not so marked in the deaths from plague in 1897; and this, after all, is probably due to errors in registration, the deaths from plague at this period having probably escaped their due amount of registration.

No. 18 (p. 85).—The strong line indicates the deaths from plague in the city of Bombay. The small dotted line shows the deaths from diseases of the respiratory organs, exclusive of phthisis; while the dash line indicates the deaths from remittent fever. It will be seen that there is a strong parallelism between these diseases, which are all more or less influenced by the hygrometric conditions of the ground. In 1890, when reporting on Bombay, I found out that diseases of the respiratory system, other than phthisis, had increased to an enormous extent in recent years, which I attribute to the filling up of the low grounds about Bombay and obstructing the natural drainage channels; and there can be little doubt that plague, remittent fever, and phthisis are also influenced by the obstruction of the natural drainage, which in Bombay still remains unremedied.

No. 19 (p. 86).—On the left-hand diagram the strong line indicates the weekly deaths from plague in London for the average of six years when plague was rife, or the years 1564, 1592, 1603, 1608, 1636, and 1642, the years selected being those when the weeks ended on the same date; and the line with a cross line upon it indicates the total weekly deaths in London for the same years. On the right hand of the diagram the strong line indicates the weekly deaths from plague in London during the Great Plague of 1665. The line with a cross line upon it indicates the total weekly deaths in London in the year 1665. On both diagrams the dash-and-dot line indicates the difference of the vapour tension between the minimum dew-point and the maximum registered temperature of the ground at 6 inches in depth at Croydon in the years 1898 and 1899. The dotted line indicates the tensional difference between the maximum registered temperature of the ground at 6 inches and the maximum dew-point; while the dash line indicates the tensional difference between the minimum temperature of the ground at 6 inches and the minimum dew-point. It will be seen from these diagrams that the tensional differences which control exhalations from the ground occur at a period immediately preceding that when plague used to be most rife in this country. There are no meteorological observations during these plague years in this country, but contemporaneous history shows that the great plagues usually occurred in, or following, dry periods.

No. 20 (p. 87).—On the left-hand diagram the strong line indicates the weekly deaths from plague in London in the years 1564, 1592, 1603, 1608, 1636, and 1642, and the dotted line indicates the total weekly deaths in London in the same years and the tensional difference due to the temperature of the ground at Croydon at the depth of 30 inches; and the minimum dew-point is shown with a strong line with cross line upon it, the tensional difference between the minimum dew-point and the temperature of the ground at 60 inches in depth being shown with a fine line. On the right-hand diagram the weekly deaths from plague in London are indicated by a strong line in the Great Plague year of 1665, and the dotted line indicates the total weekly deaths in London in the same year; the tensional difference between the dew-point and the ground at 30 inches in depth at Croydon is shown by a strong line with cross line upon it, and the tensional difference between the dew-point and the temperature of the ground at 60 inches in depth at Croydon is shown with a fine line.

No. 21 (p. 88).—The strong line indicates the weekly deaths from plague in London in 1665; the dash line indicates the total weekly deaths in the plague year of 1665; the line with crosses upon it indicates the total weekly deaths in London for the average of the years 1564, 1592, 1603, 1608, 1636, and 1642; and the dot-and-dash line indicates the deaths from plague in the same years. The strong line with a cross line upon it indicates the tensional difference between the temperature of the ground at 3·2 feet and the mean dew-point at Greenwich, while the dotted line indicates the tensional difference between the temperature of the ground at 3·2 feet in depth and the minimum dew-point at Greenwich. This diagram shows the tensional difference of the ground at Greenwich for a period extending from 1873 to 1887, while the dew-points are an average for a period extending from 1849 to 1869. These diagrams show what a strong, marked parallelism there is between the tensional differences which are the cause of vapours rising from the ground and the plague epidemics which formerly occurred in this country, but that the period of the year in which plague occurred in London was not the same as at Bombay. Yet plague is only rife when those forces are brought into play which give rise to earthy exhalations, and the fact that there is a difference in the periodicity between London and Bombay, and that these forces only come into operation in each country at the particular times the disease was prevalent, thoroughly confirms the view that plague, if not directly due to exhalations from the ground, is largely controlled by such exhalations.

No. 22 (Plate I.).—The upper diagram shows the tensional difference between the registered maximum temperature of the ground at 6 inches and the maximum dew-point at Croydon for every day from June 1898 to January 1900. The diagram shows the daily variations, and it also shows that at certain periods of the year condensation takes place; that is, all the observations above the base line represent evaporation, while those below the base line represent condensation. The lower diagram shows the tensional difference between the registered minimum temperature of the ground at 6 inches and the minimum dew-point at Croydon for every day from June 1898 to January 1900. The diagram shows the daily variations, and it also shows that condensation takes place at certain periods of the year; that is, all the observations above the base line represent evaporation, while those below the base line represent condensation.

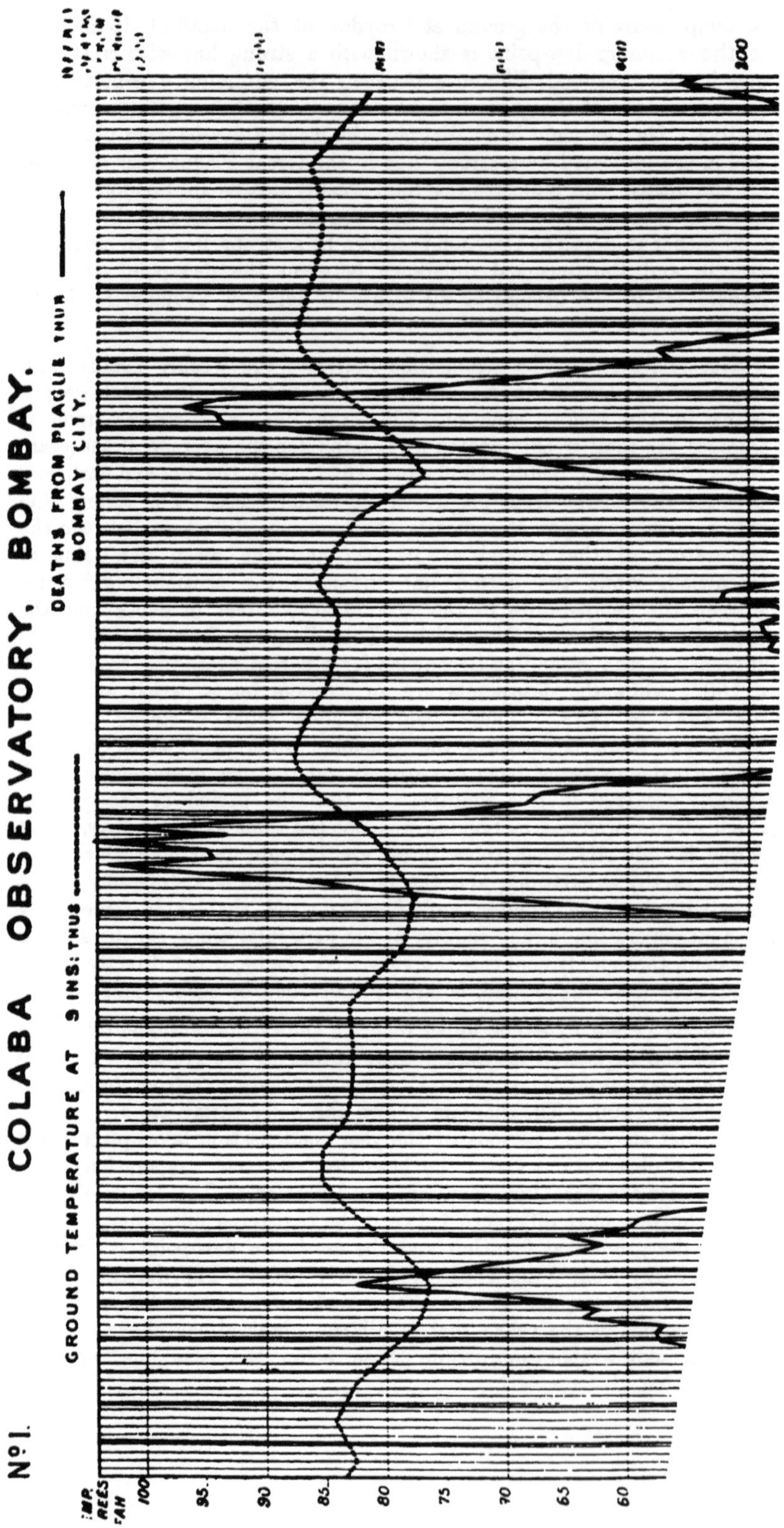
No 1.
COLABA OBSERVATORY, BOMBAY.
GROUND TEMPERATURE AT 9 INS: THUS
DEATHS FROM PLAGUE THUS
BOMBAY CITY.
100
95
90
85
80
75
70
65
60
200

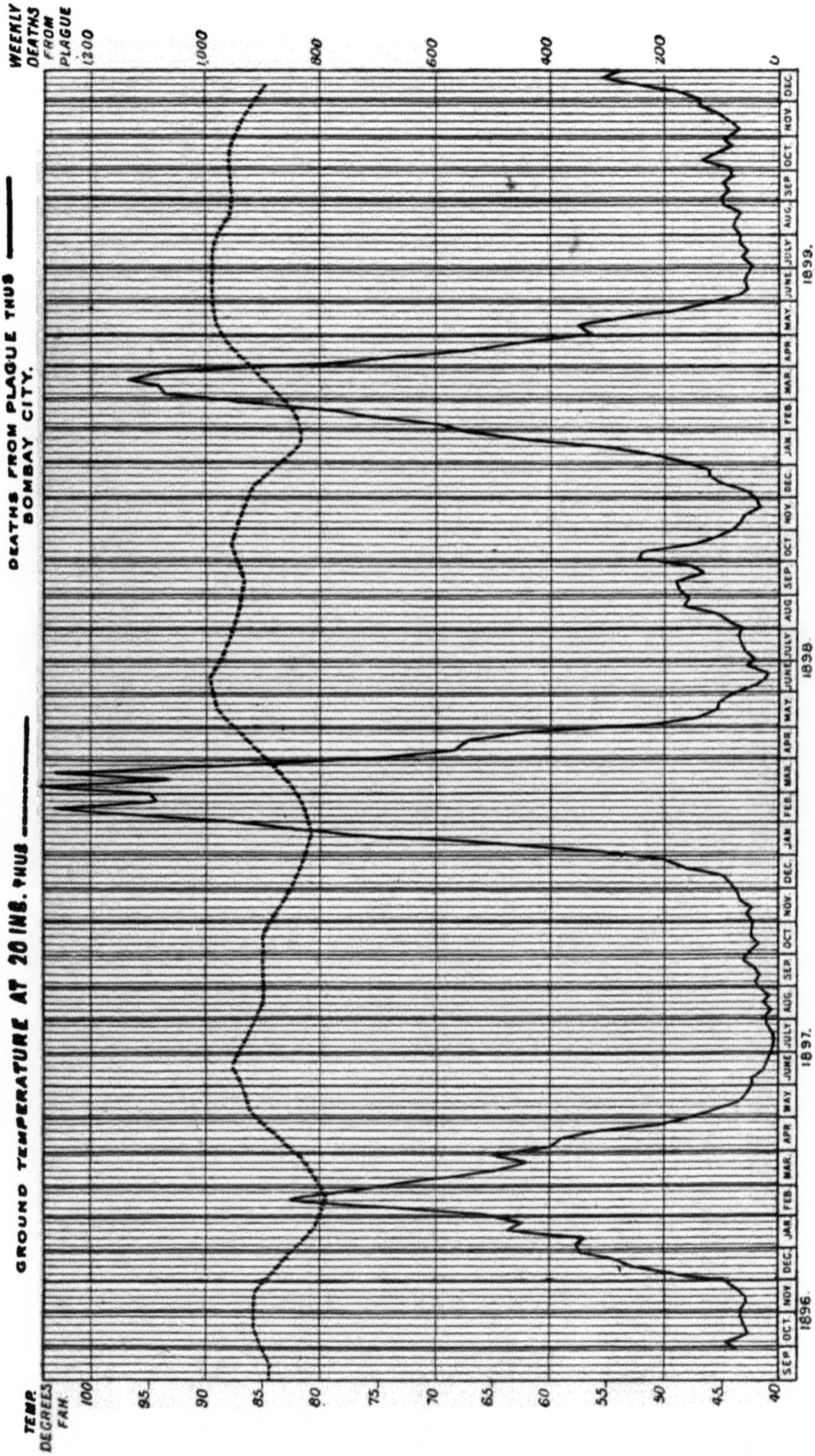
GROUND TEMPERATURE AT 20 INS. THUS
DEATHS FROM PLAGUE THUS
BOMBAY CITY.
WEEKLY DEATHS FROM PLAGUE
TEMP. DEGREES FAH.
1896.
1897.
1898.
1899.

Nº 3
COLABA OBSERVATORY, BOMBAY.
GROUND TEMPERATURE AT 60 INS. THUS
DEATHS FROM PLAGUE THUS
BOMBAY CITY.
WEEKLY DEATHS FROM PLAGUE
1,200
1,000
800
600
400
200
100
95.
90
85
80
75.
70
65
60
55
50

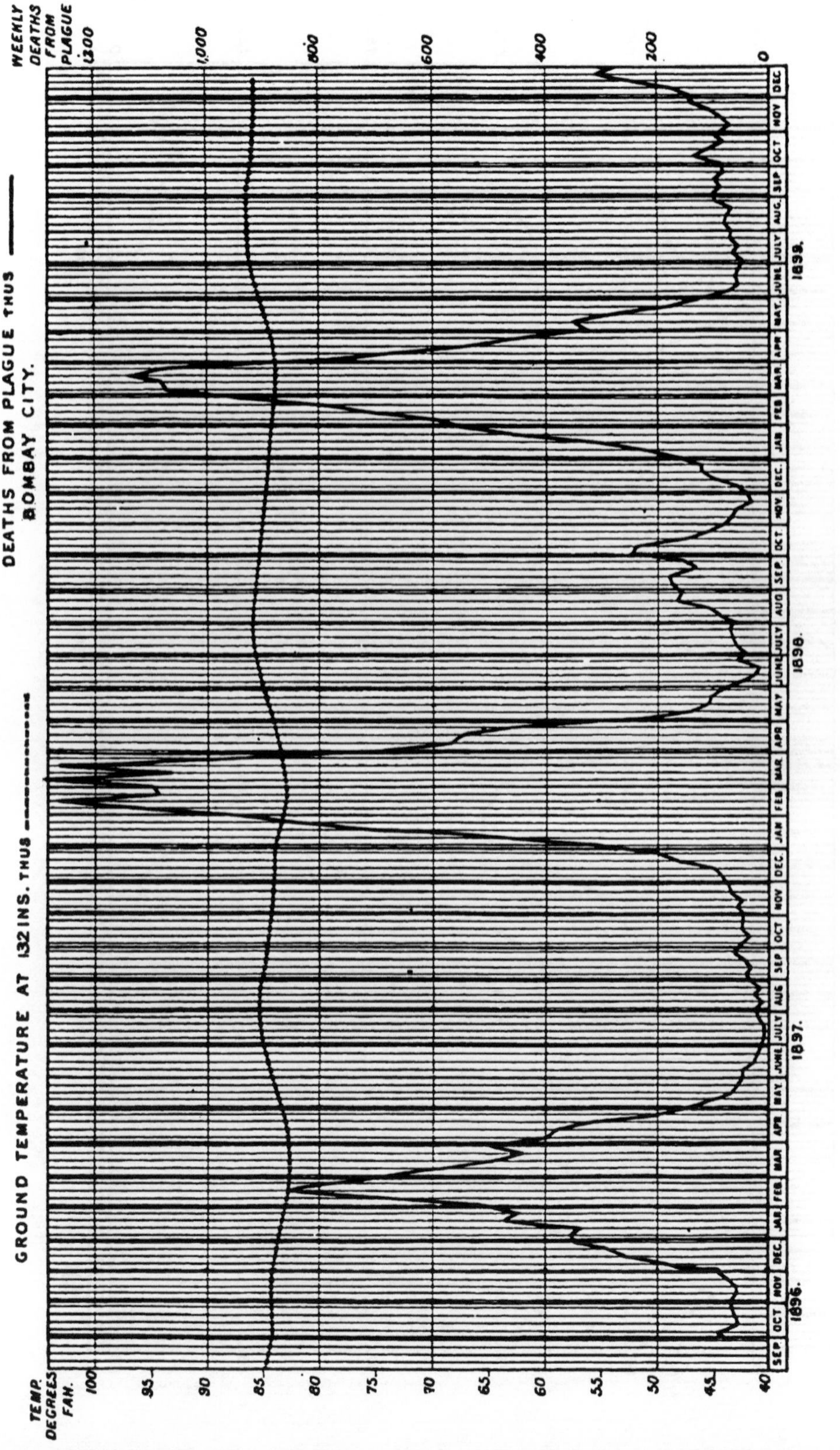
DEATHS FROM PLAGUE THUS
BOMBAY CITY.
GROUND TEMPERATURE AT 132 INS. THUS
WEEKLY DEATHS FROM PLAGUE
1,200
1,000
800
600
400
200
0
TEMP. DEGREES FAH.
100
95
90
85
80
75
70
65
60
55
50
45
40
SEP. OCT NOV DEC. JAN. FEB. MAR APR MAY JUNE JULY AUG SEP OCT NOV DEC. JAN FEB MAR APR MAY JUNE JULY AUG SEP. OCT. NOV. DEC. JAN FEB MAR. APR MAY. JUNE JULY AUG. SEP. OCT NOV DEC
1896.
1897.
1898.
1899.

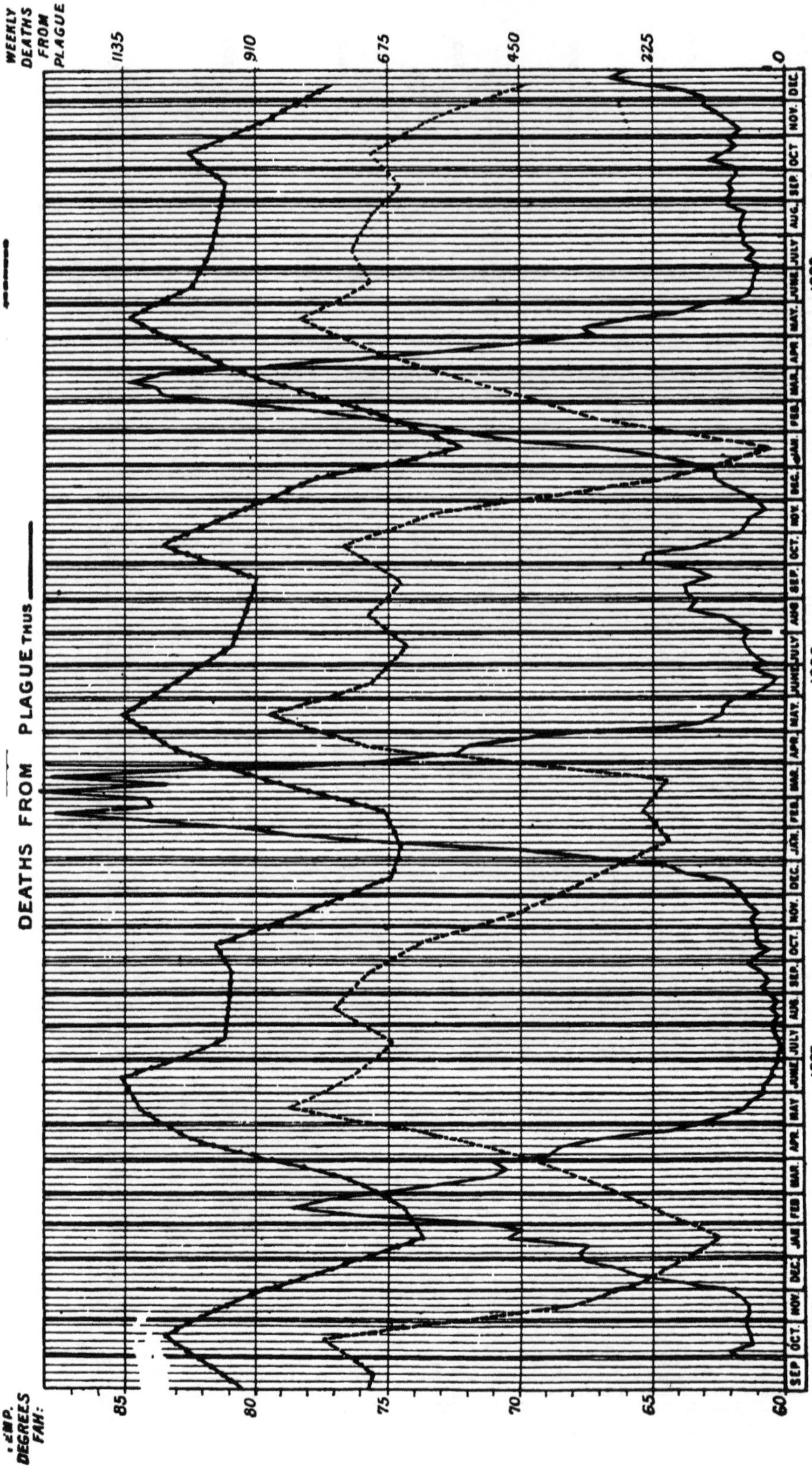
WEEKLY DEATHS FROM PLAGUE
1135
910
675
450
225
0
DEATHS FROM PLAGUE THUS
TEMP. DEGREES FAH.
85
80
75
70
65
60
SEP OCT. NOV. DEC. JAN. FEB. MAR. APR. MAY. JUNE JULY AUG. SEP. OCT. NOV. DEC. JAN. FEB. MAR. APR. MAY. JUNE JULY AUG. SEP. OCT. NOV. DEC. JAN. FEB. MAR. APR. MAY. JUNE JULY AUG. SEP. OCT NOV. DEC.
1896
1897
1898
1899

No. 7.

COLABA OBSERVATORY. BOMBAY.

MEAN BAROMETRIC PRESSURE THUS - - - - - - -

DEATHS FROM PLAGUE THUS ——— BOMBAY CITY.

BAROMETER INS	WEEKLY DEATHS FROM PLAGUE
32	1200
31	900
30	600
29	300

WEEKLY DEATHS FROM PLAGUE
1200
900
600
00
MILES PER HOUR
19
18
17
16
15
14
13
12.
11
10
9
8.

Nº 9.
COLABA OBSERVATORY. BOMBAY.
TENSIONAL DIFFERENCE 9 INS. GROUND WITH MEAN DEW POINT THUS
Dº Dº Dº MINIMUM Dº THUS
DEATHS FROM PLAGUE THUS
BOMBAY CITY.
VAPOUR TENSIONAL DIFFERENCE INS.
120
110
100
90
80
70
60
50
40
30
20
WEEKLY DEATHS FROM PLAGUE
1200
900
600

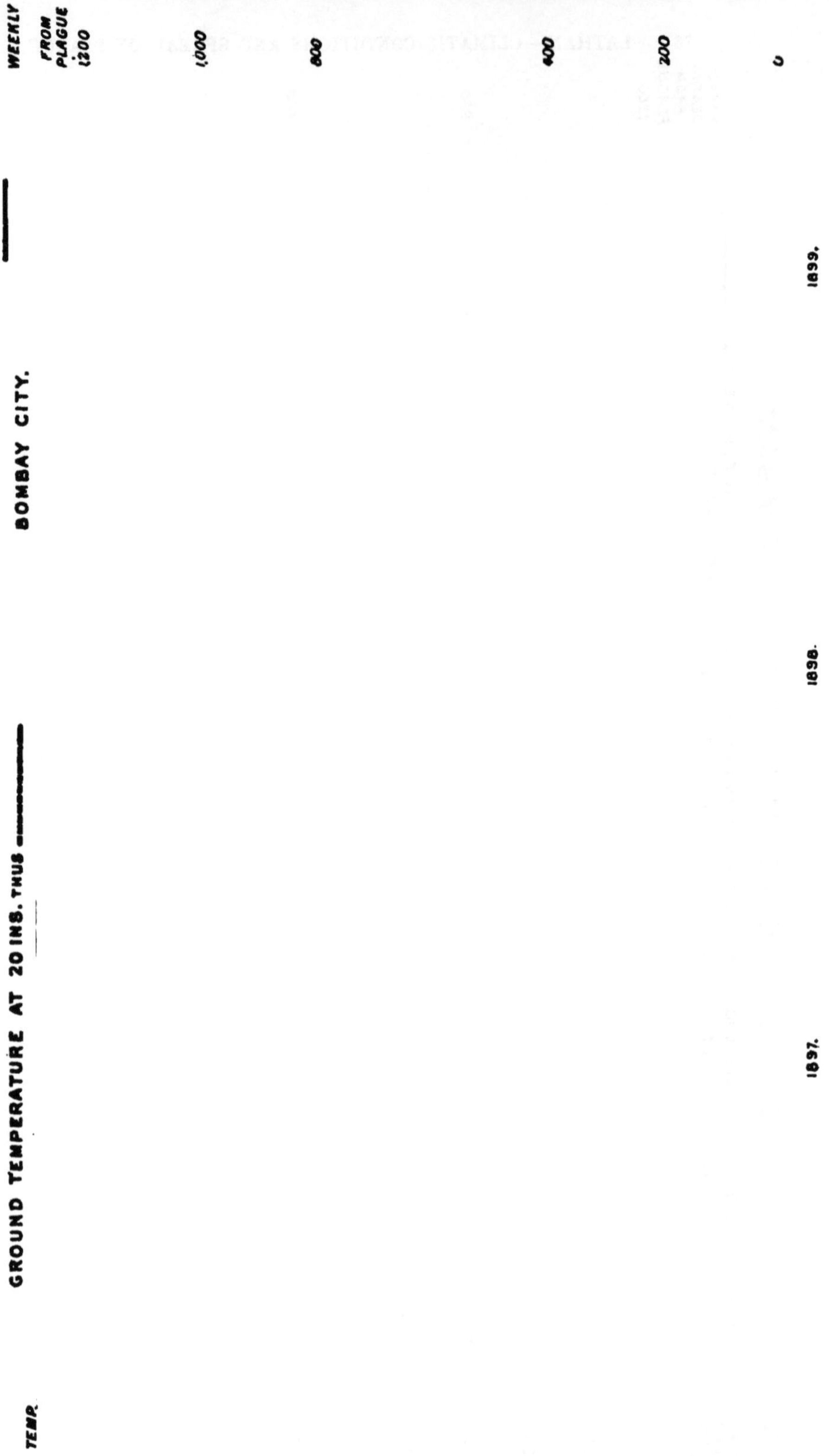
GROUND TEMPERATURE AT 20 INS. THUS
BOMBAY CITY.
TEMP.
WEEKLY
FROM PLAGUE
1200
1,000
800
400
200
0
1897.
1898.
1899.

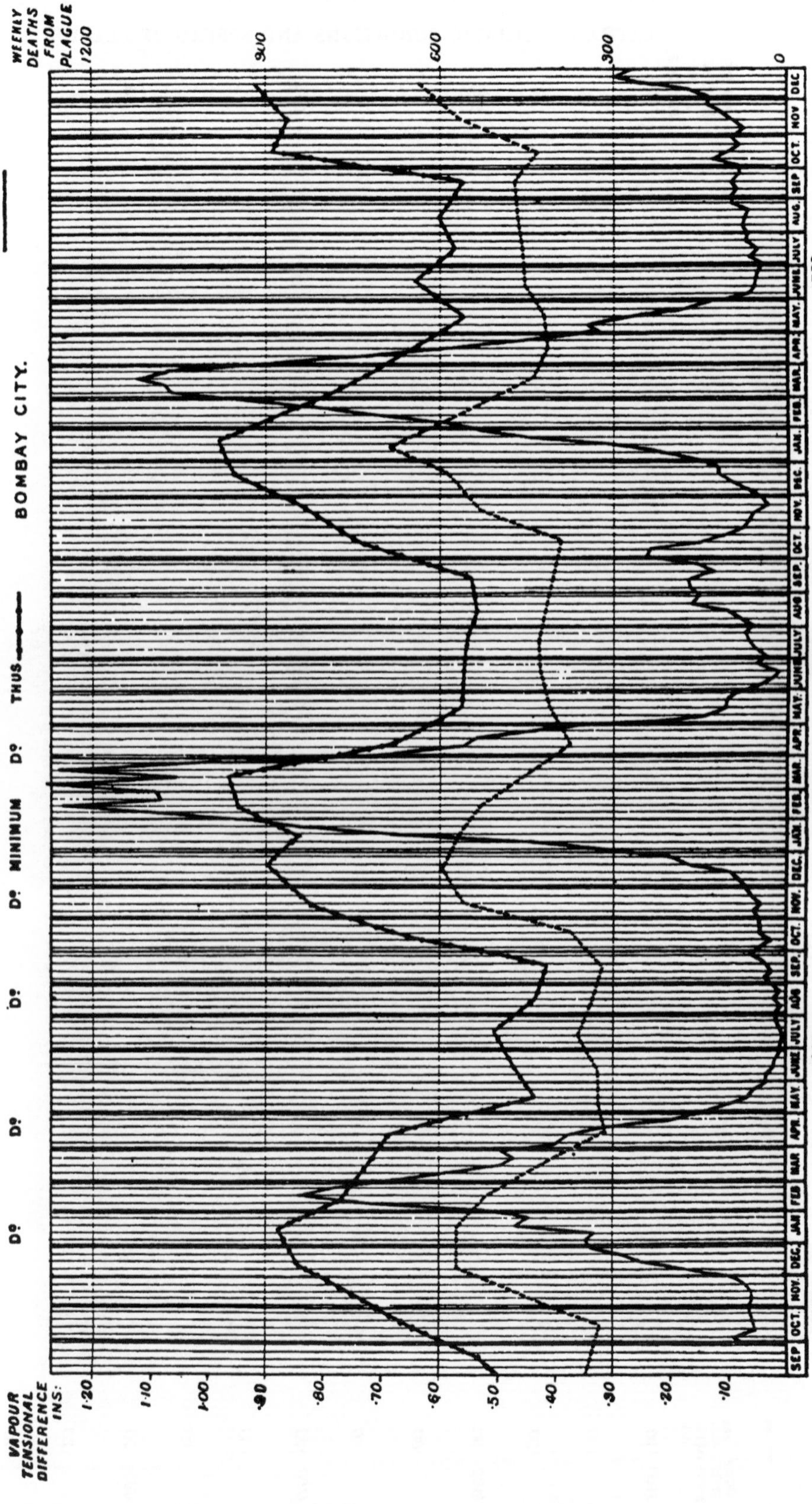

WEEKLY DEATHS FROM PLAGUE
1200
900
600
300
0
VAPOUR TENSIONAL DIFFERENCE INS.
1·20
1·10
1·00
·90
·80
·70
·60
·50
·40
·30
·20
·10
BOMBAY CITY.
Dº
Dº
Dº
Dº MINIMUM
Dº THUS
SEP. OCT. NOV. DEC. JAN. FEB. MAR. APR. MAY. JUNE JULY AUG. SEP. OCT. NOV. DEC. JAN. FEB. MAR. APR. MAY. JUNE JULY AUG. SEP. OCT. NOV. DEC. JAN. FEB. MAR. APR. MAY. JUNE JULY AUG. SEP. OCT. NOV. DEC.
1896
1897
1898
1899

WEEKLY DEATHS FROM PLAGUE
1200
900
600
00
INS
2400 1·20
1·10
1·00
1800 ·90
·80
·70
1200 ·60
·50
·40
600 ·30
·20
·10

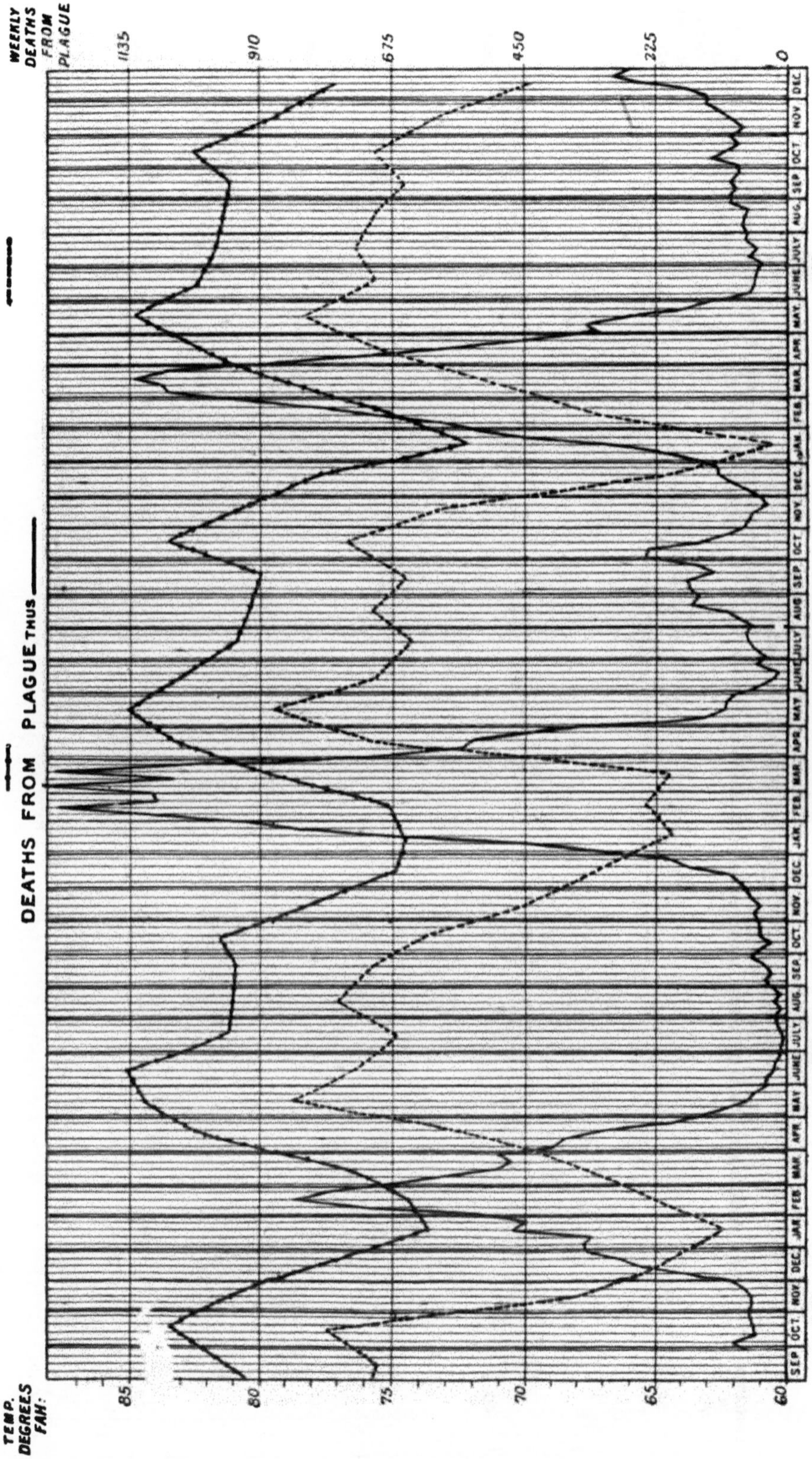
DEATHS FROM PLAGUE THUS
WEEKLY DEATHS FROM PLAGUE
1135
910
675
450
225
0
TEMP. DEGREES FAH.
85
80
75
70
65
60
SEP OCT NOV DEC JAN FEB MAR APR MAY JUNE JULY AUG SEP OCT NOV DEC JAN FEB MAR APR MAY JUNE JULY AUG SEP OCT NOV DEC JAN FEB MAR APR MAY JUNE JULY AUG SEP OCT NOV DEC
1896
1897
1898
1899

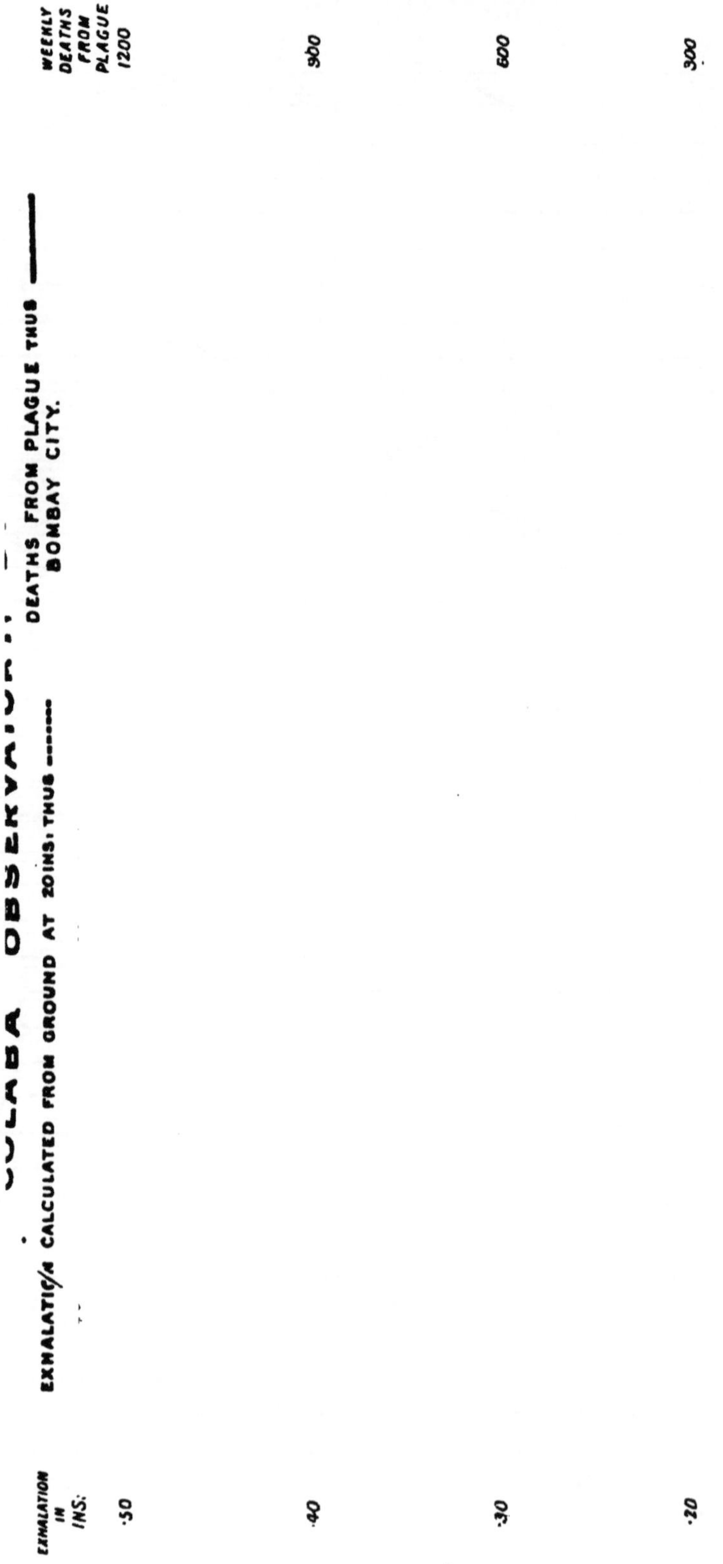
WEEKLY DEATHS FROM PLAGUE
1200
900
600
300
DEATHS FROM PLAGUE THUS
BOMBAY CITY.
EXHALATION CALCULATED FROM GROUND AT 20 INS: THUS
EXHALATION IN INS:
·50
·40
·30
·20

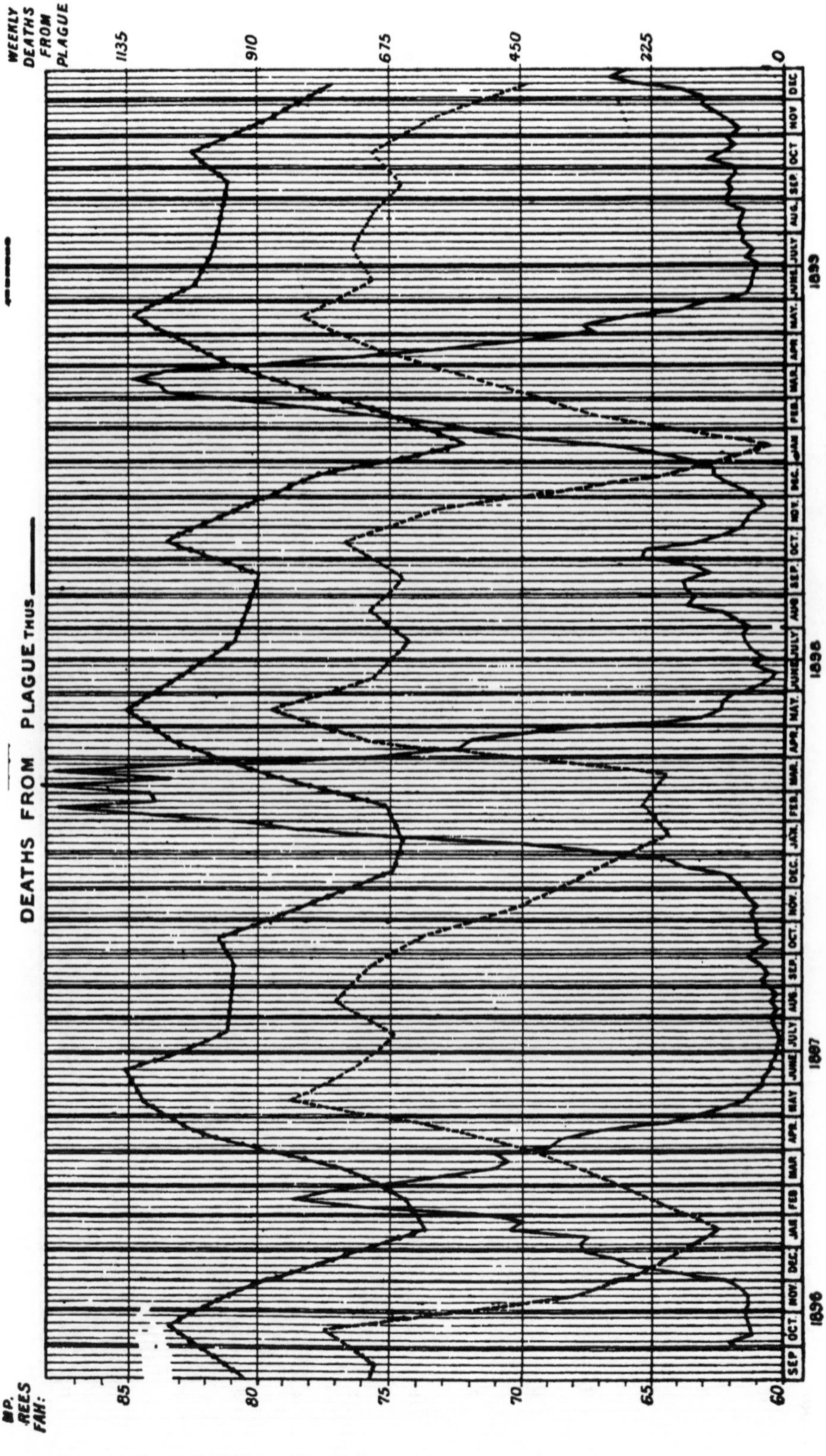
DEATHS FROM PLAGUE THUS
WEEKLY DEATHS FROM PLAGUE
1135
910
675
450
225
0
85
80
75
70
65
60
SEP OCT NOV DEC JAN FEB MAR APR MAY JUNE JULY AUG SEP OCT NOV DEC JAN FEB MAR APR MAY JUNE JULY AUG SEP OCT NOV DEC JAN FEB MAR APR MAY JUNE JULY AUG SEP OCT NOV DEC
1896
1897
1898
1899

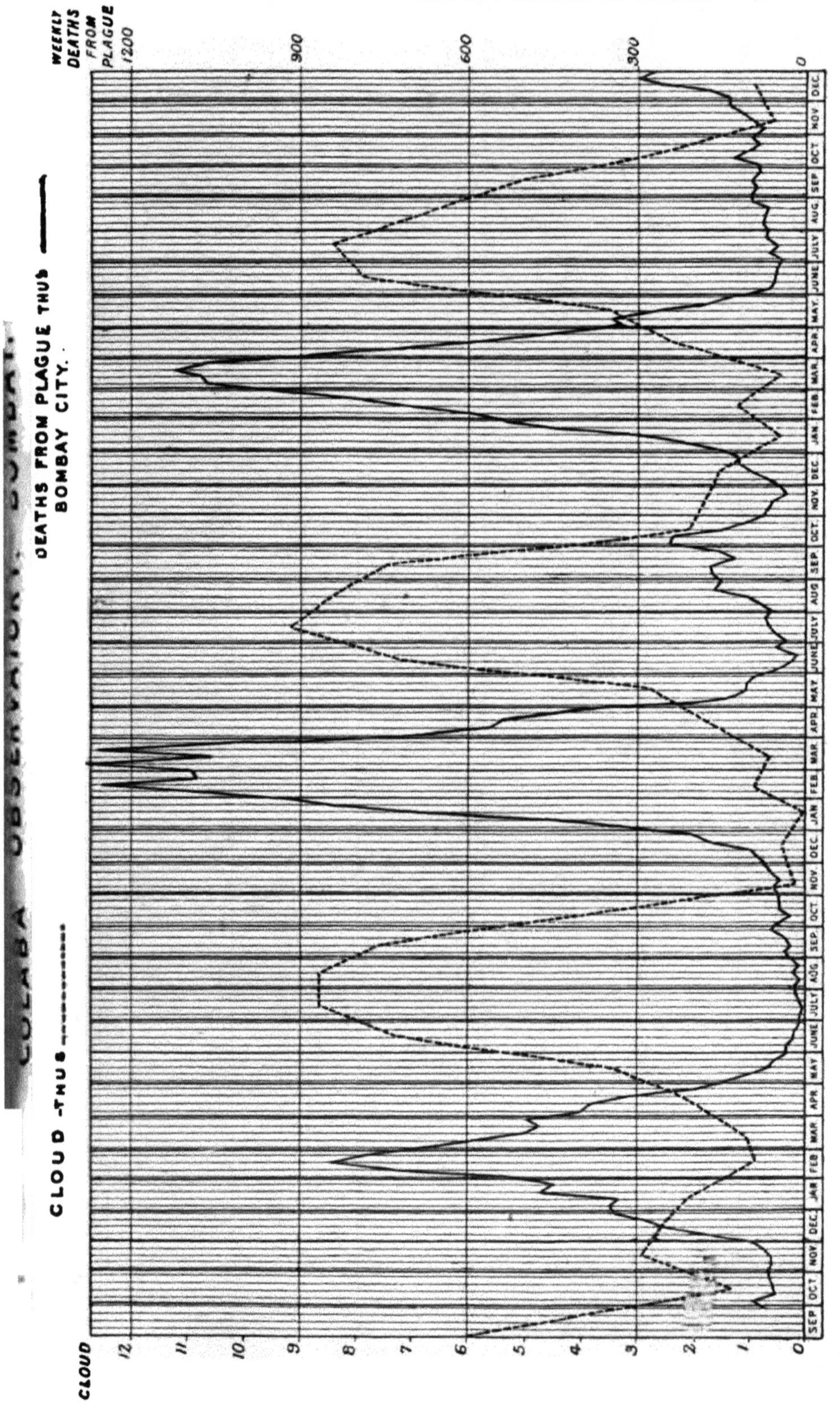
COLABA
CLOUD -THUS
DEATHS FROM PLAGUE THUS
BOMBAY CITY.
WEEKLY DEATHS FROM PLAGUE
1200
900
600
300
0
CLOUD
12
11
10
9
8
7
6
5
4
3
2
1
0
SEP OCT NOV DEC JAN FEB MAR APR MAY JUNE JULY AUG SEP OCT NOV DEC JAN FEB MAR APR MAY JUNE JULY AUG SEP OCT NOV DEC JAN FEB MAR APR MAY JUNE JULY AUG SEP OCT NOV DEC

No. 9. COLABA OBSERVATORY, BOMBAY.
TENSIONAL DIFFERENCE 9 INS. GROUND WITH MEAN DEW POINT THUS
Do. Do. MINIMUM Do. THUS
DEATHS FROM PLAGUE THUS
BOMBAY CITY.
VAPOUR TENSIONAL DIFFERENCE INS.
120
110
100
90
80
70
60
50
40
30
20
WEEKLY DEATHS FROM PLAGUE
1200
900
600
300

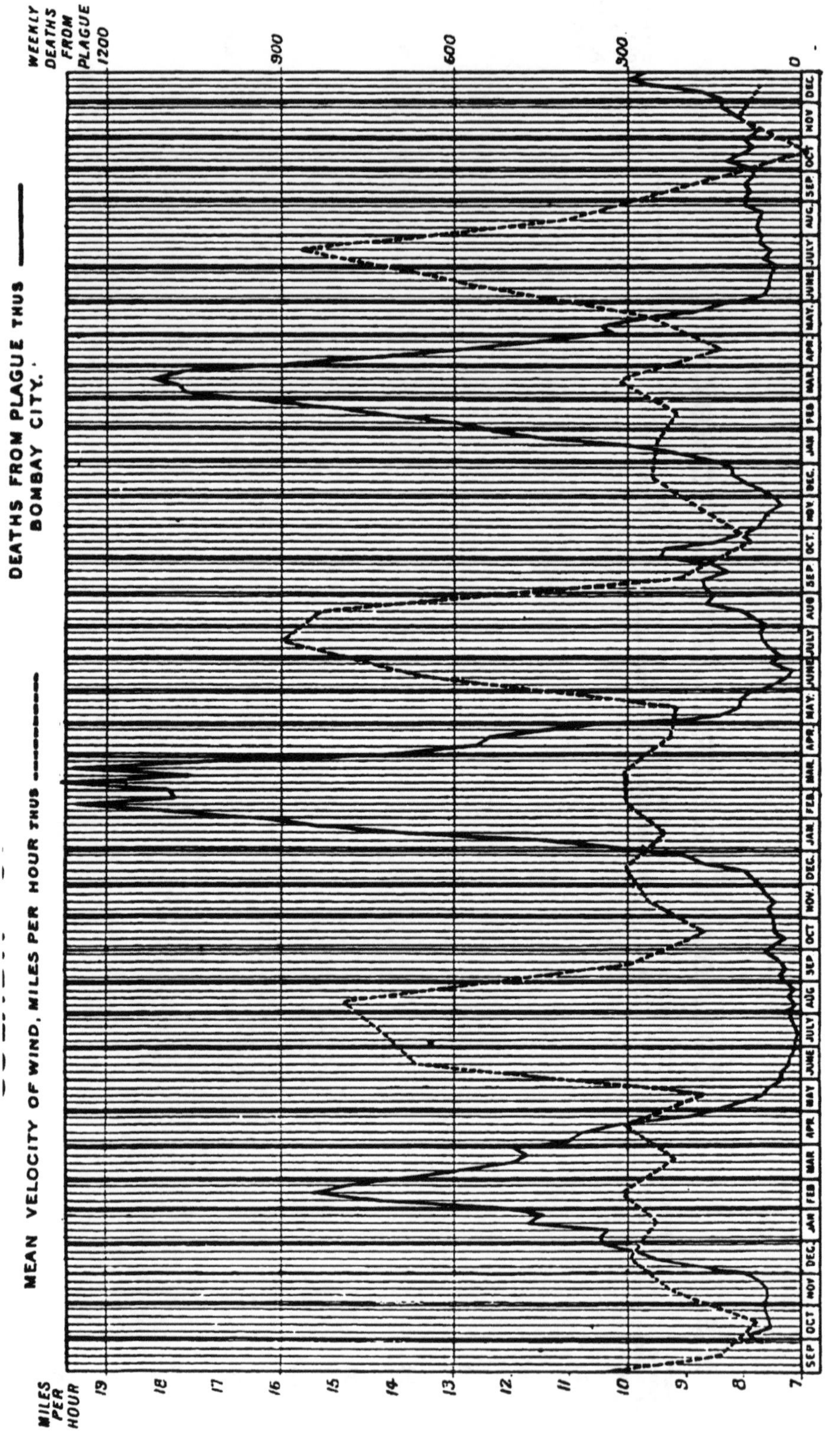
DEATHS FROM PLAGUE THUS
BOMBAY CITY.
MEAN VELOCITY OF WIND, MILES PER HOUR THUS
WEEKLY DEATHS FROM PLAGUE
1200
900
600
300
0
MILES PER HOUR
19
18
17
16
15
14
13
12
11
10
9
8
7
SEP OCT NOV DEC JAN FEB MAR APR MAY JUNE JULY AUG SEP OCT NOV DEC JAN FEB MAR APR MAY JUNE JULY AUG SEP OCT NOV DEC JAN FEB MAR APR MAY JUNE JULY AUG SEP OCT NOV DEC

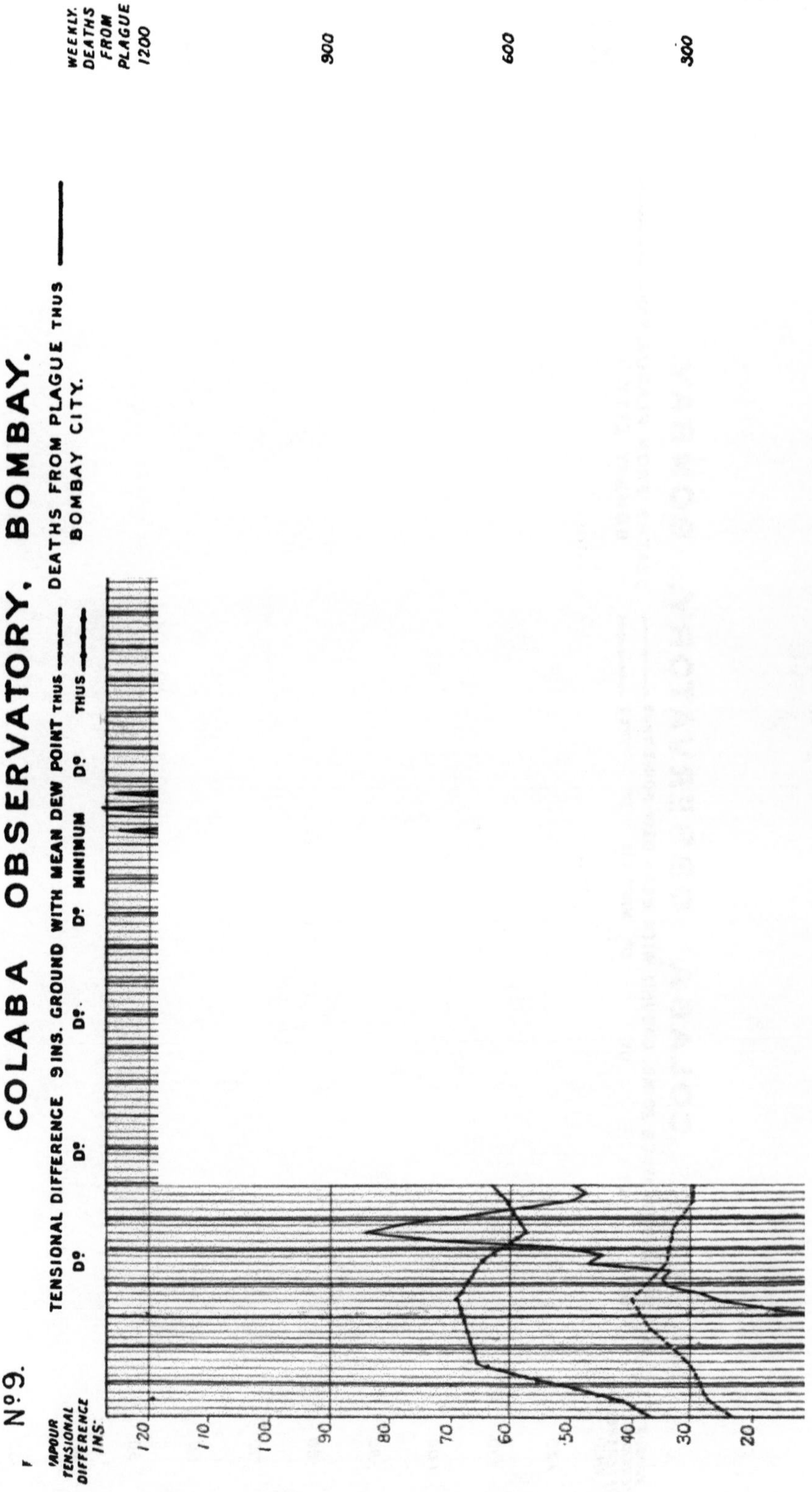

Nº 9.
COLABA OBSERVATORY, BOMBAY.
TENSIONAL DIFFERENCE 9 INS. GROUND WITH MEAN DEW POINT THUS
Dº Dº Dº MINIMUM Dº THUS
DEATHS FROM PLAGUE THUS
BOMBAY CITY.
VAPOUR TENSIONAL DIFFERENCE INS.
120
110
100
90
80
70
60
50
40
30
20
WEEKLY DEATHS FROM PLAGUE
1200
900
600
300

COLABA OBSERVATORY, BOMBAY.

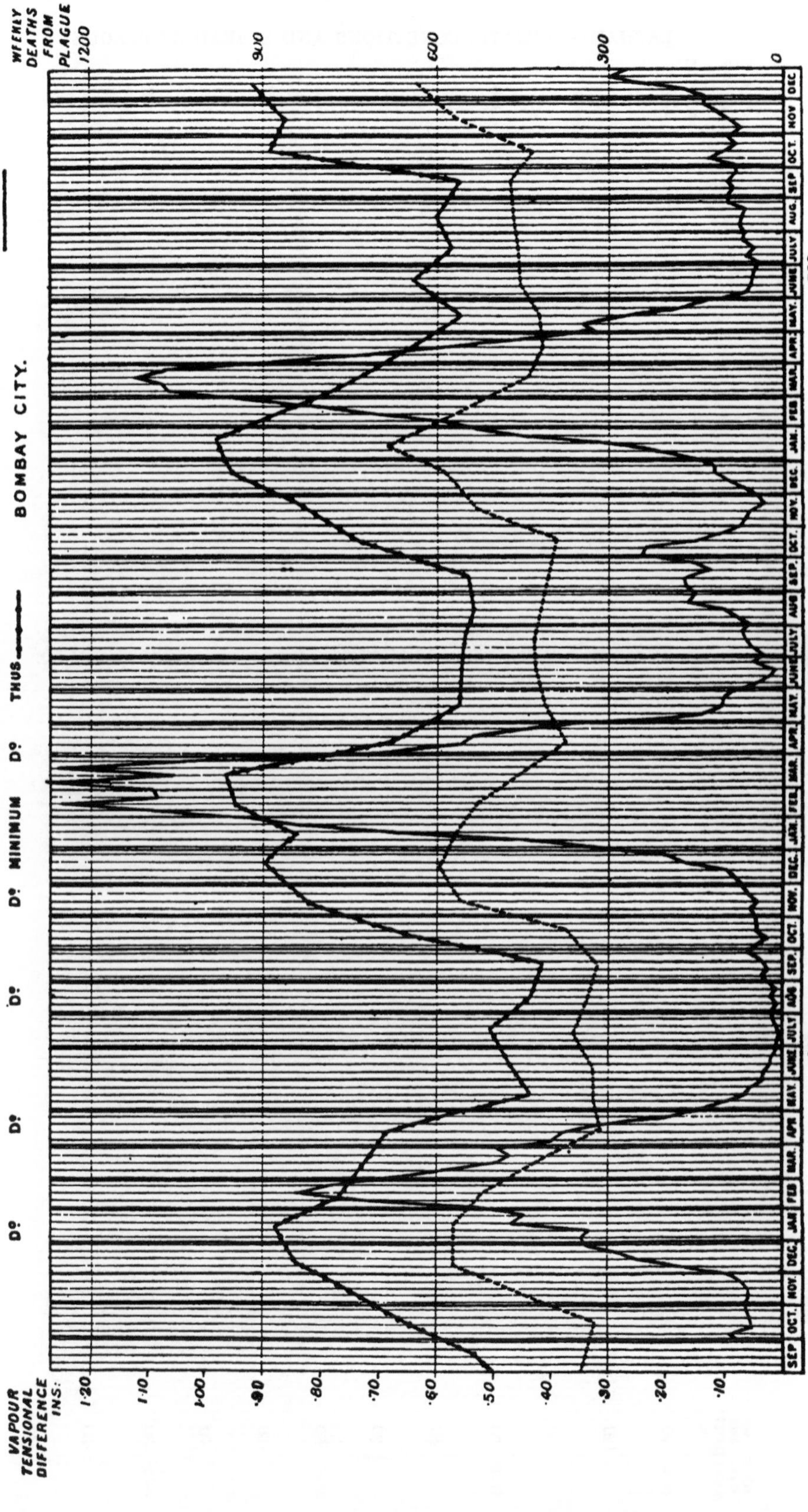
BOMBAY CITY.
Dº Dº Dº Dº MINIMUM Dº THUS
WEEKLY DEATHS FROM PLAGUE
1200
900
600
300
0
VAPOUR TENSIONAL DIFFERENCE INS:
1·20
1·10
1·00
·90
·80
·70
·60
·50
·40
·30
·20
·10
SEP OCT. NOV. DEC. JAN FEB MAR. APR MAY. JUNE JULY AUG SEP. OCT. NOV. DEC. JAN. FEB. MAR. APR. MAY. JUNE JULY AUG SEP. OCT. NOV. DEC. JAN. FEB. MAR. APR. MAY. JUNE JULY AUG. SEP OCT. NOV DEC
1896
1897
1898
1899

WEEKLY DEATHS FROM PLAGUE
1200
900
600
300
2400 1.20
1.10
1.00
1800 .90
.80
.70
1200 .60
.50
.40
600 .30
.20
.10

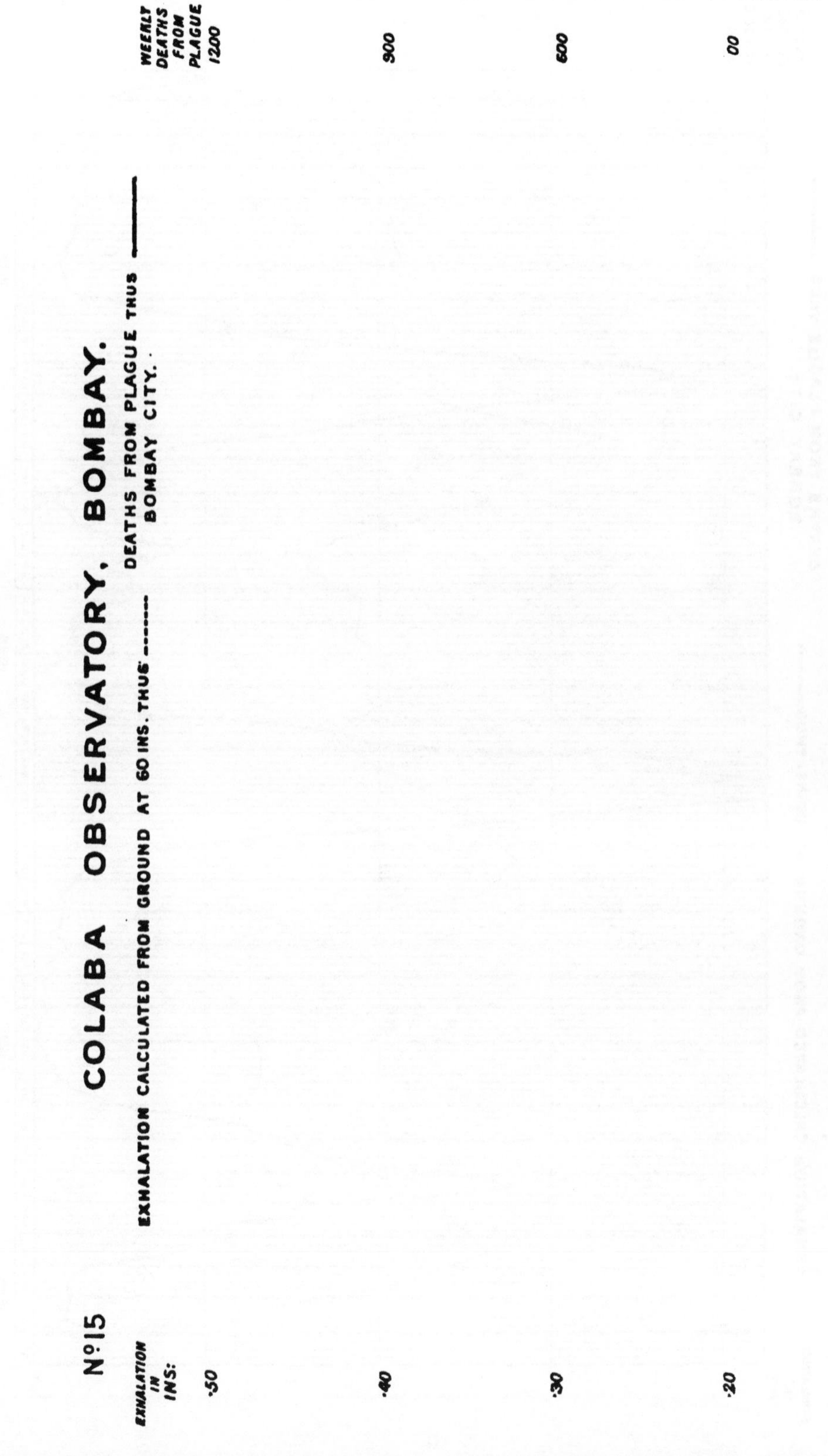
No. 15 COLABA OBSERVATORY, BOMBAY.
EXHALATION CALCULATED FROM GROUND AT 60 INS. THUS ------
DEATHS FROM PLAGUE THUS ——— BOMBAY CITY.
WEEKLY DEATHS FROM PLAGUE
1200
900
600
00
EXHALATION IN INS:
·50
·40
·30
·20

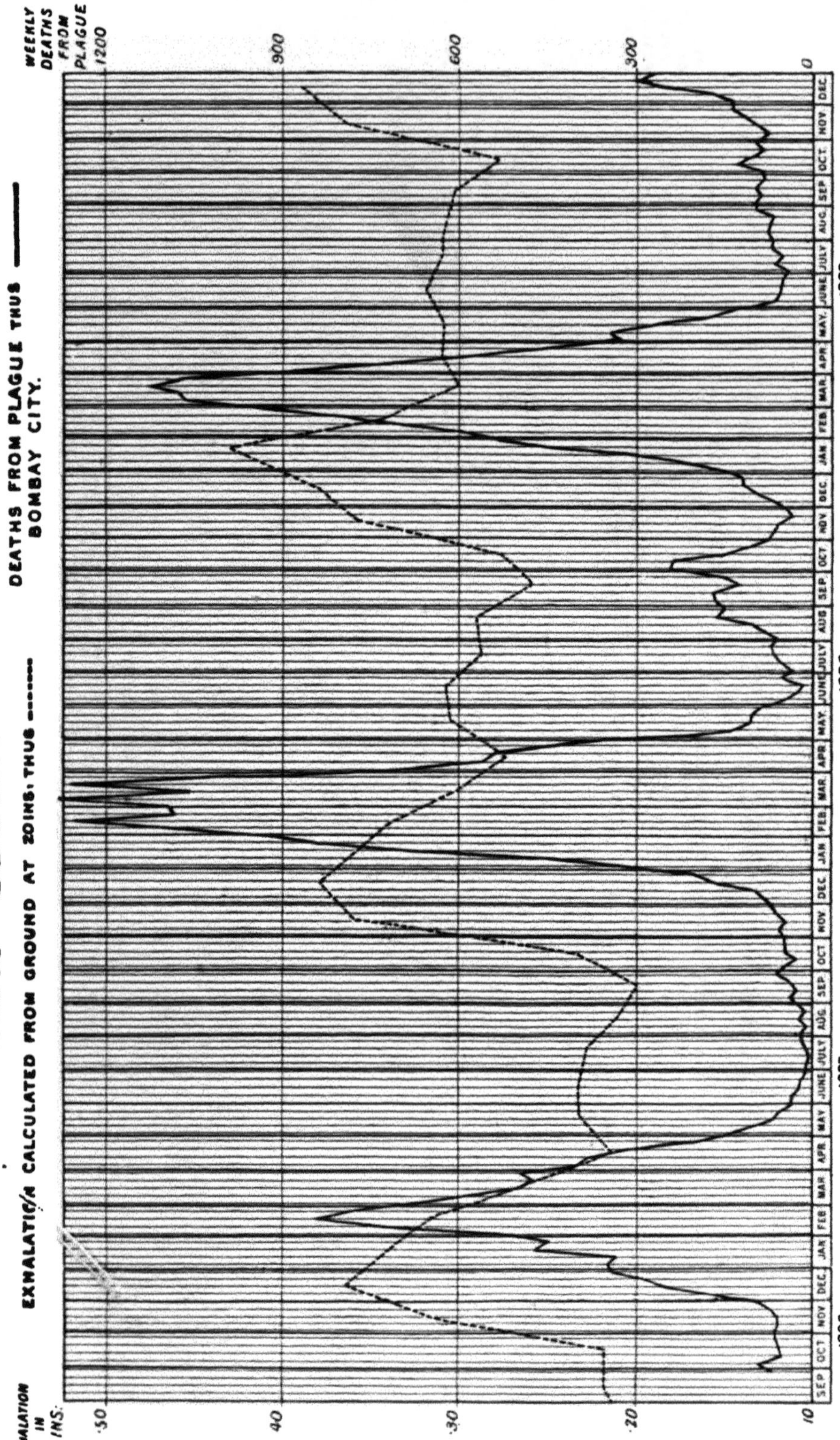
DEATHS FROM PLAGUE THUS
BOMBAY CITY.
EXHALATION CALCULATED FROM GROUND AT 20INS: THUS
WEEKLY DEATHS FROM PLAGUE
1200
900
600
300
0
EXHALATION IN INS.
50
40
30
20
10
SEP OCT NOV DEC JAN FEB MAR APR MAY JUNE JULY AUG SEP OCT NOV DEC
1896
1897
1898
1899

Nº15
COLABA OBSERVATORY, BOMBAY.
EXHALATION CALCULATED FROM GROUND AT 60 INS. THUS
DEATHS FROM PLAGUE THUS
BOMBAY CITY.
EXHALATION IN INS:
·50
·40
·30
·20
WEEKLY DEATHS FROM PLAGUE
1200
900
600
300

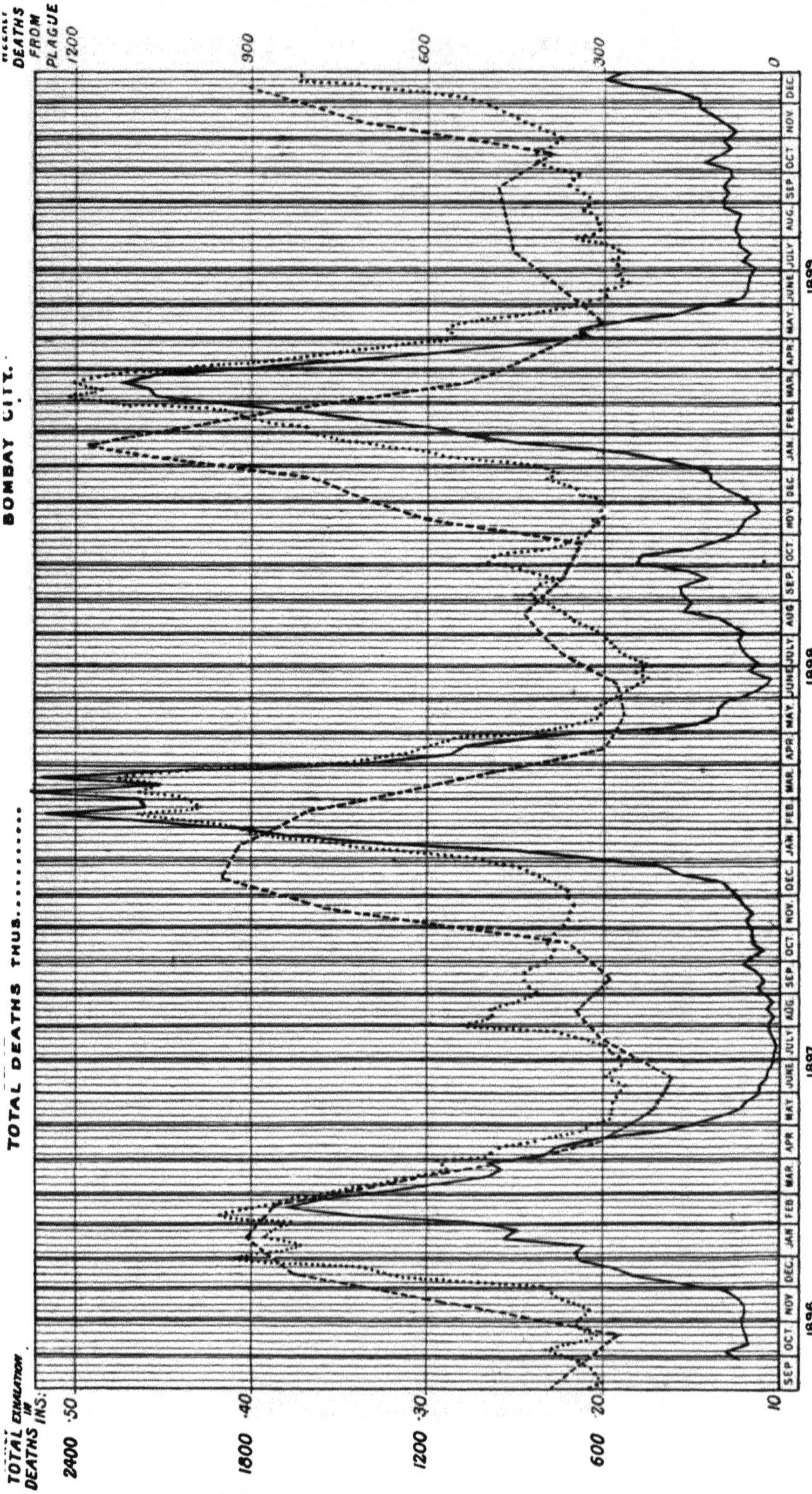
BOMBAY CITY.
TOTAL DEATHS THUS..........
DEATHS FROM PLAGUE
1200
900
600
300
0
TOTAL DEATHS
2400
1800
1200
600
EXHALATION IN INS:
·50
·40
·30
·20
10
SEP. OCT. NOV. DEC. JAN. FEB. MAR. APR. MAY. JUNE JULY AUG. SEP. OCT. NOV. DEC. JAN. FEB. MAR. APR. MAY. JUNE JULY AUG. SEP. OCT. NOV. DEC. JAN. FEB. MAR. APR. MAY. JUNE JULY AUG. SEP. OCT. NOV. DEC.
1896
1897
1898
1899

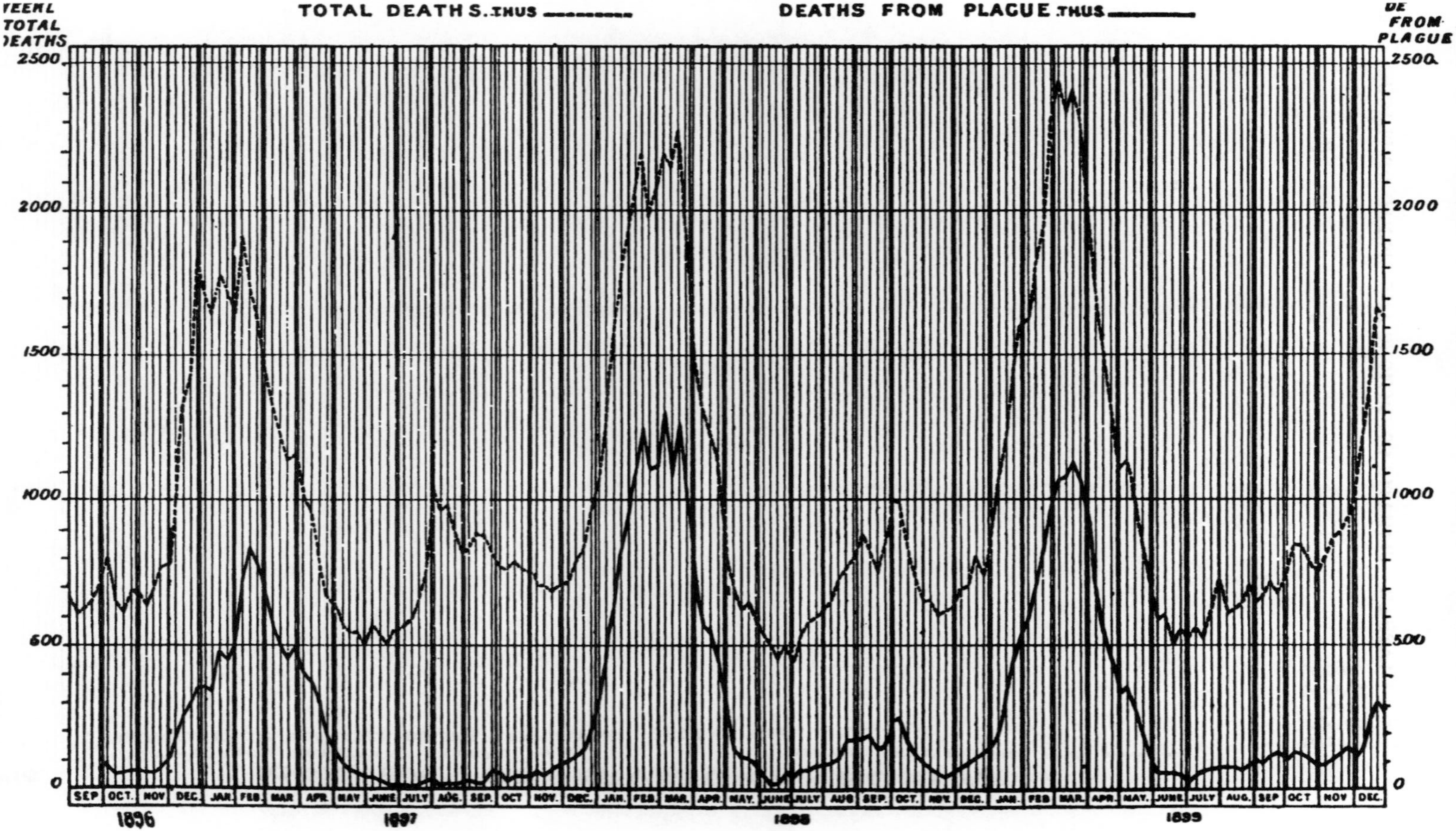
TOTAL DEATHS. THUS
DEATHS FROM PLAGUE THUS
WEEKL TOTAL DEATHS
DE FROM PLAGUE
2500
2000
1500
1000
600
0
2500
2000
1500
1000
500
0
SEP OCT. NOV DEC. JAN. FEB. MAR APR. MAY JUNE JULY AUG. SEP. OCT NOV. DEC. JAN. FEB. MAR. APR. MAY. JUNE JULY AUG SEP. OCT. NOV. DEC. JAN. FEB MAR. APR. MAY. JUNE JULY AUG. SEP OCT NOV DEC.
1896
1897
1898
1899

No. 18.
COLABA OBSERVATORY, BOMBAY.
DEATHS FROM REMITTANT FEVERS THUS
DEATHS FROM PLAGUE THUS
DEATHS FROM DISEASES OF THE RESPIRATORY ORGANS THUS
WEEKLY DEATHS REMITTANT FEVERS RESPIRATORY ORGANS DISEASE OF
600
500
400
300
200
100
WEEKLY DEATHS FROM PLAGUE
1200
900
600
300

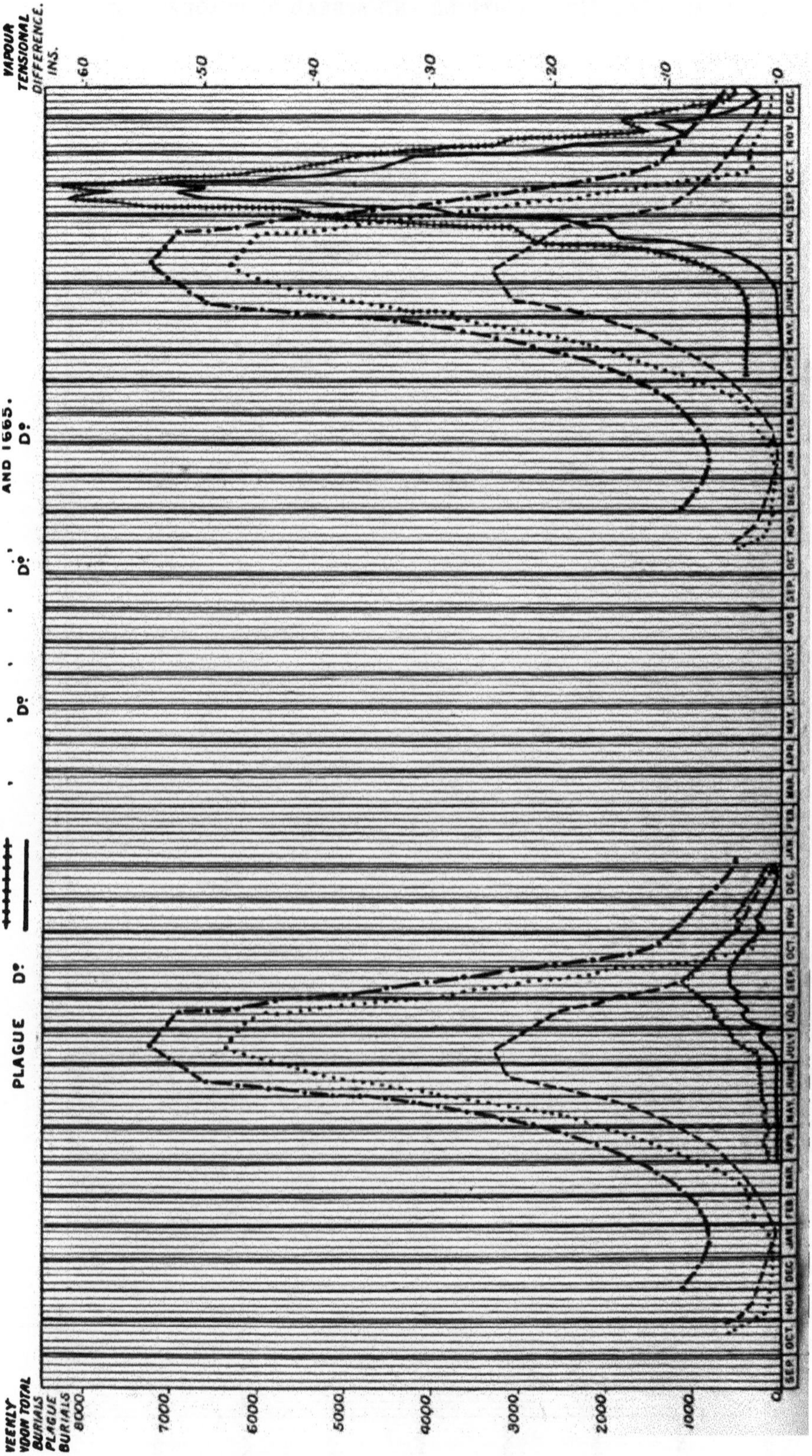
VAPOUR TENSIONAL DIFFERENCE. INS.
·60
·50
·40
·30
·20
·10
0
PLAGUE
D°
AND 1665.
D°
8000
7000
6000
5000
4000
3000
2000
1000
0
SEP. OCT. NOV. DEC. JAN. FEB. MAR. APR. MAY. JUNE. JULY. AUG. SEP. OCT. NOV. DEC.

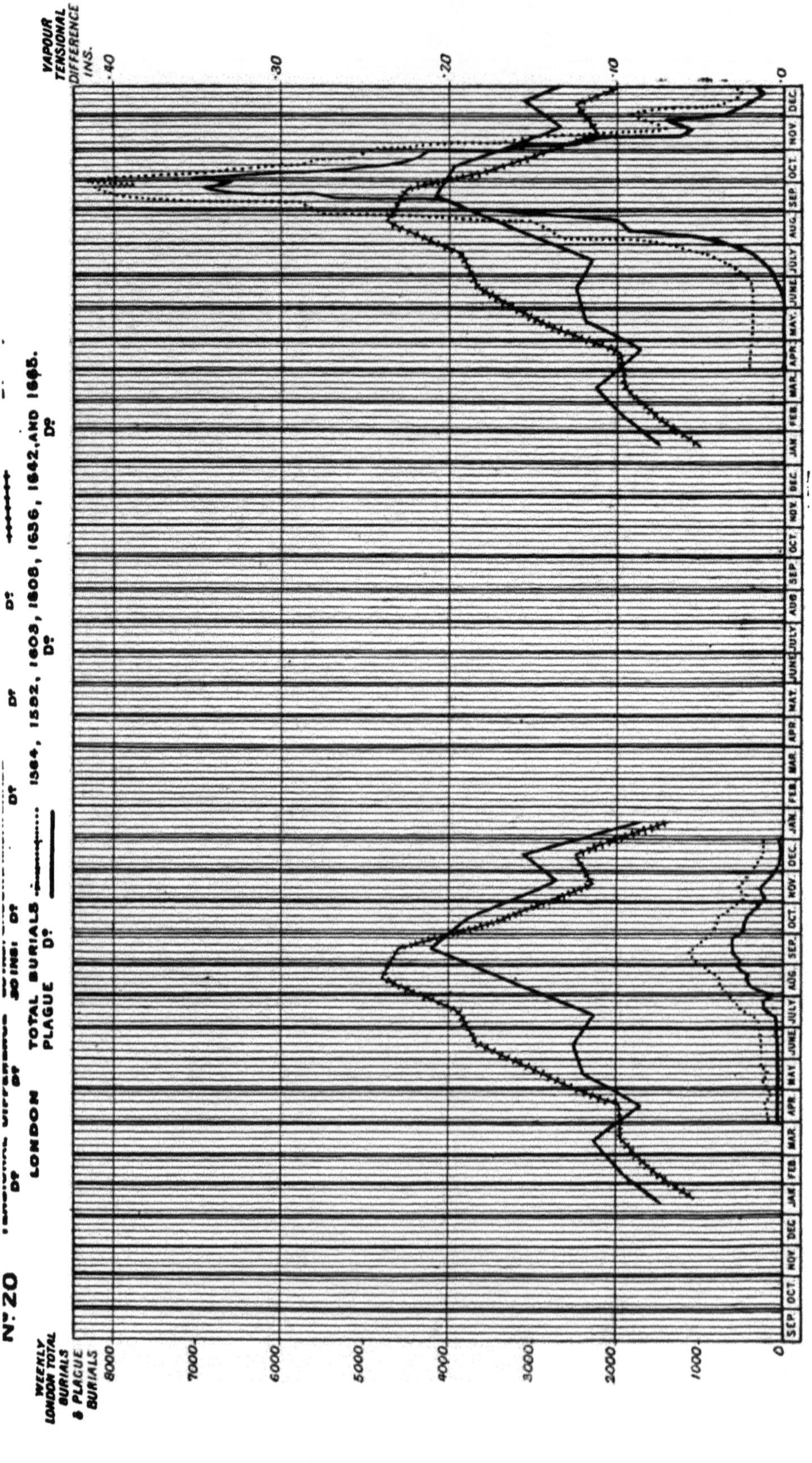
No. 20
LONDON TOTAL BURIALS 1564, 1592, 1603, 1608, 1636, 1642, AND 1665.
PLAGUE Do
WEEKLY LONDON TOTAL BURIALS & PLAGUE BURIALS
VAPOUR TENSIONAL DIFFERENCE INS.
SEP. OCT. NOV. DEC. JAN. FEB. MAR. APR. MAY. JUNE JULY AUG. SEP. OCT. NOV. DEC.
0
1000
2000
3000
4000
5000
6000
7000
8000
.10
.20
.30
.40

No. 21.

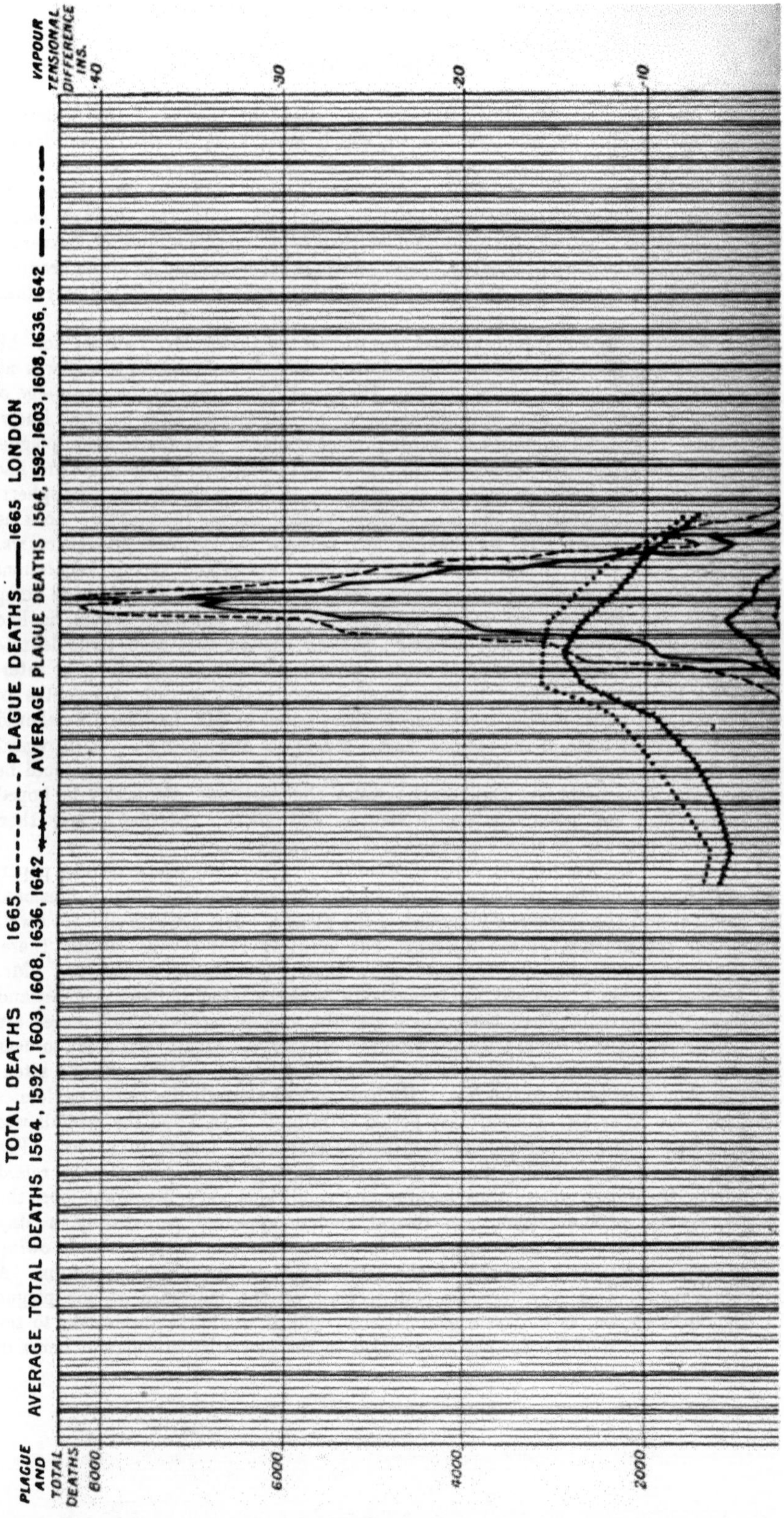
TENSIONAL DIFFERENCE 3·2 FT. GROUND AND MEAN DEW POINT GREENWICH
D° D° MIN: D° D°
TOTAL DEATHS 1665
PLAGUE DEATHS 1665 LONDON
AVERAGE TOTAL DEATHS 1564, 1592, 1603, 1608, 1636, 1642
AVERAGE PLAGUE DEATHS 1564, 1592, 1603, 1608, 1636, 1642
VAPOUR TENSIONAL DIFFERENCE INS.
·40
·30
·20
·10
PLAGUE AND TOTAL DEATHS
8000
6000
4000
2000

DISCUSSION.

The President (Mr. F. C. BAYARD) expressed the thanks of the Society to Mr. Latham for his admirable paper, which must have entailed great labour in working up. In the course of the paper, Mr. Latham often referred to the "plague," frequently meaning a different illness; and he mentioned the "sweating sickness" at York in 1604 by that name. He (Mr. Bayard) would like to know what was the definition of that term. In the table of "Average Weekly Deaths, City of Bombay," it was difficult to understand from the headings what was meant, as for three years the births were considerably lower than the deaths.

Dr. THEODORE WILLIAMS said he wished to thank Mr. Latham for his learned paper, which gave evidence of deep research and industry, and was an excellent brief history of the plague. He himself had not had the advantage of seeing a case of plague, so could not speak of the disease from personal knowledge. There was no doubt that this present epidemic was the bubonic plague, and it had also been prevalent in Egypt not long ago. Mr. Latham had first taken the negative side of the question, and had shown the atmospheric conditions not prevailing, and then those prevailing, during the plague. Looking at the subject carefully, he thought Mr. Latham had proved that there was a clear connection between the spread of the disease and vapour exhalations from the soil. At the present moment bacteriological investigations were being carried out in India by many, especially by Prof. Haffkine, whom he had hoped to see at the present Meeting; and he trusted that soon some definite theory would be forthcoming to explain plague prevalence. It would be interesting to see if the plague bacillus could be cultivated at different depths in the soil and under similar conditions to those noted by Mr. Latham; we should then ascertain some of the reasons why it multiplies and extends. With regard to the whole question, it will be a long time before anything definite could be proved. At present we could only register the outlines. Some day he hoped bacteriology and pathology would step in and fill up the blank, and then the great problem of plague prevalence would be solved.

Mr. E. D. ARCHIBALD congratulated Mr. Latham on his excellent paper, and thought he had fairly proved a connection between the vapour tensional gradient and the increase and spread of the plague. Mr. Latham did not dwell on the introduction of the microbe; but granting that it was already there, one could well imagine it would grow under favourable conditions. Mr. Latham proves a seasonal correspondence between the Indian plagues and those that have occurred here, when also the vapour tensional differences are similar, which is a "real scientific proof." He (Mr. Archibald) was sorry to hear there were no percolation gauges in India, and thought that Mr. Eliot's attention should be called to the fact. He had noticed that all the recent epidemics had come after an extraordinary period of rainfall. In 1894 the rainfall was very heavy, and during the monsoon period averaged 9 inches in excess. The plague started in 1896, the subsoil water having been considerably raised during these two years, thus making the conditions very favourable for the propagation of the plague. In Bengal, cholera appeared periodically in May and November; but in Bombay it only occurred once in May, probably owing to drier conditions prevailing in the latter place in the autumn months. A daily variation in the increase and decrease of the incidence of the plague should be shown, as well as a seasonal one; and it would be interesting to try and discover if there was also a variation in the mortality at different hours of the day.

Prof. W. J. Simpson said he had listened with much pleasure to the paper, which was very instructive and full of information. It must have cost Mr. Latham an enormous amount of labour and research to collect together so much valuable material, and every one interested in the subject of plague would appreciate his work. There were several reasons why such investigations were welcome at the present moment. Plague had been, and was still, particularly prevalent and destructive in the East. It had spread as far west as Portugal; and it was impossible to say that it would remain there, and not spread farther in Europe. The danger, therefore, was far from being imaginary, especially as very little indeed was known of the manner in which it spread. That certain climatic conditions influenced its spread in an infected locality there seemed no doubt, the plague being no exception in this respect to other zymotic or infectious diseases, all of which had a seasonal prevalence. The difficulty lay in the explanation. That given by Mr. Latham certainly was borne out most strikingly by the diagrams, showing a comparison between the vapour tension and the plague in Bombay in 1896 and the Great Plague in London in 1665-66. The explanation was given somewhat tentatively and the investigation would naturally require to be carried further, especially in the direction of discovering whether the bacillus of plague was at these times in the vapour arising from the ground in an infected house. In Bombay the bacillus had only been once found in the soil of an infected house. The bacillus might grow on the surface of the soil, or perhaps even at 9 inches depth; but it is doubtful whether it would rise in the vapour exhaled. This, however, was a matter for experiment. The seasons undoubtedly acted on the rise and fall of the plague, but he thought it was rather in the multiplication of the bacilli than their spread in the atmosphere. Further research was, however, necessary, and this paper would draw the attention of others to the subject and assist them in following on the same lines.

Mr. H. M. Birdwood, C.S.I., said that he would confine his remarks to the figured statements of plague mortality in Bombay, which Mr. Latham had found so much difficulty in collecting. There could be no question that the official registration of deaths from plague had been far from correct; for many cases of pneumonic plague, the most fatal and probably the most infectious type of the disease, were not at first recognised as plague at all. This was also the case at first even as regards the bubonic type of the disease (with its characteristic enlargement of certain glands), which was undoubtedly present in Bombay as early as in March 1896; and cases came under notice, though they were not known at the time to be plague, in the following months, until in September and October 1896 there could be no doubt that the plague had established itself as an epidemic on congenial soil. But even till early in 1897 cases of plague pneumonia were classed only as pneumonia; and there was also an abdominal type of the disease which at first it was difficult to distinguish from enteric fever. It is probable that many deaths were registered as due to diseases of the respiratory system which were really due to plague. And moreover many plague cases were concealed by the relatives or friends of patients and thus escaped official detection. Other causes also may have contributed to defective registration; and it became apparent, as time went on, that the safest way to arrive at the true plague mortality in Bombay was to deduct the average mortality, as deduced from the returns for the five years immediately preceding the first epidemic, from the total mortality from all causes, as reported during the epidemic by the Health Department. He (Mr. Birdwood) had carefully scrutinised the official returns of the total mortality in Bombay from week to week, and had framed an estimate of the plague mortality in Bombay during the three epidemics from these returns and the returns of average mortality. The result gives support to Mr. Latham's general contention that the plague has been at its worst during the driest months of the year. Of course no mere dryness of the season or any other climatic condition, or indeed any local or personal conditions of an insanitary nature, could of themselves produce plague; the essential cause of which is a vegetable organism, which must have a parent of its own kind, and cannot be evolved spontaneously or by any conditions affecting the air or the soil or the animals in whose body it finds a home; though, as just suggested by Dr. Simpson, it is possible that plague germs may thrive more vigorously at certain seasons than at others, and the Bombay figures point to such a possibility. Seasonal influences have also been noted elsewhere. At Bombay, the successive epidemics had generally established themselves unmistakably at the beginning of October (in the years 1896, 1897, and 1898), and each epidemic lasted about 30 weeks. That is, it either ceased or quickly declined towards the end of April. The official returns gave the plague mortality in the 30 weeks of the first epidemic as 10,227. The actual mortality amounted, however, according to the better method of calculation, to 20,365. For the second epidemic, the official and revised figures were respectively 15,611 and 25,059; and for the third epidemic, 12,931 and 23,988. If the periods of 30 weeks each be divided into stages of 4 weeks each, it will be found that, in the first epidemic, the worst stages were the 4th, ending January 19, 1897, during which the plague mortality amounted to more than 5000 deaths, and the 5th, when it was not much less. In the second epidemic, the 5th and 6th stages were the worst. In the 6th stage, ending March 18, 1898, the mortality exceeded 6500. In the third epidemic, the 6th and 7th stages were the worst.[1] In other words, the worst weeks in each year were those from the beginning of January to the middle of April, that is, during the driest season of the year; for, after the close of the South-west Monsoon in September, the prevailing winds on the west coast pass over the sun-baked continent of India and are necessarily dry, and it is not until April 15 that the South-west Monsoon begins again to blow, bringing with it enormous quantities of vapour from the Arabian Sea. With the increasing humidity of the air and the rise of temperature, the Bombay epidemics decline rapidly in May and the following months, when only sporadic cases occur. He (Mr. Birdwood) would be glad to show his revised figures of weekly mortality in Bombay to Mr. Latham, who would be able to say how far those figures confirmed his views as to the close connection between plague mortality and the tensional differences between the temperature of the soil at certain depths and the temperature of the dew-point. In Northern India, where there were endemic plague centres on the southern slopes of the Himalayas, and in Arabia, no particular association with the seasons had been traced; but plague seasons had been noticed in Persia and Syria, at Aleppo, Smyrna,

[1] The Secretary has received the following contrasted tabular statement prepared by Mr. Birdwood, which shows the plague mortality at Bombay in each of the stages referred to, in the epidemics of 1896-97, 1897-98, and 1898-99:—

Stages of 4 weeks each in 1st, 2nd, and 3rd Epidemics.		Plague Mortality in each Stage. First Epidemic.	Second Epidemic.	Third Epidemic.
No. 1 ending	October 27-29	784	1264	1543
" 2 "	November 24-26	945	1113	787
" 3 "	December 22-24	2681	1428	1087
" 4 "	January 19-21	*5012*	3435	2509
" 5 "	February 16-18	*4872*	*5860*	4574
" 6 "	March 16-18	3584	*6520*	*6120*
" 7 "	April 13-15	2079	4400	*5973*
" 8 (2 weeks)	April 27-29	408	1039	1395
	Totals	20,365	25,059	23,988
	Weekly Average	678	835	799

Trebizond, and Algiers. In Irak, according to Dr. Payne, the plague dies out suddenly in the summer. When the temperature rises above 86°, it begins to diminish, and it ceases abruptly at 113°. Again, some remarkable tabular statements would be found in Dr. Creighton's translation of Dr. August Hirsch's *Handbook*, which showed that plague seasons were distinctly marked at Alexandria from 1834 to 1843. An epidemic generally began between October and January, though sometimes later, and it was a matter of common observation that it ended on St. John's Day, June 24. At Cairo, the annual epidemics are said to have ended three days earlier. And then there were the facts noted by Mr. Latham in connection with the outbreaks of epidemics in this country in certain dry seasons, while sporadic cases only occurred in intermediate years. In these seasons the plague was at its worst in the hot and dry autumn months, when the conditions were perhaps not far dissimilar from those in a cold season in Bombay. There were other interesting matters dealt with by Mr. Latham to which he (Mr. Birdwood) would have wished to refer, but at that late hour it would be impossible for him to do so.

The PRESIDENT expressed the hope that Mr. Birdwood would supplement his remarks by a further statement of his views in writing, which could be published with the proceedings.

[Mr. H. M. BIRDWOOD, in a Note to the Secretary, says :—"I gladly comply with the courteous invitation of the President that I should state in writing my views on certain points to which I wished to refer at Wednesday's meeting. I will do so briefly.

"Mr. Latham has referred to various beliefs as to the cause of plague ; and I would only note as to these that the theory supported by the French Commissioners, Lagasquie and Pariset, who studied the plague in Egypt in 1828, that it is due to poisonous exhalations from corpses was shown by Dr. Hirsch of Berlin, more than eighteen years ago, to be untenable. He pointed out that for the development of the disease the access of the specific virus of plague was necessary. 'When the virus comes not, no matter how unfavourable the hygienic conditions, then the immunity from the pestilence is complete.' In 1885, Dr. Payne described the plague as depending on the reception into the body and the multiplication therein of a specific organic contagion, probably of the class Bacteria. This was indeed a 'golden guess,' for the world of science now universally recognises the *Bacillus pestis*, which is classed in the vegetable kingdom under the Bacteria, and was discovered by Dr. Kitasato at Hong Kong in 1894, as the essential cause of the plague. This essential fact must not be lost sight of in any discussion of the climatic or other conditions which favour the growth of an epidemic. Plague mortality may rise or fall under certain conditions such as those described by Mr. Latham, but that can only be in places where the plague germs are already present. In any place not already infected the virus must have been introduced before any animals can be attacked.

"With reference to Mr. Latham's remark that, so far, the sanitary measures carried out in places like Bombay appear to have been useless, though in time they may produce good results, it seems relevant to observe that, whenever infected houses had been thoroughly cleansed and vacated for a short time in Bombay, in 1896-97, fresh cases of plague rarely occurred in them, though there were some lamentable exceptions to this rule. The plague mortality in Bombay in the second epidemic only just exceeded 3 per cent of the normal population of 820,000, and was lower in the first and third epidemics. In the Great Plague of London it reached nearly 13·8 per cent of a population of 494,000. At Moscow, in 1570, the number of deaths is reported to have been 200,000. At Naples, 300,000 persons died in five months in 1656 ; in Stockholm, 40,000 in 1710 ; in Marseilles, from 40,000 to 60,000 in 1720. The lower death rate in Bombay may perhaps be fairly attributed to the vigorous sanitary measures adopted.

"With reference to Mr. Latham's remark that the plague is a disease of the poor, it may be noted that there is a fair consensus of opinion that healthy, well-nourished people are less liable to be infected; or, if infected, are better able to resist the plague than the weak or the sickly or the ill-fed. This consideration may account for the comparative immunity enjoyed by the members of certain communities in Bombay, and especially by Europeans and Mohammedans, and to a less degree by Parsis. Dr. Hirsch thinks it probable that the 'social element' gives the key to such differences,—not that they can with any confidence be attributed to degrees of racial or national predisposition. We cannot forget that, for a long series of years, the plague was practically endemic on European soil; but even then it was the poor who suffered.

"Mr. Latham thinks that the elevation of a place, as affecting its temperature, also influences plague. But it is relevant to observe that, though a high temperature destroys the plague germs, it is by no means so clear that great cold has the same effect. In Kurdistan the plague has prevailed in the severest winter weather, at an elevation of 6500 feet. In the Himalayan districts, as pointed out by Dr. Hutcheson, it occurs not only in cup-like valleys, but also on precipitous mountain ranges, in gorges reached only by cradle swings, in upland slopes close to the springs of rivers, and in an atmosphere and climate the 'finest and purest in the world,'—such advantages being apparently neutralised by the social condition of the people. No particular elevation has indeed been shown to be unfavourable to the plague bacillus.

"As to the relation of rats to the plague, I note that, in and near Bombay, the death of rats from plague has been preceded by a migration of rats. It is possible that the migration is itself a symptom of the disease; for it has been noticed that a restless desire to wander is a symptom in human beings. But that is a question for the medical expert. Anyway, the rats, in their migrations, have taken the plague with them from village to village. Villages in the neighbourhood of Bombay were not infected till the rats came; and in the city of Bombay the plague followed the migration of the rats, first from east to west and then up the sides and centre of the Island, northwards. This circumstance will perhaps explain Dr. Blaney's figures which Mr. Latham has quoted. Mr. Snow, the able Municipal Commissioner of Bombay, held that the presence of rats probably nullified to an enormous extent the advantages to be derived from ordinary remedies. Dr. Henderson of Karachi has expressed the opinion that, in cases of importation of plague, the germ is probably too weak to infect men at first, but is strong enough to attack rats, and men through them. According to Dr. Haffkine, the virulence of the microbe is supposed to depend 'on its previous passage through a susceptible animal or man.' Perhaps this last consideration may explain the circumstance that, in the earlier stages of an epidemic, the plague is not so virulent as it is afterwards. In October 1896-97 the percentage of deaths to seizures in Bombay was 70·96. In November it was 80·48; in December, 70·09. It rose in the two following months to 76·87 and 96·81, and then fell to 90·46 and 89·35, and then to 72·99 and 53·84, at which figures it stood in May and June, when only sporadic cases occurred."]

Mr. G. J. Symons concurred with the other speakers, and thought Mr. Latham's paper was worthy of great praise. Dr. Simpson half hinted that the plague might come to England, but he (Mr. Symons) thought not. The dreadfully uncleanly conditions in which the natives of plague-stricken countries live seemed to him to be the cause of the trouble; and until the natives and the Government realised this, no improvement could be hoped for. Mr. Latham had shown that those who lived on the water (which itself was not over clean) enjoyed complete immunity from the scourge. Oriental ideas differ widely from English ones, and with the advances of sanitation in this country he (Mr. Symons) felt sure that plague would find here no soil dirty enough for it to obtain a hold.

Mr. R. INWARDS remarked that in confirmation of the extract given by Mr. Latham as from the pen of Dr. Gideon Harvey, Physician to Charles II., there was a passage in that gruesome volume Defoe's *History of the Great Plague in London*, in which it was stated that the author had heard, though with doubt, that if a plague-stricken patient breathed on a piece of glass and this was examined with a microscope there might be seen "strange, monstrous, and frightful shapes, such as dragons, snakes, serpents, and devils, horrible to behold." This, though a mere invention, taken in connection with Dr. Harvey's sagacious epitome of the causes of plague, might be looked on with interest now that science had adopted the bacterial theory of the origin of the pest.

Mr. H. M. BIRDWOOD said, in reference to the remarks made by Mr. Symons as to the insanitary state of Bombay, that mortality from diseases of the respiratory system had undoubtedly increased in Bombay after the outlet for storm water from a large low-lying tract of the Island had been closed by the reclamation of the Flats, thus causing a rise of the surface level of the subsoil water. Mr. Latham had made this abundantly clear in his *Report on the Sanitation of Bombay*, with the contents of which he (Mr. Birdwood) had long been familiar; and Mr. Latham's views had attracted public attention in Bombay during the first epidemic. The necessity for a complete system of effective drainage had been strongly impressed on the Government and the Municipality. It was much to be regretted that a measure of such vital importance had been delayed so long; and other sanitary measures were also urgently needed. But these had not been lost sight of, and the responsible authorities were doing their best to overcome the difficulties of the complex problems they had to deal with. But though he had said all this, he would remind the Meeting that Bombay, judged by any sanitary standards attainable in Asia, was not an insanitary city. It was probably the cleanest and best kept city in Asia. Vigorous measures for the disinfection of streets and houses and drains, for the destruction of refuse, and the free admission of light and air into dwellings, were promptly undertaken by the Health Department of the Municipality at the very outset of the first epidemic. As observed by the Municipal Commissioner, every kind of measure known to science was tried at one time or another; and never, in the course of history, had a rising epidemic of plague in a vast city been kept within such moderate bounds. During the later stages of the first epidemic, the requisite preventive and remedial measures were carried out under the immediate control of a special Committee presided over by General Gatacre, an officer of indomitable energy and unbounded resourcefulness, who conducted plague operations not only with vigour and ability, but with tact and patience also, and succeeded in effectually conciliating the people and overcoming all the opposition which had at one time been shown to measures for the repression of the plague.

Mr. B. LATHAM, in reply, said that he had dealt only with plague in the paper, and recorded instances of plague in early times; the one exception—the sweating sickness at York in 1551—following very closely on the lines of plague. No doubt in those earlier years every epidemic was given the name of plague, but this paper only deals with bubonic plague.

PROCEEDINGS AT THE MEETINGS OF THE SOCIETY.

November 15, 1899.

Ordinary Meeting.

Francis Campbell Bayard, LL.M., President, in the Chair.

Stephen Campbell Bayard, Cotswold, Wallington;
John Chadwick, Bletchley;
Alfred Mander, Belle Vue Pharmacy, Malvern;
Charles Hubert Millard, 117 Fishergate, Preston;
Ernest Oxley, Melbourne Lodge, Clay Cross;
George Charles Walker, Jr., M.B., D.F.H., 19 Preston Road, Southport; and
Capt. Charles Louis Napoleon Wilson, Assoc.M.Inst.C.E., Bilston,
were balloted for and duly elected Fellows of the Society.

The following communications were read:—

"The Diurnal Variation of the Barometer in the British Isles." By Richard H. Curtis, F.R.Met.Soc. (p. 1).

"Note on Earth Temperature Observations." By G. J. Symons, F.R.S. (p. 27).

December 20, 1899.

Ordinary Meeting.

Francis Campbell Bayard, LL.M., President, in the Chair.

Augustus Francis Beaufort, 62 Montague Square, W.;
Herbert Stone Burbery, Trent House, Cowes, Isle of Wight;
Charles John Philip Cave, Binsted, Cambridge;
Robert Cheyne, D.P.H., Edgefield, York Road, West Norwood;
Edward Henshall, Assoc.M.Inst.C.E., Hartland House, Woolacombe;
Henry Heywood, J.P., Witla Court, near Cardiff;
Douglas M'Dougall, Logan, Stranraer, Wigtownshire;
Henry Cecil Low Morris, M.D., Gothic Cottage, Bognor;
Henry Victor Prigg, Assoc.M.Inst.C.E., 63 Craven Avenue, Plymouth;
Lieut.-Gen. John Sprot, Riddell, Lilliesleaf, Roxburghshire;
Frank Taylor, J.P., Ash Lawn, Heaton, Bolton;
William King Wilkinson, Jr., Middlewood, Clitheroe; and
Albert Wilson, 4 Eaton Road, Ilkley,
were balloted for and duly elected Fellows of the Society.

Mr. F. Gaster and Mr. M. Jackson were appointed Auditors of the Society's Accounts.

The following communications were read:—

"Note on a Remarkable Dust Haze experienced at Teneriffe, Canary Islands, February 1898." By Robert H. Scott, D.Sc., F.R.S. (p. 33).

"The Climatic Conditions necessary for the Propagation and Spread of Plague." By Baldwin Latham, M.Inst.C.E. (p. 37).

CORRESPONDENCE AND NOTES.

Retirement of Dr. R. H. Scott, F.R.S., from the Meteorological Office.—The Secretary has received the following letter on this subject:—

"DEAR SIR,—At the end of the year 1899, I had completed 33 years of service in this office, and 25 years of service as Secretary of the International Meteorological Committee.

"As I have already passed the age of retirement from Her Majesty's Civil Service, I have tendered to the Meteorological Council my resignation, to take effect as soon as the necessary arrangements can be completed on February 28.

"I take this opportunity of expressing my heartfelt appreciation of the very cordial relations which I have enjoyed, during so many years, with all my colleagues at home and abroad, and my sincere regret at their official cessation.

"My successor will be Mr. William Napier Shaw, F.R.S., Assistant Director of the Cavendish Laboratory, Cambridge, and I have every confidence in saying that my Meteorological colleagues will find him, in every way, a most valuable addition to their ranks.—Yours very sincerely, ROBERT H. SCOTT, *Secretary*.

"METEOROLOGICAL OFFICE, 63 VICTORIA STREET,
LONDON, S.W., *February* 1, 1900."

International Meteorological Congress, Paris, 1900.—The following particulars have been received of the Congress to be held in the autumn:—

An International Meteorological Congress will be held at Paris from September 10 to 16, 1900. We hope that you will readily give it your adhesion and co-operation.

The International Meteorological Committee, which met last year at St. Petersburg, decided that it would convene, at the same time as the Congress, the various Committees appointed by the Paris Conference in 1896. These Committees are the following:—

Terrestrial Magnetism and Atmospheric Electricity.
Aeronautics.
Clouds.
Radiation and Insolation.

The first of these Committees held an important meeting last year at Bristol, the proceedings and resolutions of which have been published in the Reports of the British Association.

A great number of ascents, both with free as well as captive balloons, have been made in different countries, for the systematic investigation of the upper regions of the atmosphere.

Finally, the publication and discussion of the international observations of clouds, made in 1896-97, will probably be completed in 1900, in the majority of the countries taking part in the same.

From these different points of view, we can confidently reckon on some communications of very high interest.

The questions which the Congress will be called upon to deal with are not restricted exclusively to Meteorology properly so called: they will include, generally, everything which affects the physics of the globe.

It appears to us that it will be premature to give just now a detailed programme of these different questions, and that it will be sufficient to indicate their general character by a provisional title.

In order to facilitate the compilation of a definite programme, we should be much obliged if you would send us, as soon as possible, and, in any case, before May 15, your adhesion, with the list of the questions which you propose to deal with.

The meetings of the Congress and of the Committees will be held at the House of the Société d'Encouragement, 44 Rue de Rennes, where the International Conference met in 1896.

The subscription is fixed at 20 francs (16s.). The payment of this sum will entitle the member to a ticket of admission and to the volume which will contain the proceedings of the meetings as well as the memoirs presented to the Congress. We hope that this publication will constitute a very interesting work for every meteorologist.

The adhesions and communications relating to the organisation or to the programme of the Congress should be addressed to Mons. Angot, General Secretary, 12 Avenue de l'Alma, Paris.

The subscriptions should be sent by post-office orders to Mons. Moureaux, Treasurer, 176 Rue de l'Université, Paris.—E. MASCART, *President*; A. ANGOT, *General Secretary.*

Solar Halos and Mock Suns, January 11, 1900.—We have received a number of letters giving an account of the brilliantly coloured solar halos and

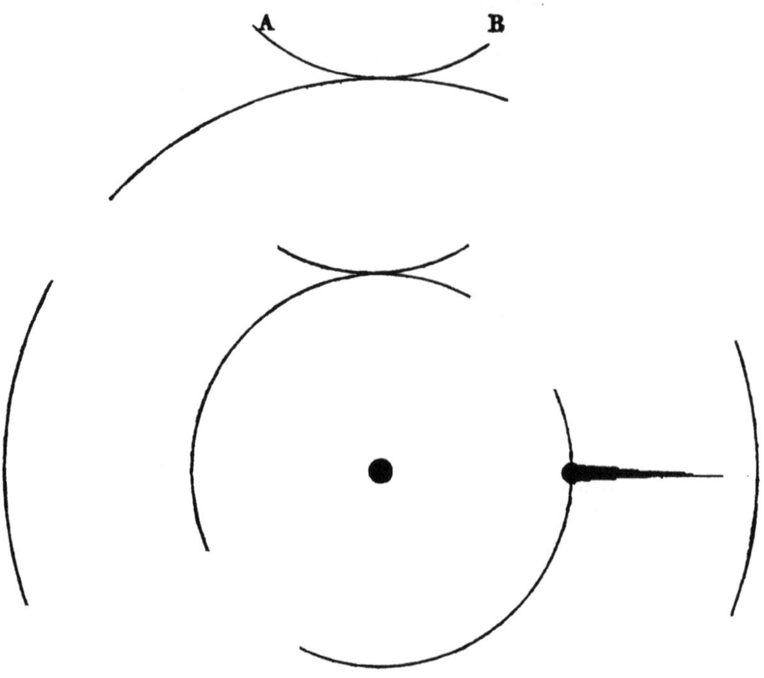

Solar Halos and Mock Sun, January 11, 1900.

mock suns which were seen on January 11, 1900. The phenomenon was visible over the greater part of the south-east of England. Several correspondents have sent coloured sketches and drawings.

The following letters from Mr. E. B. Knobel, F.R.A.S., and Mr. W. A. Macknight are of interest, and fully describe the phenomenon :—

Mr. E. B. Knobel says: "I send you a sketch of compound sun halos I saw this morning. The curious feature seems the second halo circumscribing the primary one. I carefully measured the radius of each halo, which as usual was 22° for the primary and 44° for the circumscribing one. I should have expected this latter to have been really portions of halos round mock suns east, west, and north of true sun. But the arcs seemed to be parallel with the primary halo; only one true mock sun was visible to the west. The arcs touching externally the primary and secondary halos were of the same radius as the primary halo. That marked AB was brilliant in colour—far more so than any other part."

Mr. W. A. Macknight says: "I also observed the phenomenon on January 11, while waiting in Wallington Station for the 9.22 a.m. train, and I think you will be interested in comparing the conditions attending this instance with my observations of many similar phenomena which occurred every winter during my fourteen years' residence in the Central States of the U.S.A.

"On January 11, the sun shone brightly until 8.30 a.m., when a bank of presumably sea fog, which had been hanging over the southern horizon, commenced to rise, and soon the whole sky was overcast. Between 9.20 and 9.30 a.m. the sun, though feeble, was still visible, and in shining through the mist clouds caused the prismatic effect which we observed to the right and left and above and below the sun; the sun dogs being connected to each other by, and forming part of, a visible halo; the centre of each dog being separated from the centre of the next by 90°, those to the sides of the sun being brightest; the sun being at an altitude of about 45°.

"A phenomenon of this nature is termed a 'Sun Dog,' and is entirely due to the presence of vapour or mist clouds, never occurring in a clear sky. The dog may vary slightly in length and breadth, but never in its relative position to the sun, *i.e.* taking the sun for the centre of a circle, the dog always appears at the points where a vertical and a horizontal line passing through the centre of the sun would meet such a circle. The side of the dog facing the sun is always concave, forming an arc of a sometimes visible, but most frequently invisible, circle or halo round the sun. The dogs on either side of the sun may appear together, or one alone may appear; but I have never seen a dog above or below the sun without it being accompanied by one on each side of the sun, those to the sides always being brightest. I have always noticed with this phenomenon that the sun is at an altitude of about 45°, from which I consider the effect to be due to the perspective from the point of observation causing a particular focus of the sun's rays; and as I have never observed the phenomenon except in the winter months I think, that not only a peculiar condition of cloud and temperature is necessary, but that it is due to the low position of the sun during the winter. I have also on rare occasions seen 'Moon Dogs.'

"The mock sun is a similar phenomenon in many respects, and takes the same relative position to the sun as the sun dog; but in form it differs, as it always forms a complete circle,—sometimes hollow, sometimes an exact reproduction of the sun's surface,—but it always appears to be of the same diameter and colour as the face of the sun. This phenomenon is accompanied by intense cold: it is much less frequent than the dog, but I have observed several, the best being in January 1888, the thermometer being down to 30° below zero at the time, when I observed four mock suns with hollow centres, a circle of golden light joining the four together and short horizontal lines passing through the centre of the mock suns to the right and left of the real sun, while a short vertical line passed through the centre of those above and below the sun.

"As the sun dog only appears in a cloudy sky, and forms a prismatic segment of a halo, I am of the opinion that it is caused by the sun shining through vapour. The mock sun is not prismatic; it occurs in a clear sky, with an extremely low temperature and rarefied atmosphere, and since it is a more or less perfect reproduction of the sun, it is, I believe, purely a mirage. Certainly each of these phenomena is produced under entirely different atmospheric conditions."

RECENT PUBLICATIONS.

Maryland Weather Service. The Aims and Methods of Meteorological Work. By CLEVELAND ABBE. Special Publication. Vol. I., Part IIIA. Baltimore, 1899. 8vo. 112 pp.

This elaborate and comprehensive report by Prof. Abbe was prepared at the request of Prof. W. B. Clark, and is suggestive of new lines of work for the Maryland State Weather Service. The author says: "As the weather and the climate enter intimately into every aspect of human life, the field that is before us is one of exceeding great extent, and probably no single weather bureau need attempt to compass the whole. The principal applications of meteorology to which we must call attention at present are those concerning hygiene, agriculture, commerce, and the mechanical arts." Prof. Abbe divides his report into three sections, viz. Dynamic Meteorology and its Applications; Climatology and its Aims and Methods in relation to agricultural and other interests; and Observational Appliances and Methods.

Meteorologische Zeitschrift. Redigirt von Dr. J. HANN und Dr. G. HELLMANN. December 1899. 4to.

The principal articles are:—"Die Bekämpfung der Frostgefahr": von Dr. W. Trabert (11 pp.). This is an attempt to introduce a general system of producing smoke to shelter crops from spring frosts. Dr. Trabert points out that in some communes in Germany every farmer who did not light a fire, on a signal being given, was fined. The fires are made of brushwood and weeds, and should be laid at reasonably regular intervals over the farms. Dr. Trabert, however, suggests one simple precaution when frost appears likely, and that is to water the fields copiously so that the ground shall be saturated at nightfall.—"Der Einfluss der Wärmeschwankungen des Norwegischen Meeres auf die Luftcirkulation in Europa": von Dr. E. Lesshaft (7 pp.). This is an attempt to prove that the variations in the surface temperature of the North Sea govern the frequency and the paths of cyclones over Europe.—"Zur täglichen Periode der Windgeschwindigkeit": von G. Hellmann (9 pp.). This is an investigation into the hourly wind tabulations, in order to test the question of the influence of height on the curve. The records examined are Potsdam, Magdeburg, Prague, Borkum, and Rome. Dr. Hellmann shows how the retardation in the hour of maximum increases with elevation. But he admits that we do not yet know to what level of the atmosphere the phenomenon of a night maximum, instead of the day maximum at ground level, extends. The paper is, however, very well worth careful reading.

Monthly Weather Review. Prof. CLEVELAND ABBE, Editor. Prepared under the direction of WILLIS L. MOORE, Chief U.S. Weather Bureau. August—November 1899. 4to.

Among the reports and contributions are the following articles:—"The West Indian Hurricane of August 7-17, 1899" (4 pp.).—"Conduct and the Weather": by E. G. Dexter (1 p.).—"Automatic Records of a Thunderstorm": by H. H. Kimball (3 pp.).—"Thunderstorms on August 2, 1899": by A. J. Henry (2 pp.).—"Floods and Flood Problems": by H. C. Frankenfield (4 pp.).—"Preliminary Results of Weather Bureau Kite Observations in 1898" (2 pp.).—"The Average Temperature of the Atmosphere" (3 pp.).—"The Sluggishness of Thermometers": by C. F. Marvin (4 pp.).—"The Rain Gauge and the Wind" (4 pp.).

Practical Exercises in Elementary Meteorology. By ROBERT DECOURCY WARD. Boston, 1899. 8vo. 199 pp.

This work is intended for use in schools. The author in the preface says: "The advance of Meteorology as a school study has been much hampered by the lack of a published outline of work in this subject which may be undertaken during the school years. There are several excellent text-books for more advanced study, but there is no laboratory manual for use in the elementary portions of the science. In many secondary schools some instruction in Meteorology is given, and the keeping of meteorological records by the scholars is every year becoming more general. There is yet, however, but little system in this work, and, in consequence, there is little definite result. The object of this book is to supply a guide in the elementary observational and inductive studies in Meteorology. This manual is not intended to replace the text-books, but is designed to prepare the way for their more intelligent use. Simple preliminary exercises in the taking of meteorological observations, and in the study of the daily weather maps, as herein suggested, will lay a good foundation on which later studies in connection with the text-books may be built up."

The book contains specific instructions to the student as to the use of instruments; the carrying out of meteorological observations; the investigation of special simple problems by means of the instruments; and the practical use of the daily weather maps. The appendix contains explanatory notes and suggestions for the teacher, which might be useful in directing the laboratory work of the class.

Report of the British Association for the Advancement of Science. 1899. 8vo.

This volume contains the following reports and abstracts of meteorological papers:—"Meteorological Observatory, Montreal" (1 p.).—"Meteorological Observations on Ben Nevis" (6 pp.).—"The Climatology of Africa" (12 pp.).—"Seismological Investigations" (77 pp.).—"Photographic Meteorology" (1 p.).—"Progress in Exploring the Air with Kites": by A. L. Rotch (1 p.).—"The Hydro-Aërograph": by F. N. Denison (2 pp.).—"The rainfall of the South-eastern Counties of England": by J. Hopkinson (2 pp.).—"Seismology at Mauritius": by T. F. Claxton (1 p.).

Symons's Monthly Meteorological Magazine. October—December 1899. 8vo.

The principal articles are:—"Meteorological Extremes. II. Temperature" (8 pp.). This is a continuation of a series of articles giving extremes of pressure, temperature, etc. In this article the editor deals with temperature.—"The Moon in relation to Air Temperature": by H. A. Hazen (2 pp.).—"Trees and Change of Temperature": by H. A. Hazen (1 p.).—"Results of Meteorological Observations at Camden Square for 40 years 1858-97" (3 pp.).—"The British Association at Dover" (4 pp.). This article gives the titles and short notes on the meteorological reports and papers read at the Meeting of the Association.—"Smoke fog and Maximum Temperature": by A. Wilson (1 p.).—"Flood in Cape Town" (1 p.). A flood occurred at Cape Town, and in the Worcester and Hex River districts, on August 6, 1899. The streets of Cape Town appear to have had about a foot of water, while outside the town a tramway track and the railway, at more than one place, were washed away. The rainfall at the Royal Observatory, from July 31 to August 6, was 5·31 ins.; and at Wynberg Hill, from August 1 to 10, was 7·58 ins.—"A Wet Period, October and November 1899" (1 p.). "The Moon and the Weather": by A. B. MacDowall (1 p.). "The Aims of Meteorology" (4 pp.). This article is a review of "Report on the Meteorology of Maryland. Part III."—"Lightning at Dinner" (2 pp.). [illegible] and Meteorology": by W. A. Eddy (1 p.).

QUARTERLY JOURNAL

OF THE

ROYAL METEOROLOGICAL SOCIETY

VOL. XXVI.] APRIL 1900 [No. 114.

A NEW REDUCTION OF THE METEOROLOGICAL OBSERVATIONS AT GREENWICH.

BY FRANCIS CAMPBELL BAYARD, LL.M., PRESIDENT.

An Address delivered to the Royal Meteorological Society, January 17, 1900.

(Plates II.-VII.)

I HAVE long thought that the method at present in vogue of discussing a long series of meteorological observations—and after all it is the long series that is most valuable—by simply taking a mean of the whole period and then extracting the absolute extremes, was utterly inadequate to express the salient features of such observations; and with this view I have, for my Address to-night, attempted to discuss the well-known meteorological observations of Greenwich Observatory in, I believe, an entirely new way. For the original idea of this new way, I am indebted to two short tables compiled by Mr. W. Marriott, the one on the Barometer (see *Quarterly Journal*, vol. vii. p. 57) and the other on Rainfall (see *Quarterly Journal*, vol. xxiv. p. 44). A comparison of these tables with the tables contained in this Address will, however, show that the tables in this Address contain much more information.

The Royal Observatory at Greenwich is situated on the rising ground in Greenwich Park, about six miles south-east by river from London Bridge. Its elevation above sea-level is about 157 feet, and it forms a very conspicuous object both from the river and the surrounding district. The Magnetical and Meteorological Department of the Observatory was founded in 1838, soon after the appointment of Sir G. B. Airy as Astronomer-Royal. It is about 170 feet south-south-east of the south-east Dome, and on the east stands the Library erected in 1881. "The situation is," as Mr. Inwards remarked in his Presidential Address in 1896, "much too confined, though the surrounding buildings have been erected since the Department was formed." The photograph which is shown on the screen, and which was taken in the year 1871, shows how closely the situation is enclosed by trees. Probably, as trees have a habit of growing, the situation was much more open when the Department commenced work in 1840. Sir G. B. Airy had as his Superintendents of this Department our Past Presidents Mr. James Glaisher, F.R.S., and Mr. William Ellis, F.R.S. Sir G. B. Airy retired in 1881, and was succeeded by the present Astronomer-Royal, Mr. W. H. M. Christie, F.R.S., whose Superintendents have been Mr. William Ellis and Mr. W. C. Nash.

In September 1898 the new Magnetic House, which had been erected in Greenwich Park about 350 yards east of the Observatory, was completed. It is situate in an open space in the Park, and has sufficient ground attached to it for an exceedingly good meteorological station. It is most earnestly to be hoped that duplicate instruments will be placed in the new ground, and read against the old ones in the Observatory ground, for such a length of time as may be thought necessary, in order to compute the differences between the old and new stations, so that there may be no break in continuity.

The Standard barometer to which all the observations are referred is the Newman barometer, which was mounted in 1840, and the tube has a bore of ·565 inch. The action is practically the exact reverse of the Fortin pattern, viz. for the purpose of getting the zero, the ivory point is screwed down to the mercury in the cistern, which is fixed; instead of the mercury in the cistern being screwed up to the ivory point, as in the Fortin. When the ivory point and the mercury meet, or nearly so, the reading is taken by the vernier in the ordinary way. This barometer is used for checking the records from the photographic barometer. The photographic barometer is so exceedingly difficult to describe that I shall merely confine myself to saying that it is the representation by means of photography, on a cylinder turned by a clock, of a beam of light from a slit in a mica plate connected with a siphon barometer.

With respect to the thermometers, I find that in the early years the Rutherford maximum, which has for an index a piece of blue steel wire, was used until the invention of the Negretti maximum thermometer, which came out at the Exhibition of 1851, and was subsequently used. The Rutherford minimum, a very old good pattern I presume, has been used throughout. The dry and wet-bulb thermometers call for no remark, being merely good instruments accurately divided.

The thermometers are exposed on the Glaisher stand. This is a revolving frame, fixed on a vertical axis, consisting of a horizontal board as base, of a vertical board projecting upwards from it and connected with one edge of the horizontal board, and of two parallel inclined boards (separated about 3 inches) connected at the top with the vertical board and at the bottom with the other edge of the horizontal board: the outer inclined board is covered with zinc, and the air passes freely between the two boards. The thermometers are mounted on the vertical board, the dry and wet being in the centre, the maximum and minimum on the left, and certain other thermometers on the right. A small projecting roof shelters the instruments from rain. The frame is turned several times a day, so as to keep the inclined side to the sun. In 1878 a circular board 3 feet in diameter was fixed on the supporting post, beneath the frame, to protect the thermometers against radiation from the ground; but the effect of radiation, with the board removed, was found, by experiments in 1886, to be insensible.

Osler's anemometer has been in use during the whole period, and the directions of the wind are obtained from it. It is fixed above the north-western turret of the old part of the Observatory. For the direction of the wind a large vane, from which a vertical shaft proceeds down to the registering table within the turret, gives motion by a pinion fixed at its lower end to a rackwork carrying a pencil. This pencil marks a paper fixed to a board moved horizontally by a clock in a direction transverse to that of the motion of the pencil. The paper has lines corresponding to the positions of N., E., S., and W. of the vane, with transversal hour lines. The vane is 25 feet above the roof of the Octagon Room, and 215 feet above mean sea-level. I do not propose to describe the arrangements which are attached to the Osler's anemometer for ascertaining the pressure of the wind or for measuring the rainfall.

The rain-gauges Nos. 6, 7, and 8 are the gauges used for the rain measurements. They are 8-inch circular gauges placed south of the Magnetical Observatory with their rims 6 inches above the ground. No. 6 is the old daily gauge, No. 7 the old monthly gauge, and No. 8, an additional gauge, which was brought into use in July 1881 as a check on the other two. On November 6, 1894, gauge No. 8 was shifted 61 feet eastwards. Gauge No. 6 is read at 9 a.m., 3 p.m., and 9 p.m., and Nos. 7 and 8 at 9 a.m. All the gauges are read at midnight on the last day of the calendar month.

The above particulars as to situation, personal establishment, and instruments I have, of course, obtained from the various volumes of Greenwich observations.

The meteorological records of the Observatory have been many times investigated, but, as far as I can find out, have never yet been discussed as a whole. The Greenwich authorities have themselves issued three separate volumes (I think that I may call them by this title), as follows:—

1. In the Greenwich volume for 1860 there is a supplementary appendix which gives the monthly means from 1848 to 1853 of Pressure, Temperature, Moisture, and Rain, and also a monthly statement of days of Wind from 1841 to 1860.

2. In 1878 there was issued *A Reduction of Twenty Years' Photographic Records of the Barometer and Dry-bulb and Wet-bulb Thermometers, and Twenty-seven Years' Observations of the Earth Thermometers;* and

3. In 1895 there was issued *Temperature of the Air as determined from the Observations and Records of the Fifty Years* 1841 *to* 1890.

All these discussions deal with mean values only.

Then, again, we have in our own Transactions several separate papers on different portions of these records, which I shall enumerate very shortly.

By our Past President, Mr. James Glaisher, F.R.S., we have nine separate papers, viz.:—

1. On the Determination of the Mean Temperature of every Day in the Year, from all the Thermometrical Observations taken at the Royal Observatory, Greenwich, from the Year 1814 to the end of 1856 (*Report*, 1857, p. 56).

2. On the Determination of the Mean Pressure of the Atmosphere on every Day in the Year, as deduced from all the Barometrical Observations taken at the Royal Observatory, Greenwich, from the Year 1841 to 1858 (*Report*, 1859 and 1860, p. 11).

3. On the Direction of the Wind at the Royal Observatory, Greenwich, in the Twenty Years ending 1860 (*Proc.* i. p. 21).

4. On the Mean Temperature of every Day, from all the Thermometrical Observations taken at the Royal Observatory, Greenwich, from the Year 1814 to the end of 1863 (*Proc.* ii. p. 327).

5. On the Frequency of Rain at different Hours of the Day, in the several Months and Seasons of the Year (*Proc.* iv. p. 33).

6. On the Fall of Rain at different Hours of the Day, in the several Months and Seasons of the Year (*Proc.* iv. p. 113).

7. On the Fall of Rain on every Day in the Year, from Observations extending from 1815 to 1869 (*Proc.* v. p. 87).

8. On the Direction of Wind at the Royal Observatory, Greenwich, in the Ten Years ending December 1870 (*Q. J.* i. p. 1).

9. On the Mean Temperature of every Day, from all the Thermometrical Observations taken at the Royal Observatory, Greenwich, from the Year 1814 to the end of 1873 (*Q. J.* iii. p. 198).

By our Past President, Mr. H. S. Eaton, we have two separate papers, viz. :—

1. The Average Height of the Barometer in London for Eighty-three Years (*Proc.* i. p. 273) ; and

2. The Mean Temperature of the Air at Greenwich, from September 1811 to June 1856 (*Q. J.* xiv. p. 15).

By our Past President, Mr. W. Ellis, F.R.S., we have eight separate papers, viz. :—

1. Note on the Mean Relative Humidity at the Royal Observatory, Greenwich (*Q. J.* iv. p. 194).

2. On the Greenwich Sunshine Records, 1876-80 (*Q. J.* vi. p. 126).

3. The Presidential Address on January 18, 1888, which included a Discussion of the Greenwich Observations of Cloud during Seventy Years ending 1887 (*Q. J.* xiv. p. 173).

4. On the Relative Prevalence of Different Winds at the Royal Observatory, Greenwich, 1841-89 (*Q. J.* xvi. p. 221.)

5. On the Mean Temperature of the Air at the Royal Observatory, Greenwich, as deduced from the Photographic Records for the Forty Years from 1849-88 (*Q. J.* xvii. p. 233).

6. The Mean Temperature of the Air on each Day of the Year at the Royal Observatory, Greenwich, on the Average of Fifty Years, 1841-90 (*Q. J.* xviii. p. 237).

7. The Mean Maximum and Mean Minimum Temperature of the Air on each Day of the Year at the Royal Observatory, Greenwich, on the Average of the Fifty Years 1841-90 (*Q. J.* xix. p. 211) ; and

8. Mean Amount of Cloud on each Day of the Year at the Royal Observatory, Greenwich, on the Average of the Fifty years 1841-90 (*Q. J.* xxii. p. 169).

Lastly, I must not forget to mention the Presidential Address in 1896 of our Past President, Mr. Inwards, on "Meteorological Observatories," which included a somewhat minute description of the Royal Observatory, Greenwich.

All these separate papers, however, deal with mean values only.

Having thus briefly referred to the situation, establishment, instruments, and former discussions, I shall now proceed to describe the work on which I have been engaged for several months.

I carefully examined the different Greenwich volumes, and decided to begin my work with the year 1848, because in that year the authorities commenced to take readings four times a day, owing, in all probability, to the then impending commencement of photographic registration, and to continue it on to the end of 1898—a period of 51 years. I should have liked to have taken in last year, but found it impossible to do so.

So far as I am able to judge, the observations appear throughout this long period to have been taken with great care, and to be worthy in all respects of the great Observatory at which they were made. The sets of observations that I have been able to deal with are six in number, viz.: the barometer, the maximum thermometer, the minimum thermometer, the relative humidity, the rainfall, and the direction of the wind. It has been a matter of regret to me that the observations of wind-force are in the earlier years fragmentary, and in the later years tainted with the difficulty of the question of the factors, so as to be practically useless for my purpose, and that the cloud observations have never been printed so as to be of use to me. I regret the loss of these two sets extremely, as they cause this new discussion to be incomplete.

The number of days dealt within these 51 years are:—

January March May July August October December	Each 1581 days.	April June September November	Each 1530 days.
		February, 1441 days.	

The method of dealing with the records was as follows:

Columns were ruled for the highest, lowest, and mean values of each month; and then a scale was formed in columns, in which were put the actual number of observations corresponding to the scale of days—31, 30, 28, or 29, as the case may be—for each month, and each year. At the end of the 51 years the columns were added up and means taken of the first three columns, viz. the highest, lowest, and mean, but no means or percentages were taken of the other columns. On the completion of these working tables, the six tables accompanying this Address were extracted from them, and from these tables the diagrams (Plates II.-VII.) have been constructed on a novel plan, which I think will prove very instructive.

I shall now take each of the six elements separately.

Barometer.

The readings are the mean daily value of 4 readings per diem till the end of 1876, then of 24 readings per diem till the end of 1896, then again for the last two years of 4 readings per diem. In every case the readings have been brought to two places of decimals by throwing up ·01 in. where necessary, and they have in every case been reduced to sea-level by adding a fixed correction of ·17 in. The highest and lowest values are the highest and lowest mean daily values reduced to sea-level.

On examining Table I. it will at once be noticed that the absolute highest and lowest values have occurred in the month of January; but when we look at the columns of mean values, we see that, though the highest mean value occurs in January, the lowest mean value occurs in November, the next lowest being in January. Let us now consider the question of the different seasons, and their influence—I presume that I may say so—on the question of range. If we take the absolute values, we note that in January the range is 2·40 ins., in April 1·69 in., in July

TABLE I.—Greenwich Observations, 51 Years 1848-98.
Barometer reduced to 32° Fahr. and Sea-Level.

Months.	Absolute.				Means.			No. of Days.										
	Highest.	Year.	Lowest.	Year.	Highest.	Lowest.	Mean.	in. 31·00 — 30·90	in. 30·89 — 30·70	in. 30·69 — 30·50	in. 30·49 — 30·30	in. 30·29 — 30·10	in. 30·09 — 29·90	in. 29·89 — 29·70	in. 29·69 — 29·50	in. 29·49 — 29·30	in. 29·29 — 29·10	in. 29·09 — 28·90
	in.		in.		in.	in.	in.											
	30·93	1882	28·53	1873	30·50	29·23	29·96	2	16	104	213	290	303	279	181	92	57	[illegible]
	30·86	1849	28·83	1848	30·49	29·35	29·99	...	10	99	199	300	301	249	143	89	34	[illegible]
	30·81	1854	28·74	1876	30·44	29·27	29·91	...	8	56	162	283	354	311	207	127	50	[illegible]
	30·65	1887	28·96	1876	30·34	29·38	29·92	...	...	13	95	352	407	324	207	105	23	4
	30·62	1881	29·15	1858	30·34	29·51	29·96	...	...	9	117	387	448	373	203	38	0	...
	30·56	1867	29·31	1860	30·29	29·58	29·98	...	...	4	82	400	548	357	120	19	...	...
	30·50	1848	29·25	1877	30·28	29·58	29·96	...	...	1	51	374	598	400	134	22	1	...
	30·49	1854	29·18	1876	30·27	29·54	29·95	...	...	...	49	342	583	441	126	37	3	[illegible]
	30·59	1851	28·91	1883	30·39	29·45	29·98	...	...	11	178	369	413	344	141	54	14	[illegible]
	30·67	1849	28·79	1886	30·41	29·26	29·89	...	...	22	129	303	372	321	229	146	44	[illegible]
	30·74	1857	28·78	1874	30·46	29·22	29·93	...	4	48	213	292	322	268	175	122	58	[illegible]
	30·75	1859	28·58	1876	30·47	29·24	29·95	...	7	92	224	295	283	274	221	107	50	[illegible]

1·25 in., and in October 1·88 in.; we see therefore that in the absolute values the range in summer is very nearly one-half that in winter, and that the range in autumn is about ·50 in. greater than that in spring. The column of mean values bears this statement out. In January the difference is 1·27 in., in April ·96 in., in July ·70 in., and in October 1·15 in. This result is of considerable importance, and it will be interesting to know whether the same feature is to be observed in the other elements which will be taken later on in this Address. And with reference to the "means" it appears to me that we may fairly conclude that, when the barometer either rises above the mean of the highest or sinks below the mean of the lowest, the reading is extraordinarily high or low as the case may be. The rest of Table I. is exhibited in the diagram (Plate II.), which was formed as follows: the centre line is taken as zero, and the lines on either side represent 100, 200, and 300 days. The figures, represented by solid lines, were equally divided on each side of the centre line, according to the scale which is given at the sides of the diagram. When all the solid lines were drawn, the thin line was put round their extremities to catch the eye. If we now examine the diagrams month by month we shall notice that the

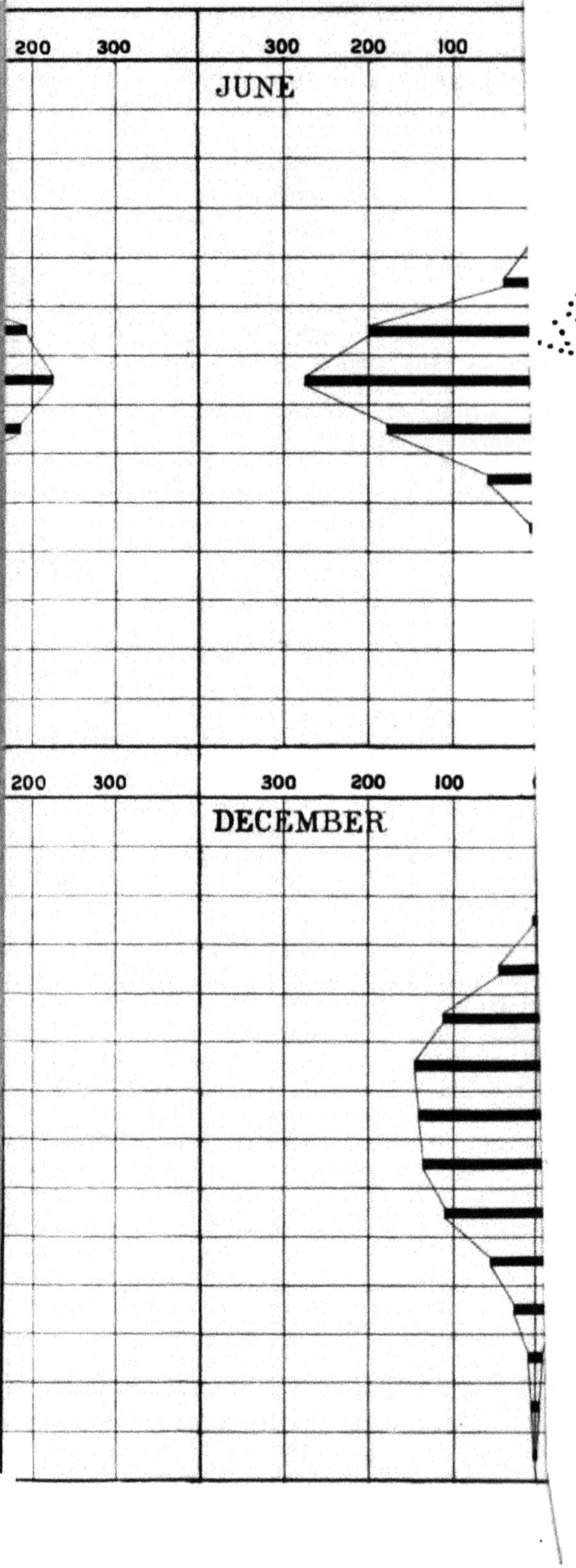

200
300
300
200
100
JUNE
200
300
300
200
100
DECEMBER

peculiar top shape of the January diagram is gradually flattened both top and bottom about the mean line on the scale 30·09–29·90 ins., the range gradually becoming less and less until we come to the July diagram, and the very extraordinary flat-topped August one, after which the range extends upwards and downwards rather rapidly until we have the December diagram, which is similar to the January one, though not quite so high.

Temperature.

The maximum temperature, the minimum temperature, and the relative humidity have been treated in a similar way to the method adopted in the case of the barometer, so that there is no necessity to describe it.

Maximum Temperature.

If we examine Table II. carefully we shall notice a somewhat different state of things to what we saw in Table I. relating to the barometer. Here we note that whilst the lowest absolute maximum

TABLE II.—Greenwich Observations, 51 Years 1848-98.
Maximum Temperature.

Absolute.				Mean.			No. of Days.													
Highest.	Year.	Lowest.	Year.	Highest.	Lowest.	Mean.	above 90°	89°–85	84°–80	79°–75	74°–70	69°–65	64°–60	59°–55	54°–50	49°–45	44°–40	39°–35	34°–30	b
56°·5	1851	19°·0	1894	53°·3	31°·6	42°·9	...	...	...	...	...	...	...	19	286	400	337	282	204	
62·1	1891	27·0	1895	55·5	35·8	45·6	...	...	...	...	...	...	5	83	359	378	302	221	80	
71·5	1848	32·1	1892	62·2	38·7	49·8	...	...	...	...	2	19	96	281	392	380	288	99	24	.
81·5	1865	36·3	1849	70·5	45·8	57·4	...	...	2	25	46	149	312	389	386	177	43	1	...	.
87·5	1880	43·2	{1866 1891	77·8	50·6	64·1	...	6	26	97	221	369	391	293	137	38	3	...	...	.
94·5	1858	52·5	1855	83·2	58·7	70·8	5	29	133	254	391	406	228	77	7	...	...	...	...	.
97·1	1881	53·9	1888	85·6	62·4	74·2	25	84	190	347	541	284	89	19	2	...	...	...	...	.
95·1	1893	55·4	1879	84·3	61·8	72·9	11	53	135	347	517	387	113	18	...	...	...	...	...	.
92·1	{1868 1898	50·8	1872	77·8	57·6	67·5	2	10	51	105	285	557	385	121	14	...	...	...	...	.
81·0	1859	39·0	{1859 1873	68·5	46·8	57·6	...	...	1	6	37	145	370	512	333	147	23	7	...	.
64·9	1894	26·9	1890	58·9	38·1	48·8	...	...	...	...	...	...	39	232	392	449	313	84	18	
62·4	1848	23·2	1855	54·8	33·0	44·2	...	...	...	...	...	...	1	74	307	418	308	290	154	

occurred in January, viz. 19°·0, the highest, 97°·1, occurred in July; and we shall also note that in January, February, November, and December the lowest absolute maximum was considerably below the freezing-point. When, however, we come to consider the influence of the seasons and the question of range a very different state of things is represented. If, in the first instance, we take the absolute values we note that the range in January is 37°·5, in April 45°·2, in July 43°·2, and in October 42°·0. We see, therefore, that there is the greatest range in the spring, the range in April being 7°·7 greater than in January, 2°·0 greater than in July, and 3°·2 greater than in October. When, however, we turn to the columns of mean value we see that the above statement is not quite borne out. In these columns the range is: in January 21°·7, in April

24°·7, in July 23°·2, and in October 21°·7, showing that the range in January and October are alike, and 3°·0 below that of April, whilst the range in April is greater than that of July by 1°·5. And lastly, as in the case of the barometer, I think that we may very fairly conclude from the columns of mean values that where an individual reading is above the mean of the highest or below the mean of the lowest it is extraordinarily high or low as the case may be.

With reference to the rest of Table II., which is graphically shown in the diagrams (Plate III.), we have an extraordinary form, something like a cup with a lid to it, which gradually expands and rises upwards during the months of February, March, April, and May. In June it commences to flatten out, a process which reaches its maximum in July, after which it gradually descends the scale, still, however, considerably flattened out, and even in December, though it is somewhat like its January shape, it has not yet come to its normal winter condition.

Minimum Temperature.

On looking over the absolute values in Table III. we note a fact which may be of some significance, viz. that the absolute lowest, viz. 6°·6, occurs in January, as in the case of the barometer and the maximum temperature, whilst the absolute highest occurs in August, and not in July as in the maximum temperature, Table II. It will also be noted that in only June, July, and August are we perfectly sure that we shall

TABLE III.—GREENWICH OBSERVATIONS, 51 YEARS 1848-98.
MINIMUM TEMPERATURE.

MONTH.	Absolute.				Mean.			No. of Days.											
	Highest.	Year.	Lowest.	Year.	Highest.	Lowest.	Mean.	above 65°	64°—60	59°—55	54°—50	49°—45	44°—40	39°—35	34°—30	29°—25	24°—20	19°—15	b
Jan.	51°·7	1883	6°·6	1867	45°·2	21°·6	33°·5	...	...	...	3	57	242	367	462	282	105	50	
Feb.	51·2	1850	6·9	1895	45·0	24·0	34·4	...	...	...	2	69	240	358	430	239	73	22	
Mar.	51·1	1872	13·1	1890	46·1	25·1	34·9	...	...	...	8	88	231	435	485	277	55	1	
April	53·0	1865	25·3	1887	48·2	29·5	38·7	...	...	...	13	190	463	508	279	77	...	...	
May	58·4	1871	28·1	1877	52·9	33·1	43·5	...	...	15	152	503	516	274	113	8	...	...	
June	63.2	1878	35·6	1869	58·0	40·9	49·8	...	15	184	566	561	177	27	...	...	...	...	
July	66·1	1872	38·7	1863	59·9	45·0	53·1	1	61	451	729	294	42	3	...	...	...	...	
Aug.	66·8	1893	38·1	1864	60·5	44·4	52·9	1	71	460	679	315	52	3	...	...	...	...	
Sept.	64·0	1898	30·6	1885	58·3	38·7	49·1	...	16	188	491	510	234	83	8	...	...	...	
Oct.	59·5	1859	24·7	1890	54·0	31·6	43·3	...	...	40	200	397	458	309	146	30	1	...	
Nov.	55·4	1857	18·3	1890	48·9	26·7	37·5	...	...	1	39	161	349	434	363	157	24	2	
Dec.	52·6	1898	8·0	1860	46·6	22·7	34·8	...	...	...	15	117	252	433	375	237	110	33	

not have a frost. When, however, we examine the columns of absolute values and mean values in order to trace the influence of the seasons on the range we find this result: in the "absolute" columns the range is in January 45°·1, in April 27°·7, in July 27°·4, and in October 34°·8, showing a state of affairs very similar to that which appears in the barometer, Table I. If we now turn to the "mean" columns we have this result, viz. that the range in January is 23°·6, in April 18°·7, in July 14°·9, and in October 22°·4. This also is very similar to the range of

he barometer in Table I. I need hardly say that this shows a state of hings very different from what has been shown in the maximum temerature, Table II. Lastly, with reference to the columns of means we nay again fairly say that where a reading is above the mean of the ighest or below the mean of the lowest, it is extraordinarily high or low s the case may be. The rest of Table III., when graphically exhibited Plate IV.), shows a distinct difference in the diagrams from those of he maximum temperature. The shape is somewhat similar to the top hape of the barometer diagram, but more angular. It gradually rises, nd at the same time begins to flatten out, the flattening becoming xtremely noticeable in April, and becoming more exaggerated until ve have the extraordinary shape of the July diagram, to which the ugust diagram is very similar. After August the diagram gradually inks down the scale, but still somewhat flattened out in every month vith the exception of November, where the diagram has a somewhat ound, even, appearance.

Relative Humidity.

This element has occasioned me much trouble and labour. The laily values had not been calculated prior to November 1857, though he mean monthly values had. I had thus to calculate the daily values rom January 1, 1848 to October 31, 1857, which I have done by lividing the elastic force of the dew-point by the elastic force of the nean daily temperature, using Crelle's *Tables*. The original calculations have placed in the library of the Society. The lowest relative humidity ccurred in December 1855, when there was a day of extremely low emperature. I do not doubt the figures printed, but may I not ask hat they be properly verified, for it seems to me that a relative humidity n December of 34 must be nearly if not quite unique? The next lowest elative humidity is 43 in May 1868, which I believe is accurate, the ame having been well investigated, as was also the reading of 44 in pril 1870. I have omitted the absolute maximum column, as I found

TABLE IV.—Greenwich Observations, 51 Years 1848-98.
Relative Humidity.

ONTH.	Absolute.		Mean.		No. of Days.												
	Lowest %	Year.	Lowest %	Mean %	% 100—95	% 94—90	% 89—85	% 84—80	% 79—75	% 74—70	% 69—65	% 64—60	% 59—55	% 54—50	% 49—45	% 44—40	% below 40
n.	51	1869 / 1879	69	87	234	380	402	288	164	72	20	14	4	3	...	...	...
eb.	52	1870	67	84	137	240	346	349	204	99	36	15	11	4	...	...	...
ar.	52	1886	65	81	70	142	303	355	323	236	100	40	11	1	...	...	...
pril	44	1870	61	78	55	122	201	273	330	272	161	78	24	13	0	1	...
ay	43	1868	59	75	39	87	137	216	295	332	272	151	40	9	2	1	...
ne	46	1887	59	74	38	74	126	245	276	285	262	162	40	16	6	...	...
ly	47	1897	59	74	24	75	152	233	297	314	246	150	61	25	4	...	...
ig.	48	1876	62	76	36	83	143	280	341	320	213	111	40	13	1	...	...
pt.	51	1898	67	80	56	136	255	353	344	247	90	36	10	3	...	...	...
t.	60	1850	72	86	211	315	369	338	220	98	22	8	...	...	...	...	...
v.	61	1866	73	87	245	351	426	314	130	49	11	4	...	...	...	...	...
c.	34	1855	71	88	283	419	406	271	122	48	19	6	3	3	0	0	1

that it was 100 in every month; but I regret that I omitted to calculate the mean maximum column, though it must be obvious that it must amount to very nearly 100 in every month. The range in the mean columns cannot therefore be shown; and, having regard to the difficulties created by the exceedingly low readings in the absolute columns, it is probably not advisable that it should be given, as it might be erroneous. It is rather remarkable that the mean of the lowest values in May, June, and July should be the same, viz. 59. It is also remarkable that the highest mean of the lowest, viz. 73, should be in November, in which month also occurred the highest value in the absolute lowest column, viz. 61. The rest of Table IV. is graphically represented (Plate V.). December is the month in which the maximum reading occurs the greatest number of times. Great difficulty is occasioned by the low reading of 34, which I have represented by a dot. If we carefully look at the diagrams, we see that the reverse of what we saw in the barometer maximum and minimum temperature holds good, viz. that in the summer time the figures are expanded instead of being flattened and contracted, as for instance in June. The result is curious, and is well worth greater attention than can be given at the present time.

Rainfall.

The rainfall has caused a good deal of trouble, for from 1848 to 1876 it was tabulated to two places of decimals, and after that date to three places. These three places have been throughout reduced to two by throwing up ·01 where necessary. There has been no month without rain; and the smallest number of rainy days in any month was in September 1864, when the number of days amounted to 1. The comparative smallness of the falls has also astonished me; for there has in the 51 years been only 1 fall, viz. July 1867, of over 3 ins., and only 4 others over 2 ins. The absolute and the mean columns explain themselves. With respect to the other columns which are graphically

TABLE V.—GREENWICH OBSERVATIONS, 51 YEARS 1848-98.
RAINFALL.

Month.	Absolute.		Mean.		No. of Days.													
	Highest.	Year.	Highest.	Mean.	in. above 3·00	in. 3·00–2·50	in. 2·49–2·00	in. 1·99–1·50	in. 1·49–1·00	in. 0·99–0·75	in. 0·74–0·50	in. 0·49–0·40	in. 0·39–0·30	in. 0·29–0·20	in. 0·19–0·10	in. 0·09–0·02	in. 0·01	Total.
	in.		in.	in.														
Jan.	1·61	1866	0·50	1·87	...	...	...	1	2	5	20	18	37	71	161	319	129	763
Feb.	0·82	1890	0·37	1·41	...	...	...	...	...	5	13	16	24	58	122	286	111	635
Mar.	1·45	1851	0·42	1·50	...	...	...	...	1	5	11	17	27	57	149	292	113	672
Apr.	2·51	1878	0·48	1·59	...	1	0	0	1	3	21	18	32	51	140	260	81	608
May	1·52	1878	0·57	1·93	...	...	...	1	7	12	27	9	41	63	118	257	74	609
June	1·70	1888	0·66	2·00	...	...	...	1	13	9	24	16	36	62	118	236	78	593
July	3·67	1867	0·84	2·50	1	1	1	1	13	13	26	32	41	74	127	227	89	646
Aug.	1·79	1865	0·73	2·30	...	...	...	1	11	14	30	28	49	66	118	245	95	657
Sept.	1·55	1859	0·62	2·19	...	...	...	1	8	14	22	30	34	88	140	219	90	646
Oct.	2·57	1857	0·73	2·77	...	1	0	1	11	16	38	42	53	85	143	254	126	770
Nov.	1·29	1861	0·54	2·12	...	...	...	...	4	7	37	19	42	79	147	255	128	718
Dec.	1·20	1898	0·44	1·87	...	...	...	...	2	6	13	20	50	74	169	302	104	740

Quart. Journ. Roy. Met. Soc. Vol. XXVI Pl. 5.

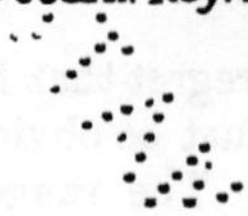

illustrated I should like particularly to call attention to the scale at the sides of the diagrams, which it will be noticed does not descend by equal steps. The total number of rainy days appears in the column headed "No. of Days," and it will be noticed that in no case does it amount to half the number of days in the month. I shall now say a few words about the diagrams (Plate VI.). The curious bottle-shaped arrangement will be noticed, and it will be observed that the capacity, so to say, of the bottle depends not so much on its height as on the length of the two lowest lines; the lowest line being longest in January and smallest in May, whilst the next line is longest in January and shortest in July when the bottle reaches its maximum height. The number of small falls and the paucity of large ones, an inch and above, is particularly noticeable. In April, May, June, and November the number of falls of over ·50 in. and under ·75 in. is well shown.

Direction of Wind.

This table, which is graphically illustrated in the diagrams, Plate VII., does not call for much remark. The great excess of South-west winds in July and August is especially noticeable, and the number of calm days in August, September, and October should be carefully considered.

TABLE VI.—Greenwich Observations, 51 Years 1848-98.
Direction of Wind.

Month.	No. of Days.								
	N.	N.E.	E.	S.E.	S.	S.W.	W.	N.W.	Calm.
January	144	165	100	133	209	497	196	74	63
February	152	184	110	97	139	428	190	82	59
March	199	227	161	97	124	387	199	122	65
April	189	281	212	106	129	314	151	96	52
May	224	316	169	87	127	376	140	85	57
June	190	201	126	89	122	462	198	95	47
July	158	162	88	70	138	544	249	114	58
August	148	134	94	75	139	568	238	105	80
September	150	204	110	96	139	481	190	76	84
October	159	178	119	123	170	462	194	93	83
November	199	186	124	123	169	406	167	95	61
December	156	128	106	110	176	511	231	91	72

The great prevalence of North-east winds in April and May is well shown, the number closely approximating to the number of the South-west winds.

The above enumeration completes the work of this new discussion, and it is a matter of regret to me that it is not possible to have the "Force of the Wind" and "The Amount of Cloud" to add to it, as I cannot help thinking that many points which are now obscure would be elucidated. The great feature which I wish to emphasise is the peculiar flattening of the diagrams of the barometer and the maximum and minimum temperatures in July and August, the roundness of the relative humidity diagrams in the same two months, and the great excess of South-west winds in the same period.

In conclusion, I desire to tender my thanks to the Astronomer-Royal, and to Mr. Nash for their willing help, to Mr. Jeffries for the loan of a number of slides illustrating the Royal Observatory, and to Mr. Marriott for kindly making the other necessary lantern slides and aiding me in other ways.

Atlas of Meteorology.—Messrs. J. G. Bartholomew and A. J. Herbertson have recently prepared and published a large and elaborate *Atlas of Meteorology* which contains a series of over 400 maps. The whole work has been edited by Dr. A. Buchan, who has also written the Introduction.

The maps deal with Climate and Weather.

The Climate Maps include :—

1. Isotherms, showing the seasonal and annual distribution of temperature over the world, to which are added in fuller detail maps of isotherms in countries such as the British Isles, Europe, Canada, United States, India, Cape Colony, and Australia. The lines show mean, isanomalous, and extreme temperatures.

2. Isobars and Arrows, showing the distribution of barometric pressure and winds.

3. Isotherms and Isobars in their relations to each other, as shown by the respective changes from month to month, and by the deviations from their averages during unusually warm and cold weather.

4. Isohels, showing the annual distribution of sunshine over Europe and North America.

5. Isonephs, showing the annual and monthly distribution of cloud over the globe.

6. Isohyets, showing the annual, seasonal, and monthly distribution of rain over the globe.

7. Maps of Hyetal Regions and the Seasonal Distribution of Rain.

8. Isobars and Isohyets, showing monthly and annual distribution of barometric pressure and rainfall as related to each other for various countries.

The Weather Maps include :—

1. Maps showing the pressure conditions and, in some cases, the accompanying temperature and rainfall in abnormally hot and cold seasons and months in different regions.

2. Maps showing the pressure conditions producing different types of winds and weather, accompanied by maps of other weather conditions.

3. Maps showing the distribution of pressure and winds in typical storms of all kinds.

4. Maps showing the tracks of the storms and the distribution of storm frequency.

5. A series of maps showing typical distributions of deviations from the normal monthly pressure.

In all the maps the metric system has been systematically employed, in conjunction with the usual English scales. Uniform gradations of distinctive colouring for the various meteorological phenomena have been strictly adhered to ; thus avoiding confusion and facilitating comparison.

A map showing, by colouring, the distribution of meteorological stations of all orders is given as the frontispiece. The number of stations is probably over 31,000.

The Appendix contains a list of Meteorological Services, with their stations and publications ; a Bibliography of the more important books and papers of special value for reference ; a Glossary of meteorological terms ; and some Meteorological Tables.

MAP SHOWING POSITION OF THE PHENOLOGICAL STATIONS, 1899.

the Names of the Stations see List of Observers, Page 121.

REPORT ON THE PHENOLOGICAL OBSERVATIONS FOR 1899.

By EDWARD MAWLEY, F.R.H.S., Secretary.

(Plate VIII.)

[Read February 21, 1900.]

The following changes have taken place in the observing stations since the last Report was issued. No returns were received during the year from Cork and Marlfield in District B; Chislehurst in District C; St. Albans (Worley Road) and Sandbeck in District D; Ellesmere and Claughton in District F; Ballynagard in District G; Thornhill, Helensburgh, and Lochbuie in District H; Great Cotes and South Milford in District I; and Horse Cross in District J. On the other hand, new stations have been started at Breamore and Weston Green in District C; and Wealdstone in District D.

The average dates for the plants in the different districts given in the present Report are the same as those used in the preceding one, viz. for the eight years ending 1898.

TABLE I.—Mean Results, with their Variations from the 8 Years' Average (1891-98), for the Thirteen Plants in those Districts where there have been sufficient Observations to warrant Comparisons being made.

Years.	Eng. S.W.		Eng. S.		Eng. Mid.		Eng. E.		Eng. N.W.	
	Day of Year.	Variation from Average.	Day of Year.	Variation from Average.	Day of Year.	Variation from Average.	Day of Year.	Variation from Average.	Day of Year.	Variation from Average.
		Days.		Days.		Days.		Days.		Days.
1891	144	+12	144	+11	150	+12	147	+12	150	+10
1892	139	+ 7	138	+ 5	144	+ 6	143	+ 8	147	+ 7
1893	118	−14	122	−11	125	−13	123	−12	128	−12
1894	126	− 6	130	− 3	135	− 3	127	− 8	137	− 3
1895	139	+ 7	138	+ 5	141	+ 3	138	+ 3	144	+ 4
1896	125	− 7	128	− 5	132	− 6	130	− 5	134	− 6
1897	130	− 2	132	− 1	136	− 2	132	− 3	142	+ 2
1898	133	+ 1	135	+ 2	138	0	136	+ 1	141	+ 1
1899	136	+ 4	136	+ 3	141	+ 3	138	+ 3	145	+ 5
Mean	132	...	133	...	138	...	135	...	140	...

Explanation of the Dates in the Tables.

1– 31	are in	January.	182–212	are in	July.
32– 59	,,	February.	213–243	,,	August.
60– 90	,,	March.	244–273	,,	September.
91–120	,,	April.	274–304	,,	October.
121–151	,,	May.	305–334	,,	November.
152–181	,,	June.	335–365	,,	December.

The Winter of 1898-99.

The weather during this quarter continued very mild in all parts of the country. December was especially warm, the departures from the average in mean temperature ranging between + 3°·8 in the north of

Scotland to as much as + 6°·3 in England south. The rainfall was very unequally distributed, but in nearly all the districts was in excess of the average. It was, however, exceptionally heavy only in England south-west, Ireland south, and Scotland north. The records of bright sunshine nearly everywhere exceeded the mean, and more particularly was this the case in the southern, eastern, and midland districts of England.

It was on the whole a very favourable winter for the farmer. Although more than the usual quantity of rain fell, the subsoil at the beginning of the season had become so dry that any superfluous moisture in the surface soil was rapidly absorbed; so that during December and the greater part of January the land was in a workable condition in a surprisingly short time after rain had fallen. Then again, notwithstanding the general mildness of the season, there occurred sufficient moderate frosts to keep the autumn-sown wheat and other winter crops from becoming unseasonably forward, while the general warmth of the ground and the unusual duration of bright sunshine enabled them to make sturdy growth and become firmly rooted. At the end of the season the young wheat especially presented a most promising appearance. The grass, moreover, remained green throughout the winter, so that there was at no time any lack of feed for sheep and cattle in the pastures. So dry had the ground become through the prolonged drought of the previous summer and autumn, that it was not until nearly the end of January that sufficient rain had fallen to saturate the heavy soils completely. On the other hand, the preparation of the land for the reception of spring corn, owing to the frequent falls of rain in February, was for a time delayed.

In the gardens the weather conditions were almost equally favourable. In the kitchen garden there never occurred sufficient frost to injure the rather scanty supply of green vegetables. Many delicate flowering plants, such as geraniums and heliotropes, remained in blossom in the more favoured districts nearly the whole of the winter.

As soon as sufficient rain had fallen to moisten the ground in December, the soil was in admirable condition for the planting of fruit and other deciduous trees and shrubs, but previous to that time the subsoil had been much too dry.

Taking the British Isles as a whole, the earlier wild plants, owing to the mild winter, flowered somewhat in advance of their average dates. For instance, the fertile flowers on the hazel made their appearance 3 days in advance of their usual time, while the coltsfoot was 2 days early.

The song-thrush began singing 10 days earlier than its mean date.

The honey-bee was first seen to visit flowers 7 days earlier than usual.

The Spring.

The spring of 1899, taken as a whole, was almost everywhere rather cold. During March and May the fall of rain was in most districts about seasonable, whereas April was more or less a wet month in all parts of the kingdom. In April there was a deficiency of sunshine, while March and May, on the other hand, proved unusually sunny.

Favoured by the dry weather that then prevailed, the arable land on the farms continued throughout the whole of March in perfect working condition. Consequently, the sowing of spring corn and other crops was carried out during that month with little labour and on an exceptionally satisfactory seed-bed; but after that time wet weather set in, and the state of the ground was much less favourable. The autumn-sown

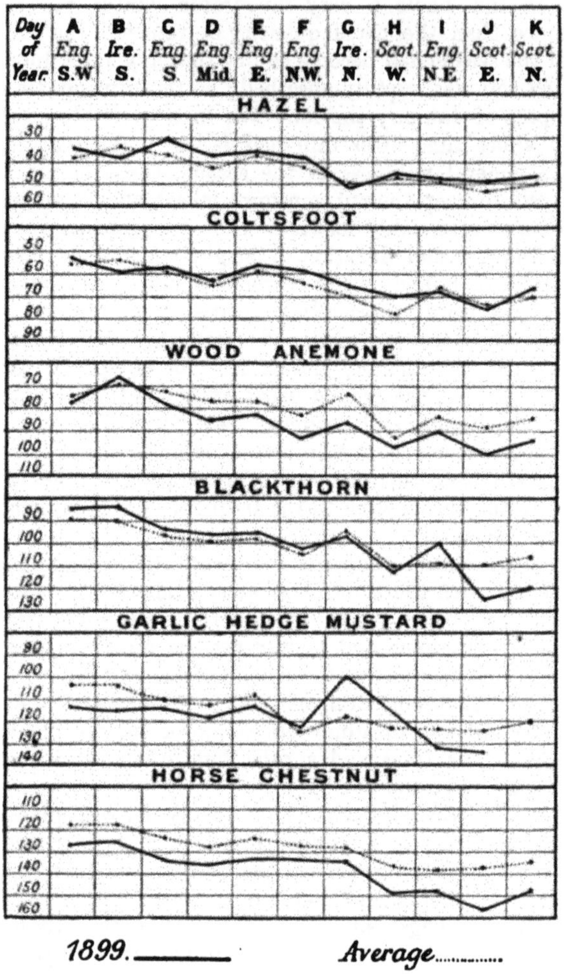

FIG. 1.—Mean dates (day of year) of flowering of plants in 1899 as compared with the eight years' average 1891-98.

cereals made little real progress until the advent of a spell of moderately warm weather in May, when all the corn crops for a time made a somewhat rapid advance. The grass, after the April rains, made excellent bottom growth, and, assisted by the subsequent short term of genial weather in May, there appeared at that time every prospect of a fairly abundant crop of hay. The pastures also became well clothed with herbage. Notwithstanding the generally low temperatures and occasional frosts, the appearance of all farm crops at the close of the spring, taking the British Isles as a whole, left little to be desired.

This quarter proved by no means a kindly one for the fruit blossom, for in each month there occurred every now and then moderately sharp frosts. Although these frosts were only here and there exceptionally

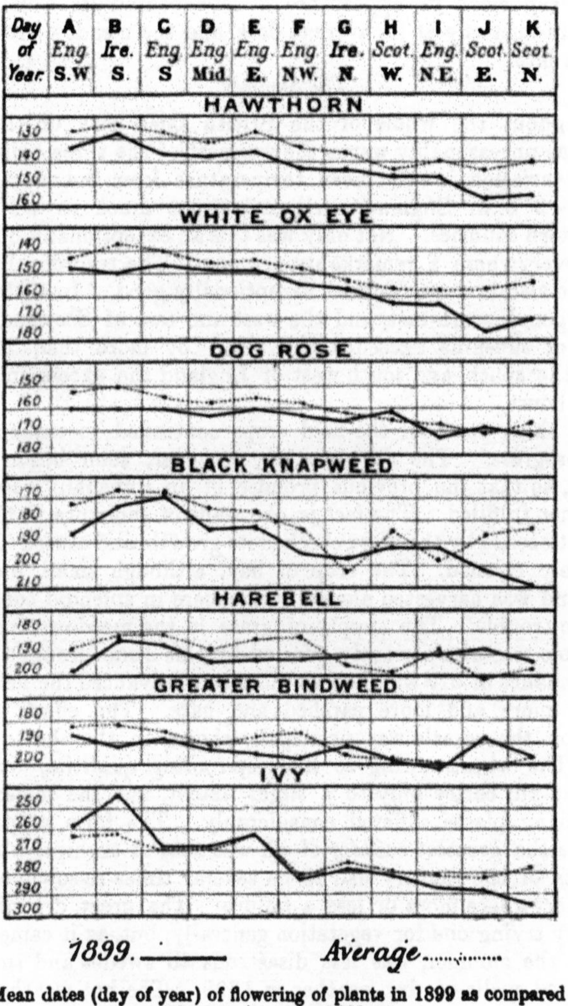

FIG. 2.—Mean dates (day of year) of flowering of plants in 1899 as compared with the eight years' average 1891-98.

keen, the cold was at times sufficiently prolonged to damage any peach, plum, pear, or apple blossoms that happened to be fully expanded at the time of their occurrence.

With the exception of the blackthorn, the time of blossoming of which was about average, the spring flowers on the list were all late in coming into bloom. The wood anemone flowered just a week later than its usual time, the garlic hedge mustard was 3 days late, the horse-chestnut 9 days late, the hawthorn 8 days late, and the white ox-eye also 8 days late.

According to the returns sent in, the spring migrants were all a few days later than usual in reaching our shores—the swallow arriving 4 days late, the cuckoo 2 days late, the nightingale 1 day late, and the fly-catcher 2 days late.

The wasp made its appearance 8 days behind its usual time, the small white butterfly at its average date, and the meadow-brown butterfly 9 days late.

The Summer.

Throughout the whole of the British Isles each of the summer months was unseasonably warm, the warmest of the three being August, when the variation in the mean temperature from the average ranged between $+2^{\circ}{\cdot}8$ in England north-east to as much as $+5^{\circ}{\cdot}0$ in the south-western counties. Not only was this an exceptionally hot summer, but also everywhere a remarkably dry one. The records of clear sunshine were also in most districts exceptionally good. In all but Ireland north, England north-east, and the west and east of Scotland, the total duration of sunshine exceeded the mean by more than 100 hours; while in the south and south-west of England the excess amounted to over 200 hours.

For a short time all the field crops continued to make very satisfactory progress. The dry weather, however, soon began to make itself felt, so that the previous promise of an unusually good yield of hay was not fulfilled. The fact is, the want of moisture in the ground, when most needed by the grass, checked its growth, and caused it to become prematurely ripened. The crop of hay, although small, was of good quality, and was harvested almost everywhere in splendid condition and with little trouble. The supply of grass in the meadows and pastures after a time was also seriously affected by this June drought, and, with the continuance of dry weather, as the season advanced the fields became gradually more and more parched and bare. The effect of the dry weather on the cereals was principally shown in the shortness of the straw. The wheat, owing to its deep-rooting qualities, was scarcely affected at all, barley only to a slight extent, but the moisture-loving oats in many places suffered considerably. The farm crop, however, which was the greatest sufferer of all was that of turnips, which in the drier parts of the country had to be several times re-sown, and proved almost everywhere more or less a failure. The great drought of 1893 was a very trying one for vegetation generally, but, as it came to an end earlier in the summer, was less disastrous to swedes and turnips than the repeated spells of dry weather in 1899. The hot weather in July, together with the parched condition of the soil, hurried the grain crops rapidly to maturity, so that although the season was really rather late a good deal of corn was cut and carried before the end of that month. Not only was the harvest an early, but also an extremely short one. Sir John Lawes, in his *Report on the Wheat Crop of* 1899, describes the weather at harvest-time as having been "as near perfection as could be desired." In the *Times* agricultural report for August the deterioration of potatoes during that month was estimated at 8 per cent, of roots at 13 per cent, and of grass at 15 per cent.

In the gardens, owing to the great heat, deficient rainfall, and singularly dry atmosphere, the summer proved a most unfavourable one. Indeed, on shallow soils it was only by constant watering that many plants and shrubs could be kept in a growing condition.

As regards insect pests, one of the most noteworthy features was the little injury done by greenfly, or by the caterpillars which in recent years have committed so much havoc on the foliage of oak and other trees. Wasps also were singularly scarce. On the other hand, the turnip-fly, assisted by the dry season, did considerable damage. The small and large white butterflies were everywhere abundant, but most other butterflies unusually scarce.

Of the 4 summer flowering plants on the list, the dog-rose was 4 days late in coming into blossom, the black knapweed 7 days late, the harebell flowered at its usual time, while the greater bindweed was 2 days late.

The meadow-brown butterfly made its appearance 3 days earlier than usual.

The Autumn.

This was another hot season. November proved a particularly warm autumn month in all parts of the country, the departures from the average in mean temperature varying only from + 4°·0 in the south-west and east of England to + 5°·4 in the west of Scotland. The fall of rain, as had been the case in the two preceding quarters, was in most districts below the mean; while there was again an unusually good record of bright sunshine.

By the end of August the harvest was practically over even in the late districts of England, and nearly over in many parts of Scotland and Ireland. So dry and hard had the ground become through the continued dry weather that it was not until the end of September that any autumn tillage operations were practicable. However, during the greater part of October, when the land had been softened by the previous heavy rains, the soil was in splendid condition for its preparation for wheat sowing. Indeed, the best seed-bed for wheat is invariably secured after the ground has been thoroughly baked by sunshine, and afterwards moistened sufficiently by rain to enable it to be cultivated. There occurred a very wet period at the beginning of November, but even after the soil had become saturated by the heavy rainfall of this period the land was seldom for long in an unworkable condition, so rapidly did the thirsty subsoil absorb the rain. In the early part of the season there appeared little prospect of any further keep in the pastures, but with the advent of sufficient rain at the beginning of November the aspect of the whole country was soon changed, so that by the end of that month the grass fields were looking greener than at any time since June. The refreshing rains here referred to came, however, too late to be of any real service to the turnips and swedes.

The same welcome rains greatly benefited the winter supply of vegetables in the kitchen garden, but in many places so stunted had these vegetables become through the long term of dry weather which preceded the rainy period, that at the close of the quarter they were little more than half their usual size. In those localities which escaped the mid-autumn frosts the gardens continued unusually gay with flowers until late in November.

In the course of the Phenological year now under review there occurred three or more distinct periods of dry weather, but as affecting farm and garden crops they may be regarded as forming together one continuous drought—lasting from the beginning of June until nearly the end of October—the wet periods separating them not being sufficiently prolonged or pronounced to be of any real service to vegetation during so warm and dry a summer.

The swallows, which are said to have been less numerous than usual in 1899, left this country a few days in advance of their regular time. The larvæ of the small and large white butterflies were singularly abundant.

The wild ivy flowered, taking its mean date for the whole country, 1 day later than usual.

The last swallows, as a rule, took their departure 2 days earlier than their average time.

According to the preliminary statement for Great Britain issued by the Board of Agriculture, the estimated yield of wheat per acre exceeded the average for the previous 10 years by nearly 3 bushels. Barley also was rather in excess of the average. On the other hand, the oat crop fell slightly short of the usual quantity. If we examine this statement a little more closely, it will be seen that the yield of all three cereals was better in England and Wales than in Scotland. Indeed, in Scotland both barley and oats were as a rule poor. In Ireland, on the other hand, the corn crops were all good. Taking the United Kingdom as a whole, the corn harvest began 5 days in advance of its average date for the previous 8 years. Beans, peas, potatoes, and mangolds were about average, but the yield of hay and turnips was very deficient. In Ireland, on the contrary, all the farm crops were good, and besides this there was throughout the summer plenty of grass in the pastures for the sheep and cattle. With the exception of 1886, there was a larger yield of hops than in any year since produce statistics were first collected, *i.e.* 15 years ago.

All the fruit crops, with the exception of the bush fruits, which were moderately good, and of walnuts, which were singularly abundant, were decidedly under average.

The autumn tints were, as a rule, remarkably fine, and in many parts of the country deciduous trees here and there retained their foliage until nearly the end of the season. Most wild fruits were abundant, especially acorns and blackberries. After the September rains, mushrooms became very plentiful in the pastures.

The Year.

The weather of the Phenological year ending November 1899 was chiefly remarkable for its high temperatures, scanty rainfall, and splendid record of sunshine. The winter and summer were singularly warm seasons, while the autumn was also warm; but during the three spring months rather low temperatures prevailed. In the early part of the flowering season, wild plants came into blossom in advance of their mean dates, but after March they were mostly late in coming into bloom. Taking the country as a whole, the best farm crop of the year was wheat. The yield of barley proved also good, while oats were slightly under average. The crops most injuriously affected by the dry weather were those of hay and turnips, the latter being in most districts exceptionally poor. The only part of the British Isles where the summer drought was not severely felt was in Ireland, throughout a great part of which there was abundant keep in the pastures during the whole summer. The year was a very bad one for fruit. The yield of apples, pears, plums, and strawberries varied greatly in different localities, but in most of them was much under average.

Observers' Notes.

December 1898.—*Aberystwith* (A)—21st. Daphne mazereon in flower. *Glendalough* (B)—Ivy-leaved geraniums and heliotrope against the house, as green and fresh as in September. *Muntham* (C)—The hazel showed fertile flowers. *Churt Vicarage* (C)—25th. Twelve different kinds of flowers in bloom, including roses and Coronilla glauca. *Berkhamsted* (D)—31st. The last rose bloom of the year was destroyed by frost and rain, or 24 days later than the average date of its destruction in the previous thirteen years, and later than in any of those years except 1885 and 1894. *Ambleside* (F)—Large flocks of gulls came inland over lake and fells.

January 1899.—*Mawnan* (A)—24th. A white azalea was seen covered with flower in a garden near here. *Aberystwith* (A)—28th. Barren strawberry in flower. *Muntham* (C)—Wild pear in blossom at the beginning of the month. *Cheltenham* (D)—8th. Winter aconite in flower. *Berkhamsted* (D)—18th. Winter aconite in flower, 4 days earlier than its average date of first flowering in the previous 10 years, but 11 days later than last year. *Hodsock* (D)—21st. Crocus Imperati in flower. *Sproughton* (E)—21st. Cut a bough of blackthorn, not in bloom, but (still more remarkable) with well-developed leaves on green shoots nearly 2 ins. long. *Brunstead* (E)—Thousands of plover at Hickling—more than the "oldest inhabitant" ever remembers. *Chirnside* (I)—20th. Winter aconite in flower.

February.—*Mawnan* (A)—Nasturtiums still alive at the end of the winter. *Falmouth* (A)—24th. A horse-chestnut noticed with buds burst and leaves just unfolding. *Altarnon* (A)—7th. Frog spawn first seen. *Aberystwith* (A)—11th. Frog spawn first seen. *Glendalough* (B)—7th. Gathered several yellow tea-roses from plants growing up the house. *Bembridge* (C)—9th. Prunus Pissardii in flower. *Muntham* (C)—17th. A stray piece of blackthorn in blossom. *Coneyhurst* (C)—Many more robins and tits than usual this winter. *Watford* (D)—7th. Daphne mazereon and winter aconite in flower. *Sheffield* (D)—3rd. A gray wagtail seen. *Brunstead* (E)—5th. Found good mushrooms. *Currygrane* (G)—25th. Frog spawn first seen.

March.—*Marazion* (A)—19th. Sand-martins first seen. *Aberystwith* (A)—26th. Wheatear first seen. *Ullenhall* (D)—Frosts on 7 successive nights (18th-24th) did much damage to the apricot blossom. *Hodsock* (D)—The remarkably severe frost of the 22nd interfered with the flowering of Banksia roses and wistaria. *Brunstead* (E)—Several wells in the district at end of month (average depth 25 feet) practically dry. *Piperstown* (G)—17th. Chiffchaff first heard. *Edgeworthstown* (G)—14th. Prunus Pissardii in flower. *Newmill* (J)—2nd. Frog spawn first seen.

April.—*Mawnan* (A)—7th. The flowering of Clematis montana spoilt for the year by heavy gale. *Bassaleg* (A)—18th. Village sycamore in full leaf. *St. Arvans* (A)—3rd. Chiffchaff first heard. 6th. Willow-wren first seen.

TABLE II.—List of the Stations with the Names of the Observers.

Station.	County.	Height above Sea-level.	Observer.
A		Ft.	
1. Marazion . .	Cornwall . .	40	F. W. Millett.
2. Mawnan . .	Cornwall . .	200	Miss R. Barclay.
3. Falmouth . .	Cornwall . .	190	Miss E. Willmore.
4. Liskeard . .	Cornwall . .	400	S. W. Jenkin, C.E.
5. Altarnon . .	Cornwall . .	600	C. U. Tripp, M.A., F.R.Met.Soc.
6. Tiverton . .	Devon . .	270	Miss M. E. Gill.
7. Westward Ho .	Devon . .	130	Miss Patterson.
8. Barnstaple . .	Devon . .	90	T. Wainwright.
9. Sidcot . . .	Somerset . .	200	W. F. Miller.
10. Long Ashton .	Somerset . .	280	Miss H. H. Dawe.
11. Clifton . .	Gloucester .	300	G. C. Griffiths, F.E.S.
12. Penarth . .	Glamorgan .	120	G. A. Birkenhead.
13. Bridgend . .	Glamorgan .	90	H. J. Randall, Junr.
14. Castleton . .	Monmouth .	80	F. G. Evans, F.R.Met.Soc.
15. Bassaleg . .	Monmouth .	125	W. J. Grant, F.R.H.S.
16. St. Arvans . .	Monmouth .	360	Miss M. Peake.
17. St. Davids . .	Pembroke .	220	W. P. Propert, LL.D., F.R.Met.Soc.
18. Aberystwyth .	Cardigan . .	30	J. H. Salter, D.Sc.
B			
19. Killarney . .	Kerry . .	100	Ven. Archdeacon Wynne, D.D.
20. Cappagh . .	Waterford .	140	R. J. Ussher.
21. Ferns . . .	Wexford . .	260	G. E. J. Greene, M.A., D.Sc., F.L.S.
22. Glendalough .	Wicklow . .	460	Mrs. W. Wynne.
23. Geashill . .	King's County .	280	Rev. Canon Russell.
C			
24. Bembridge . .	Isle of Wight .	80	C. Orchard, F.R.H.S.
25. Blandford . .	Dorset . .	270	J. C. Mansell-Pleydell, F.G.S., F.L.S.
26. Buckhorn Weston	Dorset . .	290	Miss H. K. H. D'Aeth.
27. Havant . .	Hants . .	30	H. Beeston.
28. Breamore . .	Hants . .	...	S. Bramley.
29. Muntham . .	Sussex . .	250	P. S. Godman, F.Z.S.
30. Dover . . .	Kent . .	150	F. D. Campbell.
31. Coneyhurst . .	Surrey . .	600	J. Russell.
32. Churt Vicarage .	Surrey . .	350	Rev. A. W. Watson.
32. Churt . . .	Surrey . .	300	C. Criddle.
33. Chiddingfold .	Surrey . .	230	Vice-Admiral Maclear, F.R.Met.Soc.
34. Winterfold . .	Surrey . .	580	R. Turvey.
35. Oxshott . .	Surrey . .	210	W. H. Dines, B.A., F.R.Met.Soc.
36. East Molesey .	Surrey . .	40	Lady Jenkyns, & Mrs. E. G. Johnson.
37. Weston Green .	Surrey . .	30	H. T. Potter.
38. Marlborough .	Wilts . .	480	E. Meyrick.
D			
39. Oxford . .	Oxford . .	200	F. A. Bellamy, F.R.Met.Soc.
40. Cheltenham .	Gloucester .	250	M. L. Evans.
41. Beckford . .	Gloucester .	120	F. Slade, F.R.Met.Soc.
42. Wealdstone .	Middlesex .	180	G. E. Eland.
43. Chesham . .	Bucks . .	300	Miss G. Keating.
44. Watford . .	Herts . .	240	Mrs. G. E. Bishop.
45. St. Albans (The Grange)	Herts . .	380	Mrs. Hopkinson.
46. Berkhamsted .	Herts . .	400	Mrs. E. Mawley.
47. Harpenden . .	Herts . .	370	J. J. Willis.
48. Ross . . .	Hereford . .	210	H. Southall, F.R.Met.Soc.
49. Leominster . .	Hereford . .	220	J. H. Arkwright.

TABLE II.—List of the Stations with the Names of Observers—*Continued.*

Station.	County.	Height above Sea-level.	Observer.
		Ft.	
50. Farnborough .	Warwick . .	520	Miss D. J. G. Prater.
51. Ullenhall . .	Warwick . .	340	Mrs. Coldicott.
52. Northampton .	Northampton .	320	H. N. Dixon, M.A., F.L.S.
53. Thornhaugh .	Northampton .	90	Rev. H. Slater.
54. Churchstoke .	Montgomery .	550	P. Wright, F.R.Met.Soc.
55. Thurcaston . .	Leicester . .	250	Rev. T. A. Preston, M.A., F.R.Met.Soc.
56. Beeston . .	Notts . .	210	G. Fellows.
57. Hodsock . .	Notts . .	60	Miss Mellish, F.R.H.S.
58. Macclesfield .	Cheshire . .	500	J. Dale.
59. Belton . .	Lincoln . .	200	Miss F. H. Woolward.
60. Sheffield . .	Yorks (W.R.) .	450	Miss E. F. Smith.
61. Horbury . .	Yorks (W.R.) .	100	J. Burton.
62. Ripley . .	Yorks (W.R.) .	240	Rev. W. T. Travis.
E			
63. Broxbourne .	Herts . .	120	Rev. H. P. Waller.
64. Hatfield . .	Herts . .	300	T. Brown.
65. Hertford . .	Herts . .	140	W. Graveson.
66. Sawbridgeworth .	Herts . .	350	H. S. Rivers.
67. Hitchin . .	Herts . .	220	A. W. Dawson, M.A.
68. Ashwell . .	Cambridge .	260	H. G. Fordham.
69. Bocking . .	Essex . .	240	H. S. Tabor, F.R.Met.Soc.
70. Lexden . .	Essex . .	90	S. F. Hurnard.
71. Sproughton . .	Suffolk . .	30	Rev. A. Foster-Melliar.
72. Market Weston .	Suffolk . .	150	Rev. E. T. Daubeney.
73. Tacolneston .	Norfolk . .	190	Miss E. J. Barrow.
74. Brundall . .	Norfolk . .	70	A. W. Preston, F.R.Met.Soc.
75. Brunstead . .	Norfolk . .	30	Rev. M. C. H. Bird.
76. Clenchwarton .	Norfolk . .	10	Miss E. M. Stevenson.
77. Peterborough .	Northampton .	30	J. W. Bodger.
F			
78. Palé . . .	Merioneth .	600	T. Ruddy.
79. Glan Conway .	Carnarvon .	100	A. T. Johnson.
80. Alderley Edge .	Cheshire . .	300	W. H. Pepworth.
81. Ambleside . .	Westmoreland .	260	Miss M. L. Hodgson.
82. Cronkbourne .	Isle of Man .	110	A. W. Moore. J. Murphy.
83. Orry's Dale .	Isle of Man .	70	Miss C. M. Crellin.
84. Sulby . . .	Isle of Man .	80	H. S. Clarke, F.E.S.
G			
85. Ardgillan . .	Dublin . .	210	Capt. E. R. Taylor, F.R.Met.Soc.
86. Piperstown . .	Louth . .	320	Miss E. Smith.
87. Edgeworthstown .	Longford . .	270	J. M. Wilson, M.A.
88. Westport . .	Mayo . .	10	J. M. McBride.
89. Loughbrickland .	Down . .	350	Rev. H. W. Lett, M.A.
90. Saintfield . .	Down . .	310	Rev. C. H. Waddell, M.A.
91. Antrim . .	Antrim . .	70	Rev. W. S. Smith.
92. Altnafoyle . .	Londonderry .	450	T. Gibson.
93. Ramelton . .	Donegal . .	200	Miss K. Swiney.
H			
94. New Galloway .	Kirkcudbright .	450	T. R. Bruce.
95. Jardington . .	Dumfries . .	100	J. Rutherford.
96. Port Ellen . .	Isle of Islay .	10	T. F. Gilmour.
97. Duror . . .	Argyll . .	20	R. Macgregor.

TABLE II.—List of the Stations with the Names of Observers—*Continued.*

Station.	County.	Height above Sea-level.	Observer.
I		Ft.	
98. Doddington	Lincoln	90	Rev. R. E. Cole.
99. Thirsk	Yorks (N. R.)	120	A. B. Hall.
100. East Layton	Yorks (N. R.)	570	Mrs. E. O. Maynard Proud.
101. Willington	Durham	390	Rev. W. T. Wyley.
102. Durham	Durham	350	The late H. J. Carpenter.
103. Corbridge-on-Tyne	Northumberland	200	A. W. Price.
104. Blyth	Northumberland	20	S. Dunnett.
105. Lilliesleaf	Roxburgh	530	Miss C. M. D. Sprot.
106. Chirnside	Berwick	400	C. Stuart, M.D.
J			
107. Kirriemuir	Forfar	250	T. M. Nicoll.
108. Aberdeen	Aberdeen	40	P. Harper.
109. Newmill	Banff	350	J. Ingram.
K			
110. Invermoidart	Inverness	60	S. M. Macvicar.
111. Roshven	Inverness	40	H. Blackburn.
112. Beauly	Inverness	60	A. Birnie.
113. Dingwall	Ross	10	J. P. Smith, M.D.
114. Inverbroom	Ross	50	Lady Fowler.
115. Watten	Caithness	150	Rev. D. Lillie.

The numbers before the names of the stations refer to their position on the map of the stations, Plate VIII.

22nd. Blackcap first heard. *Killarney* (B)—6th. A Northerly gale accompanied by hail did immense damage to young vegetation—leaves of horse-chestnut, hawthorn, and larch suffered much, while daffodils, etc., in full bloom were destroyed. 17th. Early potatoes cut down by frost. *Bembridge* (C)—12th. Cut first asparagus out of doors. *Coneyhurst* (C)—Blackthorn very full of bloom, but soon over. *Churt Vicarage* (C)—6th. Wheatear first seen. 13th. Wryneck first heard. *Oxford* (D)—29th. Corncrake first heard. *St. Albans* (D)—8th. Blackthorn shedding its blossoms. *Berkhamsted* (D)—20th. Wild cherry in flower, its average date for previous 13 years. *Market Weston* (E)—Not nearly so many cuckoos as usual, but nightingales are very plentiful. *Tacolneston* (E)—19th. Wryneck first heard. *Clan Conway* (F)—28th. Corncrake first heard. *Sulby* (F)—25th. Corncrake first heard. *Edgeworthstown* (G)—16th. Chiffchaff and willow-wren first heard. 23rd. Corncrake first heard. *Westport* (G)—23rd. Sand-martin first seen. 24th. Swift first seen. 25th. Corncrake first heard. *Loughbrickland* (G)—15th. Chiffchaff first heard. 28th. Corncrake first heard. *Antrim* (G)—28th. Chiffchaff first heard. *Altnafoyle* (G)—28th. Willow-wren first heard. 30th. Corncrake first heard. *Chirnside* (I)—4th. Sand-martins first seen. 5th. Wheatear first seen. 27th. Willow-wren first heard. *Newmill* (J)—27th. Corncrake first heard.

May.—*Marazion* (A)—6th. Swift first seen. 7th. Wheatear first seen. *Mawnan* (A)—11th. Swift first seen. *St. Arvans* (A)—10th. Swift first seen. *Killarney* (B)—20th. Medlar first in flower; same day as in 1898. *Coneyhurst* (C)—Flycatchers very plentiful this year. *Churt Vicarage* (C)—9th. Swift first seen. 19th. May-fly first seen. *Marlborough* (C)—27th. Potatoes badly cut

TABLE III.—DATE (DAY OF YEAR) OF FIRST FLOWERING OF PLANTS, 1899.

STATION.	Hazel.	Coltsfoot.	Wood Anemone.	Blackthorn.	Garlic Hedge Mustard.	Horse-chestnut.	Hawthorn.	White Ox Eye.	Dog Rose.	Black Knapweed.	Harebell.	Greater Bindweed.	Ivy.
A													
Marazion . .	45	47	...	72	...	...	127	156	150	181	...	185	258
Mawnan . .	47	66	...	69	...	121	136	153	156	194	...	...	...
Falmouth . .	50	18	104	70	121	110	127	148	...	174	...	172	...
Liskeard . .	43	47	103	89	...	...	...	...	...	...	...	...	...
Altarnon . .	55	87	114	100	121	134	151	162	184	198	204	206	264
Tiverton . .	24	59	85	88	112	129	132	135	156	169	...	...	256
Westward Ho .	*71*	...	...	93	*138*	127	144	154	157	196	...	187	269
Barnstaple . .	22	54	85	78	106	123	136	147	156	170	205	196	257
Sidcot . . .	19	52	65	95	120	123	130	155	153	163	...	...	...
Long Ashton .	9	...	...	...	...	128	...	...	...	...	...	...	247
Clifton . .	...	...	...	...	...	128	129	...	...	...	189	...	265
Bridgend . .	48	58	70	102	117	137	140	...	...	...	...	...	...
Castleton . .	18	50	74	76	107	118	136	140	162	186	201	182	259
Bassaleg . .	38	45	87	88	110	118	129	135	160	164	...	171	256
St. Arvans . .	19	52	79	92	122	129	132	156	158	168	191	184	255
St. Davids . .	...	63	...	108	...	128	122	...	...	...	...	191	...
Aberystwith .	45	50	95	62	106	136	133	136	167	172	...	...	267
B													
Killarney . .	23	55	61	65	114	113	119	149	158	*199*	182	181	240
Ferns . . .	43	51	85	88	...	126	130	148	160	172	182	190	245
Glendalough .	50	70	85	90	116	131	136	144	...	179	...	...	...
Geashill . .	41	...	74	91	...	131	...	157	161	170	...	201	248
C													
Bembridge . .	25	27	...	95	124	123	126	138	...	...	...	...	...
Blandford . .	18	44	72	93	89	135	142	140	161	166	183	*159*	...
Buckhorn Weston	40	*16*	86	98	105	133	134	140	159	166	180	...	258
Havant . .	42	50	...	99	...	129	138	147	153	168	...	187	275
Breamore . .	...	...	...	...	...	130	131	150	...	158	...	185	...
Muntham . .	1	41	71	61	113	130	132	...	...	...	...	...	278
Dover . . .	...	...	...	92	...	126	143	...	168	188	...	...	254
Coneyhurst . .	42	...	...	99	...	138	136	140	157	161	179	174	*236*
Churt Vicarage .	27	86	93	95	118	133	140	153	156	161	170	200	...
Churt . . .	10	86	95	102	95	129	132	150	163	179	191	199	253
Chiddingfold .	28	52	92	93	114	125	139	145	160	176	196	184	266
Winterfold . .	45	...	92	100	...	148	152	165	...	...	190	...	314
Oxshott . .	51	50	100	106	122	138	133	...	...	...	...	190	...
East Molesey .	50	56	104	104	133	132	133	146	156	167	...	198	269
Weston Green .	...	78	...	92	127	132	139	148	...	169	199	189	262
Marlborough .	8	70	70	85	110	139	142	147	162	175	189	181	250
D													
Oxford . .	...	...	...	...	...	127	139	...	...	...	207	186	260
Cheltenham .	29	55	...	78	117	124	137	150	162	...	...	197	253
Beckford . .	27	49	72	80	111	127	129	130	153	167	190	173	260
Wealdstone . .	...	...	120	98	...	134	133	...	...	...	186	...	...
Chesham . .	28	41	88	92	117	133	*113*	145	...	202	...	192	...
Watford . .	28	...	116	95	112	135	138	153	161	...	...	...	271
St. Albans (The Grange)	16	60	94	95	111	137	135	130	161	192	188	201	264

TABLE III.—DATE (DAY OF YEAR) OF FIRST FLOWERING OF PLANTS, 1899—*Continued.*

STATION.	Hazel.	Coltsfoot.	Wood Anemone.	Blackthorn.	Garlic Hedge Mustard.	Horse-chestnut.	Hawthorn.	White Ox Eye.	Dog Rose.	Black Knapweed.	Harebell.	Greater Bindweed.	Ivy.
Berkhamsted	45	65	100	92	118	134	149	145	157	176	193	190	266
Harpenden	...	...	115	100	120	...	142	...	...	...	...	...	...
Ross	45	...	...	85	120	127	127	...	...	...	...	...	...
Leominster	*61*	...	88	88	...	...	132	133	...	...	...	...	...
Farnborough	28	64	91	87	108	133	133	154	162	179	193	...	264
Ullenhall	22	...	95	102	106	129	127	155	160	174	193	198	284
Northampton	56	...	74	105	121	135	140	150	162	186	190	198	*248*
Thornhaugh	46	*97*	89	96	122	134	137	138	152	179	192	202	260
Churchstoke	27	71	...	99	...	140	139	...	165	...	...	...	...
Thurcaston	55	89	100	110	119	138	141	153	159	174	198	201	257
Beeston	...	65	...	101	129	141	140	161	169	204	*161*	...	...
Hodsock	43	72	91	90	119	120	136	157	165	178	194	170	269
Macclesfield	48	71	98	109	136	144	148	161	171	185	187	190	271
Belton	...	43	*68*	98	121	137	132	...	...	...	...	...	...
Sheffield	44	...	...	...	...	141	145	160	174	202	195	204	294
Horbury	...	...	92	*122*	*149*	153	149	156	173	183	191	187	284
Ripley	36	...	91	111	137	149	151	...	...	...	...	...	...
E													
Broxbourne	57	*102*	92	92	111	136	134	...	...	...	...	...	253
Hatfield	24	...	...	...	...	130	129	157	159	...	...	...	...
Hertford	29	50	78	71	106	...	131	143	155	178	195	191	261
Sawbridgeworth	...	54	...	93	98	135	...	...	156	...	...	196	...
Hitchin	...	66	...	...	116	135	131	147	...	...	...	204	265
Ashwell	20	...	...	98	...	...	139	...	158	...	...	...	...
Bocking	44	42	105	99	110	130	137	159	159	181	190	191	250
Lexden	40	...	92	93	120	130	132	140	158	...	...	182	262
Sproughton	29	46	72	95	119	133	135	138	159	...	...	...	...
Market Weston	49	81	102	96	108	140	136	152	159	173	195	207	271
Tacolneston	41	...	...	...	108	120	138	...	...	...	...	...	...
Brundall	59	...	92	109	106	138	141	152	166	...	197	190	...
Brunstead	25	...	97	99	114	125	134	149	160	183	184	205	253
Clenchwarton	18	...	...	105	...	...	...	...	166	197	...	201	284
Peterborough	36	...	102	87	124	131	135	152	167	*166*	...	184	...
F													
Palé	44	65	106	102	132	140	149	154	164	194	194	209	*303*
Glan Conway	...	...	...	101	...	...	...	...	...	...	...	...	...
Alderley Edge	41	57	101	...	130	124	143	153	*173*	188	190	...	...
Ambleside	30	55	...	89	128	141	141	...	...	189	...	198	283
Cronkbourne	...	58	100	...	96	132	142	...	...	203	193	205	283
Orry's Dale	...	*102*	...	115	...	125	134	...	160	...	...	181	279
G													
Ardgillan	46	52	93	100	...	129	140	150	165	193	...	195	283
Piperstown	*5*	*100*	...	79	...	121	144	158	163	196	...	193	...
Edgeworthstown	...	...	...	102	...	...	...	...	164	...	...	...	...
Westport	...	...	...	99	...	*117*	135	...	...	...	...	...	...
Loughbrickland	...	77	100	101	...	134	147	162	168	188	...	182	274
Saintfield	...	...	...	98	...	140	146	159	167	...	...	...	...
Antrim	56	...	...	92	100	142	144	...	167	197	...	193	...

TABLE III.—DATE (DAY OF YEAR) OF FIRST FLOWERING OF PLANTS, 1899—*Continued.*

STATION.	Hazel.	Coltsfoot.	Wood Anemone.	Blackthorn.	Garlic Hedge Mustard.	Horse-chestnut.	Hawthorn.	White Ox Eye.	Dog Rose.	Black Knapweed.	Harebell.	Greater Bindweed.	Ivy.
Altnafoyle	...	...	96	115	...	143	146	...	165	209	...	...	...
Ramelton	*88*	...	...	99	...	132	143	153	...	207	...	...	...
H													
New Galloway	52	...	119	114	...	154	155	168	160	...	198	...	...
Jardington	43	92	93	111	...	150	149	159	163	200	188	...	...
Port Ellen	25	59	...	...	...	144	148	160	161	191	193	199	...
Duror	59	58	...	110	...	...	130	...	...	182	182	...	281
I													
Doddington	58	68	103	98	110	138	140	155	166	...	...	207	266
Thirsk	32	67	74	71	123	143	131	163	167	185	193	185	285
East Layton	...	...	...	...	...	148	152	...	...	...	...	...	...
Willington	65	61	102	108	146	151	150	162	164	189	192	192	...
Durham	...	72	108	...	...	154	154	172	176	195	185	220	...
Corbridge-on-Tyne	38	66	105	112	144	...	151	163	176	200	186	...	281
Blyth	...	51	...	...	...	...	...	...	...	...	...	...	...
Lilliesleaf	...	...	119	110	...	...	...	...	186	...	194	...	...
Chirnside	*89*	94	91	100	*163*	155	150	*196*	171	187	*224*	*242*	317
J													
Kirriemuir	...	84	...	120	...	...	155	...	167	201	182	...	...
Aberdeen	...	73	110	...	...	155	156	184	*193*	...	196	...	*331*
Newmill	49	69	110	130	134	158	160	167	171	...	187	189	289
K													
Invermoidart	49	...	103	...	...	...	153	172	173	217	...	...	282
Roshven	44	55	98	105	...	142	148	160	166	208	...	198	281
Beauly	53	73	*124*	139	...	152	159	167	176	197	195	...	303
Inverbroom	38	*80*	...	...	...	...	...	...	...	...	...	...	...
Dingwall	50	65	107	115	...	151	155	161	169	...	191	195	312
Watten	...	73	...	...	...	...	161	189	...	216	...	...	...

The dates in *italics* have not been taken into consideration when calculating the means given in Table IV.

by the frosts of the last two nights. *Beckford* (D)—28th. Potato-tops blackened by frost. *Wealdstone* (D)—12th. Corncrake first heard. *Chesham* (D)—7th. Orange-tip butterflies unusually abundant. *Farnborough* (D)—28th. Sharp frost cut off nearly all early potatoes. 31st. Latest date for orange-tip butterfly during last 15 years. *Beeston* (D)—27th. Strawberries blackened by frost. *Ripley* (D)—This has been the worst spring for bees that I can remember. *Lexden* (E)—Singular absence of aphis. 13th. Swift first seen. *Palé* (F)—No wasps to be seen until the end of first week, afterwards plentiful. *Piperstown* (G)—Hawthorn blossom abundant. *Altnafoyle* (G)—Hawthorn in splendid bloom. *New Galloway* (H)—5th. Corncrake first heard. *Lilliesleaf* (I)—26th. Corncrake first heard. *Chirnside* (I)—1st. Corncrake first heard. 12th. Swift

TABLE IV.—Mean Dates (Day of Year) for the First Flowering of Plants in 1899, and their Variations from the Eight Years' Average (1891-98).

Plants.	A England, S.W. 1899.	A Average for 8 Years.	A Variation from Average.	B Ireland, S. 1899.	B Average for 8 Years.	B Variation from Average.	C England, S. 1899.	C Average for 8 Years.	C Variation from Average.	D England, Mid. 1899.	D Average for 8 Years.	D Variation from Average.
Hazel	34	38	− 4	39	*34*	+ 5	30	36	− 6	37	42	− 5
Coltsfoot	53	55	− 2	59	*54*	+ 5	58	59	− 1	62	64	− 2
Wood Anemone	87	84	+ 3	76	*79*	− 3	88	82	+ 6	95	86	+ 9
Blackthorn	85	89	− 4	84	*90*	− 6	94	96	− 2	96	99	− 3
Garlic Hedge Mustard	114	104	+ 10	115	*104*	+ 11	114	110	+ 4	119	112	+ 7
Horse-chestnut	126	118	+ 8	125	*118*	+ 7	133	124	+ 9	135	128	+ 7
Hawthorn	134	127	+ 7	128	*124*	+ 4	137	128	+ 9	138	131	+ 7
White Ox Eye	148	143	+ 5	150	*138*	+ 12	147	140	+ 7	149	147	+ 2
Dog Rose	160	152	+ 8	160	*150*	+ 10	160	155	+ 5	163	158	+ 5
Black Knapweed	178	172	+ 6	174	*167*	+ 7	170	169	+ 1	184	175	+ 9
Harebell	198	188	+ 10	182	*181*	+ 1	186	181	+ 5	193	189	+ 4
Greater Bindweed	186	182	+ 4	191	*181*	+ 10	189	186	+ 3	192	191	+ 1
Ivy	259	263	− 4	244	*262*	− 18	268	269	− 1	268	269	− 1
Mean for the 13 Plants	136	132	+ 4	133	*129*	+ 4	136	133	+ 3	141	138	+ 3

Plants.	E England, E. 1899.	E Average for 8 Years.	E Variation from Average.	F England, N.W. 1899.	F Average for 8 Years.	F Variation from Average.	G Ireland, N. 1899.	G Average for 8 Years.	G Variation from Average.	H Scotland, W. 1899.	H Average for 8 Years.	H Variation from Average.
Hazel	36	37	− 1	38	42	− 4	51	50	+ 1	45	47	− 2
Coltsfoot	57	59	− 2	59	64	− 5	65	70	− 5	70	78	− 8
Wood Anemone	92	86	+ 6	102	92	+ 10	96	83	+ 13	106	102	+ 4
Blackthorn	95	97	− 2	102	103	− 1	98	97	+ 1	112	110	+ 2
Garlic Hedge Mustard	112	109	+ 3	122	123	− 1	100	*118*	− 18	...	*122*	...
Horse-chestnut	132	123	+ 9	132	127	+ 5	134	128	+ 6	149	137	+ 12
Hawthorn	135	128	+ 7	142	134	+ 8	143	136	+ 7	146	143	+ 3
White Ox Eye	149	144	+ 5	154	149	+ 5	156	153	+ 3	162	*156*	+ 6
Dog Rose	160	155	+ 5	162	159	+ 3	166	162	+ 4	161	164	− 3
Black Knapweed	182	177	+ 5	194	184	+ 10	198	202	− 4	191	*185*	+ 6
Harebell	192	184	+ 8	192	182	+ 10	...	*195*	...	190	*199*	− 9
Greater Bindweed	195	188	+ 7	198	186	+ 12	191	*195*	− 4	199	*199*	Av.
Ivy	262	262	Av.	282	280	+ 2	279	*276*	+ 3	281	*280*	+ 1
Mean for the 13 Plants	138	135	+ 3	145	140	+ 5	140*	139*	+ 1*	151*	150*	+ 1*

Plants.	I England, N.E. 1899.	I Average for 8 Years.	I Variation from Average.	J Scotland, E. 1899.	J Average for 8 Years.	J Variation from Average.	K Scotland, N. 1899.	K Average for 8 Years.	K Variation from Average.	British Isles. 1899.	British Isles. Average for 8 Years.	British Isles. Variation from Average.
Hazel	48	49	− 1	49	*54*	− 5	47	*50*	− 3	41	44	− 3
Coltsfoot	68	66	+ 2	75	*74*	+ 1	67	*70*	− 3	63	65	− 2
Wood Anemone	100	93	+ 7	110	*99*	+ 11	103	*95*	+ 8	96	89	+ 7
Blackthorn	100	109	− 9	125	*110*	+ 15	120	*106*	+ 14	101	101	Av.
Garlic Hedge Mustard	131	*123*	+ 8	134	*124*	+ 10	...	*120*	...	118	*115*	+ 3
Horse-chestnut	148	139	+ 9	157	*138*	+ 19	148	*134*	+ 14	138	129	+ 9
Hawthorn	147	140	+ 7	157	*144*	+ 13	155	*140*	+ 15	142	134	+ 8
White Ox Eye	163	158	+ 5	176	*158*	+ 18	170	*154*	+ 16	157	149	+ 8
Dog Rose	172	168	+ 4	169	*170*	− 1	171	*166*	+ 5	164	160	+ 4
Black Knapweed	191	198	− 7	201	*187*	+ 14	210	*183*	+ 27	189	182	+ 7
Harebell	190	189	+ 1	188	*201*	− 13	193	*197*	− 4	190	*190*	Av.
Greater Bindweed	201	*200*	+ 1	189	*201*	− 12	197	*197*	Av.	193	*191*	+ 2
Ivy	287	*281*	+ 6	289	*282*	+ 7	295	*278*	+ 17	274	*273*	+ 1
Mean for the 13 Plants	150	147	+ 3	155	*149*	+ 6	156*	*147*	+ 9	143	140	+ 3

* For 12 Plants.

+ indicates the number of days later than the average date.
− " " " earlier " "
Av. " average date (1891-98).
The dates in *italics* are approximate averages.

first seen. *Newmill* (J)—Butterflies scarce. 11th. Swift first seen. 26th. Potatoes blackened by frost. *Watten* (K)—31st. Corncrake first heard.

June.—*Mawnan* (A)—15th. Hay harvest began. *Bembridge* (C)—25th. Saw a clouded yellow butterfly. *Coneyhurst* (C)—17th. Sand-martin first seen. 20th. Swift first seen. *Churt Vicarage* (C)—The bloom of flowering shrubs such as rhododendrons, guelder roses, wistaria, and clematis montana very much poorer than usual. 15th. Potatoes, scarlet runners, etc., cut down by frost in the lower parts of the district. *Marlborough* (C)—White butterflies exceptionally plentiful. *Harpenden* (D)—12th. First wheat ear out of its sheath, or 4 days later than its average date in the previous 7 years. *Leominster* (D)—The feature of the year has been the scarcity of greenfly, and the almost total absence of caterpillars on forest trees. Leaves of oak, lime, and beech, generally the most liable, have been practically untouched. There should be a very deep growth in the timber ring this year. 21st. Have only seen 3 wasps as yet. *Macclesfield* (D)—3rd. Potatoes cut down by frost. *Hatfield* (E)—The oaks have been almost entirely free from injury by caterpillars. *Bocking* (E)—Lime trees flowered abundantly. *Market Weston* (E)—Sulphur butterflies unusually abundant. *Clenchwarton* (E)—Wild roses were very abundant. *Edgeworthstown* (G)—Hawkmoth often seen. *Port Ellen* (H)—3rd. Have not yet seen either a wasp or butterfly. *East Layton* (I)—9th. Humming-bird hawkmoth seen. *Willington* (I)—Wild roses very plentiful. *Durham* (I)—Small white butterfly very plentiful. *Newmill* (J)—12th. Humming-bird hawkmoth seen, rare here.

July.—*Mawnan* (A)—25th. Corn harvest began. *Coneyhurst* (C)—7th. Cuckoo last heard. *Chiddingfold* (C)—Lawn too dry to mow after 23rd. *Oxford* (D)—Limes flowering with unusual freedom. The small white butterfly very numerous. *Wealdstone* (D)—22nd. Oats first cut. *Market Weston* (E)—Small white butterflies very numerous, from 10 to 20 eggs on every cabbage leaf I examined at the end of the month. *Brunstead* (E)—I never remember the birds so ravenous for fruit—red currants stripped up to our back door ere half ripe. *Clenchwarton* (E)—A great many white butterflies this season. *Palé* (F)—Flowers on Portugal laurels, wild roses, honeysuckle, and elder unusually abundant. *Ambleside* (F)—8th. First hay cut. *Cronkbourne* (F)—Very few wasps. *Chirnside* (I)—Summer migrants scarcer than usual, especially redstarts and swifts.

August.—*Marazion* (A)—16th. Swift last seen. *Altarnon* (A)—26th. Pastures bare and brown, and water is being carried to the cattle for great distances on the uplands. *St. Arvans* (A)—Butterflies numerous, especially meadow-brown and large white. Not many wasps. Pasture lands very brown. *Killarney* (B)—No wasps, and but few moths. Numerous green caterpillars on geraniums and mignonette. Leaves of lime falling freely at end of month. *Geashill* (B)—Very few wasps. Number of small white butterflies unusually large. No earwigs seen this year. *Churt* (C)—All kinds of butterflies rather scarce. *Chiddingfold* (C)—All ponds in neighbourhood dry. *Oxford* (D)—17th. Swift last seen. *Cheltenham* (D)—Very little aphis. Wasps very scarce. Corn harvest finished even on the hills by the 25th. *Watford* (D)—Pastures and lawns very brown. Large white butterflies numerous. *Hodsock* (D)—Corn harvest began on 1st and ended on 30th. *Macclesfield* (D)—14th. Leaves of lime began to fall. 24th. Oats stacked. *Lexden* (E)—Butterflies and wasps have been very abundant. *Market Weston* (E)—Very few wasps. Walnuts plentiful. Many ponds dried up. The foliage of apple trees has not suffered much from the attacks of insects. *Clenchwarton* (E)—2nd. Corn harvest commenced. *Palé* (F)—An exceptional number of the large white butterfly. *Cronkbourne* (F)—White butterflies very numerous. *Ardgillan* (G)—5th. Several trees struck by lightning. Severe thunderstorm lasting 12 hours.

TABLE V.—DATE (DAY OF YEAR) OF SONG AND MIGRATION OF BIRDS, AND FIRST APPEARANCE OF INSECTS, 1899.

STATION.	Song.	Migration.					Insects.				
	Song-Thrush first heard.	Swallow first seen.	Cuckoo first heard.	Nightingale first heard.	Flycatcher first seen.	Swallow last seen.	Honey Bee.	Wasp.	Small White Butterfly.	Orange Tip Butterfly.	Meadow Brown Butterfly.
A											
Marazion	4	105	109	...	...	297	*107*	...	76	154	173
Mawnan	...	*123*	118	...	...	319	56	60	92	131	168
Falmouth	...	106	122	...	...	...	59	50	72	127	...
Liskeard	...	105	107	...	...	...	48	...	69	127	...
Altarnon	5	104	110	...	*105*	285	49	60	120	122	120
Tiverton	...	...	...	...	...	325	58	...	...	...	...
Westward Ho	34	115	112	...	142	279	63	*152*	73	...	*86*
Sidcot	...	107	103	111	120	289	48	...	112	125	122
Long Ashton	1	109	108	...	...	...	40	73	...	...	...
Clifton	...	112	115	120	...	...	...	...	120	148	...
Penarth	...	...	...	...	...	...	68	91	101	112	171
Bridgend	39	105	113	...	...	...	50	142	117	...	...
Castleton	5	101	108	...	141	291	50	75	97	117	177
Bassaleg	8	100	105	123	126	282	42	47	93	110	128
St. Arvans	1	109	110	108	139	282	38	77	91	128	164
St. Davids	38	100	104	...	...	284	79	...	...	136	175
Aberystwith	...	106	119	...	142	279	64	136	75	120	162
B											
Killarney	...	*122*	...	...	...	...	60	121	113	118	121
Cappagh	...	110	106	...	132	...	...	...	...	...	...
Ferns	4	98	108	...	...	285	94	110	101	101	127
Glendalough	...	103	109	...	110	...	46	116	116	115	118
Geashill	...	107	121	...	...	285	48	...	114	127	174
C											
Bembridge	1	105	106	108	...	302	45	...	96	...	176
Blandford	12	108	103	109	109	...	48	119	72	106	166
Buckhorn Weston	12	98	106	117	127	291	47	...	73	107	...
Havant	8	95	103	117	143	296	8	...	68	...	168
Breamore	...	103	107	112	131	...	...	120	119	127	...
Muntham	1	105	102	105	132	284	49	...	100	131	...
Dover	...	115	...	...	...	327	...	...	...	...	...
Coneyhurst	20	104	104	109	131	...	45	...	57	162	...
Churt Vicarage	7	104	108	115	134	285	47	119	96	141	166
Churt	11	108	104	105	136	301	15	85	84	140	162
Chiddingfold	1	108	103	107	*100*	283	...	128	96	121	...
Winterfold	18	107	104	106	...	296	14	117	...	...	...
Oxshott	42	116	107	113	...	280	...	...	...	...	...
East Molesey	4	98	118	122	135	283	41	45	...	...	...
Weston Green	...	104	109	105	133	276	40	147	61	...	...
Marlborough	18	108	111	...	140	...	48	...	73	123	169
D											
Oxford	...	112	112	112	...	...	...	...	...	...	...
Cheltenham	...	117	110	120	146	285	48	70	75	161	...
Beckford	4	108	105	110	133	281	40	149	109	156	166
Wealdstone	...	113	112	120	...	281	...	...	...	...	...
Chesham	27	110	110	125	...	282	*120*	124	72	127	126
Watford	8	117	109	121	145	275	...	144	125	...	...
St. Albans (The Grange)	...	108	107	112	...	...	54	...	99	146	...
Berkhamsted	14	107	102	107	...	285	41	70	76	...	...

TABLE V.—Date (Day of Year) of Song and Migration of Birds, and First Appearance of Insects, 1899—*Continued.*

Station.	Song.	Migration.					Insects.				
	Song-Thrush first heard.	Swallow first seen.	Cuckoo first heard.	Nightingale first heard.	Flycatcher first seen.	Swallow last seen.	Honey Bee.	Wasp.	Small White Butterfly.	Orange Tip Butterfly.	Meadow Brown Butterfly.
Harpenden	...	108	110	113	...	...	...	...	109	...	...
Ross	17	...	119	...	142	...	45	18	100	...	...
Leominster	19	105	114	122	133	...	41	131	129	127	...
Farnborough	15	108	109	...	109	281	45	...	86	151	163
Ullenhall	*89*	112	115	112	...	286	...	83	81	118	127
Thornhaugh	3	105	109	110	136	282	48	49	89	125	181
Churchstoke	41	105	111	...	...	275	...	...	128	127	170
Thurcaston	...	...	...	...	...	...	...	...	125	...	...
Beeston	...	114	115	...	133	...	...	110	126	...	...
Hodsock	...	110	119	115	132	284	4	114	102	149	...
Macclesfield	25	111	107	...	...	279	...	...	*151*	159	...
Belton	...	110	110	112	135	...	...	...	119	...	...
Sheffield	...	*132*	...	...	...	277	...	...	...	...	...
Horbury	...	115	120	...	127	282	43	66	127	...	...
Ripley	9	100	114	...	141	279	41	124	120	...	...
E											
Broxbourne	...	106	104	109	149	...	...	93	109	141	...
Hatfield	19	119	106	110	...	...	...	...	...	...	...
Sawbridgeworth	9	108	107	110	132	278	48	41	72	140	190
Hitchin	15	...	115	109	123	285	...	...	...	...	127
Ashwell	...	110	116	109	139	283	47	...	...	...	...
Bocking	...	...	113	111	...	...	...	...	...	...	...
Lexden	14	108	110	110	138	288	41	45	107	131	180
Sproughton	8	116	110	110	134	...	42	111	96	150	157
Market Weston	7	116	114	108	135	275	46	122	109	130	179
Tacolneston	...	...	...	117	...	...	...	...	...	138	...
Brundall	...	...	108	117	...	...	...	...	...	...	...
Brunstead	6	107	109	...	139	276	41	...	89	155	189
Clenchwarton	...	116	118	...	...	...	...	...	...	...	...
Peterborough	36	102	100	102	*154*	305	38	*221*	107	153	...
F											
Palé	22	94	116	...	132	276	48	131	121	149	175
Glan Conway	...	106	113	...	...	...	...	60	...	...	...
Alderley Edge	6	116	119	...	127	287	...	98	116	121	...
Ambleside	20	117	119	...	118	278	46	137	120	151	...
Cronkbourne	9	98	120	...	...	...	4	122	76	...	*75*
Orry's Dale	...	121	121	...	...	280	57	115	108	...	...
Sulby	17	109	*141*	...	...	298	109	90	*132*	...	157
G											
Ardgillan	9	108	121	...	...	277	...	93	116	128	135
Piperstown	9	109	109	...	...	...	5	91	112	116	122
Edgeworthstown	...	114	111	...	...	281	60	...	106	...	...
Westport	...	99	110	...	...	...	...	106	...	...	...
Loughbrickland	...	105	124	...	...	282	75	122	124	130	170
Saintfield	...	112	107	...	...	274	...	...	123	147	...
Antrim	20	109	111	...	148	274	50	123	114	145	...
Altnafoyle	...	121	120	...	...	...	*125*	149	118	149	182
Ramelton	...	103	113	...	...	274	...	144	...	146	...

TABLE V.—Date (Day of Year) of Song and Migration of Birds, and First Appearance of Insects, 899—*Continued.*

Station.	Song.	Migration.					Insects.				
	Song-Thrush first heard.	Swallow first seen.	Cuckoo first heard.	Nightingale first heard.	Flycatcher first seen.	Swallow last seen.	Honey Bee.	Wasp.	Small White Butterfly.	Orange Tip Butterfly.	Meadow Brown Butterfly.
H											
New Galloway	22	111	115	...	...	269	44	...	127	...	...
Jardington	...	113	110	...	142	...	...	125	120	...	186
Port Ellen	...	127	118	...	...	...	50	...	...	...	...
Duror	43	110	119	...	...	285	57	...	125	...	...
I											
Thirsk	13	120	115	...	...	276	...	...	94	149	...
East Layton	22	118	118	...	...	...	41	...	...	157	...
Willington	49	119	120	...	*157*	272	40	113	71	...	...
Durham	43	126	125	...	...	...	73	...	148	156	...
Corbridge-on-Tyne	42	118	...	...	...	272	...	...	...	...	...
Blyth	38	...	...	...	...	...	...	...	...	...	...
Lilliesleaf	42	118	121	...	...	298	57	127	122	...	126
Chirnside	24	111	118	...	145	279	84	120	144	...	155
J											
Kirriemuir	...	127	114	...	...	270	43	126	...	...	...
Aberdeen	40	135	137	...	138	269	93	151	151	...	...
Newmill	*89*	120	121	...	...	281	58	150	146	...	160
K											
Invermoidart	40	...	122	...	...	...	...	125	123	...	...
Roshven	1	113	118	...	...	...	...	125	124	...	...
Beauly	...	131	130	...	139	303	68	168	*174*	...	...
Inverbroom	...	...	...	...	...	...	43	...	...	...	...
Dingwall	43	130	124	...	148	258	50	147	149	...	...
Watten	...	...	*160*	...	...	...	54	...	138	...	112
Mean Dates for the British Isles in 1899	18 Jan. 18th.	110 Apl. 20th	113 Apl. 23d	112 Apl. 22d	134 May 14th	284 Oct. 11th	49 Feb. 18th	106 Apl. 16th	104 Apl. 14th	135 May 15th	157 June 6th
Mean Dates for 1891-99	Jan. 28th.	Apl. 16th	Apl. 21st	Apl. 21st	May 12th	Oct. 13th	Feb. 25th	Apl. 8th	Apl. 14th	May 6th	June 9th

The dates in *italics* have not been taken into consideration when calculating the means for the British Isles.

Piperstown (G)—5th. Very heavy thunderstorm. *Edgeworthstown* (G)—Very early harvest. Oats cut on 10th. *Lilliesleaf* (I)—No wasps were seen previous to this month, and then only about half a dozen. A plague of small black house-flies. *Newmill* (J)—26th. Corn harvest began.

September.—*Marazion* (A)—The dry season has rendered it necessary for the growers at a great expense to water the broccoli plants. Caterpillars have

TABLE VI.—ESTIMATED YIELD OF FARM CROPS IN 1899.

Description of Crop.	England.						Scotland.			Ireland.	British Isles.
	A S.W.	C S.	D Mid.	E E.	F N.W.	I N.E.	H W.	J E.	K N.	B and G S. and N.	
Wheat	Av.	O. Av.	Av.	O. Av.	Av.	O. Av.	Av.	U. Av.	Av.	O. Av.	O. Av.
Barley	U. Av.	U. Av.	U. Av.	U. Av.	Av.	Av.	Av.	Av.	Av.	O. Av.	U. Av.
Oats	U. Av.	U. Av.	U. Av.	U. Av.	Av.	U. Av.	U. Av.	U. Av.	Av.	O. Av.	U. Av.
Corn Harvest began, average Date	212 (July 31)	209 (July 28)	213 (Aug. 1)	213 (Aug. 1)	224 (Aug. 12)	227 (Aug. 15)	241 (Aug. 29)	243 (Aug. 31)	... ...	228 (Aug. 16)	223 (Aug. 11)
Beans	U. Av.	U. Av.	U. Av.	Av.	Av.	Av.	Av.	O. Av.	...	O. Av.	U. Av.
Peas	Av.	U. Av.	U. Av.	U. Av.	U. Av.	Av.	...	O. Av.	...	Av.	U. Av.
Potatoes	Av.	U. Av.	U. Av.	U. Av.	O. Av.	Av.	Av.	O. Av.	O. Av.	O. Av.	O. Av.
Turnips	Much U. Av.	Much U. Av.	Much U. Av.	Much U. Av.	Much U. Av.	Much U. Av.	Much U. Av.	Much U. Av.	Much U. Av.	U. Av.	Much U. Av.
Mangolds	Av.	Av.	O. Av.	Av.	O. Av.	Av.	Av.	...	...	O. Av.	O. Av.
Hay (Permanent Pastures)	Much U. Av.	Much U. Av.	Much U. Av.	Much U. Av.	U. Av.	U. Av.	U. Av.	U. Av.	...	U. Av.	Much U. Av.
Hay (Clover, etc.)	Much U. Av.	Much U. Av.	Much U. Av.	Much U. Av.	U. Av.	U. Av.	U. Av.	U. Av.	Av.	U. Av.	Much U. Av.

The variations from the average for the above crops have been obtained from the returns which appeared in the *Agricultural Gazette*, August 14 & 21, 1899.

TABLE VII.—ESTIMATED YIELD OF FRUIT CROPS IN 1899.

Description of Crop.							Scotland.	Ireland.	British Isles.
	A S.W.	C S.	D Mid.	E E.	F N.W.	I N.E.	H, J, and K W. E. and N.	B and G S. and N.	
Apples	U. Av.	U. Av.	U. Av.	U. Av.	U. Av.	U. Av.	U. Av.	U. Av.	U. Av.
Pears	U. Av.	U. Av.	U. Av.	U. Av.	U. Av.	U. Av.	U. Av.	U. Av.	U. Av.
Plums	U. Av.	U. Av.	U. Av.	U. Av.	U. Av.	U. Av.	U. Av.	U. Av.	U. Av.
Raspberries	O. Av.	O. Av.	O. Av.	Av.	Av.	Av.	O. Av.	O. Av.	O. Av.
Currants	O. Av.	O. Av.	O. Av.	Av.	Av.	Av.	O. Av.	O. Av.	O. Av.
Gooseberries	O. Av.	O. Av.	O. Av.	Av.	Av.	Av.	O. Av.	O. Av.	O. Av.
Strawberries	Av.	U. Av.	U. Av.	U. Av.	O. Av.	Av.	O. Av.	O. Av.	U. Av.

TABLE VIII.—APPROXIMATE VARIATIONS FROM THE AVERAGE IN MEAN TEMPERATURE, RAINFALL, AND SUNSHINE, 1898-99.

WINTER 1898-99.

Temperature.

MONTHS.	Eng. S.W.	Ire. S.	Eng. S.	Eng. Mid.	Eng. E.	Eng. N.W.	Ire. N.	Scot. W.	Eng. N.E.	Scot. E.	Scot. N.
	°	°	°	°	°	°	°	°	°	°	°
December . .	+5·8	+5·0	+6·3	+5·8	+5·5	+5·8	+5·3	+5·8	+5·5	+5·5	+3·8
January . .	+3·3	+1·0	+5·0	+3·5	+4·8	+2·5	+0·5	+0·8	+2·3	−1·0	−1·0
February . .	+2·3	+0·8	+3·0	+2·0	+3·3	+1·8	+0·3	+0·5	+1·8	+0·5	+0·5
Winter . .	+3·8	+2·3	+4·8	+3·8	+4·5	+3·4	+2·0	+2·4	+3·2	+1·7	+1·1
Rain.											
	in.	in.	in.	in.	in.	in.	in.	in.	in.	in.	in.
December . .	+0·8	−0·2	0·0	+0·2	+0·1	+0·1	0·0	+0·7	−0·8	+0·3	+5·2
January . .	+3·2	+2·2	+0·3	+1·2	+0·2	+2·0	+0·7	+1·1	+0·5	+1·1	+0·4
February . .	+1·3	+1·4	+0·4	+0·5	−0·2	−0·3	−0·4	−1·4	−0·4	−0·2	−1·8
Winter . .	+5·3	+3·4	+0·7	+1·9	+0·1	+1·8	+0·3	+0·4	−0·7	+1·2	+3·8
Sunshine.											
	hrs.	hrs.	hrs.	hrs.	hrs.	hrs.	hrs.	hrs.	hrs.	hrs.	hrs.
December . .	+ 6	− 8	+ 2	+ 8	+13	+ 5	− 3	− 2	+ 3	− 4	+ 2
January . .	+ 1	+ 5	+23	+15	+28	+ 9	+10	+ 1	0	+ 9	+13
February . .	+ 6	− 6	+22	+12	+25	+11	+ 3	+ 1	+11	+ 7	+16
Winter . .	+13	− 9	+47	+35	+66	+25	+10	0	+14	+12	+31
SPRING 1899. *Temperature.*											
	°	°	°	°	°	°	°	°	°	°	°
March . .	−0·6	+1·0	−0·8	−0·8	−1·4	+0·2	+1·2	+0·6	0·0	+0·4	+0·4
April . .	0·0	+0·3	−0·3	0·0	+0·8	−0·8	−1·0	−1·0	+0·3	−1·3	−2·0
May . .	−0·4	−0·8	−0·2	−1·4	−0·8	−1·4	−0·8	−2·0	−1·2	−3·2	−2·0
Spring . .	−0·3	+0·2	−0·4	−0·7	−0·5	−0·7	−0·2	−0·8	−0·3	−1·4	−1·2
Rain.											
	in.	in.	in.	in.	in.	in.	in.	in.	in.	in.	in.
March . .	−1·8	−1·0	−1·5	−1·0	−0·6	−0·5	−0·5	+0·2	−0·3	+0·1	+1·3
April . .	+1·6	+1·2	+1·1	+0·5	+0·9	+1·6	+2·3	+2·2	+0·5	+1·4	+1·8
May . .	+0·1	+0·2	−1·0	−0·1	−0·1	+0·1	+0·3	+1·0	+1·0	+1·0	+0·1
Spring . .	−0·1	+0·4	−1·4	−0·6	+0·2	+1·2	+2·1	+3·4	+1·2	+2·5	+3·2
Sunshine.											
	hrs.	hrs.	hrs.	hrs.	hrs.	hrs.	hrs.	hrs.	hrs.	hrs.	hrs.
March . .	+50	+41	+55	+59	+52	+54	+49	+20	+22	+16	+ 3
April . .	−34	−12	−27	−27	−39	−21	−14	−26	−22	− 1	− 7
May . .	+19	+40	+37	+33	+29	+24	+24	+ 6	+ 8	+ 1	+25
Spring . .	+35	+69	+65	+65	+42	+57	+59	0	+ 8	+16	+21

+ indicates above the average, − below it.

TABLE VIII.—Variations from the Average—*Continued.*

Summer 1899.

Temperature.

Months.	Eng. S.W.	Ire. S.	Eng. S.	Eng. Mid.	Eng. E.	Eng. N.W.	Ire. N.	Scot. W.	Eng. N.E.	Scot. E.	Scot. N.
	°	°	°	°	°	°	°	°	°	°	°
June . .	+2·8	+2·5	+1·8	+1·8	+0·5	+2·0	+2·0	+2·3	+1·2	+2·3	+2·3
July . .	+2·0	+1·5	+3·8	+2·8	+3·3	+1·3	+1·5	+1·5	+2·8	+1·5	+2·0
August . .	+5·0	+4·4	+4·6	+4·4	+3·0	+3·6	+4·4	+3·8	+2·8	+3·2	+4·2
Summer . .	+3·3	+2·8	+3·4	+3·0	+2·3	+2·3	+2·6	+2·5	+2·3	+2·3	+2·8

Rain.

Months.	Eng. S.W.	Ire. S.	Eng. S.	Eng. Mid.	Eng. E.	Eng. N.W.	Ire. N.	Scot. W.	Eng. N.E.	Scot. E.	Scot. N.
	in.	in.	in.	in.	in.	in.	in.	in.	in.	in.	in.
June . .	−0·4	−0·5	−0·4	−0·1	−0·6	+0·4	+0·4	+0·4	+0·2	−0·2	−1·0
July . .	−1·5	−0·2	−1·3	−1·6	−0·9	−0·5	−1·3	−0·4	−0·4	0·0	−0·4
August . .	−1·9	−0·5	−1·4	−1·8	−2·0	−1·9	−1·7	−3·4	−1·9	−2·5	−3·1
Summer . .	−3·8	−1·2	−3·1	−3·5	−3·5	−2·0	−2·6	−3·4	−2·1	−2·7	−4·5

Sunshine.

Months.	Eng. S.W.	Ire. S.	Eng. S.	Eng. Mid.	Eng. E.	Eng. N.W.	Ire. N.	Scot. W.	Eng. N.E.	Scot. E.	Scot. N.
	hrs.	hrs.	hrs.	hrs.	hrs.	hrs.	hrs.	hrs.	hrs.	hrs.	hrs.
June . .	+ 44	+ 13	+ 40	+ 48	+ 17	+ 54	+ 11	+ 11	+ 20	+ 15	− 8
July . .	+ 39	− 32	+ 60	+ 39	+ 32	− 13	− 46	− 27	− 16	− 30	− 37
August . .	+ 123	+ 120	+ 103	+ 94	+ 91	+ 103	+ 109	+ 50	+ 50	+ 57	+ 147
Summer . .	+ 206	+ 101	+ 203	+ 181	+ 140	+ 144	+ 74	+ 34	+ 54	+ 42	+ 102

Autumn 1899.

Temperature.

Months.	Eng. S.W.	Ire. S.	Eng. S.	Eng. Mid.	Eng. E.	Eng. N.W.	Ire. N.	Scot. W.	Eng. N.E.	Scot. E.	Scot. N.
	°	°	°	°	°	°	°	°	°	°	°
September .	+2·3	+0·8	+1·0	+0·8	+0·5	−0·3	+0·8	−0·3	+0·3	−1·0	−0·5
October . .	+1·3	+0·8	+0·8	−1·0	−0·5	+0·3	+1·8	+0·8	+0·5	+1·8	+2·0
November .	+4·0	+4·2	+4·4	+4·2	+4·0	+4·8	+4·6	+5·4	+4·8	+5·2	+4·8
Autumn . .	+2·5	+1·9	+2·1	+1·3	+1·3	+1·6	+2·2	+2·0	+1·9	+2·0	+2·1

Rain.

Months.	Eng. S.W.	Ire. S.	Eng. S.	Eng. Mid.	Eng. E.	Eng. N.W.	Ire. N.	Scot. W.	Eng. N.E.	Scot. E.	Scot. N.
	in.	in.	in.	in.	in.	in.	in.	in.	in.	in.	in.
September .	−0·7	−1·1	+0·3	+0·6	+0·1	+1·1	+0·7	+1·0	+0·3	+0·9	+3·5
October . .	−1·2	−1·9	−1·4	−0·4	−0·6	−1·5	−1·7	−1·5	−0·6	−1·8	−0·3
November .	−0·9	0·0	+1·2	−0·6	+0·2	−0·4	0·0	+1·5	−1·6	+0·4	+3·6
Autumn . .	−2·8	−3·0	+0·1	−0·4	−0·3	−0·8	−1·0	+1·0	−1·9	−0·5	+6·8

Sunshine.

Months.	Eng. S.W.	Ire. S.	Eng. S.	Eng. Mid.	Eng. E.	Eng. N.W.	Ire. N.	Scot. W.	Eng. N.E.	Scot. E.	Scot. N.
	hrs.	hrs.	hrs.	hrs.	hrs.	hrs.	hrs.	hrs.	hrs.	hrs.	hrs.
September .	+ 7	− 14	+ 21	+ 21	+ 21	− 4	− 6	− 5	+ 18	− 4	− 1
October . .	+ 20	+ 29	+ 31	+ 21	+ 24	+ 43	+ 31	0	+ 21	+ 11	+ 2
November .	− 8	0	− 4	− 6	− 1	+ 5	− 17	− 12	+ 12	− 2	− 14
Autumn . .	+ 19	+ 15	+ 48	+ 36	+ 44	+ 44	+ 8	− 17	+ 51	+ 5	− 13

The above Table has been compiled from the variations from the mean, given in the *Weekly Weather Reports* issued by the Meteorological Office.

been very numerous and destructive to all plants of the cabbage family. *Mawnan* (A)—Blackberries especially good and plentiful. *Geashill* (B)—The haws in great beauty. Cabbages suffered much from the larvæ of the small white butterfly. *Bembridge* (C)—Mushrooms very plentiful after rain had set in. Apples greatly thinned by maggot of codlin moth. *Churt Vicarage* (C)—Very few wasps this season. 22nd. A late brood of swallows still in nest at Vicarage. *Churt* (C)—A marked scarcity of holly-berries, but heavy crops of acorns and sweet chestnuts. Large quantities of mushrooms. Wasps very scarce. *Marlborough* (C)—Tomatoes and grapes in the open ripened unusually well owing to excess of sunshine. *Beeston* (D)—Very few wasps this season, but a large quantity of gnats. *Hodsock* (D)—29th. Dahlias spoilt by frost. *Hitchin* (E)—The spring at Wellhead, about a mile south-west of Hitchin, has again been dry for some months this year, as it was in 1898. As far as I can ascertain, this has not occurred before in living memory. *Market Weston* (E)—Blackberries abundant. *Clenchwarton* (E)—7th. Corn harvest ended. 8th. Laburnum again in flower. *Palé* (F)—About the middle of the month a few wasps were seen, but none at all previously. *Piperstown* (G)—Blackberries abundant and fine. Numerous hips on wild roses. *Antrim* (G)—Wasps remarkably scarce. *Duror* (H)—A plague of wasps last year, a dearth of them this year. *Willington* (I)—Wasps very scarce this year. *Kirriemuir* (J)—Very few wasps indeed were seen. *Newmill* (J)—Wasps scarce, earwigs numerous. *Beauly* (K)—Hardly a wasp to be seen.

OCTOBER.—*Marazion* (A)—The main body of the swallows left on the 13th, but a small number remained until the 24th. *Altarnon* (A)—8th. Dahlias killed by frost. *Havant* (C)—Around this district water has been very scarce, especially among the hills. *Churt Vicarage* (C)—The autumn tints very fine. *Tacolneston* (E)—19th. First Royston crow seen. *Palé* (F)—The foliage of the trees ripened to charming tints of colour. Such wild fruits as mountain-ash berries, haws, rose-hips, elder-berries, and acorns abundant, but there was only a light crop of beech-mast. *Ambleside* (F)—10th. Autumn colouring magnificent. *Jardington* (H)—Great scarcity of wasps during the summer and autumn. *Chirnside* (I)—The abrupt departure of swallows on or before October 6 is noteworthy. This was most likely owing to the destruction of insects by frost previous to that date.

NOVEMBER.—*Mawnan* (A)—30th. Leaves still remaining on the trees in the valleys. *Altarnon* (A)—30th. Some oaks and elms still in partial foliage. *St. Arvans* (A)—18th. Picked ripe raspberries. 19th. Dahlias blackened by frost. *Churt Vicarage* (C)—4th. Many oaks and some elms still in full leaf. Chiddingfold Ponds at last filled, but the ditches are still dry. *Chesham* (D)—5th. Gathered a ripe alpine strawberry. *Watford* (D)—Trees quite bare of leaves at end of month. *Berkhamsted* (D)—18th. Dahlias killed by frost—14 days later than average date for previous 14 years. *Beeston* (D)—24th. Some roses still in flower. *Hodsock* (D)—Grass very green at end of month. *Sheffield* (D)—27th. Geraniums flowering in a window-box facing south in an exposed situation. *Tacolneston* (E)—19th. First fieldfare seen. *Ambleside* (F)—Acorns and holly-berries very abundant. *Cronkbourne* (F)—30th. Dahlias still in flower. *Loughbrickland* (G)—Many trees retained their leaves until the frost on the 30th. *Ramelton* (G)—30th. Roses still in flower. *Duror* (H)—30th. Dahlias still in flower. *Lilliesleaf* (I)—The foliage remained on the trees until the middle of this month. *Chirnside* (I)—Haws plentiful, but holly-berries scarce.

DISCUSSION.

The Chairman (Mr. R. BENTLEY) said that a double meed of thanks seemed due to Mr. Mawley, firstly for the very interesting survey which he had given of the preceding twelve months, and secondly for the labour involved for some years in training a staff of observers to collect data upon the subject. The history of Phenological observation appeared to divide itself into three periods: the earliest, until after the time of Sir Thomas Browne, was based upon isolated or casual observations scattered through the works of a large number of writers; the second period was a very fertile one, inasmuch as it included the work of Linnæus, Gilbert White in his fascinating *History of Selborne*, Leonard Jenyns, Caroline Molesworth in the *Cobham Journals*, Thos. Forster, Heinrich Gätke, and others, all of great value. Despite, however, the enormous care and industry bestowed upon these, they suffered from the disadvantage of being too largely founded upon the records of a single individual, or of one with but few correspondents. Under the third, or present, régime the observations were conducted on a systematic plan simultaneously over a large area, and their accuracy was thereby increased. With the present organisation for Phenological research, Mr. Mawley was fortunate, he understood, in having upwards of a hundred expert observers constantly at work, which gave great interest to a Report such as they had before them.

Mr. F. C. BAYARD remarked that Mr. Mawley had taken over the work from the Rev. T. A. Preston, who for many years had done a great deal of it, and who was really the first worker for the Society in this subject. Mr. Mawley had taken it on when it was likely to fall through about 10 or 11 years ago, and had worked it up to its present point. He (Mr. Bayard) was greatly indebted to Mr. Mawley for much information contained in these Reports. One especially good feature was the photographs exhibited on the screen, which showed the exact conditions prevailing, and which brought the state of things before the Meeting in a way that no figures or diagrams could possibly do. For instance, the illustration of the canal all overgrown with grass and quite empty of water, which was the result of two seasons' drought, graphically showed how very dry and hot the weather must have been. It can be shown in the diagrams and tables that certain plants and products do not come out well, but that does not appeal to the eye so well as the illustration of the dry canal. The pictures of the ivy-leaf geranium also clearly proved how mild the winters must have been, as it was well known that this plant could not stand frost.

Mr. J. HOPKINSON remarked that the Rev. T. A. Preston's list of plants, birds, and insects was a large one, well keeping up the interest of the observers, but some species might have been better chosen. With Mr. Mawley's much smaller list a long interval sometimes elapsed between one observation and another, which would tend to slacken the observers' interest; but the species were all well selected, and there could be no mistake in their identification. Although Mr. Preston was the first who worked up the results of Phenological observations for the Society, Mr. Mawley had given to the observations that degree of accuracy and uniformity which was essential in all meteorological work.

Mr. H. MELLISH said that in his district (Nottinghamshire) the crops did not quite correspond with the results given by Mr. Mawley, and that the straw yield was a very large one for oats and barley as well as for wheat. This was possibly the results of the thunderstorms in July, which did not come south. The weather during hay-making also was not very good, but was unsettled and thundery. He had noticed too that farther north the harvest was much delayed, much corn in Scotland being still out late in September.

Dr. R. H. SCOTT remarked that apparently they had not noticed that neither

Mr. Mawley nor the Rev. T. A. Preston was the originator of the Phenological Reports. In 1874, after the Vienna Congress, a meeting of representatives from a number of Societies was held in the Society's rooms, and out of that meeting the scheme for the Phenological observations arose. Many plants were given for observation, and afterwards birds and insects were added—the late Mr. Cordeaux taking great interest in the scheme. Mr. Eaton took part in the work of organisation. There was a question as to whether or not it would be well to adopt the plan followed in Germany by Dr. E. Ihne, which included the observing of a very limited number of species of plants in all the districts.

Mr. J. E. Clark drew attention to the essential conditions laid down by Mr. Mawley that the same selected plants should be observed from year to year. With his own series (1877-97) this could hardly be done, as the observers were chiefly in schools and ever shifting. Therefore, earliest observations were requested. Yet a rough comparison indicated little difference in results. Geranium plants he had found most luxuriant at Christmas 1898, so far east as Street, Somerset, but hardly a flower was seen. It would be interesting to know what would be considered a drought in the Yorkshire dales. They were complaining last August in Wensleydale, yet the "fog," or meadow-land, was of the most vivid green. As illustrating how wheat had suffered less than other grain, he had passed through a field under the escarpment of the North Downs, east of Merstham, where the wheat was more than 5 feet high, so that one hardly saw over it.

Mr. W. B. Tripp remarked that in the Isleworth district, in his kitchen garden, in rather a dry situation, there was little or no produce during the season, and the fruit on some chestnut trees in the neighbourhood was very scanty and small sized. Could Mr. Mawley give any explanation of this?

Mr. F. A. Bellamy said that he had taken observations for the past 18 years, and was sorry when the list of plants was so cut down. The list now included chiefly large trees and shrubs, and the climatic effect on large trees was hardly to be trusted. A few days' sunshine, irrespective of temperature, sufficed to bring them into flower, especially the chestnut and blackthorn; while a mild and less sunny period would hardly affect the time of flowering. He would like to know if Mr. Mawley had incorporated sunshine and earth temperatures in his Report as before? Their influence acted differently on trees and small shallow-rooted plants; for example, one sharp frost would kill the whole plant, but, if the days were sunny, the trees would blossom without such a severe check as would affect small plants. Last year both the small and large butterflies were unusually abundant, more particularly in June and July; wasps seemed scarce about Oxford.

Mr. J. E. Clark believed another butterfly had been unusually abundant, —the Azure Blue—noticed by him around Croydon, and especially in Somerset.

Mr. E. Mawley said that the principal difference between his own and Mr. Preston's method was that on Mr. Preston's list there appeared a large number of plants, birds, and insects, whereas under the present method the list of plants, etc., had been considerably reduced. Under the previous system it was difficult to obtain sufficient observers, as only skilled naturalists were available, but now any one with a good knowledge of ordinary country objects could take the observations required. His experience had shown that a fairly large staff of observers was necessary in order to keep the balance true between the early and late localities in each district, and to counteract the disturbing effects of sudden changes of temperature, such as so often occurred during the spring. No doubt the taller growth made by the corn crops in the localities mentioned by Mr. Mellish and by Mr. Clark than represented in the Report for the country generally, was due, as surmised by Mr. Mellish, to the occurrence of welcome rains, at some critical period of their growth, which most other places had missed. It was by no means easy to condense into a few paragraphs the general effect of the weather upon farm and other crops in any year. He (Mr. Mawley), however, endeavoured, by the study of the observers' notes and the weekly reports which appeared in the agricultural and other papers, to ascertain as far as possible what had taken place over the British Isles as a whole; and, where marked differences from these average conditions occurred in any large section of the country, to mention briefly the character of those differences. He was sorry to say that Mr. J. Cordeaux, the eminent ornithologist, whose name had been mentioned, had died only last year. In the earlier Reports he had had charge of the ornithological section, and since then had been one of the Society's most valued observers. With regard to Mr. Tripp's inquiries as to the non-fruiting of the horse-chestnut trees in his neighbourhood last year, he thought that this perhaps might be explained by the weakened condition of the trees through the combined influence of the dry weather and local drainage. Remarks on the duration of sunshine in the different seasons would be found in the Report, where it would be seen that in the south-west and south of England the mean duration exceeded the average during the summer by as much as 200 hours, which he thought must be a remarkable record.

Circulation of the Atmosphere in the Southern Hemisphere.—"I have just seen the *Geographical Journal* for October 1899, which contains a paper by H. Arctowski on Antarctic Climate. His tables of barometric pressure show readings of from 30·0 ins. to 30·4 ins. occasionally in the winter months. All through the year, however, there were very low readings (near 28 ins.) occasionally, and the mean for the year was low—29·39 ins. It is not clear from the report how the direction of the wind corresponded with high or low pressures, but apparently high pressure occurred with Westerly winds, and low pressure most frequently with Easterly winds.

"It seems evident that the cyclonic and anticyclonic alternations observed by the Belgian Expedition so far south as lat. 70° cannot be due to the system of anticyclones and cyclones which we experience in lats. 35° to 45°, but to two additional belts of anticyclones and cyclones existing in Antarctic regions, as I was led to infer from the ship's logs. These far south cyclones and anticyclones are subject to displacement northwards and southwards in the same way as those in our latitudes, and they are specially subject to a Poleward displacement in winter.

"Probably the central line of the Antarctic cyclones is normally farther from the Pole than is indicated on my diagram. I show it in lat. 75° S. The Belgian observations would indicate that it was nearer 70° S., perhaps 72°.

"I think that the low mean barometer at 70° S. shows that the centres of the cyclones are often near that latitude, and I would infer that the low mean barometer which has always been observed in Antarctic regions is mainly due to the cyclonic circulation of the atmosphere in that belt of latitude.

"Other minds may see reason to doubt my conclusions, but it seems to me that they are strongly supported by the Belgian observations."—H. SCHAW, Major-General R.E., Wellington, New Zealand, November 23, 1899.

RESULTS OF PERCOLATION EXPERIMENTS AT ROTHAMSTED, SEPT. 1870—AUG. 1899.

BY ROBERT H. SCOTT, D.Sc., F.R.S.

[Read February 21, 1900.]

IN the *Proceedings of the Institution of Civil Engineers*, vol. xlv. p. 61, and again in the same *Proceedings*, vol. cv. p. 31, will be found some remarks by Sir J. Henry Gilbert on the experiments in percolation which have now been carried on for nearly thirty years by Sir J. B. Lawes and himself at Rothamsted, with tabular results.

These tables give the yearly and monthly figures from 1870-71 to 1889-90.

Sir Henry Gilbert has lately placed in my hands, for submission to the Society, the figures down to the end of August 1899, completing the harvest year 1898-99.

As the values from August 31, 1890, have not yet been published, I venture to submit the entire series of 29 years with the present communication.

In the first of the papers cited Sir Henry Gilbert gives a brief account of the mode in which the observations were carried out. He says, speaking of Sir J. B. Lawes and himself :—

"We took the soil just as it was; we dug down and undermined it, putting iron plates which were drilled with holes underneath. We gradually got it underpinned in this way, and built it in with brick and cement, so that we had an isolated square of soil entirely undisturbed.

"The area of each gauge was one-thousandth of an acre.[1] We had one such gauge with 20 inches, one with 40 inches, and one with 60 inches depth of soil."

The rain gauge has the same area as the percolation blocks, viz. one-thousandth of an acre.

Views of the rain gauge and of the percolation gauges are given in Figs. 1 and 2 (p. 140).

The years are counted as harvest years, from September 1 to August 31. The figures are all inches and decimals of an inch.

In the original papers Sir. H. Gilbert has given columns for evaporation in addition to those for percolation, but as the former are obtained by subtracting the amount of percolation from the amount of rain, it does not appear necessary to reproduce them.

In Table I. will be found the annual amounts of rain, and of percolation, as measured at the three depths above mentioned.

In Table II. the monthly averages for the entire period are given, and also the same grouped into half-yearly periods.

The interval from September till February, inclusive, is counted as winter, and the remaining six months, March to August, as summer.

Finally, Table III. gives the actual monthly measurements for each year of the series.

On looking at the average results in Table II., it will be seen that in the yearly figures, and those for the winter and summer respectively, the

[1] The gauges were rectangular, being 7 feet 3·12 inches by 6 feet.

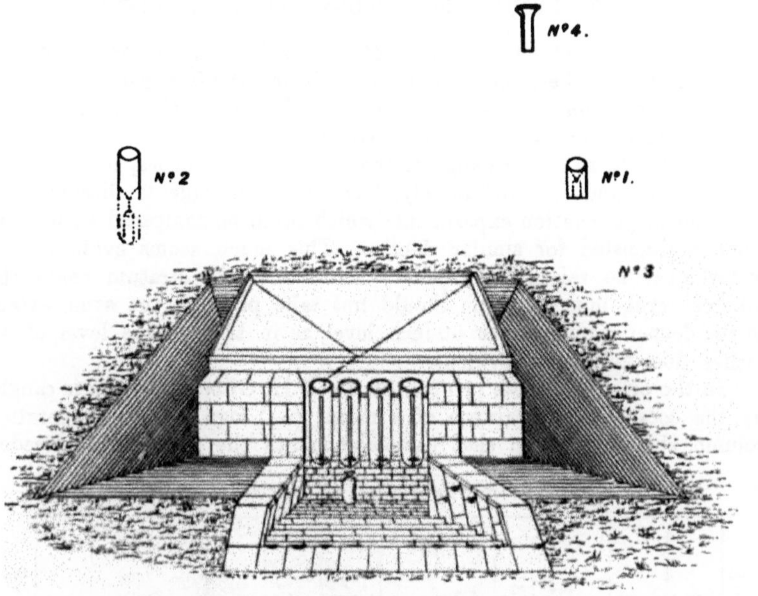

FIG. 1.—View showing the Rain Gauges.

No. 1.—Small Funnel-gauge, 5 ins. diameter.
No. 2.—Small Funnel-gauge, 8 ins. diameter.
No. 3.—Large Gauge—
Size—7 ft. 3·12 in. × 6 ft.
Area—One-thousandth of an acre.
4 Collectors, each holding rain = 0·500 in.
Gauge-tubes graduated to 0·002 in.
Overflow tank to hold rain = 2·000 ins.
Small cylinder tube graduated to 0·001 in. (for quantities less than 0·05 in.).
No. 4.—Stand with level marble top, for measuring.

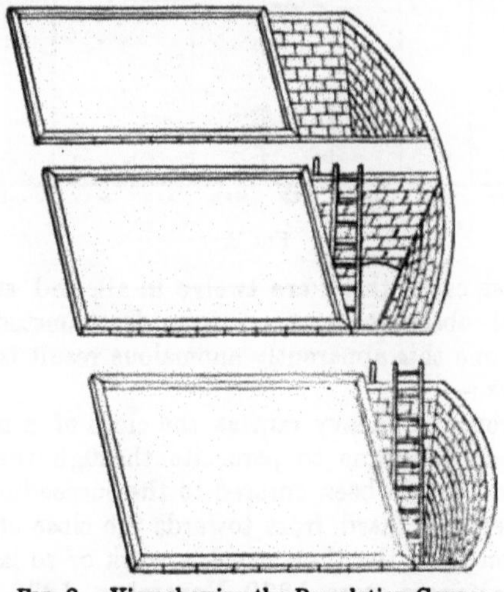

FIG. 2.—View showing the Percolation Gauges.

Each 7 ft. 3·12 ins. × 6 ft. = $\frac{1}{1000}$th acre area.
Respectively 20, 40, and 60 ins. depth of soil.
2 Collectors, each holding drainage = 0·500 in.
Gauge-tubes graduated to 0·002 in.
Overflow tank to hold drainage = 2·000 ins.

amount collected at the depth of 40 inches is always in excess of that collected at 20 inches, and also of that collected at 60 inches.

In the autumn, August to November, the percolation at 20 inches is above that at either of the other depths.

This result, as to the gauge at the depth of 40 inches, seems rather unexpected; and I, unfortunately, have not been able to discover any other set of percolation experiments which could be compared with those from Rothamsted for similar depths. This much seems evident, that water must be raised by capillary action into the stratum below the 20-inch level, but why this should not take place to the same extent in the deeper gauge, at the 60-inch level, as in that at the level of 40 inches, does not appear evident.

In the original figures printed by Sir J. H. Gilbert, the eye is caught by the occasional appearance of a minus (–) sign in the evaporation column, showing that in that particular month the percolation exceeded

PERCOLATION AT 20 INS., 40 INS., AND 60 INS.

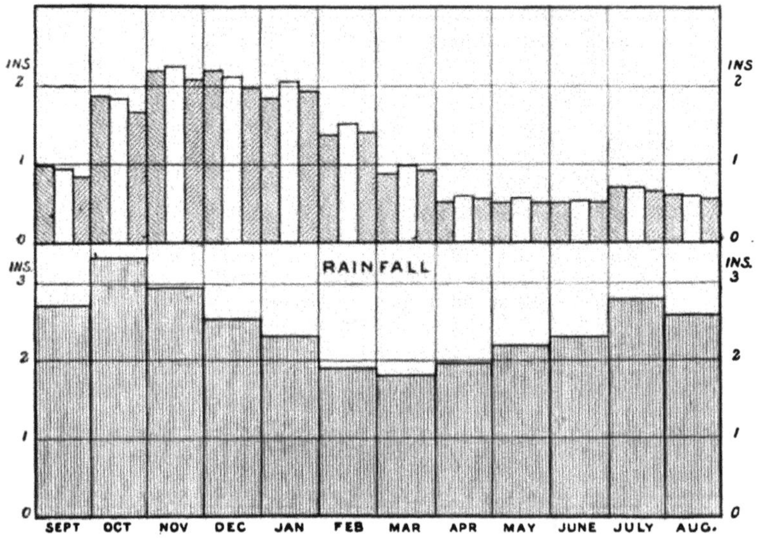

FIG. 3.

the rain. Of these cases there are twelve in all, and an examination of the meteorological observation sheets from Rothamsted shows that in every case except one this apparently anomalous result is to be explained in one of two ways :—

1. The occurrence of heavy rain at the close of a month, the water from which has not had time to percolate through the soil before the month was out, and so has been entered to the succeeding month.

2. The prevalence of hard frost towards the close of a month, which checked percolation until the thaw came, a week or so later.

The twelve instances were 1870 November, 1879 February, 1880 January, 1884 December, 1886 January and February, 1887 January, 1888 March, 1891 February, 1893 March, 1895 January, and 1897 February.

To return to the consideration of the monthly results given in Table II. The diagram Fig. 3 shows the monthly averages of rain and of percolation at the three depths. It will be seen that the maximum of percolation occurs in November, a month later than the maximum for rain.

This is to be anticipated, as the water must require some time to soak through the soil. It is, however, remarkable that the secondary maximum of rain in July makes its influence distinctly felt in the percolation curves.

In order to show the relation between percolation and rain, I have calculated for each month, for the entire 29 years, the percentage which the mean percolation, that is, the mean of the three depths, bears to the rain for that month.

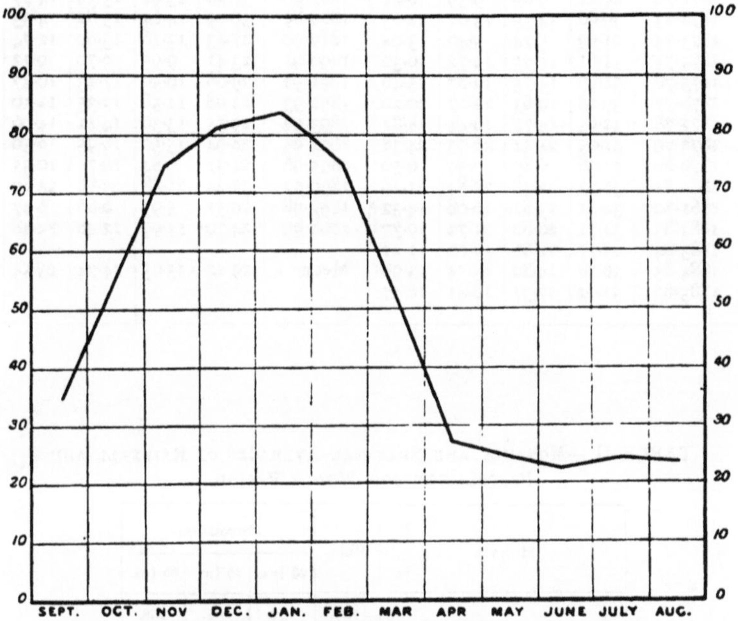

FIG. 4.—Monthly Percentages of Rainfall measured by Percolation.

The figures are shown in Table IV., and graphically in Fig. 4. It will be seen that the curve is simple, with a maximum in January.

It is therefore obvious how the progressive saturation of the soil, as winter comes on, facilitates the access of water to springs.

The year divides itself into two portions, the values for October and March being reasonably coincident. In this curve too the temporary rain maximum in July makes itself felt.

We may say that, on the whole, in the winter months more than half the amount of rain penetrates into the soil and is available for springs, while in summer this amount only reaches a quarter of that of the rain.

In conclusion, I can only say that we all owe a deep debt of gratitude to our respected Fellow, Sir J. B. Lawes, Bart., the owner of Rothamsted, who has for such a lengthened period maintained these observations at his own unaided cost, and has thereby placed meteorologists and engineers in a position to know something of what happens to the rain when it falls.

TABLE I.—Rainfall and Percolation, Annual Amounts, Harvest Years.

Year.	Rain.	Percolation.			Year.	Rain.	Percolation.		
		20 Ins.	40 Ins.	60 Ins.			20 Ins.	40 Ins.	60 Ins.
	ins.	ins.	ins.	ins.		ins.	ins.	ins.	ins.
1870-71	27·55	9·64	9·42	5·81	1886-87	23·61	10·64	12·58	11·72
1871-72	29·02	9·69	9·39	8·24	1887-88	30·50	13·96	15·58	14·67
1872-73	30·66	14·35	13·67	12·03	1888-89	30·09	14·64	15·82	14·33
1873-74	21·69	5·74	5·40	3·94	1889-90	27·43	13·16	13·60	12·74
1874-75	31·61	12·25	12·72	10·30	1890-91	23·41	9·95	9·70	9·73
1875-76	31·98	14·75	16·87	15·46	1891-92	29·68	16·50	17·43	16·47
1876-77	39·28	19·63	22·07	20·20	1892-93	24·08	11·58	12·35	12·10
1877-78	32·65	14·72	16·44	14·84	1893-94	29·55	13·36	14·11	14·06
1878-79	41·05	24·44	26·03	24·38	1894-95	28·94	15·50	16·95	16·30
1879-80	21·36	6·89	7·39	6·50	1895-96	24·37	9·84	10·75	10·35
1880-81	36·77	22·38	22·84	21·26	1896-97	37·24	21·88	23·86	22·80
1881-82	32·31	15·81	16·08	14·32	1897-98	19·51	5·95	6·66	6·47
1882-83	34·71	20·82	21·72	19·72	1898-99	24·70	11·99	12·48	12·48
1883-84	25·77	11·86	12·00	11·21					
1884-85	26·78	14·82	15·14	13·98	Mean .	29·22	13·93	14·74	13·54
1885-86	31·02	17·37	18·41	16·57					

TABLE II.—Monthly and Seasonal Averages of Rainfall and Percolation for Whole Period.

Month.	Rain.	Percolation.		
		20 Ins.	40 Ins.	60 Ins.
	ins.	ins.	ins.	ins.
September	2·69	0·98	0·93	0·83
October	3·27	1·86	1·83	1·65
November	2·94	2·19	2·25	2·07
December	2·51	2·00	2·13	1·97
January	2·31	1·81	2·05	1·93
February	1·87	1·35	1·49	1·38
March	1·81	0·87	1·00	0·93
April	1·96	0·52	0·59	0·55
May	2·17	0·51	0·58	0·52
June	2·29	0·51	0·53	0·49
July	2·79	0·71	0·72	0·65
August	2·59	0·62	0·61	0·56
Year	29·20	13·93	14·71	13·53
Winter (Sept.-Feb.) .	15·59	10·19	10·68	9·83
Summer (Mar.-Aug.) .	13·61	3·74	4·03	3·70

TABLE III.—Monthly Amount of Rainfall and Percolation for each Harvest Year (September 1—August 31).

Month.	Rain.	Percolation.			Rain.	Percolation.		
		20 Ins.	40 Ins.	60 Ins.		20 Ins.	40 Ins.	60 Ins.
		1870-1871.				1871-1872.		
	ins.	ins.	ins.	ins.	ins.	ins.	ins.	ins.
September	2·31	0·22	0·06	0·02	4·74	1·82	1·43	1·08
October	4·13	1·07	0·45	0·18	1·12	0·12	0·24	0·23
November	1·40	1·84	1·42	0·71	0·66	0·07	0·14	0·35
December	2·65	2·10	1·95	1·07	1·43	0·82	0·76	0·48
January	1·45	0·25	1·12	0·72	4·67	3·64	3·55	3·13
February	1·63	0·91	1·13	0·71	1·52	0·64	0·77	0·58
March	1·50	0·34	0·43	0·23	2·12	0·92	0·82	0·83
April	2·89	0·81	0·80	0·63	1·61	0·09	0·16	0·13
May	0·96	...	0·05	0·04	2·90	0·77	0·75	0·63
June	3·87	1·29	1·15	0·90	3·25	0·77	0·74	0·76
July	3·99	0·81	0·85	0·60	2·72	0·01	0·01	0·01
August	0·77	...	0·01	...	2·28	0·02	0·02	0·03
Year	27·55	9·64	9·42	5·81	29·02	9·69	9·39	8·24
		1872-1873.				1873-1874.		
September	1·37	0·01	0·02	0·01	2·38	0·70	0·38	0·20
October	4·67	3·13	2·68	2·10	2·82	0·99	0·83	0·29
November	4·03	2·85	2·80	2·44	1·99	1·08	1·11	0·86
December	4·16	3·38	3·40	3·04	0·71	0·15	0·11	0·04
January	3·74	2·77	2·73	2·71	1·93	1·22	1·35	1·21
February	1·34	0·71	0·54	0·55	1·73	0·85	0·84	0·73
March	2·05	0·88	1·02	0·80	0·65	0·01	0·04	0·03
April	0·64	...	0·01	0·01	2·14	0·32	0·29	0·25
May	1·87	...	...	...	1·19	...	...	...
June	1·76	...	...	...	1·59	...	...	...
July	2·39	0·62	0·47	0·37	2·81	0·42	0·45	0·33
August	2·64	...	...	...	1·75	...	...	...
Year	30·66	14·35	13·67	12·03	21·69	5·74	5·40	3·94
		1874-1875.				1875-1876.		
September	3·62	0·63	0·25	0·21	2·80	0·89	0·83	0·71
October	3·22	1·52	1·26	1·02	5·90	3·72	3·95	3·55
November	2·34	1·21	1·04	0·69	4·43	3·24	3·54	3·26
December	1·80	1·16	1·34	1·04	1·19	0·78	1·01	0·97
January	3·99	2·87	3·39	2·62	1·81	1·46	1·76	1·67
February	1·18	0·34	0·44	0·38	3·05	1·87	2·20	1·94
March	0·87	0·50	0·57	0·46	2·90	1·28	1·74	1·58
April	1·56	0·09	0·11	0·06	3·33	1·36	1·66	1·72
May	2·74	0·29	0·37	0·30	0·78	...	0·04	0·03
June	3·53	0·35	0·26	0·14	1·35	...	...	...
July	5·66	3·29	3·66	3·35	1·46	...	...	...
August	1·10	...	0·03	0·03	2·98	0·15	0·14	0·03
Year	31·61	12·25	12·72	10·30	31·98	14·75	16·87	15·46
		1876-1877.				1877-1878.		
September	5·02	2·30	2·24	2·04	1·53	0·21	0·26	0·21
October	1·52	0·82	1·10	0·96	1·95	0·58	0·51	0·39
November	4·20	2·89	2·99	2·66	5·16	4·03	4·20	3·82
December	6·00	5·21	5·74	5·25	2·28	1·74	1·98	1·75
January	4·99	3·79	4·41	4·11	1·75	1·10	1·36	1·20
February	2·10	0·87	1·19	1·23	1·80	1·01	1·20	1·13
March	2·55	1·01	1·25	1·10	0·98	0·27	0·50	0·46
April	2·76	1·33	1·61	1·49	4·09	2·35	2·52	2·43
May	2·82	0·44	0·55	0·51	4·97	1·48	1·85	1·50
June	1·44	0·03	0·09	0·10	2·51	0·61	0·86	0·76
July	3·28	0·56	0·51	0·44	0·65	0·01	0·03	0·06
August	2·60	0·38	0·39	0·31	4·98	1·33	1·17	1·13
Year	39·28	19·63	22·07	20·20	32·65	14·72	16·44	14·84

TABLE III.—*Continued.*

Month.	Rain.	Percolation.			Rain.	Percolation.		
		20 Ins.	40 Ins.	60 Ins.		20 Ins.	40 Ins.	60 Ins.
		1878-1879.				1879-1880.		
	ins.	ins.	ins.	ins.	ins.	ins.	ins.	ins.
September	1·46	0·07	0·12	0·11	3·13	1·11	1·00	0·92
October	2·99	1·37	1·39	1·10	0·82	0·22	0·42	0·43
November	4·55	3·77	4·07	3·66	0·81	0·20	0·12	0·10
December	1·60	1·11	1·37	1·54	0·82	0·41	0·49	0·44
January	2·85	2·47	2·65	2·47	0·55	0·48	0·61	0·46
February	3·80	4·44	4·44	4·22	2·90	2·36	2·59	2·30
March	1·18	0·14	0·28	0·26	1·13	0·04	0·09	0·09
April	2·79	1·27	1·51	1·38	2·16	0·49	0·53	0·43
May	3·48	1·22	1·39	1·30	0·74	...	0·02	0·03
June	5·55	2·15	2·24	2·18	1·97	0·01	0·01	0·02
July	4·24	1·83	1·97	1·81	5·26	1·35	1·23	1·06
August	6·56	4·60	4·60	4·35	1·07	0·22	0·28	0·22
Year	41·05	24·44	26·03	24·38	21·36	6·89	7·39	6·50
		1880-1881.				1881-1882.		
September	5·86	3·96	3·93	3·78	2·17	0·81	0·81	0·70
October	5·94	4·47	4·45	4·07	0·05	1·76	1·73	1·53
November	2·92	2·25	2·39	2·14	3·47	2·49	2·50	2·29
December	3·47	2·82	2·85	2·68	4·38	3·95	4·04	3·65
January	1·14	1·01	1·12	1·32	1·57	1·24	1·38	1·23
February	3·70	3·43	3·71	3·29	2·02	1·15	1·13	1·01
March	2·15	1·66	1·78	1·65	1·57	0·45	0·58	0·49
April	1·00	...	0·01	0·03	3·92	1·87	1·77	1·57
May	1·38	...	0·01	0·04	2·07	0·74	0·85	0·74
June	1·63	0·01	0·02	0·04	3·93	1·25	1·15	0·99
July	1·76	...	0·01	0·01	2·09	0·10	0·12	0·10
August	5·82	2·77	2·56	2·21	2·07	...	0·02	0·02
Year	36·77	22·38	22·84	21·26	32·31	15·81	16·08	14·32
		1882-1883.				1883-1884.		
September	2·29	0·71	0·57	0·40	3·99	1·63	1·43	1·32
October	6·52	5·46	5·55	5·10	2·49	1·39	1·50	1·38
November	3·44	2·49	2·65	2·41	3·52	2·77	2·71	2·47
December	3·28	3·00	3·22	2·98	1·16	0·79	0·97	0·95
January	3·30	2·89	3·11	2·81	2·56	1·87	1·81	1·65
February	4·34	3·76	4·01	3·70	1·42	0·72	0·92	0·86
March	0·89	0·02	0·06	0·09	1·66	1·13	1·18	1·10
April	1·48	0·28	0·26	0·22	1·79	0·24	0·18	0·19
May	1·89	0·63	0·70	0·62	0·64	0·04	0·09	0·11
June	2·23	0·13	0·11	0·09	2·50	1·09	1·06	1·04
July	4·21	1·44	1·42	1·25	2·44	0·16	0·10	0·10
August	0·84	0·01	0·06	0·05	1·60	0·03	0·05	0·04
Year	34·71	20·82	21·72	19·72	25·77	11·86	12·00	11·21
		1884-1885.				1885-1886.		
September	2·18	1·29	1·26	1·11	4·39	1·55	1·42	1·25
October	1·70	0·52	0·47	0·41	4·82	3·41	3·51	3·14
November	2·05	0·72	0·69	0·61	3·77	3·41	3·59	3·31
December	3·06	3·22	3·23	3·01	1·33	1·00	1·04	0·91
January	2·99	2·59	2·60	2·43	3·44	3·58	3·91	3·92
February	2·85	2·43	2·60	2·45	0·61	0·58	0·71	0·60
March	1·46	0·63	0·71	0·67	1·59	0·83	0·93	0·69
April	2·88	1·04	1·05	0·92	1·96	0·59	0·73	0·58
May	2·88	0·91	0·98	0·87	4·24	2·12	2·29	1·93
June	2·76	1·46	1·52	1·46	1·23	0·08	0·12	0·10
July	0·38	0·01	0·03	0·04	2·42	0·21	0·14	0·11
August	1·59	...	...	...	1·22	0·01	0·02	0·03
Year	26·78	14·82	15·14	13·98	31·02	17·37	18·41	16·57

TABLE III.—*Continued.*

Month.	Rain.	Percolation.			Rain.	Percolation.		
		20 Ins.	40 Ins.	60 Ins.		20 Ins.	40 Ins.	60 Ins.
		1886-1887.				**1887-1888.**		
	ins.	ins.	ins.	ins.	ins.	ins.	ins.	ins.
September	1·51	0·01	...	0·01	3·11	0·36	0·26	0·19
October	3·94	2·16	1·99	1·74	1·69	0·35	0·26	0·20
November	2·77	2·40	2·62	2·43	3·41	2·70	2·82	2·65
December	4·21	2·46	2·58	2·36	1·66	1·19	1·31	1·23
January	2·39	2·32	3·83	3·78	0·94	0·46	0·56	0·50
February	0·95	0·48	0·55	0·51	1·03	0·27	0·43	0·45
March	1·76	0·21	0·22	0·18	3·13	3·16	4·05	3·99
April	1·19	0·13	0·22	0·18	2·14	0·76	0·93	0·88
May	2·35	0·04	0·06	0·07	1·28	0·07	0·09	0·09
June	0·71	0·43	0·50	0·45	4·87	2·38	2·49	2·40
July	0·79	...	0·01	0·01	3·86	0·76	0·83	0·68
August	1·04	...	...	...	3·38	1·50	1·55	1·41
Year	23·61	10·64	12·58	11·72	30·50	13·96	15·58	14·67
		1888-1889.				**1889-1890.**		
September	1·03	0·08	0·12	0·09	2·44	0·77	0·73	0·63
October	1·09	0·07	0·03	0·02	3·62	2·45	2·47	2·28
November	4·45	3·51	3·51	3·29	1·21	0·93	0·98	0·91
December	1·69	1·51	1·60	1·54	1·46	1·29	1·46	1·34
January	1·29	0·82	1·06	0·82	2·94	2·42	2·62	2·52
February	1·95	1·53	1·74	1·61	0·82	0·48	0·60	0·54
March	1·89	0·83	0·85	0·82	2·78	1·71	1·83	1·69
April	2·47	0·35	0·42	0·35	1·31	0·01	0·06	0·06
May	5·00	3·06	3·32	2·85	1·38	0·12	0·10	0·10
June	1·38	0·41	0·53	0·47	2·40	0·06	0·03	0·04
July	5·67	2·43	2·58	2·42	4·56	2·76	2·61	2·54
August	2·18	0·04	0·06	0·05	2·51	0·16	0·11	0·09
Year	30·09	14·64	15·82	14·33	27·43	13·16	13·60	12·74
		1890-1891.				**1891-1892.**		
September	1·20	0·18	0·11	0·11	1·39	0·14	0·13	0·13
October	1·57	0·17	0·05	0·04	6·76	5·59	5·72	5·48
November	2·76	2·05	2·10	1·94	2·25	1·72	1·74	1·67
December	0·56	0·13	0·15	0·13	4·13	3·70	3·92	3·77
January	2·25	1·85	1·47	2·14	1·01	0·90	1·05	0·95
February	0·09	0·13	0·31	0·21	1·48	0·93	1·21	1·14
March	1·76	1·34	1·46	1·34	1·22	0·42	0·56	0·47
April	1·50	0·68	0·72	0·68	0·79	0·01	0·05	0·06
May	3·46	1·10	1·08	1·02	1·40	0·01	0·01	0·03
June	1·89	0·39	0·42	0·41	2·56	0·27	0·24	0·16
July	2·34	0·21	0·12	0·13	3·00	1·34	1·36	1·28
August	4·03	1·72	1·71	1·58	3·69	1·47	1·44	1·33
Year	23·41	9·95	9·70	9·73	29·68	16·50	17·43	16·47
		1892-1893.				**1893-1894.**		
September	2·46	1·02	0·98	0·88	1·14	...	...	...
October	3·99	2·89	2·95	2·87	4·46	2·75	2·66	2·51
November	2·06	1·62	1·81	1·82	2·92	1·84	2·05	2·29
December	1·63	1·40	1·53	1·54	2·63	2·27	2·48	2·48
January	2·05	1·26	1·43	1·40	2·38	1·75	1·89	1·88
February	3·62	2·89	3·12	3·05	1·96	1·11	1·18	1·18
March	0·42	0·38	0·50	0·49	2·19	1·26	1·43	1·38
April	0·25	...	...	0·02	1·71	0·01	0·03	0·04
May	1·22	...	...	0·01	2·07	0·01	0·01	0·01
June	1·00	...	...	...	2·01	0·64	0·71	0·70
July	3·00	...	...	...	2·40	0·07	0·06	0·08
August	2·38	0·12	0·03	0·03	3·68	1·65	1·61	1·51
Year	24·08	11·58	12·35	12·11	29·55	13·36	14·11	14·06

TABLE III.—*Continued.*

MONTH.	Rain.	Percolation.			Rain.	Percolation.		
		20 Ins.	40 Ins.	60 Ins.		20 Ins.	40 Ins.	60 Ins.
		1894-1895.				**1895-1896.**		
	ins.	ins.	ins.	ins.	ins.	ins.	ins.	ins.
September	2·22	0·74	0·75	0·71	1·06	0·10	0·12	0·08
October	3·45	2·18	2·15	2·13	2·69	0·82	0·84	0·72
November	4·98	4·44	4·70	4·50	4·96	4·04	4·13	4·16
December	2·18	1·46	16·5	1·58	2·34	1·84	2·04	2·01
January	2·23	2·20	2·55	2·47	1·12	0·70	0·86	0·81
February	0·19	...	0·04	0·10	0·59	0·04	0·13	0·11
March	1·91	0·84	1·15	0·97	3·75	2·06	2·20	2·13
April	1·47	0·13	0·20	0·20	0·95	0·02	0·13	0·08
May	0·69	...	0·04	0·05	0·48	...	0·01	0·03
June	0·45	...	0·01	0·01	2·25	0·07	0·11	0·11
July	5·12	1·99	2·09	1·99	1·27	...	0·01	0·01
August	4·05	1·52	1·62	1·59	2·91	0·15	0·17	0·10
Year	28·94	15·50	16·95	16·30	24·37	9·84	10·75	10·35
		1896-1897.				**1897-1898.**		
September	8·08	6·14	6·45	6·36	2·44	0·91	0·96	0·87
October	4·13	2·82	3·06	2·99	0·96	...	...	...
November	1·39	0·78	0·92	0·83	1·05	0·22	0·14	0·11
December	4·42	3·83	4·00	3·81	3·50	2·96	3·09	3·06
January	2·03	1·42	1·66	1·59	0·80	0·65	0·83	0·82
February	2·92	3·20	3·58	3·26	1·01	0·01	0·05	0·05
March	4·20	2·54	2·69	2·59	1·06	0·36	0·50	0·49
April	1·91	0·23	0·37	0·32	1·44	0·05	0·09	0·08
May	1·72	0·01	0·05	0·05	2·89	0·78	0·95	0·92
June	2·73	0·77	0·95	0·87	1·61	...	0·02	0·03
July	0·47	...	0·02	0·02	1·45	0·01	0·01	0·02
August	3·24	0·14	0·11	0·11	1·21	...	0·02	0·02
Year	37·24	21·88	23·86	22·80	19·51	5·95	6·66	6·47

MONTH.	Rain.	Percolation.		
		20 Ins.	40 Ins.	60 Ins.
		1898-1899.		
	ins.	ins.	ins.	ins.
September	0·60	...	...	...
October	2·89	1·22	1·16	1·06
November	2·44	1·87	1·81	1·72
December	3·01	2·37	2·44	2·47
January	2·96	2·46	2·71	2·75
February	2·44	2·08	2·13	2·12
March	0·87	...	0·04	0·04
April	2·73	0·67	0·76	0·82
May	2·81	1·12	1·18	1·22
June	1·58	0·04	0·04	0·07
July	1·28	0·16	0·21	0·21
August	1·09	...	...	...
Year	24·70	11·99	12·48	12·48

TABLE IV.—MONTHLY MEAN PERCOLATION AND CORRESPONDING PERCENTAGE OF RAIN.

	Sept.	Oct.	Nov.	Dec.	Jan.	Feb.	Mar.	Apr.	May.	June.	July.	Aug.
	in.	in.	in.	in.	in.	in.	in.	in.	in.	in.	in.	in.
Mean Percolation .	0·91	1·78	2·17	2·03	1·93	1·41	0·93	0·55	0·54	0·51	0·69	0·60
Percentage of Rain .	34	54	74	81	83	76	51	28	25	23	25	23

	Year.	Winter.	Summer.
	ins.	ins.	ins.
Mean Percolation	14·06	10·07	3·82
Percentage of Rain	48	65	28

DISCUSSION.

The Chairman (Mr. R. BENTLEY) said that the thanks of the Society were due to Dr. Scott for the time he had bestowed upon the analysis which had just been read of the experiments at Rothamsted, which would be of great service to meteorologists, engineers, and agriculturists alike.

Mr. A. BREWIN inquired whether the different nature of soils would not affect the results, and whether the amount of percolation would not be different with chalk and clay soils?

Mr. E. MAWLEY said that in regard to the greater percolation through the 40-inch gauge at Rothamsted, he was of opinion that Sir H. Gilbert's explanation was the correct one, and that the circumstance was entirely due to the greater number of stones in the soil of that gauge. In proof of this he might instance his own percolation gauges at Berkhamsted, which contained the natural soil of the district, and this had in it a large number of flints of various sizes. Through both these gauges the rain passed much more freely than through either of the Rothamsted gauges. As it happened, the two sets of gauges were at about the same height above sea-level, were only about 10 miles apart, and were bare of vegetation. Taking the 11 harvest years ending 1898-99, the mean annual rainfall at Berkhamsted fell short of that at Rothamsted by 1·41 in. On the other hand, the percolation through the Berkhamsted gauge, containing 30 ins. of the surface soil of the neighbourhood (disintegrated clay and flints), exceeded that through the Rothamsted gauges, which were 20 ins. and 40 ins. deep by respectively 4·04 ins. and 3·19 ins. Then again, the percolation through the Berkhamsted gauge, containing the subsoil of the district (yellow clay and flints), exceeded that through the Rothamsted gauges, which were 20 ins. and 40 ins. deep, by respectively 4·41 ins. and 3·56 ins. He (Mr. Mawley) could not understand why the percolation should be rather greater through his own gauge containing the heavier soil than through the light soil gauge, unless it was that the latter soil presented more evaporating surfaces than the heavier soil. The fact appeared to be that stones on the surface of land helped to conserve the moisture in it by checking evaporation, whereas stones incorporated with the soil itself tended to drain it.

Mr. R. H. CURTIS suggested that it would be well to give Sir Henry Gilbert's letter to which Dr. Scott had referred.

Mr. J. HOPKINSON exhibited and explained the following table, which shows certain comparative results for the last 24 years in periods of 6 years each :—

Period.	Herts Mean Rainfall. Winter.	Herts Mean Rainfall. Year.	Rothamsted Percolation, 5-feet Gauge.	Flow of the Chadwell Spring.
	%	%	%	%
1875-81 . .	+11	+20	+20	+ 1
1881-87 . .	+12	+ 5	+ 1	-15
1887-93 . .	- 8	- 4	-11	-27
1893-99 . .	+ 3	- 6	- 7	-43

He stated that the years in the first column were from April 1 to March 31 ; the next two columns gave the difference from the mean rainfall in Hertfordshire for the 57 years ending March 31, 1899, the winter six months and the year both ending on this day ; the fourth column gave the difference from the mean of the 24 years in the percolation through 5 feet of soil, the deepest gauge only being utilised in his investigations ; and the last column gave the difference in the yield of the Chadwell Spring from the average of 3,600,000 gallons per diem accepted as approximately correct by all the engineers of the New River Company up to a few years ago. He wished to draw attention to the very great falling-off in the yield of this spring, which ceased to flow for some months last year, and also during the year 1898 for the first time on record. With an annual rainfall for the last 6 years only 6 per cent below the average, and a winter rainfall, which is much more telling upon our chalk springs, 3 per cent above the average, the yield of the Chadwell Spring had fallen to nearly half the average which it maintained before the excessive pumping of the New River Company began to tell upon it ; the increase in this draught upon our underground water-supplies was thus graphically shown in the greatly decreased flow of this spring compared with the rainfall or the percolation. In this table he had purposely commenced with the year 1875-76, as the percolation through the 60-inch gauge in the years 1871-75 did not tally with the subsequent percolation, being very much less in comparison with the rainfall. It seemed that the soil of this gauge had taken 5 years to consolidate, or else there must have been some error in the observations. He most strongly protested against Dr. Scott's statement that in the winter more than half, and in the summer a quarter, of the rain which falls "penetrates into the soil and is available for springs," the fact being that in nature not a quarter of the year's rainfall gets down into the chalk to feed the springs, as shown by percolation experiments at Nash Mills and Lea Bridge. The Rothamsted gauges were constructed for the purpose of analysing the water in order to determine the amount of foreign ingredients which it takes up in passing through different depths of soil : not to show the amount of water which passes through soil in its normal condition in Hertfordshire. The surface of the soil was kept in an artificially porous condition, being frequently hoed, and no vegetation whatever being allowed to grow upon it, whereas in the other series of experiments, which corroborate each other, grass was allowed to grow, and the soil remained in its natural state. There was a generally prevalent impression that we were having a very dry time, but that was in comparison with the very wet period of 20 or 25 years ago, the fact being that we had lately had dry summers but wet winters.

Dr. R. H. SCOTT, in reply, said he thought that none of the explanations given were very satisfactory, and he could not see why, if the underground water rose in the 40-inch gauge, it should not do so at 60 inches. The gauges at Rothamsted touch each other, and therefore the soil of each must be the same.

[Mr. R. H. CURTIS, in a note to the Secretary, sent in subsequent to the meeting, remarks: "With reference to the peculiar fact brought out by the figures given by Dr. Scott, viz. that the total amount of water which passes through the 40-inch gauge is greater than that which passes through either the 20-inch or the 60-inch gauges, it is important to bear in mind that each of the gauges is completely isolated from the ground beneath it and surrounding it, and that therefore any capillary action is confined strictly to the depth of the strata enclosed in each gauge respectively. But it appears to me that the amount of moisture the earth in each gauge is capable of absorbing, and the effect of evaporation in restoring some of this again to the air, are important points to bear in mind.

"Supposing the earth in the 20-inch gauge to have become quite dry during a spell of warm and dry weather, it is evident that the first rain which falls upon it will be retained by the earth, and until a certain minimum amount of water has been absorbed none will be available to pass through to be measured as percolation. This is a condition which seems, from the monthly figures, to have occurred several times during the period they cover. But in the deeper gauges there is a greater reserve of water retained by the earth, and the effect of capillary action, under the influence of evaporation, will be to keep the earth in these gauges moist for a longer period; and since, owing to their greater mass, their general temperature would also in all probability be lower, one would further expect that both the relative and also the actual amount of water lost from them by evaporation would be smaller than from the shallower gauge.

"Bearing this in mind, it is easy to understand how the 40-inch gauge would oftentimes be more nearly in a condition for passing water through it than the shallower one would be, and would begin to record percolation earlier; and also how from this cause, combined with a smaller loss of water by evaporation, the total amount of water which would pass through the 40-inch gauge should generally be greater than in the case of the 20-inch gauge.

"This supposition is, I think, supported by the fact that in nearly every case where percolation entirely fails during a month in both the 20-inch and the 40-inch gauges, and when, therefore, it may be assumed that both have become nearly or quite dry, and are each in a similar condition as regards their capacity for absorbing water, the amount of water which passes through the shallower gauge when rain next falls is greater than that which passes through the deeper 40-inch gauge.

"To properly investigate the point, the detailed observations are needed, together with particulars as to temperature and the character of the weather, and these I have not got. But as far as can be seen from the figures given in the paper, it would appear that with the masses of earth in these gauges there is a minimum depth at which the reserve of moisture is usually sufficient to maintain the soil in the condition of dampness necessary to facilitate the passage of water through them; and since the 60-inch gauge almost invariably gives a smaller amount of percolation than the 40-inch, it is probable that the latter depth is not far from the minimum required.

"Referring now to Table I., it seems to me that the facts indicated by the figures would have been more readily appreciated if the percolation had been given as a percentage of the amount of rainfall, instead of giving the result in inches. I have grouped the figures in the table according to the amount of the rainfall, instead of in order of date, and have given the result in percentages in the way I suggest, and the results are as follows:—

Amount of Rainfall measured in the Year.	Percentage of Percolation to Rainfall in 20-inch Gauge.	40-inch Gauge.	60-inch Gauge.	Number of Years grouped.
	%	%	%	
Below 23 ins. . .	29·7	31·2	27·3	3
From 23 to 26 ins. .	45·1	47·9	46·3	6
From 26 to 29 ins. .	48·0	49·8	44·1	4
From 29 to 32 ins. .	46·3	48·8	44·5	9
From 32 to 35 ins. .	51·4	54·3	48·9	3
Above 35 ins. . .	57·3	61·4	57·5	4
Mean difference .	2·6 per cent		4·0 per cent.	

"From this table it can at once be seen how not only the actual, but also the relative amount of percolation increases with an increased rainfall; and this, I think, may be regarded as due to the fact that in wet seasons the earth is more constantly fully charged with moisture, so that less of the rainfall is required for absorption and a larger proportion is available to pass through the gauges.

"Whether it is safe to assume, with Dr. Scott, that the proportion of rain available for springs is one-half the total fall in winter, and one-fourth of that in summer, is doubtful. The tables show that the amount of percolation diminishes as the depth increases; but, in addition to this, it must be remembered that the soil in these gauges is kept bare, whilst in nature it is, as a rule, covered with vegetation, which actively assists evaporation in abstracting moisture from the ground and restoring it again to the atmosphere; and each of these facts should probably modify our estimate of the percentage of the rainfall which may be expected to reach the springs and deeper wells."]

Meteorology of Tropical Africa.—The Eighth Report of the British Association Committee on the Climatology of Africa, drawn up by Mr. Ravenstein, is published in the recently issued General Report of the Association for 1899. The number of stations from which returns have been received reaches the total of 40 as compared with 26 during the previous year. The most valuable work has perhaps been done in Nyasaland, where the meteorological service has been organised by Mr. J. M'Clounie, head of the scientific department. The very complete series of observations inaugurated by Mr. John Moir at Lauderdale in 1894, of which only two years' results had been previously published, has been continued without a break, being now brought down to 1898 by the publication of three additional years' records. The series now bears comparison with those obtained by the Germans at the Cameroons and elsewhere, and the hours of observation (6 a.m., 2 p.m., and 9 p.m.) agree with those adopted by the latter, except the first, which is an hour earlier at Lauderdale. At the new stations at Zomba and Fort Johnston the first observation is made, as by the Germans, at 7 a.m. At Mombasa a continuous record (though not so detailed) has been kept by Messrs. Pigott and Craufurd since 1894, but the full observations begun in 1896 by the Scotch missionaries at Kibwezi have been interrupted by the removal of the mission from that station. They are being continued, however, at the new station in Kikuyu. A record has been kept by Mr. Ormerod of the level of the Tana River at Golbanti, which shows that the floods reflect two rainy seasons, which are not those of the lower river, but of the country at its source near Mount Kenya. The Tana is therefore a miniature Nile, and offers great potentialities for irrigation.—*Geographical Magazine*, April 1900.

PROCEEDINGS AT THE MEETINGS OF THE SOCIETY.

January 17, 1900.

Ordinary Meeting.

FRANCIS CAMPBELL BAYARD, LL.M., President, in the Chair.

CUTHBERT ELLISON CARR, 1 Collingwood Street, Newcastle-on-Tyne;
AUGUSTUS ERNEST CHEETHAM, Strayfield, Church Road, Urmston;
ADOLPHUS COLLENETTE, Beaulieu, Hauteville, Guernsey;
F. NAPIER DENISON, Meteorological Office, Victoria, British Columbia;
GEORGE SOMES EUNSON, 17 Albion Place, Northampton;
DANIEL HALL, Lynwood, Smallshaw, Ashton-under-Lyne;
CHARLES HAWKSLEY, M.Inst.C.E., 30 Great George Street, S.W.;
ARTHUR BASSETT JONES, M.B., M.R.C.S., 37 Marine Terrace, Aberystwith;
G. W. KÜCHLER, M.A., Presidency College, Calcutta;
WILLIAM HENRY LEETE, Assoc.M.Inst.C.E., Shire Hall, Bedford;
FRANK GARDINER LINNELL, 6 Cromwell Street, Stretford, Manchester;
EUSTACE HENRY LIPSCOMB, M.B., Holywell Hill, St. Albans;
LEONARD SWAINE MORTLOCK MARSH, M.Inst.C.E., Birley Edge, WadsleyBridge;
ARTHUR MARSTON, Levant Lodge, Earls Croome, Worcester;
WILLIAM ERNEST MILNER, Rose Cottage, Berkhamsted;
ARTHUR LATHAM ORMEROD, M.B., Banbury Road, Oxford;
EDWIN JOSIAH POYSER, F.Z.S., Dungburgh House, Geldeston, Beccles;
CHARLES NELSON TWEEN, Assoc.M.Inst.C.E., 12 Finsbury Circus, E.C.; and
MARCUS WARREN ZAMBRA, Fontenoy, Finchley Road, Hampstead, N.W.
were balloted for and duly elected Fellows of the Society.

January 17, 1900.

Annual General Meeting.

FRANCIS CAMPBELL BAYARD, LL.M., President, in the Chair.

Mr. J. E. CLARK and Mr. F. DRUCE were appointed Scrutineers of the Ballot for Officers and Council.

Mr. E. MAWLEY read the Report of the Council and the Balance-Sheet for the year 1899. [This will appear in the next number of the *Quarterly Journal.*]

It was proposed by the PRESIDENT, seconded by Mr. E. MAWLEY, and resolved: "That the Report of the Council be received and adopted, and printed in the *Quarterly Journal.*"

It was proposed by Dr. J. W. MOORE, seconded by Mr. W. M. BEAUFORT, and resolved: "That the thanks of the Society be given to the Officers and other Members of the Council for their services during the past year."

It was proposed by Mr. H. S. EATON, seconded by Capt. M. W. C. HEPWORTH, and resolved: "That the thanks of the Society be given to the Standing Committees and to the Auditors, and that the Committees be requested to continue their duties till the next Council Meeting."

It was proposed by Mr. R. BENTLEY, seconded by Major L. FLOWER, and resolved: "That the most cordial thanks of the Royal Meteorological Society be communicated to the President and Council of the Institution of Civil Engineers for having granted the Society free permission to hold its Meetings in the rooms of the Institution."

The PRESIDENT then delivered an Address on "A NEW DISCUSSION OF THE GREENWICH METEOROLOGICAL OBSERVATIONS, 1848-1898" (p. 101).

It was proposed by Mr. G. J. SYMONS, seconded by Mr. B. LATHAM, and resolved: "That the thanks of the Society be given to Mr. FRANCIS CAMPBELL BAYARD for his services as President during the past year, and for his Address, and that he be requested to allow it to be printed in the *Quarterly Journal.*"

The Scrutineers declared the following gentlemen to be the Officers and Council for the ensuing year:—

PRESIDENT.

GEORGE JAMES SYMONS, F.R.S.

VICE-PRESIDENTS.

RICHARD BENTLEY, F.L.S., F.R.G.S.
Capt. ALFRED CARPENTER, R.N., D.S.O., F.Z.S.
HENRY NEWTON DICKSON, B.Sc., F.R.S.E., F.R.G.S.
Sir CUTHBERT EDGAR PEEK, Bart., M.A., F.R.G.S., F.R.A.S.

TREASURER.

CHARLES THEODORE WILLIAMS, M.A., M.D., F.R.C.P.

SECRETARIES.

FRANCIS CAMPBELL BAYARD, LL.M.
EDWARD MAWLEY, F.R.H.S.

FOREIGN SECRETARY.

ROBERT HENRY SCOTT, M.A., D.Sc., F.R.S.

COUNCIL.

FREDERICK JOHN BRODIE.
RICHARD HENRY CURTIS.
WILLIAM HENRY DINES, B.A.
WILLIAM ELLIS, F.R.S., F.R.A.S.
Major LAMOROCK FLOWER.
Capt. MELVILLE WILLIS CAMPBELL HEPWORTH, F.R.A.S.
JOHN HOPKINSON, F.L.S., F.G.S., Assoc.Inst.C.E.
RICHARD INWARDS, F.R.A.S.
BALDWIN LATHAM, M.Inst.C.E., F.G.S.
HUGH ROBERT MILL, D.Sc., F.R.S.E., F.R.G.S.
ROBERT COCKBURN MOSSMAN, F.R.S.E.
Capt. DAVID WILSON-BARKER, F.R.S.E., F.R.G.S.

Mr. F. C. BAYARD having left the Chair, it was taken by Mr. G. J. SYMONS, the newly elected President, who thanked the Fellows for having a second time elected him to that office.

February 21, 1900.

Ordinary Meeting.

RICHARD BENTLEY, F.L.S., Vice-President, in the Chair.

The CHAIRMAN stated that owing to very serious illness Mr. G. J. SYMONS, F.R.S., had been obliged to resign the office of President, to which he was elected at the last Meeting, and that the Council had with very great regret accepted his resignation.

The Chairman further stated that the Council had that day, under Bye-Law 5, appointed Dr. C. THEODORE WILLIAMS President, to hold office until the next General Meeting.

It was proposed by Mr. A. BREWIN, seconded by Mr. W. B. TRIPP, and resolved: "That a letter be sent to the relatives of Mr. SYMONS expressing the sympathy of the Fellows with them in the serious illness of the late President."

OTTO BERNARD COLE, 551 Boylston Street, Boston, Mass.;
EDWARD LEIGH MANSELL COLVILE, Kempsey, Bournemouth;
THOMAS JONES GIBB DUNCANSON, Nutwood, Bickley Park;
STEPHEN ALBERT MARSHALL, J.P., Skelwith Fold, Ambleside;
ANDREW NOBLE, Sydney Observatory, New South Wales; and
WILLIAM NAPIER SHAW, M.A., F.R.S., 63 Victoria Street, S.W.,

were balloted for and duly elected Fellows of the Society.

The following communications were read:—

1. "REPORT ON THE PHENOLOGICAL OBSERVATIONS FOR 1899." By EDWARD MAWLEY, F.R.Met.Soc. (p. 113).

2. "RESULTS OF PERCOLATION EXPERIMENTS AT ROTHAMSTED, 1870-1899." By ROBERT H. SCOTT, D.Sc., F.R.S. (p. 139).

Hurricanes and Birds.—Mr. T. Digby Pigott, C.B., writes from the Carlton Club:—"I have received from a friend who has lately returned from an annual visit to St. Vincent, where he owns a property, a curious account of the effects of the hurricane of September 1898 on the bird-life of that island. A strange fact which he mentions would, I think, if you can spare a corner in your columns, interest many of your readers. Among the tamest and commonest birds before the hurricane was a small bronze-green humming-bird. My correspondent, in his earlier visits, had been accustomed to see these birds in numbers in every direction, often sitting—like house martins and swallows in English summers—in parties on the telephone wires. During a seven weeks' stay in the island, just finished, he saw none, and was informed by Mr. Thompson, the Administrator, that, so far as he had been able to learn, the bird, since the hurricane, had entirely disappeared. The disappearance is the more remarkable as other humming-birds less common are still to be seen in St. Vincent, though in diminished numbers. Volumes have been written, and have yet to be written, on the altering conditions of animal life on the earth, and the constant gradual removal of birds and beasts from spots where they were once at home. But it would not, I think, be very easy to find another instance of the obliteration of a numerous species from the avifauna of an island in something under an hour and a half."—*Times.*

GEORGE JAMES SYMONS, F.R.S.

(*President* 1880-1 and 1900)

BORN AUGUST 6, 1838. DIED MARCH 10, 1900.

George James Symons, F.R.S.

(PORTRAIT—Plate IX.)

GEORGE JAMES SYMONS was the only son of Joseph and Georgiana Symons, and was born at Pimlico on August 6, 1838. He was educated at St. Peter's Collegiate School, Eaton Square, and also by a private tutor in Leicestershire.

As a lad he was interested in natural phenomena, and while quite young commenced regular observations of the weather. His love of this was so strong that his parents were ultimately obliged to allow him to follow this branch of science.

He was elected a Fellow of this Society as early as March 25, 1856; and from 1860 to 1863 he served under Admiral FitzRoy in the Meteorological Department of the Board of Trade. While there, in addition to other useful work, he reduced, tabulated, and discussed the anemometrical observations made at Bermuda in 1859-60; these appeared in the eighth number of *Meteorological Papers* published by authority of the Board of Trade, 1861. In 1862 he was sent by Admiral FitzRoy to superintend the erection of the anemometer entrusted to the care of the late Rev. C. Clouston, Sandwick Manse, Orkney. In 1857 he became one of the meteorological reporters to the Registrar-General, and continued to be so up to the last. During his spare time from his duties at the Meteorological Department he occupied himself with collecting information about English thunderstorms, and the accidents produced by them; and his first paper, "On the Thunderstorms of 1857," was read before this Society on June 9, 1858. One of his early reports, which had been communicated to the British Association about the year 1860, was, at the request of the Thunderstorm Committee of the Royal Meteorological Society, read at the meeting of the Society on November 21, 1888, and printed in the *Quarterly Journal*, vol. xv. p. 1. In the introductory note to that paper Mr. Symons said: "It will, however, probably be well to explain that it was the fourth report, and the summary of work upon thunderstorms to which I had devoted much time in the years 1857, 1858, and 1859, having established a small organisation analogous, but naturally inferior, to the one recently started by the Royal Meteorological Society."

Out of this early thunderstorm inquiry Mr. Symons was led to collect statistics of rainfall, which henceforth became his life-work. His first annual volume of *British Rainfall* was for the year 1860, and contained records from 168 stations. He was soon obliged to devote his whole time to the work, and so had to sever his connection with the Meteorological Department.

How this rainfall organisation grew under his guidance and unceasing energy will be seen from the fact that in the volume of *British Rainfall* for 1871 he published records from 1504 stations; for 1881, from 2145 stations; for 1891, from 2709 stations; while for 1898 he was able to publish records from 3404 stations. The collection, examination, and tabulation of these records occupied considerable time and also entailed a vast amount of correspondence. In the early years of this work his chief assistant, or rather coadjutress, was his mother.

When Mr. Symons began the collection of rainfall statistics there was much diversity in the method of observing; but by dint of great perseverance and by the personal inspection of as many stations as possible, he was able in the course of time to secure general uniformity of practice in the time of measurement, the mode of entry, the size, height, and form of gauge, etc.

In 1866 he commenced the publication of *Symons's Monthly Meteorological Magazine*, which incorporated and superseded the *Rainfall Circular* which had been issued monthly since 1863; and this has been continued up to the present time.

The information and statistics of rainfall which Mr. Symons collected soon became of much assistance to civil engineers and others engaged in questions of water supply; and in the course of time he became the greatest authority on the distribution of rainfall over the country, and was an indispensable witness at Parliamentary Committees on questions of the water supply of our principal towns.

From the hands of H.R.H. the Prince of Wales Mr. Symons received the Albert Gold Medal of the Society of Arts, which had been awarded to him in 1897 "for the services he had rendered to the United Kingdom by affording to engineers engaged in the water supply and the sewage of towns a trustworthy basis for their work, by establishing and carrying on during nearly forty years systematic observations (now at over 3000 stations) of the rainfall of the British Isles, and by recording, tabulating, and graphically indicating the results of these observations in the annual volumes published by himself."

With the view of ascertaining the variation in the amount of rain collected by gauges at various heights above the ground, and also in determining whether gauges of different sizes and shapes yielded different results, Mr. Symons initiated several series of experiments between 1863 and 1872, which were carried out first by Col. M. F. Ward at Calne; then by the Rev. C. H. Griffith at Strathfield Turgiss; and subsequently by the Rev. F. W. Stow at Hawsker, near Whitby. As the result of these experiments, Mr. Symons ultimately recommended the adoption of rain-gauges with funnels 5 or 8 ins. in diameter, having deep rims (now called Snowdon gauges), and that they should be placed with their rims at the height of 1 ft. above the ground.

Mr. Symons designed two patterns of storm-gauges to enable observers to note the most minute details of heavy rain during thunderstorms. These gauges can be observed at a distance of 20 or more feet. With one of these gauges at Camden Square, Mr. Symons, on June 23, 1878, ascertained rain to be falling for 30 seconds at the rate of 12 ins. an hour.

In conjunction with Mr. Rogers Field, Mr. Symons arranged for an elaborate set of experiments to be carried out with different patterns of evaporators. The observations were made at Strathfield Turgiss by the Rev. C. H. Griffith during 1870-73. The result was that the pans or dishes of small size were found to be worthless, chiefly owing to their becoming heated by the sun. The gauge which gave the best results was a tank made of stout galvanised iron, 6 ft. square and 2 ft. deep;

it was sunk in the ground so that the rim was 3 ins. above the grass. The water was usually kept 3 ins. below the top. Observations were also made of the temperature of the water in the tank and in the neighbouring river Loddon. Mr. Symons's conclusion from these records was "that the evaporation from the tank accurately represents that from the surface of a large body of nearly stagnant water, such as a pond, lake, or reservoir, but is rather larger than occurs from rivers, and to a less extent than from canals, where the water is in progressive motion." In 1884 this tank was removed from Strathfield Turgiss and placed in Mr. Symons's garden at 62 Camden Square, where daily observations on evaporation have since been made.

As many different thermometer-stands were in use in the early years, Mr. Symons considered that the results from them were not comparable. Having obtained a grant from the Royal Society, he arranged for a series of comparisons to be carried out to ascertain their relative merits. Eleven screens of various patterns (open, closed, wall, etc.) were made and set up at Strathfield Turgiss; and the thermometers in them were read three times daily by the Rev. C. H. Griffith from November 1868 to April 1870. The results of these observations were discussed by Mr. F. Gaster, F.R.Met.Soc., and published by the Meteorological Council as Appendix II. to the *Quarterly Weather Report* for 1879. As the result of these comparisons and the outcome of a discussion on the subject at the meeting of this Society in November 1873, the Stevenson thermometer-screen was recommended for general adoption in this country.

About 1876 Mr. Symons brought out a new thermometer for observing earth temperature. This consists of an iron tube closed at one end, and sunk in the ground to any required depth; a thermometer fastened in a stick is attached to a chain and let down to the bottom of the tube, and a cap is placed on the top of the tube to prevent any exchange of air and to keep out the rain. This pattern of earth thermometer is now in general use at the Society's stations.

About the same time he also brought out his "unmistakable true north compass," which, by allowing for the difference between the magnetic and astronomical north, shows by a black cone the true north.

When the second order stations of this Society were started in 1874-75, Mr. Symons took a leading part in their organisation, and personally inspected the stations during the first two or three years. At the meeting on February 19, 1879, a Testimonial Album was presented to Mr. Symons, containing nearly 200 photographs of the Fellows, in "recognition of the valuable work done by him for the Society by inspecting its stations and testing the instruments used by the observers, independently of the services rendered by him as one of the Secretaries for several years."

Mr. Symons was for a long time engaged in devising an instrument to show the sequence of the various phenomena occurring during thunderstorms, and in 1890 MM. Richard Frères, of Paris, made for him the Brontometer, which he subsequently had in use at Camden Square as occasion required. A considerable proportion of the cost of this apparatus was defrayed by grants from the Government Grant Fund, and the Donation Fund, of the Royal Society. This instrument is provided with endless paper, 12 ins. wide, travelling under the various recording pens at the rate of 1·2 in. per minute, or 6 ft. per hour. The velocity of the wind is continuously recorded by one of Richard's anemo-cinemographs, and the atmospheric pressure by a modified form of their statoscope, which is so delicate as to give 30 ins. for each inch of the mercurial barometer. There are mechanical arrangements whereby the observer records: (1) the commencement, variation in intensity, and termination of rain; (2) the instant of each flash of lightning; (3) the commencement and duration of each clap of thunder; and (4) the commencement, variation in intensity, and termination of hail.

Mr. Symons served on the Council of this Society from 1863. He was President 1880-81, and Secretary in 1873-79, and also in 1882-99. He was elected President a second time in January 1900, in view of the Jubilee of the Society taking place during the year; but, owing to his being seized with paralysis on February 14, he had, to the great regret of his colleagues, to resign this office at the following Council meeting. He never rallied from this attack, but passed peacefully away on March 10, 1900. He was buried at Kensal Green Cemetery on March 16, after a Memorial Service had taken place at Holy Trinity Church, Marylebone, at which a large number of friends and many eminent representatives of science were present, including Lord Lister, the President of the Royal Society.

Mr. Symons was elected a Fellow of the Royal Society in 1878, and was made a member of the Council at the last anniversary meeting. He was Chairman of the Krakatoa Committee of the Royal Society (the first suggestion for which inquiry came from himself), and edited their comprehensive and valuable report published in 1888, *The Eruption of Krakatoa, and subsequent Phenomena.*

When the Lightning Rod Conference was formed in 1878, Mr. Symons was appointed the Secretary. He took great interest in the work of the Conference, and was the editor of the *Report* which was published in 1882, and for which he was pecuniarily responsible.

Mr. Symons was a great authority on bibliography. He collected the titles of all books and pamphlets bearing on meteorology of which he could gain intelligence, and, at the time of his death, these titles amounted to about 60,000. In 1882 he had furnished about 20,000 titles to the Chief Signal Office, Washington, U.S., with the view of their being printed, but this was not fully carried out. It is to be hoped that this bibliography may come into the possession of this Society.

Mr. Symons had an extensive and valuable library, and delighted in collecting old and rare books, and in some instances he published reproductions of them; *e.g.* Merle's MSS. *Consideraciones Temperiei pro 7 annis, 1337-1344.*

He also published *Rain: how, when, where, why it is measured* (1867); *Pocket Altitude Tables* (1876), three editions; *The Floating Island in Derwentwater* (1888); *Cowe's Meteorological Register, 1795-1839* (1889).

Mr. Symons was a regular attendant at the meetings of the British Association, and served on various committees. For several years he organised a Breakfast on the morning when papers on meteorological subjects were to be read, in order to promote friendly intercourse amongst observers.

He was for some years a member of the Council of the Royal Botanic Society, and took a leading part in organising the Evening Fêtes. He also served on the Council of the Sanitary Institute, and was Registrar for a considerable period. He was also a Fellow of other scientific societies, and a honorary or corresponding member of several foreign societies.

In 1876 he received a Telford premium of the Institution of Civil Engineers for his paper "On the Floods in England and Wales during 1875"; and in 1894 he received a silver medal of the Society of Arts for his paper "Rainfall Records in the British Isles."

In 1891 he became a Chevalier de la Legion d'Honneur.

Mr. Symons was a frequent correspondent of the *Times* newspaper, writing upon meteorological phenomena of exceptional interest. His letters often contained observations carried on up to nearly midnight, when he would walk to the newspaper office and deliver them personally.

In 1866 he married Miss Elizabeth Luke, who helped him very considerably in his clerical work. The only child of the marriage died in infancy, and Mrs. Symons died in 1884.

Mr. Symons was a most genial and amiable man, and had the power of drawing around him a vast number of friends and voluntary observers. He was ever ready to help any one needing advice or information—in fact, he spared neither trouble nor money so long as he could render any one a service. By his death the Society has lost a beloved President, and the science of meteorology a most indefatigable worker.

[It is satisfactory to know that the rainfall work so long and ably carried on by Mr. Symons will, by his wish, be continued by his coadjutor, Mr. H. Sowerby Wallis, F.R.Met.Soc.]

At the Meeting of the Society held on Wednesday evening, March 21, 1900:—

The President (Dr. C. Theodore Williams) said it was his sad duty to announce the loss of one of the greatest supporters and active workers of the Society. At the last meeting it was given out from the Chair how seriously ill Mr. Symons was, and he had since passed away on March 10. What he had done and what projected was really wonderful, and in his sixty years he had proved himself one of the most active men of the century. The list of new Fellows to be elected that night—most of them proposed by Mr. Symons—was a testimony to his activity. He did not propose to say much about Mr. Symons that evening, but at the Jubilee Meeting next month he would have the privilege of reading Mr. Symons's own address which he had specially prepared for that occasion, and which was probably the last piece of literature he had composed. Mr. Symons joined the Society at the early age of eighteen, and had taken part in every branch of meteorology, though his principal work was his rainfall organisation. His ingenuity was remarkable, and enabled him to successfully surmount all difficulties; and if an instrument required for a special purpose was not available, he immediately set to work and invented one. He has left us his work to carry on, and also his great example. Not only did he possess the faculty of working himself, but he raised up around him a great army of co-workers, which at the time of his death numbered over 4000. We all feel much poorer since we have lost a great friend and the Society one of its leading spirits. As a rule, a vote of condolence was sent by the Council only, but as Mr. Symons's prominence and his personality were so remarkable, and also in view of the coming Jubilee in which he was to have played so important a part, it has been felt by the Council that the Fellows should take part in expressing their sympathy to his relatives, and their tribute to his memory.

Dr. Williams then read the following resolution, which he asked Mr. C. Harding to propose:—

> "The Council and Fellows of the Royal Meteorological Society have heard with deep regret of the death of their beloved Past-President, Mr. George James Symons, F.R.S., which took place on March 10.
>
> "He joined the Society on March 25, 1856, and served on the Council from 1863. He held the office of Secretary from 1873 to 1879, and from 1882 to 1899; and of President for 1880 and 1881. In view of the approaching Jubilee of the Society, the Fellows, at the Annual General Meeting on January 17, elected him President for the second time, but, owing to his being seized with paralysis on February 14, he was obliged to resign this office at the last Council Meeting.
>
> "The Council and Fellows desire to record their deep sense of the irreparable loss the Society has sustained in Mr. Symons's death, and their appreciation of the wise counsels and generous support he gave, and the ceaseless energy and unfailing courtesy he displayed in the conduct of its affairs.
>
> "The Council and Fellows desire to express their sincere sympathy with his relatives in their bereavement."

Mr. C. HARDING, in proposing the resolution, said that he shared in common with every Fellow of the Society the deep sense of loss that they had sustained. His acquaintance with Mr. Symons extended for nearly forty years. As far back as February 1861, he worked in the same room with Mr. Symons in the Meteorological Office, and he there learnt to respect him thoroughly, and had never had occasion to lessen that feeling. Mr. Symons was always ready to assist any one, especially when making a research, and would always place at their disposal any information and data that he might have received. It is frequently stated that meteorologists, as a rule, live long, but it has not proved so in this case, and he (Mr. Harding) was sure he was expressing the wish and feeling of all meteorologists in proposing this vote of condolence.

Mr. F. B. EDMONDS seconded the resolution.

Mr. E. MAWLEY said that it was almost impossible to over-estimate the loss the Society had sustained in the death of Mr. Symons, and he felt all present would agree with him in thinking that there was no one connected with the Society who could have been as ill spared. Whether at the Council table or at the ordinary meetings, he would be greatly missed, for at both everything appeared to turn upon Mr. Symons. Indeed, it seemed impossible to realise, after the number of years he had worked for the Society, the keen interest he always took in its welfare, and his regular attendance at its meetings, that his genial presence, ready judgment, and clear expositions were things entirely of the past, and that he would never take his place among them again. His death, occurring as it did so soon after his re-election as President, and just before the Jubilee celebrations, rendered his loss doubly sad.

Mr. J. HOPKINSON said that he had known Mr. Symons intimately for about twenty-six years, and he wished to bear testimony to his extreme conscientiousness and great kindness. Some years ago he himself invited Mr. Symons to be President of the Hertfordshire Natural History Society, of which he was an Honorary Member, but he (Mr. Symons) declined because he could not spare the time to attend the meetings regularly, and he considered that it would not be doing justice to the Society to fulfil only the *necessary* duties—to deliver an address once a year. For twenty-five years the returns of the rainfall in Hertfordshire which he received had been compared with those sent to Mr. Symons, and he could testify to the care which was exercised in checking the returns and correcting any mistakes, no corrections being made without the corroboration of the observers. This was a work of considerable labour even for one small county alone, the number of rainfall observers in which had increased from 15 to 50 since 1874, partly owing to the County Society but more to the efforts of Mr. Symons. What then must it be with an army of 3000 observers?

Then as to his kindness. He had found Mr. Symons to be ever willing to give information required to aid any investigation; for instance, he readily supplied any observations which, through being received too late for publication, were omitted from the monthly tables in his *Meteorological Magazine*. He thus made all working meteorologists who came in contact with him his friends, and his death was undoubtedly the greatest loss which could have befallen the Society.

Mr. W. MARRIOTT said that he would like to add his testimony to the memory of Mr. Symons. Since 1873 he had sat by the side of Mr. Symons at the meeting table, and had always looked up to him with great respect. The assistance which Mr. Symons was continually rendering the Society could never be known by any of the Fellows. In organising and inspecting the Society's stations he had given the greatest help both in time and money; and in recognition of this work a Testimonial Album containing nearly 200 photographs of Fellows was presented to him on February 19, 1879. At the Lightning Rod Conference and in the preparation of its Report his help and advice were most valuable. At the various Exhibitions held by the Society he rendered great assistance both in their preparation and in the loan of exhibits. When new premises were required by the Society, Mr. Symons had been foremost in looking out for rooms and in attendance at the various Committee meetings. His kindly spirit and genial nature were well known. He was always regular and punctual in his attendance at Council and Committee meetings. Mr. Symons had entered heartily into the preparations for the forthcoming Jubilee Celebration, which he wished to be a great success. The Society, by his death, had lost a great friend and worker.

Mr. F. C. BAYARD spoke of the great help which Mr. Symons had given him when the Croydon Microscopical Society started their rainfall observations, and it was principally due to his assistance that that branch of its work had attained its present standing. Mr. Symons had also rendered him valuable assistance when he (Mr. Bayard) was elected to follow Dr. Tripe as one of the Secretaries to the Society.

The PRESIDENT, in conclusion, said he was much pleased at what had been said in praise of Mr. Symons. At his funeral on the previous Friday he had been glad to notice, in addition to the representatives of other Societies, the good attendance especially of the older Fellows of this Society and of personal friends of Mr. Symons who were paying him their last tribute of respect. It was impossible to take up meteorology without coming across Mr. Symons, and once meeting him was to ensure his friendship. The President then put the resolution to the meeting, which was unanimously adopted.

CORRESPONDENCE AND NOTES.

Minimum Temperatures on Mountain Peaks.—In the August Report of the California Section, Mr. M'Adie publishes a note from Prof. J. N. Le Conte, Professor of Engineering in the University of California, giving the results of observations on the summit of Mount Lyell, on the Sierra Nevada Mountains of Central California, lat. 37° 44′ N.; long. 119° 16′ W.; altitude, 13,041 feet:—

"On July 8, 1897, Prof. Le Conte left a minimum thermometer of the United States Weather Bureau pattern on the summit. It was enclosed in a thin wooden box about 6 inches square and 2 feet long, one side of which was laid exactly in line with the edge of the great southern precipice, over 1500 feet high. Large stones were laid upon it, but one side was exposed to the weather, and in no way could it become entirely covered with snow. On June 5, 1898, the mountain was revisited, and the thermometer box was carefully uncovered. The thermometer was in perfect condition and registered −13°·6 F. It was reset and left upon the mountain a second year. Prof. Le Conte was unable to make the ascent of the mountain in 1899, but Prof H. I. Randall of the Civil Engineering Department of the State University visited the spot in July and obtained the reading. In this case it was −7°·6 F.

"It would be instructive to obtain the minimum winter temperatures of a number of high peaks distributed along the crest of the range from Lake Tahoe to Mount Whitney."

In reference to these, Mr. M'Adie writes as follows:—

"The above experiments were made under the auspices of this office with a view of determining the minimum winter temperatures at the top of the Sierra Nevada Mountains. Mr. J. N. Le Conte, son of Prof. Joseph Le Conte, is an instructor in mechanical engineering in the University of California, and also one of the officers of the Sierra Club. He is an acknowledged authority upon the High Sierra, and I consider that the Bureau has been fortunate in obtaining the services of this gentleman for the experiment.

"It is very interesting to note that the minimum temperature on Lyell, elevation 13,040 feet, was −17°; while at Bodie, elevation 8248 feet, the lowest temperature was −30°. One of the objective points of meteorological investigation at present is the determination of the thickness of the stratum of air in which cold waves are thought to have their origin. I believe it is an accepted fact that the mean temperature of the Plain region is lower than that of the Rocky Mountains, although the latter are from 5000 to 6000 feet high. The experiment on the Sierras seems to confirm this. From many other standpoints the experiment is also interesting."

The accuracy of these results depends in part upon the assumption that the thermometer was well ventilated at the time of minimum temperature. So many accidents are liable to occur that it would be desirable to expose two or more thermometers in different places as a check on each other.—*U.S. Monthly Weather Review.*

Kite and Balloon Station near Berlin.—The Berlin correspondent of the *Standard* announces that the Royal Prussian Meteorological Institute in Berlin is about to make arrangements for the systematic examination of the higher strata of the atmosphere by means of special apparatus. In the grounds of the Aeronautical Observatory at Tegel—a suburb of Berlin, where Alexander and William von Humboldt were buried—registrations of the atmospheric conditions at a height of three to five thousand metres will be carried on, if possible, day and night with kites and kite-balloons. The registering apparatus, which automatically records the pressure, temperature, humidity, and wind velocity at these heights, is taken up by a kite-balloon connected with the earth by piano wire. An elevation of 4500 metres has been attained by a train of kites even without balloons when there was sufficient wind.—*Nature*, February 8, 1900.

Vertical Circulation of the Atmosphere.—I hope that I may be permitted to make a short reply to the very interesting discussion which took place at the meeting of the Royal Meteorological Society on May 17, 1899, after the reading of my paper on "Some Phenomena connected with the Vertical Circulation of the Atmosphere."[1]

I am not surprised that many Fellows should have expressed doubts as to the possibility of upward and downward currents in the atmosphere being indicated by a balanced wind-vane. The reasons assigned for the doubt are very difficult to answer in the present state of our knowledge. Yet that such currents do exist and are made manifest by a balanced wind-vane, is a fact now well established by observation. The observations made in Wellington Harbour, it is true, sometimes show the influence of the hills, and of land and sea breezes, but thoroughly reliable observations have been made during the last four months at Farewell Spit, a low-lying, long, level, sandy spit, the most north-westerly point of the Southern Island of New Zealand, where there is no obstruction to the free motion of the wind. There the upward motion connected with cyclonic circulation and the downward motion connected with anticyclonic circulation are generally shown very distinctly, and correspond with the downward and upward variations in barometric pressure.

I am not able to picture in my own mind *how* the atmosphere over a large area can move upwards or downwards at a considerable angle of inclination; but I think that it certainly does so. How the vacancy is filled up below the ascending current, and how the air escapes below the descending current, I do not see clearly. Expansion or compression of the elastic air may be, and possibly are, associated with the movements; but the motions of isolated clouds seem to indicate that there are numerous small whirls within the larger circulations, producing both upward and downward motions in the particles of air, combined with their onward motion in the direction of the wind. The up and down motions are shown, on the balanced wind-vane, by slow or quick oscillations; sometimes these oscillations are about equal up and down, but in

[1] *Quarterly Journal*, vol. xxv. p. 305.

a cyclonic circulation they show a more or less decided preponderance of upward motion—and in anticyclonic circulation the preponderance is more frequently downwards. In the calm centre of both circulations the balanced wind-vane generally shows a light, steady current, either upwards, in the centre of a cyclone, or downwards, in an anticyclonic calm. Near the sea-level these *upward* motions are more frequently exhibited than the *downward* motions, and this is what we might expect, seeing that the upward motions originate generally at a low level and the downward motions at a high level. The observations hitherto recorded at Farewell Spit seem to indicate, however, that the down current from the following anticyclone under-runs the rear of a cyclone, and this probably is the cause of the sudden rise in the barometer which occurs when the centre of the cyclonic circulation has passed.

It was observed in the discussion that flags and smoke give indications of a similar nature to those given by a balanced wind-vane; but in both cases gravity acts against ascending currents, and, in the case of smoke, heat acts in the upward direction. The information given by these means is neither so reliable nor so accurate as that given by the balanced wind-vane, and I am sure that any meteorologist who observes for a short time the indications of a balanced wind-vane in a freely open situation, will be so interested in the story it tells, that he will pursue the quest for more knowledge in this direction. When a Southerly storm with falling barometer reached Wellington lately, I noticed that the flags of all the shipping in the harbour were pointing upwards; the smoke and the dust also showed that the air motion was upwards over a very wide area. But my balanced wind-vane showed that the upward inclination was frequently as great as 40° from the horizontal. So when in anticyclonic weather, with high barometer, the balanced wind-vane shows a downward air motion at an inclination of from 5° to 15°, the smoke from the steamers in the harbour and all the chimneys in the city is forced downwards. It is clear, therefore, that upward and downward motions of the air take place in some way over considerable areas, and it is also a matter of observation that these upward and downward motions are associated with downward and upward fluctuations of barometric pressure. It was remarked in the discussion that the temperature of the air influenced barometric pressure, which undoubtedly is a fact. A certain volume of warm air is lighter than the same volume of cold air; but if this were the direct cause of the fluctuations in barometric pressure, we should have always a low barometer in hot weather and a high barometer in cold weather, and we know that this is not so. My view is that variations in temperature cause upward and downward currents in the air, and these motions cause the fluctuations in barometric pressure at any particular place.

As regards the interaction of cyclones upon one another, my observations agree with those of some of the speakers at the meeting that the occurrence of a collision between two storms moving in opposite directions is a rare phenomenon, and probably much more rare in England than it is here on the border of the anticyclonic belt. But I have observed two such cases of which I have given full particulars in papers published in the *Transactions of the New Zealand Institute* in 1897, 1898, and they seem to me valuable as throwing some light upon the nature of the wave motion of translation of a cyclonic circulation, although it is still very difficult to understand.

Since I wrote the paper which has been discussed, I have derived some fresh light on the subject of the circulation of the atmosphere in the Southern hemisphere south of latitude 45° from the logs of a number of voyages of steamers trading with New Zealand, which I have embodied in a paper published in the *Transactions of the New Zealand Institute* for 1898, of which a copy is enclosed. The theory which I deduced from these logs has received remarkable confirmation from the meteorological records of the late Belgian Antarctic Expedition, which show that although a very low barometer prevails during the summer months in high southern latitudes—as all Antarctic voyages (necessarily conducted during these months) have shown to be the case—yet in the winter months a very high barometer was not infrequently observed. I infer that the cause of the low barometer is the cyclonic circulation which prevails in a belt situated near the 70th parallel of south latitude with its upward air motion, and that anticyclonic circulations prevail north of that latitude, and probably south of it also. In fact, it would appear that alternate belts of anticyclones and cyclones exist in this Southern Hemisphere, as indicated in the diagram illustrating the above paper, but that these belts alter their positions notably in winter as compared with summer, and less distinctly at other times. This certainly is the case in the latitude of New Zealand, cyclonic storms belonging to the belt of cyclones south of New Zealand being much more frequently and severely felt in winter than in summer.

This new light on the system of circulation of the atmosphere in the Southern Hemisphere obliges me to relinquish the hypothesis I ventured to put forward in the paper—that our Antarctic cyclones had their origin near the icy regions, and that their eastward motion was accelerated by the so-called counter Trade Winds. These counter Trade Winds are really the northern parts of cyclones, and they become Easterly winds in the southerly parts of the cyclones; and south of these cyclonic circulations lies another belt of anticyclones between them and the cyclones of the 70th parallel.

The cause of both cyclones and anticyclones must, I believe, be somewhat as I have attempted to describe—the upward and downward motions of the air due to variations of temperature, combined with the rotation of the earth; the variations in temperature being produced chiefly by sun heat in the direction of the equator and by latent heat in water converted into vapour, when it is made apparent again by condensation in the regions near the pole. The down rush from the anticyclones feeds the cyclones, and the up rush from the cyclones feeds the anticyclones. Cyclones move eastward more vigorously than anticyclones, probably because they are more closely influenced by the rotation of the earth, and by its heat.—H. Schaw, Major-General R.E., Wellington, New Zealand.

Hurricanes of the Far East.—In the *Meteorologische Zeitschrift* for February 1900 there appeared the report of a lecture given by Dr. Paul Bergholz before the German Association in Munich in 1899 upon the places of origin, paths, and zones of the hurricanes of the Far East, the gist of which was as follows:—

In the year 1897 a work by Señor P. Algué, entitled *Baguios ó Ciclones Filipinos*, was published, which brought together and worked up in a clear manner the existing material available from such important observatories as those of Manilla, Shanghai, Hong-Kong, and Tokio; and as scarcely any of the larger atmospheric disturbances are experienced in the Far East without making themselves felt in the Philippine Islands, those observations which have been collected in Manilla must therefore be especially numerous. Dr. Bergholz says that in the book in question, which aims at being purely practical, the general points of view are drawn attention to, such as the places of formation, the paths, and the zones of the hurricanes (reference is then made to his *Die Orkane des fernen Ostens*, 1900). "According to Viñes," he continued, "the cyclonic regions of the tropics unite in themselves, in a more or less conspicuous manner, the following geographical conditions:—

"To large continents, rich in bights and bays whose coasts run north and south, there are joined in the East wide extents of sea, which are sown with islands. These conditions are more or less completely fulfilled in the cyclonic regions of Central America, the Philippines, the China Sea, and the seas of India and—turning to the Southern Hemisphere—of South Africa with the neighbouring islands of Madagascar, Mauritius, Réunion, etc. Different conditions prevail in these regions at different times."

He considers that, to be enabled to follow to their places of origin the hurricanes of East Asia, observations must, in the first instance, be obtained from the Caroline and Marianne Islands, and from that part of the sea which lies to the east of Mindanao; which observations are now being made in sufficient numbers for the purpose, if supplemented by those recorded in recent years.

Should the paths of the hurricanes which are accurately known from June 1878 and onwards be grouped according to the months, not only the tropical places of origin are brought to our notice, but one sees that hurricanes of certain monthly grouping have much similarity in their positions of origin as well as in the paths they pursue. Sharp lines of difference cannot be drawn, it is true, as the places of origin and paths of the hurricanes of adjacent months must naturally lie close together: those, for example, of September and October. Taking this into account in corresponding cases, the hurricanes can be grouped together in three monthly groups, the first of which comprises the months of December to March inclusive; the second, April, May, October, and November; and the third the remaining months of the year, which are the so-called typhoon months. Many of the tropical cyclones are formed south of 10° N. lat., none north of 20° N., and the place of origin of by far the greater number of them lies eastward of the Philippine Islands.

In the first group of the year the greatest number of hurricanes arises in lower latitudes than 10° N., but at the beginning of December and the end of March the place of origin extends itself a little farther north, so that for this group it lies between 5° and 12° N. lat., 145° and 143° E. long. In the second group the place of formation lies between 17° and 6° N. and 142° to 149° E. In the third group the limits are 20° to 8° N. and 139° to 126° E.

By consulting the isobaric and isothermal charts of the Manilla Observatory, 1894, it will be found that in the first monthly group the position of origin lies between the isobars 757 mm. (29·804 ins.) and 759 mm. (29·882 ins.) and the isotherm 27° C. (80·6 Fahr.) and 30° C. (86° Fahr.). The same isobars will be seen over the area allotted to the second monthly group associated with the isotherm 28° C. (82°·4 Fahr.) and 30° C. (86° Fahr.). In September the zone of formation is in the isobar 757 mm. (29·804 ins.), and in the remaining months of the third group between the 757 mm. and 759 mm. isobars (29·804 ins. and 29·882 ins.). In all months of this group we hit upon the isotherm 28° C. and 29° C. (82°·4 Fahr. and 84°·2 Fahr.). The hurricanes appear, therefore, to be formed in regions where neither barometric nor thermal gradients of any importance exist—in, as it were, a neutral zone. Their places of origin migrate from February to July or August north-north-west, after which they return south-south-eastward until January. In this periodic migration a relation between the sun's declination and the place of cyclonic origin may be recognised.

Dr. Bergholz shows how the paths of the tropical hurricanes of East Asia arrange themselves into two groups, viz. those of the Pacific Ocean and those of the China Sea, by pointing out that the former do not cut the 130° E. long., but that those of the China Sea cross this longitude, but incidentally are formed actually in the China Sea.

The following is the table he quotes :—

	Month.	Direction of first branch.	Mean latitude of vortex. N. Lat.	Direction of second branch.
First Group.	December, January, February, March	N.N.W.	15° to 19°	N.N.E.
Second Group.	April, May, October, November	N.W.	16° to 21°	N.E. .
Third Group.	June, July, August, September	N.W. by N.	21° to 25°	N.E. by N.

In general, all the paths of the hurricanes are parabolic, and the mean inclination of their paths where they cross the latitude of Manilla is much greater than the mean inclination of their paths in their first branch, *i.e.* before they commence to curve. This is especially striking during the months of the first group, and it corresponds very well with the fact that the latitude of the vertex comes very near to the latitude of Manilla.

In regard to the paths of the hurricanes of the China Sea, Dr. Bergholz pointed out that none of the hurricanes forming in the first monthly group of this division appear to recurve or have a parabolic path, but that it is possible they may recurve in the interior of the Asiatic Continent; the observations necessary for ascertaining whether this be the case are, however, wanting. Some hurricanes of the second group have a parabolic path, and in the China Sea they recurve in the south of the Formosa Channel; but, in consequence of the paths in their first branch having a less northerly inclination, while still in the Pacific the curve completes itself in relatively low latitudes. The hurricanes which belong to the typhoon months proper, that is to say to the third group, recurve much more frequently and also reach much higher latitudes: the recurving hurricanes of this group have many of the attributes which belong to those of the Pacific of the same group.

"If," said the lecturer, "we follow the course of the China Sea hurricanes which do not recurve, there results the following:—Hurricanes which form in the months of December and March have from the beginning a direction west by north, which they maintain on their way through the southern part of the China Sea. They land in December and January on the continent in French Cochin China and South Annam, and in February and April move to the north, almost exclusively in Annam."

He concludes from this that the zone in which these hurricanes originate lies between the parallels of 5° and 12° N., and its place of landing is situated between 18° and 15°. He finds that the hurricanes of April and May start in a north-west by north direction and reach the land—North Annam—in April; in May they enter the Gulf of Tonquin or Straits of Hainan, visiting at the end of May the neighbourhood of Macao.

The October cyclones, which take a west-north-west course, reach the continent to the north of Hong-Kong in the first days of the month, but later in the month they move in a more southerly direction into the Gulf of Tonquin.

The direction of the hurricane paths is again west by north in November, and their place of landing Annam; the place of origin of this group lies between 6° and 17° N. lat., and their landing-place between 12° and 23°. Of the hurricanes of the third group he states that the June hurricanes progress in a north-westerly direction to the south coast of China through the Straits of Hainan, but some recurve when south of the Formosa Channel.

Dr. Bergholz divides the July typhoons, which he states take a north-westerly direction to begin with, into three classes. Those of the first class progress like those of June; those of the second land on the coast of China between Amoy and Shanghai, or recurve in a north-north-east direction, traversing the Yellow Sea; and those of the third recurve opposite—and to the eastward of—Formosa, and run up the Sea of Japan.

The direction of the August cyclones is north-west, otherwise their behaviour is like that of the July cyclones. In September the initial direction is north-west by north, the same as the first and third classes of July.

In regard to the zone of hurricanes of the months of the third group he shows that their place of origin lies between 8° and 20°, and their landing-place between 30° and 18°. If, with the help of the isobaric chart, the conditions under which the cyclones form themselves in the different months and groups of months are traced, the hurricanes of the Pacific of group one will be seen to have their origin between two centres of high pressure, of which one is on the continent and one in the Pacific Ocean. They run to the centre of low pressure, which takes in a portion of the Behring Sea.

The hurricanes of the China Sea follow lower latitudes, which are reached by the extreme isobars of the centre of high pressure lying over Asia; and according as this centre flattens and withdraws from January to March, the extreme isobar pushes northward, and the tracks gain in latitude accordingly.

The hurricanes of the Pacific during April and May, if traced on the isobaric chart, will be found to move between the extreme isobars of the high-pressure areas of the Pacific Ocean and of Asia; but those of the China Sea move south of the isobar 760 mm. (29·922 ins.) of the high-pressure district of Asia, skirting the low-pressure district of Hindustan.

The lecturer then went on to show that during October and November, as the high-pressure district in Asia develops the hurricanes "are pushed more into the lower latitudes," but the direction of their paths is controlled by the development of the district of low pressure in Hindustan.

"The hurricanes of the Pacific Ocean have for their course, especially during October, the great region between the Philippines, Japan, and the 760 mm. isobar of the high-pressure district of the Pacific." Consequent on the further development of the continental high-pressure area in November the zone becomes more restricted. The paths of the hurricanes of the Pacific belonging to this group are directed towards depressions in high latitudes north-north-eastward of Manilla. The withdrawal of the centre of high pressure from the coast of Asia in January, and its disappearance until at least the middle of September, was given as a characteristic of the months of the third group, and in connection with this it was shown that these hurricanes reach high latitudes: those of the Pacific recurve near the 125 meridian east of Greenwich, that is to say, nearer to the Philippine Islands than those of the earlier months.

The hurricanes of the second half of September constitute a special exception to the above, as they commence to curve 5° or 8° more to the eastward.

Dr. Bergholz is of opinion that all the hurricanes of the Pacific Ocean have for their object the northern centre of low pressure. The hurricanes of the China Sea move along a path persistently more northward until the end of August or the beginning of September, as the high-pressure area of the continent advances towards the north; but when, about the middle of September, the low pressure migrates farther south, the paths of these cyclones follow. Some of the July hurricanes, after recurving, follow a path which has a strong northerly tendency, cross the Yellow Sea, and migrate to a centre of low pressure which has been formed in Siberia.—CAMPBELL HEPWORTH.

RECENT PUBLICATIONS.

Annals of the Astronomical Observatory of Harvard College. Vol. XLII. Part II. Observations made at the Blue Hill Meteorological Observatory, Massachusetts, U.S.A., in the years 1897 and 1898, under the direction of A. LAWRENCE ROTCH, M.A. 4to. 147 pp. Cambridge. 1900.

Routine observations and automatic records at the three stations on the summit and the base of Blue Hill and in the Naponsel Valley have been maintained as in previous years, and the two following investigations mentioned in the introduction to the *Observations* for 1896 have been continued. As already stated, Blue Hill was one of the stations co-operating in the work of the international "Cloud Year," which commenced May 1, 1896. The measurements with theodolites of the heights and velocities of the clouds ceased April 30, 1897, but the usual observations of the level, kind, and amount of the clouds, and their direction of motion and relative velocity with a nephoscope, are still being made, although their publication ended with the year 1897. These measurements and observations, reduced in the form recommended by the Cloud Committee, preceded by a description of the methods used and by a brief discussion of the results by Mr. Clayton, constitute Appendix C. Some of the tables include also the measurements made in 1890-91. A summary of the observations with the nephoscope during the "Cloud Year" will probably be published by the United States Weather Bureau with the similar observations at its own stations.

The exploration of the air by means of kites has been prosecuted with great success. In consequence of improvements devised by Messrs. Clayton and Fergusson, the kites now fly through larger ranges of wind velocity, and also attain greater heights, while at these heights in the free air the meteorographs, perfected by Mr. Fergusson, record accurately four elements, namely, atmospheric pressure, air temperature, relative humidity, and wind velocity. Thirty-eight flights were made during 1897, and the average height of the meteorograph above the sea was 4557 feet, the maximum height being 11,716 feet. During 1898 there were 35 flights, of which the average height was 7350 feet, and the maximum was 12,070 feet. Throughout several nights the meteorograph was maintained at a nearly constant height, and by frequent ascents and descents during consecutive days the conditions prevailing in the different strata were determined.

Ice and Ice Movements in Bering Sea during the Spring Months. 8vo. 19 pp. Washington Hydrographic Office. 1900.

The increasing commercial importance of Bering Sea has led to many inquiries at the Branch Hydrographic Offices on the Pacific coast for information as to the earliest date at which navigation of the sea is practicable. The present pamphlet is published in response to these inquiries. It has been prepared by Mr. James Page, of the Division of Marine Meteorology.

Meteorologische Zeitschrift. Redigirt von Dr. J. HANN und Dr. G. HELLMAN. January—March, 1900. 4to.

The principal articles are :—" Ergebnisse der internationalen Ballonfahrten," von H. Hergesell (28 pp.). This is the continuation of the paper noticed in the number for February 1899. In it he deals with three questions: (1) The determination of temperature; (2) The temperature above and below; and (3) The actual results of the ascents. The paper is not yet complete. (1) As to temperature observations, he recommends a metallic thermometer carefully tested beforehand in baths of known temperature. He says the instrument behaved admirably, but is somewhat sluggish when compared with ventilated thermometers, owing to radiation from the car and other parts of the balloon. One important matter comes out—that the descending curve is not so true as the ascending one, owing to this radiation. (2) As to the temperature, the ascents have proved the existence of enormous variations of temperature at the very highest levels reached. Dr. Hergesell says that apparently the temperature oscillations rather increase than decrease with altitude. (3) As regards the actual ascents, three are described, and weather charts given for the 1500 and 8000 feet levels. It appears from these—based on nearly a dozen observations partly with manned, and partly with unmanned, balloons sent up simultaneously over Europe on May 13, 1897, March 24, 1899, and October 3, 1899—that the systems of depression over the earth's surface were reproduced in a general sort of way at the highest levels reached, at least in the first and third cases. This is extremely interesting. The balloons always drifted along the supposed isobars at the upper level.—"Temperatur und Bewolkung um Ufer des Baikal und auf den benachbarten Höhen," von A. Woeikof (5 pp.). This is an account of three years' observations at five stations near Lake Baikal, one of them the highest station in the Russian system (3000 feet).—In the Reviews for the January number there is a notice by Dr. Sprung of Dr. Schreiber's paper "On the Modes of determining Wind Force." Dr. Sprung gives a detailed criticism of the work of the Wind Force Committee of the Royal Meteorological Society which is well worth reading. He comes to the conclusion that, after all, an electrical Robinson's instrument of small size is the best, and he maintains that the Dines Pressure Tube arrangement cannot be used in cold climates, owing to the freezing of the water cylinder.—"Ueber den taglichen Gang der Sommerregen bei verschiedenen Wetterlagen," von Dr. E. Lees (22 pp.). This is a discussion of rain records with reference mainly to quantity, and it does not deal with the total amounts falling in a short period. Dr. Lees firstly treats of the fall according to the wind, as to whether it was Northerly or Southerly. He found that these showed distinct differences, but these did not explain the double daily maximum. He then took the days of heavy rain (Platzregen) on which a minimum of say 0·2 in. fell in an hour, and found that their maximum fell decidedly later than that on ordinary rain days. He shows how this fact is mainly attributable to the supersaturation of the air with vapour, due either to abnormal heating of the lower strata, or to abnormal cooling of the upper strata. He then illustrates this by data from Chemnitz, Hohenheim, and other localities. At the end he deals with frequency, and shows that at Berlin the quantity and frequency are greatest in the forenoon with Northerly, and in the afternoon with Southerly winds.—"Ueber Bildungstätten, Bahnen und Zonen der Orkane des 'Fernen Ostens,'" von P. Bergholz (4 pp.). This is a paper read at the meeting of the German Association at Munich in 1899 (see note on p. 165). The author has also published a book on the same subject, basing it mainly on Padre Algué's book, *Baguios ó Ciclones Filipinos.* Dr. Bergholz's book will appear shortly in an English translation.—"Arktis und Antarkis," von A. Woeikof (5 pp.). In this paper Dr. Woeikof discusses the results of Nansen's observations on his expedition, and compares these with the figures given by the Belgian South Pole Expedition as published by Arktowski. These latter are the first winter temperatures we possess for those regions. The annual mean for 70° 2′ S. is 14°·7 F.; that for 70° N., according to Spitaler's calculation, is 14°·0, and to Mohn's, 13°·5. It is, however, doubtful if the year of the Belgian visit was too cold or too warm. On the whole, Dr. Woeikof maintains that the ocean climate of the Southern Hemisphere on the parallels of 45°, 50°, and 55° is, on the whole, about 3° lower than that of the Northern. He concludes the paper by anticipating that the results of Borchgrevink's observations will probably show extremely low readings of the thermometer.—"Das dynamische Princip der Cirkulations-bewegungen in der Atmosphäre," von V. Bjerknes (10 pp.). This is, as its title shows, a mathematical investigation into atmospherical circulation. The present paper is only the first instalment.—"Die Ergebnisse der Beobachtungen der Wolken in Manila in dem internationalen Wolkenjahre," von P. Bergholz (10 pp.). This is a German abstract of Padre Algué's *Las Nubes en el Archipiélago Filipino*, published in 1898. The Jesuits have managed to keep up their work despite the troubles of the war, as the production of this discussion of their very careful cloud observations proves.—"Mitteltemperaturen von Ostsibirien," von A. Woeikof (9 pp.). This is the reproduction of a paper by *Iwitzky*, published in the Annual Report of the Cabinet for Physical Geography of the St. Petersburg Academy. There are tables for 31 stations, for varying lengths of duration, from 21 years (1875-95) for Irkutsk, Nertschinsk, Nikolajewsk, and Wladiwostok; for Werchojansk only 11 years (1884-94) are available. The tables are very useful, as the figures have not been previously collected from the successive yearly volumes.

Monthly Weather Review. Prof. CLEVELAND ABBE, Editor. Prepared under the direction of WILLIS L. MOORE, Chief, U.S. Weather Bureau. November 1899—January 1900. 4to.

Among the articles and reports are the following:—"Rivers and Floods" (4 pp.).—"Climate and Crop Service" (6 pp.).—"Observations at Rivas, Nicaragua" (1 p.).—"Ratio of the Discharges of the Chagres River at Gamboa and Bohio to the Rainfall in the Watershed above these places" (2 pp.).—"History of the Barometer" (1 p.).—"Meteorological Observations at Public Schools" (1 p.).—"Precipitation" (1 p.).—"Contributions to the Meteorology of Panama" (1 p.).—"Some of the Results of the International Cloud Work for the United States" (5 pp.).—"South African Meteorology" (1 p.).—"Climatology of San Diego Cal." (1 p.).—"Artificial Rain" (2 pp.).

Nautical-Meteorological Annual, 1899. Published by the Danish Meteorological Institute. 4to. 244 pp. Copenhagen. 1899.

The *Annual* is published this year in the same compass as the last two preceding years, only the title has been changed to *Nautical-Meteorological Annual* instead of, as previously, *Nautical-Meteorological Observations.* At the same time English text has been adopted instead of French along with the Danish text, the Institute presuming that those who abroad take an interest in the *Annual*, and particularly in the accompanying treatises, are more versed in the English than in the French language. This volume contains, in addition to the tables of observation, two papers by V. Garde on "The State of the Ice in the Waters E. and W. of Greenland, 1899" (23 pp.) and "Windcharts of the Northernmost Part of the Atlantic and of Davis Strait" (18 pp.).

Symons's Monthly Meteorological Magazine. January—March 1900. 8vo.

The principal articles are:—"Low Barometric Pressure on December 29, 1899" (3 pp.).—"Royal Meteorological Society" (3 pp.).—"Severe Frost in December 1899" (2 pp.).—"Results of Meteorological Observations at Camden Square for 40 years, 1858-97" (1 p.).—"Our Climatological Records for the

British Empire for 1898" (3 pp.). The Editor publishes from month to month a Climatological Table of Observations at various places in the British Empire. In this article he gives the results for 1898, together with a Summary showing extremes of temperature, etc., at all the stations.—"The Meteor of January 9, 1900" (2 pp.).—"George James Symons, F.R.S." (1 p.). This is a very brief Obituary Notice of the Editor of the Magazine.—"The Snow and Floods of February 1900" (9 pp.). This article deals with the heavy snowfall and floods which occurred during the month of February. In a large number of places the total rainfall for the month exceeded double the average. One of the most striking effects of the flood was the destruction of the old bridge at Guildford.

The Diurnal Range of Rain at the Seven Observatories in connection with the Meteorological Office, 1871-90. By R. H. SCOTT, D.Sc., F.R.S. 8vo. 48 pp. London. 1900.

A discussion of the diurnal march of the fall of rain from the ten years 1871-80 was published in 1885 as Appendix II. to the *Quarterly Weather Report* for 1877. The expiration of another decade has rendered it desirable to ascertain if any features of periodicity, which had not come out in the interval of ten years, would show themselves when that interval was doubled. The results are represented graphically in seven plates.

The curves do not exhibit any marked character as regards quantity, except in the summer months, when at four of the stations—Armagh, Aberdeen, Stonyhurst, and Kew—there is a decided increase of quantity in the early afternoon hours. It is therefore clear that even twenty years are not sufficient to show any definite periodicity, should such exist, in the amount of rain which falls during the twenty-four hours.

However, at several of the stations there is a decided falling off in quantity between 10 and 11 a.m. At Armagh this decrease occurs between 8 and 9 a.m., and there is no depression at 11 a.m.

The papers are changed at 10 a.m., but this does not seem sufficient to account for the diminution in quantity, as at more than one of the stations the reduction of quantity is continued till noon, and even later.

QUARTERLY JOURNAL

OF THE

ROYAL METEOROLOGICAL SOCIETY

VOL. XXVI.] JULY 1900 [No. 115.

ROYAL METEOROLOGICAL SOCIETY JUBILEE CELEBRATION—APRIL 3–4, 1900.

THE Royal Meteorological Society attained its Jubilee on Tuesday, April 3, having been founded on April 3, 1850. This Fiftieth Anniversary was celebrated in the following manner:—

TUESDAY, APRIL 3.

A COMMEMORATION MEETING was held at the Institution of Civil Engineers, Great George Street, Westminster, at 3 p.m.

The President, Dr. C. Theodore Williams, delivered an Address, and Delegates from other Societies were received.

A CONVERSAZIONE was held at the Royal Institute of Painters in Water Colours, Piccadilly, at 8.30 p.m.

In addition to the Pictures in the Galleries, there was also an Exhibition of Meteorological Instruments, Models, and Photographs, and Lantern Demonstrations were given by Mr. T. C. Porter (of Eton), Col. H. M. Saunders, and Mr. W. Marriott.

Short Concerts were given by the "Schartau" Part-Singers, and Instrumental Music was performed by the Royal Artillery String Band.

WEDNESDAY, APRIL 4.

An EXCURSION was made to the Royal Observatory, Greenwich, by permission of the Astronomer-Royal (Mr. W. H. M. Christie, F.R.S.), followed by a visit to the Painted Hall and Naval Museum of Greenwich Hospital. About ninety Fellows joined in the excursion.

A DINNER was held at the Westminster Palace Hotel, Victoria Street, S.W., at 7 p.m.[1]

[1] A list of the guests will be found on p. 192.

COMMEMORATION MEETING,

APRIL 3, 1900.

Dr. C. THEODORE WILLIAMS, President, in the Chair.

The PRESIDENT announced that the following Delegates from other Societies had been appointed to represent them at the Jubilee Celebration, and that he was glad to see that nearly all of these were present :—

The Royal Society.—Prof. J. J. Thomson, M.A., D.Sc., LL.D., F.R.S.
Royal Astronomical Society.—Mr. E. B. Knobel, President.
Royal Geographical Society. — General Sir Henry W. Norman, G.C.B., G.C.M.G., C.I.E.
Geological Society.—Mr. J. J. H. Teall, F.R.S., President.
Institution of Electrical Engineers.—Prof. Silvanus P. Thompson, D.Sc., F.R.S., President.
Royal Agricultural Society.—Sir Ernest Clarke, Secretary.
Royal Horticultural Society.—Sir Trevor Lawrence, Bart., President.
Royal Botanic Society.—Major J. W. N. Cotton.
Scottish Meteorological Society.—Mr. R. C. Mossman, F.R.S.E.
Sanitary Institute.—Mr. A. Wynter Blyth, M.R.C.S.
Hertfordshire Natural History Society.—Mr. J. Hopkinson, F.L.S.
Oxfordshire Natural History Society.—Mr. H. Balfour, President.
German Meteorological Society.—Prof. Dr. G. Hellmann.

Mr. F. C. BAYARD read the following extracts from letters and telegrams which had been received from some of the Honorary Members and other institutions :—

AUSTRIAN METEOROLOGICAL SOCIETY, Vienna.—The Austrian Meteorological Society sends to its sister, the English Society, on the occasion of its Jubilee, its warmest greetings and its most sincere congratulations. The Society looks back on the long period of active work in Meteorology carried out by eminent students of the science which has redounded to the credit of the Royal Meteorological Society, and it expresses its hope that the future may be as fruitful as the past.—VICTOR VON LANG, President; J. M. PERNTER, Vice-President.

ROUMANIAN METEOROLOGICAL INSTITUTE, Bucharest.—In the name of the Roumanian Meteorological Institute at Bucharest, I have the distinguished honour of presenting to the Royal Meteorological Society its heartiest congratulations on the occasion of its Jubilee of fifty years.

Long live the Royal Meteorological Society, which has always been in the first rank for the advancement of our science !—Prof. Dr. S. HEPITES, Director.

Prof. R. BILLWILLER, Zürich.—The Royal Meteorological Society can look back on its fifty years' activity with pride and satisfaction. It established itself as a private Society in order to organise meteorological observations, and to turn them to account for the science, long before the Government had called any office into being for the purpose. It is this natural development of the subject which has also been the case in this country, where the Government did not take up the matter until a private Society had proved its practical importance.

Your Society, of which I have the high honour of being an Honorary Member, has shown that, notwithstanding the existence of a Government office, there is still room for active work and prosecution of the science; and I am convinced that in the future the co-operation of the Government office and the private Society will work together for the common weal of our science, and will secure its solid advancement.

With these words, I beg you to convey to the Royal Meteorological Society my warmest congratulations on its Jubilee.

Dr. A. BUCHAN, F.R.S., Edinburgh.—Kindly convey to your Council my extreme regret that I am prevented from expressing on the occasion my profound sense of the services which have been rendered to Meteorology by the Royal Meteorological Society.

Dr. N. EKHOLM, Stockholm.—I wish to express my best wishes and salutations to the Fellows of the Society, and I will send you, as a humble expression of homage to the Royal Meteorological Society and the science it so successfully has been working for during the past half-century, a paper entitled, "On the Variations of the Climate of the Geological and Historical Past and their Causes."

Prof. Dr. JULIUS HANN, Graz.—I wish you to express my congratulations to the Royal Meteorological Society.

Prof. H. H. HILDEBRANDSSON, Upsala.—I beg you to lay before the Royal Meteorological Society my humble and sincere congratulations on the good work done during half a century, and my best wishes for the future.

Dr. W. KÖPPEN, Hamburg.—Sends his warmest congratulations to the Royal Meteorological Society.

Dr. H. MOHN, Christiania.—Convinced that your Society in the future will be, as now, in the van in all meteorological progress, I send the best and most heartfelt wishes for its future.

Geheimrath Dr. G. NEUMAYER, Hamburg.—I have the honour to send to the Royal Meteorological Society on the occasion of its Jubilee my sincerest congratulations, and my hopes for its future progress and success.

Dr. M. SNELLEN, de Bilt, Utrecht.—I wish the Royal Meteorological Society great prosperity, and a long and glorious life.

Dr. H. WILD, Zürich.—I hope that the Royal Meteorological Society will be as prosperous in the future as in the past, in furthering the progress of Meteorology.

The Society can look back on the past fifty years with much satisfaction; and the meteorologists of the whole world will take this opportunity of recognising the Society's past activity, and of offering their good wishes for the future.

The President (Dr. C. THEODORE WILLIAMS) expressed his great pleasure and satisfaction in receiving the good wishes and congratulations from so many friends, and especially from foreign meteorologists and foreign meteorological societies. He would like to make a few remarks on the circumstances which led up to the present Jubilee Celebrations. It was decided in January last by the Council and Fellows to elect Mr. Symons as President for the forthcoming Jubilee year, and it was unanimously agreed that no one could carry out the work in a better or more able manner. Mr. Symons had entered into the matter with great spirit, but was to their great sorrow struck down with paralysis, which resulted in his death on March 10. It was Mr. Symons' expressed wish, whilst lying ill, that another President should be elected in his place, and the Council had conferred on him

(Dr. Williams) a great honour by appointing him for a second time to that responsible position. Mr. Symons, with his usual readiness, had, before his illness, prepared an Address for this occasion, which he (Dr. Williams) would now have the melancholy privilege of reading, afterwards adding a few remarks of his own on Mr. Symons himself and his work.

JUBILEE ADDRESS.

Prepared by the late G. J. SYMONS, F.R.S., President.

We are to-day concerned chiefly with the events of April 3, 1850, with the progress of our Society in the subsequent half-century, and with thoughts as to its future.

But I think that it will be well to devote a few minutes to earlier times, and so to lead up from the very earliest efforts to the date at which our Society was formed out of the shipwrecked fragments of its predecessor.

The earliest English meteorological observer and recorder of whom the work has come down to the present day was the Reverend William Merle, Fellow of Merton College, Oxford, and Rector of Driby, near Alford, Lincolnshire. He was admitted to the benefice May 13, 1331, in the reign of Edward III., and his record of observations for the seven years 1337-1344 is still preserved in the Bodleian Library at Oxford, and was in 1891 reproduced by photography, translated, and published. Of course it contained no instrumental results, but the descriptions of the weather were in some respects better than any published now. A reproduction of the MS. is in the Exhibition.

Two hundred years have to pass before we can trace anything except stray notes of floods, famines, snows, and storms : no observer's name is known to me, nor the title of any book published in England upon the subject.

The earliest English book on the weather was, I believe, issued about 1530, but it has no date ; its title is "GODFRIDVS : Here begynneth THE BOKE OF KNOWLEDGE OF THYNGES VNKNOWEN APPERTEYNYNGE TO ASTRONOMYE, with certayne necessary Rules," etc., 16mo. It is largely astrological, but contains weather proverbs based on Aratus, Aristotle, Bonatus, and others. This book was extremely popular, and thousands of copies of it, or modifications of it, were sold by pedlars even down to the present century. This was followed about twenty years later by another book of weather proverbs by Leonard Digges, entitled "A prognostication everlasting of right good effect, fruitfully augmented by the author, containing plaine, briefe, pleasant, chosen rules to judge the weather by the Sunne, Moone, Starres, Comets," etc., London, 4to, 1555.

I must not occupy time with notes on subsequent publications, except in as far as they bear upon that with which we are more concerned namely, recorded facts.

Not being sure as to the precedence, in starting weather records, of the following men, I am reduced to the necessity of mentioning them in the order of their birth and stating what little I know of the work of each.

The Rev. Dr. JOHN GOAD was born in London, February 15, 1615, and educated at the Merchant Taylors' School. From 1643 to 1646 he was Vicar of St. Giles's, Oxford, and subsequently for twenty years Head-master of Tonbridge and of the Merchant Taylors' Schools. He drew up reports of the weather and presented them personally once a month to King James II. Mr. Bentley informs me that some of his MS. records are still preserved at the Ashmolean Museum at Oxford. His records formed the basis of his "Astro-Meteorologia" published in 1686, but he does not appear to have possessed any instruments, although oddly enough the following advertisement is found at the end of his book, p. 508:—

"The Truest and Best approved Weather-Glasses, both Baroscopes and Thermometers, are accurately made by John Warner, a Maker of Mathematical Instruments at the East end of Portugal Row, near adjoining to Lincolns-Inn-Fields, London."

The Hon. Robert Boyle was born at Lismore in 1627. Although this distinguished physicist left no long series of meteorological observations, he certainly made a great many on barometric pressure (as early as 1659), temperature, and humidity, as is proved by several of his almost innumerable tracts.

Dr. Robert Plot, Secretary to the Royal Society, was born at Borden in Kent in 1641. He made a series of observations for the year 1683-4, which, together with a diagram of the barometer for every day in that year, is printed in one of the early volumes of the *Phil. Trans.* I notice that a remark made by Dr. Plot destroys a theory which I once held, and it may be well to mention it. When the readings of an instrument are marked by a line upon squared paper, they are often said to be "plotted"; as I had never seen the process employed previous to the above diagram, I traced the word "plotted" to Dr. Plot—but he distinctly ascribes it to Dr. Lister, so that we ought apparently to say "listered" instead of "plotted."

The whole paragraph, written by Dr. Plot more than two centuries since, is worthy of reproduction:—

"I here give you the Observations of a full Year, made by Order of the Philosophical Society at Oxford, not only of the Rise and Fall of the Quicksilver (mark'd by the wandring prickt Line, after Dr. Lister's Method) and the Weather; but also how the Wind stood each Day. If the same Observations were made in many foreign and remote Parts at the same Time, we should be enabled with some Grounds to examine, not only the Coastings, Breadth, and Bounds of the Winds themselves, but of the Weather they bring with them; and probably in Time thereby learn to be forewarned certainly of divers Emergencies (such as Heats, Colds, Dearths, Plagues, and other epidemical Distempers) which are now unaccountable to us; and by their Causes be instructed for Prevention, or Remedies. Thence too in Time we may hope to be informed how far the Positions of the Planets, in Relation to one another, and to the fixed Stars, are concerned in the Alterations of the Weather, and in bringing and preventing Diseases, or other Calamities; for by this means it is, doubtless, that the Learned Dr. Goad of London, has arriv'd to that Pitch of Knowledge he already has in predicting Weather. This, no Question, was the Opinion of the industrious Walter [should have been William—G. J. S.] Merle, Fellow of Merton College, who thus observed the Weather here at Oxford every Day of the Month seven Years together, viz. from January 1337 to January 1344; the MS. Copy of which Observations are yet remaining in the Bodleyan Library. And doubtless it was some such Consideration as this, that moved Erasmus Bartholin to make Observations of the Weather every Day through the whole Year 1671, which are printed inter Acta Medica Tho. Bartholini."

Sir Christopher Wren was born at E. Knoyle in Wiltshire in 1632. He is so well known as the architect of St. Paul's Cathedral that few persons regard him as Professor of Astronomy at Gresham College, as President of the Royal Society, or as the inventor of the first recording rain-gauge, yet on the latter account he certainly merits mention here.

A few years later (in 1697) several instrumental records were being kept, including rainfall, at one station in Essex and at another in Lancashire. It is not now necessary to trace these records further.

I must turn to the history of organisations for securing uniformity of procedure among observers.

The honour of priority of suggestion in this respect rests, according to the last quotation, with Dr. Plot, and it was followed by Dr. Jurin, Secretary of the Royal Society, whose paper in the *Phil. Trans.* for 1723 shows remarkable knowledge and judgment. A few new stations were started, but in fifteen years all but one had stopped. Twenty years later (in 1744) Mr. Roger Pickering, F.R.S., published a paper on a "Scheme of a Diary of the Weather," but this produced no perceptible effect.

Gilbert White's enthusiasm and example seem to have proved more powerful, for his record at Selborne extended from 1780 to 1793, and the number of observers during the ten years 1785 to 1794 was greater than in any previous ten years, or indeed than in any other ten years up to 1808-17.

The first English Meteorological Society was founded in 1823 on the suggestion of Mr. J. G. Tatem, an observer then living at Harpenden, St. Albans, but subsequently of High Wycombe. The first meeting was held at the London Tavern, October 15, 1823, Luke Howard, Thomas Forster, and Dr. Birkbeck being among the founders. Sir Benjamin Brodie, Sir Henry de la Beche, and Prof. Daniell were members of this Society. Very shortly afterwards Luke Howard left London for Yorkshire, and the Society went to sleep. It was not wound up, but it did so little that in 1836, when Mr. W. H. White proposed the formation of a Meteorological Society, Mr. Tatem, the founder of the 1823 Society, did not know whether that Society was alive or dead. This proposal seems to have so far roused the 1823 Society that it passed on its property to the 1836 one, but I cannot trace any formal resolution as to the relations of the two Societies.

The Society formed in 1836 called itself by many names, but generally "The Meteorological Society of London." During its whole career Mr. W. H. White acted as Secretary, and eventually its death was, I think, due to the ever-increasing domination of the astro-meteorological views which he entertained. During its period (1836-1842) many meetings were held and much good work was done, details of which are given in our *Quarterly Journal* for 1881. Sir John Herschel, Sir James Ross, and Mr. Ruskin were all members of this Society, and contributed to its *Transactions.*

Just as in 1836 the prior existence of the Society of 1823 was ignored, so when the present Society was founded on April 3, 1850, the Society of 1836 was itself in turn ignored. This is the more remarkable because out of the Council of the 1850 Society no fewer than five were office-bearers in the 1836 Society, which, though it had done nothing for six years, had not been formally dissolved. The announcement of the establishment of the 1850 Society aroused the old officials, and, as far as I am able to judge, their offers and proposals of help towards the 1850 Society did not meet with the response which might have been expected. The result was that the 1850 Society got neither the minute books, the MSS., nor the library of the 1836 Society; but in the course of years these have mostly been purchased by a former President of the 1850 Society and are now in its library.

We are now in a position to deal with our present Society (the 1850 one) alone.

First as to when, where, and by whom, it was started. The "when" is soon disposed of—on April 3, 1850, and I believe, but am not sure, in the afternoon of that day. The "where" and the "by whom" had better be taken together, because they were mutually dependent. The late Dr. Lee, F.R.S., was a member of many learned societies, and had two (if not more) residences—an official one under the shadow of St. Paul's Cathedral, and the somewhat important one of Hartwell House, Aylesbury. He and Admiral Smyth, F.R.S., worked much together, and Dr. Lee had a good private observatory at Hartwell. Moreover, I believe that the worthy old Doctor (of Laws, not Medicine) liked to have scientific friends staying with him. And so it came about that, fifty years ago, a little gathering of ten meteorologists and astronomers assembled in the library of Hartwell were the founders of this Society, and it is not a little remarkable that two of them have lived to see the jubilee of that day.

[Since this Address was prepared by Mr. Symons, Mr. E. J. Lowe, F.R.S., has died, so that Mr. J. Glaisher, F.R.S., is now the sole survivor. —EDITOR.]

In our *Quarterly Journal* for 1881 will be found a full account of the work of the Society during the first thirty years of its existence; it is therefore inexpedient to repeat details then given, and it will perhaps be better to give a few personal recollections of early days for comparison with present-day facts known to all the Fellows.

During the first half of its career the Society was largely guided by its original Secretary and our oldest Fellow, Mr. James Glaisher, F.R.S., who nursed it through its infancy and youth and left it to other hands only when it was old enough and strong enough to walk alone.

What small beginnings it had may be illustrated by my own recollection of one of the earliest meetings which I attended. It was early in 1857, *i.e.* when the Society was scarcely seven years old. Dr. Lee, F.R.S., was President. I rang the bell at what appeared to be a private house in Cavendish Square, and was ushered into a small sitting-room where the total attendance was far less than is now usual at a Council Meeting. Dr. Lee, tall and stately as ever, was sitting in an arm-chair at the end of a dining-table as President, Mr. Glaisher (Secretary) by his side, with a pile of papers before him, and the other members seated round the table.

After the midsummer of 1857, for reasons which I forget, we were unable to meet in that room; happily we had then for President the distinguished engineer Robert Stephenson. He obtained from the Council of the Institution of Civil Engineers the great kindness of permission to meet in their rooms. But in 1858 the Institution was not possessed of a palace with marble halls, but only of a private house, 25 Great George Street, and our meetings used to be held in the old library, *i.e.* the front room on the first floor.

Officials in this country generally try to stop scientific work. This time it was, I believe, the Westminster Vestry; but it does not matter, for as far as my experience goes, all public bodies are alike. Somebody, however, took legal proceedings against the I.C.E. for rates or taxes or something, and the result was, that until the Institution came out triumphant, they had to stop their kind and wholly gratuitous hospitality, and as regards meetings we were homeless and destitute. We held our meetings for a time on Adelphi Terrace, as guests of the Victoria Institute. Happily the Law Courts found against the officials, the Institution renewed its hospitality, and both in its old building and in the new has done everything for us that was possible ever since.

I have said nothing about our library, our staff, or our rooms.

Up to 1858 we had practically no library: Mr. Glaisher had some books at Blackheath, Dr. Lee had some at Doctors' Commons, and some were in a loft at the old house in Cavendish Square. In 1862 our Past President, Mr. Eaton, collected them and prepared a catalogue,—about 200 entries,—not a tithe of the very fine collection which we now have.

From the very first the Society had an assistant, who (as the Society had no home) used to work at Mr. Glaisher's residence; but it is from the appointment of Mr. Marriott as Assistant-Secretary, and the taking of a room for library, office, and workroom in the spring of 1872, that progress has been most rapid. It is needless to set out the details: those who remember Mr. Marriott, all alone, with a few shelves of books in the garret of 30 Great George Street, and see our present suite of rooms, our library, and our staff, will need no further evidence of progress.

I must also refer to our Charter. Originally we were merely a voluntary association, but in 1866 we obtained a Royal Charter whereby the Members of the British Meteorological Society were all changed into Fellows of the Meteorological Society. In 1882 our then President, Mr. J. Knox Laughton, carried us a step further, for he obtained from our beloved Queen permission to use the prefix of Royal. Thus we arrive at our present status of The Royal Meteorological Society. Most persons would hold that we could not desire more; I do—and I do not think that justice will be done until we get it.

When old Burlington House (which I well remember) was pulled down and the present one was erected, the Government provided comfortable accommodation for the Royal Academy, the Royal Society, and five or six other of the richest of the scientific societies. That was quite right, and, if our rulers did but know it, was one of the best investments that Government ever made. But can anybody say why the rich societies ought to have quarters free and the (relatively) poor ones be made to pay rent, rates, etc.? The sooner the nation appreciates science at its true value, and builds a proper centre for the smaller societies, the better will it be for the country.

It would take too long to epitomise our work. We claim for ourselves, and we grant to all who attend our meetings, absolute freedom of discussion; and we leave our publications, Reports, Proceedings, Quarterly Journal, and Record as the best evidence of what we have done. Perhaps, however, I ought, for the benefit of our newer Fellows, to mention some of the steps taken by the Society in order to advance and popularise the science.

In 1878 the President (Mr. C. Greaves) and Council arranged for the delivery of a course of six free public lectures upon Meteorology by experts in various branches. These were published in 1879 under the collective title of *Modern Meteorology,* and were so appreciated upon the Continent that they were translated into German and published at Brunswick in 1882.

In 1881 we commenced our series of annual or triennial Exhibitions of Instruments ancient and modern,—typical, and frequently remarkably ample, illustrations of the development of single instruments, such as barometers, thermometers, hygrometers, anemometers, etc., from the earliest to those of the present day,—these exhibitions being accompanied by a unique series of monographs by our successive Presidents. Fourteen of these exhibitions have been held, and the series of catalogues is a perfect store of information as to instruments ancient and modern.

Another recent addition to our work is the forming and classifying a collection of many hundred photographs of meteorological interest, from which again a further branch has been organised for the preparation and storage of lantern photographs of meteorological subjects, which are lent to our Fellows for lecture purposes.

Of our research and organising work I have not time to speak fully, but among the former I ought to mention the temperature observations on Boston Church Tower and on the tower of Lincoln Cathedral, and those on wind-force at Hersham and on H.M.S. *Worcester.* Of organisations I may quote the Conferences on Phenological Observations, and on Lightning Conductors; and I personally, as Chairman of the Committee of the Royal Society upon the Eruption of Krakatoa, feel bound to express our indebtedness to the two representatives of the Royal Meteorological Society upon that Committee, viz. the Hon. Rollo Russell and Prof. Archibald—our report sufficiently shows the extent and the quality of their work. Very much remains to be done, but there is not time to deal with that to-day.

I hope that this retrospect will stimulate our younger Fellows to see to it that the Centenary may show even a better record than the Jubilee.

JUBILEE ADDRESS.

(Complementary to Mr. Symons'.)

By C. THEODORE WILLIAMS, M.D., F.R.C.P., President.

And now that I have read to you the last sentences which Mr. Symons wrote, I will say a word on the man and his work. Symons was a man of unceasing energy, of extreme ingenuity and foresight and great industry, and withal possessed of a heart as kindly and free from self-seeking as it is possible to conceive. His humility about his achievements was remarkable, but his good-nature and readiness to help other workers, even at a cost of his own valuable time, was more striking still.

Symons was brought up with but small educational advantages, and these only enjoyed early in life. No public school or university education fell to his lot, but having been taught in his early days how to learn, his own dogged perseverance and the school of adversity did the rest. He once related to me that after his father's death, in order to assist his mother, he had to engage in trade, and found it a most uncongenial occupation for a student of science; and when, to his delight, he managed to save enough money, he attended a course of lectures on physics Professor Tyndall was then giving at the Normal School, South Kensington. This course was so well mastered by young Symons, that at the examination at its close he came out first, and naturally attracted the Professor's attention and his kindly interest, and afterwards, on Symons asking his help towards a scientific career, Tyndall persuaded Admiral FitzRoy to give him an appointment in the newly-organised Meteorological Department, where he remained for some years, thus reminding us of the well-known introduction of Faraday to Sir Humphry Davy.

But the trammels of official life could not long bind such an independent spirit as Symons', which burned to investigate the universe in his own way, and foreseeing the enormous importance a knowledge of the rainfall would prove, when questions of supplying large towns with water arose, he began his observations on rainfall, and by example and perseverance enlisted a vast number of observers all over the country, himself inspecting the gauges and collating all the observations; and year by year the numbers of stations and observers increased, so that at the time of his death there were 3414 stations scattered throughout England and Wales, Scotland and Ireland, garrisoned by the largest army of voluntary observers ever known in any country. The results of all the records are embodied in the volumes of *British Rainfall*, which is a standard work, indispensable not only to meteorologists, but also to civil engineers, horticulturists, and sanitary experts among others.

Mr. Symons, like many distinguished men, owed much to his mother, who was evidently a woman of considerable intellect and power, and, as Mr. Charles Harding informs me, in the early days of the rainfall organisation assisted her son greatly in clerical work and in discussion of the results.

Mr. Symons was a pleasant speaker and a fluent and easy writer, and his letters to the *Times* on meteorological subjects were welcome to that journal and its large circle of readers, while his own *Magazine* was always well worth reading. His ingenuity was shown in the number of improvements he introduced into meteorological instruments—witness the earth-thermometers and the rain-gauges.

He devised the brontometer which was exhibited at the Royal Society in 1890, a rather complex instrument which registers each lightning flash, measures the interval before the thunderclap, and records (1) the duration of the latter, (2) the time and duration of the rain and hail, also (3) the variations in atmospheric pressure, as well as the wind pressure.

In Mr. Symons' garden was a complete station abounding in ingenious contrivances, and in his house was one of the best—perhaps the very best—meteorological library in existence, containing many curious old works, besides the modern literature of the subject in all languages; but he did not restrict himself to meteorology, but collected books generally with all the ardour of a bibliophile. But, in describing Mr. Symons, we must never forget how the goodness of his heart enhanced the greatness of his genius, and rendered it doubly useful to his fellow-workers, and it was this Society which profited most largely by the generous combination. If ever, through illness or absence, the promised paper or address were not forthcoming, Mr. Symons was always ready with a contribution, which was sure to be instructive and edifying, and would lead to a good discussion. By his will Mr. Symons bequeaths to the Society £200, the great bulk of his library, and the album of photographs presented to him by the Fellows in 1879.

When we review his life and work, we cannot but come to the conclusion that he has not lived in vain, that while himself actively urging on the progress of meteorological science, he organised his large body of efficient workers to pursue his labours after him, and he bequeaths to us —most precious legacy of all—his own bright example.

In addition to the work mentioned in Mr. Symons' Address, our Society maintains a number of meteorological stations, and these are of two kinds.

1. Second order stations organised in 1874, where regular observations on pressure, temperature, humidity, wind, cloud and rain, etc., are conducted twice a day, viz. at 9 a.m. and p.m. The number of these is 23.

2. Climatological stations started on January 1, 1880. Of these there are 70, where the observations are only taken once a day, at 9 a.m. All these stations are regularly inspected by our Assistant-Secretary and reported on to the Council. The returns are received in our office and then checked and printed in the *Meteorological Record.*

Phenological observations have been carried on for many years, first under the superintendence of the Rev. T. A. Preston, and subsequently under Mr. Mawley's direction.

The Society has of late years made several scientific investigations, two of which call for special notice.

1. Thunderstorm investigations. This resulted in a most interesting collection of photographs of lightning, and it has demonstrated that the old conventional form of flash, as seen in many well-known paintings, is erroneous, and that it really resembles the discharging spark or stream to be seen at the pole of an electric battery. Moreover, that when a photograph of an electric spark is compared with a lightning flash, they are seen to be almost identical. Turner, of all landscape painters, as Mr. Inwards has shown, seems to have most truthfully portrayed the lightning flash.

2. The wind-force experiments, on which a Committee has been engaged for some years, are at the present moment being continued on H.M.S. *Worcester*, under the superintendence of Captain Wilson-Barker. An outcome of this research has been the invention of an entirely new form of anemometer by Mr. Dines, which has now been largely tested, and found of superior efficacy to its predecessors. In order to assist such investigations, the Society has founded a Research Fund, grants from which have been made for this and like work, and at times grants have also been obtained from the Government Grant Committee.

To promote the study of Meteorology among the rising generation, the Society yearly awards a medal to the Cadet on board H.M.S. *Worcester* who displays the greatest knowledge of Meteorology.

With regard to publications—we began by publishing, for 10 years, *Reports of the Council;* we then changed to *Proceedings*, of which we brought out 5 volumes; but in 1872 the *Quarterly Journal* of the Society was successfully evolved, and has continued to the present time. Our *Meteorological Record* began in 1881 and is therefore in its 19th year of existence. Two other publications deserve special notice:—The *Hints to Meteorological Observers*, by the Assistant-Secretary, Mr. Marriott, which has gone through four editions, and *Instructions for the Observation of Phenological Phenomena*, which has reached two editions. The Society has a large and valuable Library, and in 1890 published an excellent *Catalogue*.

Much we owe to Dr. Scott, F.R.S., our Foreign Secretary, for invaluable help in the way of papers, whether from his own pen or contributions from the Meteorological Office with which he was for so many years connected, and we trust we may look to his successor in the Office, Mr. Shaw, for a continuance of kind assistance. Also to Mr. Bayard, our late President (and present Honorary Secretary), for utilising the Society's records on the climatology of Great Britain in various valuable papers.

The office establishment of the Society consists of the Assistant-Secretary and four Computers, and, as may well be imagined, their hands are always full. Our finances are satisfactory, and we have some invested funds, and had we more money at our disposal we should undertake fresh lines of investigation and further advance our science.

Meteorology appeals to all classes, high and low, rich and poor. Its subject, the weather, entwines itself into every one's life, and, no matter what the proposed plan of action may be, it claims recognition. A sound knowledge of Meteorology is of practical use to the civil engineer, the horticulturist, the agriculturist, the mariner, and to many others, but this is only to be obtained by regular and patient observation of the face of nature and of her smiles and frowns. I will not conclude with my own words, however, when I can quote those of an old meteorologist and a member of one of the Societies which preceded ours, the late John Ruskin, the master of poetical prose, who says of Meteorology:—

"But it is a science of the pure air and the bright heavens; its thoughts are amidst the loveliness of Creation; it leads the mind as well as the eye to the morning mist, and the noon-day glory, and the twilight cloud—to the purple peace of the mountain heaven—to the cloudy repose of the green valley; now expatiating in the silence of stormless æther—now on the rushing of the wings of the wind. It is indeed a knowledge which must be felt to be, in its very essence, full of the soul of the beautiful. For its interest, it is universal, unabated in every place, and in all time. He whose kingdom is the heaven, can never meet with an uninteresting space—can never exhaust the phenomena of an hour: he is in a realm of perpetual change,—of eternal motion—of infinite mystery. Light and darkness, and cold and heat, are to him as friends of familiar countenance, but of infinite variety of conversation; and while the geologist yearns for the mountain, the botanist for the field, and the mathematician for the study, the meteorologist, like a spirit of a higher order than any, rejoices in the kingdoms of the air."

The PRESIDENT then presented to each of the Delegates a Bronze Commemoration Medal, bearing on the obverse a portrait of Luke Howard, F.R.S., which had been struck as a memento of the Jubilee of the Society.

Prof. J. J. THOMSON rose on behalf of the Royal Society to convey the congratulations of that body to the Royal Meteorological Society, and to express their sympathy on the death of Mr. Symons, who was latterly a member of the Council of the Royal Society. He said there was hardly a department of science that was not connected in some way with Meteorology, and some of the most difficult problems were those suggested by its study. Some of these questions dealt equally with other branches of science, making the task of solving them more difficult to the meteorologist, for unfortunately nature would mix up her forces, and thus prevented her problems being dealt with one at a time. It would thus be seen of what great importance an established laboratory for making investigations would be, and the great help that would be afforded in knowing what to look for when carrying out research. It was surprising to find that in a science that appealed so greatly to every one, no Chair of Meteorology was maintained at any of the teaching centres in the kingdom, and he would recommend that a proposal for remedying that defect should be put forward for the greater advancement of meteorological knowledge generally.

Mr. E. B. KNOBEL, President of the Royal Astronomical Society, spoke on behalf of that Society. He pointed out a curious error in Admiral Smyth's work, *Speculum Hartwellianum*, p. 385, where the formation of the British Meteorological Society is described as taking place on April 4, not April 3, 1850. The subject of Meteorology was extremely interesting to all, and the late Prof. Daniell once said man may with propriety be said to be a meteorologist by nature. This was doubtless true, with the notable exception of Dr. Johnson, who professed his inability to understand the subject. The science of Astronomy was closely connected with Meteorology, and depended greatly on the refined character of meteorological instruments in the reduction of observations. There was one branch of Meteorology, namely refraction, which had not received the attention it deserved, and which had made no advance during recent years. Manuel Johnson, in his observations at St. Helena, pointed out that the refraction for observations made over the land was not the same as for observations made over the sea, and no doubt many points would be cleared up were the subject given more prominence. This Society had always struck him (Mr. Knobel) by its great number of disinterested men, and it might fairly be said that this country was the home of amateur science and research. As recently as the previous evening news had been received of the discovery of the South Magnetic Pole by the Southern Cross Expedition. Mr. Gladstone had remarked thirty years ago that it was the distinction and pride of England to do by individual effort what in other countries is only attained by influence and patronage. This trait was very remarkably exemplified in the late Mr. Symons and his work, and reflected greatly to his credit.

Mr. J. J. H. TEALL, as representative of the Geological Society, referred to the interesting observations made by Dr. Plot two hundred years ago, and spoke of the climatic effect of the weather on the composition of geological formations and on the forms of the earth's surface. He was deeply interested in the work and the progress of the Royal Meteorological Society, and esteemed the invitation to be present as a great favour.

Dr. G. HELLMANN said :—Herr President! Meine Herren!—Die Deutsche Meteorologische Gesellschaft hat mich entsandt, um ihrer ältesten Schwestergesellschaft, der Royal Meteorological Society, zu deren fünfzigjährigen Stiftungsfeste die herzlichsten und die aufrichtigsten Glückünsche auszusprechen und zugleich eine Adresse zu überreichen, in der diese Wünsche dauernden schriftlichen Ausdruck gefunden haben.

Indem ich mich dieses ehrenvollen Auftrages hiermit erledige, sei es mir gestattet, den Inhalt der Adresse mit einigen Worten in englischer Sprache zu erläutern.

DER ROYAL METEOROLOGICAL SOCIETY IN LONDON ZUM 3 APRIL 1900.

Die Feier des funfzigjahrigen Bestehens, welche die Royal Meteorological Society am heutigen Tage begeht, giebt der Deutschen Meteorologischen Gesellschaft willkommene Gelegenheit, ihrer altesten Schwestergesellschaft die herzlichsten Glückwunsche darzubringen und zugleich der hohen Achtung Ausdruck zu geben, welche die Royal Meteorological Society in deutschen Fachkreisen geniesst.

Die Gründung der Royal Meteorological Society fallt in eine Zeit, in der Grossbritannien eines Sammelpunktes für die meteorologischen Arbeiten und Bestrebungen des Landes dringend bedurfte.

Die Meteorologie erfreute sich damals in England noch keiner staatlichen Fürsorge, dagegen stand, merkwurdig genug, die Astro-Meteorologie wieder in hohem Ansehen.

Da war es ein erstes, grosses Verdienst der neu gegründeten British Meteorological Society, dass sie diesen Einflüssen nachdrucklich entgegentrat und durch ernste, wissenschaftliche Arbeit die Bestrebungen der nach solchen Zielen gerichteten Vereine zu nichte machte.

Dazu traten bald weitere, positive Leistungen von hervorragender Bedeutung für die Meteorologie im Allgemeinen wie für die klimatologische Erschliessung des Inselreiches.

Die stattliche Reihe der Veröffentlichungen der Gesellschaft, die eine Fülle der werthvollsten Abhandlungen und Discussionen in sich bergen, spricht am besten für das zielbewusste Streben und für den streng wissenschaftlichen Geist der Gesellschaft.

Durch die Einrichtung verschiedener Netze von Beobachtungsstationen mit mustergultiger Aufstellung der Instrumente sowie durch die Untersuchung wichtiger meteorologischer Fragen in Sonderausschüssen, hat die Royal Meteorological Society in vorzüglicher Weise viel von dem geleistet, was in anderen Ländern den Staatsinstituten zu erledigen zufällt.

Möge dieser rege wissenschaftliche Geist auch fernerhin in der Gesellschaft walten, möge es ihr vergönnt sein, sich in der Zukunft stets neue grosse Aufgaben zu stellen und einer glücklichen Lösung zuzuführen: der Meteorologie zum Nutzen und Frommen, den Mitgliedern zur Ehre und zur Befriedigung.

Die Deutsche Meteorologische Gesellschaft.

Dr. v. BEZOLD. Dr. W. KÖPPEN.

O. BEHRE. G. HELLMANN. V. KREMSER. A. SPRUNG.

[*Translation.*]

TO THE ROYAL METEOROLOGICAL SOCIETY IN LONDON ON APRIL 3, 1900.

The occasion of its fiftieth anniversary, which the Royal Meteorological Society celebrates on this day, gives an opportunity to the German Meteorological Society to express to its eldest sister Society its most hearty congratulations, and also to assure it of the very high esteem which the Royal Meteorological Society has gained for itself among the students of the science in Germany.

The foundation of the Meteorological Society occurred at an epoch when the want of a central organisation to collect and systematise meteorological works and investigations was most urgently felt in the British Isles. At that date no Government support was available for Meteorology, and, on the other hand, Astro-Meteorology was in very considerable repute.

It is a great merit of the newly-established British Meteorological Society that it set itself decidedly against such theories, and that by dint of careful scientific work it succeeded in putting a stop to the operations of the Association for the prosecution of Astro-Meteorology.

In addition, the Society was able to show more extensive and careful investigations which were of the highest importance for the development of the climatology of the United Kingdom.

The noble series of publications of the Society, which contain stores of papers and discussions of very high value, is the best proof of the persistent activity and the strict scientific spirit of the Society.

The Society has itself been able to do much of the work which falls on Government institutions elsewhere. It has organised networks of observing stations and enforced uniform conditions of instrumental exposure, and it has entrusted to various special committees the examination of numerous scientific problems.

We can only express the hope that this spirit of scientific inquiry will live on in the future, and that it may be granted to it to achieve still more important results in the furtherance of our science which may redound to the honour of its future Fellows.

The German Meteorological Society.

Dr. v. Bezold. Dr. W. Köppen.

O. Behre. G. Hellmann. V. Kremser. A. Sprung.

Dr. G. Hellmann continued:—Mr. President, Gentlemen—After having thus far performed my official duties, I may be allowed to address to the honourable assembly some words in English, asking at the outset your kind indulgence to all linguistic blunders I may commit.

The Royal Meteorological Society was founded at a time when a centre of union for the meteorological work done in Great Britain was much needed. The Government had then not yet provided for an official meteorological service—that of the Board of Trade being established only in 1855—whereas, curiously enough, Astro-Meteorology began anew to come into favour in this country. Already the original "Meteorological Society of London" was much influenced with such ideas, as has been also pointed out in the interesting address prepared by your late President (Mr. Symons) for the Commemoration Meeting of to-day; and other Societies of a similar character were hereafter founded, as the "Astro-Meteorological Society" and the "Copernican Meteorological Society," both of which have been forgotten long ago.

Under these circumstances it can be considered to have been the first great merit of the newly-formed "British Meteorological Society" that it wholly ignored the old one, and that it combated those perverse astro-meteorological efforts and tendencies by really scientific work.

Indeed, gentlemen, your Society has from its beginning always deserved well of Meteorology in general, and in later years also of the Climatological Survey of Great Britain.

By the organisation of several systems of well-equipped stations, and by the institution of special committees for inquiry into important meteorological questions, the Royal Meteorological Society has done in the best way a good deal of that work which in other countries is incumbent upon the meteorological offices of the Government. And the splendid series of the Society's publications, which contain numerous valuable papers with their no less valuable discussions, most clearly prove that the Royal Meteorological Society is in the best sense of the word a learned Society, highly esteemed all over the world, wherever scientific

Meteorology is cared for and cultivated. May—this is the hearty wish of the German Meteorological Society, which I have the honour of representing here—may, I say, the scientific spirit prevailing in your work be maintained, may also in the future the Society be able to put forward new great problems and to solve them: for the benefit of the science, and for the honour and satisfaction of the Royal Meteorological Society.

Mr. R. C. Mossman, as delegate of the Scottish Meteorological Society, spoke of the mutual relations existing between the two Societies. He regretted the absence of Dr. Buchan, whose substitute he was, and who was prevented from appearing through serious domestic illness. He wished to express his congratulations and best wishes to the Royal Meteorological Society.

Mr. A. Wynter Blyth spoke of the connection between Meteorology and Hygiene, and offered his congratulations on behalf of the Sanitary Institute. The effect of the weather on health was very pronounced: the advent of either cold or hot weather produced marked changes in the death-rate. There were no extensive Bills in Parliament that did not deal in some way with the two sciences, and the late Mr. Symons was always in request at the House in connection with questions dealing with meteorological and sanitary matters.

The President (Dr. C. Theodore Williams), in reply, said he was much gratified to receive the congratulations and good wishes of the various Delegates, and hoped that all present would be able to take part in the Conversazione and the Dinner.

Mr. W. Marriott referred to the apparent discrepancy in the date of the formation of the Society in Admiral Smyth's book, mentioned by Mr. Knobel, and stated that the original meeting was held on April 3, but adjourned to the next day, April 4. Mr. Marriott also announced the arrangements for the evening and the following day, and hoped that all the Fellows would find instruction as well as pleasure in the various interesting objects which had been prepared for them.

CONVERSAZIONE,

April 3, 1900.

The President and Mrs. Theodore Williams received the Guests in the Central Gallery at the Royal Institute of Painters in Water Colours, Piccadilly

Lantern Demonstrations were given in the East Gallery as follows:—

9.15—Mr. T. C. Porter (of Eton).
Views showing the growth of Eclipse of the Shadow of the Peak of Teneriffe by the Shadow of the Earth.

Col. H. M. Saunders.
Clouds.

10.15—Mr. W. Marriott.
(*a*) Slides illustrating Meteorological Phenomena.
(*b*) Portraits of Presidents of the Royal Meteorological Society.

Refreshments were served in the West Gallery.

PROGRAMME OF MUSIC

PLAYED BY

THE BAND OF THE ROYAL ARTILLERY IN THE EAST GALLERY.

1.	MARCH	"El Capitan"	*Sousa.*
2.	OVERTURE	"La Couronne d'Or"	*Herman.*
3.	IDYLL	"Evening Breeze"	*Langey.*
4.	SELECTION	"The Belle of New York"	*Kerker.*
5.	GAVOTTE	"La Princesse"	*Czibulka.*
6.	SONG (Cornet Solo)	"Songs of Araby"	*Clay.*
7.	VALSE	"Verborgene Perlen"	*Ziebrer.*
8.	SELECTION	"San Toy"	*Jones.*
9.	PIZZICATI	"Sylvia"	*Delibes.*
10.	MARCH	"A Frangesa"	*Kaiser.*
11.	INTERMEZZO	"Danse des Bacchantes"	*Gounod.*
12.	UNGARISCHER TANZ (No. 2)		*Brahms.*
13.	LIED	"Gute Nacht"	*Kucken.*
14.	SELECTION	"Gems of England"	*Binding.*

"God Save the Queen."

Conductor . . . . Sergt.-Major W. SUGG.

PROGRAMME OF MUSIC

PERFORMED BY

THE "SCHARTAU" PART-SINGERS (under the direction of Mr. Herbert Schartau).

BOAT SONG	"Row, gently Row"	*Cowen.*
GLEE	"My Celia's Arbour"	*Horsley.*
PART-SONG	(*a*) "The Soldier's Farewell"	*Kinkel.*
HUMOROUS RECITATIVE	(*b*) "Three Little Kittens"	*M.S.*
BALLAD (*with vocal accompaniment*)	"Thinking of Home"	*Millard.*
MADRIGAL	"This pleasant Month of May"	*Beale.*
THURINGIAN VOLKSLIED	(*a*) "My flaxen-hair'd Nanny"	*S.A.*
HUMOROUS QUARTET	(*b*) "Only Once"	*M.S.*
SWEDISH MELODY	(*a*) "Come, Zephyr, gently"	*Jüngst.*
HUMOROUS QUARTET	(*b*) "Master Johnny Horner"	*M.S.*
HARMONISED MELODY	"On the Banks of Allan Water"	*Scotch.*
HUMOROUS QUARTET	"The Chafers"	*Trühn.*
PART-SONG	"Ladybird, fly away Home"	*Cowen.*

CATALOGUE OF THE METEOROLOGICAL INSTRUMENTS, &c.,

EXHIBITED IN THE BANQUETING-ROOM.

CAMBRIDGE SCIENTIFIC INSTRUMENT CO.

- Callendar's Recording Thermometer.
- Callendar's Sunshine Recorder.

MR. C. F. CASELLA, F.R.Met.Soc.

- Maximum Thermometer.
- Minimum Thermometer.
- Dry and Wet Bulb Thermometers.
- Bifurcated Grass Minimum Thermometer.
- Black and Bright Bulb Maximum Thermometers *in vacuo.*
- Earth Thermometers, 6 in. and 1 ft.
- Case for holding Meteorological Instruments under a Thatch Shelter at Stations in Tropical Africa.
- Fortin Barometer.
- Kew Barometer.

Mountain Barometer.
Boylean-Mariotte Barometer.
Collie's Barometer for Travellers.
Aneroids.
Snowdon Rain Gauge.
Meteorological Office Rain Gauge.
Symons' Mountain Rain Gauge.
Engineer's Large Mountain Float Rain Gauge.
Dines' (G.) Dew-Point Hygrometer.
Lambrecht's Polymeter.
Well Thermometer.
Miller-Casella Deep-Sea Thermometer.
Whipple-Casella Sunshine Recorder.
Dines' (W. H.) Ether Sunshine Recorder.
Dines' (W. H.) Portable Pressure Tube Anemometer.
Richards' Recording Instruments :—
Barograph.
Dry and Wet Bulb Thermograph.
Hair Hygrometer.
Rain Gauge, float pattern.
Anemometer.

Mr. W. H. Dines, B.A., F.R.Met.Soc.
Apparatus for Illustrating the Formation of the Tornado Cloud. (Demonstrations were given at intervals during the evening.)

Mr. W. H. George.
Instruments used by Dr. Livingstone and Captain Cameron :—
Pocket Compass.
Boiling-Point Thermometer.
Photographs of Dr. Livingstone and Dr. Moffat.

Mr. Walter M. Gibson.
Five Medals awarded to the late Prof. J. F. Daniell, F.R.S.
Photographs of Prof. Daniell and Prof. Faraday.
Bust of Prof. Daniell.

Mr. James Glaisher, F.R.S.
Aneroid Barometer used by Mr. Glaisher and Mr. Coxwell in their Balloon Ascent from Wolverhampton, on September 5, 1862, when they attained an altitude of seven miles from the earth.
Portrait of Mr. James Glaisher, F.R.S., Founder of the Royal Meteorological Society.

Mr. Alfred J. Hands, F.R.Met.Soc.
Model of Chimney Shaft, fitted with Lightning Conductors.
Coronal Band, with points for top of Chimney, as recommended by the Lightning Rod Conference.
Specimens of Copper Tape, etc., for Lightning Conductors.

Mr. J. J. Hicks, F.R.Met.Soc.
Mountain Barometer.
Watkin Aneroid.
Clinical Thermometers, with magnifying fronts.
Alarm Thermometer.
Grass Minimum Thermometer with Shield hermetically sealed over the divisions.
Circular Maximum and Minimum Thermometers.
Solar-radiation Thermometer.
Solar-radiation Thermometer with Radiometer.
Phillips' Maximum Thermometer, made by Prof. J. Phillips, F.R.S., 1832.
George's Artificial Horizon.
Clinometer for use on board ship.
Sphygmometer.

Meteorological Council.
Campbell Wooden Sunshine Bowls.

Mr. R. C. Mossman, F.R.S.E.
Meteorograph for use with Kites.

Mr. R. W. MUNRO, F.R.Met.Soc.

Dines' Pressure-tube Recording Anemometer.
Dines' Pressure-tube Sight-Indicating Anemometer.

Messrs. NEGRETTI & ZAMBRA.

Maximum Thermometer.
Minimum Thermometer.
Grass-Minimum Thermometer with Link Bulb.
Solar-radiation Thermometer with Mercurial Test Gauge.
Black and Bright Bulb Thermometers, as used at the Montsouris Observatory, Paris.
Negretti & Zambra's Electrical Turnover Dry and Wet Bulb Thermometers.
Negretti & Zambra's Marine Thermometer for shallow depths.
Negretti & Zambra's Recording Deep-Sea Thermometer.
Magnaghi's Frame for Negretti & Zambra's Reversing Thermometer.
Long-Range Mercurial and Glycerine Barometer.
Morland's Diagonal Barometer.
Combined Barograph and Thermograph.
Symons' Storm Rain Gauge.
Negretti & Zambra's Self-recording Rain Gauge.
Campbell-Stokes Sunshine Recorder.
Jordan Photographic Sunshine Recorder.
Robinson Anemometer.

ROYAL GEOGRAPHICAL SOCIETY.

Aneroid used by Lieut. Grandy, R.N., on his journey in the Lower Congo region, 1873, in search of Dr. Livingstone.
Two Aneroids carried by Lieut. Cameron, R.N., on his journey across Africa, 1874.
Watkin Aneroid, recently carried by Mr. H. J. Mackinder to the top of Mount Kenia.

ROYAL METEOROLOGICAL SOCIETY.

Climatological Station.—Enclosure with instruments necessary for the equipment of a Climatological Station of the Royal Meteorological Society.
Models of Hailstones, 7 inches in circumference, which fell near Montreaux, France, August 15, 1888.
Albums containing photographs of the Stations of the Royal Meteorological Society, taken by Mr. W. Marriott, 1884-99.
Album containing photographs of Clouds, taken by the late Hon. R. Abercromby.
Jubilee Commemoration Medal, April 3, 1900.
Lantern Slides.
Frames of photographs illustrating Meteorological phenomena :—

1. Lightning Flashes.
2. Damage caused by Lightning, Wind, and Tornadoes.
3. Damage caused by Floods.
4. Frost, Snow, and Hail.
5. Instruments and Kite Experiments.
6–9. Clouds.

The late Mr. G. J. SYMONS, F.R.S. (the Executors of).

A Meteorologist's Library, A.D. 1500.
Alleged "Thunderbolts" exposed at the Meeting of the Royal Meteorological Society, March 21, 1888.
The first Rainfall Map.
First Daily Weather Maps, Volume of.
Testimonial Album presented to Mr. G. J. Symons, F.R.S., by the Fellows of the Royal Meteorological Society, 1879.
Portion of Tree damaged by Tornado in Wiltshire, October 1, 1899.

Mr. W. H. TINGEY, F.R.Met.Soc.

Tingey's Electrical Anemometer Recorder.

Mr. FRANK WILSON.

Several Instruments used by Dr. Livingstone.

COMMEMORATION DINNER,

April 4, 1900.

The concluding function of the Jubilee Celebration was a Dinner held at Westminster Palace Hotel, Victoria Street, S.W., on Wednesday evening, April 4. The company included :—

Dr. C. Theodore Williams, President, in the Chair.

Mr. R. Alford
Dr. Clifford Allbutt
Dr. R. Barnes
Mr. F. C. Bayard
Mr. S. C. Bayard
Mr. L. Beard
Mr. R. Bentley
Mr. A. W. Blyth
Mr. J. W. Bolton
Mr. F. J. Brodie
Mr. C. J. Bromhead
Mr. A. H. Brown
Dr. K. Buée.
Mr. W. H. Butlin and friend
Capt. A. Carpenter
Mr. G. Charsley
Dr. Church, President, Royal College of Physicians
Sir Ernest Clarke
Mr. R. S. Clarke
Mr. A. Collenette
Major J. W. N. Cotton
Mr. R. H. Curtis
Mr. H. N. Dickson
Mr. J. Dover
Mr. F. Druce
Mr. F. B. Edmonds
Mr. A. T. Flagg
Major L. Flower
Mr. W. L. Fox
Mr. W. H. Gunner
Mr. H. Harries
Mr. C. Hawksley
Mr. K. Hawksley
Dr. G. Hellmann
Capt. M. W. C. Hepworth
Mr. J. Hunter
Mr. R. Inwards
Mr. H. Gwyn Jeffreys
Major E. Jones
Mr. B. Latham
Prof. J. K. Laughton
Mr. W. Marriott
Mr. W. J. Marriott
Mr. E. Mawley
Mr. W. B. Myers-Beswick
Gen. Sir H. W. Norman
Dr. Pavy, President, Royal Medical and Chirurgical Society
Mr. F. J. Ratcliffe
Mr. T. F. Read
Mr. T. F. Read, Jun.
Mr. H. Rofe
Mr. W. N. Shaw
Mr. W. F. Stanley
Mr. J. J. Steward and friend
Dr. J. T. Thomas
Prof. S. P. Thompson, President, Institution of Electrical Engineers
Dr. B. A. Whitelegge
Dr. D. Williams
Dr. J. R. Williams
Mr. C. J. R. Wilson
Mr. C. L. N. Wilson
Capt. D. Wilson-Barker
Mr. E. Worrall
Mr. Wynne-Williams
Daily Chronicle
Daily Graphic
Daily News
Daily Telegraph
Morning Post
Standard
Times

MENU.

Appetisers in variety.

Soups.

Clear Turtle. Barley Cream.

Fish.

Turbot with Cardinal Sauce. Fillets of Soles à la Normande.

Entrées.

Chickens à la Demi-deuill.
Stuffed Quails with Perigueux Sauce.

Joint.

Roast Saddles of Mutton.
Spinach. Potatoes. French Beans.

Punch à la Romaine.

Roast.

Roast Ducklings and Peas. Salads.

Sweets.

Fruit Cakes with Cream Sauce.
Stewed Apples and Rice with Whipped Cream.

Ice.

Noyeau Ice Bomb.

Savoury.

Mushrooms with Soft Roes.

Dessert.

After Dinner, the PRESIDENT said :—Gentlemen—It is my privilege to begin the toasts this evening by proposing that toast which is of course most acceptable to us all, that is the health of Her Majesty the Queen and their Royal Highnesses the Prince and Princess of Wales. We need not say much about Her Majesty, who is endeared to our hearts, and whom we respect for her many acts of kindness to all her subjects. It is curious that the older she grows the more interest she takes in her kingdom and her subjects. Apart from the fact that she brings sunshine and happiness wherever she goes, she is a woman of the greatest tact and knowledge. It is said she is the first foreign minister in Europe, and knows more about foreign affairs than any living minister. She is a model sovereign, and we obey her slightest wishes because we not only respect, but love her.

As a meteorologist I have tried to discover the reasons for Her Majesty's high standard of life, and have noticed in reading the *Court Journal* that Her Majesty goes out in her donkey-chair in the morning and takes drives every afternoon. She is a great worshipper of open air. She is in fact a true meteorologist, going out in all weathers. You will be glad to hear too that she maintains a good meteorological station at Osborne, and in addition to that keeps a private diary where meteorological observations are recorded every evening. In addition, at Braemar there is a well-known station, which was originally started by the late lamented Prince Consort (reporting to our sister Society of Scotland). I hope now I have convinced you that, in addition to her other virtues, Her Majesty is a good meteorologist.

As regards the Prince and Princess of Wales, they enter into all our work and our pleasures. If there is a good deed to be done in starting a hospital-ship, inspecting volunteers, laying the foundation-stones of public institutions, there the Prince and Princess are to be found, ready to do all good work, and to do it thoroughly. No other nation is equally blest with such a Royal Family. I have great pleasure in giving the health of Her Majesty and the Prince and Princess of Wales.

The toasts having been honoured, the company sang "God Save the Queen."

Prof. J. K. LAUGHTON.—The toast I have the honour to propose is one that perhaps eighteen months or two years ago might have called forth quite other remarks than it does at the present time. Naval men, from the circumstances of their profession, are meteorologists, and soldiers on active service have the pleasure of spending days and nights in the open air, and studying the book of the sun, moon, and stars, in their relation to the weather; so that as practical meteorologists both sailors and soldiers come in the first rank. But I think at the present time our thoughts on the Navy, the Army, and the Reserve Forces run in a different direction. We do not consider them in their secondary capacity as meteorologists, but in their primary capacity as fighting men. At the present time our hearts are full of the gallant deeds of the sailors and soldiers of the regular and auxiliary forces—the British born or Colonial. I have the honour of asking you to drink to "The Navy, the Army, and the Auxiliary Forces." I am permitted to couple with the Navy the name of Capt. Carpenter, and with the Army that of Gen. Sir Henry Norman.

Capt. A. CARPENTER.—On behalf of the Navy I thank Prof. Laughton for the encomiums he has passed on that branch of H.M. forces to which I belong, and you gentlemen for the hearty manner in which you echoed the toast. I think the Navy just now is a service to which any man may be proud to belong, and that we may surely trust it with the safety, honour, and welfare of this country.

There is, however, a pernicious motto floating about, rather popular just now, "Si vis pacem para bellum"—"If you wish for peace be prepared for war." You must remember that if all nations followed that maxim the state of tension would become dangerous, and that it leads to increased armaments.

But the Navy has a peaceful as well as a warlike side, and I should like to deal with the former to-night. We have our surveying-ships all over the world, charting the coasts, discovering hidden dangers in the ocean, and opening up new ports; indeed they may be called the pioneers of commercial prosperity. On board of these surveying-vessels there are officers who specially devote their time to meteorological research, and, situated as they are where the aerial and liquid oceans meet, they are in an exceedingly good position to note the phenomena of both. While on the China station for some ten years I owed my life, and the safety of my ship, on more than one occasion to the splendid researches made by the older meteorologists into the course, direction of wind, and special characteristics of the violent typhoons that rage in those seas; and I may here remark that among those who made these researches were many distinguished officers of the Mercantile Marine.

I am of opinion that in times of peace our Navy should devote more time than it does to geographical and meteorological research; and it seems as if the old roving, pioneering spirit was dying away when the Admiralty permit a Nansen or a Borchgrevink to secure the laurels that lie within our reach.

Gen. Sir Henry Norman.—I am extremely obliged for what has been said about the Army. I do not think I need mention any of its ancient performances. It has been distinguished in every part of the world, from Paris to Pekin, from Copenhagen to Abyssinia, and the present Army is now well upholding the credit gained by its ancestors. We never had such an Army in the field, for size; and I do not know that we have had one with a more difficult task to perform—with a brave, skilful enemy, and difficult country. That Army is composed in a way we have never seen before—not only are there a number of Volunteers, Militia, and Yeomanry, but the Army has never been so representative of the possessions of Her Majesty from Australia, Canada, and the Cape. All these Auxiliary Forces have distinguished themselves immensely; they seem to be admirably suited for the kind of warfare in which they are engaged. What can I say of the Regular Forces of Her Majesty: they have distinguished themselves on every sort of occasion. The other day under Buller, when, after an heroic service, one regiment had only 100 men left unwounded, these 100 men volunteered to lead the assault, although they had scarcely any officers. On that occasion we lost eleven guns and suffered most severely, and I happen to know that the military attaché of a great foreign army wrote to his sovereign and said there was nothing to equal the dash and determination of the British soldier. On the whole, I think we have raised the credit of the British Army to a very high point indeed. We all have many friends in South Africa, and do not know at what moment we may hear that they are killed or wounded, but we know they will do their duty thoroughly. I may mention, as a matter of interest, that the commander of that force was my comrade in many fights: I saw him the first time he was under fire. He has a clear head and a brave heart, and you may depend upon it he will lead the war to a successful and satisfactory issue.

But I came here not to return thanks for the Army, but as a Delegate from the Royal Geographical Society to the Royal Meteorological Society, and I must deliver the message entrusted to me. The President of the Royal Geographical Society desires to congratulate the Royal Meteorological Society on this auspicious occasion. Atmospheric phenomena are so closely connected with questions in physical geography, that geographical science is largely benefited by the prosperity of the Royal Meteorological Society.

There have always been the most friendly relations between the Societies, and I have no doubt these relations will continue.

I think I ought to say something about my humble connection with Meteorology. In the two Colonies of which I was Governor great attention was paid to Meteorology. In Jamaica both Mr. Maxwell Hall and Mr. Johnston took voluntarily a great interest in Meteorology. They established stations, and started Dr. Morris, our Botanist, in an observatory on the top of Blue Mountain Peak, 7300 feet above the sea, by far the highest station in the British West Indies. Meteorological observations have been carried on for a series of years.

In Queensland the meteorologist is Mr. Clement Wragge, who started the observatory on Ben Nevis. He has a network of meteorological observing stations throughout Queensland, and has brought them into communication with the French Colony of New Caledonia. He issues Weather Reports every day, with information from every part of the world, and these are taken advantage of by captains of ships and others, who do not put to sea when Wragge has prophesied a hurricane. I hope his work will go on and prosper.

I am exceedingly obliged for the opportunity this Society has afforded me of going over the Royal Observatory at Greenwich to-day.

Mr. W. N. Shaw, F.R.S.—It falls to me to propose the important toast of "The Royal Meteorological Society." In doing so it is natural to turn one's attention to the future, and only to recall the past in order to derive example and encouragement. The last fifty years have been years of co-operation in meteorological research. Development has chiefly been in the direction of combining the work of many observers in different places for the single purpose of advancing our knowledge of the atmosphere and its phenomena. That was conspicuously the case with the organisation our late lamented President carried through for the observation of rainfall. It is equally manifest if we regard the enormous development of synoptic Meteorology in the United States of America, or the smaller but nevertheless substantial organisations for the same purpose in this country and on the Continent.

It may be said that the chief characteristic of meteorological advance during the last fifty years is co-operation between meteorologists for the purpose of obtaining satisfactory data; and in looking to the future it is quite evident that, stimulated by the example of those who have gone before, we may develop still more the co-operation between meteorologists and between societies and organisations for meteorological research, in order to push further into the region of the unknown and realise the true state of meteorological phenomena. Our late President has practically carried out a meteorological survey of the British Isles, so far as regards rainfall. There are other elements which might be similarly investigated. A complete meteorological survey is greatly to be desired, and it can only be carried out by the most energetic co-operation.

There is, moreover, another point to which I should like to direct your attention. During the last fifty years there has been enormous development in the sciences of physics, chemistry, and biology, and this has given us entirely new ideas about the constituents and modes of action of the atmosphere. In the coming fifty years we may look forward to the application of these ideas to meteorological problems with great expectation of success. Perhaps when these applications are carried out we shall find that some opinions we have carried with us for years require modification if we are to get hold of what Maxwell would have called the "real go" of meteorological phenomena. To take only one example, I am informed that it is possible to find a specimen of air at a temperature of 127°·4 F. if you go to the right place to look for it; and also, without leaving the surface of the earth, it is possible to find a specimen of air with a temperature of -90°·4 F. Now I have a feeling that there is no distinction of caste in the atmosphere, and that the same specimen of air might at one time be at 127°·4, and at another at −90°·4 F., and that the transfer might take place under natural laws. But to change the temperature of a mass of air is a most difficult matter. Air has very little conductivity, so it is difficult to communicate heat to it, and unless you can put it into immediate contact with some body of higher temperature the greater part of the atmosphere has no chance of getting hot. I am aware that if you raise the position of the air it becomes cooled, if you depress it again, it becomes warm. We used in old days, in explaining the trade-winds, to say that the air at the Equator got warmed, and rose in consequence. It then flowed over at the top, cooled, and came down again as a cold current. But I would like to ask how it managed, in coming down, to avoid being warmed to at least the same extent as it was cooled on going up. Indeed, on its way the air very probably lost a certain amount of its moisture as rain, and in doing so appropriated the "heat of evaporation." Without much exaggeration of theory, it would indeed be easy to say that the hot air rising at the Equator gets rid of its moisture, comes down in Siberia with the heat it originally possessed, and with some more besides derived from condensation, and that therefore the temperature of the air in Siberia must be largely in excess of the temperature at the Equator. Somehow, however, it manages to lose heat on the way. Of course one can say "radiation," but the question is not so easy to deal with as it appears. Anybody who will tell us exactly where the radiation comes in, where the heat is lost, and how the air manages to cool itself to such an extent that when it comes to the surface again it has such a very low temperature, will have added a substantial piece of knowledge to meteorological physics.

There are many other questions associated with physics, chemistry, or biology, and for the solution of these we require the co-operation of these sciences in order that we may really explain many meteorological phenomena with which we are in practice extremely familiar. Therefore, in putting before you the toast of "The Royal Meteorological Society," I should like to suggest it to you as the symbol and embodiment of the co-operation of meteorologists and meteorological organisations with each other, and of Meteorology with other sciences, for the purpose of elucidating problems connected with the atmosphere. Such co-operation is happily suggested at a dinner like the present, where we have not only meteorologists, but representatives from other Societies representing sciences with which we are closely associated. I therefore give you the toast of "The Royal Meteorological Society."

It is unnecessary for me to couple any name with this toast. The toast is naturally associated with the President of the Society; but I cannot sit down without thanking him for the able and distinguished way in which he has carried out the difficult task that devolved upon him, under circumstances which no one could have foreseen. I would also mention the admirable manner in which the Secretaries and the Assistant-Secretary have carried out the arrangements of this festival.

The PRESIDENT (Dr. C. THEODORE WILLIAMS).—I feel quite unworthy to reply to this toast, which Mr. Shaw has so kindly connected with my name. The only thing I can say is that I am an old Fellow, and that I have had the pleasure of being President before. I felt it as a great honour when the Society, on the loss of one of our most distinguished Fellows, called upon me to supply his place. I agree with Mr. Shaw that there are many problems to be worked out, and that the important Office of which he is the head should take part in them; but besides, I should like to say a few words as to the features of our Society, and to point out some of its advantages. Meteorology is a science easily cultivated, provided the observations are taken correctly; they can be taken by a man without a high standard of education at all—many excellent observations are taken by gardeners and coachmen—provided the instruments are good and they are regularly inspected. This inspection is attended to by our excellent Assistant-Secretary. I would commend the Society to all those who live in the country. As one of our late Presidents said to me: "It is necessary to take the observations at 9 a.m. and 9 p.m.—that means, the observer must be up before 9 o'clock in the morning, and he cannot be sitting over his cups at 9 o'clock at night, as then he would not be in a fit state to take his observations." Another thing is that, as you must go into the open air for everything, so you become fond of the weather, and your life is exceedingly healthy. To prove that fact, only yesterday we had a message from our senior Fellow, and one of our founders, Mr. James Glaisher, F.R.S. He still goes on with his work and continues his observations, and his report appears every quarter; and I understand that, on Saturday next (April 7), if he lives, as we all hope he will, he will reach the age of ninety-one. Again, our excellent Treasurer (Mr. H. Perigal) who passed away some few years ago, used to be pointed to as a fine example. When he was ninety-two, I had the honour of presiding at a dinner given to him by the various Societies of which he was a member. He made an excellent speech, and was even a little heterodox in the opinions of his old age. He used to attend all the meetings of the Society, and, as far as I remember, died at the ripe age of ninety-seven.

As regards the utility of our Society, you will admit that it takes up the questions of water-supply, ventilation, and climate, and there is no doubt that the knowledge collected by our stations helps a great deal in the advance of sanitary science.

I should like to say a word about other Societies, especially as we are honoured by the presence of representatives from several. I am pleased to see them here, because these Societies are always kind to us, and nothing can be more helpful than the information they give to us. One of the most important is the Royal Astronomical Society: it deals with matter more or less fixed, whereas we unfortunately deal with matters not by any means fixed. One day we have one set of phenomena, the next day another. Still it would be wise for the astronomers to make friends with the meteorologists, for we know that now and then an expedition goes out to observe an eclipse of the sun. When all the instruments are ready Meteorology misbehaves itself and diffuses a fog round the astronomers, or a great nimbus comes down, with thunder, lightning, hail, and rain, and spoils everything. Then we have Sir Henry Norman, who so well represents the Royal Geographical Society. He has told us several things that some of us did not know before. I think he will admit that if there had not been Meteorology, there could not have been Geography. If you had not rainfall you would not have rivers, nor the changes in the earth's crust caused by them, so we are to some extent the parents of Geography. Then there are our botanical and agricultural friends, who will see at once the close connection between Meteorology and Botany, between the supply of rain and the growth of the crops. I have to thank you most warmly for the way you have received this toast, and am sorry that there is not a more able meteorologist in the chair to-night, but there is no one I would yield to in my earnest devotion to the science.

Mr. F. C. Bayard.—I rise, at the command of our President, to give you the toast of "The Delegates from other Societies," who have so kindly honoured us with their presence at our Meeting yesterday, and at our Dinner this evening. I regret to say that he has already taken some of the words I should liked to have said out of my mouth. He has referred to our relations with other Societies, but there is another way of looking at the question. We are all, as it were, parts of one great whole—that is, Science pure and simple. The Geological

Society deals with the subject of the earth; the Institution of Electrical Engineers with the subject of the air; the Royal Agricultural Society deals with the subject of the surface of the ground; the Sanitary Institute deals with problems partly under ground, and partly above. They all come to us for observations of different sorts, and we say we will do our best to supply them. Sometimes these things are very difficult, sometimes very simple. It is not easy to supply the wants of many Societies working on different lines. The President of the Royal Astronomical Society suggested yesterday that we should take up the subject of the refraction of the air. Well, it is a very difficult subject, but it is one of those we are asked to take up. Then the Royal Geographical Society asks us to give it the temperatures of the different lands in South Africa, Central Africa, the middle of the Soudan, and the Sahara. We are willing to do these things, but we have no observations. We hope to do better as time goes on, but we are all learning, and the Meteorological is not ashamed to send this answer to its sister Society. I am asked to couple this toast with the name of the President of the Institution of Electrical Engineers, Prof. Silvanus Thompson. Electricity is a subject with which we are all very nearly concerned in our work. It is very erudite and difficult to deal with, and we are continually called upon to answer questions which we have to refer to the electricians. We go to them and ask for information; they come back to us and say they have none. Then we have to go on our own lines, and do the best we can. In some ways we give the lead to the gentlemen who are Presidents and Secretaries of these different Societies. We are very grateful to them for the information they have given us, and for their co-operation; and we ask for that co-operation in future, and hope that we shall receive it.

Prof. SILVANUS THOMPSON, F.R.S.—I thank you exceedingly for the very kind way in which you have drunk this toast. I thank you on behalf of the Delegates from the various Societies, and more particularly of that Institution which I have the honour to represent here. It was a matter of regret to me that I should be present for so short a time yesterday, as I missed a very pleasant afternoon. I had the opportunity of hearing read the discourse prepared by our late dear friend, your late President, Mr. Symons. It struck me as very remarkable, and it indicated in no uncertain way the progress that has been made in the science of Meteorology. I regret that the responsibility for this toast falls exclusively on me. I understood it was to have been replied to in the first instance by Prof. Joseph J. Thomson, who is the Delegate for the Royal Society, but he is unfortunately absent.

As I have the honour of being a Fellow of that Society, I will only say that the Royal Society of London takes the very deepest interest in all meteorological questions, and in any question of collaboration between the Royal Meteorological and the Royal Societies you may rely on the Royal Society helping you in every way it can. Though I am Delegate for the Institution of Electrical Engineers, I should like to say I am still connected with some other Societies perhaps even more intimately connected with Meteorology. I refer to two of those local Societies which are doing such admirable and not properly valued work—the Yorkshire Philosophical Society and the Bristol Naturalists' Society. It is now nearly a quarter of a century since I actively served the Yorkshire Philosophical Society, when for nearly two years I undertook the meteorological work in the grounds of the Society at York. The way in which all students of physics, and particularly students of electricity, come into contact with meteorological matters is no new affair. People are in the habit, I suppose, of thinking of electricity as one of the most modern developments of science. But if you look back through the history of electricity you will discover that many of those men who did most to promote the progress of magnetic and electrical science were keenly interested in Meteorology. Most of them played their part in the development of Meteorology in their time. Boyle, Franklin, Gauss, Sabine, Humboldt, Volta, Dove, Dalton, were all interested in the development of Meteorology. If the name of Daniell is endeared to every electrical engineer, it is well known to every meteorologist on account of his hygrometer; and Lord Kelvin, the authority to whom we look, has worked at meteorological problems, has studied the question of atmospheric electricity, and improved the instruments for making observations. Then we may remember that the man who invented the first British electrical telegraph, and laid a cable about eight miles long in his garden at Hammersmith, Sir Francis Ronalds, whose library is the glory of electrical engineers, was a keen meteorologist. So one might go over the names of men who have taken this interest in the science which I am here to represent, and also in Meteorology. In fact, no man works at physics without coming across those problems in the physics of the air, earth, or sea that come within your province. Perhaps I speak in the presence of biologists who can correct me, but it seems to me that your science differs from the more immediately physical in one important respect—its extraordinary complexity. You have to deal with phenomena which are wrapped up in one another, and which it is exceedingly difficult to unravel, and to determine amongst a multitude of possible causes the one, or two, or three efficient causes of the moment. And in a science of that complexity it is absolutely necessary you should have not only an army of observers, but also a man of clear head and strong brain, a man of logical mind, who can from time to time generalise on the phenomena and extract the simple general laws that underlie them. If we honour that man we must also, however, honour those workers whose names are legion and whose labours have been absolutely necessary to enable the one man to arrive at scientific generalisations. Now, I believe, in many minds the name of electrical engineer is not held in good odour. You curse us under your breath when you reflect how the introduction of electric light and traction has upset some of your observations, and how some of your observatories have had to be broken up to get away from the disturbing effects of electrical machinery. I suppose it is the necessary consequence of the progress of that branch of engineering. People will have the means of locomotion; and if you have magnetic observatories placed near the large centres of population, you cannot expect that people living near them will not desire to move about in the most expeditious way. I read a paragraph not long ago which recounted how the whole soil of New York was teeming with wild-cat electricity. All water-pipes and gas-pipes and iron bridges were corroded, and you could not put a wire anywhere into the soil without catching the current. Indeed, it seemed as if life would not be worth living in New York on account of the strong electric currents that ran riot in its soil. The evening papers do not always represent things, however, in their true proportion. I should like to say a word on this matter as to the interference with magnetic observations caused by the leakage of electric currents. There is no necessary leakage of electricity, no necessary interference. The whole thing has arisen from the adoption—the hasty adoption—of methods of propulsion and the supply of electricity in forms which are not of the best. In America, a very go-ahead country, where there are no vestries or local government boards to interfere much with new schemes, you do find crude inventions going ahead and developing, even though they interfere with the interests of others. But allow me to assure you that there is no necessary interference; because it is possible to propel tramcars and distribute currents round a whole community for the purpose of lighting and power without any of the distressing wild-cat effects, and without eating up the gas- or water-pipes. Let me give you a little hint. If any of you are connected with electrical tramways which might endanger the safety of any observatory, do not buy your machinery in America from the first pushing engineer who offers it to you. Insist on its being made and carried out in England; for there are kinds of electric currents and arrangements of circuits which do not play havoc in this way with magnetic observatories; and the fact that they can propel something heavier than a tramcar is admitted by those who have visited the railways that climb the Jungfrau and the Gorner Grat; and it would be easy for the Kew Electric Tramway to be designed so as to run without giving any cause of complaint from the Kew Observatory. I have in my small way the honour of being a collector, and I am going to appeal to any meteorologist who may have a fellow-feeling. I am, I believe, the only man in England who is a collector of rainbows—I mean anything bearing upon rainbows—particulars, pictures, records, photographs. Have any of you ever photographed a rainbow? I believe there are details in its structure which will be seen by the camera, but which cannot be seen by the naked eye, in the same way as invisible stars can be seen by photography. If you can enable me to enrich my collection I shall be glad. To return again to the connection of our Societies with one another, Mr. Shaw and Mr. Bayard spoke of collaboration; anything we can do to promote collaboration between the workers of one Society and another is for the good of us all. It is necessary for progress that we should be kept acquainted with what our fellows are doing, but our efforts must be international. Our collaboration must extend through the whole world, in order to be aided by the effort of every worker; for it is by collaboration, by united effort, and by mutual assistance which we give to one another, that science will progress.

Mr. E. Mawley.—After the excellent repast of which we have so recently partaken, it may seem idle for me to try and convince you that the English meteorologist exists as a rule almost exclusively upon air. Nevertheless such is undoubtedly the case. In the first place, the thoughts of meteorologists are always wandering about somewhere in the atmosphere. It may be now and then fruitlessly among the clouds, but be this as it may, the air with its problems is their natural dwelling-place. Then in another way the British meteorologist may be said to rely upon little but air for his existence, in that the science of Meteorology is generally acknowledged to be one of the least remunerative of them all. And need this be wondered at when we consider that the earth's atmosphere may be ransacked for months together without sufficient gold or other precious metal being extracted from it to cover even a sixpence. I mention these facts in order to show that considerable credit is due to our Royal Meteorological Society for the position it has already attained. For although nourished almost exclusively on this meagre diet it has nevertheless been in existence for fifty years, and now at the end of the half-century it is in a more flourishing and prosperous condition than ever before. If we trace back the history of the Society from the beginning, its present state of prosperity will be found to have been in a very great measure owing to the untiring efforts of those who have had nothing whatever to gain by forwarding either the best interests of Meteorology itself or of the Society representing it in this country. I have been asked to propose the last and shortest toast of the evening, that of "The Visitors." This I do with considerable pleasure, and desire on behalf of the Society to accord to all our guests the heartiest welcome. Our thanks are also due to them for so kindly coming here this evening to countenance with their presence and sympathy a Society which, as I have endeavoured to point out, has existed for so long on such a fickle and unsubstantial element as air. I have much pleasure in coupling with this toast the name of one of the most distinguished of our visitors, Dr. Pavy.

Dr. Pavy.—I am conscious of the privilege which has been conferred upon me; I am also conscious of the responsibility of the task, especially looking at the distinguished guests present here this evening. You, sir, have referred to your science as being a healthy science, necessitating as it does the regularity of life involved in the recording of observations at 9 o'clock in the morning and at 9 in the evening. Now this applies to the votaries or devotees of your science, but it does not apply to the public generally. I am afraid there are many persons who do not consult their health by placing themselves under such regular conditions. We look to science to afford the means of conferring benefit upon the public generally. Now there is no doubt that the Royal Meteorological Society can contribute to this, but not by altering the conditions dealt with—your Society's work appertains to conditions of too cosmical, too comprehensive a nature to permit of your being able to alter them as we strive to do in the profession to which I belong. In my profession we seek for knowledge as you do, but we seek it not simply for its own sake, but with the practical view of conferring benefit around. We seek for knowledge so as to acquire power, and to be able to control conditions and bring about the results which we desire. These results are for the benefit of the health of mankind. I am afraid, Sir, that with your science you stand in much the same position as does the astronomical science. You are not able to control conditions, but you may study them, and through the study confer a benefit by giving us knowledge of the variations of meteorological conditions which are in prospect before us. It is a maxim that to be fore-warned is to be fore-armed, and if we have a knowledge of the conditions which are before us we can provide ourselves suitably to meet the circumstances. In this way your science may be a benefit to humanity. I will give a simple illustration: take the affection with which, Mr. President, your life has been closely associated, that of consumption. This, as we now know, depends upon a microbe. Now this microbe may enter a system which is not vulnerable, or it may enter one which is. Your Society, by fore-warning us, may keep us from taking cold, and by avoiding taking cold we may maintain ourselves in an invulnerable state. It is quite possible, looking at the advance you have made during the last fifty years, that you may in the years to come, by your knowledge of the conditions and circumstances likely to arise, put humanity in a much more favourable position than it is at present for guarding itself against conditions which prove unfavourable to health. With conditions over which you have control you have shown you can very largely contribute to the happiness of those around you. Looking at the repast which has been provided for us this evening, over which you have had the power of exercising control, you have shown us you can use your endeavours in the right direction for contributing to the pleasure of others. I am sure I express the feeling of all present when I thank you for the way in which your guests have been entertained this evening.

Dr. G. Hellmann.—Not being familiar with the English manner of toasting, and after having heard so many able toasts, it is of course very difficult for me to propose a new one. Notwithstanding, I will try it, as the President permits me to do so. It seems to me that one point of view has not been alluded to this evening—I mean the cosmopolity of Meteorology. Except perhaps Astronomy, there is no other science so dependent upon co-operation as Meteorology: it has no nationality. A friend of mine whom you know very well, Professor Mohn of Christiania, on a similar occasion said to me: "My dear friend, do you know what is the best of Meteorology?" and at once he replied, "Its internationality, its international character"; and he is quite right. Without co-operation—international inter-oceanic co-operation—we cannot make progress, and therefore I drink to "The Progress and Prosperity of the International Science of Meteorology."

LIST OF PRESIDENTS, 1850-1900.

(PLATES X. and XI.)

Since the founding of the Society on April 3, 1850, twenty-four gentlemen have been elected President, most of whom have served for the usual term of two years, Dr. R. D. Thompson died during his year of office, when the Council appointed Mr. S. C. Whitbread to the Presidential Chair for the remainder of the year. In view of the Jubilee of the Society, the late Mr. G. J. Symons was elected President for the second time, on January 17, 1900, but owing to being seized with paralysis on February 14, he was obliged to resign this office at the next Council Meeting, when Dr. C. Theodore Williams was appointed President for the remainder of the year.

Date of Election.		
1850	Apr. 3.	SAMUEL CHARLES WHITBREAD, F.R.S., F.R.A.S.
1853	May 24.	GEORGE LEACH, F.Z.S.
1855	May 22.	JOHN LEE, LL.D., F.R.S., F.R.A.S.
1857	May 27.	ROBERT STEPHENSON, M.P., F.R.S., M.Inst.C.E.
1859	June 8.	THOMAS SOPWITH, M.A., F.R.S., M.Inst.C.E.
1861	June 12.	NATHANIEL BEARDMORE, M.Inst.C.E., F.R.A.S.
1863	June 17.	ROBERT DUNDAS THOMPSON, M.D., F.R.S.
1864	Oct. 19.	SAMUEL CHARLES WHITBREAD, F.R.S., F.R.A.S.
1865	June 21.	CHARLES BROOKE, M.A., F.R.S., F.R.C.S.
1867	June 19.	JAMES GLAISHER, F.R.S., F.R.A.S.
1869	June 16.	CHARLES VINCENT WALKER, F.R.S., F.R.A.S.
1871	June 21.	JOHN WILLIAM TRIPE, M.D.
1873	June 18.	ROBERT JAMES MANN, M.D., F.R.A.S.
1876	Jan. 19.	HENRY STORKS EATON, M.A.
1878	Jan. 16.	CHARLES GREAVES, M.Inst.C.E., F.G.S.
1880	Jan. 21.	GEORGE JAMES SYMONS, F.R.S.
1882	Jan. 18.	JOHN KNOX LAUGHTON, M.A., F.R.G.S.
1884	Jan. 16.	ROBERT HENRY SCOTT, M.A., F.R.S.
1886	Jan. 20.	WILLIAM ELLIS, F.R.S., F.R.A.S.
1888	Jan. 18.	WILLIAM MARCET, M.D., F.R.S.
1890	Jan. 15.	BALDWIN LATHAM, M.Inst.C.E., F.G.S.
1892	Jan. 27.	C. THEODORE WILLIAMS, M.A., M.D., F.R.C.P.
1894	Jan. 17.	RICHARD INWARDS, F.R.A.S.
1896	Jan. 15.	EDWARD MAWLEY, F.R.H.S.
1898	Jan. 19.	FRANCIS CAMPBELL BAYARD, LL.M.
1900	Jan. 17.	GEORGE JAMES SYMONS, F.R.S.
1900	Feb. 21.	C. THEODORE WILLIAMS, M.A., M.D., F.R.C.P.

Portraits of all the Presidents, but with two exceptions, are given on Plates X. and XI. It has not been possible to obtain a portrait of Mr. G. Leach, nor of Dr. R. D. Thompson.

THE ROYAL METEOROLOGICAL SOCIETY
R.STEPHENSON. F.R.S.
1857-8.
T. SOPWITH. F.R.S.
1859-60.
Dr. J. LEE. F.R.S.
1855-6
N. BEARDMORE
1861-2
C. BROOKE. F.RS.
1865-6
S. C. WHITBREAD. F.R.S.
1850-2-1864.
C.V. WALKER. F.R.S.
1869-70.
Dr. J.W. TRIPE
1871-2
J. GLAISHER F.R.S.
1867-8
Dr. R.J. MANN
1873-5
H.S. EATON
1876-7
PRESIDENTS
OF THE
ROYAL METEOROLOGICAL
SOCIETY.

C. GREAVES.
1878-9.
G. J. SYMONS, F.R.S.
1880-1; 1900.
J. K. LAUGHTON,
1882-3.
R. H. SCOTT, F.R.S.
1884-5.
W. ELLIS. F.R.S.
1886-7.
Dr C. T. WILLIAMS,
1892-3: 1900.
Dr W. MARCET, F.R.S
1888-9.
B. LATHAM,
1890-1.
F. C. BAYARD.
1898-9.
R. INWARDS.
1894-5.
E. MAWLEY.
1896-7.
PRESIDENTS
OF THE
ROYAL METEOROLOGICAL
SOCIETY.

REPORT OF THE COUNCIL

FOR THE YEAR 1899.

THE most noteworthy event in connection with the Society has been the removal of the Society's Offices and Library from 22 Great George Street to its new rooms at 70 Victoria Street.

After much discussion between the Society's legal advisers (Messrs. Fladgate and Co.) and its Surveyor (Mr. Penfold) on the one part, and the representatives of the Commissioners of Her Majesty's Works and Public Buildings on the other, the sum of £800 was awarded to the Society by the Government as compensation for the compulsory removal of the Offices and Library, and for the purchase of the Leasehold interest of the Society in No. 22 Great George Street. In addition to this, the costs of the negotiations were paid by the Government, and the Council were allowed to remove, without charge, some of the bookcases which were required.

The Council regret having been obliged to remove so far from the premises of the Institution of Civil Engineers, where the Meetings of the Society have been held for so many years. On the other hand, they cannot but regard the present Offices, now that they have been, at considerable expense, altered and fitted up to meet their requirements, as in many respects the most suitable the Society has yet occupied. The new rooms are larger and more lofty than the old ones, and, among other advantages, afford better accommodation for the Fellows and for the rapidly increasing Library. The principal room is sufficiently large to allow of the Society's Meetings being held there whenever, as occasionally happens, the Meeting Room at the Institution of Civil Engineers is not available. A comfortable and suitably furnished Reading Room is set apart for the use of Fellows consulting the Library.

The Council trust that the work of the House Accommodation Committee in carrying out the alterations and arrangement of the new Offices will meet with the approval of the Fellows.

The removal of the Library, Manuscripts, and Records from Great George Street, and the rearrangement of the Library, necessarily threw additional work on the staff and somewhat delayed the issue of the Society's publications, particularly of the *Meteorological Record.*

The Council desire to place on record their appreciation of the zeal with which the staff have carried out their work.

When all the alterations had been completed, the President gave a reception to the Fellows in the New Rooms on May 16, and this was numerously attended.

The Council mention with special regret the deaths of two of the oldest Fellows, viz. the Rev. Canon Slatter, F.R.A.S., who was one of the founders of the British (now the Royal) Meteorological Society; and Mr. C. L. Prince, F.R.A.S., who was elected in its first year (1850). At the present time the only original founders in the ranks of the Society are Mr. J. Glaisher, F.R.S., Mr. W. Johnson, F.R.A.S., and Mr. E. J. Lowe, F.R.S.

Committees.—The Council have been materially assisted during the year by the under-mentioned Committees:—

EDITING COMMITTEE.—The President, Messrs. Bentley, Inwards, and Dr. Scott.

GENERAL PURPOSES COMMITTEE.—The President, three Secretaries, Treasurer, Messrs. Ellis, Inwards, and Latham.

HOUSE ACCOMMODATION COMMITTEE.—The President, three Secretaries, Treasurer, Messrs. Heberden, Inwards, and Latham.

WIND FORCE COMMITTEE.—The President, Secretaries, Messrs. Chatterton, R. H. Curtis, Dines, C. Harding, Munro, Capt. Wilson-Barker, and Dr. Scott.

Meetings.—With the exception of the May and June Meetings, which were held in the afternoon in the Society's own rooms, the Meetings of the Society were held as usual, by the courtesy of the President and Council of the Institution of Civil Engineers, in their Meeting Room.

Quarterly Journal.—This publication has contained papers of unusual interest, among which may be mentioned the Presidential Address by Mr. Bayard on "The Government Meteorological Organisations in various Parts of the World"; Mr. F. J. Brodie on "The Prolonged Deficiency of Rain in 1897 and 1898"; Mr. H. Mellish on "Soil Temperatures"; and Mr. H. N. Dickson on "The Mean Temperature of the Surface Waters of the Sea round the British Isles and its relation to that of the Air."

Meteorological Record.—This publication has been increased from 12 to 16 pages, as the records of earth temperature and of sunshine had increased in number. The reason for its issue having temporarily fallen in arrear has already been stated.

Wind Force Experiments.—In continuation of the Wind Force experiments carried out at Greenhithe in 1897-98 on H.M.S. *Worcester*, an anemometer has been erected, under the direction of the Wind Force Committee, at Stone Ness Point, on the north side of the river, and 800 yards from the ship.

Research Fund.—A welcome contribution of £10 to this Fund has been received during the year from a Member of Council. The cost of providing anemometers and of their erection on H.M.S. *Worcester* for the Wind Force experiments above mentioned has recently been met out of this fund; and the Council trust that further contributions will be received, to enable them to undertake fresh investigations.

Medals to Cadets on H.M.S. Worcester.—The first Silver Medal struck from the die presented to the Society by the President was awarded, on the recommendation of the examiner appointed by the Council (Dr. R. H. Scott, F.R.S.), to Cadet A. E. C. Harris for the best essay sent in on "The Meteorology of the Atlantic."

Stations.—Observations have been accepted from the following new Stations, viz. Southwold, Suffolk; Cahir, Tipperary; Bath, and Ilton, Somerset; Roden, Shropshire; and Ravenscar, Yorkshire.

Inspection of Stations.—All the Stations in the north and north-east of England were inspected and found to be on the whole in a satisfactory condition. Mr. Marriott's Report is given in Appendix.

Phenological Report.—This was as usual prepared by Mr. Mawley and read at the February meeting. There is a satisfactory increase in the number of observers, and the distribution of the stations has been still further improved.

Library.—Advantage has been taken of the removal of the Society's books from Great George Street to rearrange the whole Library, and steps are being taken to check it against the MS. Catalogue. It was also found that much space was occupied by books containing little or no information upon Meteorology. These were put aside, and a Committee of the Council examined them and disposed of what was considered useless to the Society.

Bequests.—The Council are glad to report that in addition to the numerous books presented by Mr. C. L. Prince before his death, and reported last year, he has by his will left to the Society his remarkably long and interesting MS. and printed record, extending from 1841 to 1899, and also authorised the Society to make a further selection from his library. The Society is also indebted to the Rev. Canon Slatter for the bequest of his MS. records and some additions to the Library.

A list of the books, etc., received by purchase or presentation will be found in the Appendix.

Fellows.—The changes in the number of Fellows are given in the following Table, which shows an increase of one during the year:—

Fellows.	Annual.	Life.	Honorary.	Total.
1898, December 31	400	146	18	564
Since elected . . .	+ 28	+ 4	...	+ 32
Since compounded .	− 1	+ 1	...	0
Deceased	− 9	− 4	...	− 13
Retired	− 13	...	...	− 13
Struck off	− 5	...	...	− 5
1899, December 31	400	147	18	565

Deaths.—The Council have to announce with much regret the deaths of the following Fellows:—

Elizabeth Brown.	elected April 19, 1893.
Edward Case, J.P., Assoc.M.Inst.C.E.	„ May 17, 1899.
Laurence Trent Cave.	„ May 19, 1886.
Capt. Sir Douglas Galton, K.C.B., D.C.L., LL.D., F.R.S., Hon.M.Inst.C.E., F.G.S., F.L.S.	„ June 18, 1879.
Arthur Greg.	„ Dec. 17, 1890.
James Stewart Hodgson, J.P.	„ Mar. 19, 1879.
Joseph Horrocks.	„ Nov. 19, 1890.
James Wallace Peggs, Assoc.M.Inst.C.E.	„ April 21, 1880.
Charles Leeson Prince, M.R.C.S., F.R.A.S.	„ May 7, 1850.
Rev. Canon John Slatter, M.A., F.R.A.S.	„ April 3, 1850.
Thomas Taylor Smith, M.Inst.C.E.	„ May 17, 1876.
Capt. Samuel Trott.	„ Dec. 15, 1886.
Hale Wortham, F.R.A.S.	„ Feb. 11, 1851.

APPENDI

STATEMENT OF RECEIPTS AND EXPENDITUR

RECEIPTS.

	£	s.	d.	£	s.	d.
Balance from 1898				£85	1	
Subscriptions for 1899	£682	0	0			
Do. for former years	66	3	4			
Do. paid in advance	27	0	0			
Life Compositions	105	0	0			
Entrance Fees	28	0	0			
				908	3	
Meteorological Office—Copies of Returns	£106	6	6			
Do. Grant towards Inspection Expenses	25	0	0			
				131	6	
Dividend on Stock (including £40 : 18 : 2 from the New Premises Fund)				131	3	
Sale of Publications, &c.				47	17	
Compensation for Surrender of Lease of Rooms at 22 Great George Street to the Commissioners of Her Majesty's Works and Public Buildings				800	0	
Repayment from Research Fund—						
(1) Per Account	£13	7	8			
(2) Sale of £16 : 6 : 11 Consols at 101⅛	16	6	7			
				29	14	
				£2133	7	

I.

FOR THE YEAR ENDING DECEMBER 31, 1899.

EXPENDITURE.

Journal, &c.—		
Printing Nos. 109 to 112	£168 6 6	
Illustrations	31 5 11	
Authors' Copies	10 13 6	
Meteorological Record, Nos. 72 and 73	35 14 6	
Reprints from Registrar-General's Reports	3 8 11	
		£249 9 4
Printing, &c.—		
General Printing	£24 8 6	
Forms	17 8 6	
Stationery	22 18 8	
Books and Bookbinding	16 12 10	
		81 8 6
Office Expenses—		
Salaries	£461 18 4	
Rent and Housekeeper	200 0 0	
Coals, Lighting, &c.	12 9 6	
Postage	62 8 0	
Petty Expenses	19 2 7	
Refreshments at Meetings	13 10 6	
Medals	2 8 6	
		771 17 5
New Offices—		
Fitting up new Bookcases and Cupboards	£201 1 9	
Alterations, Furnishing, Removal, &c.	262 10 0	
Architect's Fees and Plans	18 13 11	
Gratuities to Staff	25 0 0	
		507 5 8
Observations—		
Inspection of Stations	£54 9 11	
Observers	9 2 0	
Instruments	16 17 10	
		80 9 9
Stock—		
Purchase of £234 : 2 : 11 South Australian Inscribed Stock at 106⅞		250 0 0
		£1940 10 8
Balance—		
At Bank of England	£181 10 0	
In hands of Assistant-Secretary	11 6 4	
		192 16 4
		£2133 7 0

Examined and found correct,

FREDc. GASTER, M. JACKSON, } *Auditors.*

January 10, 1900.

APPENDI.

ASSETS AND LIABILITIE

LIABILITIES.

To Subscriptions paid in advance	£27 0 0	
,, Rent for quarter ending December 25, 1899	50 0 0	
		£77 0
,, Excess[1] of Assets over Liabilities		3631 1
		£3708 1

[1] This excess is exclusive of the value of the Library and Stock of Publications.

WM. MARRIOTT, *Assistant-Secretary.*

NEW PREMISES FUNI

Amount paid to the Society's Funds towards the rent of rooms at 70 Victoria Street	£40 18

RESEARCH FUNI

Amount paid to the Society's Funds	£13 7

I.—Continued.

ON JANUARY 1, 1900.

ASSETS.

By Investment in Great Central Railway 4½ per cent Debenture Stock, £800 at 143 xd	£1144	0	0				
,, Investment in New South Wales 4 per cent Inscribed Stock, £654 : 18s. at 113	740	0	9				
,, Investment in London & North-Western Railway Consolidated Stock, £350 at 198	693	0	0				
,, Investment in 2½ per cent Annuities, £231 : 11 : 9 at 97	224	12	10				
				£2801	13	7	
,, Subscriptions unpaid, estimated at	£40	0	0				
,, Entrance Fees unpaid	9	0	0				
,, Interest due on Stock	56	14	7				
				105	14	7	
,, Furniture, Fittings, &c.	£464	15	10				
,, Instruments	143	1	3				
				607	17	1	
,, Cash at Bank of England	£181	10	0				
,, Cash in hands of the Assistant-Secretary	11	6	4				
				192	16	4	
				£3708	1	7	

Examined,

January 10, 1900.

FRED^C. GASTER, M. JACKSON, } *Auditors.*

DECEMBER 31, 1899.

Interest received on investment	£40	18	2

Note.—The Society holds on account of this Fund £1443 : 7 : 9 South Australian 3½ per cent Inscribed Stock.

Examined,

January 10, 1900.

FRED^C. GASTER, M. JACKSON, } *Auditors.*

DECEMBER 31, 1899.

Contribution by Mr. R. Bentley	£10	0	0
Interest received on investment	3	7	8
	£13	7	8

Note.—The Society holds on account of this Fund £107 : 17 : 9, 2¾ per cent Consols.

Examined,

January 10, 1900.

FRED^C. GASTER, M. JACKSON, } *Auditors.*

APPENDIX II.

INSPECTION OF STATIONS, 1899.

All the stations north of 52° N. latitude, and east 2° W. longitude, which were not inspected last year, as well as several others, have been visited, and were found to be generally in a satisfactory condition.

The number of thermometers which have been tested has been 150, in 22 of which there was an alteration of zero. Twenty-one rain-measuring glasses have also been tested, one of which was not satisfactory.

At two or three stations the index in the minimum thermometer has occasionally got out of the spirit, and the instrument has consequently been out of order. This seems to be due to the inside of the tube not being clean, as the index does not slide down the tube freely when the thermometer is inclined.

I am glad to say that, in accordance with my recommendation, the Hospital authorities at Buxton made fresh arrangements for the carrying on of the observations and appointed a chemist in the town as the observer. I believe the observations will now be satisfactory. Owing to these changes the barometer had to be moved to another place. The returns sent into the Society showed that the readings were too high. On examining the adjustment of the barometer, I found that it was greatly out of the perpendicular, this being due to the settlement on one side of the post on which it was suspended. I got a carpenter to set the post upright and to make it thoroughly secure. From readings taken before and after the operations, I found that the barometer, owing to being out of the perpendicular, had been reading ·024 in. too high.

I regret that the Scarborough observations have been unsatisfactory. After seeing the observer I wrote to the Town Clerk stating that the Society could not continue to accept observations from Scarborough unless they were satisfactory, and recommending that the Corporation should thoroughly reorganise the meteorological station. I am glad to say that this matter has been favourably considered, and that the Corporation have transferred the meteorological observations to the Borough Engineer's Department.

For some time past I have been doubtful about the amount of sunshine recorded at Regent's Park, as it seemed to be much lower than that at surrounding stations. The glass ball is apparently losing its power to record the sunshine, as will be seen from the following figures :—

Difference from the Sunshine Recorded at

	Kew.	Bunhill Row.
1894	−212 hours.	− 74 hours.
1895	−292 ,,	− 68 ,,
1896	−423 ,,	−123 ,,
1897	−402 ,,	−126 ,,
1898	−500 ,,	−184 ,,

These figures show a distinct falling off in the amount of sunshine recorded at Regent's Park. The ball is very dull, and the surface of the glass appears to be eaten into, or affected by the atmosphere. As this seems to be somewhat similar to what occurred at Greenwich a couple of years ago, I think the matter should be inquired into, so that, if possible, the cause of the change may be ascertained.

WM. MARRIOTT.

October 17, 1899.

NOTES ON THE STATIONS.

APPLEBY, *July* 7.—The thermometer screen required strengthening. As the maximum was placed near the top of the screen, I recommended that it be lowered and mounted just above the minimum. On comparing the thermometers it was found that the dry and wet had gone up 0°·1 and the maximum 0°·2.

BELPER, *August* 24.—The thermometers were in the same place as formerly, but the rain-gauge had been discontinued and a 5-inch gauge started at Mr. Hunter's new house, "Quarry Bank," which is 60 feet above the former site.

BLACKPOOL, *July* 12.—The minimum had some spirit up the tube. The thermometer screen required painting. On comparing the thermometers it was found that the minimum had gone down 0°·1. Owing to alterations at the Sanatorium it will be necessary to move the instruments to another site. Dr. Anderson suggested a fresh site which seemed very good. He also wished to bring the sunshine recorder there, as the cards were occasionally tampered with on the pier. A good exposure would be obtained if the recorder were mounted about 20 feet above the ground.

BOWNESS, *July* 10.—The sunshine recorder is mounted on the roof of the Hydropathic Hotel. In the winter months it is placed on the roof of the water tower. I re-adjusted the instrument, as it was neither level nor set to the proper latitude, but could not examine it for time, as there was no sunshine.

BRUNDALL, *September* 14.—The thermometer screen required strengthening. On comparing the thermometers it was found that the minimum had gone up 0°·2.

BURTON-ON-TRENT, *August* 25.—I called on Mr. Wells and found that the observations had been regularly taken, but that he had not time to copy them out and send them to the Society, owing to his new duties. He, however, agreed to arrange for the readings to be sent from January 1. The instruments appeared to be in good order.

BUXTON, *July* 25.—In accordance with my recommendation, the Devonshire Hospital Authorities had recently made fresh arrangements for the carrying on of the observations, and had appointed Mr. Pilkington as observer. I gave him instruction on various matters of detail. The screen required painting. I recommended that the grass plot containing the instruments should be railed off. The sunshine recorder required re-adjusting. The barometer was not hanging vertically.

I visited this station again on August 23, and found that the recommendations which I had previously made had not all been carried out. The barometer was still out of perpendicular. This, I found, was due to the settlement of the hut in which it is mounted. I engaged a carpenter, who succeeded in making the board quite perpendicular, so that the barometer hung freely in the ring round the cistern. From readings taken before and after the operation I found that the barometer, owing to being out of the perpendicular, had been reading ·024 in. too high.

CHEADLE, *August* 22.—The barometer had some globules of mercury up the tube. These I removed by running the mercury up to the top of the tube. The grass minimum had some spirit up the tube.

CORTON, *September* 14.—The sunshine recorder was in good condition, but was about 5 minutes fast in time. I recommended that the tops of some trees should be cut off, so as not to intercept the sun's rays.

DERBY, *August* 24.—The screen required painting. I altered the position of the dry and wet thermometers in the screen. It is proposed very shortly to have a 4-foot earth thermometer.

DRIFFIELD, *September* 4.—I called on Mr. Lovel to see if he could not continue to send returns to the Society. After some persuasion, he agreed to do so for a time.

ELY, *September* 14.—On comparing the thermometers it was found that the dry and wet had gone up 0°·1. I suggested that the screen should be washed.

GRANGE-OVER-SANDS, *July* 11.—The Jordan sunshine recorder at Charnley Hall is mounted on a post on the lawn at the southern corner of the house. The exposure is good except on the west and north-west, where the trees make an angle from 7° to 10°. The instrument required re-adjusting.

HARROGATE, *July* 20.—I called on Mr. Paul and found that he had recently been appointed meteorologist by the Corporation. The thermometers were to be sent to Kew for re-verification.

HILLINGTON, *September* 12.—The minimum had an air-bubble in the spirit, just below the index, and was apparently acting as an ordinary thermometer. The muslin on the wet bulb was not working properly.

HODSOCK, *August* 28.—On testing the thermometers it was found that both the earth-thermometers had gone up 0°·1. Trees on the east and east-north-east intercept a little of the early morning sunshine.

IPSWICH, *September* 15.—I called at the Museum, but found that the instruments had not yet been moved to a more open situation as recommended at my last visit.

LANCASTER, *July* 11.—The minimum had 0°·8 of spirit up the tube. The column of mercury in the maximum separated and ran up the tube when the screen was shaken. I instructed the observer always to tilt the thermometer gently before reading. The screen required painting. The hook to the funnel of the Glaisher rain-gauge prevented the water from running into the can below. I recommended that this be replaced by a straight tube. The sunshine recorder required re-adjusting, as the ball had been clamped much too low and the instrument had been set for latitude 48° instead of 54°.

LINCOLN, *August* 30.—There was no change in any of the instruments. The electrical thermometer on the tower of the Cathedral seemed to be in good order. The screens on the turret required painting.

LLANDUDNO, *August* 19.—The minimum had 0°·8 up the tube. As the mercury in the cistern of the Fortin barometer was very dirty, I recommended that the instrument be sent to the makers to be cleaned.

LLANERCHYMEDD, *August* 18.—This station is at Llwydarth Esgob, which is about two and a half miles from the sea at its nearest point. The instruments are on a lawn with a good exposure, but somewhat protected by trees from west to north. The thermometers required re-arranging in the screen. I recommended that a deputy be trained to take the readings when the observer is away.

LOWESTOFT, *September* 13.—Mr. Miller has transferred his instruments to the Corporation with the view of securing the continuity of the observations. A good site has been secured in the Belle Vue Park, and the instruments are placed in a railed-off enclosure. The sunshine recorder is mounted on a post about 20 feet high.

MACCLESFIELD, *August* 23.—On testing the thermometers it was found that the minimum had gone up 0°·2.

OLD STREET, E.C., *September* 21.—Owing to the growth of trees it was considered desirable to have a second set of instruments placed in another position in the churchyard. I found that the new screen was placed close to a tombstone, and was not in the spot which I had previously selected. The screen was subsequently removed to the selected site.

RAVENSTHORPE, *September* 26.—The indices of the maximum and minimum both had a tendency to go up the tube when shaken. I recommended that the thermometers be mounted more inclined, and also that fresh back-plates, with a hole and slot, be put on. The tube of the maximum was liable to slip down 5° when shaken for setting. This was due to the knob at the end of the tube having been broken off. I refixed the thermometer tube and made it firmer. I urged the observer to give careful attention to the wet bulb.

REGENT'S PARK, N.W., *September* 21.—The ball of the sunshine recorder was very dull, and the surface of the glass appeared to be eaten into or affected by the atmosphere. This seems to be somewhat similar to the old ball at Greenwich. Two trees required to have their tops cut, as they subtended a considerable angle above the horizon. The minimum had been broken, and another thermometer, which did not always work properly, was used in its place. I recommended that a better thermometer be obtained. The screen required painting, Three of the earth thermometers had some mercury up the tube. I succeeded in getting this down in two of them, but the 3-inch thermometer still has 1°·8 of mercury detached.

RODEN, *August* 21.—Roden is 6 miles east-north-east of Shrewsbury and 8 miles north-north-west of Wellington. The station is at the Roden estate, which has recently been opened by the Co-operative Wholesale Supply, Limited, of Manchester, for growing strawberries, tomatoes, and other kinds of fruit. The screen was placed close to a temporary roadway. I recommended that it be moved to another site, and that grass should be laid down round it. The thermometers required re-arranging in the screen. I recommended that the pipe in the Glaisher rain-gauge be straightened, and that holes be made in the groove outside.

ROUNTON, *July* 20.—The index of the maximum is very short, being only 4½° in length. The earth thermometer needed some rubber over the bulb, as the bottom of the stick was worn away and the glass bulb exposed.

SCALEBY, *July* 15.—The posts of the screen had become rotten and required strengthening. The wet bulb was not working properly. I impressed upon the observer the necessity of paying great attention to the working of this instrument. On comparing the thermometers it was found that the dry and wet bulbs had gone up 0°·1.

SCARBOROUGH, *July* 21.—Owing to the unsatisfactory manner in which the observations had been kept, and after consulting with the Chairman of the Meteorological Sub-Committee, I wrote to the Town Clerk recommending that the Corporation should take steps for the equipment and maintenance of a thoroughly good station.

SEATHWAITE, *July* 14.—I took with me a new Stevenson thermometer screen, which I put up on the same site as the old one. At the request of Mr. Symons I also set up a Negretti and Zambra self-recording rain-gauge. The 5-inch rain-gauge needed some repairs, which I had done in Keswick.

SOUTHWOLD, *September* 15.—The instruments are placed in an enclosure in a garden near the church. The enclosure is 30 feet square and is surrounded by wire-netting 5 feet high. The exposure is good. The grass minimum had 5° of spirit up the tube. Mr. Herbert has a full equipment of instruments, including an evaporation tank 4 feet square.

STRELLEY, *August* 25.—On comparing the thermometers it was found that the dry and wet had gone up 0°·1. A more open exposure for the sunshine recorder is desirable (but not obtainable), as the trees on the east and west make an angle of 10°.

USHAW, *July* 19.—A new rain-gauge had been obtained since the last inspection. On comparing the thermometers it was found that the dry bulb had gone up 0°·1.

WAKEFIELD, *August* 29.—I found that the rain-gauge had not been examined that morning, although there had been rain the previous day. I urged very strongly that the gauge should be examined every morning. I also recommended that great attention should be paid to the wet bulb. On comparing the thermometers it was found that the wet had gone up 0°·1.

WRYDE, *September* 5.—The maximum sets very stiffly and requires a good deal of shaking to get the mercury down. This may possibly account for some high readings, if it is not well shaken down. The tube of the minimum apparently has some dirt or deposit in it, as the index does not slide freely.

APPENDIX III.

OBITUARY NOTICES.

Miss E. BROWN.—On March 5, 1899, Miss Elizabeth Brown, one of our few lady Fellows, was suddenly called away from an active scientific life.

Her astronomical work in connection with the Liverpool Astronomical Society, and, later, in the formation of the British Astronomical Association, in both of which Societies she held the responsible post of Director of the Solar Section, was fully commented on in the public papers and in scientific journals at the time of her death, but her meteorological work was only slightly noticed.

She much prized her Fellowship in the Royal Meteorological Society, an honour offered her by the late Mr. G. J. Symons, with whom she had long corresponded, as also her father, Mr. T. C. Brown. It was in taking up her father's work, who had supplied Rainfall Observations from 1845 to 1871, after which increasing infirmities caused him to pass over the daily record to his daughter, that Miss E. Brown felt she really had a solid connection with Meteorology; and Mr. Symons, in a letter of December 12, 1882, expressed his delight that no break in the long record had occurred. One of her chief characteristics—that of quiet perseverance in whatever she undertook—was fully shown in this work. The 9 a.m. visit to the rain-gauges was the regular beginning of every day. She also recorded temperature, noted deep-well measurements, and for some years undertook to report thunderstorms. Trained from childhood to make the watching of the sky and of the sunset a daily pleasure, she was ever keenly alive to the absorbing interests of Meteorology, a keen watcher of the tokens of the clouds and the lessons of the winds, and the strong bent of her mind towards science was combined also with that desire for accuracy and truth which is so essential to the value of any report.

This scientific turn of mind coloured the pleasures of her home life and of her many travels; it gave her constant occupation, and linked her to many friends. Correspondents with whom she seldom or never exchanged a word miss her now.

Humble and quiet, simple in her tastes, and constant in her love for the good and the true, she has left behind her an example of the gentle life which will not soon be forgotten. Her death was in harmony with her life. She was spared long illness, the shadow of fear, and the bitterness of parting; being called away in a moment, before anxiety had time to awaken.

The very last effort of her active pen was the adding up in her Rainfall book of the record of April 1899.

She was elected a Fellow of this Society on April 19, 1893.

EDWARD CASE was born on September 6, 1842, and was educated at the Maidstone Grammar School and at the Queenwood College, Hants. After serving a pupilage in the office of Mr. Whichord, County Surveyor of Kent, he was appointed in 1866 an engineer in the Public Works Department of Ceylon. Whilst in Ceylon he had charge of large and important districts, constructed 10 miles of mountain railway, designed and erected several bridges and public buildings, and carried out important drainage, irrigation, and water-supply works. In 1883 Mr. Case retired from the public service, returned to his native town, Maidstone, and there practised as an engineer. In the following year he was appointed local engineer to the Maidstone Waterworks Company, and was engaged for that Company in 1885 and 1886 on a Parliamentary Bill for a large extension of the Works.

In May 1890 Mr. Case was appointed to the office of Expenditor of the Romney Marsh Level, and on him then devolved the charge of the important sea-defences at Dymchurch. He applied himself to this difficult task with characteristic vigour and determination, and the results have been particularly satisfactory; for the shore, which in 1894 consisted of pools of water standing low in the sluggish mud and sand, was in 1897 a fine stretch of sand. The engineering difficulty had been overcome, a heavy beach had been formed, and low-water mark, which formerly touched the foot of the paving, had been pushed 400 feet seawards. This system of groyning, with which Mr. Case's name will be chiefly associated, is remarkable for its simplicity of design, the economy it effects in time, labour, and cost of materials, and its successful results at Dymchurch and elsewhere.

Mr. Case, who was an Associate Member of the Institution of Civil Engineers, died on September 23, 1899.

He was elected a Fellow of this Society on May 17, 1899.

Sir DOUGLAS STRUTT GALTON, K.C.B., D.C.L., F.R.S., was born in 1822, and was the second son of Mr. John Howard Galton of Hadzor House, Droitwich, Worcestershire. He went from Rugby to the Royal Military Academy at the age of 15, and when he obtained his commission in the Royal Engineers he passed the highest examination on record, taking the first prize in every subject. Although a soldier, his career was almost entirely a civil one; indeed, he never attained a higher rank in the army than that of captain.

In 1847 he acted as Secretary to the Commission that investigated the application of iron to railway structures, and soon after became an Inspector of Railways and Secretary of the Railway Department of the Board of Trade. This position he resigned in 1860, but his knowledge of railway matters led to his still carrying out a good deal of important work in connection with railways. Perhaps the most important of these was the series of experiments for testing automatic brakes carried out in 1878 and 1879. In 1860 he was appointed Assistant Inspector-General of Fortifications, and two years later he became Under-Secretary of State for War. After his retirement from this post he became Director of Works and Public Buildings in Her Majesty's Office of Works, an appointment which he held until 1875.

To the general public he was best known as an eminent sanitarian. For the greater part of his life he devoted himself to the investigation of sanitary questions, and of late years these attracted his attention almost to the exclusion of other matters. The first important occupation in his life was immediately after joining the Army, when he became engaged under Sir C. W. Pasley in the attempt to raise the *Royal George*, which had sunk with great loss of life in August 1782; and for two or three years after this time he was abroad on business connected with the fortifications at Malta and Gibraltar. Afterwards he visited the United States and took the opportunity of studying the railway system in use there. He was one of the referees when the Metropolitan Drainage Scheme was under consideration in 1857, and after the Crimean War he took part in preparation of a report on military sanitation. It may certainly be said with truth that in recent years no movement of any importance for the improvement of public hygiene occurred in which Sir Douglas did not take an active share. Another subject which he took up energetically was the study of submarine telegraphy. He was a leading member of the various sanitary institutions; he took a prominent part in the Health Exhibition of 1884; he was a prime mover in the International Congress on Hygiene held in London in 1891; and was always ready to devote his time and trouble to any project which seemed to hold out a prospect of benefit to public health. Sir Douglas Galton took the deepest interest in methods to promote the care and suitable education of defective brain power, and it is due to this that he assisted in founding the Childhood Society, of which he was elected Chairman, Earl Egerton of Tatton being President. Dr. Francis Warren and Dr. G. E. Shuttleworth were among the Members of the Council.

He was long and closely associated with the British Association, acting as one of its General Secretaries for twenty-five years, and it was only in 1895 that he gave up that office to become President of the Association. He was elected a Fellow of the Royal Society in 1863, and an Honorary Member of the Institution of Civil Engineers in 1894. He was a D.C.L. of Oxford, and an LL.D. of several other universities. He was made a C.B. in 1865, and a K.C.B. in 1887.

He died on March 10, 1899.

He was elected a Fellow of this Society on June 18, 1879.

James Stewart Hodgson was born in 1827, and was the younger son of the late Mr. J. Hodgson of Hampstead, and the brother of Kirkman

Daniel Hodgson, some time Governor of the Bank of England and M.P. for Bristol. Mr. Stewart Hodgson had for many years lived at Haslemere, where he built for himself a noble house on Lythe-hill, one of the loveliest positions in the South of England, and where, in his days of great prosperity, his kindliness of heart and his wise generosity made him universally beloved. He was a keen sportsman and an excellent shot, and at one time preserved largely. But his interest in sport never led him to use his position as a landowner to restrict public rights or interfere with the public enjoyment of the beautiful country in which he lived. In politics he was a hearty Liberal, was on the Commission of the Peace for Surrey, and some years ago served as high sheriff; and he was lord of the manor of Haslemere and Godalming. He was a patron of art and artists, and was the original owner of Leighton's "Daphnephoria," the picture with regard to which Mr. Holman Hunt once wrote in the *Times* in terms of enthusiastic praise. Mr. Hodgson, as a man of business, was always on the side of caution, but (like the other Baring partners) he was overborne by the stronger will of the late Lord Revelstoke, and, of course, had to share with him the responsibility for the great collapse. He bore this sudden adversity with great courage; left Lythe-hill, sold all cherished treasures, moved into the small manor-house, and, though he was already fairly advanced in years, set himself to aid the liquidation with all the strength at his command. It is satisfactory that his efforts, and those of his associates, met with remarkable success. He died on July 14, 1899.

He was elected a Fellow of this Society on March 19, 1879.

James Wallace Peggs was born in London on September 3, 1848, and was educated at King's College School. In 1865 he was articled to Mr. J. W. Grover, and in 1867 and 1868 he was employed as resident engineer on the construction of the Clevedon Pier. He was engaged in the same capacity in 1869 and 1870 on the new pier at the Royal Arsenal, Woolwich, and from 1870 to 1872 he designed and carried out a dock and sea-wall at Garston, near Liverpool, for Hamilton's Windsor Ironworks Company. From about 1884 to 1887 Mr. Peggs acted as engineer to the Metropolitan Asylums Board, and carried out amongst other works an ambulance station and pier at Fulham, dry earthworks near Long Reach, and various matters in connection with the Board's fleet of hospital ships and ambulance boats. About this period he carried out various works for the Guardians of the Poor of the Parish of St. Leonard, Shoreditch.

In 1888 Mr. Peggs was elected a Member of the Council of the Sanitary Institute, but owing to ill-health resigned his connection a few months previous to his death. He designed and presented to the Parkes Museum an interesting model showing the cone of depression produced in water-bearing strata caused by pumping from a deep well. He took great interest in experiments on the action of the wind on cowls, and was for many years one of the judges in connection with the annual exhibitions of the Sanitary Institute, in which capacity he took a deep interest and rendered much valuable service. He died on February 24, 1899.

Mr. Peggs was an Associate Member of the Institution of Civil Engineers.

He was elected a Fellow of this Society on April 21, 1880.

Charles Leeson Prince was born at Uckfield, Sussex, June 15, 1821, where he passed the greater portion of his life; and he died, April 22, 1899, at his residence, The Observatory, Crowborough, in the same county, and but seven miles distant from his birthplace.

His father, Charles Prince, originally of Cambridgeshire, settled in Sussex and practised as a medical man in Uckfield and the surrounding districts. From Uckfield to Tunbridge Wells *via* Crowborough, a ride of fourteen miles, was a common professional round in the early part of the century now closing, and Mr. Prince would often relate how his uncle, his father, and another doctor used to meet at Crowborough—then a bare hilltop and not considered safe, being frequented by highwaymen—who on seeing Charles Prince would pounce out and say, "Oh! it's the doctor, let him go."

He was educated primarily at the Uckfield Grammar School, and subsequently at Lewes, and received his medical training at Guy's Hospital like his father before him; and so became the fifth surgeon in the family by direct descent from father to son. He settled at Uckfield, and practised with his father till the death of the latter, after which he remained in the same place till 1872, when he removed to Crowborough, at that time a barren common, but now, largely through Mr. Prince's influence, a health resort of no small repute. As a physician Mr. Prince paid special attention to the treatment of both epilepsy and hydrophobia. In the British Medical Association's *Journal* of May 16, 1874, appeared an account of his treatment of the latter disease.

Mr. Prince was a man of many parts: up to his last illness he took a keen and active interest in such widely diverse pursuits as medicine and surgery (though he had retired from practice some ten years), astronomy, meteorology, photography, botany (which he studied practically in his beautiful gardens at Crowborough), archæology, and numismatics. Furthermore, he had a very fine library, containing some rare and valuable books, some of the more famous editions of the Bible, and the earliest printed copies of the classics.

He was the inventor of *Prince's Perpetual Calendar*, by which the day of the week on any date, past or future, may be found through an arrangement of the Sunday letters. Of this calendar he caused a silver casting to be made, which he left as an heirloom to his infant grandson, Christopher Switzer.

He studied photography practically from the cradle of that science and has left on record descriptions of many early examples now difficult to procure, and he had a unique collection of old paper negatives dating from the forties. His coins also formed a most interesting collection, well worth studying. His bookplate was a very beautiful production, and may be found in an early number of *Ex Libris*.

In 1882 he issued *The Illustrated Account given by Hevelius in his "Machina Celestis" of the Method of Mounting his Telescopes and Erecting an Observatory*. This work consists of a reprint of chapters xviii., xx., and xxii., from an original copy of Hevelius, together with a translation and some remarks.

In 1883 he published his *Observations upon the Great Comet and Transit of Venus, made at Crowborough, Sussex, in the year* 1882. With illustrations.

And in 1895 he brought out *A Literal Translation of the Astronomy and Meteorology of Aratus, with some Bibliographical Remarks.* With regard to illustrations Mr. Prince says in the preface to this work: "As a frontispiece to this little volume I have given a representation of the revolution of the planets around their supposed primary, in the order designed to them by the Ancients in the time of Aratus. This engraving appears first, as far as I know, in the edition of Hugo Grotius, publisher at Leyden, in the year 1600; while Cellarius, in his *Harmonia Macrocosmica*, 1661, has given the same on a much larger scale, and it is from this latter plate that I have taken a photograph."

Mr. Prince contributed to the Royal Astronomical Society papers on cometary, stellar, and other observations. He had several telescopes and other instruments at his observatory, which he greatly prized; the chief was an equatorial with an object-glass of 6·8 inches aperture and 12 feet focal length, which had formerly belonged to Dr. Pearson, and was originally made by Tulley about the year 1823.

His chief contributions to the science of Meteorology were his two books on *The Climate of Uckfield and its Neighbourhood*, published in 1871 (with a second edition in 1886), and his *Observations upon the Topography and Climate of Crowborough Hill, Sussex* (the second edition of which appeared in 1898, not twelve months before his decease). For more than forty years Mr. Prince assiduously carried on an unbroken series of meteorological observations.

Mr. Prince's illness became acute in November 1898, and he underwent a considerable amount of suffering till finally released by his death in April 1899.

He was elected a Fellow of this Society on May 7, 1850.

John Slatter was born at Iffley, near Oxford, April 9, 1817. He went up to Oxford in 1835, and entering at Lincoln College, he became one of Lord Crewe's exhibitioners and graduated in 1838. In 1841 he took his M.A. degree and was ordained. For some years he worked at Leeds under Dr. Hook, then Vicar of Leeds. He subsequently had charge of Sandford-on-Thames, near Oxford, during the years 1852-61, residing at Iffley. In 1861 he was appointed Vicar of Streatley, Berks, and in 1880 Rector of Whitchurch, Oxon, where he remained until the time of his death, April 7, 1899. In 1876 he was appointed Honorary Canon of Christ Church, Oxford.

Canon Slatter had a private observatory at Rose Hill, Iffley, where he worked a good deal. He was obliged to give this up when he went to Streatley, but he still kept up much interest in Astronomy and Meteorology. He communicated two papers to the Royal Astronomical Society, relating to the observations of the aurora of February 4, 1872, and containing some interesting remarks as to the height of the aurora as deduced from observations of an auroral arch made at Streatley simultaneously with observations at Greenwich, October 24, 1870. Canon Slatter deduced a height of 118 miles above the earth's surface, on the assumption that the same phenomenon was observed at both places. He mentions one other case in which the identity of the phenomenon observed was satisfactorily established, and in this case, with a base of nineteen miles, a height of less than three miles was deduced.

He was an original Fellow of this Society, having been elected on April 3, 1850.

HALE WORTHAM was born at Royston, July 1822, and was the son of the late Thomas Wortham, Solicitor, of Royston. He was educated at Mr. Carver's school at Melbourn, Cambs, and King's College, London. In 1844 he was admitted to practice, and on the death of his father, which occurred shortly afterwards, he succeeded to his business, living alone at Royston. In December 1871 he was appointed Clerk of the Peace for the County of Cambridge.

When the Local Government Act came into operation in 1888, and many of the functions discharged by Quarter Sessions were transferred to another authority, an enormous amount of work devolved upon Mr. Wortham. He was appointed Clerk to the newly constituted County Council, and occupied that post until his death. He was also Clerk to the Magistrates of the Arrington and Melbourn Division, and of the Odsey (Hertford) Division; and was a Deputy-Lieutenant for Cambridgeshire. Mr. Wortham owned considerable property in Royston, where he had lived all his life. He died, after a short illness, April 18, 1899.

He was elected a Fellow of this Society on February 11, 1851.

APPENDIX IV.

BOOKS, ETC., PURCHASED DURING THE YEAR 1899.

BOOKS AND PAMPHLETS.

ARCANA OF SCIENCE AND ART. 8° (1838).

BARÉTY, A.—Nice and its Climate. Translated, with additions, by Charles West. 8° (1882).

BARTHOLOMEW'S PHYSICAL ATLAS, vol. iii. Atlas of Meteorology. A series of over four hundred maps. Prepared by J. G. Bartholomew and A. J. Herbertson, and edited by A. Buchan, F.R.S. F° (1899).

BARTON, J.—A Lecture on the Geography of Plants. 8° (1827).

CAMBRIDGE, AMERICAN ASSOCIATION FOR THE ADVANCEMENT OF SCIENCE.—Proceedings at the Tenth Meeting, held at Albany, New York, Aug. 1856; and Twelfth Meeting, at Baltimore, Maryland, May 1858. 8° (1857 and 1859).

CHRISTIAN ALMANACK, 1837. 8° (1837).

CROYDON'S Handbook for Torquay and its Neighbourhood, with the natural history of the district. 8°.

HALL, T. B.—A Flora of Liverpool, and an Appendix containing Meteorological Tables and Observations for the year 1838 by W. Armistead. 8° (1840).

HASSALL, A. H.—San Remo and the Western Riviera, Climatically and Medically considered. 8° (1879).

HELLMANN, G.—Neudrucke von Schriften und Karten über Meteorologie und Erdmagnetismus. No. 12. Wetterprognosen und Wetterberichte des XV. und XVI. Jahrhunderts. Facsimiledruck mit einer Einleitung. 4° (1899).

LARDNER, D.—Handbook of Natural Philosophy. Hydrostatics, Pneumatics, and Heat. 8° (1855).

LESLIE, JAMESON, and MURRAY, H.—Narrative of Discovery and Adventure in the Polar Seas and Regions, with illustrations of their climate, geology, and natural history, and an account of the whale fishery. 8° (1830).

LONDON, RIVERS POLLUTION COMMISSION (1868).—Sixth Report of the Commissioners appointed in 1868 to inquire into the best means of preventing the pollution of rivers. Domestic Water Supply of Great Britain. Presented to both Houses of Parliament by command of Her Majesty. F° (1874).

LONDON, SOCIETY OF ARTS.—Transactions, 1846-47, part i. 4° (1847).

M'I., J.—Summer and Winter Yachting in the *Meteor* and *Hebe*, 1872-73. 8° (Privately Printed.)

M'Nicoll, E. D.—Handbook for Southport, Medical and General, with copious notices of the natural history of the district. 3rd ed. 8° (1883).

Mudie, R.—The World, familiarly, but philosophically described; being a companion to Gilbert's illustrated Map of the World. 8° (1840).

Sargeaunt, R. A.—Notes on the Climate of the Earth, past and present. 8° (1875).

Stabel, E.—The Mineral Waters of Kreuznach (1888).

Rhind, W.—Studies in Natural History, exhibiting a popular view of the most striking and interesting objects of the Material World. 2nd ed. (1838.)

Veraguth, C.—The Baths of St. Moritz, Upper Engadine, Switzerland. 8° (1890).

Year-Book of the Scientific and Learned Societies of Great Britain and Ireland, 1899. 8° (1899).

Zoinlin, R. M.—Recreations in Physical Geography; or, the Earth as it is. 8° (1840).

APPENDIX V.

DONATIONS RECEIVED DURING THE YEAR 1899.

Books and Pamphlets.

Presented by Societies, Institutions, etc.

Adelaide, Marine Board of South Australia.—Information as to the Principal Ports of South Australia, 1899.

Adelaide, Observatory.—Meteorological Observations made at Adelaide Observatory and other places in South Australia and the Northern Territory, 1895 and 1896.

Aix-la-Chapelle, Meteorologische Station.—Die Niederschlagsverhältnisse der Rheinprovinz.—Die Strömungen der Luft in den barometrischen Minima und Maxima, von P. Polis.—Die Strömungen der Luft in den Cyclonen und Anticyclonen, von P. Polis.—Die Temperaturverhältnisse von Aachen, von P. Polis.—Ergebnisse der meteorologischen Stationen I. Ordnung, Aachen und deren Nebenstation im Jahre 1898.—Uebersicht der Witterung des Monats Feb.-March 1899.

Allahabad, Meteorological Office.—Annual Statement of Rainfall in the North-West Provinces and Oudh, 1898.

Athens, Observatoire National.—Annales, tome i.

Bangalore, Central Observatory.—Meteorology in Mysore, 1898.—Report on the Rainfall Registration in Mysore, 1897 and 1898.

Barbados, Colonial Secretary's Office.—Returns of Rainfall in Barbados, 1899.

Batavia, Magnetical and Meteorological Observatory.—Observations, vol. xx., 1897.—Rainfall in the East Indian Archipelago, 1897.

Berlin, Deutsche meteorologische Gesellschaft.—Meteorologische Zeitschrift, Dec. 1898 to Nov. 1899.

Berlin, Gesellschaft für Erdkunde.—Verhandlungen, Band xxv. No. 10 to Band xxvi. No. 9.—Zeitschrift, Band xxxiii. No. 5 to Band xxxiv. No. 4.

Berlin, Königlich-Preussisches meteorologisches Institut.—Bericht über die Thätigkeit des Königlich-Preussischen meteorologischen Instituts im Jahre 1898.—Ergebnisse der Beobachtungen an den Stationen II. und III. Ordnung, 1894, Heft 3; 1898, Heft 1 and 2.—Ergebnisse der magnetischen Beobachtungen in Potsdam, 1897 and 1898.—Ergebnisse der meteorologischen Beobachtungen in Potsdam, 1897.

Bidston, Liverpool Observatory.—Report of the Director, 1898.

Bombay, Government Observatory.—Magnetical and Meteorological Observations, 1897.

Bombay, Meteorological Office.—Brief Sketch of the Meteorology of the Bombay Presidency, 1898-99.

Bremen, Meteorologische Station.—Ergebnisse der meteorologischen Beobachtungen, 1898.

Brisbane, General Register Office.—Annual Report on the Vital Statistics of Queensland, 1898.—Report on Vital Statistics, Oct. 1898 to Sept. 1899.

Brisbane, Royal Geographical Society of Australasia (Queensland Branch).—Proceedings and Transactions, 1897-98 and 1898-99.

Brisbane, Weather Bureau.—Meteorology of Australia; Kosciusko and Merimbula Meteorogram, Jan. 1898.

Brussels, Académie Royale de Belgique.—Annuaire, 1898 and 1899.—Bulletins,

3rd série, tome xxxiv to xxxvi.—Tables Générales du Recueil des Bulletins, 3rd série, tome i. to xxx.

BRUSSELS, OBSERVATOIRE ROYALE DE BELGIQUE.—Annales, Observations météorologiques d'Uccle, July 1897 to May 1898; Sept. and Oct. 1898.—Annuaire, 1899. —Bulletin Mensuel du Magnétisme Terrestre, Jan. to July 1899.—Bulletin Météorologique, Dec. 1898.

BUCHAREST, INSTITUT MÉTÉOROLOGIQUE DE ROUMANIE.—Annales, tome xiii., 1897. —Buletinul Observatiunilor Meteorologice din Romania, 1898.—Climatologie du littoral Roumain de la mer noir, par C. Hepites. — Éléments magnétiques de Bucharest.— Repartitiunea ploaiei pe districte si pe Basinuri in România, Anul 1897.

BUDAPEST, KÖNIGL.-UNG. CENTRAL-ANSTALT FÜR METEOROLOGIE UND ERDMAGNETISMUS. — Beobachtungen angestellt am astrophysikalischen und meteorologischen Observatorium in O-Gyalla, Bander xix.-xxi.—Jahrbuch, 1897, Theile i. und iii.; 1898, Theil ii.

BUXTON, DEVONSHIRE HOSPITAL.—Annual Report, 1898.

CAIRO, SOCIÉTÉ KHÉDIVIALE DE GEOGRAPHIE.—Bulletin, Vme série, Nos. 2 and 3.

CALCUTTA, METEOROLOGICAL DEPARTMENT OF THE GOVERNMENT OF INDIA.—Daily Weather Charts of the Indian Monsoon Area, July 1, 1898 to May 31, 1899.—Indian Daily Weather Reports, Dec. 1, 1898 to Nov. 30, 1899.—Indian Meteorological Memoirs, vol. vi. parts 4 and 5; vol. x. parts 2, 3, and 4.—Memorandum on the Snowfall in the mountain-districts bordering Northern India, etc., 1899.— Monthly Weather Review, Aug. 1898 to Apr. 1899.—Rainfall Data of India, 1897.— Report on the Administration of the Meteorological Department, 1898-99.

CALCUTTA, ST. XAVIER'S COLLEGE OBSERVATORY.—Meteorological Register, July 1898 to June 1899.

CAMBRIDGE (MASS., U.S.), ASTRONOMICAL OBSERVATORY OF HARVARD COLLEGE.— Annals, vol. xxxix. part 1, Peruvian Meteorology, 1888-90.

CAMBRIDGE (MASS., U.S.), BLUE HILL METEOROLOGICAL OBSERVATORY.—Bulletin, 1899, Nos. 1-3.

CAPE TOWN, METEOROLOGICAL COMMISSION.—Report, 1898.

CAPE TOWN, SOUTH AFRICAN PHILOSOPHICAL SOCIETY.—Transactions, vol. x. parts 2 and 4.

CARDIFF, ASTRONOMICAL SOCIETY OF WALES.—Cambrian Natural Observer, vol. ii. Nos. 1-3.

CARLSRUHE, CENTRALBUREAU FÜR METEOROLOGIE UND HYDROGRAPHIE IM GROSSHERZOGTHUM BADEN.— Die Ergebnisse der meteorologischen Beobachtungen, 1898.—Niederschlagsbeobachtungen der meteorologischen Stationen im Grossherzogthum Baden, 1898, part 2.

CHEMNITZ, KONIGL.-SÄCHSISCHES METEOROLOGISCHES INSTITUT.—Jahrbuch, 1896, Abth. iii.; 1897, Abth. i. and ii.

CHRISTIANIA, NORSKE METEOROLOGISKE INSTITUT.— Jahrbuch, 1898.— Klima Tabeller for Norge V-XII., af H. Mohn.— Nedboriagttagelser i Norge, Aargang I.-III., 1895 Juli eni 1897 Dec.—Oversigt over Luftens Temperatur og Nedborden i Norge, 1898.

CHRISTIANIA, NORWEGIAN NORTH ATLANTIC EXPEDITION, 1876-78.—XXV. Zoologi. Thalamophora.—XXVI. Zoologi. Hydroida.

COPENHAGEN, DANSKE METEOROLOGISKE INSTITUT. — Annuaire météorologique, 1894 and 1896.—Bulletin météorologique du Nord, Dec. 1898 to Nov. 1899.—Meteorologisk Aarbog, 1895, part 2; 1897, part 1.—Meteorologiske Middeltal og Extremer for Faeroerna, Island og Gronland.— Observations météorologiques-nautiques, 1897 and 1898.

CORDOBA, ACADEMIA NACIONAL DE CIENCIAS.—Boletin, tomo xvi. entrega 1.

COSTA RICA, INSTITUTO FISICO-GEOGRAFICO NACIONAL.—Annales, tome vii., 1894. —Informe sobre los Trabajos practicadas en el Instituto Fisico-Geografico Nacional durante el ano 1896-97; 1897-98.

CRACOW, K. K. STERNWARTE.—Meteorologische Beobachtungen, Nov. 1898 to Sept. 1899.

CROYDON, MICROSCOPICAL AND NATURAL HISTORY CLUB.— Daily Rainfall in the Croydon District, Dec. 1898 to Oct. 1899. — Report of the Meteorological Sub-Committee, 1898.

DUBLIN, GENERAL REGISTER OFFICE.— Weekly Returns of Births and Deaths, 1899.

DUBLIN, ROYAL IRISH ACADEMY.—Proceedings, Third Series, vol. v. Nos. 2 and 3.—Transactions, vol. xxxi. part 7.

DUBLIN, ROYAL SOCIETY.— Proceedings, vol. viii. part 6.—Transactions, vol. vi. parts 14-16, and vol. vii. part 1.

DURANGO (MEXICO), OBSERVATORIO METEOROLÓGICO DEL SEMINARIO CONCILIAR.— Boletin Mensual, Jan. to Oct. 1899.

EDINBURGH, GENERAL REGISTER OFFICE.—Quarterly Returns of the Births, Marriages, and Deaths registered in Scotland, Dec. 31, 1898 to Sept. 30, 1899.

EDINBURGH, ROYAL SCOTTISH GEOGRAPHICAL SOCIETY.—Scottish Geographical Magazine, 1899.

EDINBURGH, SCOTTISH METEOROLOGICAL SOCIETY.—Quarterly Returns of Births, Deaths, and Marriages, Scotland, for the quarters ending Sept. 30, 1859; Sept. 30, 1860; and Supplements for 1880 and 1881.

FIUME, I. R., ACCADEMIA DI MARINA.—Meteorological Observations, Nov. 1898 to Sept. 1899.

GENEVA, SOCIÉTÉ DE GÉOGRAPHIE.—Le Globe, tome xxxvii. No. 12.

GLASGOW, PHILOSOPHICAL SOCIETY.—Proceedings, 1898-99.

GREENWICH, ROYAL OBSERVATORY.—Magnetical and Meteorological Observations, 1896.—Report of the Astronomer-Royal to the Board of Visitors, June 3, 1899.

GUATEMALA, INSTITUTO NACIONAL DE GUATEMALA.—Resumen general de las Observaciones meteorológicas desde el año de 1857 hasta en año de 1898.

GUATEMALA, LABORATORIO QUIMICO CENTRAL.—Observaciones meteorológicas, 1898.

HALIFAX, NOVA SCOTIA, NOVA SCOTIAN INSTITUTE OF SCIENCE.—Proceedings and Transactions, vol. ix. part 4.

HAMBURG, DEUTSCHE SEEWARTE.—Aus dem Archiv, 1898.—Deutsche Ueberseeische meteorologische Beobachtungen, Heft VIII.—Ergebnisse der meteorologischen Beobachtungen an 10 Stationen II. Ordnung und an 48 Signalstellen, sowie stündliche Aufzeichnungen an 4 normal Beobachtungens-stationen, 1897.—Jahresbericht über die Thätigkeit der Deutsche Seewarte, 1898.—Wetterbericht, 1899.

HONG-KONG, OBSERVATORY.—China Coast Meteorological Register, 1898.—Extract of Meteorological Observations, Nov. 1898 to Oct. 1899.—Observations and Researches, 1898.

INNSBRUCK, UNIVERSITAT.—Beobachtungen des meteorologischen Observatoriums, 1898.

JAMAICA, GOVERNMENT METEOROLOGIST.—Jamaica Rainfall, 1898.—Meteorological Results, 1898.—Weather Report, Oct. 1898 to Oct. 1899.

JERSEY, OBSERVATOIRE ST. LOUIS.—Bulletin des Observations météorologiques, 1898.

JURJEW (DORPAT), METEOROLOGISCHES OBSERVATORIUM DER KAISERLICHEN UNIVERSITÄT.—Meteorologische Beobachtungen, Apr. to July 1896, Oct. to Dec. 1898.

KAZAN, OBSERVATOIRE MAGNÉTIQUE DE L'UNIVERSITÉ IMPÉRIALE.—Observations, July 1897 to Dec. 1898.

KEW, OBSERVATORY.—Experiments on Aneroid Barometers at Kew Observatory, and their Discussion.—Report of the Kew Committee, 1898.

KIEW, METEOROLOGICAL SERVICE OF THE DNIEPER.—Information relating to the Condition of the Beetroot Plantation in connection with the Weather, Apr. 1 to Oct. 15, 1898.

KIEW, OBSERVATOIRE MÉTÉOROLGIQUE DE L'UNIVERSITÉ.—Meteorological and Rural Economical Bulletin of the Kieff Meteorological Observatory, Année ii. Nos. 10-12; Année iii. Nos. 1-12.; and Année iv. Nos. 1 to 4.—Observations, Jan. 1896 to June 1897.

LEON, OBSERVATORIO METEOROLOGICO.—Boletin Mensuale, Nov. 1898 to Sept. 1899.

LISBON, OBSERVATORIO DO INFANTE D. LUIZ.—Boletin Meteorologico, Jan. 1899.

LISBON, SOCIEDAD DE GEOGRAPHIA.—Boletin, 16a serie, Nos. 10 to 12.

LONDON, AERONAUTICAL SOCIETY.—Aeronautical Journal, vol. iii. No. 10.

LONDON, BRITISH ASSOCIATION.—Report, 1898.—Committee on the Climate of Tropical Africa, Seventh Report.

LONDON, BRITISH BALNEOLOGICAL AND CLIMATOLOGICAL SOCIETY.—The Journal of Balneology and Climatology, vol. iii., 1899.

LONDON, BRITISH SOUTH AFRICA COMPANY.—Reports on the Administration of Rhodesia, 1897-98.

LONDON, CAMERA CLUB.—Journal, 1899.

LONDON, GENERAL REGISTER OFFICE.—Quarterly Returns of Marriages, Births, and Deaths for the year ending Sept. 30, 1899.—Weekly Returns of Births and Deaths, 1899.

LONDON, GEOLOGICAL SOCIETY.—Quarterly Journal, vol. lv., 1899.

LONDON, INSTITUTION OF CIVIL ENGINEERS.—Minutes of Proceedings, vol. cxxxv., 1898-99, part i.

LONDON, INSTITUTION OF ELECTRICAL ENGINEERS.—Journal, Nos. 137-141.

LONDON, INSTITUTION OF JUNIOR ENGINEERS.—Record of Transactions, 1897-98.

LONDON, METEOROLOGICAL OFFICE.—Daily Weather Report, 1899.—Weekly Weather Reports, 1899.—Accessions to Library during the years ending March 31, 1895 and 1896.—Report of the Meteorological Council for the year ending March 31,

1898.—Meteorological Charts of the Southern Ocean between the Cape of Good Hope and New Zealand.—Meteorological Observations at Stations of the Second Order, 1895.—Hourly Means from the five Observatories under the Meteorological Council, 1895.—Bulletin-quotidien de l'Algérie, Jan. to June and Aug. to Nov. 1899.—Annual Report Royal Cornwall Polytechnic Society, 1898.—Annual Meteorological Report, Straits Settlements, 1898.—Climate of Cuba, by W. F. R. Phillips.—Clock-rates and Barometric Pressure as illustrated by the Mean-Time Clock and Three Chronometers at Mare Island Observatory, by E. Hayden.—Commissã Geographica e Geologica de Sao Pauli, Seccas Meteorológica Dados Climatologuos, 1893-96.—Comparative Rainfall, Colony of the Gambia.—Colony of Lagos, General Abstract of Registration, 1890.—Die Meteorologie der Sonne und das Wetter in Jahre 1889 zugleich Wetterprognose für das Jahr 1899, von Prof. K. W. Zenker.—Die Temperaturverhältnisse von Berlin, von R. Bornstein und E. Lees.—Die Vertikalbewegungen eines Freiballons, von H. Hergesell.—Ergebnisse siebenjähriger Niederschlags-Registrierungen in Basel, von A. Riggenbach.—Ein Verfahren zur harmonischen Analyse erdmagnetischer Beobachtungen nach einheitlichem Plane, von A. Nippoldt.—Informe Sobre los trabjos practicados en el Instituto Fisico-Geográphico Nacional de Costa Rica durante el año 1895-96, 1896-97.—Magnetische Declinationsbeobachtungen zu Klagenfurt, Sept. 1898 to Aug. 1899.—Minerva. Jahrbuch der gelehrten Welt, 1896-97.—Notes on Malaria in connection with Meteorological Conditions at Sierra Leone, by Surg.-Maj. E. M. Wilson.—Osservazioni di Temperatura e del Calore delle Acque, di A. Riccò e di G. Saya.—Osservazioni Meteorologiche orarie simultanee. Nota A. Riccò e di G. Saya.—Report of the Registrar-General, Bermuda, 1898.—Return of Rainfall in Ceylon, 1898, and means during different periods.—Wolkenhöhenmessungen, von E. Kayser.

LONDON, PHYSICAL SOCIETY.—Proceedings, Nos. 91 and 94.

LONDON, ROYAL AGRICULTURAL SOCIETY.—Journal, third series, vol. ix. part 4.

LONDON, ROYAL ASTRONOMICAL SOCIETY.—Monthly Notices, 1899.—Memoirs, vols. lii. and liii.

LONDON, ROYAL BOTANIC SOCIETY.—Quarterly Record, March 1899.

LONDON, ROYAL GEOGRAPHICAL SOCIETY.—Geographical Journal, 1899.

LONDON, ROYAL INSTITUTION.—Proceedings, vol. xv. part 3.

LONDON, ROYAL SOCIETY.—Proceedings, Nos. 406 to 421.

LONDON, ROYAL STATISTICAL SOCIETY.—Quarterly Journal, Dec. 1898 to Sept. 1899.

LONDON, SANITARY INSTITUTE.—Journal, vol. xix. No. 4 to vol. xx. No. 3.

LONDON, SOCIETY OF ARTS.—Journal, 1899.

MADRID, INSTITUTO CENTRAL METEOROLÓGICO.—Boletin, Jan. 1 to Oct. 15, 1899.

MADRID, OBSERVATORIO.—Observaciones meteorológicas, 1896-97.—Resumen de la observaciones meteorológicas efectuadas en la Peninsula y algunas de sus Islas adyacentes, 1895-96.

MADRID, SOCIEDAD GEOGRAPHICA.—Boletin, tomo xl. No. 7 to tomo xli. No. 3.—Revista de geografia colonial y mercantil publicada por la sección de geografia comercial. Actas de la sesiones celebradas por la sociedad por la junta directiva y por les secciones, Nos. 16 to 23.

MAGDEBURG, WETTERWARTE DER MAGDEBURGISCHEN ZEITUNG.—Jahrbuch, 1897.

MANCHESTER, LITERARY AND PHILOSOPHICAL SOCIETY.—Memoirs and Proceedings, vol. xliii. parts 1 to 4.

MANILA, OBSERVATORIO METEOROLÓGICO.—Boletin Mensuale, Sept. 1897 to March 1898.—La Erupcion del Volcan Mayon en los dias 25 y 26 de Junio de 1897.—Las Nubes en el Archipielago Filipino.

MARLBOROUGH COLLEGE NATURAL HISTORY SOCIETY.—Annual Report, 1898.

MARSEILLES, COMMISSION DE MÉTÉOROLOGIE DU DÉPARTEMENT DES BOUCHES-DU-RHÔNE.—Bulletin Annuel, 1897 and 1898.

MAURITIUS, OBSERVATORY.—Mauritius Magnetical Reductions, 1896.

MELBOURNE, OBSERVATORY.—Record of Results of Observations in Meteorology, Terrestrial Magnetism, etc., July 1897 to June 1898.

MERZIFUN (ASIA MINOR), ANATOLIA COLLEGE.—Meteorological Records, 1898.

MEXICO, OBSERVATORIO METEOROLÓGICO-MAGNÉTICO CENTRAL.—Boletin Mensual, Sept. 1898 to June 1899.—Red. Meteorológica del Estado de Mexico.

MEXICO, SOCIEDAD CIENTIFICA "ANTONIO ALZATE."—Memorias y Revista, tomo xi. No. 9 to tomo xii. No. 10.

MILAN, R. OSSERVATORIO ASTRONOMICO DI BRERA.—Osservazioni meteorologiche, 1898.

MONTEVIDEO, OBSERVATORIO METEOROLÓGICO DEL COLEGIO PÍO DE VILLA COLÓN.—Boletin Mensual, Anno x. Nos. 7 to 12; Anno xi. No. 8.

MOSCOW, OBSERVATOIRE MÉTÉOROLOGIQUE DE L'UNIVERSITÉ IMPÉRIALE DE MOSCOW.—Observations, July 1896 to Nov. 1898.

MOSCOW, SOCIÉTÉ IMPÉRIALE DES NATURALISTES.—Bulletin, 1898, Nos. 2-4.

MUNICH, K.-B. METEOROLOGISCHE CENTRAL-STATION.—Beobachtungen der meteorologischen Stationen im Kön. Bayern, Jahrgang xix. Heft 4; Jahrgang xx. Heft 1-3; Jahrgang xxi. Heft 1.—Uebersicht über die Witterungsverhältnisse im Kön. Bayern, Nov. 1898 to Oct. 1899.

MYSORE, GOVERNMENT METEOROLOGICAL DEPARTMENT.—Report on the Rainfall Registration in Mysore, 1897.

NATAL, OBSERVATORY.—Report of the Government Astronomer, 1898.

NEW YORK, ACADEMY OF SCIENCES.—Annals, vol. xi. parts 2 and 3; vol. xii. part 1.

NEW YORK, CENTRAL PARK OBSERVATORY.—Abstracts of Registers from Self-recording Instruments, Nov. 1898 to Oct. 1899.

ODESSA, OBSERVATOIRE MAGNÉTIQUE ET MÉTÉOROLOGIQUE.—Vie Physique de notre Planète devant les lumières de la Science Contemporaine, par A. Klossovsky.

O-GYALLA (HUNGARY), METEOROLOGISCHES MAGNETISCHES CENTRAL-OBSERVATORIUM.—Beobachtungen, Dec. 1898 to Oct. 1899.

OÑA (SPAIN), COLEGIO MAXIMO DE LA COMPAÑIA DE JESUS.—Observaciones Meteorológicas, 1897 and 1898.

PARIS, BUREAU CENTRAL MÉTÉOROLOGIQUE DE FRANCE.—Bulletin International, 1899.—Bulletin Mensuel, Nov. 1898 to Oct. 1899.

PARIS, OBSERVATOIRE MUNICIPAL DE MONTSOURIS.—Annuaire, 1898.

PARIS, SOCIÉTÉ MÉTÉOROLOGIQUE DE FRANCE.—Annuaire, April 1898 to June 1899.

PERTH (WESTERN AUSTRALIA), OBSERVATORY.—Meteorological Observations made at the Perth Observatory and other places in Western Australia during the years 1897 and 1898.

PHILADELPHIA, AMERICAN PHILOSOPHICAL SOCIETY.—Proceedings, Nos. 158 and 159.

POLA, K.-K. HYDROGRAPHISCHES AMT.—Meteorologische Termin-Beobachtungen in Pola und Sebenico, Nov. 1898 to Oct. 1899.—Jahrbuch der meteorologischen und erdmagnetischen Beobachtungen, Gruppe iii. Heft 2, Gruppe iv. Heft 2.—Jahrbuch, 1898.

PRAGUE, K.-K. STERNWARTE.—Magnetische und meteorologische Beobachtungen, 1898.

PUEBLA.—Boletin de Estadistica del Estado de Puebla, ii. Epoca, No. 6.

RIO DE JANEIRO, COMMISSÃO GEOGRAPHICA E GEOLOGICA.—Boletim, No. 5.

RIO DE JANEIRO, MINISTERIO DA MARINHA.—Boletim Semestral, Nos. 2 and 3.

RIO DE JANEIRO, OBSERVATORIO.—Annuario, 1899.

ROCK ISLAND (ILL., U.S.A.), AUGUSTANA COLLEGE.—The Mechanical Composition of Wind Deposits.

ROME, SOCIETÀ SISMOLOGICA ITALIANO.—Bollettino, vol. iv. Nos. 5 to 9; vol. v. Nos. 1 to 4.

ROME, UFFICIO CENTRALE DI METEOROLOGICA E DI GEODINAMICA.—Revista Meteorica-Agraria, vol. xix. No. 35 to vol. xx. No. 34.—Annali, serie seconda, vol. xvi. part 2; vol. xvii. parts 1 and 2; vol. xviii. part 2.

ST. PETERSBURG, PHYSIKALISCHES CENTRAL-OBSERVATORIUM.—Annalen, 1897.—Cyclone Tracks in European Russia, by P. Rybkin [in Russian].—New Evaporation Gauge for Observations on Evaporation from Grass, and the First Observations therewith at the Constantine Observatory in 1896, by M. Rykatcheff.—On the Prediction of Lowest Night Temperatures, by N. Korosteleff [in Russian].—On the Relation between the Amount of Cloud and the Duration of Sunshine, by J. Figourovsky.—Prediction of Weather for Different Places from the Point of View of Synoptic Meteorology, by S. D. Griboyedeff [in Russian].—Report of the Central Physical Observatory, 1897, by M. Rykatcheff [in Russian].—Results of Meteorological Observations at the Stations of the Central Physical Observatory at the time of the Solar Eclipse, Aug. 9, 1896, by J. Shukevick.—Thunderstorms in European Russia and in the Caucasus, by N. Komoff.

SALONICA, GYMNASE BULGARE DES GARÇONS "ST. CYRILLE ET METHOD."—Bulletin Annuaire, 1898.

SALTILLO (MEXICO), OBSERVATORIO METEOROLÓGICO DEL COLEGIO DE SAN JUAN NEPOMUCENO.—Boletin Mensual, tomo iii. No. 1.

SAN FERNANDO, INSTITUTO Y OBSERVATORIO DI MARINA.—Annales, sección 2a, Observaciones meteorológicas y magnéticas, 1897-98.

SAN PAULO, COMMISSÃO GEOGRAPHICA E GEOLOGICA.—Secção meteorológica, Dados climatológicos, 1897.

SANTIAGO DI CHILE, OBSERVATORIO ASTRONOMICO.—Annuario, tomo primero.

SCARBOROUGH, TOWN COUNCIL.—Report of the Scarborough Observatory, 1898.

SOPHIA (BULGARIA), STATION CENTRALE MÉTÉOROLOGIQUE.—Bulletin Mensuel, Nov. 1898 to Oct. 1899.

STA. LUCIA, BOTANIC GARDENS.—Synopsis of Meteorological Observations.

STOCKHOLM, ACADÉMIE ROYALE DES SCIENCES DE SUÈDE.—Études sur diverses méthodes servant à calculer la moyenne diurne de la température, par R. Rubenson.—La Pression Atmosphérique moyen en Suède, 1860-95, par H. E. Hamberg.—Ueber die

Nahzen 26-tägige Periode der Polarlichter und Gewitter, von N. Ekholm und S. Arrhenius.—Ueber den Einfluss des Mondes auf die Polarlichter und Gewitter, von N. Ekholm und S. Arrhenius.

STOCKHOLM, METEOROLOGISKA CENTRAL-ANSTALTEN. — Månadsöfversigt af Väderleken i Sverige, Nov. 1898 to Oct. 1899.—Meteorologiska Iakttagelser i Sverige, 1893.

STONYHURST, COLLEGE OBSERVATORY.—Results of Meteorological and Magnetical Observations, 1898.

STRASBURG, METEOROLOGISCHES LANDESDIENSTS IN ELSASS-LÖTHRINGEN.—Ergebnisse des Meteorologischen Beobachtungen im Jahre 1896.

SYDNEY, OBSERVATORY.—Meteorological Observations, 1897.—Results of Rain, River, and Evaporation Observations in New South Wales, 1897.—Weather Charts, 1898.

SYDNEY, ROYAL SOCIETY OF NEW SOUTH WALES.—Journal and Proceedings, vol. xxxii.

TACUBAYA, OBSERVATORIO ASTRONÓMICO NACIONAL.—Observaciones Meteorológicas, 1895.

TOKIO, CENTRAL METEOROLOGICAL OBSERVATORY.—Annual Report, 1897, part i.

TOKIO, IMPERIAL UNIVERSITY.—Calendar, 1897-98.

TORONTO, METEOROLOGICAL OFFICE.—Monthly Weather Review, Oct. 1898 to Sept. 1899.—Report of the Meteorological Service of Canada, 1896.—Toronto General Meteorological Register, 1898.

TRIESTE, I. R. OSSERVATORIO ASTRONOMICO METEOROLOGICO.—Osservazioni meteorologiche, Oct. 1898 to July 1899.—Rapporto annuale, 1896.

TRINIDAD, ROYAL BOTANIC GARDENS.—Meteorological Return.

TURIN, OSSERVATORIO CENTRAL DEL R. C. CARLO.—Annuario Storico-meteorologico Italiano, 1898.

TURIN, OSSERVATORIO DELLA R. UNIVERSITÀ.—Effemeridi del Sole e della Luna per l'orrizonte di Torino e per l'anno 1899.—Notize sui lavori della Commissione eletta dal Club Alpino per lo studio dei Ghiacciai Italiani.—Sulla eclisse totale di Luna del 27mo Dicembre 1898.

TURIN, R. OSSERVATORIO ASTRONOMICO.—Osservazioni meteorologiche, 1897-98.

TURIN, SOCIETÀ METEOROLOGICA ITALIANA.—Bollettino Mensuale publicata per cura dell' osservatorio centrale del Real Collegio Carlo Alberto, vol. xviii. No. 9 to vol. xix. No. 7.

UPSALA, OBSERVATOIRE MÉTÉOROLOGIQUE DE L'UNIVERSITÉ.—Bulletin Mensuel, 1898.—Études internationales des Nuages, 1896-97.—Observations et mesures de la Suède, iii.

UTRECHT, K.-NEDERLANDSCH METEOROLOGISCHE INSTITUT.—Ouweders in Nederland, 1898.

VIENNA, K.-K. CENTRALANSTALT FÜR METEOROLOGIE UND ERDMAGNETISMUS.—Beobachtungen, Oct. 1898 to July 1899.—Bericht des Sonnblick-Vereines, 1898.—Jahrbuch, 1895, 1896, and 1898. Theil i.

VIENNA, K.-K. HYDROGRAPHISCHEN CENTRAL-BUREAU.—Jahrbuch, 1897.

VIENNA, OESTERREICHISCHE GESELLSCHAFT FÜR METEOROLOGIE.—Meteorologische Zeitschrift, Dec. 1898 to Nov. 1899.

VIZIGAPATAM, G. V. JUGGA ROW OBSERVATORY.—Notes on the Meteorology of Vizagapatam, by W. A. Bion: part i., Rainfall; part ii., Report, 1897.

WASHINGTON, GEOLOGICAL SURVEY.—Report, 1896-97, parts 1-5; 1897-98, parts 1, 4, and 6 continued.—Mineral Products of the United States, 1888-97.

WASHINGTON, HYDROGRAPHIC OFFICE.—Pilot Chart of the North Atlantic Ocean, 1899.—Pilot Chart of the North Pacific Ocean, Jan. to April and June to Dec. 1899.

WASHINGTON, SMITHSONIAN INSTITUTION.—Excerpt Papers from the Smithsonian Report, 1896, Nos. 1096-1100, 1102, and 1106.—Explorations of the Upper Atmosphere.—Letters from the Andrée Party.—On Soaring Flights, by E. C. Huffaker.—Story of Experiments in Mechanical Flight, by S. P. Langley.

WASHINGTON, U.S. NAVAL OBSERVATORY.—Report of the Superintendent for the year ending June 30, 1898.

WASHINGTON, WEATHER BUREAU.—Lightning and the Electricity of the Air.—Monthly Weather Review, Sept. 1898 to Sept. 1899.—Proceedings of the Convention of Weather Bureau Officials held at Omaha, Nebr., Oct. 13-14, 1898.—Report of the Chief, 1897-98.

WATFORD, HERTFORDSHIRE NATURAL HISTORY SOCIETY.—Transactions, vol. x. Nos. 2-4.

WELLINGTON COLLEGE, NATURAL HISTORY SOCIETY.—Report, 1898.

WELLINGTON (N.Z.), GENERAL REGISTER OFFICE.—Official Year-Book, 1898-99.—Statistics of the Colony of New Zealand, 1897.

YALE (U.S.), UNIVERSITY OBSERVATORY.—Report, 1898-99.

Zi-ka-wei, Observatoire Magnétique et Météorologique.—Bulletin Mensuel, 1896.—La Navigation à Vapeur sur le Haut Yang-tse, par P. S. Chevalier, S.J.

Zürich, Schweizerischen meteorologischen Central-Anstalt.—Annalen, 1896.

Presented by Individuals.

Aburrow, C.—Annual Report relating to the Public Works Department of the Stadsraad, Johannesburg, S.A.R.—Meteorological Observations taken at Joubert's Park, Johannesburg, S. Africa, Nov. 1898 to Aug. 1899 (MS.).

Agamennone, G.—Sopra un sistema di doppia registrazione negli strumenti sismici.

Baracchi, P.—Cloud Observations in Victoria.

Baxendell, J.—Meteorological Observations at Southport, Dec. 31, 1898 to Dec. 16, 1899.—Results of Observations at the Fernley Observatory, Southport, 1898.—The Weather of 1898: Main features of the months at Southport.

Bebber, Dr. J. van.—Wissenschaftliche Grundlage einer Wettervorhersage auf mehrere Tage voraus.

Bell, Major.—Charts from a Richard Barograph at Yewhurst, East Grinstead, 1898.

Bentley, R.—A Quarter of a Century's Rainfall at Upton (Bucks), 1874-99.

Black, Dr. W. G.—Summer Meteorology—Sea-side, with Diagrams.

Boffito, Padre G.—Un Porta della Meteorologia.

Brown, A., and Boobbyer, Dr. P.—The Meteorology of Nottingham, 1898.

Brown, W. P.—The Climbers' Club Journal, vol. i. No. 3.

Callendar, H. L., and M'Leod, C.—Observations of Soil Temperatures with Electrical Resistance Thermometers.—Preliminary Results of Observations of Soil Temperatures with Electrical Resistance Thermometers.

Chandler, A.—Meteorological Report, Borough of Torquay, 1898.—Seventeenth Report (Third Series) of the Committee on the Climate of Devon.—The Average of Temperature, Rainfall, and Sunshine of Devon.

Chapman, Dr. T. A.—Lepidoptera with a General Inland Distribution in Europe, but confined to Coast Habitats in England.

Clayton, H. H.—Investigations on Periodicity in the Weather.

Clifford, H.—Annual Report of the State of Pahang, 1898.

Colborne, Dr. H.—Annual Report of the Meteorological Observations for the year 1898 at Hastings.

Cooke, R.—Return of Rainfall for 1898 at Detling, Maidstone.

Coventry, F. (the late).—Diagram of Readings of the Barometer and Thermometer at Duddington, Stamford, Jan. to Nov. 1899 (MS.).

Coxen, Mrs.—Records of Meteorological Observations at Bulimba, Queensland, July 1898 to June 1899 (MS.).

Cresswell, A.—Records of Meteorological Observations taken at the Observatory of the Birmingham and Midland Institute, 1898.

Dechevrens, P. M.—Les variations de la température de l'air dans les tourbillons atmosphériques et leur véritable cause.

Dixon, C.—Results of Meteorological Observations taken at Holland House, Middlesex, Dec. 1898 to Nov. 1899 (MS.).

Doyle, P.—Indian Engineering, 1899.

Eaton, H. S.—Returns of Rainfall, etc., in Dorset, 1898.

Editor.—Ciel et Terre, 1899.

Editor.—Electrical Review, 1899.

Editor.—Home Counties Magazine, vol. i. No. 1 to vol. ii. No. 1.

Editor.—Nature, 1899.

Editor.—Travel, Jan. 1899.

Editors.—Observatory, 1899.

Fowler, T. W.—A Contribution to Australian Oceanography.—Determination of Latitude by Observations in the Prime Vertical.—Observations with Aneroid and Mercurial Barometers and Boiling-point Thermometers.—Observed Variations in the Dip of the Horizon.—The Determination of Heights by Barometric Methods.

Fox, W. L.—Meteorological and Magnetical Tables at Falmouth, 1898.

Gautier, B.—Résumé Météorologique pour Genève et le Grand St-Bernard, 1897-98.

Ginn & Co.—Practical Exercises in Elementary Meteorology, by R. de C. Ward.

Glyde, E. E.—Meteorological Observations at Whitchurch, Tavistock, Nov. 1898 to Oct. 1899.

Greenwood, W. N.—Greenwood's Kludonometric Tide Tables, 1899.

Hamberg, H. E.—Om Skogarnes inflytande på Sveriges Klimat.

Hardwick, Dr. A.—Annual Report of the Medical Officer of Health, and Meteorological Report, Newquay, 1898.

HARRIS, Dr. S.—A Guide to Guimar Hospital for Tuberculosis, with an Appendix on Teneriffe and Grand Canary.

HAWORTH, Dr. F. G.—Report of the Medical Officer of Health for Darwen, 1898.

HAZEN, H. A.—Forests and Rainfall.—Meteorologic Waves.—Some Consideration as to the Mechanism of Highs and Lows.—The Distribution of Moisture in the United States.—The Moon and the Aurora.

HELLMANN, Dr. G.—Regenkarte der Provinz Schlwien.

HEYWOOD, H.—Meteorological Observations in the Cardiff Naturalists' Society's District, 1898.

HILDEBRANDSSON, Dr. H. H.—Quelques recherches sur les centres d'action de l'atmosphère. II. La Pluie.

HILL, G. H.—Returns of the Rainfall in the Glasgow, Manchester, Ashton, Dewsbury, Stockport, Halifax, Blackburn, Holme Reservoirs, Oldham and Batley Waterworks Districts, 1898.

HOPKINSON, J.—Report on the Rainfall in Hertfordshire, 1898.—Meteorological Observations taken in Hertfordshire, 1898.—The Chadwell Spring and the Hertfordshire Bourne.

HUNTER, J.—Meteorological Observations at Belper, 1899.

KELLY, Dr. C.—Weather Report for Worthing for the month and for the half-year ending Dec. 31, 1898.—Weather Report for Worthing, Jan. to Oct. 1899.

LECKY, J.—MS. Observations taken by the late Mr. Lecky, May 1799 to May 1804.

M'LANDSBOROUGH, J.—The Meteorology of Bradford, 1898.

MACLEAR, Vice-Admiral J. P.—Études sur les mouvements de l'air, par Lartigue.—Études sur l'origine des courants d'air principaux, par Lartigue.—Figures to denote the Force of the Wind.—Geometrical Investigations concerning the Phenomena of Terrestrial Magnetism, by T. S. Davies.—Hygrometrical Tables adapted to the use of the Dry and Wet Bulb Thermometers, by J. Glaisher (3rd ed.).—Letters to denote the State of the Weather.—Mean Temperature of the Day, and Monthly Fall of Rain, at 127 Stations under the Bengal Presidency, from Official Registers kept by Medical Officers for the year 1861, by W. H. Sykes.—Memoirs (4 to 14) with reference to the Law of Storms in India, by H. Piddington. -Meteorological Instructions of the Cape Town Meteorological Committee.—Note on the Laws which regulate the Distribution of Isothermal Lines, by H. Hennessy.—On a Differential Barometer, by W. H. Wollaston.—On Periodical Laws discoverable in the Mean Effects of the larger Magnetic Disturbances, by E. Sabine.—On the Annual Variation of the Magnetic Declination at different Periods of the Day, by E. Sabine.—On the Diurnal Variation of the Magnetic Declination at St. Helena, by E. Sabine.—On the Evidence of the Existence of the Decennial Inequality in the Solar-diurnal Magnetic Variations, and its Non-existence in the Lunar-diurnal Variation of the Declination at Hobarton, by E. Sabine.—On the Laws of the Deviation of Magnetised Needles towards Iron, by W. H. Christie.—On the Means adopted in the British Colonial Magnetic Observatories for determining the Absolute Values, Secular Change, and Annual Variation of the Terrestrial Magnetic Force, by E. Sabine.—On the probable Electric Origin of all the Phenomena of Terrestrial Magnetism, by P. Barlow.—On the Westerly Route for crossing the Line, by H. Toynbee.—Paper on Meteorology, by R. FitzRoy.—Probabilités météorologiques pour l'année 1864, par M. Bulard.—Remarks on Revolving Storms.—Système d'observations météorologiques continues annonçant les époques de changements de temps, par C. Bulard.—The Probable Weather and Storm Periods in 1870, by "B."—Treatise on the Motions of the Earth and Magnet.—Uses to which Mason's Hygrometer is applicable.—"Vox Stellarum," or a Loyal Almanack for the years 1808 and 1822, by F. Moore.

MARKHAM, C. A.—Meteorological Report for Northamptonshire, Oct. 1898 to Sept. 1899.

MARSHALL, S. A.—Rainfall in the Lake District, Dec. 1898 to Nov. 1899.

MAWLEY, E.—Lessons from the Great Drought of 1898.—Meteorological Observations at Berkhamsted, Dec. 14, 1898 to Dec. 6, 1899.—The Rosarian's Year-Book, 1899.

MELLISH, H.—The Weather of 1898 at Hodsock Priory, Worksop.

MIDGLEY, W. W.—Annual Report of the Museums and Meteorological Observatory of the Borough of Bolton, 1898.

MITCHELL, Rev. J. C.—Results of Meteorological Observations taken in Chester during 1898.

MOHN, H.—Das Hypsometer als Luftdruckmesser und seine Anwendung zur Bestimmung der Schwere-Korrektion.

MOSSMAN, R. C.—Report on the Meteorology of Scotland for the year ending Sept. 30, 1898.—Results of Meteorological Observations taken at Edinburgh during 1898.

ORMEROD, Miss E. A.—General Index to Miss Ormerod's Reports on Injurious Insects, 1877-98.

PARNABY, J. M.—Meteorological Report for Albert Park, Middlesborough, Dec. 1898 to Nov. 1899.

PEEK, Sir C. E.—Meteorological Observations at Rousdon Observatory, 1898.

PERCY, C. W.—Kite-flying by Steam Power.

POLIS, P.—Die Niederschlagsverhältnisse der Rheinprovinz.—Die Strömungen der Luft in den barometrischen Minima und Maxima.—Die Strömungen der Luft in den Cyclonen und Anticyclonen.—Die Temperaturverhältnisse von Aachen.

PRESTON, A. W.—Meteorological Notes, 1898, from Observations taken at Brundall, Norfolk.

ROTCH, A. L.—Exploration of the Free Air by means of Kites at Blue Hill Observatory.

RUSSELL, Hon. F. A. R.—London Fog and Smoke.

RUSSELL, H. C.—Current Papers, No. 3.—Waterspouts on the Coast of New South Wales.

SALLE, O.—Das Wetter, 1899.

SCHAW, Maj.-Gen. H.—Australasian Weather Charts and New Zealand Storms.—Notes on the Vertical Component of the Motions of the Earth's Atmosphere.—On the Interaction of Cyclones upon one another.

SLADE, F.—Meteorological Observations at Beckford, Tewkesbury, 1898.

SMELT, Rev. M. A.—Rainfall at Heath Lodge, Cheltenham, 1867-98.

STOKES, J.—Annual Report on the Health of Margate, and Meteorological Report, 1898.

SWETTENHAM, F.—Report by the Resident General of the Federated Malay States to His Excellency the High Commissioner, 1899.

SYMONS, G. J.—Annuaire de la Société Météorologique de France, tome viii., 1860.—Bulletin of International Meteorology, 1875-82.—Karte zu von Mollendorffs Regenverhältnisse Deutschlands. — Symons's British Rainfall, 1898. — Symons's Monthly Meteorological Magazine, 1883 and 1899.—U.S. Monthly Weather Review, 1881-82.

SYMONS, Dr. W. H.—Annual Report of the Medical Officer of Health to the Bath Urban Sanitary Authority, 1896 and 1898.

TAYLOR, Capt. E. R.—Report and Results of Meteorological Observations made at Ardgillan, Co. Dublin, Ireland, during the year 1898.

TAYLOR and FRANCIS, Messrs.—Calendar of the Meetings of the Scientific Bodies of London, 1899-1900.

TEISSERENC DE BORT, L.—Sur les ascensions dans l'atmosphère d'enregistreurs météorologiques portés par des cerfs-volants.

TINSLEY, G. W.—The Mechanics of a Cyclone, by a Mechanic.

TYRER, R.—Annual Report on the Meteorology of Cheltenham, 1898.—Climate of Cheltenham, 1898.—Rainfall in the County of Gloucester, Dec. 1898 to Nov. 1899.

USBORNE, Miss.—Charts from a Richard Barograph at Writtle, Chelmsford, 1898 and 1899.

VALLOT, J.—Annales de l'Observatoire Météorologique physique et glaciaire du Mont Blanc.

VAUGHAN, J. D. W.—Meteorological Observations at Suva, Fiji, Feb. to July 1898.

VINCENT, J.—Comment on photographie les nuages.

WAGSTAFFE, W. W.—Report of the Weather, Sevenoaks, 1898.

WARD, R. DE C.—The Equipment of a Meteorological Laboratory.

WATERS, R.—Sunshine in the English Lake District, 1898.

WHIPPLE, R. S.—Meteorology and Seismology.

WILMSHURST, A. J.—Rainfall at Manor Park, Essex, 1898.

LANTERN SLIDES.

BAYARD, F. C.—Alipor Observatory, Calcutta.—Burketown Observatory, Queensland.—Capemba Observatory, Brisbane.—Chemnitz, Royal Saxon Meteorological Institute (2 slides).—Deutsche Seewarte, Hamburg (2 slides).—Eidgenössisches Physikgebäude in Zurich.—Hobart Observatory, Tasmania (2 slides).—Institutul Meteorological Romaniei.—Hong-Kong Observatory (2 slides).—Moncalieri Observatory, Italy.—Mount Kosciusko Observatory, New South Wales.—Mount Wellington Observatory, Tasmania.—Observatoire de Athenes.—Observatoire du Infante D. Luiz, Lisbon.—Perth Observatory, Western Australia (2 slides).—Royal Meteorological Institute, Utrecht.—Toronto Observatory, Canada.—Upsala Observatory, Sweden (2 slides).—Weather Bureau, Washington.—Portraits of Dr. R. Billwiller (Zürich).—T. F. Claxton (Mauritius).—W. E. Cooke (West Australia).—W. G. Davis (Cordoba).—Dr. W. Doberck (Hong-Kong).—D. Eginitis (Athens).—J. Eliot, F.R.S. (Calcutta).—R. L. J. Ellery, F.R.S. (Melbourne).—H. C. Kingsmill (Hobart).—Dr. H. Mohn (Christiania).—Prof. W. L. Moore (Washington).—Dr. A. Paulsen (Copenhagen).—Dr. R. Rubenson (Stockholm).—H. C. Russell, F.R.S. (Sydney).—Prof. Dr. P. Schreiber (Chemnitz).—Dr. R. H. Scott, F.R.S. (London).—C. M. Stewart (Cape Town).—Dr. J. P. Van der Stok (Batavia).—C. L. Wragge (Brisbane).

LATHAM, B.—Climatic Conditions necessary for the Propagation and Spread of Plague: 15 slides showing temperature of ground and relation to mortality, Bombay.

E. MAWLEY.—Grand Junction Canal and Tring Reservoir: normal condition and drought, 1898 (4 slides).

APPENDIX VI.

BEQUESTS.

BEQUEST BY THE LATE C. L. PRINCE, F.R.A.S.

ABBE, C.—Cloud Observations at Sea.

BARKER, T. H.—Results of Meteorological Observations at Bedford, 1861.

COXWORTHY, F.—On the Constitution of the Atmosphere, geologically considered.

CRALLAN, T. E.—Meteorological Observations taken at the County Lunatic Asylum, Haywards Heath, 1871, 1878, and 1879.

LIDDELL, J.—Meteorological Register kept at Bodmin, 1885 and 1886.

LONDON, ROYAL NATIONAL LIFEBOAT INSTITUTION.—Directions for fixing Coast Barometers and for keeping a Barometer Chart, by J. Glaisher.

[LUCAS, W.]—Forty Years' Temperature and Rainfall at Hitchin, 1850-89.

MALDEN, C.—Rainfall at St. Lawrence Rectory, Isle of Wight, 1868-77.

MILNER, W. R.—Meteorological Table for the year 1855 at Wakefield Prison.

MOYLE, M. P.—Meteorological Summary of the Weather at Helston from 1845 to 1855, both inclusive, in Quarterly Periods.—Meteorological Summary of the Weather at Helston for the year 1855.

PIM, W. H.—Summary of Meteorological Observations for 1861, taken at Monkstown, Co. Dublin.

POINTER, J.—A Rational Account of the Weather.

PRINCE, C. L.—Meteorological Journal kept at Uckfield, July 1, 1842 to May 15, 1872; and at Crowborough Hill, from May 16, 1872 to Nov. 15, 1898 (MS.)—Meteorological Report for Crowborough, Dec. 1876.—Summary of a Meteorological Journal for Jan. 1851, observed at Uckfield.

PRINCE, L.—Meteorological Observations, Jan. 1, 1846 to Oct. 31, 1854 (MS.).

S. M.—Summary of Meteorological Observations made in Kendal in 1866.

SAINT-HILAIRE, J. B.—Météorologie d'Aristote.—Traduite en français pour la première fois et accompagnée de notes perpétuelles, avec le petit traité apogryphe du monde.

SMELT, M. A.—Synopsis of Rainfall, on the Surface of the Ground, registered at Twenty-four different Meteorological Stations in England during the year 1861.

SYMONS, G. J.—Barometrical Depression, Dec. 23-27, 1859.

WHISTLECRAFT, O.—The Weather Record of 1856, being Extracts from the Journal of Orlando Whistlecraft, Thwaite, Suffolk.

BEQUEST BY THE LATE CANON J. SLATTER, F.R.A.S.

ALLNATT, H.—Monthly Meteorological Tables for the year 1857; together with a Summary showing the Fall of Rain at about Thirty Localities in England, Ireland, and Scotland.

BARKER, T. H.—Results of Meteorological Observations at Bedford, 1859 to 1861.—The Weather at Bedford for the years 1860 and 1864.

BURROW, W. and J.—Summary of Meteorological Observations taken at Malvern, 1868.

CHISWICK.—The Weather of 1864 at Chiswick, by R. T.

DREW, J.—Results deduced from a Meteorological Register kept at Southampton during the years 1851 and 1853.

GLAISHER, J.—Remarks on the Weather during the quarter ending Dec. 31, 1851.

MOYLE, M. P.—Meteorological Summary of the Weather at Helston, 1861.

OXFORD, MAGDALEN COLLEGE LABORATORY.—Meteorological Register for the months July 1875 to Oct. 1876, Dec. 1876, April and June 1877, March and July to Oct. 1878, Jan. to March 1880, Jan. to March and Sept. to Dec. 1881, and Dec. 1891 (MS.).—Rainfall registered at Magdalen College 1875, 1876, 1878 to 1881, and 1885 to 1886.

OXLEY, W.—Anemometer for Self Registering the Daily Pressure and Mean Variable Directions of the Wind.

PLANT, T. L.—Meteorological Report for 1861, from observations taken at Camp Hill, Birmingham.

SLATTER, J.—Meteorological Journal kept at Iffley, Oxford, Nov. 3, 1847 to Dec. 31, 1861; at Streatley, Jan. 1, 1863 to May 23, 1880; and at Whitchurch, Reading, May 24, 1880 to April 5, 1899 (MS.).

SMELT, M. A.—Synopsis of Rainfall registered at Twenty-three different Meteorological Stations in England during the year 1862.

SYMONS'S RAINFALL CIRCULAR, 1864 and Feb. and April 1865.

APPENDIX VII.

REPORTS OF OBSERVATORIES, ETC.

THE METEOROLOGICAL OFFICE.—Lieut.-Gen. Sir R. Strachey, R.E., G.C.S.I., F.R.S., Chairman of Council; Robert H. Scott, D.Sc., F.R.S., Secretary; Capt. M. W. Campbell Hepworth, R.N.R., F.R.A.S., Marine Superintendent.

Considerable changes have occurred in the administration of the Office since the last Report was printed.

On June 24, Lieut. C. W. Baillie, R.N., the Marine Superintendent, died quite suddenly, of heart affection. His place was filled by the appointment of Capt. M. W. Campbell Hepworth, F.R.Met.Soc., who took up his duties on October 1.

At the end of the year Mr. Scott's resignation of his Secretaryship took effect. His successor is Mr. William Napier Shaw, F.R.S., Assistant Director of the Cavendish Laboratory, Cambridge.

MARINE METEOROLOGY.—*Meteorological Charts of the Southern Ocean between the Cape of Good Hope and New Zealand.*—These charts were published during the past summer, and it is hoped that they will prove of considerable value to seamen navigating the Southern Ocean.

South Atlantic Ocean and West Coast of South America.—Steady progress has been made in the discussion of the observations which have been extracted from the Office logs and from those of Her Majesty's ships, and the method of exhibiting the results on charts has been practically decided.

The Weather of the Winter 1898-99 *over the North Atlantic.*—Daily synoptic charts have been prepared for a period of sixty days, from December 18, 1898, to February 15, 1899, to illustrate the exceptionally stormy character of the weather along the trans-Atlantic routes during that period. These charts are now being lithographed, so that the work may be expected to appear shortly.

WEATHER TELEGRAPHY.—Considerable reductions have been made in the number of reporting stations, owing to the necessity of retrenchment in order to arrange for a pension fund. Some of the members of the staff, after more than forty years' service, are approaching the age at which retirement is enforced.

The stations which have been discontinued for daily reports are Ardrossan, York, Cambridge, The North Foreland, Hurst Castle, and Prawle Point; but in place of the two last, Portland Bill has been established, as about half-way between Dungeness and Scilly.

In addition it should be mentioned that the reporting station in the west of Co. Mayo has been moved from Belmullet to Blacksod Point.

LAND METEOROLOGY OF THE BRITISH ISLES.—The volume of *Results of Observations from Stations of the Second Order* for 1896 has appeared. The volume of *Hourly Mean Readings for the Five Observatories* for 1896 has been published.

In connection with the anemometer experiments which have for some time been in progress at Holyhead, it may be mentioned that the Robinson Cup instrument has been removed to a position closely adjoining the other instruments, with which its records will in future be more strictly comparable. The non-oscillating pressure-plate erected two years ago has yielded some interesting results. So far the observations appear to confirm those obtained with the bridled and the pressure-tube anemometers, and at the same time they show that the high pressures frequently recorded by freely oscillating plates are fallacious, the latter being in some cases as much as 200 per cent in excess of the truth.

Atmospheric Electricity.—The Royal Society have continued the grant for a research into this intricate subject for another year. Mr. Wilson has handed in the account of his work in 1898-99 in the form of a paper "On the Comparative Efficiency of Condensation Nuclei of Positively and Negatively Charged Ions," which was communicated by the Council to the Royal Society and appears in volume 193 of *Philosophical Transactions.*—*January* 9, 1900.

ROYAL OBSERVATORY, GREENWICH.—W. H. M. Christie, C.B., M.A., F.R.S., Astronomer-Royal.

The meteorological work of the Royal Observatory in 1899 has been maintained on the usual plan, with such modifications and extensions as have been rendered necessary by the development of the scheme of observations for the new observing station in the Magnetic Pavilion enclosure.

Temperature of the air ranged between 90°·0 on August 15 and 19°·3 on December 16. The yearly mean was 50°·7, being 1°·2 above the average. The monthly means were in excess in all months except March, May, October, and December: in January the excess amounted to 4°·2; in August to 8°·9; and in November to 4°·8. The recorded sunshine amounted to 1704 hours, exceeding the amount recorded in 1898 by 289 hours. In the summer months, May to August, the excess was particularly marked, amounting to 253 hours as compared with the record for the corresponding months in 1898. The rainfall for the year amounted to 22·33 ins., being 2 ins. below the average. In the five years 1895-99, which have all been dry, the total deficiency of rainfall amounts to 17 ins. The rainfall in August, 0·35 in., was the smallest August fall on record, the smallest fall in the preceding fifty-eight years having been 0·45 in. in 1849. Among the occasional phenomena observed during the year, the remarkable exhibition of parhelia with brilliantly coloured halos, and inverted arcs, on October 11, may be particularly noted.—*April* 18, 1900.

ROYAL OBSERVATORY, EDINBURGH.—Ralph Copeland, Ph.D., F.R.S.E., Astronomer-Royal for Scotland.

The meteorological observations have been made by the staff, under the same conditions as in former years. The bi-daily readings of the barometer, dry and wet bulb thermometers, wind and cloud, and daily readings of the shaded and exposed maximum and minimum thermometers have been continuous throughout the year. The Robinson anemometer and King's barograph have also been in operation without interruption. A monthly copy of the daily readings has been supplied, as usual, to the Scottish Meteorological Society for the use of the Registrar-General for Scotland, and the monthly means have been published in the Registrar's Quarterly Reports. The weekly readings of the rock thermometers at Calton Hill have been continued. The observations since 1879 are now being prepared for publication by Mr. Heath, along with a summary of the whole series from the commencement in 1837 to the end of 1899.—*January* 29, 1900.

KEW OBSERVATORY, RICHMOND, SURREY.—Charles Chree, Sc.D., F.R.S., Superintendent.

The several self-recording instruments for the continuous registration of atmospheric pressure, temperature of air and wet bulb, wind (direction and velocity), bright sunshine, and rain have been maintained in regular operation throughout the year, and the standard eye observations for the control of the automatic records duly registered.

The tabulations of the meteorological traces have been regularly made, and these, as well as copies of the eye observations, with notes of weather, cloud, and sunshine, have been transmitted, as usual, to the Meteorological Office.

The electrograph worked generally in a satisfactory manner during the year.

The "setting" of the electrometer needle, mentioned in last year's Report, has been considerably reduced, and the working of the instrument improved, by the removal of the large glass cup with a diameter of 100 mm.—used for holding the sulphuric acid—and the substitution for it of a small glass beaker with a diameter of 40 mm., resting upon a disc of paraffin, and containing 10 drachms of acid only. The acid and accumulated moisture is removed at frequent intervals.

Scale value determinations were made on January 24, May 12, July 21, and November 7, and in addition the potential of the battery has been tested weekly. Forty cells only have been employed throughout the year. A battery of thirty-six Clark cells has been purchased from Messrs. Muirhead, on behalf of the Meteorological Council, with the hope of thereby introducing greater certainty into the interpretation of the records.

The comparisons of the potential, at the point where the jet from the water-dropper breaks up, and at a fixed station on the Observatory lawn, referred to in last year's Report, have been continued, and the observations have been taken three or four times every month.

The observations of a series of distant objects, referred to in previous Reports, have been continued. A note is taken of the most distant of the selected objects which is visible at each observation hour.

The results of the comparison of platinum and gas thermometers at Sèvres were analysed by Dr. Chappuis and Dr. Harker, and embodied in a paper which was read before the Royal Society in June, and which will appear in the *Philosophical Transactions*.

The experiments which were begun in 1895 into the constancy and general behaviour of platinum thermometers have led to the accumulation of a large number of results. These have been dealt with by the Superintendent in a critical paper which was recently read before the Royal Society.

Towards the end of the year an oil-bath was constructed, from the designs mainly of Dr. Harker, for the purpose of comparing thermometers at high temperatures. Some preliminary comparisons have already been made in it of a few German and English mercury standards with a platinum thermometer.

During the year 1899, the air temperature ranged from 21°·3 on December 14 to 87°·3 on August 15. The mean was 50°·6. The maximum temperature in the sun's rays (black bulb *in vacuo*) was 147° on July 9, whilst the lowest temperature on the ground was 6° on December 14.

1763 hours of sunshine were recorded, giving a mean percentage of the total possible of 37, which is 8 per cent above the average for the 20 years 1877-96, and is the largest yearly value yet registered, the next largest being 35 per cent in 1893. Values above the average were obtained every month, with the exception of April and November, and the totals for February, June, and August were the largest yet recorded for those months.

The total rainfall was 20·845 ins., which is 3·19 ins. below the average for the past 35 years. The greatest and least monthly falls were respectively 3·980 ins. in November, and 0·445 in. in August, this latter total being the lowest August value since 1859. In the 10 days between October 27 and November 5 there were three falls exceeding one inch, viz. 1·055, 1·350, and 1·250 in.

Parliament having, on the motion of Her Majesty's Ministers, voted a sum of money for the establishment of a National Physical Laboratory, to be under the management of a committee nominated by the Council of the Royal Society, the Royal Society have drawn up, and the Government have approved, a scheme for the organisation of the Laboratory. In accordance with this scheme, the Kew Observatory is incorporated with the National Physical Laboratory, and becomes part of the organisation thereof as from January 1, 1900. The Kew Observatory Committee as hitherto constituted ceases to exist at the same date, and its property is to be transferred to the Royal Society. The work of the Observatory will, however, proceed as heretofore, and will be carried on by the existing staff.

The scheme of organisation already mentioned constitutes an Executive Committee, as the authority having the immediate management of the National Physical Laboratory, and this Committee includes at present six members of the Kew Observatory Committee. The scheme also provides for the appointment of a Director, who, subject to the authority of the Executive Committee, is to have sole control and direction of the officials of the National Physical Laboratory and of the work done within it. Mr. R. T. Glazebrook, F.R.S., has been appointed to this office.—*March* 28, 1900.

The Circulation of Water in the North Atlantic.—The Gulf Stream is to be distinguished from the broad drift into which it merges. The former has an inner circulation, which reaches to the Azores and to the region of the Trades, and circles round the Sargasso Sea; the Gulf Stream drift is a vast movement of the warm superficial waters of the Atlantic, driven by the prevail- South-west winds towards the north and east. The limit between the two, as determined by the directions taken by floating bottles, may be placed between 43° and 47° N. The drift spreads out in a fan shape, and branches into four streams, of which each goes towards one of the four straits which unite the North Atlantic with the Polar seas, viz. Davis Strait, Denmark Strait, the channel between Iceland and the Faeroes, and that between the latter and Shetland. The circulation of the North Atlantic is strongly influenced by the conformation of the bottom of the sea. Other factors which enter into these movements are the melting of the polar ice, the relative salinity and temperatures of the various streams; and the seasonal variations in the circulation have a profound effect on the climate of these waters and the neighbouring lands. The complex relations of these various conditions are the subject of a study by Dr. C. Pettersson in *Petermann's Mitteilungen*, Nos. 3 and 4 of the present year. This essay, which is itself too condensed to admit of any shorter abstract, brings together the results of research in the North Atlantic until last summer, and is illustrated by charts and diagrams.—*Scottish Geographical Magazine.*

The Riviera in the Last Century.—The observations taken by Tobias Smollett at Nice, and printed in his *Travels through France and Italy*, extend from November 1763 to April 1765, and from February 1764 to April of the year following are very fully recorded. The thermometers Smollett employed were one of mercury, graduated on the Réaumur scale, and one of spirits of wine constructed by Chateauneuf and graduated in the same manner. They were placed in the shade in a room without a fire, with a southerly exposure, and the readings were taken between ten and eleven in the forenoon.

REMARKS ON THE WEATHER CONDITIONS OF THE STEAMSHIP TRACK BETWEEN FIJI AND HAWAII.

By Capt. M. W. CAMPBELL HEPWORTH, F.R.Met.Soc.

(Plate XII.)

[Read March 21, 1900.]

Having in view the fact that to the seafarer generally the intertropical regions of the Pacific Ocean are at least comparatively unknown, I venture to hope that the following remarks upon the Trade Winds of the Pacific, as experienced on the Canadian-Australian Steam Route, may be useful to those navigators who are called upon to make the passage under sail between Australia and the North American Continent, and, moreover, perhaps interesting and acceptable to the Fellows of the Royal Meteorological Society.

The following records are taken from a journal of my voyages, which followed in regular sequence, an interval of five months excepted (viz. from the end of November 1896 to the beginning of May 1897), and deal with observations of wind, its force and direction, made and recorded by my officers and myself every four hours during twenty passages between Australasia and British Columbia in the steamships *Warrimoo* and *Aorangi*, commencing May 1896 and extending to August 1899.

Although the track which must be taken by a sailing vessel differs very largely from that of the steamers on which the observations referred to were made, I contend that no very appreciable difference will be found to exist in the direction and force of the wind over an area extending many hundreds of miles east and west of it, excepting in the vicinity of island groups; and that, at any rate, such knowledge as my records supply should be of some service as indicating the seasonal variations of the Trade Winds of those regions and their mean limits at different periods of the year.

I have endeavoured to embrace these observations within as small limits as intelligibility would allow; and therefore, instead of drafting them on charts for each month of the year, I have employed four charts in their delineation, each exhibiting the observations which belong to their allotted quarter.

It may appear at first sight that instead of adhering to the conventional division of the year, a more efficient grouping of the months might be adopted for the purpose under discussion, bracketing, for instance, the summer and winter months respectively, and, in like manner, those months during which in temperate climates spring ushers in the summer, and those again when autumn merges into winter. This grouping of the seasons was at first contemplated, but subsequently, on a closer examination, it was found, as regards the Southern Hemisphere, to display serious faults —should the plan contemplated, of drafting the observations on four charts, each containing as far as practicable about the same number of observations, be carried into effect. For instance, the month of May, when the South-east Trade Winds blow steadily, would be classed on a chart with March and April, months during which the winds are very variable; and in like manner the month of September would be found with those of October and November, an analogous case, for the South-east Trade Wind still holds its own in September, whereas during the two succeeding months it is found to be giving way to the Monsoon of summer.

In accordance with the method adopted, we have on separate charts (Plate XII.): (1) January, February, March, monsoonal and variable; (2) April, May, June, variable and South-east; (3) July, August, September, South-east; (4) October, November, December, variable and monsoonal.

The direction and force of the wind is shown by arrows which fly with the wind, each arrow bearing a symbol denoting the force of the wind.

In making the passage between the straits of Juan de Fuca and Honolulu it has usually been found that the first indication of the expected North-east Trade Wind, and preceding it often by as much as 300 miles, is a long swell from the north-eastward, although the wind be not, and has previously not been, experienced from that quarter to the North-eastward, but, on the contrary, has probably been from some Westerly point. Let me make myself clearly understood.

Approaching the edge of the North-east Trade Winds from the north-eastward, the atmospheric conditions for a considerable area to the north-eastward being known for some time past, and these conditions not being North-easterly, it appears reasonable to suppose that the wind would first be experienced, and with no accompanying swell, until such time as the wind should have been of sufficient strength to account for a corresponding disturbance of the sea surface; this, it is contended, is the reasonable assumption, but the reverse happens.

A swell is experienced that has no wind at its back, and not infrequently it is quite a heavy swell.

The opportunity is here taken for proclaiming this apparent anomaly, which has not, to the best of my belief, been brought forward hitherto, for it is a phenomenon which may be found associated not only with the North-east Trade Winds of the North Pacific Ocean, but also with other strong winds blowing over extensive areas in all parts of the globe. Sailors usually take into consideration the advent of a swell or swells when forecasting the weather. Thus when a swell from a certain direction is encountered, and decreases as his vessel proceeds, he conjectures that the cause of disturbance is becoming more remote; and conversely, when it increases, it augurs, in his opinion, a nearer approach, and he assumes that before long the wind may be expected to come from the quarter from which the swell is making, because the sea surface is being impelled in such a direction by the wind "at the back of it,"—to use a sailor's expression,—but it is my desire to show that a swell is frequently experienced *in rear of the wind that produced it.* The occurrence has often puzzled me. When a high, increasing head-swell has led one to expect before long the gale which caused it, the expectation has frequently been unfulfilled. When it has been anticipated from an increasing sea disturbance following, quartering, or on the beam, that its correlative in wind would be forthcoming, it has, in many instances, not arrived.

In the first instance the gale may have been blowing over areas many hundreds of miles ahead of the vessel experiencing the sea disturbance it

JI AND HAWAII.

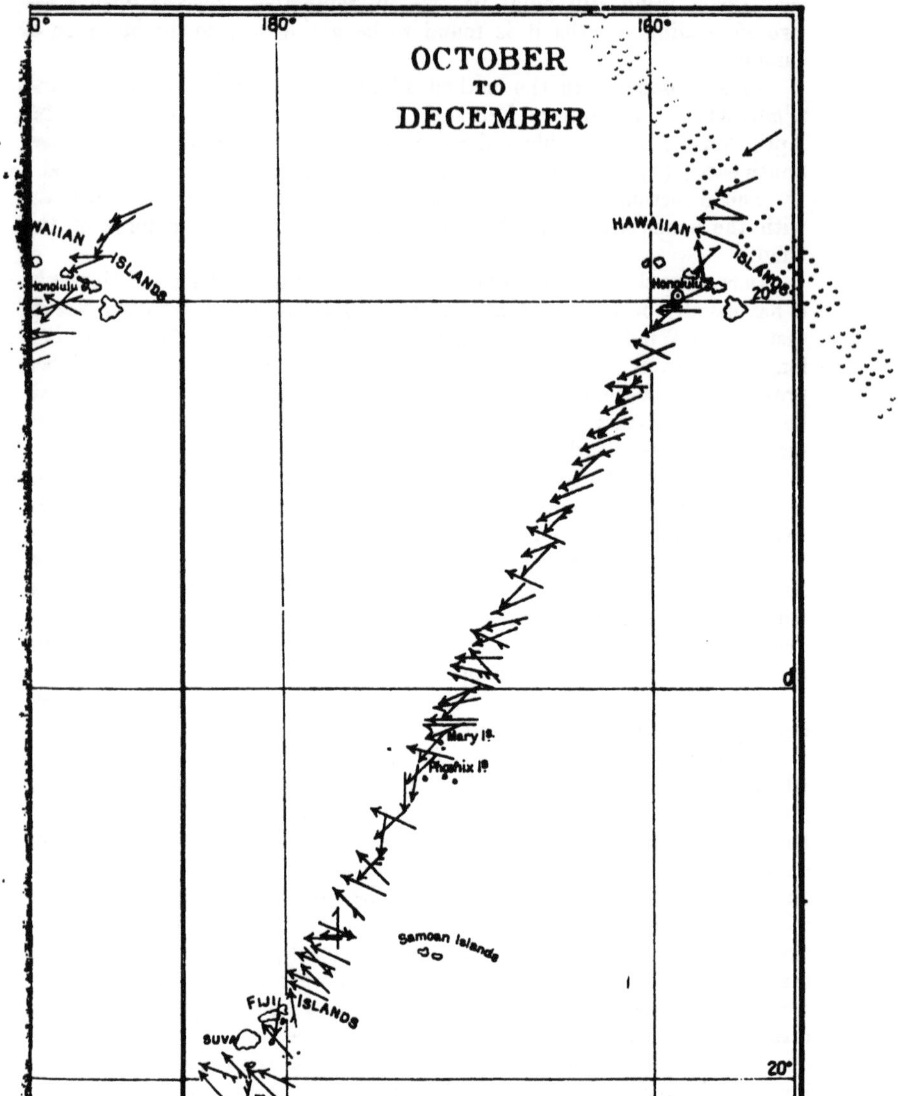

lm & Variable.

Malby & Sons, Lith.

produced, and many have "taken off" suddenly. In the second case a fitting explanation would be that the vessel had run out of the area of disturbance; but when it can be reasonably assumed that for a vast expanse of water rearward of a long ocean swell there exists no dominating power, some other explanation must be sought. The explanation, in my opinion, is that the waves caused by the impact of air in motion upon an expanse of water induce undulations upon its surface in rear as well as in front of the impelling power whenever the vibrations are set in motion.

As has already been stated, then, the first intimation of the North-east wind comes in a long swell from that quarter, and during the months of January, February, and March these Trade Winds rarely extend to the northward of the 24th parallel of North latitude upon the route which we are following, and its mean limit may be stated as 22½° N. At this period of the year, as also during December and the latter part of November, strong Southerly winds are occasionally experienced as far south as the 13th degree of North latitude, resulting from the passage of low-pressure systems to the northward, traversing the Pacific from west to east. These Southerly winds are attended by rainy weather, and have an enervating and depressing effect upon the white population of the Hawaiian Island.

According to the published report of Mr. Curtis J. Lyons, Director of the Hawaiian Weather Bureau, the average yearly rainfall at Honolulu, from 1894 to 1897 inclusive, was 35·4 ins. The largest rainfall in one day in 1894 occurred in February, and was 2·7 ins.; the smallest in May, and was 0·13 in. In 1895 the largest rainfall in one day occurred in December, and was 6·15 ins.; the smallest, in July, being 0·21 in. In 1896 and in 1897 the largest rainfalls in one day occurred in December and in September, being 5·00 ins. and 1·64 in. respectively; the smallest, occurring in July and in August, being 0·16 in. and 0·19 in. respectively. During the years 1894 to 1897, inclusive, the North-east Trade Wind was experienced during 20 days and upwards each month from March to October inclusive, and on 24 days and upwards each month from May to September inclusive; for the remaining months of the year much less frequently.

During January, February, and March moderate Trade Winds, with occasional showers, may be expected from the 20th parallel southward to the Equator, thence lighter North-easterly winds and fine weather through the Phœnix Group to 5° S., the wind retaining its North-easterly direction, but associated, as a rule, with unsettled squally weather to 20° S. Thus it will be seen that the winds become monsoonal between the Equator and 20° S. during these months, as also during the latter part of December; but instead of the wind being North-west, as it is found to be at this period of the year in the Indian Ocean and Java and Arafura Seas, it here takes a North-easterly direction.

By way of accounting for the existence of the Monsoon over the area under discussion, it may here be appropriately stated that during passages made in the months of January and February 1897, 1898, and 1899 the mean temperature of the air between the parallels of 5° N. and 5° S. was found to be 79°·8, and it was of course considerably lower to the northward; and between the parallels of 15° and 20° S. the mean temperature was found to be 81°, and again between 16° and 26° S. it was found to be 81·5·. These months may be considered as representing the height of the Monsoon season. It will be seen that at this season the temperature of the belt 5° each side of the Equator was nearly 2° (1°·7) less than that of a belt contained between the 16th and 26th parallels; whereas during the months of May, June, and July of the same years, when the Trade Wind was blowing steadily, the mean temperature of the Equatorial belt alluded to was 82°·1, and of the belt contained between the 16th and 26th parallels 74°·8, and was of course considerably lower to the southward. That is to say, the Equatorial belt, which during January and February was the cooler, during May, June, and July became the warmer by 7°·3. The observations from which the mean of the temperature was obtained were taken on board the *Aorangi* by my officers and myself every four hours, and the readings are from one of Casella's thermometers, supplied by the Meteorological Office. The thermometers were located in the screen supplied for the purpose in a favourable situation.

In a paper which I read before the Royal Society of New South Wales upon "Current Observations on the Canadian-Australian Route," I endeavoured to show that the position and limits of the counter current of the Pacific on this route, and presumably for hundreds of miles east and west of it, changed during different seasons of the year, and that during the Monsoon season it was absent. It may be well, however, to give a portion of the text in full, which runs as follows:—

"My records show that during the months of May, June, and July the counter current may be met with between the parallels of 1° and 6° N., and during August, September, and October between the parallels of 5° and 9° N.; and it should be noted that during these months the South-east Trade Winds blow without intermission.

"During December we find two observations of counter currents between the Equator and the 4th parallel, and three observations of currents flowing to the north-eastward and east-north-eastward between the 8th and the 11th parallels of North latitude, which will not, for reasons given hereafter, be considered as belonging to the counter current proper.

"During February and March no eastward-moving currents have been recorded; but in April two observations of counter current are recorded, one between the 3rd and 5th parallels, and one between the 8th and 10th.

"Disregarding these last two observations, which may be looked upon as exceptions to prove the rule, we find that from December to March inclusive, *i.e.* during the Monsoon season in the region about Fiji and westward to the Coral Sea, when the wind between this and the Equator is drawn to the North-eastward, the Equatorial counter current slackens, or is altogether absent, and that it is questionable whether it has much value during April."

Now, in addition to the rise in the temperature of the air during the spring and summer months over that area of water so thickly interspersed with islands which lies between the 16th and 24th parallels of South latitude, and between the 170th meridian of East longitude and the Australian coast, owing to the superheating of the islands and of the comparatively shallow, and thus more easily heated, waters by which they are surrounded, it may be assumed that the warm water of the Equatorial current, taking at this season of the year a more southerly course and—due in some measure, no doubt, to the absence of the counter stream—having a greater volume and velocity, also causes a rise in temperature of the air lying over these regions, and thus it will appear that wind and current act and react one upon the other.

The Monsoon season is the hurricane season, December and March being the months during which hurricanes most frequently occur, and at an interval, it is said, of about three or four years. Although, from such information as I have been able to gather, the force of the wind during the passage of one of these revolving storms does not attain, as a rule, so high a velocity as it usually attains in visitations of a similar nature in most other tropical regions where they may be looked for, yet they do an incalculable amount of damage to property, unroofing many of the settlers' houses and often laying low those of the native population, felling and uprooting cocoa-nut and banana trees and wrecking the sugar-cane. Copra, sugar, and bananas being the chief product of these islands, upon which their prosperity mainly depends, these visitations are as much dreaded by the white population as by the native.

From the data supplied to me by Mr. J. D. W. Vaughan, F.R.Met.Soc., Government Meteorologist at Suva, and Captain Woolley, Harbour-master at that port, it appears that previous to the advent of a hurricane at that place the indications, in addition to a falling barometer, usually are a steady freshening of the wind at South-east associated with much rain, heavy banks of clouds to the south-eastward, and a high swell which breaks over the barrier reef and rolls into the harbour. As a rule, the wind blows strongest after the passage of the lowest pressure from some Northerly point, when the track of the storm centre lies to the north-westward.

During the five years 1894 to 1898 inclusive, the mean temperature of the air at Suva, Fiji, was 79°, the mean monthly maximum temperature was 83°·8, and the mean monthly minimum temperature was 72°·3: the highest temperature being 98°, occurring on March 14, 1897; and the lowest temperature being 61°·5, occurring on October 27, 1898.

The mean humidity of the air was 73 per cent. The mean rainfall was 100·6 ins. for twelve months. The greatest yearly rainfall was 111·8 ins. in 1894; the smallest rainfall being 79·7 ins., and occurring in 1896. The mean height of the barometer from 1894 to 1898 was 29·95 ins., the lowest reading being 28·60 ins., which occurred when a hurricane was being experienced on January 7, 1895, at 9 a.m., during a partial lull, soon after the passage of the centre of the storm, the wind being North at the time, force 9. The highest reading was 30·29 ins., which occurred on June 29, the wind being South-east at the time and the humidity 58 per cent.

Amongst the Fiji Group the South-east Trade Wind is liable to interruption at all times of the year. From the beginning of April to the end of November it is most constant.

In January, February, and March, between the 20th and 24th parallels, the South-east Trade Wind prevails, but is liable to interruptions.

During April, May, and June the limits of the North-east Trades appear to be from 24° N. lat. to 2° N. lat., but between this and 5° S. lat. the winds retain for the most part their North-easterly direction and are associated with a good deal of rain. Between the 5° S. and 25° S. the South-east Trades blow steadily, as a rule, during these months. From the end of June to the beginning of October the North-east Trade Wind is met with in about 25° N. lat., and extends south of the Equator. During these months very little rain is experienced near the Equator, and it is difficult to define the southern limits of the North-east Trades and the Northern limits of the South-east, as they merge into one another without interruption, and south of the 5th parallel to the 20° S. the latter blows very steadily.

During October, November, and December the North-east Trades extend from about 30° N. to 3° N. on the Canadian-Australian Route, and the South-east Trades from about the latter parallel to 23° S. during October and part of November; but during the latter half of November and in the month of December the Easterly wind has frequently more Northing than Southing in it, and the weather is, as a rule, squally and unsettled. At all times the belt of calms and variable winds between the North-east and South-east Trades is far more circumscribed in its limits than those of the corresponding belts in the Atlantic and Indian Oceans, and, as before stated, during July, August, and September it can hardly be considered to exist.

DISCUSSION.

THE PRESIDENT (DR. C. THEODORE WILLIAMS) said he wished to thank Capt. Hepworth for his valuable and interesting paper.

Commander W. F. CABORNE, C.B., said that as he had never navigated the particular waters dealt with by the lecturer in his paper, his remarks would necessarily be of little value. At the same time, it was a fact that a heavy swell was frequently met with in different parts of the world, which was not found to be the precursor of winds. Capt. Hepworth's remarks regarding swell after a breeze were curious, and this point would seem to call for further investigation.

Mr. E. D. ARCHIBALD said he had twice taken the journey between Fiji and Hawaii. It was an interesting part of the world, and in the Pacific conditions were less circumscribed by land than anywhere else, and consequently the Trade Winds were more free and less interrupted by doldrums. With regard to the question of the swell following after the wind, it was no doubt quite possible that if the swell were the result of vibrations set up by the wind they should emanate from the centre of the disturbance, but it was certainly remarkable that they should have the power of spreading in the reverse direction to their apparent motion of translation. While at Hawaii, he (Mr. Archibald) had met Mr. Lyons the director of the U.S. Weather Bureau Service there, who had particularly drawn his attention to the unique advantages possessed by a volcano named Halcakalà on the island of Maui. This mountain was an ideal position for taking observations of the trade winds. It was an isolated cone rising 10,200 feet above the sea-level, and a good comparison could thus be made between the anti-Trade Winds and the lower currents. This he (Mr. Archibald) had suggested to the American Weather Bureau. The temperature of Hawaii was much lower than that of Fiji, the mean being 74°, and the island never felt too hot, although it was in the same latitude as Bombay. In crossing the Equator in the Pacific the belt of warmth was hardly noticeable, which was very different from the crossing in the Atlantic and Indian Oceans. The Trade Wind was generally distinguishable by its regularity. In the Monsoon months the Trade Winds shown on Capt. Hepworth's charts had a distinct deflection southwards towards the Australian land area similar to what occurred in a reverse direction towards Asia in the Indian Monsoon months.

Mr. W. H. Dines said he did not consider that there was anything remarkable in the wave disturbance travelling backwards against the wind; for if a stone were thrown into the water the ripples spread out on all sides, and why should not this be the case for waves that were caused by other means? He would like to draw Capt. Hepworth's attention to a very common example on the English coast. There was often in summer, with continuously calm weather or light Westerly winds, a heavy ground swell on the north-east coast of England, and this could nearly always be traced to a gale on the Norwegian coast. The swell was of very common occurrence, and was not looked upon by the fishermen as a sign of bad weather, probably because of the well-known fact that in temperate latitudes a barometric depression with its accompanying strong winds seldom travels from east to west.

Capt. D. Wilson-Barker remarked that he agreed with Capt. Hepworth and Capt. Caborne with regard to the prevalence and curious nature of the swell, and thought it was due entirely to the propagation of the waves from centres of disturbance, for it must not be forgotten that the disturbances and the observers were both in movement. He had taken the trip once in a sailing ship, but had gone by the inner course through the islands, and had made a much quicker passage than the other vessels that had taken the outer route. With regard to the smallness of the doldrum belt, he could confirm Capt. Hepworth's explanation by the exceedingly good conditions for extension of the Trade Winds.

Capt. M. W. C. Hepworth, in reply, said he was pleased to have heard the remarks of the Fellows. The temperatures for Hawaii in the paper were taken from Mr. Lyons's printed reports. With reference to the passages taken by vessels, he had sketched out tracks for different seasons, and they varied greatly according to the time of the year. Occasionally, the steamship track through the islands could be taken as Capt. Wilson-Barker had done, with success, and he had in fact recommended it to be taken at certain seasons of the year. He thanked the Fellows for listening so patiently to his paper, which he had feared could claim but little interest for landsmen.

Climatology of the Sonnblick Group.—Dr. Fritz Machaček contributed a paper on the climatology of the glacier region of the Sonnblick to the report of the *Sonnblickverein* for 1899, dealing specially with Eduard Richter's observations of the remarkably low level of the snow-line in the eastern part of the Hohe Tauern. The recent considerable developments in the system of observations, especially the increase in the number of summit stations, has provided a large quantity of new material. The glaciers cover, or covered in 1871, an area of 16 square kilometres (6·2 square miles) on the north side of the group, and about half as much on the south side. The mean elevation of the glaciers on the two sides is 2680 metres (8800 ft.) and 2730 metres (9000 ft.) respectively, the same as the position of the "climatic" snow-line. Above this level, say 2700 to 3100 metres (8900 to 10,200 ft.), lie the catchment basins of the glaciers. Calculating from the rainfall, the yearly increase in thickness corresponds to from 14 to 17 metres (46 to 56 ft.) of freshly-fallen snow—as much as Heim allows for the Western Alps, and twice as much as von Schlagintweit estimated at a time when few observations at high-level meteorological stations existed. The annual mean of temperature is +0°·1 C. (32°·2 F.), and the summer mean 7° C. (44°·6 F.), at an elevation of 2200 metres (7200 ft.); at 2700 metres (8900 ft.) the summer mean is 3°·6 C. (38°·5 F.); and at the top of the Sonnblick, 3106 metres or 10,190 feet, the annual mean is −6°·1 C. (21° F.), summer mean +0°·4 C. (32°·7 F.). The new observations confirm Hann's supposition that the level of the snow-line changes from month to month within comparatively narrow limits. The lower edge of the snow covering the temporary snow-line rises from 1400 to 1600 metres (4600 to 5200 ft.) in April, to 2400 to 2700 metres (7900 to 8900 ft.) in July; and snow disappears from the valley slopes almost entirely in August. The rule that the snow limit rises towards the centre of the mountain mass holds good for the temporary as well as for the climatic snow-line. Slopes with southerly exposure are specially favoured; they are clear of snow half the year up to 2000 metres (6600 ft.), and for 140 days to 2400 metres (7900 ft.), while northerly exposures are only clear for 60 days at the same elevation. The proportion of snow removed from the "Firn" region by melting, estimated from the air temperatures above freezing, is markedly greater in the glaciers exposed to the south than in those exposed to the north, notwithstanding similar precipitation and mean temperatures—a significant example of the importance of this element. The cause of the low level of the climatic snow-line—2700 metres (8900 ft.)—is therefore primarily the abundant precipitation, which favours large Firn deposits; but the low summer temperature, preventing extensive melting of snow, is also an important factor. Great local variations of level—2600 to 2900 metres (8500 to 9500 ft.)—are due to the conditions of exposure and the shadows thrown by the mountain masses.—*Geographical Journal.*

Temperature of the Free Air.—"The Temperature of the Free Air" is the title of a paper communicated by Dr. Hergesell to Part V. of *Petermann's Geographische Mitteilungen.* We have frequently referred to the great importance of this subject and to the valuable work performed by Dr. Hergesell in organising ascents of manned and free (or unmanned) balloons, and in discussing the results of the observations obtained. In the present paper he collects and discusses the most recent materials, and deals especially with the daily range and the vertical decrease of temperature in the upper strata of the atmosphere. The observations show that even at a height of a few hundred metres there is a very small diurnal range: at night-time it amounts, in some ascents, to only a few tenths of a degree, and in the day-time, at about 800 metres, to some 3° or 4° centigrade, when solar radiation is unobstructed. On cloudy days, and in the mean values, the daily amplitude is much less. With respect to the vertical decrease of temperature, the results of thirty sets of observations show that in all levels up to 10,000 metres an extremely varying temperature obtains, according to the season of the year and the conditions of weather. The decrease at that height reached or exceeded 40° C. in all cases, but no fixed rule could be laid down as to the regular decrease with altitude.—*Nature,* July 12, 1900.

THE ETHER SUNSHINE RECORDER.

By W. H. DINES, B.A., F.R.Met.Soc.

[Read March 21, 1900.]

SINCE there are already two sunshine recorders in common use in England, it may seem superfluous to describe another; but as I have had a different kind of instrument in use for four years, which possesses the advantage of requiring very little expense to keep it going, I have thought it well to give this description of it.

The instrument is an electrical one, and consists of two parts—the one to be exposed to the sun; the other, which registers on ordinary paper the amount of sunshine, to be put indoors in any convenient position. Without entering into details, the parts may be described thus:—

The sun shines upon a bent glass tube, one end of which is blackened. The tube contains a small quantity of mercury and some ether, but is completely exhausted of air. The result of the sun shining upon this tube is that the blackened end is warmed more than the other, the pressure of the ether vapour in this end is therefore greater than in the other, and the mercury, which naturally lies in the bottom of the bend, is driven away from the blackened end. The tube being mounted in a metal holder, which can turn a short distance on pivots, the change of position of the mercury overbalances the holder, which falls over, and is stopped by an electric contact piece against which it falls. When the sun ceases to shine, the mercury returns to its lowest position, and the holder also returns to its normal position.

The metal holder which contains the glass tube is in metallic connection with an electric battery, and the result may be summarised thus:—

When the sun is shining the battery is in connection with an insulated wire which we may call the "sunshine wire"; and when it is not shining the battery is in connection with another wire, the "non-sunshine wire."

These two insulated wires and the return circuit, in which the battery is placed, run from the sunshine recorder to the registering apparatus.

The registering apparatus consists of a clock drum mounted on a spiral; the drum makes a complete turn each day, and also drops about one-sixth of an inch. It runs for a week, and requires a fresh paper and winding only weekly. The registration is effected by a siphon pen on ordinary paper, the pen being on the paper when the sun is shining, and not on the paper when the sun is not shining. This is effected by two electro-magnets round which the "sunshine" and the "non-sunshine" wires are coiled. When the current passes through the "sunshine" wire and magnet, the pen is pressed on the paper; when the current goes through the other magnet, the pen is withdrawn from the paper.

To save battery power the following arrangement is added. The "sunshine" wire has a break in it, but this break is bridged over by the mechanism which carries the pen in such a manner, that when the pen is not on the paper the break or gap in the wire is bridged over, but the bridge fails just before the pen reaches the paper. Thus on the sun beginning to shine, a current passes round the sunshine magnet, and draws over the pen; as soon, however, as the pen is over, the circuit is broken, and the current ceases, but the pen remains in contact with the paper. A similar arrangement is introduced into the "non-sunshine" wire. Thus the battery simply shifts the pen, and has no time to run down; and a single Leclanché cell, value about 1s., will work the apparatus for two or three years.

The week's trace consists of a series of parallel lines lying over each other on the paper. The time of sunshine for any given day is obtained by adding up the total length, just as in the Campbell-Stokes or Jordan recorders, but the beginning and the end of the trace are always perfectly definite.

The advantages of this instrument seem to me to be:—

1. The very trifling expense and trouble in the use of the instrument, since the record is on common paper, and only 52 instead of 365 sheets are required per year.

2. The recorder itself can be put on a pole, since when once set it

The Ether Sunshine Recorder.

requires no attention, and thus the trouble of finding an unshaded spot can be partially avoided.

The necessity for a clock is certainly a disadvantage, since no clock can equal the sun itself as a timekeeper. The use of electricity is in some ways objectionable; but considerable experience has convinced me that the trouble that so often accompanies its use in meteorological instruments is due for the most part to faulty design. If the contacts are of platinum; if the magnets are arranged, as they easily may be, to work with small battery power; and if the design is such that it is practically impossible for the circuit to remain on and the battery run down, then there is not, as a rule, any trouble.

There is one other point about this instrument, perhaps the most important of all, which must be mentioned. The instrument can be made to register any degree of sunshine, or more strictly of sun-heat; if, however, it be made to register when the sun is low down or half hidden in a bank of cirrus cloud, it will also register in summer when the sun is high and almost or quite hidden by fog, or low thin cloud.

The point, however, at which registration commences is settled by the maker, and cannot be fairly altered by the observer. What this precise point should be is more or less a matter of opinion. The instruments made by Mr. Casella are designed to agree with the Campbell-Stokes recorder, since, whatever my own opinion on this point may be, I consider that uniformity in meteorological observations is of more importance than anything else. There is no difficulty about testing the similarity of one of these instruments to a standard. It is easily done by placing it in a room of given temperature, and at a given distance from a standard source of heat, such as a candle, or blackened copper globe of a definite size containing boiling water, and noting how long it takes for the tube and holder to fall over, or preferably, how far off the standard source of heat must be, so as to make the holder just, but only just, fall over.

DISCUSSION.

THE PRESIDENT (Dr. C. THEODORE WILLIAMS) thanked Mr. Dines for his admirable paper and expressed the appreciation of the Society for his very ingenious instrument.

Capt. D. WILSON-BARKER inquired whether Mr. Dines had experienced any difficulty owing to the heat caused by the glass globe over the instrument.

Mr. R. BENTLEY—while recognising the advantage of the electrical attachment when the recorder had to be placed on a roof, or out of easy reach of examination—inquired whether Mr. Dines would issue the instrument in an alternative form for use in ordinary positions. In this last case it might be practicable to attach the recording pen to the tilting (or expansion) chamber impinging directly upon the cylinder revolving by clockwork. This would obviate any risk from batteries running down, and also, by the simplification of the instrument, reduce its cost under ordinary conditions—the electric attachment being reserved for special use.

Mr. R. H. CURTIS said there were two points about Mr. Dines's instrument in which it possessed a decided advantage over either of the sunshine recorders at present in use. The first of these lay in the fact that the recording portion could be placed indoors in any convenient position, and at any reasonable distance from the exposed part, so that the difficulty of changing cards each night in what is in some cases an awkward, or even a dangerous, position is entirely obviated; whilst the second point is found in the compactness of the record, since the trace for seven days occupies less space and is more readily stored than the Campbell-Stokes record for one day. This latter advantage specially appealed to the speaker, because he had to face each year the difficulty of finding storage space at the Meteorological Office for the cards from a large number of stations; and when it is remembered that for each station there are 365 cards of three different shapes, it will be readily seen that the additional space required annually is considerable. Mr. Dines had mentioned another point in favour of the instrument which, however, the speaker did not think was an unqualified advantage, namely, that "the end of the trace was always perfectly definite." That was so, but on the other hand it should be said that the trace affords no indication whatever of the intensity of the solar heat, which the Campbell-Stokes instrument does give at any rate to some extent; and, after all, the gradual tapering off of the record of the latter at sunrise and sunset, and its varying width at other times of the day, speaks to a phase of the phenomenon which is not without some value. But in the speaker's judgment a really grave drawback to the instrument lay in the danger there was of its being made to suit the requirements of those who asked makers for the instrument which would yield the largest record of sunshine for the district in which they were interested. He was afraid, speaking from experience, that there were those who, whilst they would not falsify an observation, were yet quite content to quote results yielded by a peccant instrument. It was a point very strongly in favour of the Campbell-Stokes recorder, and possessed by no other, that if the instrument fulfilled the conditions which had been already laid down for it, it supplied a definite standard which could scarcely vary, and which secured practically the uniformity of result it was so desirable to get. These conditions were that the lens should be of crown glass, 4 inches in diameter, and 3 lbs. in weight, and that it should be properly mounted and adjusted in a bowl made to fit it. Such a lens will not record the faintest sunshine; but whenever the sun's rays acquire a certain minimum power a record will be made, and that minimum is sufficiently low to embrace all sunshine of any practical value.

Mr. E. D. Archibald said he thought that the glass cover would probably store up the heat, and might possibly make the instrument register even dark heat as well as sunshine. Mr. Blanford used to say that two similar solar radiation thermometers with black bulb *in vacuo*, placed side by side, would occasionally give results differing by as much as 10°. These instruments, which were very ingenious, might be liable to similar errors.

Mr. F. C. Bayard said he thought that the clockwork arrangement, by which, by the descent of a small space each day, the traces were arranged directly over each other, was an extremely good one, and greatly superior to most clockwork mechanisms. Mr. Dines had said that the instrument could be made to agree with the Campbell-Stokes recorder, or even made to register just as one pleased, and it would be a very good thing if a proper standard were determined and each instrument tested and set in a laboratory before being issued. There were several difficulties in connection with the Campbell-Stokes recorder, and recently two of the balls in London had come to grief, and probably some of the Fellows present had examined the curious markings on the Greenwich globe, no doubt caused by atmospheric impurities. Mr. Dines placed his apparatus under a glass cover, thereby ensuring it being kept clean. He wished to know whether the apparatus would be likely to deteriorate, say after being ten years in use. One great advantage of the instrument was that it could be placed in any position, while the recording part could be kept in the house.

Mr. R. Stanley Clarke inquired whether electrical disturbances were likely to affect the instrument.

Mr. W. H. Dines, in reply, said that there were two reasons for the glass cover. It was necessary for protection from the wind, and, being fixed on, it prevented any one from tampering with the instrument. Glass did not obstruct the direct rays of the sun, so that he did not think it should make any practical difference. As it had been pointed out, the electrical registration could be avoided, but as a matter of fact he (Mr. Dines) had used the instrument for several years and experienced no trouble from the electrical part. He fully agreed with the remarks made by Mr. Curtis; but, after all, one must trust to the honesty of the observer. All returns might be falsified; in the photographic recorder much depended on the sensitiveness of the paper, and recent experience had shown that the diathermancy of the glass ball of the Campbell-Stokes was not, at least in large towns, unalterable. Periodical inspection was doubtless necessary for sunshine recorders, as well as for other meteorological instruments.

COMPARISON BY MEANS OF DOTS.

By ALEX. B. MACDOWALL, M.A., F.R.Met.Soc.

[Read March 21, 1900.]

THERE is a simple method of representation by means of dots (a development of the graphic method), in which a dot is used to indicate two things: one by its relation to the line of abscissæ, the other by its relation to the line of ordinates. Thus two numerical series may be easily compared. Two lines may be drawn, one from each scale, to represent the two averages. These, crossing at right angles, divide the space into four parts, and the dots in these rectangles may then be counted.

This method, which does not seem to have been much used by meteorologists, is capable, I think, of many useful applications. If to some minds it presents a little initial difficulty, this may be soon overcome by familiarity and practice. I propose to submit to the Society a few examples of the method for consideration and criticism. These are all drawn from one field of investigation, viz. that relating to our winters and summers in London (Greenwich) since 1841.

I. *Comparison of the number of frost days with that of hot days (max. temp. 80° or more) in each year.*

Here we use the line of abscissæ for the frost days, and that of ordinates for hot days. The average of the former is 55; that of the latter 15; and from the corresponding points in the two scales two lines are drawn which cross at right angles. We may call the two upper rectangles *a* and *b*, and the two lower *c* and *d*. The first year, 1841, had 62 frost days and only 2 hot days. So, finding the point where a vertical line from 62 in the upper scale and a horizontal one from 2 in the lateral scale meet, we put a dot there. The same with other years. The number of dots in each rectangle is indicated at the outer corner, and their significance below the diagram (Fig. 1).[1]

Premising that the few remarks made on each diagram are merely by way of suggestion, not of full discussion, we may proceed to note the following features in this first diagram:—

1. The six hottest summers (over 27 hot days) all occurred in mild years (frost days *under* average).

2. Seven out of the nine coolest summers (6 hot days and less), were in cold years (frost days *over* average).

3. The rarity of a hot summer in a cold year may be put thus:—There were 27 cold years, and 22 of these had summers with less than 18 hot days (15 being the average), while only 5 summers had more than 18. These five summers, curiously, come very close together in number of hot days. They are as follows:—1847 (26 hot days), 1858 (26), 1870 (27), 1887 (27), and 1895 (26).

A mild year may have a hot or cool summer indifferently, but (unlike the case of cold years), the summer may be extremely hot (say over 27).

As a practical deduction from what has been said, if great cold in the

[1] In the diagrams as originally drawn cross-ruled paper was used; but the lines are here omitted, in order to show the distribution of dots more plainly.

early part of the year is followed by a hot summer, the cold in the end of the year is likely to be under average.

II. *Comparison of the number of hot days* (80° *or more*) *in a summer season with that of frost days in the winter following* (*September-May*).

The line of abscissæ here measures the former, and the line of ordinates the latter (Fig. 2). Averages as before.

1. The rarest case here is evidently a hot summer followed by a

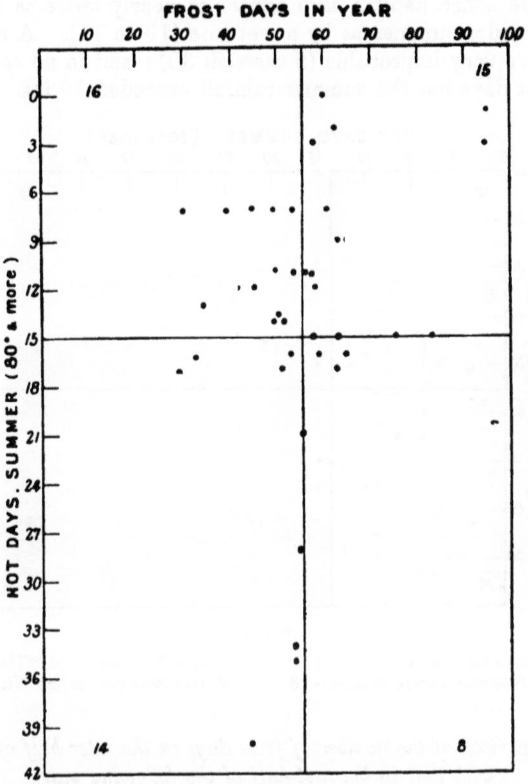

FIG. 1.

a. Winter half mild, Summer cool—16 *b*. Winter half cold, Summer cool—15
c. Winter half mild, Summer hot—14 *d*. Winter half cold, Summer hot—8

severe winter (7 instances); and the most frequent a cool summer followed by a severe winter (18 instances).

2. A hot summer has been followed by a mild winter more than twice as often as by a severe winter (16 to 7), and a cool summer by a severe winter more frequently than by a mild one (18 to 12). It is curious, however, that 3 out of the 4 hottest summers have been followed by severe winters.

3. This statement may be made:—There are 27 cold winters, and 22 of these were preceded by summers having not over 16 hot days: only 5 by summers with more than 16 hot days.

III. *Comparison of the number of frost days in winter (September to May), with rainfall in the summer following (May to August).*

The averages here are 55 frost days and 8·75 ins. rainfall.

1. Five out of the six wettest summers (over 13 ins.) were preceded by severe winters, and eight out of the twelve driest summers (under 6 ins.) were preceded by mild winters (*i.e.* 2 out of 3).

2. A severe winter may be followed by a wet or a dry summer (over or under average), almost indifferently, and the summer may be extremely wet. On the other hand, a mild winter is nearly twice as likely to be followed by a dry summer as by a wet one (19 to 11). A rainfall over 10 ins. is here very improbable (5 cases in 30); and in no case with less than 43 frost days has the summer rainfall exceeded 10 ins.

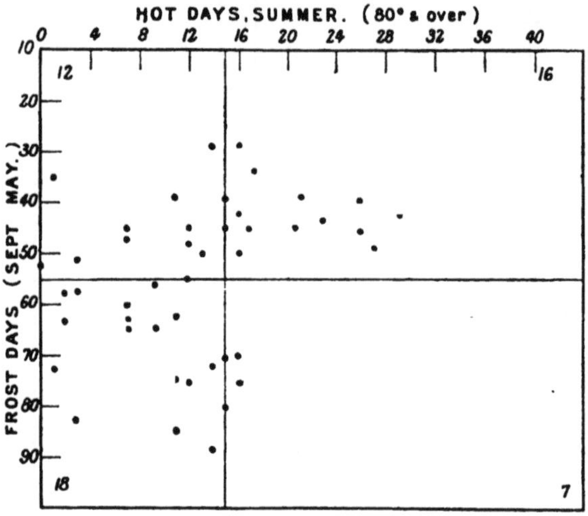

FIG. 2.

a. Cool Summer, mild Winter—12
b. Hot Summer, mild Winter—16
c. Cool Summer, severe Winter—18
d. Hot Summer, severe Winter—7

IV. *Comparison of the number of frost days in the later half of the year with that in the first half of the following year.*

The averages are here 18 and 38 respectively.

1. It will be seen that the instances in which the two halves have been similar (both severe or both mild), viz. 39, are just three times as numerous as those in which they have been different, viz. 13.

2. The rarest case is a mild second half followed by a cold first half. There have been only five instances of this; while the sequence, cold second half, mild first half, has occurred eight times.

V. *Comparison of the cold (frost days) in thirty successive first halves of the year with the first half following in each case.*

This diagram apparently illustrates the principle of compensation in weather. After a long time of one kind of weather we expect, in a vague way, some of the opposite kind to restore equilibrium. Perhaps the principle might be utilised to obtain some light on the character of coming seasons. We may compare a pretty big "block" of cold, say the total frost days in thirty consecutive winters, with the total frost days in the winter just following. In the present case we select the total frost days in the first half of the year, and proceed thus. We add the frost days in the thirty first halves of (*a*) 1841-70, (*b*) of 1842-71, (*c*) of 1843-72, and so on; then compare the first of these sums (*a*) with the total frost days in the first half of 1871, the second (*b*) with the same in 1872, the third (*c*) with the same in 1873, etc.

Using the abscissæ for the larger set of values, having an average of about 1100, and the ordinates for the smaller (average 38), we put dots as before. The dots here are not very numerous (29 in all), and therefore do not warrant a very confident statement; but so far as they go, we see that in general the cold thirty-year groups tend to be followed by mild first halves, and the mild thirty-year groups by cold first halves. Thus: (1) Of twelve thirty-year groups with more than 1100 frost days, only two were followed by cold first halves. (2) Of nine thirty-year groups with less than 1090 frost days only one was followed by a mild first half.

Should a more copious supply of data present the same kind of dot distribution as that here shown, it seems as if one might obtain some clue as to the limits, at least, within which a coming winter would probably fall.

As to the current season (Feb. 20, 1900), the total frost days in the 30 first halves ending 1899 is 1099, and looking at the diagram we might at least, I think, perceive that an extremely severe season was improbable.

VI. *Comparison of total frost days in thirty successive winters (December-February) with frost days in the following winter.*

This is merely another example of the kind of comparison just considered, the data being those for winter proper; and the results, which appear to be of the same order as above, need not be here enlarged upon.

These diagrams may suffice to show the general scope of the method; and while it might have been better, on some accounts, to have recourse to a variety of subjects widely apart, what has been said may perhaps prompt some students of weather among us, to whom the method may be new, to try its capabilities on some more of the numberless subjects to which it may be applied.

PROCEEDINGS AT THE MEETINGS OF THE SOCIETY.

March 21, 1900.

Ordinary Meeting.

Dr. C. THEODORE WILLIAMS, President, in the Chair.

CHARLES HENRY ALDERSON, Effingham, Woodridings, Pinner;
FREDERICK JOHN BARCLAY, Vronvelin, Lovelace Road, Surbiton;
Rev. HERBERT ARNOLD BOYS, M.A., North Cadbury, Somerset;
JOHN CHARLTON, Denton House, Low Road, Carlisle;
ALEXANDER MITCHELL DAWSON, Shu-le-Crow House, Keswick;
Capt. WILLIAM A. DOBIE, New Lodge, Ryde, Isle of Wight;
AMBROSE THOMAS FLAGG, M.A., Westoe, South Shields;
THOMAS JAMES GUILBERT, Colborne Villa, Rohais, Guernsey;
WILLIAM AINGE GUNNER, Ashleigh, Taunton;
PERCY CRAVEN HALL, M.A., The Nook, Gateacre, Liverpool;
GEORGE HOWARD HARRISON, J.P., Thornton, Ryde, Isle of Wight;
CHARLES PAGET HOOKER, L.R.C.P. Ed., Dollarward House, Cirencester;
DONALD W. HORNER, 82 New Park Road, Clapham Park, S.W.;
CECIL EDWARD MAPLES, Aughton Springs, Ormskirk;
FRANK JOHNSTONE MITCHELL, F.G.S., Llanfnechfa Grange, Caerleon;
THOMAS PRICHARD NEWMAN, Hazelhurst, Haslemere;
HENRY HAMILTON PALAIRET, J.P., Caltistock Lodge, Dorchester;
Sir JAMES RANKIN, Bart., M.P., Bryngwyn, Hereford;
M. B. SUBHA RAO, B.A., The Observatory, Madras;
HENRY ROFE, M.Inst.C.E., 8 Victoria Street, S.W.;
HENRY JOHN ROFE, M.A., F.G.S., 8 Victoria Street, S.W.;
JOHN WILLIAM SHEPHERD, Settle;
EDWARD SIMPSON, J.P., Walton Hall, Wakefield;
JOHN TERTIUS SOUTHALL, J.P., Parkfield, Ross;
GEORGE WELLER, J.P., The Plantation, Amersham, Bucks;
ARTHUR J. WILMSHURST, 6 Albany Road, Manor Park, E.; and
GEORGE ALEXANDER YOOL, Field Place, Weybridge,

were balloted for and duly elected Fellows of the Society.

Monsieur ALBERT LANCASTER, Royal Observatory, Uccle, Brussels; and
General MIKHAIL A. RYKATCHEFF, Central Physical Observatory, St. Petersburg,

were balloted for and duly elected Honorary Members of the Society.

The PRESIDENT stated that he had to announce with deep regret the death of Mr. G. J. SYMONS, F.R.S., which occurred on March 10 (see p. 159).

The following communications were read:—

"REMARKS ON THE WEATHER CONDITIONS OF THE STEAMSHIP TRACK BETWEEN FIJI AND HAWAII." By Capt. M. W. C. HEPWORTH, F.R.Met.Soc. (p. 235).

"THE ETHER SUNSHINE RECORDER." By W. H. DINES, B.A., F.R.Met.Soc. (p. 243).

"COMPARISON BY MEANS OF DOTS." By A. B. MACDOWALL, M.A., F.R.Met.Soc. (p. 247).

CORRESPONDENCE AND NOTES.

Kite Experiments at Blue Hill Meteorological Observatory.—At the Blue Hill Meteorological Observatory, on June 19, a kite used in the exploration of the air was sent up to the height of 14,000 feet, thus exceeding the greatest height previously obtained there by 1440 feet. The temperature at this height was 15° below freezing-point, the wind velocity was about 25 miles an hour from the North-east, and the air was extremely dry, although clouds floated above and below that level. The kites remained near the highest point from 5 to 8 p.m. On the way down the kites passed through a stratum of thin ragged clouds at the height of 1½ mile. These were moving with a velocity of about 30 miles an hour. At this time the wind at the Observatory, about 600 feet above the general level of the surrounding country, had fallen to a calm. The highest point was reached with 4½ miles of music wire, as a flying-line, supported by five kites attached to the line at intervals of about three-quarters of a mile. The kites were Hargrave, or box, kites of the improved form devised at the Observatory. They have curved flying surfaces modelled after the wings of a bird. The three kites nearest the top of the line had an area of between 60 and 70 square feet each, and the two others about 25 feet each. The total weight lifted into the air, including wire, instruments, and kites, was about 130 lbs.

Vertical Gradients of Temperature, Humidity, and Wind Direction.—A preliminary report by Mr. H. C. Frankenfield on the U.S. Weather Bureau Kite Observations of 1898 has recently been published. This paper discusses probably the largest amount of free air meteorological observations ever taken within a like space of time over so large an area, and adds to the general knowledge of temperature and hygrometric conditions of the lower levels of the air. An introductory chapter on the Kite Meteorograph, Construction and Operation, is added by Prof. C. F. Marvin.

Kite ascensions were commenced at seventeen stations in April 1898, and were continued to November 1898, but only those for the months of May to October inclusive have been used for the preparation of this report.

Temperature conditions at all elevations and under varying conditions of weather and time have been computed in terms of the gradient in degrees Fahrenheit for each 1000 feet, and the increase of elevation necessary to cause a fall of 1° in the temperature. The mean results are only given to degrees per thousand feet. Attention has also been devoted to the question of wind directions, relative humidity, and vapour pressure.

The results may be summarised as follows :—

Temperature.—The mean rate of diminution of temperature with increase of altitude, as determined from 1217 ascensions, and 3838 observations, taken at elevations of 1000 feet or more, was 5°·0 for each 1000 feet, or 0°·4 less than the true adiabatic rate. The largest gradient, 7°·4 per thousand feet, was found up to 1000 feet, and thereafter there was a steady decrease up to 5000 feet, the rate of decrease becoming less as the altitude increased. The gradient up to 5000 feet was 3°·8 per thousand feet. Above this altitude there is a tendency toward a slow rise, but the lack of a sufficient number of observations above 6000 feet forbids a definite statement to that effect. The morning gradients were also greatest up to 1000 feet, and least up to 5000 feet, and the rate of decrease was about the same as the mean rate, the curves showing a very close agreement in this respect. The average morning gradient was 4°·8 per thousand feet. The afternoon gradients were larger, but not decidedly so, the average value being 5°·8 per thousand feet. The greatest rate of decrease is still found at 1000 feet, and the least up to 5000 feet, if the few observations at 7000 feet are not considered as of equal rate.

Relative Humidity.—The relative humidities at and above the surface of the earth differed but little except at 7000 feet, where the surface humidity was 11 per cent less than that above. With this exception, the greatest difference was 3 per cent, and, except at 2000 and 8000 feet, the upper air percentages were the lower. The mean result obtained from all the observations showed 60 per cent at the surface and 58 per cent above—a difference of 2 per cent.

The stations at which there were marked differences were Washington, where the mean difference was 14 per cent; Omaha, where it was 29 per cent; Springfield, Ill., where it was 21 per cent; and Fort Smith, where it was 12 per cent—the surface humidity being the higher, except at Fort Smith. At the remaining thirteen stations, except Lansing, the upper air humidity equalled or exceeded that at the surface, but the difference at no place exceeded 10 per cent. At nine stations the difference was 5 per cent or less.

Vapour Pressure.—The vapour pressures are expressed in percentages obtained by the formula $\frac{p}{p^{\circ}}$, in which p represents the vapour pressure at any given altitude, and p° that observed simultaneously at the earth's surface. The mean of the percentages thus obtained was 59, and there was a steady, though not by any means uniform, decrease with increase of altitude. The percentage at 1500 feet was 82, and at 8000 feet 44. The decrease was most rapid between 2000 and 5000 feet, where it averaged 9 per cent for each 1000 feet. The decrease between 5000 and 6000 feet was only 3 per cent, while between 6000 and 7000 feet it was 10 per cent. The lowest percentage (52) was found at Omaha, and the highest (77) at Pierre.

Tule Fog.—In our search for local meteorological terms not widely known, but sometimes worthy of broader usage, we have come upon the expression "tule fog" as used by Mr. M'Adie in a recent number of the Report of the California Section.

According to the botanical dictionary, "tule" is a species of bulrush occupying large areas of swamp and overflowed bottom lands in California. Of course, therefore, we infer that "tule fog" is meteorologically equivalent to fogs over marshes and swamps, or the fogs of the lowlands and the valleys. It is essentially due to the cooling by radiation during clear nights. At first the vegetation cools by its own radiation; then the adjacent air cools by contact with the leaves and branches; after this cool air has settled quietly to the ground it cools still further by its own radiation and by contact with the cooling grass and leaves until fog is formed; the particles of fog then cool by their own radiation, and thus the layer of cold air grows upward, and the fog grows higher and higher until a little after sunrise.

Observers who look down upon such marshes and valleys from elevated stations would do well to keep a record of the depth of the accumulated layer of fog by noting the points that are still uncovered at its upper edge.—*U.S. Monthly Weather Review*, December 1899.

Meteorological Charts of the Southern Ocean between the Cape of Good Hope and New Zealand.—The Meteorological Council have published a set of Meteorological Charts for the above district, which show for each month of the year the direction and force of the wind for areas of 3° of latitude by 10° of longitude; also the barometrical pressure by isobars, and the temperature of the air and sea surface by isotherms. The regions of excessive range of sea-surface temperature are indicated by shading; and the amount of fog is shown by percentages of the total number of weather observations, and also, graphically, by curves. The currents are given in separate Monthly Charts.

The preparation of these Charts was carried out under the superintendence of the late Lieut. C. W. Baillie, who also made some remarks on the Charts.

Barometer.—The broad features of the barometric system exhibited on the Charts are the following :—

1. An area of high barometer lies over the sea, between the African Continent and Australia, throughout the year. It alters its position, slightly, from month to month, and, generally, the central portion of the system, which is sometimes divided into two parts, is situated more to the east and south during the six months November to April than in any of the other months.

2. Over the relatively small region of the Great Australian Bight, there is also evidence of a seasonal variation in the distribution of pressure, but the changes are not so regular as over the open sea. In the summer months, December to March, the barometer is lower over the land than over the sea, but during the winter the contrary is generally the case.

3. In the Tasman Sea, the changes from month to month are of a much less defined and regular character than those to the westward. Usually, the barometer is highest over the northern parts of this region, anticyclonic systems appearing in February and March.

4. In the far south the barometer is comparatively low throughout the year.

Winds.—The winds of the Southern Indian Ocean are subject to very similar seasonal movements as the areas of high and low barometer.

South of the parallel of about 35° S. the winds are mainly the result of cyclonic systems travelling to the eastward. As the centres of the depressions are generally far to the southward the resulting winds in the portion of the ocean shown on these charts are principally from the Western quarter.

As in similar latitudes in the North Atlantic and Pacific, the actual track of the depression may be considerably to the North or South of East, the rates of progression will vary, and the shape of the depression will greatly affect the veering of the wind, so that while one vessel may carry a wind from the West for great distances, another may experience constant shifts when comparatively small depressions moving in different tracks pass her in her course.

The high-pressure areas being farthest north during the winter months, winds from points in the Western half of the compass generally prevail from May to November. Off the African coast, however, North-easterly winds are experienced in nearly all months, but they are least marked in June and July.

As the high-pressure areas move southward the winds over the northern part of the sea, in the neighbourhood of about lat. 30°, become more variable in direction. By December, however, North-easterly and South-easterly winds are increasing in frequency, and in the first three months of the year they are the prevailing winds between the 30th and 36th parallels of latitude. This is therefore the best period for attempting a homeward voyage round the Cape of Good Hope. The winds off Cape Leeuwin are also, usually, favourable at this time.

In April the Easterly winds, although still experienced, are not so prevalent, and they do not extend so far south as in the preceding months. In May they are north of lat. 30°.

In the Tasman Sea during the summer months, January to March, winds blow from every quarter of the compass, but off the Australian coast the prevailing winds are Northerly to North-easterly, and off Bass Strait and Tasmania South-westerly. On the New Zealand side of the sea, Southerly to Easterly winds prevail. During the remaining nine months of the year the winds over this region are very variable in direction.

In all months, and practically all over the ocean, by far the greater proportion of winds are those ranging in force from 4 to 7 of Beaufort's scale, and calms are comparatively rare. During the summer months light winds are common over the northern parts of the sea.

Gales are not of frequent occurrence in January, and those encountered are mainly confined to the southern parts of the sea, south of about lat. 42°. As the year advances, however, they become more frequent and they are experienced farther north, until in June and July they are met with up to the 30th parallel. They then recede about as regularly southward towards the end of the year.

Air Temperature.—The general distribution of air temperature is very similar to that of the sea water, being fairly uniform throughout the year in the neighbourhood of Kerguelen, while in the more northern latitudes there is a difference of about 10° between the summer and winter mean temperatures. Over these northern localities, however, the temperature of the air is generally lower than that of the sea to the extent of a few degrees.

Fog.—Only the most northern parts of the sea are free from fog. South of about lat. 40°, over the western part of the sea, in the neighbourhood of the areas where the range of sea-surface temperature is great, fog is of frequent occurrence, amounting to as much as 10 per cent of the weather observations. South of New Zealand, from November to April, and also in August, fog is often experienced.

Sea Temperature.—The mean temperature of the sea surface, in the more southern latitudes, does not undergo any very important change during the year; the temperature near Kerguelen being approximately 40° in all months, but farther north there is a greater variation depending on the season.

From January to March the temperature of the sea surface off the west coast of Australia is about 5° lower than on the east coast, and the difference ranges from 5° to 10° in October, November, and December, but there is little or no difference during the six months April to September.

The difference in the temperature on the western and eastern sides of New Zealand is less marked, but there is a general tendency for a somewhat higher temperature down the east coast of North Island, and lower up the east coast of Middle Island.

Throughout the year the temperature off Cape Colony is about 10° lower on the west coast than it is on the east coast.

The regions of greatest range of temperature, 20° and upwards, are situated west of the 70th meridian, between the latitudes of about 39° and 45° S. In January, February, and March, areas of great range are also found along the south coast of Cape Colony, and in May there is a similar small area off Sydney, New South Wales.

RECENT PUBLICATIONS.

British Rainfall, 1899. Compiled by H. Sowerby Wallis, F.R.Met.Soc. 8vo. 307 pp. 1900.

This is the thirty-ninth consecutive volume of *British Rainfall*, and is the first one that does not contain an article from the pen of the founder of the Rainfall Organisation, the late Mr. G. J. Symons, F.R.S.

The number of perfect rainfall records published in this volume is 3501, being an increase of 86 upon the previous year. The rainfall for 1899 was again greatly deficient. The largest rainfall was at Ben Nevis Observatory, where the total fall amounted to 187·31 ins.; the least rainfall was recorded at

Moulton, Norfolk, where the total only amounted to 17·31 ins. In addition to the rainfall statistics and notes on the meteorology of 1899, the volume contains an Obituary Notice of the late Mr. Symons, and various papers and reports.

Journal of the Scottish Meteorological Society. Vol. XII. Third Series. Nos. XV. and XVI. 8vo. 1900.

In addition to the Reports of the Council and the meteorological tables for the years 1897 and 1898, this contains four papers, viz.—(1) "The Annual Rainfall of Scotland from 1800 to 1898," by Dr. A. Buchan, F.R.S. (33 pp.) In the *Journal*, vol. iii. pp. 202-211, there appeared a paper on the Annual Rainfall of Scotland, which contained a table giving the yearly totals at 47 stations for the years from 1815 to 1870. In this paper yearly totals are dealt with, and the returns of 296 rainfall stations representing all districts of Scotland, during various terms of years from 1800 to 1898. These records extend from 99 years at Rothesay to 19 years at some other stations. The results are given in two tables. It appears that in the years 1861, 1862, 1872, 1877, and 1882 the rainfall was practically above the average over the whole of Scotland. In 1872 the excess was very large, amounting to as much as 50 per cent and 70 per cent in various districts. The rainfall was practically under the average over the whole of Scotland in the years 1855, 1857, 1858, 1865, 1870, 1871, 1880, and 1885 to 1889. The rainfall was from 30 per cent to 50 per cent below the average over extensive areas in the years 1855, 1870, 1887, and 1889. At 126 stations the year of maximum rainfall was 1872, and at 67 stations in 1877. These two years the rainfall of Scotland was much in excess of the average. The year of minimum rainfall occurred at 53 stations in 1887, 52 in 1870, 34 in 1855, 17 in 1895, and at 14 in 1865, 1885, and 1889. The years 1856, 1871, 1879, 1880, and 1897 were also dry years. The variability of the rainfall from year to year ranged between one-fifth to one-seventh of the average annual fall. It was, on the whole, somewhat greater south of the Grampians than to the north of this range of mountains.—(2) "Further results of Mr. Wragge's Ben Nevis Observations, taken in the year 1882. Humidity and Temperature Variability," by R. C. Mossman (6 pp.). The more prominent results (dealing with temperature, pressure, and rainfall) of Mr. Wragge's observations were given in a paper by Dr. Buchan on the Meteorology of Ben Nevis in vol. vii. of the *Scottish Meteorological Journal.* In this paper Mr. Mossman discusses the variability of humidity and temperature. The mean daily temperature variability has been computed from the Fort-William and Ben Nevis observations with a view to finding out how far the values of this element are affected by height. The variability or inter-diurnal change of temperature is quite distinct from the daily range of temperature, which is merely the difference between the highest and lowest readings, whereas the former is the difference between the temperature at the same hour on successive days, and may be said to measure the changeableness of the weather from day to day. From June to August there is a well-marked minimum of temperature variability in the early morning hours, and a maximum in the afternoon about 1 p.m. In September and October these conditions were reversed, the maximum occurring in the early morning or forenoon, and the minimum in the evening. As regards the influence of height on the variability of temperature, it cannot be said, from an examination of the data, that the variability at high levels on the mean differs much from sea-level values taken in the vicinity. It is well known that the variability of temperature increases as we proceed from the sea inland, as does also the daily range; but in taking observations on a mountain we obtain the somewhat paradoxical result that, while the daily range of temperature steadily diminishes as we proceed upwards, the variability of temperature at the various stations changes but little, if indeed it does not increase. As regards the daily range of variability at the hill stations little can be said, owing to the paucity of observations; but in nearly every case, except in October, the observations indicate an increase as the day proceeds. This is probably due to the circumstance that a variation between the temperature of two days, brought about say by a change from cloudy to clear weather, would be much greater about noon than in the early morning, owing to the greater insolation which would then prevail.—(3) "Barometric and Thermometric Gradients between London and Edinburgh 1864-98," by R. C. Mossman (8 pp. and coloured plate).—(4) "The Temperature Correction of Barometers," by R. T. Omond (1 p.).

Maryland Weather Service. Vol. I. 8vo. 565 pp. Baltimore. 1899.

This is the first of a series of reports dealing with the climatic features of Maryland. Much work has already been done in the preparation of the subsequent volumes, and they will follow from time to time as the investigations are completed.

The Introduction, prepared by Wm. Bullock Clark, and constituting Part I., is devoted mainly to a discussion of the plan of operation of the Maryland Weather Service, together with a recital of the facts connected with its organisation. A history is given of the work and publications of the Service since May 1891, when the Bureau was established, as well as the scope of the proposed publications.

The chapter on the Physiography of Maryland, which forms Part II., has been prepared by Cleveland Abbe, jun., and embraces a general statement regarding the more important physiographic features of the State. To this is appended a detailed discussion of stream development in the Piedmont Plateau.

The report on the Meteorology of Maryland, which comprises Part III., is the joint work of Cleveland Abbe, F. J. Walz, and O. L. Fassig, all of whom are members of the staff of the U.S. Weather Bureau. (See note, p. 99.)

The succeeding chapters, relating especially to Maryland meteorology, are prepared by Messrs. Walz and Fassig of the Baltimore Office of the U.S. Weather Bureau; the former being the Local Forecast Official and Section Director of that Bureau as well as Meteorologist of the State Weather Service, while the latter, in addition to being a Section Director of the U.S. Weather Bureau, is also instructor in Meteorology in the Johns Hopkins University. The chapter by Dr. Fassig, which follows that of Prof. Abbe, deals with the history of the development of knowledge regarding Maryland meteorology from early colonial times to the present. The final chapter, by Mr. Walz, is an exhaustive study of Maryland meteorology, based upon the records of past years. This work has required the critical examination of a vast amount of recorded data, in which all the members of the Baltimore Office have been engaged.

Meteorologische Zeitschrift. Redigirt von Dr. J. HANN und Dr. G. HELLMANN. April—June 1900. 4to.

The principal articles are:—"Das dynamische Princip der Cirkulationsbewegungen in der Atmosphäre," von B. Bjerknes (12 pp.). This is the completion of the paper noticed in the number for March. Prof. Bjerknes goes on in this to account for most of the atmospheric movements, such as Trade Winds, Monsoons, Land and Sea Breezes, Cyclones, and Anticyclones, by the existence of solenoids in the atmosphere, and gives diagrams illustrative of V-shaped depressions, etc. The whole paper deserves careful study; but we can hardly expect the realisation of the Professor's dream, that as a result of the Conference at Stockholm last year, the different naval expeditions sent out to explore the

North Atlantic will include in their *personnel* meteorologists fully provided with apparatus for work in the upper atmosphere, we suppose by kites and captive balloons!—"Klima von New-Guinea," von Dr. A. v. Danckelman (8 pp.). A new work by Dr. Max Krieger, which has come out in the *Bibliothek der Länderkunde*, gives Baron v. Danckelman material for a paper on the climate of New Guinea, which is far fuller than anything yet in print. The observations are irregular and scanty, owing to repeated interruptions by illness. The coast of Kaiser Wilhelms Land is best represented. For Dutch New Guinea there is nothing but a few travellers' notes, except a short record from Geelvuik Bay. In the deficiency of information about all the East Indian Archipelago in general, any contribution like the present is most acceptable. Most of the statistics refer to rain.—"Klima von Luktschun, Centralasien," von A. Woeikof (10 pp.). The late Baron v. Tillo published, in the *Comptes Rendus* of the Russian Academy for 1899, a paper on the climate of this district, which is a depressed valley below sea-level in Eastern Turkestan. Its level is not quite certain, but is assumed at nearly 400 feet below that of the sea. Prof. Woeikof proceeds to give an abstract of v. Tillo's results, and compares the climate with that of Death Valley, California, which is the region most closely resembling that under consideration. Death Valley is rather the more excessive climate of the two. The annual range of pressure is greater at Luktschun than anywhere else in the world, and the annual range of temperature is also greatest for the same latitude. The non-periodic changes of pressure and temperature are not great, and the same may be said of temperature variability. The paper winds up with tables for 1894 and 1895, and a comparison of data from the Azores so as to exhibit the contrast between typical continental and typical oceanic climates.—"Der Luftdruck und die atmosphärische Cirkulation in Asien," von A. Woeikof (5 pp.). This is a paper closely connected with the foregoing. Dr. Woeikof remarks that besides the Luktschun depression there are others among the mountain chains of Central Asia which allow of the efflux of air eastwards and westwards, as they in former years afforded passage to invading hordes. He says that these facilities for efflux probably render the pressure less excessive in winter than at Luktschun. He then argues that we really do not know much about the conditions of the whole central region of Asia, and urges the importance of systematic observations on the Pamir plateau, where levels are accessible which are comparable with those reached by balloons in the temperate zone.—"Wo ist der höchste Luftdruck der Erde, mit und ohne Reduktion auf das Meeresniveau?" von A. Woeikof (2 pp.). This is a discussion of the question as to whether the sea-level reductions for Siberian stations are to be trusted, as the altitudes are unknown. He takes the reading of 31·84 ins. at Barnaoul as the best which has been reasonably accurately determined, but he says that at the Dead Sea, and also at Luktschun, both below sea-level, readings of about 31·97 ins. ought to be observed.—"Beiträge zur Frage der Kälterückfälle im Mai," von V. Kremser (6 pp.). This is an attempt to settle the question of the cold days in May by the evidence of the Forest stations in Germany. The observations only extend for 17 years up to 1897. The present paper deals with 14 years' observations of minimum temperature at 1·2 metre above ground, and so nearly exactly at our 4 feet level. The observations were taken at Marggrabow. For the period quoted, the predominance of cold nights from May 11-13 is most striking. It is, however, very remarkable that this particular interval of years is most favourable to the cold day theory at most stations in Germany; but if a longer period is taken the figures do not at all support the theory so strongly. Tables are given at the end of the paper for Klaussen and Berlin, extending over 50 years, and from these it appears that at Klaussen the eleven years 1888-98, and at Berlin the decade 1878-87, were more favourable to the theory than the other decades.—"Eine einfache Methode zur Berechnung klimatologischer Mittelwerthe von Flächen," von Dr. W. Meinardus (17 pp.). The author raises serious objections to the method of giving the arithmetical mean of all the rain values for a district as the real fall for that district, and the present paper is to prove the value of the interpolation method for the same object. For this method you require a correct map of the country, with the values and isohyetals inserted. On this you lay down a sheet of tracing millimetre paper, or a glass plate finely divided with rectilinear lines into squares. For the precise details of the work we must refer to the paper, but Dr. Meinardus assumes the process is very rapid and the results very satisfactory.—"Ein neues Barometer," von Dr. K. T. Fischer (18 pp.). This is an account of an instrument, called the "Pressure Aremometer," which Dr. Fischer, after seven years' work, has succeeded in bringing into a useable form for balloon ascents. This is a most important acquisition if it proves to possess all the advantages claimed for it. The final name of the apparatus is the "Pressure Weight Areometer."

Symons's Monthly Meteorological Magazine. Edited by H. SOWERBY WALLIS. April—June 1900. 8vo.

The principal articles are:—"The Jubilee of the Royal Meteorological Society" (2 pp.).—"A Curious Fact about London Summers" (1 p.).—"The Snow and Floods of February 1900" (7 pp.). This is a large collection of notes from the newspaper press of the heavy snowstorm and floods which occurred in February.—"Meteorological Extremes. III. Wind Force" (7 pp.). This is one of a series of articles appearing in the Magazine dealing with meteorological extremes. The two previous articles which have appeared dealt with barometer and temperature extremes, this article deals with wind force. The highest velocity in a gust which the author has seen recorded is that registered by Sir Cuthbert Peek, at his Rousdon Observatory in South Devon, in March 1897, by a Dines pressure-tube anemometer, which amounted to a rate of 101 miles per hour.—"Indian Famine-Causing Droughts and their Prevision" (3 pp.). This is the first part of an interesting article dealing with the general causes of Indian famines and their relation to the prevision of Indian weather. The general causes of Indian famine have been summarised by Mr. Eliot, the head of the Indian Meteorological Service, as follows:—(1) Prolonged delay in the commencement of the rains more especially of the summer monsoon; (2) a prolonged break in the middle of the South-west monsoon rains; (3) scanty rainfall during the greater part or whole of the season; and (4) unusually early termination of the South-west monsoon rains.—"Meteorological Observations during the Eclipse" (1 p.).

The Meteorology of Ben Nevis in Clear and in Foggy Weather. By J. Y. BUCHANAN, F.R.S. Transactions of the Royal Society of Edinburgh. Vol. XXXIX. Part III. (No 31.) 4to. 48 pp. Edinburgh. 1899.

The author says: "The Ben Nevis observations show very clearly the nocturnal heating in the winter months, which has been observed before, both on mountains and in balloons. This occurs in both clear and foggy weather, though it is more pronounced in the clear weather.

"No distinction is made between one kind of fog and another, and they are not distinguished in the monthly sheets of the observatory. There are, however, several different kinds of fog, and these are clearly distinguished by the observers living on the mountain. There is the very wet fog, which is called 'mist' in the log; and there is the comparatively dry fog, which is logged 'fog.'

Then both the fog and mist in winter seem to be much denser than in summer. These belong to the elements of meteorology which cannot be expressed in numbers. They are as important as those which can be so expressed; and they can be brought into the discussion of the meteorology of the mountain with their due weight and importance only by men who have spent a considerable time there as observers.

"Whether wet or dry, the fog which characterises the climate of the mountain is nothing but cloud under another name. The lower surface of the clouds, which form on the hills rising out of the Western Ocean, is found generally at a height of about 3000 feet above the sea. On the west coast of Scotland the air is very damp and the clouds abundant, consequently the observatory on the summit of Ben Nevis is usually situated in the heart of the common clouds of the country. It may therefore be claimed that it is in reality an observatory established in the clouds, and that the observations made in it furnish a record of the meteorology of the clouds. In this respect the observatory of Ben Nevis is unique."

The Relative Humidity of our Houses in Winter. By R. DE C. WARD. 8vo. 11 pp. Boston. 1900.

This is an article reprinted from the *Boston Medical and Surgical Journal*. The author says: "The present methods of heating our houses are wretchedly inadequate from the point of view of supplying sufficient moisture. Undoubtedly, the relative humidity of the air coming from an ordinary furnace may be somewhat increased by increasing the size or the number of the evaporating pans in the furnace, or by placing pans of water on, or, better still, within the registers. As to the precise amount of increase in the relative humidity as the result of either of these methods, I am not yet able to give any definite results."

Transactions of the South African Philosophical Society. Vol. XI. Part I. 8vo.

This part contains two papers of meteorological interest, viz.:—"Do the Mining Operations affect the Climate of Kimberley?" by J. R. Sutton. (11 pp.). The author draws the following general conclusions:—(1) The air is always warmer above the surface of the blue ground than it is above the red sand; (2) beneath the surface the blue ground is always warmer by night and cooler by day than the red sand; and (3) blue ground is the better reflector and therefore the worse absorber—heat passes less readily, in or out, across the bounding surfaces of its particles. The uniformly greater temperature of the air just above its surface is a reflection effect by day, and an effect of actual warming by contact and conduction during the night.—"The winds of Kimberley," by J. R. Sutton (38 pp. and 8 plates). This is a discussion of the direction and velocity of the wind, from records of Osler's and Robinson's anemometers at Kenilworth, Kimberley, February 1896 to February 1899.

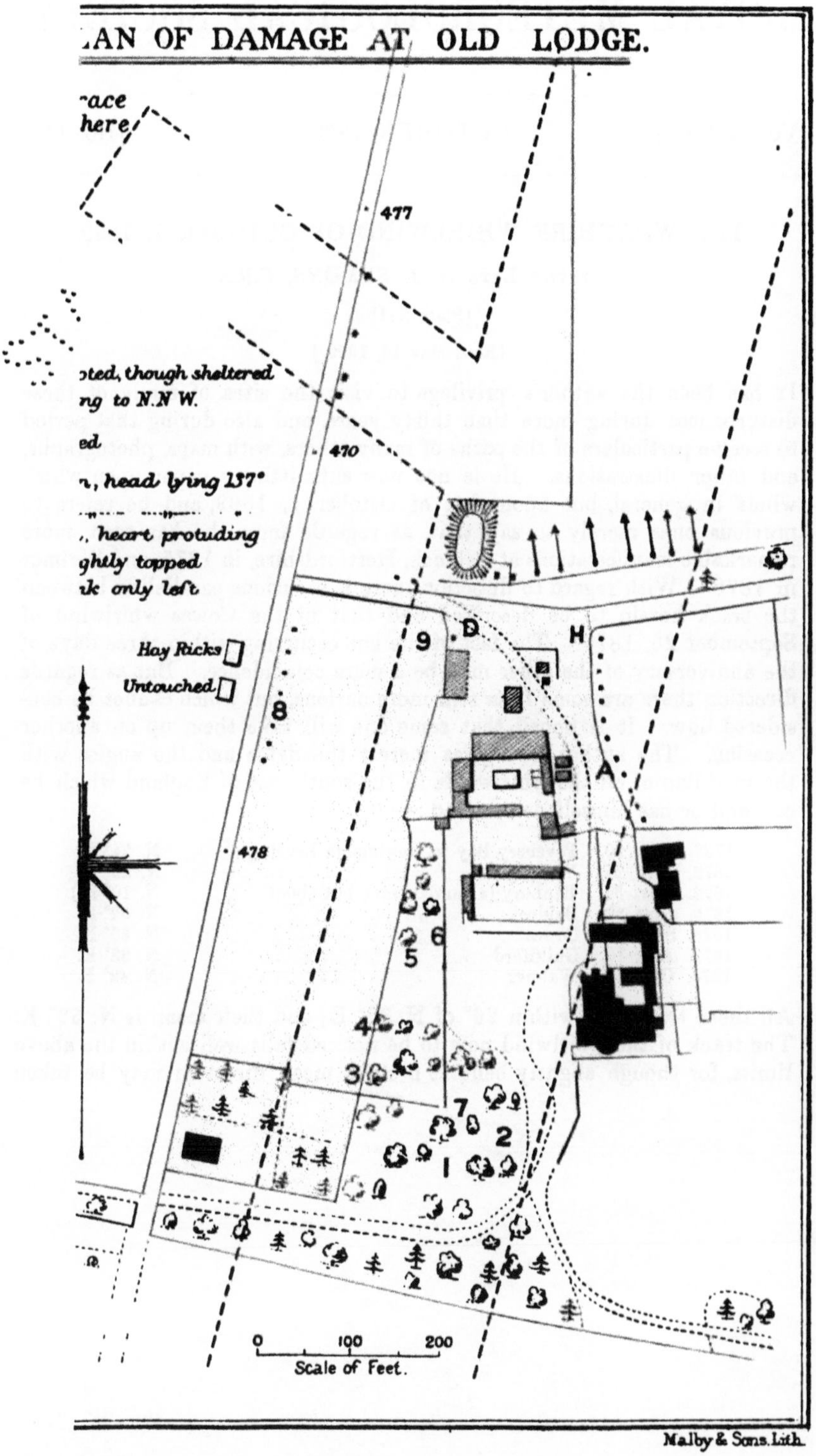
LAN OF DAMAGE AT OLD LODGE.
race
here
477
470
478
oted, though sheltered
ng to N.N.W.
ed
n, head lying 137°
, heart protuding
ghtly topped
k only left
Hay Ricks
Untouched
9
D
H
8
A
6
5
4
3
7
2
1
0 100 200
Scale of Feet.

Malby & Sons. Lith.

QUARTERLY JOURNAL

OF THE

ROYAL METEOROLOGICAL SOCIETY

VOL. XXVI.] OCTOBER 1900 [No. 116.

THE WILTSHIRE WHIRLWIND OF OCTOBER 1, 1899.

BY THE LATE G. J. SYMONS, F.R.S.

(Plate XIII.).

[Read May 16, 1900.]

IT has been the author's privilege to visit the sites of many of these disturbances during more than thirty years, and also during that period to receive particulars of the paths of many others, with maps, photographs, and other illustrations. He is not now submitting a paper upon whirlwinds in general, but upon that of October 1, 1899, and he refers to previous ones merely to say that, as regards force, he has seen more remarkable manifestations at Baldock, Hertfordshire, in 1875, and Walmer in 1878. With regard to direction there is a curious parallelism between the track herein to be described and that of the Cowes whirlwind of September 28, 1876. The fact of the one occurring within three days of the anniversary of the other may be a mere coincidence. But as regards direction there are some facts still more curious, but which cannot be considered now. It is hoped that some one will take them up on another occasion. The author now gives merely the dates and the angles with the meridian of all the whirlwinds in the south-east of England which he can find or has himself determined:—

1729.	May 20.	Pevensey Bay to Newingden Level	N. 24° E.
1872.	July 25.	Wantage	N. 22° E.
1872.	Nov. 30.	Banbury (a curved track but about	N. 10° E.)
1875.	June 12.	Baldock	N. 62° E.
1876.	Sept. 28.	Cowes	N. 30° E.
1877.	Aug. 10.	Guildford	N. 33° E.
1878.	Oct. 24.	Walmer	N. 42° E.

All these tracks are within 26° of N. 36° E., and their mean is N. 32° E. The track of the whirlwind now to be noticed falls well within the above limits, for though slightly bent at first its mean direction may be taken as N. 20 E. Why do whirlwinds in the south-east of England generally go from south-south-west to north-east?

This, however, is a digression—the author's present object is to describe what occurred along the track, the longest one he ever followed, and this he does chiefly from personal observation, but largely aided by the extreme kindness of many residents on or near the track. Among them should be especially mentioned Mr. T. T. S. Metcalfe, F.R.Met.Soc., of Roche Court, Salisbury; Major Poore, of Old Lodge, Salisbury (several of whose farm buildings were destroyed); and all the clergy through whose parishes it passed, especially the Rev. A. G. Lawe of Fosbury and the Rev. W. E. Burkitt of Buttermere.

Owing to this kindness and hospitality he was able to almost live upon the track for several days, and to determine its direction and limits with a precision rarely attainable. The 6-inch Ordnance map shows every barn and stable and clump of trees, and having joined up the entire series of maps, he took them with him, and either by tape or by azimuth instruments determined the track with all possible accuracy, generally within 100 ft.

The general atmospheric conditions at the time of the passage of the whirlwind cannot be accurately determined, as very few observations are made between 9 a.m. and 6 p.m. on a Sunday; but Dr. Scott, F.R.S., has very kindly supplied a map drawn for 2 p.m. from all the data received by the Meteorological Office, and the Radcliffe observer at Oxford (Dr. Rambaut, F.R.A.S.) has supplied copies of the exquisitely sharp records of pressure, temperature, wind, and rain which are reproduced in Plate XIII. Records from various private observers are given in Appendix A (p. 268).

From these and other sources it appears that on October 1, at 8 a.m., the centre of a depression (29·1 ins.) was off the extremity of Cornwall in about long. 6° W. and lat. 49° N.

At 2 p.m. the centre had moved only about 60 miles (10 miles an hour) towards north-east, and was nearly due south of Falmouth, and nearly 200 miles south-west of where the whirlwind was being formed. It was a squally day, with the winds lying well along the isobars.

By 6 p.m., according to the map supplied to *The Times* by the Meteorological Office, this centre (29·1 ins.) is shown as being near Bristol, having thus advanced in these four hours three times as far as in the previous six hours—or at the rate of 45 miles an hour instead of 10.

At 8 a.m. on the 2nd, the centre (29·3 ins.) is shown off Whitby, say in long. 1° E. and lat. 54° N., having slackened its motion to about 16 miles an hour. From this it is evident that the whirlwind occurred considerably in front of the centre, and north-east of it.

At first sight it seems remarkable that not one of the author's correspondents reported the storm at the time of its occurrence, and that no reference to it appeared in any London newspaper.[1] But a little calculation supplies the explanation. The length of the damage was nearly 20 miles, but the average breadth was only about 100 yards, therefore the area was very little over one square mile, and we are far from having one observer to each mile or even to each ten miles.

[1] It was, however, one of my correspondents, Mr. Knowles of Conholt Park, Andover, who eventually called my attention to it, he having seen the storm travelling along the valley below him.

It was a wild, squally day, with about an inch of rain in the west and centre of England, and with thunderstorms in many places.

Miles from Origin 0.

The first trace of the storm is afforded by Mr. Charles Yates, who states that the trees in a copse near Middle Winterslow were violently agitated and twisted about in a manner which he had not before seen, but that no breakage occurred. This spot is in 1° 39′ 40″ W. and 51° 5′ 25″ N.; it is 1⅓ miles south by west of the first recorded damage, and about 200 yards west of a prolongation backwards of the path eventually taken: it is rare to obtain details so near the commencement.

The next spot on the path was determined backwards from Gutridge's Farm. At the cottage by the farm was a man named Horne, who, struck by the darkness, went to the cottage door about 2.15 p.m. and saw "a mass like smoke rolling over the hill." He was asked to point out the part of the hill over which it came by identifying certain trees, and shown how to point a portable altazimuth at the spot, afterwards he did so and it read 204°, *i.e.* (allowing 17° for variation) 7° W. of S., therefore according to him the path was to N. 7° E.; obviously he would be so astonished that he might easily be a few degrees out, but he seems to have been correct.

Miles from Origin 1·3.

Horne's cottage was untouched, but about 150 ft. north-west of it was a large, nearly new timber barn, resting on brick footings, and with a heavy tiled roof. The north-east corner of this large structure was lifted off the brickwork and pushed 2½ ft. to the north-west, whereas the north-west corner was not appreciably moved. North-westward from the barn was a group of ricks; most of these were stripped, but the farthest to the north-west, about 180 ft. north-north-west of the barn, suffered very slightly.

Miles from Origin 2·0.

For half a mile the path crossed bare down, and then it reached a clump of trees, mostly Scotch firs; it went almost through the centre of the clump, wrecking all but the two outside ones. Close by, a shepherd, John Harroway, was sheltering behind a bush, but the wind tore him out and flung him round with considerable force into another bush, hurting his arm, but not affecting his breathing that he can recollect. The breadth here was apparently 150 ft. This clump is about N. 2° E. from Gutridge's barn.

Miles from Origin 2·8.

N. 12° E. from the clump of trees just described, in a wooded hollow, is Old Lodge, where the havoc was greater than at any other place in the path. Although Major and Mrs. Poore were both at home, and saw the storm rush by, it was so sudden (like the passage of an express train) that they naturally could not observe the details, but two of their remarks are of especial interest. They were standing at the Hall door, and they said that while many of the trees in front of them were uprooted or beheaded, they all bent down extraordinarily as the storm came upon them. Subsequently, when examining the trees, one was found which, at 3 ft. above the ground, was 5 ft. 11 ins. in girth, and which had two nearly vertical cracks on its east side and one on the west side, so that probably one crack went right through. The longest crack reached from the ground to the height of 8 ft. Perhaps the most remarkable proof of the strain to which this tree had been subjected was afforded by the fact that a strip (about ¼ in. square) of the interior wood protruded through the bark at the before-mentioned crack, having been nipped there by the return of the tree to its normal position.

Another noteworthy observation was the fate of a pet cockatoo, which spends much time flying about the grounds. The centre of the storm was passing roughly from south to north about 150 ft. west of the Hall door (where the wind was by no means violent). The cockatoo flew westwards towards the track; the owners saw him caught in the storm, and rolled over and over amid the shower of branches and leaves. Immediately that the storm had passed they went to look at the wreck of the farm buildings, and there was the cockatoo sitting on a rail, covered with mud, but quite uninjured.

Only those who have visited the sites of explosions of gunpowder, gas, or steam, or the tracks of storms like this, can realise the wreckage which may be produced in from 60 to 90 seconds, and it is extremely difficult to convey the impression to others. The accompanying photographs do not fully do it, and the plan does not, because it is not easy to realise the size of the buildings. The fact that nearly half a mile north of the Lodge, wood, slate, and glass from the barns and gardens were strewn along the track, will give some idea of the shower of materials which was blown away; and the portion of a perfectly strong and healthy ash which is exhibited, shows by the disintegration (splintering does not express it) of the wood, the terrific strain to which it has been subjected.

The usual puzzles connected with storms are presented by the facts of this one, *e.g.* the trees thrown down are not those which one would have expected. The storm track met a wood at a right angle, passed over the first 150 ft. of the wood, then threw down a tree quite sheltered by others, and in the next 600 ft. threw down 40 or 50 large ones.

The track opposite Old Lodge was about 200 ft. wide, but slight damage extended about 50 ft. farther on each side, giving a total breadth of 300 ft. Five hundred feet farther north, *i.e.* just beyond the ruined yard, a row of trees running nearly east and west affords another measure of breadth, and they give 360 ft.; and another belt 900 ft. farther north gives a breadth of 318 ft.

The farmyard was so wrecked that it was not easy to trace exactly what had happened, and it cannot be dealt with systematically. In among the buildings, in a little garden, were two cucumber frames and a small greenhouse; the lights of the cucumber frames were carried away and have not been found, yet the greenhouse was damaged only by falling material.

There is the usual ample evidence of the lifting power of confined air. Several sheds were lifted and twisted round towards the north-west, the big barn fell all to pieces, the roofs were taken off all the piggeries. Why then did not the roof go off the greenhouse?

Perhaps the most striking evidence of the lifting power developed by the passage of a whirlwind over even a small volume of air, is afforded by the fact that the air below the barn floor, though less than 2 ft. thick and open to expand laterally (only it had not time), sufficed to lift the whole floor and carry it laterally about 20 ft., depositing it at an angle of nearly 45° with its original position.

A shed near the northern extremity of the yard, built of wood, on a brick foundation, and which was about 11 ft. square and 10 ft. high, was lifted up and dropped down 5 ft. west of its original position. Another wooden shed 12 ft. 6 ins. square and about 9 ft. high was lifted off its brick base, its centre moved about 7 ft. to north-west, and its sides deposited at an azimuth 37° W. with their original position. (See sketch, Plate XIII.)

Little can be said about the trees, because there were so many down that time could not be spared to measure them all, and the writer's experience leads him to believe that the character of the root-hold largely influences the direction in which trees fall; but several were marked on the 25-inch map, and the majority appear to lie towards north-north-west or north-west, *i.e.* about 40° W. of the azimuth in which the whirlwind was travelling. This agrees singularly well with the twist given to the barn and to the last-described shed.

Serious as is the wreck of the farm buildings, it is some consolation that Old Lodge itself lost only two chimneys: the stables, bailiff's house, and cottages, though within 100 yards of the storm, were all untouched.

Miles from Origin 4·1.

We here come to "Martin's Farm" on the Ordnance map, but now known as "The Warren." The previous mile had been bare, treeless down, so that no trace was to be expected, and a similar treeless track extends from 4·5 miles to the 6th mile. At or near "The Warren" many trees were damaged, and the wire fencing of a large pheasantry was blown down.

Miles from Origin 6·0.

From the 5th to the 10th mile there was scarcely a tree or object along the path, but where there was any object damage is found. For instance, at the 6th mile the line crosses the western extremity of the wood round Quarley Camp, and the trees are damaged. At 7·5 miles it passes just west of Thruxton Down Farm, and though no damage was done there, the residents said that they thought that the house would go down.

Miles from Origin 9·1.

About three miles N. 19° E. from Quarley Hill a shepherd's hut on wheels was standing in a field; it was blown over on to its side, and while so lying was pushed about 10 ft. to north-west. A few hundred yards north of this hut were some ricks which were slightly damaged.

Miles from Origin 10·4.

N. 17° E. of the shepherd's hut is the farm of Great Shoddesden, where the damage was nearly equal to that at Old Lodge. The following account appeared in the *Andover Advertiser*, and so accurately describes the damage, that no attempt is made to re-write it:—

At Shoddesden, shortly before 3 o'clock, when Mr. Fowler and family were sitting quietly at home, an unusually heavy peal of thunder was heard, and his daughter, looking through the window, exclaimed in astonishment that the large barn was gone. And so it proved, for a subsequent examination revealed that the wind had struck the building with such force that the whole, from about a yard above the ground, had been demolished. Great rafters were carried in the air and deposited fully 100 yards away; while the roof was borne bodily to a wood nearly half a mile distant across several meadows and there fell. Other farm buildings were similarly treated, and under the ruins were buried about 300 sacks of barley, pigs, and other stock. Within the course the cyclone had taken there was similar and quite as complete destruction. A large elm was snapped off straight and the upper portion smashed to fragments, which were carried by the wind to a considerable distance and scattered in all directions, great branches being subsequently found twisted like wire. Ricks were literally cut to pieces and the straw borne away on the wind till only fragments could afterwards be found. From others the thatch was torn bodily and carried on the wind like so many derelict umbrellas. In one meadow on the farm the waggons, carts, ploughs, elevators, etc., had been arranged in lots on Saturday ready for the sale by auction to take place on Monday, as Mr. Fowler's tenancy has expired. With these the wind played like so many feathers. Large corn bins were lifted up and carried over the hedges into the adjoining road, which was strewn with debris of every kind. Heavy carts and waggons were broken to pieces, and, doubtless, through contact with other things, ploughs were broken; while a large elevator was turned completely over and considerably damaged. The whole place within the area of the wind passage was in fact a complete wreck, so great had been the devastating power of the cyclone. Fortunately it does not appear to have been of long duration, and seems to have been the final concentration of the storm, for shortly afterwards the wind dropped and the rain ceased, so that those on the farm and in the neighbourhood could turn out and render what assistance was possible in the saving of property. Attention was turned to the excavation of the pigs and other live stock from their unpleasant positions, and strange to say, none had been killed. The preservation of the barley under the debris of the demolished barn was also an important consideration, because it was feared that it would be damaged almost beyond use should the rain come on again. What could be removed was taken to another barn, and the remainder so covered as to protect it until it also could be placed under permanent cover. This, however, was not accomplished until Wednesday; while it took a considerable time to remove the corn bins and other obstructions from the road. It is calculated that it will cost Sir J. Pollen, the owner of the farm, considerably over £1000 to replace the damaged buildings; while Mr. Fowler's loss must be considerable, as the amount realised at the sale must have been very materially reduced through the breaking of waggons, implements, and machinery. It is remarkably fortunate that the storm did not occur on the previous day, as then it must have been attended with fatal results, as several men were at work in the barn.

It was more than a month after the event when the writer was able to visit the farm, but even then the ruins were not all cleared away, rebuilding had not begun, and the lane by the side of the farm was blocked by large trees lying across it, mostly towards north-west.

Little can be added to the newspaper account, except that the breadth of the track was about 270 ft.

Miles from Origin 11·0.

About half a mile N. 24° E. is Chopwood Copse, in which trees are reported to be damaged.

Miles from Origin 11·5.

Another half mile N. 10° E. brings us to the junction of Ball's Drove with Biddenden Lane, and here a well-known oak was badly damaged, and the hedge near it was reported to look "as if boiling water had been poured over it."

Miles from Origin 12·9.

A mile and a third N. 20° E. of this tree, on the east side of Collingbourne Wood, in Honey Bottom, several trees were pulled up by the roots.

Miles from Origin 13·7.

A mile and a half N. 18° E. is the west end of the village of Chute. The path here was about 200 ft. wide, and the damage was not serious. A disused windmill lost part of one sail. The hood of a carrier's cart, which was standing in his yard, was picked up, blown across two or three fields, and smashed. The remaining portion (about ¼) of a hay rick in the Vicar's meadow was blown away. The thatch was blown from some wheat ricks, and about 30 sheaves were carried to a hedge 100 yards off. At two cottages the galvanised iron roofs of pig-styes were carried away.

Miles from Origin 15·9.

The track here crosses Newfield Copse, with the usual result of broken trees, followed in 300 yards by Tummer Copse, where many trees are down, notably one very large ash, the head of which lay exactly lengthwise in the track of the storm.

Miles from Origin 16·7.

Passing two arable fields, we come to Little Heath Copse (close to Fosbury House), where the wreckage is severe—some dozens of trees being overthrown or hopelessly injured. The storm crossed the road (blocking it with a fallen tree) happily almost midway between Fosbury House and the Vicarage, so that neither was damaged. It wrecked a few trees in the Vicarage grounds, and then did no damage for nearly a mile.

Miles from Origin 17·7.

The track here crossed the road from Fosbury to Rivar at an angle of 37°. Two thorn bushes on the west side of the road were thrown over, and a hay rick about 100 yards east of the road had the upper half blown off, whereas another rick only 29 yards south-east of the above rick was uninjured.

Miles from Origin 17·9.

The track here enters Apsley Copse, and for nearly half a mile there is a track of damaged or destroyed trees finishing only when the track leaves the wood at its northern extremity, which is called Grubground Copse.

Miles from Origin 18·6.

Crossing the small grass field north of the wood, it scattered a pile of hurdles, damaged a tree in the hedge, and crossing the road, which is

740 ft. above sea-level, came upon a rick of oats, a considerable portion of which it carried right over the village of Ham and deposited in a field belonging to "Prosperous Farm," one and two-thirds of a mile (say 3000 yards) from where it had been picked up.

APPENDIX A.—Records of Private Observers.

Kent	Tenterden	T.S. with heavy R. (·82 in.) and high wind.
,,	Leysdown, Sheerness	Showery, very rough and windy.
Sussex	Isfield Place	Misty rain early, harder at 7.30, cleared by 9.15 a.m.
,,	Crowborough	Cloudy and rain all day.
,,	West Dean	1st and 2nd, white frost, dull and foggy, followed by S.W. gale.
Hants	Emsworth, Redlands	T., L.
Herts	Kensworth	Heavy thunderstorm, 3 to 4 p.m.
Bucks	Slough, Upton	Rain variable, averaging ·14 in. per hour, subdued T. during the downpour. Quantity of rain = 1·36 in.
,,	Winslow, Addington	Wet forenoon.
Oxford	Oxford, Mag. Coll.	Overcast and very wet the greater part.
,,	,, St. Giles	T., R., H.
,,	Swerford, Oxon.	Showery, T. and L.
Suffolk	Bury St. Edmunds, Westley	Distant T.
Norfolk	Norwich, Brundall	Rough and rainy.
Dorset	Winterbourne Steepleton	R. till 11 a.m., windy.
,,	Blandford, Whatcombe	Cloudy, and strong E. wind.
Devon	Druid, Ashburton	Heavy rain early, showers during the day.
,,	Tavistock, Statsford	Heavy R. 6 to 7.50 a.m., 9.30 to 11 a.m., 6.30 to 9.17 p.m., heavy 10.50 to 11.45 p.m.
,,	Polapit Tamar	Heavy showers; raw and cold. Strong E. wind. R. 1·13.
Somerset	North Cadbury	Strong gale, especially from noon to 6 p.m.
Gloucester	Stroud, Upfield	Wind S.E., S.W., N.W. Gale.
,,	Further Barton	T. 2 to 3 p.m.
Hereford	Ross, The Graig	Rain 9.15 a.m. to 0.15 p.m., ·67; 0.15 to 2.15 p.m., ·26.
Stafford	Wolverhampton, Tettenhall	R. ·87.
Warwick	Coventry, Priory Row	R. all day, ·41 in.
Lincoln	Hemingby	Wet most of the day, ending with L. and T.

APPENDIX B.—Hourly Readings at the Radcliffe Observatory, Oxford, October 1.

Hour.	Sea-Level Pressure.	Temperature. Dry Bulb.	Temperature. Wet Bulb.	Wind. Direction.	Wind. Motion since previous hour.	Rain since previous hour.
	ins.	°	°			in.
Noon	29·189	51·4	50·7	E.	...	...
1 p.m.	29·160	53·0	52·2	E.S.E.	18	·00
2 p.m.	29·145	55·9	55·0	S.E.	13	·00
3 p.m.	29·141	56·7	55·9	S.S.W.	7	·04
4 p.m.	29·095	54·8	54·2	S.S.E.	8	·21
5 p.m.	29·099	57·0	53·8	S.	17	·00

Remarks.—*Barometer*—Fell to 29.083 ins. at 2.50 p.m. *Dry Bulb*—Fell to 52°.3, and *Wet Bulb* fell to 51°.5 at 3.25 p.m. *Wind*—The direction made rather more than a complete rotation from S.E. through S.W., N.W., N.E., to S.E. again between 3 and 3.30 p.m.—the velocity at 3 p.m. was for a few minutes very high. *Rain*—During a T.S. at 3 p.m. hail and heavy rain fell, .25 in. falling between 2.40 and 3.45 p.m.

DISCUSSION.

The President (Dr. C. Theodore Williams) remarked that this paper, in its lucidity and directness, was typical of Mr. Symons and all his work.

Mr. H. Sowerby Wallis said that the paper was the last piece of work done by Mr. Symons before he was stricken down with paralysis, he being engaged on it the day before his illness. It was practically complete as he left it, but any letters received subsequent to his illness had been incorporated in the context by himself (Mr. Wallis). It had often struck him as a curious fact that nearly all the known instances of destructive British whirlwinds occurred in the south-east of England, and travelled in a somewhat similar direction. About the atmospheric conditions during the present whirlwind there was not much information. Mr. Symons had written to many observers along the track, but with little success. The Oxford barogram showed the time of the occurrence very clearly, the disturbance of the trace being precisely similar to that with which he was familiar in the case of thunderstorms. With regard to the remark about the shepherd not experiencing any difficulty in breathing when struck by the storm, he was probably too much astonished to notice it. Another feature common in whirlwinds was the manner in which the severest damage was concentrated at isolated spots along the track, as though at times the whirlwind came in contact with the ground and then rose into the air. This was in accordance with the general description of waterspouts, in which the column was said to be continually changing in length. Amongst Mr. Symons's papers was found evidence of an attempt to determine the rate of progression of the disturbance, but the idea was apparently given up, the reports being contradictory.

Mr. F. J. Brodie said that in listening to the paper one was reminded of the fact that the collection of rainfall statistics was by no means the only good service rendered by the author to the cause of meteorology. The stations established by Mr. Symons were so numerous, and the network they covered so fine, that events of considerable importance which had eluded the more widely spread organisations of the Society and of the Meteorological Office were often rescued from the oblivion in which they might otherwise have remained buried. So far as he (Mr. Brodie) could see, the ordinary isobaric charts for the day threw no light whatever upon the origin of the whirlwind, beyond showing that the weather over England was in a very unsettled state. In a similar way the tornado which passed over Camberwell in October 1898 was altogether unaccounted for by the current weather charts, the stations plotted being too widely scattered for the elucidation of phenomena such as these, which are in nearly all cases of a purely local character. The Oxford curves also seem to throw very little light upon the matter. The only place at which any striking barometrical change occurred on this day was apparently at Rochford, near Tenbury, where the tracing of a Richard aneroidogram showed at 2·15 p.m. a sudden fall of about a tenth of an inch. The station is, it is true, a long way from the path of the whirlwind, but the fact of the sudden change occurring at about the same time as the violent wind seems to point to some connection between the two events.

Mr. R. H. Curtis said it was to be regretted that no instrumental observations made at the spot were available to assist in throwing light upon the origin of this disturbance, because owing to the purely local character of such whirlwinds the general conditions of pressure and temperature over a large extent of country, such as is shown by the *Daily Weather Report* map, does not go much further than to show that the general state of things at the time of their occurrence was unsettled. Such a disturbance may have received its first impulse owing to an invasion of temperature over the place of origin, by which an initial indraught of air was set up at the earth's surface. Its rotatory motion was then possibly due to the friction caused by bodies of air moving inwards in opposite directions, and the gyration thus set up may have been able to propagate itself along a certain line, and to develop energy up to a certain point as it progressed. But for the proper investigation of these points not only are observations required at places close together along the track of the storm, but we also need to know something of the temperature and the hygrometric condition of the upper air; and since such observations can only be made by the aid of kites, the chance of their being forthcoming, when and where they are wanted for this special purpose, is somewhat remote.

The instrumental indications shown by the Oxford instruments are, as Mr. Wallis has pointed out, typical of those commonly observed in thunderstorms, and they may have been due on this occasion to a local storm and only indirectly connected with the whirlwind described. The only reference in the paper to the weather which accompanied the storm is that given in the extract from the *Andover Advertiser*, from which it appears there was thunder and heavy rain; and from the notes as to weather in the Appendix it appears that thunderstorms were prevalent over a great part of Southern England on the day in question. Much larger oscillations of pressure and temperature than those shown are occasionally found with thunderstorms when there is no indication of a whirlwind anywhere near. What Mr. Symons had found to be the usual direction of the path of these disturbances was very interesting. He might mention that a small whirlwind was observed a few years ago in the west of London, which apparently originated over the grounds of the London Athletic Club at Fulham, during the progress of some sports connected with King's College. Amongst other damage it stripped the bandsmen's stands of their sheets of music, and these, with some ladies' sunshades and other odds and ends picked up by the whirl, served to indicate its course for many minutes. He had found from information given to him that its path was north-east from the grounds, and the whirl could be distinctly seen travelling away over London, but at a considerable altitude, until it became lost to view owing to the distance. As far as he could ascertain nothing was felt of this whirlwind along its course over the west of London after it had left the grounds, and this fact was of interest, because it seemed to show that such a whirlwind might, under certain conditions, propagate itself along a path through the upper air without being felt at the earth's surface.

Capt. A. Carpenter mentioned that he had recently observed two small whirlwinds from his house in Surrey, one occurring at 10 minutes before noon, and the other precisely at noon. The direction in which they were travelling was south-south-west. Some papers were carried away from the verandah on which he was sitting, and he also saw some brown paper whirling round in the air to a great height, which evidently had been taken up from a neighbouring house. He agreed with Mr. Wallis's suggestion with regard to the funnel or tongue shape of the whirlwind as was met with in the waterspout. He also thought that the reason why some of the farm buildings at Old Lodge were twisted and others not was accounted for by the fact that those not directly in the path of the whirlwind only experienced the tangential direction of wind, whereas those in the centre experienced the twisting action of the revolving funnel.

Mr. W. Marriott said that some years ago the Society, at the request of the late Hon. Ralph Abercromby, undertook an investigation on the phenomena of thunderstorms, but in consequence of Mr. Abercromby's removal to Australia the discussion of the observations devolved upon him (Mr. Marriott). It was originally intended that the observations should be confined to the south-east of England, but it was soon found that the area was too limited, so that the whole country had to be included. The stations, however, were really not sufficiently numerous to show all the minute changes which take place during thunderstorms. He had tried to improve upon the *Daily Weather Charts* by preparing isobaric maps for 9 a.m. and 9 p.m. during the month of June 1888 with the isobars drawn for each ·02 inch. These to a large extent indicated the localities where thunderstorms were in progress; but the direction of the wind was the most important factor, for where there was any deflection of the arrows it was a sure indication of the presence of a thunderstorm in that locality. The thunderstorm formations were really very small cyclonic disturbances, the wind circulating round them in the same way as in ordinary cyclones. These thunderstorm formations were only a few miles in diameter, and often several would be travelling along at but short distances from each other. He did not think that whirlwinds were confined exclusively to the south-east of England, for on one occasion, when visiting Brigg in Lincolnshire, he had learned that a whirlwind had passed over the town a few hours previously; and on another occasion, when at Ashburton in Devonshire, he had learned that a small whirlwind had passed over a field, carrying up the hay to a considerable height. Mr. Symons's charts and plans were very valuable, as they showed the lifting and twisting power of the wind. He (Mr. Marriott) was of opinion that the greatest force of the wind would be on the right hand or eastern side of the whirlwind, rather than on the left or western side, owing to the progressive motion of the phenomena.

Mr. H. N. Dickson said he would like to ask Mr. Brodie or Mr. Curtis whether any systematic examination had been made of the general atmospheric conditions under which these disturbances occurred in this country. If, as seemed likely, they were associated with cyclonic systems having light gradients, this might suggest an explanation of their being most frequently observed in the south and east of England, and also of their tendency to move north-eastward.

Dr. H. R. Mill remarked that the whole report read like the descriptions of a United States tornado on a small scale, the phenomena being the same in kind, but less intense. In the Mississippi and Ohio valleys tornadoes generally occurred in the afternoon, and with a track of from 20 to 30 miles in length, and a breadth of about a quarter of a mile—in fact, similar in every way to the cyclone studied by Mr. Symons, only on a larger scale. Possibly the reason why the south-east of England was more liable to these visitations than other parts of the country was, that the configuration of the ground there was more favourable, and the general trend of the valleys and escarpments might account for the prevailing course of these cyclones towards the north-east, this being also the usual course of storms traversing the island. Mr. Symons's closely-planted rainfall stations were of great use in discussions such as these, and recently he had found them of extreme value in making investigations into the detailed climate of a small portion of Sussex.

Mr. R. Bentley stated that he had referred that morning to the dates and localities of over fifty whirlwinds in the United Kingdom—some in the last century, and some in this. August was the month in which the largest number occurred, but they were also very numerous in the months of June, July, and October, and comparatively few in September. They happened most frequently in the Midland Counties, and very frequently also on the east side of England, between Yorkshire and Kent, and more rarely in other parts.

Mr. R. Inwards said it would be interesting if a careful observer could go to these places directly after such an occurrence and plot the positions of the fallen trees and the directions in which they fell.

Mr. F. J. Brodie, in reply to Mr. Dickson's inquiry as to whether any investigation had been made into the conditions of barometrical pressure at the time of this and similar events, said that the great difficulty was to obtain observations in sufficient numbers and sufficiently close together. The difficulty was increased by the fact that such phenomena usually occurred in the afternoon, —a time when, in the ordinary course of things, very few meteorological observations were made. He (Mr. Brodie) had observed that in this country whirlwinds and tornadoes usually occurred during the prevalence of a cyclonic distribution of pressure of a complex nature. In the case under discussion, however, the distribution, though cyclonic, was fairly simple, the depression which lay over England at the time being of considerable depth, and attended by gales on many parts of our southern coast.

Mr. W. H. DINES remarked that tornadoes generally occurred in America, on the south-east side of a low pressure system, and he thought that most damage was generally done on the south-east side of the track. It appeared, however, as though this whirlwind had occurred in front of, instead of on the flank of, the main depression.

Memorial to the late Mr. G. J. Symons, F.R.S.—On May 31 a Meeting was held at the rooms of the Royal Meteorological Society to consider the question of a Memorial to the late Mr. G. J. Symons, F.R.S., the distinguished Meteorologist and Founder of the British Rainfall Organisation.

It was resolved unanimously that the Memorial should take the form of a Gold Medal, to be awarded from time to time by the Council of the Royal Meteorological Society for distinguished work in connection with Meteorological Science.

An Executive Committee was appointed to take the necessary steps to raise a Fund for that purpose. We have now much pleasure in stating that their appeal has been very heartily responded to, not only by meteorologists, engineers, and representatives of other branches of science and industry, but also by personal friends and admirers of the late Mr. Symons in all classes.

The Committee have decided to keep the list open until the end of January 1901, in order to allow all who have in any way benefited by Mr. Symons's advice and assistance to contribute to the Memorial Fund.

C. THEODORE WILLIAMS, M.D., *Treasurer.*
R. MELDOLA, F.R.S., } *Secretaries.*
WM. MARRIOTT., }

70 Victoria Street, Westminster, S.W.

RAINFALL IN THE WEST AND EAST OF ENGLAND IN RELATION TO ALTITUDE ABOVE SEA-LEVEL.

By WILLIAM MARRIOTT, F.R.Met.Soc.

[Read June 20, 1900.]

In 1883 the Meteorological Council published a work entitled *Rainfall Tables of the British Isles for* 1866-80, *compiled from the Records of* 366 *Stations by G. J. Symons, F.R.S.* These Tables gave the monthly and annual rainfall for every year, as well as the means for each lustrum and for the whole period. In 1897 the Meteorological Council published another volume, *Rainfall Tables of the British Islands*, 1866-90, which were compiled by Mr. F. Gaster from information supplied chiefly by Mr. Symons, and by Dr. Buchan, and also from the reports furnished directly to the Meteorological Office. Part III. of this volume contains an abstract of the mean monthly and annual rainfall for the 10 years 1881-90 at 492 stations. This is a very valuable table, as it permits a strict comparison to be made of the rainfall at those places for the same period.

Some time ago I extracted the mean monthly and annual rainfall at the English and Welsh stations, and grouped them according to the altitude of the stations above sea-level. The results of this grouping I now wish to lay before the Society. It is necessary, however, to point out that the means apply only to the ten-year period, 1881-90, and that the results may perhaps be modified when a much longer series of observations is employed.

As the annual rainfall is heavier in the western part of the country than in the eastern part, it seemed desirable to separate the western from the eastern stations. I ultimately decided to consider all stations as "western" which drained to the west, and all stations as "eastern" which drained to the east. The stations were then grouped together for each 50 feet up to 500 feet, and above that altitude for each 100 feet. The number of stations was as follows:—

Altitude. feet	West.	East.	Total.	Altitude. feet	West.	East.	Total.
1- 50	16	31	47	401-450	6	5	11
51-100	13	24	37	451-500	12	4	16
101-150	16	23	39	501-600	11	5	16
151-200	18	17	35	601-700	5	3	8
201-250	8	17	25	701-800	5	3	8
251-300	17	6	23	801-900	2	0	2
301-350	9	14	23	901-1000	3	1	4
351-400	3	7	10	Above 1000	3	2	5

There were therefore 147 "western" stations, and 162 "eastern" stations; the total being 309.

The mean annual rainfall at the various altitudes was as follows:—

Altitude. feet	West. ins.	East. ins.	Altitude. feet	West. ins.	East. ins.
1- 50	32·79	24·36	401-450	56·26	27·73
51-100	33·59	25·39	451-500	41·00	32·54
101-150	35·40	25·76	501-600	38·08	35·84
151-200	36·28	26·14	601-700	41·25	35·27
201-250	36·50	26·35	701-800	58·83	45·12
251-300	35·36	28·41	801-900	55·01	...
301-350	41·05	28·30	901-1000	59·54	49·33
351-400	35·10	28·75	Above 1000	45·51	44·27

It will be seen that there is a general increase in the amount of rainfall as the altitude increases. The irregularities at the higher altitudes are no doubt due to the small number of stations employed. The values have been plotted on the diagram (Fig. 1), which shows in a very striking manner that the rainfall is considerably greater in the west than in the east, the excess being nearly a quarter.

If, however, the west and east values be combined the curve becomes much smoother, the increases of rainfall according to altitude being much more uniform (Fig. 2, p. 276).

The accompanying table gives the mean monthly rainfall grouped according to altitude for west and east:—

MEAN MONTHLY RAINFALL, 1881-90, GROUPED ACCORDING TO ALTITUDE FOR WEST AND EAST.

ALTITUDE.	WEST.												
	Jan.	Feb.	Mar.	Apr.	May.	June.	July.	Aug.	Sept.	Oct.	Nov.	Dec.	Year.
feet	ins.	ins.	ins.	ins.	ins.	ins.	ins.	ins.	ins.	ins.	ins.	ins.	ins.
1– 50	2·81	2·14	2·35	1·93	2·19	2·19	3·07	2·84	2·93	3·41	3·89	3·04	32·79
51–100	2·97	2·45	2·35	2·03	2·19	2·16	3·10	2·67	2·91	3·52	4·04	3·20	33·59
101–150	3·10	2·45	2·64	2·10	2·45	2·23	3·46	3·08	3·15	3·47	4·03	3·24	35·40
151–200	3·29	2·64	2·59	2·19	2·41	2·33	3·49	2·89	3·16	3·67	4·29	3·33	36·28
201–250	3·37	2·86	2·73	2·38	2·44	2·42	3·22	2·66	2·89	3·69	4·33	3·53	36·50
251–300	3·16	2·63	2·53	2·18	2·44	2·40	3·19	2·80	3·08	3·64	4·11	3·21	35·36
301–350	3·66	3·05	3·01	2·39	2·67	2·65	3·70	3·21	3·58	4·40	4·68	4·05	41·05
351–400	3·00	2·43	2·52	2·27	2·49	2·66	3·56	3·10	3·03	3·27	3·77	3·00	35·10
401–450	5·81	4·60	4·40	3·13	3·69	3·11	4·94	4·29	4·67	5·33	6·68	5·58	56·26
451–500	3·70	3·20	2·95	2·61	2·81	2·63	3·59	3·25	3·44	4·13	4·83	3·85	41·00
501–600	3·48	2·88	2·82	2·28	2·58	2·44	3·40	3·15	3·03	3·94	4·44	3·66	38·08
601–700	3·75	3·28	3·01	2·51	2·70	2·53	3·47	3·42	3·25	4·43	5·02	3·89	41·25
701–800	5·55	4·33	4·43	3·27	3·51	3·53	5·38	4·93	5·25	5·91	6·90	5·85	58·83
801–900	5·56	4·10	4·31	3·32	3·55	3·21	4·65	4·19	4·22	5·68	7·01	5·21	55·01
901–1000	6·16	4·87	4·42	3·41	3·76	3·07	4·71	4·81	4·82	6·08	7·38	6·05	59·54
Above 1000	4·03	3·06	3·04	2·69	2·99	3·10	4·02	3·98	3·87	5·11	5·18	4·45	45·51

ALTITUDE.	EAST.												
	Jan.	Feb.	Mar.	Apr.	May.	June.	July.	Aug.	Sept.	Oct.	Nov.	Dec.	Year.
feet	ins.	ins.	ins.	ins.	ins.	ins.	ins.	ins.	ins.	ins.	ins.	ins.	ins.
1– 50	1·78	1·57	1·66	1·59	1·83	1·68	2·47	2·07	2·29	2·89	2·53	2·00	24·36
51–100	1·94	1·65	1·81	1·69	1·94	1·77	2·54	2·15	2·30	2·94	2·59	2·09	25·39
101–150	1·91	1·71	1·84	1·75	1·97	1·82	2·62	2·21	2·32	2·87	2·67	2·07	25·76
151–200	2·04	1·75	1·88	1·78	2·00	1·84	2·59	2·21	2·29	2·85	2·80	2·12	26·14
201–250	1·92	1·78	1·91	1·76	2·10	1·92	2·67	2·30	2·35	2·83	2·74	2·05	26·35
251–300	2·01	1·81	2·18	1·83	2·14	1·88	2·77	2·53	2·59	3·15	3·17	2·35	28·41
301–350	2·28	1·96	2·08	1·89	2·17	2·06	2·76	2·31	2·46	2·94	3·05	2·35	28·30
351–400	2·25	1·94	2·15	2·04	2·09	1·99	2·98	2·40	2·47	3·17	3·02	2·26	28·75
401–450	2·26	1·90	1·98	2·03	2·20	1·99	2·73	2·26	2·32	2·84	3·02	2·20	27·73
451–500	2·77	2·25	2·51	2·01	2·26	2·31	3·12	2·92	2·67	3·25	3·42	2·79	32·54
501–600	2·81	2·17	2·93	2·21	2·52	2·48	3·62	3·32	3·28	3·70	3·72	3·09	35·84
601–700	3·16	2·32	2·60	2·04	2·24	2·34	3·18	3·07	3·25	3·96	3·93	3·19	35·27
701–800	4·47	3·16	3·67	2·66	2·74	2·52	4·25	3·78	3·77	4·72	5·16	4·21	45·12
801–900	...	...	...	...	...	...	...	...	...	...	...	...	...
901–1000	4·65	3·52	3·96	2·47	3·24	3·25	4·43	4·26	3·83	5·23	5·70	4·79	49·33
Above 1000	4·09	2·87	3·43	2·95	3·25	2·86	3·94	3·30	3·31	5·48	4·88	3·90	44·27

The figures in thick type indicate the greatest monthly rainfall. The figures in italic type indicate the least monthly rainfall.

If these values are thrown into diagrams [1] some very interesting features are brought out.

1. The greater rainfall in the west than in the east is at once apparent.

2. The monthly rainfall in the west is subject to a much greater range than in the east.

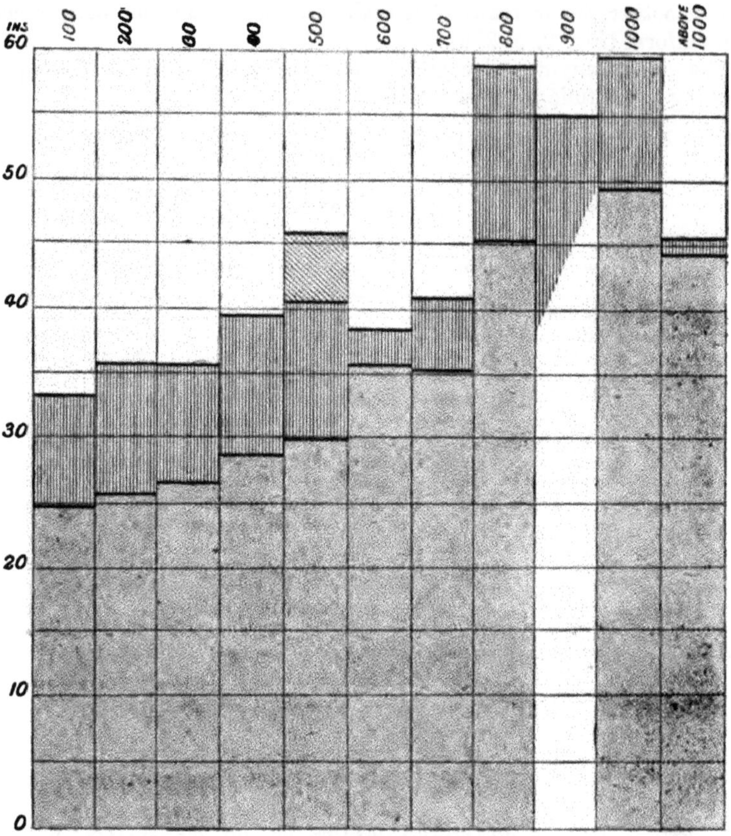

Fig. 1.—Mean Annual Rainfall in the West and East of England, grouped according to Altitude.

The light shading shows the rainfall in the east, while the vertical shading shows the excess of the rainfall in the west over that in the east. The cross shading under 500 ft. indicates the excess due to the rainfall at Seathwaite.

3. In the west the maximum at all altitudes occurs in November (and not in January as is popularly supposed), but in the east generally in October.

4. In the west the three spring months, April, May, and June are very dry.

5. One of the most marked features in all the diagrams both west and east is the great rise in the rainfall from June to July.

[1] These diagrams were exhibited at the Meeting, but were too numerous to be reproduced.

The prevailing winds over the British Isles are south-westerly. These come from the Atlantic as moist winds, and as soon as they strike the land they are forced upwards and, owing to the consequent reduction of temperature, have to part with some of their moisture in the form of rain; and so the rainfall in the west is greater than in the east. The greater the velocity of the wind the more rapid will be the condensation of the moisture, and consequently the heavier the rainfall.

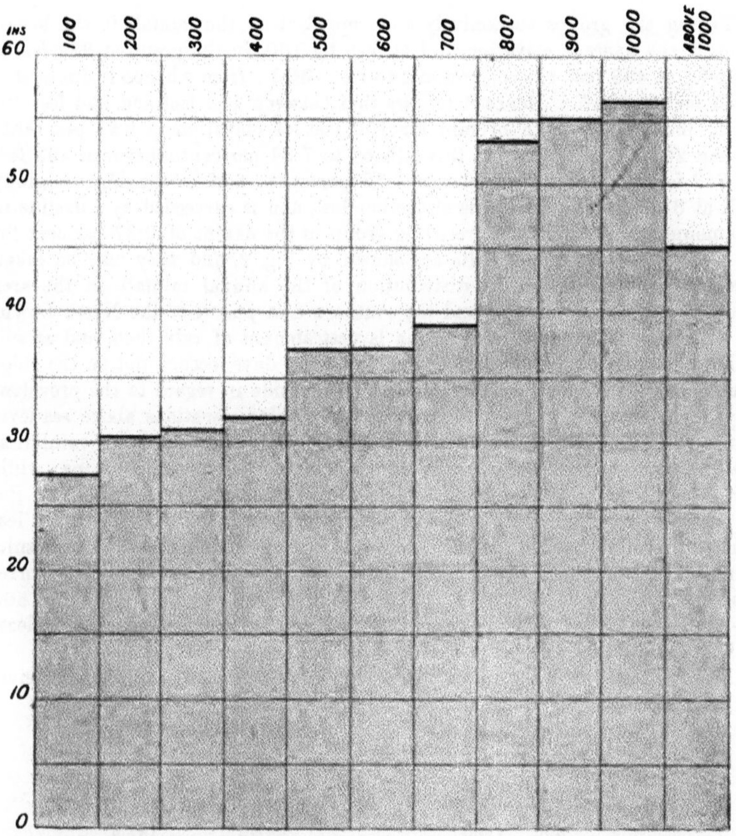

FIG. 2.—Mean Annual Rainfall (West and East combined) grouped according to Altitude.

When the current of air has passed over high ground it descends on the east side of the range a drier air, as it has parted with a great deal of its moisture. Consequently the conditions are not so favourable for the formation of rain on the east as on the west.

In the spring months there is a great prevalence of north-east winds. These as a rule are drier than the south-west winds, as they are often associated with anticyclonic conditions. And if rain does occur, it is mostly confined to the neighbourhood of the east coast, and does not extend very far inland.

With regard to the heavy rainfall in July, this is no doubt due in a large measure to the prevalence of thunderstorms. If, however, the isobaric and wind charts be examined, it will be seen that the prevailing winds for this month are decidedly Westerly, whereas in the spring months the winds are light and more from the Northward.

Very little has been written on the subject of the increase of rainfall with altitude above sea-level. Mr. H. S. Eaton, in his "Report on the Temperature and the Rainfall of the Croydon District for the five years 1881-85,[1] dealt with the question as referring to that district. He said :—

Taking the groups successively and representing the rainfall in the lowest group at the average elevation of 124 feet by 100, in the group at 234 feet it is 109·1; at 493 feet 129·4; and at 648 feet 136·1; from whence it diminishes at 841 feet to 134·7. Hence it follows that between 124 feet and 234 feet the rate of increase of depth of rain for 100 feet of elevation is 8·27 per cent; between 234 feet and 493 feet this falls off to 7·84 per cent; between 493 feet and 648 feet it further diminishes to 4·32 per cent; and in the highest group of all at 841 feet the increase is altogether lost, and is succeeded by a decline in the amount of rain from the preceding group to the extent of 0·37 per cent for 100 feet. The foregoing results are shown by Fig. 2, and they may be taken as representing generally the distribution of the annual rainfall on the area included between the Thames and the southern escarpment of the North Downs and the rivers Mole and Darent. The largest amount of rain then, and as will be shown presently, the greatest number of rainy days, occurs, not on the ridge of the North Downs, but some distance on the lee side in regard to the prevalent rainy South-westerly winds. The amount at similar elevations above sea-level seems also to diminish from west to east; in Surrey the mean annual rainfall at nineteen stations, having an average elevation of 322 feet, was 26·68 ins., while in Kent, at nine stations having an elevation of 313 feet, it was 25·29 ins. The number of rainy days, a rainy day being reckoned as one on which not less than 0·005 in. of rain is measured, has been similarly examined; the results given in Table X., and shown graphically by Fig. 3, indicate a close correspondence with the depth of rain. In the zone of greatest rainfall—600 to 800 feet—the number of rainy days in the year was 178·9, and in that of least rainfall—below 200 feet—it was 165·0 days.

Briefly summarised, the rainfall in the district from 1881 to 1885 inclusive, was as under :—

Elevation above Sea-level. ft.	Depth of Rain. ins.	Rainy Days.
Above 800	31·36	178·3
Between 600 and 800	31·66	178·9
,, 400 ,, 600	29·12	173·7
,, 200 ,, 400	25·39	167·8
Below 200	23·27	165·0

The last point of consideration is the monthly rainfall in connection with the altitude of the stations above sea-level, and for this purpose they have been grouped separately into those above and those below 400 feet. The result is that in every month the depth of rain is greater in the upper group, which includes ten stations at an average elevation of 594 feet. But the table of ratios of the monthly to the annual fall shows that in spring and summer there is a larger amount of rain proportionately in the lower group of eleven stations at an average elevation of 193 feet. This condition of the rainfall is associated with the relative humidity of the atmosphere. When that is low, or, in other words, when the air is dry, a relative excess of rain is experienced at the lower stations, while a high degree of humidity is favourable to a more copious

[1] *Transactions of the Croydon Microscopical and Natural History Club*, 1886.

precipitation at the upper stations. Numerically, the proportion of the rainfall of the upper to that of the lower group for the five months, November to March, was as 106 to 100, the number of rainy days being as 107·7 to 100; and for the seven months, April to October, it was as 96 to 100, and the number of rainy days as 105·3 to 100, the relative humidity of the air for the corresponding periods being respectively 87 and 78.

The late Mr. Thomas Hawksley, C.E., many years ago laid it down as a rule that for engineering purposes the increase of rainfall with altitude might be taken as 3 per cent for every 100 feet. This, I believe, has been generally adopted by the engineering profession in Parliamentary inquiries on water supply. I do not think, however, that it is correct.

From the data which I have given in this paper the increase of rainfall with altitude comes out as follows:—

100 feet	+ 9 per cent.	600 feet	+ 5 per cent.
200 ,,	+ 8 ,,	700 ,,	+38 ,,
300 ,,	+ 3 ,,	800 ,,	+ 3 ,,
400 ,,	+14 ,,	900 ,,	+ 4 ,,
500 ,,	+ 1 ,,	1000 ,,	−21 ,,

With a much longer period of observations and a larger number of stations these percentages might be considerably modified, and certainly would be more uniform.

Each individual case must, however, be judged on its own merits, as exposure, position, and surroundings, as well as altitude, greatly affect the rainfall.

As the late Mr. G. J. Symons, F.R.S., said in *British Rainfall*, 1896, p. 24, "the influence of position with respect to hills and valleys is far greater than that of altitude."

DISCUSSION.

The President (Dr. C. Theodore Williams) said the paper was a very valuable one, and he specially commended the way in which the matter had been handled. By grouping the stations into east and west he thought the subject could be more readily grasped.

Mr. Baldwin Latham said the question of the increase of rainfall with altitude was a very important one to engineers, and often had to be considered, especially when going into a strange country. If only more observations and more calculations of the same kind were made, the benefits to engineers generally would be greatly enhanced. He thought that each district should be dealt with by itself if any definite conclusion was to be arrived at. For instance, in the Breconshire hills district, and on the hills round Snowdon the increase of rainfall with elevation was enormous, and greatly in excess of anything to be met with in the east of England, where no such elevations could be found. He would like to see each district mapped out separately, and he hoped some one would be able to go into the matter more fully.

Mr. H. Sowerby Wallis said the Fellows were much indebted to Mr. Marriott for his most interesting paper. There was one point which he thought Mr. Marriott had overlooked, that was, as to how far many places in the eastern portion were dependent on North-east winds for their rainfall. He had heard a good deal of discussion on rainfall matters in Parliamentary Committee rooms, and was of opinion that engineers generally had not accepted the rule of three per cent increase for each 100 feet of elevation. Mr. T. Hawksley arrived at it in connection with the Vartry works for Dublin, and did not contend that it was applicable in all cases. He (Mr. Wallis) had tried working with small areas, and various periods, but could get no uniform result. The influence of position was the all-important fact.

Mr. E. Mawley said that Mr. Marriott had undertaken the preparation of this paper at the request of the Council. If some one could be prevailed upon to take up the subject he thought Mr. Marriott would be glad, and he was sure Mr. Wallis would give all the information in his power. If there was no increase of rain with elevation there certainly was an increase of wind; and he did not think the gauges caught the full amount of rainfall when a strong wind was blowing. Unfortunately, the higher one ascended the greater influence the wind exerted.

Rev. Dr. J. D. Parker said that at Hawes Junction, which was over 1000 feet in altitude, the rainfall was very heavy; while at Hawes, Yore Bridge, and Aysgarth Vicarage the fall went down by steps; and still lower down the dale the amount greatly decreased. Recently he had been brought into personal contact with the power of the rain-storms amongst the hills, for at Fossdale farm in Wensleydale a storm had completely wrecked the garden, yard, and outhouses, doing also an enormous amount of damage to the tenant's cattle, sheep, and implements; destroying at the same time the picturesque gorge of the well-known Hardraw Scarr—all in half an hour.

Dr. H. R. Mill said that greater clearness would have resulted if the observations had been subdivided into small groups, not into counties, which were artificial units, but into natural regions. The artificial character of county divisions was very probably the reason why satisfactory results had not been obtained by Mr. Wallis. The exposures should have been taken into consideration. It would be very interesting to group the stations into natural districts, such as the Lake district, the hilly portion of Wales, the Pennine Chain, and other regions of England; and then to divide the stations in each district into two groups, those facing east and those facing west. From these it would be possible to get a better approximation to the average change of rainfall with elevations in different types of country. He was certain there was an increase of precipitation with a rise in altitude; the Ben Nevis observations placed the fact beyond doubt.

Rev. Dr. J. D. Parker said he thought that rainfall did not always increase with elevation, for at his house at Bennington the fall was frequently heavier down in the village than on the hill where he lived, and showers were often experienced in the valley that did not reach him at all.

Mr. R. H. Curtis said the rainfall of any place depended upon other factors besides its height above sea-level, and its position east or west of the watershed; and therefore it was unsafe to group together a number of stations spread over a considerable range of latitude without having regard to their geographical positions, and to the features of the districts in which they were severally situated. In the present paper stations in Cornwall had probably been grouped, with others in Westmoreland, and possibly with others at intermediate latitudes; and since the rainfall at each of the stations was probably influenced to some extent by its own local surroundings, the mean result derived from the grouping could hardly be regarded as a true exponent of the effect due to altitude alone, or to any other single cause. In his recent discussion of the meteorology of a position of Sussex Dr. Mill had shown how largely rainfall was affected, not only by height above mean sea-level, but also by the geological character of a district, the rainfall on the same contour line varying as the position of the stations changed relatively to other and purely local features of the country.

Mr. F. J. Brodie agreed with previous speakers in the opinion that variations in the amount of rainfall are due not merely to the effect of altitude, but to the actual situations of the gauges with regard to hill and valley systems. He had long been of opinion that in order to obtain anything like an intelligent explanation of local differences in rainfall the values must be plotted on orographical maps of the largest scale available. It must, however, be remembered that to indulge with any success in work of this kind it is absolutely essential that the exact positions of the gauges should be known, and that in many cases such information is not readily available. The information is, of course, best obtained by personal inspection; but, where this is impossible, it might in many cases be had from carefully drawn plans supplied by the various observers. He (Mr. Brodie) concurred in the hope that Mr. Wallis might, at some future date, find time for an inquiry of the kind so much desired by meteorologists.

Mr. J. Hopkinson said that he had been working for some time with the Tables used by Mr. Marriott, but only with the view of deducing the mean monthly and annual county rainfall in England and Wales, dividing England into four districts—north, midland, south-east, and south-west. In the last conversation he had with Mr. Symons he mentioned the increase of rainfall with elevation, and from east to west, and Mr. Symons remarked that the observed increase was due neither to the height nor the longitude, but to the aspect of the stations. He was sure that they were all much indebted to Mr. Marriott for this paper, which must have involved a great amount of tedious labour. He (Mr. Hopkinson) had sometimes spent hours in finding out and correcting a mistake detected by the sum of the monthly falls not agreeing exactly with the yearly fall for a number of years at several stations. By such non-agreement he had already detected about a dozen mistakes in the printed Tables referred to for the years 1881-90. He doubted whether deductions derived from the suggested classification of the gauges according to their aspect would repay the labour which would be entailed by such an investigation.

The President (Dr. C. Theodore Williams) said that Mr. Symons had supplied him with rainfall records from Wales, and it had struck him from these that the matter was purely one of condensation. When the station was high and facing west a heavy fall of over 50 ins. was to be expected; but when low, and even if still facing west, only from 25 to 30 ins. would probably be measured. He had learnt much from the discussion, and he was sure it was one which Mr. Symons himself would have thoroughly appreciated.

Mr. W. Marriott, in reply, said that he had extracted the figures some time ago, but that the paper had only been prepared for the meeting. He had experienced some difficulty in grouping the stations, and had found it best to arrange them under "west" and "east." He had only used those stations which continued for the whole 10 years. He would have liked to have gone into the matter more thoroughly, and he hoped that some one else would deal with the subject in a much more exhaustive manner than he had done.

HALLIWELL'S SELF RECORDING RAIN GAUGE.

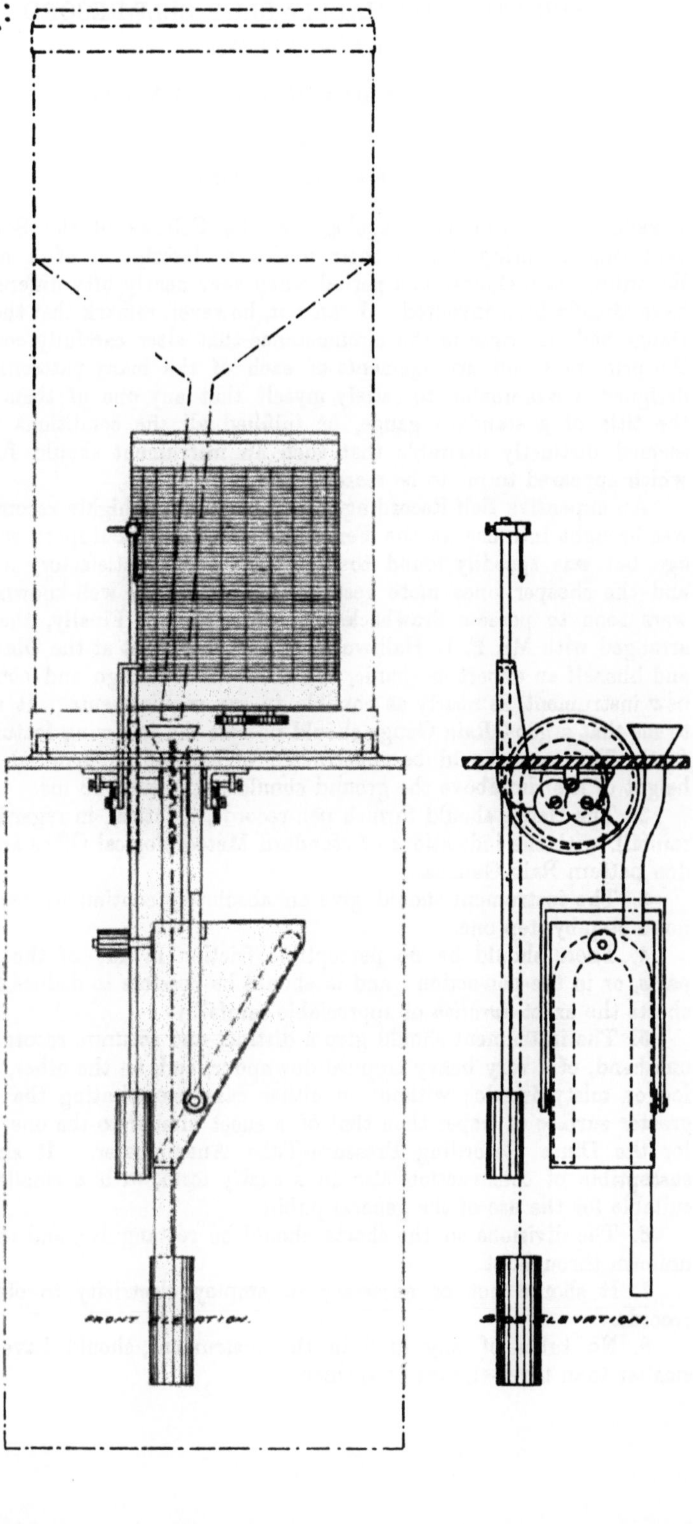

DESCRIPTION OF HALLIWELL'S SELF-RECORDING RAIN GAUGE.

By JOSEPH BAXENDELL, F.R.Met.Soc.

(PLATE XIV.).

[Read June 20, 1900.]

I FEEL that I owe some apology to the Fellows of the Society for venturing to bring before their notice a description of a new Self-Recording Rain Gauge, at a period when very nearly fifty different kinds have already been invented. I can but, however, remark that the present Gauge had its origin in the circumstance that after carefully considering the principles and arrangements of each of the many patterns already designed, I was unable to satisfy myself that any one of them merited the title of a standard gauge, or fulfilled all the conditions which it seemed distinctly desirable that such an instrument should fulfil, and which appeared to me to be reasonable.

An expensive Self-Recording Rain Gauge, most highly recommended, was brought into use at the Fernley Observatory, Southport, some time ago, but was speedily found to be by no means satisfactory in action; and the cheaper ones more recently introduced by well-known makers were seen to possess drawbacks of other kinds. Finally, therefore, I arranged with Mr. F. L. Halliwell, the chief assistant at the Observatory, and himself an expert mechanic, to endeavour to design and construct a new instrument, as nearly as possible to my requirements. It appeared to me that a good Rain Gauge should possess the following features :—

1. The case should be constructed of substantial material, and the height of the rim above the ground should not exceed 18 ins.

2. The Gauge should furnish pen-records, identical, in regard to total rainfall, with the indications of standard Meteorological Office and Snowdon pattern Rain Gauges.

3. The instrument should give an absolutely continuous record, and not a step-by-step one.

4. There should be no perceptible friction in any of the working parts, or in the pen-action; and it should be possible to deduce from the charts the exact *duration* of appreciable rainfall.

5. The instrument should give a distinct and accurate record, on the one hand, of a very heavy tropical downpour, and, on the other, of a wet fog or misty drizzle; without in either case necessitating the use of a greater surface of paper than that of a sheet similar to the one required for the Dines Recording Pressure-Tube Anemometer. It should be susceptible of construction also in a *weekly* form, with a smaller chart, suitable for the use of the general public.

6. The divisions on the charts should be rectangular, and the scales uniform throughout.

7. It should not be necessary to employ electricity to obtain the records.

8. No tubes of any kind in the instrument should have a bore smaller than three-eighths of an inch.

9. The working parts should require little or no attention, after once being properly placed in position at the Station.

10. The Gauge should contain apparatus for melting falling snow, with a minimum amount of evaporation.

11. Everything should be as simple as possible, but each detail should be carefully thought out and tested, and accurately finished.

12. The total cost of the Gauge, complete, should not exceed £10.

After experiments extending over nearly two years, Mr. Halliwell has now produced a Self-Recording Rain Gauge which I have accepted, and which, indeed, approaches much more closely to my ideal standard than I had dared to hope would be practicable. I therefore venture to communicate the following description of it to the Society:—

An 8-inch Meteorological Office pattern Rain Gauge receiver, of copper (having the usual deep rim, capped by a stout brass ring ground at the top to a sharp edge), is borne upon a cylinder of the same diameter, and this covers a vertical clock-drum of the usual Richard type. The cylinder and the clock spindle are secured to the lid of a rectangular galvanised iron "well," 9 ins. square and 21 ins. deep, which is sunk in the ground; and, when all is fixed in position, the upper edge of the rim of the daily Gauge is 18 ins., and that of the weekly one only 15 ins., above the ground, the exposure of the instruments being therefore virtually identical with that of an ordinary standard Rain Gauge. The cylinder is detachable, and is lifted off when the chart requires changing. Both it and the "well" may, if preferred, be replaced by an iron frame-box fitted with four plate-glass sides, in order to render the recording arrangements visible; but this necessitates slightly increasing the height of the rim above the ground, and also adds somewhat to the otherwise low cost of the instrument.

From the funnel the rain is conveyed by a half-inch brass pipe to the well, where it falls into a modified partially tipping bucket, in one side of which is brazed a half-inch or other large-bore siphon. The bucket is suspended, at a suitable point, on knife-edges, in a hanger, which in turn depends from a pulley-wheel by a snake-pattern chain secured to the groove of the wheel and coiled partly round it. The pulley-wheel is rigidly attached to its axis, and immediately behind it, similarly fastened to the same axis, is a good-sized cam, carefully balanced, however, by a false one; and in the rear of these again is a second pulley-wheel. A line suspended from the part of the grooved periphery of the cam nearest to its axis carries a suitable weight. A chain upon the second pulley raises or lowers a rod, which simply bears against the pulley, and is kept vertical by being weighted at the bottom. On the top of the rod is a new kind of frictionless pen. The joint axis of the cam and two pulleys revolves on anti-friction rollers; and, in actual use, practically no frictional effect is apparent in any part of the instrument.

As water falls into the bucket the latter descends, the line carrying the weight being gradually wound upon the periphery of the cam; at the same time the pen is being vertically raised. The divisions on the chart are rectangular, and the scale uniform throughout.

Immediately half an inch of rainfall has been collected, in the case of the daily form of the instrument, or one inch in that of the weekly pattern, the bucket quietly turns through a moderate angle, bringing the large siphon at once into action, *full* bore. The amount of return-water from the short leg of the siphon at the end of the discharge is found to be on all occasions the same, and hence the zero is constant. The bucket of course automatically rights itself. There is no possibility of the half-inch siphon dribbling, of its starting before the time, or of its continuing to carry off the water during a tropical downpour after the end of the proper discharge.

This combination of a moderately vibrating bucket and a large-bore siphon is found to be decidedly preferable to any tipping bucket alone, the latter entailing the provision of a plunger working in glycerine, or some similar attachment, for the purpose of preventing the instantaneous return of the pen to zero, by which ink would be jerked out, and the chart otherwise spoiled.

The bucket of the daily Gauge is completely emptied in six seconds; for the weekly one a rather larger siphon is employed to secure the same result, the discharges in its case only occurring half as frequently as in that of the daily one. The quantity of incoming rain lost during six seconds, and this but once for each half-inch (or inch) of rainfall, is, under all ordinary circumstances, entirely inappreciable; nevertheless, a double bucket, with a pair of siphons, can, if required, be fitted to the gauge in place of the single one, without material effect upon the total cost, and then nothing whatever will escape collection.

The indications of the instrument in its present form are identical with those of the standard Meteorological Office and Snowdon Rain Gauges. The water passing through it can, however, be retained, and subsequently measured by hand.

The rain scale adopted for the daily Gauge is 0·50 in. to five inches of paper; that for the weekly is 1·00 in. of rain to three inches of paper. The time scale of the daily one is made to correspond exactly with that employed for the Dines Pressure-Tube Anemometer and for the Recording Anemoscope described on pp. 326-328 of the last volume of the *Quarterly Journal*. The time scale for the weekly one is that generally used by Richard of Paris, and other makers, with, however, the substitution of straight abscissæ for Richard's curved ones. The instruments could, if desired, be constructed for any given scales. The charts are printed on waterproof paper.

The rain in the bucket is most readily prevented from freezing in winter, and moderate falls of snow melted, by the use of a small gas burner, which entails very little expense in cases where gas is laid within a reasonable distance of the Rain Gauge. Otherwise, special dwarf candles, to burn 26 hours, can be obtained.

I cannot conclude without acknowledging the very great assistance which has been afforded to Mr. Halliwell and myself by the late Mr. G. J. Symons' absolutely unique series of articles on Self-Recording Rain Gauges in the volumes of *British Rainfall* for 1878, 1879, 1884, and 1898.

Addendum.—Since the above was written, it has been found possible to suspend from the same pulley-wheel both the bucket and the rod carrying the pen, thus dispensing with one wheel, and rendering the instrument even more simple than before.

DISCUSSION.

THE PRESIDENT (Dr. C. THEODORE WILLIAMS) said that he was sure the Fellows would record their thanks to Mr. Baxendell and Mr. Halliwell for this interesting paper.

Mr. W. H. DINES said that the instrument seemed to him, so far as he could judge from the drawings, to be in every way satisfactory; and he much liked the plan of combining a tipping bucket and siphon. Referring to self-recording rain gauges in general, he said that the precise determination of heavy falls of short duration depended on the time scale. With the clock drum used in this case an interval of one minute of time corresponded to about one-hundredth part of an inch, and with a fine pen kept in good order it was possible to determine the interval in which any given amount fell without much chance of the error exceeding two minutes.

Mr. R. H. CURTIS said that as he had had a great deal of experience with another form of self-registering rain gauge, and had also seen Mr. Halliwell's gauge and some of its records, he would like to call attention to one or two points which appeared to be specially good features in the latter. The first was the rapidity of its discharge; and on this head he might mention that at Plymouth, in August 1898, during a very heavy thunderstorm, the Beckley gauge had, after recording the first two-tenths of an inch, gone on indicating *no rain*, owing to the fact that the rain was actually falling faster than the siphon could discharge it from the float. The Corporation had bought the gauge as one result of a lawsuit they had had, in the course of which the need had been felt of data such as it was intended to supply; and therefore this result, in the first heavy storm after its erection, was particularly disappointing. A similar accident could not occur with Halliwell's gauge. The open scale of the record was another advantage of this gauge, because it enabled one to follow easily every variation in the rate of fall; and this open scale, combined with the sensitiveness of the bucket, allowed small amounts of precipitation to be measured which might otherwise be lost, but which in the aggregate might amount to a considerable quantity in a month. The fact that heat could be applied in times of frost and snow was also an advantage which could not be secured in some forms of gauge; and he had personally had a good deal of trouble in allocating falls of snow to the hours at which it had fallen, because it had not been possible to melt it as it fell. He understood from Mr. Baxendell that the dwarf candles acted satisfactorily; and, in reply to a question, he added that he did not think any difficulty need be anticipated with respect to the clock, as he had found similar clocks to work quite satisfactorily under conditions as severe as those to which these were likely to be subjected. He was sorry no specimens of the trace had been sent, but he could speak to the satisfactory character of those he had himself seen. He thought the inventor had shown great ingenuity in contriving the mechanism of the instrument, and from its simplicity it was not likely to get out of order easily; whilst its price, he thought, was remarkably low.

Mr. H. SOWERBY WALLIS remarked that he had not seen the rain gauge, but thought that it possessed an advantage in the fact that the bucket did not tip with a small amount of rain. He had had no experience of the Beckley self-recording gauge, but had obtained good results from the Casella instrument. If the working pen was kept in good order it was possible to read off to intervals of two minutes.

Dr. R. H. SCOTT inquired if any one present had had experience with any of the heating arrangements for the melting of snow, as it entered the gauge. Lamps had been used in the Babinet self-recording gauge which was mentioned by Prof. Fradesso de Silveira at the Leipzig Conference in 1872, but as far as he (Dr. Scott) was aware, that form of rain gauge was not now in use, so that presumably its action had not been satisfactory.

Mr. H. Sowerby Wallis said that he had worked a Casella gauge for 14 or 15 years, and during that period had obtained reasonably good records in all ordinary falls of snow. He had used night-lights for warming the funnel, and on appearance of snow at night always put in two at 9 p.m. Some amount was evaporated by the heat, and this loss probably amounted to as much as 5 per cent.

Mr. E. Mawley said that judging from the diagram he thought very highly of the instrument, but wished some tracings had also been exhibited. He himself had used a Casella recording rain gauge for some years, and had always found it work satisfactorily. The trouble was to keep it in good working order, and it should be frequently overhauled and the pencil looked to. By greasing down the sides where the roller moves it was found to work much more easily. He had tried to devise a plan for suspending a lamp from a kind of diaphragm, so as to shut off the heat from the bucket, but could not get the lamp to burn. During the heavy snowstorms of January 1881, Mr. Latham seemed to be the only observer to get good results, and he thought it must have been through constantly watching his gauge. He could not make out how Mr. Wallis's gauge had worked so well.

Mr. Baldwin Latham remarked that during the heavy snowstorm of January 1881 he had stayed up all night and thus secured his record. In snowy weather he used a petroleum lamp with a $\frac{3}{4}$-inch flame, which was sufficient to melt the snow as it fell into the gauge, providing the fall was not too heavy. Of course some was always lost by evaporation owing to the large amount of heat used, and the total amount measured on the diagram was generally a little behind what would be recorded when rain only falls.

Dr. R. H. Scott inquired about the measurement of hail, which would probably take longer to melt than snow.

Mr. Baldwin Latham thought there would be no difficulty with hail, as it was generally associated with thunderstorms, and usually fell in the summer months when the gauge was warm. Mr. Baxendell had given great attention to that branch of rainfall which was especially valuable to engineers, namely, the rate of fall and the actual time occupied in falling. The new recording gauge was certainly a very ingenious instrument, its action depending upon a cam with a bucket for containing the rain at one side, with a counterweight on the other side, so arranged that as the bucket increased in weight with the volume of rain falling the leverage diminished and the counterweight still equipoised the weight of rain, and therefore there was no liability for the instrument to race. The shape of the bucket showed considerable ingenuity, as it was not until it had got its full charge of water, of half an inch, that it tilted and started the siphon suddenly to work so as to completely empty it, and on being emptied it resumed its former position, and the instrument started to again record from zero.

Mr. F. Campbell Bayard inquired if a pendulum clock could be substituted for the French clock, as the latter did not go well out of doors.

Mr. J. Baxendell, in a note to the Secretary, in reply, said that the method of heating by means of a gas-jet had proved to give decidedly more satisfactory results than either the dwarf candles or ordinary night-lights, but that since the paper was written a special adjustable paraffin lamp had been arranged which was found to answer very well; and as it could be constructed to burn satisfactorily inside the gauge for three days without attention, it should be useful in the many localities where gas is not available. Pendulum clocks could readily be substituted for the French spring ones, if preferred, but, with care, the latter (somewhat improved) seemed to work sufficiently well. He much regretted that no specimen traces were sent with the paper; some should, however, be submitted to the inspection of the Fellows at the next opportunity. He might add that, in addition to the weekly pattern of the gauge, mentioned in the paper, it had been thought desirable to construct another, with a more open scale, viz. 1 inch of rain to 5 inches of paper, and a length of about 14 inches to the week.

Heavy Rainfall in Local Storms.—We are sometimes asked where all the rain comes from that falls during a short time in a thunderstorm or cloud-burst. Three inches of rain in an hour makes a very heavy local rain. Rainfalls from 3 inches in half an hour up to 12 or 15 inches in an hour are spoken of as cloud-bursts. The heaviest rains are those recorded at Cherrapunji, amounting to 30 or 40 inches in a day. It is very rare that rain falls from absolutely still air. In general, there is a horizontal movement, which we detect by the motions of the clouds, and an ascending movement which is easily seen if we study the phenomena going on within the clouds. This ascending movement is very violent in thunderstorms and tornadoes, is always present in waterspouts, and in the general heavy rains attending areas of low pressure. In studying the thunderheads, or great cumulus clouds, of a thunderstorm, we see a rapid ascension going on at the top of the cloud, nearly over the region where hail and the heaviest rain occur. Evidently the quantity of rain that falls upon any given area represents, not merely the vapour precipitated from the air over that area at any moment, but from the successive masses of air that flow over it during any given time. Thus at Cherrapunji, India, the heavy rains drop from a rapidly moving South-west Monsoon current flowing over the Khasia Hills. It is not improper to assume that the heavy rainfalls that we call local rains are also due to the supply of moisture brought by rapid currents flowing over any given spot. Thus, in the hailstorm, and in the centre of a large cumulus cloud, the currents of air ascend rapidly, while in the general widely extended rains they ascend slowly. One can easily calculate the total depth of rainfall in the column of air extending from the ground to the upper limit of the atmosphere, with results as shown in the accompanying table, prepared in 1883, but published in the *Smithsonian Report* for 1888, p. 410.

Height of column.	Depth of water in the atmosphere corresponding to the respective dew points at the earth's surface.			
feet	80°	70°	60°	50°
	ins.	ins.	ins.	ins.
6,000	1·3	1·0	0·7	0·5
12,000	2·1	1·5	1·1	0·8
18,000	2·5	1·8	1·3	0·9
24,000	2·7	2·0	1·4	1·0
30,000	2·8	2·1	1·5	1·1

These figures apply only to still air, and are to be modified to an indefinite extent if horizontal or vertical movements are taking place.—*U.S. Monthly Weather Review*, May 1900.

PROCEEDINGS AT THE MEETINGS OF THE SOCIETY.

May 16, 1900.

Ordinary Meeting.

Dr. C. THEODORE WILLIAMS, President, in the Chair.

JAMES DUNN, Brunswick House, Cambridge ;
T. ALMOND HIND, Goldsmith Buildings, Temple, E.C. ;
RICHARD HUNTER MAUND, O'Connell, New South Wales ;
FRANCIS DAVIDSON OUTRAM, Assoc.M.Inst.C.E., The Manor Lodge, Worcester Park, Surrey ;
Rev. HARCOURT CHARLES VAUX SNOWDEN, St. Peter's, Kent ;
PROSPER CHARLES TREBECK, 2 O'Connell Street, Sydney, N.S.W. ; and
WILLIAM JOHN TREVASKIS, Georgetown, Demerara, British Guiana,
were balloted for and duly elected Fellows of the Society.

The following communications were read :—

"THE WILTSHIRE WHIRLWIND OF OCTOBER 1, 1899." By the late G. J. SYMONS, F.R.S. (p. 261).

"THE VARIATIONS OF THE CLIMATE OF THE GEOLOGICAL AND HISTORICAL PAST AND THEIR CAUSES." By Dr. NILS EKHOLM, Hon. Member Roy. Met. Soc. [This paper will appear in next number.]

June 20, 1900.

Ordinary Meeting.

Dr. C. THEODORE WILLIAMS, President, in the Chair.

THE PRESIDENT announced that the late Mr. G. J. SYMONS, F.R.S., had bequeathed to the Society the Album presented to him by the Fellows in 1879, his Medals, a portion of his valuable Library, and the sum of £200.

The following letter was read :—

MAURITIUS METEOROLOGICAL SOCIETY,
ROYAL ALFRED OBSERVATORY, MAURITIUS,
May 7, 1900.

DEAR SIR—I am requested by the President and Council of the above Society to inform you that at a meeting of the Society on Thursday last, May 3, 1900, referring to the death of Mr. G. J. Symons, it was unanimously resolved :

That the Society should record their deep sense of regret at the lamented death of so distinguished a Meteorologist whose labours had been of such benefit to science, and who had always taken a kindly interest in the welfare of the Mauritius Meteorological Society.—I am, your obedient servant,

T. F. CLAXTON,
Hon. Secretary.

THE PRESIDENT,
ROYAL METEOROLOGICAL SOCIETY.

MURRAY L. ALLEN, Kosciusko Observatory, Jindabyne, N.S.W. ;
NICHOLAS CULLINAN, M.D., Pontymister, Monmouth ;

Arthur John Leopold Evans, Town Hall, Luton ;
John St. Clair Gunn, M.B., Bloomsbury, Kaikowra, New Zealand ;
Capt. William Perfect Lapage, 69 Gordon Road, Ealing, W. ; and
John Little, Low Friar Street, Newcastle-on-Tyne,
were balloted for and duly elected Fellows of the Society.

The following communications were read :—

"Rainfall in the West and East of England in Relation to Altitude above Sea-Level." By William Marriott, F.R.Met.Soc. (p. 273).

"Description of Halliwell's Self-Recording Rain Gauge." By Joseph Baxendell, F.R.Met.Soc. (p. 281).

CORRESPONDENCE AND NOTES.

The Climate and Diseases of Northern Brazil.—The most northern of the United States of Brazil is the State of Pará, which occupies a vast region of that Republic comprised between 3° 11′ and 15° 20′ of longitude West of the meridian of Rio de Janeiro and between the 4° 22′ of North latitude, and 9° 15′ of South latitude, also wholly in the tropical zone. The city of Pará lies very near the Equator at 1° 28′ S. lat. The State is bounded on the north by the Atlantic Ocean, French, Dutch, and English Guianas ; on the east by the States of Maranham and Goyaz ; on the south by the State of Matto-Grosso ; and on the west by that of Amazon. In extent its territory is the third State of Brazil, and corresponds to one-seventh of the Brazilian territory and to one-thirteenth of the surface of South America. Though there has been lately a decided increase of population, especially of the town of Pará, the numerical value of the population of the whole State is small, less than 500,000. In the different rivers of the neighbourhood of Pará, as well as on the maritime coast, there are numbers of islands, some of which are exceedingly large. Opposite Pará there is the so-called "Panther Island" (Isla do Onça), and a little farther on the island of Catnoca. The latter is so situated that it commands the port of Pará, and is particularly suitable for a sanitary station. The establishment of such a station was very much needed in order to avoid the very great inconvenience of ships that are obliged to be quarantined, having to go to Ilha Grande, situated to the south of Rio de Janeiro. For instance, in August 1899 several cases of bubonic plague having been noticed in Portugal, the different ships coming from Europe, which had touched in Lisbon, were not allowed to land, but were sent to the only quarantine station for the whole of Brazil at Ilha Grande. In consequence of this Pará was without letters from Europe for many weeks, whilst with a sanitary station at Catnoca island the quarantine might have been reduced to one or two weeks. Quite recently a sanitary station has been established at Catnoca island.

Mosqueiro is situated on the right bank of the river of Pará. This place has become a favourite resort for the people of Pará ; Pinheiro, about half the distance from Pará to Mosqueiro, is also a very much frequented and popular locality. Opposite Pará, but hidden by the Panther Island, is the large island of Marajo. According to the waters which bathe them, the shores of these islands differ one from the other. On the west coast, bathed by the Amazon, are found lowlands, muddy and clayey, whilst on the northern part of the coast, blown over by winds, the shores present a reddish sand, which becomes hard and cemented by clay, forming blocks over which the shallow water rolls. On the contrary, the northern and southern coasts are characterised by the frequent presence of coarse beds: ferruginous sandstones on one hand and white sand on the other. In a longitudinal band, which does not extend three miles in its greatest width, based on the reefs, the eastern coast rises with some little interruption to a superior height to the general level of the island, but without reaching a sufficient height to form a hill. The largest layers of the complicated Amazonian deposits are plainly visible in the island of Marajo. They are lying from west to east with a slight declivity. At the bottom they are clays and marls, in a fine state, without granulation, so that the mass is absolutely uniform and homogeneous. Then appears a mixture of clay and sand, in thin regular layers, the sand growing coarser and coarser. Above this first system appears another deposit of gravel and grains of different rocks: silica, limestone, and oxide of iron, the latter sometimes in such a proportion that the coarse sandstone looks like an iron ore. The characteristics of these layers are the great variety of materials forming the sandstone. They present nearly everywhere the same parallelism, sometimes 90 feet, and even more, in thickness. Above them is placed the result of conglomeration of very fine sandy clays which present vestiges of stratification.

There are two entirely opposite ideas on the climate of the State of Pará. According to some Pará would appear to be a relatively healthy place, but according to others it would be a deadly place for the Europeans. Why do we have such a difference of opinion? Those who speak of the relatively low death-rate take of course the death-rate on all the population. They might see, for instance, that the monthly death-rate varies between 0·2 and 0·3 per cent. This taken on the whole population would not appear exceedingly high, but it is high when we take the proportion of diseases not on the whole population, but on the immigrants and travellers. So far as it is known it is those who have to suffer most.

Now, if we look at the statistics of the diseases we see that the infectious ones are the most prominent, and, above all, the yellow fever. The deaths due to yellow fever amount yearly to something like 300 (sometimes even more). This disease is specially fatal to the newly-arrived European, often soon after his arrival, or after a few weeks or months. However, those cases could be reduced if the quantity and the quality of food and drink were carefully regulated so as to be appropriate to the local conditions of an equatorial country. By carefully avoiding gastrointestine and hepatic troubles, and by taking more or less vegetable food, a good deal of those infectious diseases would never appear. Local statistics do not give the proportion of Europeans who arrive and who die; they give the number of Europeans who passed away, but they give only the total number of passengers, including Brazilians and passengers of every nationality. However, it could be recognised without difficulty that the death-rate for foreigners is greater than a few per cent. And that is why this climate is considered as a centre of fevers in general.

It has been said that the temperature of Pará varies between the narrow limits of 70° and 90°, and that there is a great regularity in the variation of temperature. No doubt this might be for some months of the rainy season, but is surely wrong when taken in general. For the last three months of 1899 the temperature of the air in the shade was near 100°, and that of the grass in the shade over 104°. Then the rain did not fall in the afternoon as ordinarily, and thus did not soften the climate. The period from October 1 to December 31, 1899, has been exceedingly dry; in all other so-called dry seasons there had always been more rain than in this period. The total amount of the rain of the last three months of 1899 shows how far from reality are the so-called "perpetual rains" on the Equator and on the sea-shore. When the rain is very abundant it is chiefly in the first months of the year, but even here we see that 1900 has been exceptionally dry. What is certain is that the temperature of Pará in the so-called dry season is something quite different from that of the rainy season. How far does this agree with other statements according to which the wet period would be the hottest? In the so-called rainy season, immediately after a rain, the temperature seems relatively somewhat higher (may this be due to the absence of wind or to some other reason?), but the temperature of the whole of the rainy season is much lower than that of the dry season. If the day temperatures are high, the nights are, however, very agreeable, and in general as mild as in the temperate zones. The minimum is the temperature of a part of the night, generally a little before sunrise, whilst the maximum is the temperature of the early afternoon, very frequently about 2 p.m. The clouds form in the course of the day, whilst in the early morning the sky is generally without clouds. On the days when there has been some rain the clouds begin to form in the forenoon, condense in the afternoon, and in the nights the sky is generally without clouds. In the dry season most evenings are splendid owing to the freshness and brilliancy of the atmosphere. The winds blow more or less constantly from East and North-east, but it is specially in the late afternoon that they are well marked.

For the last months of 1899 it does not appear at first sight that there is equality between the rain and the evaporation from the surface of free water. This year has been relatively dry, but as a rule, in this equatorial zone, the rainy season lasts from October till May, and the quantity of rain that falls is very considerable in all the Amazon basin and all along the Northern coast. This abundant rain gives rise to inundations over a great part of the Amazon basin. The Amazon river deposits a quantity of fish and other aquatic animals which are unable to go back, when the level of the river is diminishing. The temporary swamps give rise to most unhealthy emanations, and this not only on the banks of the river, but equally in the plains of the interior.

In the temperate climates the barometric pressure varies considerably with the changes of weather, and the variation may amount to over 0·78 in. On the contrary, in Pará, the barometric variations due to the influence of the change of weather are much less, and amount to something like 0·0975 or 0·117 in. But, on the other hand, there are daily periodic variations which repeat themselves with great regularity. Those daily periodical variations appear everywhere with the alternation of day and night, and are produced with a great regularity wherever this alternation between day and night is itself very regular, as it is at and near the Equator. The regularity of the daily oscillation exists in Pará, and this can be seen on examination of the tables giving the barometric pressure at the different hours of the day, and is quite clearly noticeable, when account is taken of all other elements, temperature, rains, etc. It is specially the amount of vapour of water present in the atmosphere which should not be overlooked, and by deducting from the barometric pressure (on Dove's principle) the amount of inches due to the tension of this water vapour, we might perhaps have had an even greater regularity. Whatever it might be, we see that, in January for instance, there is a maximum at about 10 a.m. and a minimum at 4 or 5 p.m., the daily difference between the extreme oscillations being 0·078 or 0·117 in. There is equally a maximum and a minimum during the night; the difference, however, is much smaller than that of the day. The movement of the barometer is greater by day than it is by night; the morning maxima and the afternoon minima differ respectively more from the mean than the other oscillations. The night maximum is at 10 or 11 p.m. and the minimum at 3 or 4 a.m. So the barometer rises from 3 or 4 a.m. to between 9 and 10 a.m., then falls to between 4 and 5 p.m., rises again at 10 p.m., and again falls till about 3 a.m. When greatest, and this is in the day and not at night, the fall from the forenoon to the afternoon amounts to

0·117 in. Besides, those hours may vary more or less from season to season, from month to month, from fortnight to fortnight, but the oscillations of the barometric pressure of February and March are after all very similar to those of January, especially with regard to the maxima and minima.

The barometer is usually low; this is in accordance with the general experience of equatorial countries.

It has been said that the foreigner who wishes to live in Pará will find a benign climate, which will guarantee him health and strength. However, this is not so certain. No doubt on the finest of the summer days the temperate climate is sometimes far warmer than Pará, but what makes Pará's climate trying for many of the European constitutions is the continuity of temperature, whilst changes, such as are frequent in the temperate countries, would be most welcome. As a result of this temperature being continuously high, the quantity of microbes of the air and of the water is quite astonishing.

EUGENE ACKERMANN,
Engineer and Chief of the Chemical Laboratory of the Sanitation Commission of Pará.

[In Vol. VIII. of the *Meteorologische Zeitschrift* (1891) Dr. Hann gives a summary of what is known of the climate of Pará. Dove, in his *Klimatologische Beiträge*, prints some figures, but without giving any authority. The hours were sunrise, noon, and 8 p.m.; the results for temperature are therefore too high. The number of years were 4½ for temperature, 1½ for rain.

Dr. Englenberg, who accompanied Dr. van Ryckevorsel on his magnetic expedition to Brazil, carried out regular observations for 12 months, December 1882 to November 1883, in a garden. The screen was louvred, and the thermometers were about 4 ft. 6 ins. above the ground. Dr. Hann gives data for diurnal range, and we must refer to his paper for these data. The accompanying table gives a brief summary of the principal mean results:—

Months.	Pressure. 9 a.m. and 4 p.m.	Temperature. 6 a.m., 2 and 6 p.m.	Daily Range.	Vapour Tension. 6, 9 a.m. and 2, 10 p.m.	Rain.
	ins.	°	°	in.	ins.
December	29·73	79·2	15·8	·81	(5·51)
January	29·78	77·2	10·6	·83	(18·29)
February	29·76	77·7	13·1	·83	8·98
March	29·79	76·5	9·9	·84	17·82
April	29·77	77·4	10·3	·86	11·14
May	29·77	79·5	16·9	·85	6·73
June	29·84	79·9	18·9	·83	3·70
July	29·85	79·2	19·3	·80	3·74
August	29·87	79·8	20·5	·80	1·89
September	29·84	79·3	19·8	·79	(2·20)
October	29·77	78·4	20·5	·76	(0·67)
November	29·76	78·6	19·6	·74	(4·45)
Year	29·79	78·4	16·2	·81	85·12

The figures in brackets indicate the rain was not measured daily.

One interesting remark made by Dr. Hann is that sunstroke appears to be unknown at Pará.—EDITORS.]

Radcliffe Observatory, Oxford.—The meteorological observations and automatic registrations have been maintained as usual, and the results have been regularly sent, as heretofore, to the Meteorological Office (by telegram), the Registrar-General, the local newspapers, the *Windsor Chronicle* (rainfall only), and to sanitary and other public authorities on request, as well as to some private inquirers.

The underground platinum resistance thermometers have worked very satisfactorily. Readings of the 5 thermometers buried in the soil at depths of 6 ins.,

1 ft. 6 ins., 3 ft. 6 ins., 5 ft. 10 ins., and 10 ft. respectively, and of a similar one "A" suspended in air in the observing room, have been taken every day and reduced to the air scale. In October, thermometer "A" and the upper one of the buried instruments were carefully re-standardized, and as the fundamental points were found to have remained practically stationary during the year elapsed since their previous standardization (the greatest difference being 0°·03 C.) it was not thought advisable to go to the labour of exhuming the deeper ones for the present.

The following are the chief characteristics of the weather noted at Oxford in the year 1899:—

The mean reading of the barometer for the year was 29·759 ins., being 0·034 in. above the mean for the preceding 44 years. The highest reading, 30·485 ins., occurred on November 17; the lowest 28·201 ins. on December 29, a range of 2·284 ins.

The mean temperature of the air was 50°·4, being 1°·6 above the mean for the preceding 71 years. The maximum in the air was 86°·0 on July 20; the minimum 14°·9 on December 16; the lowest on the grass 7°·0 on December 14.

The following table shows the differences of the mean monthly temperatures from the corresponding means deduced from the observations of the preceding 71 years:—

	°		°		°
January	+4·1	May	−1·1	September	+1·4
February	+2·4	June	+3·1	October	−1·5
March	−0·4	July	+3·9	November	+4·0
April	+0·4	August	+5·7	December	−3·1

Very warm weather was experienced in July and August, the thermometer in the screen recording over 80° on 8 days in July and 9 days in August, whilst the mean of the daily maxima for the 7 successive days ending August 5 works out as high as 82°·0.

The amount of bright sunshine registered during the year by a Campbell-Stokes recorder was 1810 hours, or 382 hours above the mean of 19 years. The following table gives the monthly differences from the average:—

	hours.		hours.		hours.
January	+28	May	+ 8	September	+32
February	+46	June	+71	October	+21
March	+44	July	+85	November	− 6
April	−22	August	+80	December	− 3

The rainfall during the year amounted to 22·024 ins., or 4·164 ins. below the mean for the preceding 84 years; the monthly differences from the mean appear in the subsequent table, which also indicates a defect of rainfall during the whole period, May to October:—

	in.		in.		in.
January	+1·031	May	−0·482	September	−0·398
February	+0·404	June	−1·482	October	−0·118
March	−1·280	July	−0·900	November	+0·244
April	+0·135	August	−0·607	December	−0·711

ARTHUR A. RAMBAUT, M.A., D.Sc., *Radcliffe Observer.*

The "Southern Cross" Expedition to the Antarctic, 1898-1900.—Mr. C. E. Borchgrevink recently read before the Royal Geographical Society a paper describing the results of his expedition to the Antarctic regions in the "Southern Cross." This paper has now been printed in the *Geographical Journal*, from which the following account of the meteorological portion has been reproduced:—

The meteorological observations were taken at Cape Adare in lat. 71° 18′ S. during an entire year, from February 1899 to February 1900. They were conducted on nearly the same lines as at a station of the first order, and as accurately and regularly as possible. During nine months of the year readings were taken two-hourly, from 9 a.m. to 9 p.m.; and during the three winter months, June, July, and August, two-hourly observations were made day and night. Besides these readings and those of maximum and minimum thermometers, the self-registering instruments furnished barograph and thermograph curves for the whole period, and records of the amount of sunshine were made by the Campbell-Stokes sunshine recorder. The tables given below, although only first approximations, are sufficiently exact to indicate the general nature of the climate. Observations taken at Cape Adare are possibly affected to a certain degree by local accidents, such as the contour of the country and proximity to the sea, but the record for the year has the great advantage of being taken at the one spot.

Meteorological observations were taken on board ship every two hours, night and day, during the month (January 1899) she was beset in the ice pack. The geographical area over which the observations were taken was between the parallels 63° 38′ S. and 66° 46′ S., and the meridians 160° 6′ E. and 166° 56′ E.

The mean temperature of air for January was 29°·9, and of the sea 29°·6. The mean temperature for the second week being the highest in both cases.

TABLE I.—*Weekly Mean Temperature for January* 1899.

	Air.	Sea.
	°	°
1st week	30·2	29·8
2nd ,, ...	31·9	30·1
3rd ,, ...	29·4	29·5
4th ,, ...	28·4	29·2

The lowest temperature for the month, which occurred on the 29th at 3 a.m., was 16°·8 in lat. 66° 45′ and long. 165° 25′ E., off one of the Balleny Islands. The highest temperature for the month was 36°·4 at 5 p.m. on the 12th, lat. 65° 3′ and long. 161° 42′ E. The mean diurnal oscillation of temperature for the month was 5°·2. The greatest range between the maximum and minimum of one day was 16°, the least 1°.

Light and variable winds prevailed during most of the month; the force was rarely greater than 4, Beaufort's scale. Gales blew on the 9th, 16th, 22nd, and 23rd, when the velocity of the wind exceeded 30 miles an hour.

The weather may be summarised as 5 days' clear bright sunshine; 13 days' snow and sleet; 2 days' rain, when temperature rose above 32°; 4 days' mists and fogs; and the rest overcast.

As will be seen from the table given below, the mean temperature at Cape Adare is above zero for six months in the year, and below zero for six months.

TABLE II.—*Monthly Mean Temperatures.*

Month.	Mean Temperature.	Date of Maximum.	Maximum.	Date of Minimum.	Minimum.
1899.	°		°		°
February . .	26·4				
March . .	17·7	5th	31·1	25th	− 2·5
April . .	10·3	2nd	30·0	19th	−10·0
May . . .	− 4·6	4th	23·2	13th	−31·1
June . .	−11·8	11th	14·1	3rd	−36·0
July . . .	− 8·6	18th	23·8	9th	−39·9
August . .	−13·4	15th	18·9	4th	−43·1
September .	−11·9	7th	11·5	30th	−36·1
October . .	− 1·8	15th	19·6	2nd	−35·5
November .	+17·8	28th	45·7	1st	− 4·0
December . .	31·8	25th	42·2	11th	+20·4
1900.					
January . .	33·0	23rd	48·9	10th	22·5

Mean temperature for the year = 7°·05.

August was the coldest month, the mean temperature being $-13°{\cdot}4$.

The extreme minimum temperature occurred on August 4 at 9 p.m. during perfectly calm and clear weather.

Table III. shows the fall of temperature during the afternoon of that day with the accompanying barometric pressure:—

TABLE III.

Time.	Temperature. °	Barometer (cor.) ins.
1 p.m.	$-36{\cdot}0$	29·292
3 ,,	$-40{\cdot}0$	29·312
5 ,,	$-41{\cdot}5$	29·324
7 ,,	$-42{\cdot}0$	29·344
9 ,,	$-43{\cdot}1$	29·355

At these temperatures the mercury froze in the ordinary thermometers, and spirit ones had to be used. The above temperatures are means derived from three thermometers. At these low temperatures there was a slight diversity in the indications of the respective thermometers, even after applying the corrections as given upon the Kew Certificates. The maximum temperature observed at Cape Adare, 48°·9, occurred during a very heavy storm from the East-southeast on January 23, 1900; but this is quite exceptional. The mean monthly temperature is above freezing-point during only one month of the year, viz. January.

The relatively high mean temperature for July is due to the number of gales from East-south-east and South-east during that month, temperature invariably rising with these winds. The extreme range of temperature was 92°, and the mean temperature for the year $+7°{\cdot}06$, which, compared with the mean annual temperature for the same northern latitude, is extremely low. The mean temperature for Lapland, in 71° N., is about 32°, and the mean temperature for the north of Spitzbergen, which extends as far north as 82° N., is about 10°.

The temperature of the sea during the greater part of the year, that is, while the surface of the sea was frozen over, remained constant at 27°·8. In the summer months, December, January, and February, it rarely rose above 32°.

During the winter months, or at least during the 71 days that the sun remained constantly below the horizon, the diurnal variations of the thermometer and barometer were scarcely perceptible, being almost, if not quite, concealed by the oscillations due to the passage of storms.

The intensity of solar radiation was measured with the black bulb thermometer *in vacuo*. This instrument was freely exposed to the sun by fixing it horizontally above the ground at the same height as the thermometer screen, viz. 4 ft. 6 ins. A temperature above 80° was frequently recorded by this thermometer, whilst the temperature in the shade remained below freezing-point. These high readings were probably due to the hygrometric conditions of the atmosphere; the air, on account of the intense cold, being extremely dry.

Table IV. gives some of the highest readings with the solar radiation thermometer and the temperature of air in the shade observed at the same time:—

TABLE IV.

Date.	Solar Thermometer.	Temperature in Shade.
March 3	88°	24°
,, 6	92	22·4
,, 14	88·3	20·9
,, 16	92·2	24·5
,, 26	104·2	8·0

Relative humidity between 40 and 50.

The most remarkable feature in the meteorological conditions of the Antarctic is the wind. The prevailing East-south-east and South-east winds at Cape Adare, which is within the area of abnormally low pressure, tend to prove the existence of a great anticyclone stretching over the polar area, which in its turn necessarily implies the existence of upper currents from the Northward, blowing towards and in upon the polar regions, to make good the drain caused by the surface out-blowing South-easterly winds. The frequency and force of these gales, and the persistency with which they blew—always from the same direction, East-south-east—the invariably high rise in temperature, and the sudden fall and rise of the barometer, the dryness of the winds—the relative humidity, generally between 40 and 50 per cent—and the motion of the upper clouds from the north-west, point to the fact that the south pole is covered by what may be regarded practically as a great permanent anticyclone, more extensive in the winter months than in the summer. Nothing more appalling than these frightful winds, accompanied by tons of drift-snow from the mountains above, can be imagined. On 92 days, or 26 per cent of the time spent at Cape Adare, the wind blew from the East-south-east and South-east, with a velocity above 40 miles an hour, and on one or two occasions above 90 miles an hour, at which stage our Robinson anemometers were demolished. A proper table of wind directions, velocities, and thermal wind-roses is not available, but the following tables will suffice to convey some idea of the conditions:—

TABLE V.—*Number of Days in each month when Velocity of the Wind was above 40 miles an hour.*

1899.	No. of days.	1899.	No. of days.
February	5	September	6
March	11	October	7
April	8	November	5
May	7	December	9
June	7		
July	12	1900.	
August	6	January	[illegible]

TABLE VI.—*Conditions during a storm on April 2, 1899.*

Time.	Barometer (corrected).	Temperature of Air.	Direction of Wind.	Velocity of Wind.
	ins.	°		Miles per hour.
April 1, 9 p.m. .	29·599	12·2	W.	5·7
,, 2, 9 a.m. .	29·199	17·0	Whirlwinds	
,, ,, 11 ,, .	29·064	22·6	E.S.E.	82
,, ,, 1 p.m. .	28·919	24·0	,,	83
,, ,, 3 ,, .	28·916	26·9		102 (?)
,, ,, 5 ,, .	28·880	24·3	..	88
,, ,, 7 ,, .	28·880	25·3	,	90
,, ,, 9 ,, .	28·917	27·9	,,	82·5
,, 3, 9 a.m. .	29·208	19·5	S.	40·6

The maximum temperature during the gale was 31°·5. During a gale of March 19 a Robinson anemometer was demolished, the velocity of the wind exceeding 90 miles an hour; and another was destroyed on the night of May 18, when it was impossible to estimate the velocity of the wind. The anemometers used were tested at the Kew Observatory prior to the departure of the expedition from England, and were found to give results within 97 per cent of the Kew instruments. It is evident, however, that the action of wear and tear on the instrument by these gales must have a very material influence on its indications.

The barograph and thermograph curves during a storm from the East-south-east on May 4, 1899, show very clearly that the temperature commences to rise before the barometer commences to fall; indeed, it was often possible to predict an approaching gale by the thermometer alone, long before the barometer showed any sign of the disturbance.

The mean barometric pressure for the winter months is much lower than the mean for the summer, but the means have not yet been determined. The highest barometric pressure occurred on July 22, 1899, when the barometer registered 30·182 ins., and the lowest 27·860 ins. on September 9, 1899.

On the journey from Cape Adare southwards, some remarkably low temperatures were observed for the time of the year. Thus, off Mount Erebus on February 11, 1900, the temperature sunk to $-6°$ with a wind from the South straight off the great ice barrier. Again, on February 19, the minimum temperature was $-12°$, with clear sky and light wind from the South. It is possible to form an idea from these temperatures what one would be likely to encounter in the way of cold on a sledge journey southwards from the edge of the great ice barrier in the middle of the Antarctic summer.

The Geographical Distribution of Relative Humidity.—At the Meeting of the British Association at Bradford in September, Mr. E. G. Ravenstein read a paper on this subject. He stated that the importance of relative humidity as a climatic factor was fully recognised. Having illustrated its influence upon organic life, upon agriculture and human industries, he expressed his regret that neither in number nor in trustworthiness did humidity observations meet the requirements of a person desirous of illustrating its distribution over the globe by means of a map. This was owing largely to defects in the instruments employed, incompetence of the observers, and unsuitability of the hours chosen for the observations. As to the humidity over the ocean, we were still dependent upon the observations made on board passing vessels, and he was afraid the time had not yet come when floating meteorological observatories would be stationed permanently throughout a whole year at a few well-chosen localities in mid-ocean. Notwithstanding this paucity of available material he had ventured, in 1894, to publish in Philip's *Systematic Atlas* a small chart of the world, showing the distribution of humidity. The subject had not been lost sight of by him since then, and he now placed the results before the meeting. He did so with some diffidence, and over-cautious meteorologists might condemn his action, but they must remember that when Berghaus, in 1838, acting upon suggestions made by Zimmermann and Humboldt, published the first isothermal chart, the observations on temperature were even less numerous than those on humidity were at present. His charts, of course, must be looked upon as sketches, but he felt confident that they brought out the broad features of the subject, and, to reduce the sources of error, he had limited himself to indicating four grades of mean annual humidity, the upper limits of which were respectively 50 per cent (very dry), 65 per cent, 80 per cent, and 100 per cent (very damp). The relative humidity over the oceans might exceed 80 per cent, but in certain regions ("horse latitudes") it was certainly much less, and in a portion of the Southern Pacific it seemed not to exceed 65 per cent, a feature seemingly confirmed by the salinity of that portion of the ocean, which exceeded 3·6 per cent.

His second chart exhibited the annual range of humidity, viz. the difference between the driest and the dampest months of the year. In Britain, as in many other parts of the world, where the moderating influence of the ocean was allowed free scope, this difference did not exceed 16 per cent, but in the interior of the continents it occasionally exceeded 45 per cent, spring or summer being exceedingly dry, whilst the winter was excessively damp, as at Yarkand, where a humidity of 30 per cent in May contrasted strikingly with a humidity of 84 per cent in December.

This great range directed attention to the influence of temperature (and of altitude) upon the amount of relative humidity, for during temperate weather we were able to bear a great humidity with equanimity, whilst the same degree of humidity, accompanied by great heat, such as is occasionally experienced during the "heat terms" of New York, and recently visited London, may prove disastrous to men and beasts. Hence, combining humidity and temperature, the author suggested mapping out the earth according to sixteen *hygrothermal types*, as follows:—

1. Hot (temperature 73° and over) and very damp (humidity 81 per cent or more)—Batavia, Camaroons, Mombasa.
2. Hot and moderately damp (60-80 per cent)—Havana, Calcutta.
3. Hot and dry (51-65 per cent)—Bagdad, Lahore, Khartum.
4. Hot and very dry (50 per cent or less)—Disa, Wadi Halfa, Kuka.
5. Warm (temperature 58°-72°) and very damp—Walvisch Bay, Arica.
6. Warm and moderately damp.—Lisbon, Rome, Damascus, Tokio, New Orleans.
7. Warm and dry.—Cairo, Algiers, Kimberley.
8. Warm and very dry.—Mexico, Teheran.
9. Cool (temperature 33°-57°) and very damp.—Greenwich, Cochabambo.
10. Cool and moderately damp.—Vienna, Melbourne, Toronto, Chicago.
11. Cool and dry.—Tashkent, Simla, Cheyenne.
12. Cool and very dry.—Yarkand, Denver.
13. Cold (temperature 32° or less) and very damp.—Ben Nevis, Sagastyr, Godthaab.
14. Cold and moderately damp.—Tomsk, Pike's Peak, Polaris House.
15. Cold and dry.—
16. Cold and very dry.—Pamir.

The actual mean temperature of the earth amounted, according to his computation, to 57°, and this isotherm, which separated types 8 and 9, also divided De Candolle's *Mikrothermes* from the plants requiring a greater amount of warmth.

The author further illustrated this paper by a number of diagrams giving the curves of the temperature, rainfall, and humidity, as also by a chart of the world exhibiting the number of rainy days.

Rainfall of the Central Rhine Provinces.—The latest addition to the *Forschungen zur deutschen Landes- und Volkskunde* is a paper by Dr. P. Polis, director of the meteorological station at Aix-la-Chapelle, on the rainfall of the Central Rhine provinces and the surrounding regions. The period covered by the material used is only the one decade 1886 to 1895, but the discussion has the merit, all too rare in such investigations, of attempting to estimate the probable errors of the results: the mean uncertainty in differentiating one station with another is found to amount to about 5 per cent. A very clear set of maps shows the distribution of rainfall in the four seasons, and the percentage of the total annual fall received during each. The special points of local importance are pointed out, but some conclusions of general interest, based on the examination of this particular area, are suggestive when compared with the rainfall types recognisable in the British Isles. The rainfall is in the first instance determined by the distribution of pressure, condensation occurring in the ascending currents associated with low barometric pressure; and along with this the temperature and humidity, largely depending on the position with regard to sea and land, must be taken into account. Given the general conditions controlled by these factors, the local inequalities are primarily regulated by the surface relief of the region. Mountains cause a general increase of rainfall on their weather side and diminution on their lee side; an increase of winter and autumn rainfall, and a diminution of summer rainfall. A maximum in October is due to the greater humidity of the atmosphere, and the larger numbers of cyclones, during that month. The increase of rainfall with height is closely connected with open position of mountains concerned; sheltered elevations of equal height diminish the rainfall. A mountain range diminishes the annual range of temperature on its weather side, and increases it on its lee side; hence on the former the winter rainfall, on the latter the summer rainfall, is increased. We may compare this with the west coast, and the midland and eastern counties, of England. The alteration of weather and lee sides due to the seasonal changes in the direction of prevailing winds tends to increase the winter rainfall on south-west exposures, and the summer rainfall on north-east exposures. Spring rainfall is increased on eastern slopes by the prevailing Easterly winds. The long period records of Aix show that snow falls most frequently in March, January coming second, and February third; but for the 1889-95 period January and February are the months of most frequent snow. The number of days of snowfall increases rapidly with increase of height. Old snow may give as much as 3·5 mm. of water per centimetre of depth, equivalent to nearly one-third.—*Geographical Journal*, June 1900.

The Climate of the Valley of the Joux (Jura).—The *Scottish Geographical Magazine* for November 1900 contains an interesting article on the valley of the Joux, from which the following notes on the climate have been taken:—

The valley of the Jura is situated on the west-south-west corner of Switzerland. It extends between lat. 46° 33′ and 46° 31′ N., and long. 3° 47′ and 4° 0′ E. As compared with the Alps, the air of the Jura at a corresponding altitude may be generally pronounced as colder and as less dry and constant. It is invigorating, brisk, and stimulating, it does not agree with over-delicate persons, but it greatly benefits consumptives. The extreme range of temperature is 120°, the maximum going up to 80°, while the minimum falls as low as − 40°. The cold season is the most agreeable and most healthy. The winter is mostly dry and sunny; the snow which is generally abundant clears the air, and covers fields and forests from the beginning of December to the end of March. While the plain to the north of Geneva Lake is lost in fog, rising up to 2500 and 2900 feet, the valley is all splendour and sunshine. The nights are cold, but as soon as the sun appears on the horizon the air is softened and the temperature, even in January, rises to 37° and sometimes 41°. The effect of the sun increases with altitude. In sunny days the thermometer in Sentier and Chez-le-Maitre registers a minimum of 10°·5, and even lower, while that in Risoux, 1280 feet higher, indicates at the same time a minimum of 23° only. This season is very healthy, few cases of sickness occurring. The extreme cold attains − 26° and exceptionally − 40°, and is attained by the North-east wind ("la bise"), which lowers the temperature. The mean winter temperature is 21°·5.

The spring is less healthy and agreeable. Thawing snows chill the air, and the return of warmth is checked by hail showers and sleet. There is a great range of temperature, the minimum falling as low as 12° and even 5°, while the maximum rises to 62° in April, 65°·5 in May, and 73° in June. The mean spring temperature is 37°. The summer weather is very variable. The maximum temperature rises to 79°·7 and 80°·6 in July and August respectively; these high temperatures are invariably followed by cool nights. Dew is abundant, and the grass remains always green. The mean summer temperature is 53°·2.

The autumn is sometimes rainy, but mostly dry, warm, and fine. The air is brisk and fresh in the morning, but towards mid-day the sun becomes genial, although there is a great difference between the sunny and shady sides of the valley. The nights are frosty. The mean autumn temperature is 41°·2. The mean annual temperature 38°·2.

From the region of the Lake of Geneva north-westwards towards Jura the rainfall steadily increases with altitude from 35·37 ins. annually on the Lake of Geneva, up to 57 ins. on the Lake of Joux, and continues to increase with altitude in the mountain chains surrounding this lake. While the mean annual rainfall in Sentier is about 58 ins., it is 77 and 84 ins. respectively in the Post des Mines and Châlet Capt, situated on the crest of Risoux, some 1600 feet higher. Considerable variations are recorded in the amount of rain from year to year, and from month to month, in different years in the same place. This amount varies in the first case from 1 to 1·5 ins., and in the second from 1 to 20 ins. The average number of rainy days is 165. March, May, July, August, and October have the greatest rainfall, while January, February, and September have the least. The mean for the greater part of the country is about 65 ins., and for the region of Risoux about 79·25 ins. The rain is distributed according to the seasons, thus: winter 17 per cent, spring 27 per cent, summer 30 per cent, autumn 26 per cent. A considerable part of the rainfall is in the form of snow. It may snow in every month of the year, although in the summer months, of course, it occurs very rarely. February, March, April, and December are the real snow months. The mean annual depth of snowfall is about 18½ feet on the Risoux, and a little more than half, viz. 9·3 feet, in the valley proper. The mean number of days of snow is 68 in the mountains and 50 in the valleys. Wind:—Two principal winds predominate "la bise," or North wind, which blows from North-west, North, and North-east, and is generally dry and cold; and "le vent" which blows from South-west, South, and South-east, and is generally damp and warm. There are in the mean about 123 days in the year with the former and 196 with the latter, 46 days remaining comparatively calm. Hurricanes come from the South-west, and on this side houses are specially protected by bardeaux (tiles of wood). These Southern winds predominate in May, August, and December. Besides the predominating "la bise" and "le vent" there blow occasionally some local winds, such as North-west ("Joran"), bringing cold and snow, and West-south-west ("Moussillon"), bringing storm and shower, and so on.

RECENT PUBLICATIONS

Journal and Proceedings of the Royal Society of New South Wales for 1899. Vol. XXXIII. 8vo. 1899.

Contains the following papers bearing on meteorology:—"Suggestions for depicting diagrammatically the character of Season as regards Rainfall, and especially that of Droughts," by H. Deane (6 pp.).—"Observations on the determination of Drought-intensity," by G. H. Knibbs (17 pp.).—"Current Papers, No. 4," by H. C. Russell (9 pp.).—"On a remarkable increase of temperature after dark at Seven Oaks, Macleay River," by H. C. Kiddle (3 pp.). During a moderate heat wave on November 25-27, the maximum thermometer recorded 90° to 91°·8 at about 10 a.m.; then a sea breeze came in, and by mid-day the temperature fell to what it had been at 7.30 a.m., and continued to fall under the same influence till at 7 p.m. it stood at 75°. On the 27th, shortly after 7 p.m., a thunderstorm which had been working up from the west for half an hour reached Seven Oaks, but instead of the usually cool breeze which a thunderstorm brings there was a blast as from a furnace. In a few minutes the temperature rose from 75° to 86°, and during the blast reached 95°·5, or 3°·7 higher than it had been at the hottest part of the day. The phenomenon is the more remarkable when it is remembered that it occurred after dark. This hot wind came from the West-north-west, and reached a force from "fresh" to "strong." Seven Oaks is situated on the Macleay River, approximately in lat. 31° 2′ S., long. 151° 3′ E., and is about seven miles in a direct line from the coast.— "Records of Rock Temperatures at Sydney Harbour Colliery Birthday Shaft, Balmain, Sydney," by J. L. C. Rae, E. F. Pittman, and Prof. T. W. E. David (17 pp.). The deep sinking now being carried on at the Sydney Harbour Colliery, Balmain, with which one of the authors is actively associated, affords a very favourable opportunity of noting the nature and temperatures of the various rocks underlying the neighbourhood of Sydney, and this the authors are utilising. The paper deals with the temperatures noted to a depth of 1450 feet, which was the depth reached in the shaft at the middle of November. The thermometers used were specially supplied by Prof. Everett, F.R.S., Secretary of the British Association Committee on the subject of Underground Temperatures. The sinking of the Birthday Shaft had reached a depth of 600 feet before the thermometers were available, but since then observations have been made at intervals of practically 50 feet, and an opportunity will be got of recording temperatures at less depth than 600 feet when the sinking of the Jubilee Shaft is gone on with. From 600 feet down to 1100 feet two slow-action thermometers were used, and the horizontal holes which were drilled into the walls of the shaft for their reception were put in a distance of 3 feet down to 950 feet, and 4 feet from that to the 1100 feet level. Beginning at the 1150 feet level, two maximum thermometers were used in addition to the slow-action instruments, and the practice has been to place one instrument of each type in each of the holes, which have been put in to a distance of 5 feet. The plugging in each case consisted of about 6 inches of greasy cotton waste placed next to the thermometers, the remainder of the hole being filled up with plastic clay rammed into the hole. Every precaution was taken to ensure accuracy of results. If the mean annual temperature of Sydney be taken as 63°, the rate of increase is shown, by the observations made, to be at the rate of 1° for every 90½ feet, which is fairly low, and may be taken as a favourable indication for the future ventilation of the mine. A remarkable increase of temperature was noted as the sinking passed from the Hawkesbury Sandstones into the Narrabeen Beds, the upper section of which consists of chocolate shales. These shales, which outcrop on the sea coast at Narrabeen, some 8 miles to the north of Manly, were struck in the shaft at a depth of 1024 feet 9 inches, or at practically the same depth from the surface as in the Cremorne Bore, the exact difference being 59 feet 7½ inches measured from mean low-tide level in Sydney Harbour, the shaft being the deeper of the two. This is a very slight difference in 3¼ miles, which is the distance from the shaft to the bore.

Meteorologische Zeitschrift. Redigert von Dr. J. Hann und Dr. G. Hellmann. July—September 1900. 4to.

The principal articles are :—'Klimatische Verhältnisse des Memel-, Pregel-, und Weichsel-Gebietes," von V. Kremser (48 pp.). No detailed account of the climate of Eastern Prussia has hitherto appeared. Some fifty years ago Dove published a summary in tables with hardly any text. The present is much more detailed, the first instalment appears in the July number, the second in that for August. The first is almost entirely taken up with the rain and snow statistics, and the second with temperature. It is, however, only an abridgment of the original publication, several tables and illustrated maps being omitted. The separate branches of the subject are treated in detail, and it would not be possible to condense the results for a notice like the present. The entire paper gives an interesting picture of the effect of proximity to the sea on one side and the Carpathians on the other, the intervening extensive area being nearly flat.—"Elektrizerung durch Eisreibung," von H. Ebert und B. Hoffmann (9 pp.). This is an account of a series of experiments carried out at the Laboratory of the Technical High School in Munich, *inter alia*, to test the several applications of Faraday's statements as to the production of electricity by steam impinging on solid bodies. This was fully confirmed, and then the authors proceeded to experiment with liquefied air, and they found that if any body was plunged into the air it was negatively electrified by friction against the fragments of ice contained in the air. Accordingly, they say that almost any body touching very dry ice at a temperature like that of liquid air will be negatively electrified.—"Ueber den Einfluss des Waldes auf die Lufttemperatur nach den in Eberswalde an verschieden aufgestellten Thermometern gemachten Beobachtungen," von Prof. Dr. Müttrich (17 pp.). The interest in this paper consists in the comparison of what is termed the English screen (presumably the modified Stevenson approved by the Royal Meteorological Society), with the Forest screen, a zinc screen, and finally with the aspirated thermometer. The comparison is carried out in great detail, and Dr. Müttrich concludes the paper by saying that the differences between the temperatures taken outside and inside the forest is greatest with the zinc screen; then follow in order the Forest screen, the English screen, and the aspirated thermometer. He announces that more elaborate comparisons between the English screen and the aspirated thermometer are in progress.—"Ueber Abhängigkeit des Fruhlingseintritts von der geographischen Breite in Deutschland," von Prof. Dr. Ihne (3 pp.). This paper is of special interest for the Phenological Observers. The plants on which the observations were made were all trees, or shrubs, 7 for early spring, and 6 for full spring.—"Untersuchungen über das Wetterschiessen," von J. M. Pernter und W. Trabert (30 pp.). This is an account of a very careful series of experiments on the possibility of averting damage from hail by means of firing at the clouds. The apparatus was very elaborate, and it was satisfactorily proved that the smoke rings were propelled to a height of 800 metres (say 2500 feet), while, according to most careful observations, the clouds in a thunderstorm never exceed that level. The conclusion arrived at is, that inasmuch as damage by hail occurred while the firing was in progress, it cannot be maintained that the firing is prophylactic.

Monthly Weather Review. PROF. CLEVELAND ABBE, Editor. Prepared under the direction of WILLIS L. MOORE, Chief U.S. Weather Bureau. February—August 1900. 4to.

Among the articles and reports in this publication are the following:—"Anemometer tests," by Prof. C. F. Marvin (6 pp.).—"Kite observations at Bayonne, N.J." (1 p.).—"Loss of life by lightning," by A. J. Henry (1 p.).—"A partial explanation of some of the principal ocean tides," by R. A. Harris (5 pp.).—"Special report on the floods in the Colorado Valley, Texas, April 7 to 17, 1900, and other floods during the same period," by I. M. Cline (4 pp.).—"Special report on the floods in the Brazos River Valley, Taxas, April 27 to May 17, 1900; also freshets in other streams," by I. M. Cline (3 pp.).—"Droughts, famines, and forecasts in India," by E. D. Archibald (3 pp.).—"Prevention of hail by cannonading" (1 p.).—"Fog studies on Mount Tamalpais," by A. G. M'Adie (3 pp.).—"Climatology of St. Kitts, West Indies," by W. S. Alexander (3 pp.).—"The hot weather of August 1900," by A. J. Henry (3 pp.).

Rainfall of India, 1898. Published by the various Provincial Governments, and issued under the Authority of the Government of India by the Meteorological Department, Calcutta. 1899. Folio.

This volume, which is the eighth, contains the monthly statements of rainfall published by the various Local Governments, and gives practically the whole of the rainfall data available for the Indian Empire for the year 1898. Symons's rain gauges were used at the majority of the stations, the only important exception being in Mysore, where gauges of local construction were used. The whole of the available rainfall data of the Indian Empire has been recently collected and tabulated in the Meteorological Office at Calcutta, and the average monthly rainfall and number of rainy days in each month were calculated from this tabulated information for all stations, for which at least five years' rainfall statistics were available. In the majority of cases the rainfall data extends back to 20 or 30 years. The averages thus obtained have been utilised for the comparison of normal with actual data.

Symons's Monthly Meteorological Magazine. Edited by H. SOWERBY WALLIS. July—September 1900. 8vo.

The principal articles are:—"Indian Famine-causing Droughts and their Prevision," by E. D. Archibald (5 pp.). This is the concluding part of an article, the first part of which appeared in the June number. The author summarises his facts as follows:—(1) Extensive droughts occur in the dry area of Southern India, embracing in particular Northern Mysore, South Deccan, South-west Hyderabad, but occasionally reaching Guzerat and parts of the Bombay and Madras Presidencies at intervals of 9 to 12 years, and usually, but not regularly, about a year before the sunspot minimum. When the conditions are sufficiently acute, famine occurs in the ensuing year. (2) A severe drought in the Peninsula of Southern India is followed by a severe drought and ensuing famine in Northern India in about 5 cases out of 7. (3) Summer droughts tend to occur in Northern India alone, in years of maximum sunspot, connected in some way with the abnormal high pressure over Western Asia, which prevails at such epochs.—"Meteorological Extremes. III. Wind Force" (2 pp.).—"Thunderstorms of June 11th and 13th 1900" (2 pp.).—"The Visitation of the Royal Observatory" (3 pp.).—"July 1900" (12 pp.). The month of July yielded so many exceptional phenomena that the Editor inserts this article, in which reference is made to its great heat, its thunder, and hailstorms of exceptional severity, and the Cloud-burst on Rombald's Moor.—"August 1900" (3 pp.). The month of August was, speaking of the United Kingdom generally, decidedly wet, with a considerable number of rainy days in addition to the heavy thunderstorm rains which usually make up the larger part of the total in a wet August.—"Mean Temperature Southern Counties 17–18 years, January 1883—August 1900" (2 pp.)—"Studies of Cyclonic and Anticyclonic Phenomena with Kites" (2 pp.). This is the first part of an article based on a memoir by Mr. H. H. Clayton, issued by the Blue Hill Meteorological Observatory.

INDEX

Address from the German Meteorological Society, 186
Address, Jubilee, 176, 181
Africa, Tropical, Meteorology of, 151
Air currents in thunderstorms, 32
Air, Temperature of the free, 242
Alderson (C. H.), elected, 251
Allen (M. L.), elected, 287
Altitude above sea-level, Relation of rainfall to, 273
Annual General Meeting, 152
Antarctic, "Southern Cross" expedition to the, 292
Atlantic, North, Circulation of water in the, 234
Atlas of Meteorology, 112
Atmosphere, Circulation of, in the Southern Hemisphere, 138
Atmosphere, Vertical circulation of the, 163
Auditors, 95

Balance-Sheet, 206
Balloon and kite station near Berlin, 163
Barclay (F. J.), elected, 251
Barometer, Diurnal variation of, in the British Isles, 1
Baxendell (J.), Description of Halliwell's self-recording rain gauge, 281
Bayard (F. C.), A new reduction of the meteorological observations at Greenwich, 101
Bayard (S. C.), elected, 95
Beaufort (A. F.), elected, 95
Bequests, 230, 287
Berlin, Kite and balloon station near, 163
Birds and hurricanes, 154
Blue Hill Meteorological Observatory, Kite experiments at, 252
Books purchased, 220
Boys (Rev. H. A.), elected, 251
Brazil, Northern, The climate and diseases of, 288
British Isles, Diurnal variation of the barometer in the, 1
Brown (Miss E.), Obituary notice of, 214
Burbery (H. S.), elected, 95

Cape of Good Hope and New Zealand, Meteorological charts of the southern ocean between, 253
Carr (C. E.), elected, 152
Case (E.), Obituary notice of, 215
Cave (C. J. P.), elected, 95
Celebration, Jubilee, April 3-4, 1900, 173
Central Rhine Provinces, Rainfall of the, 297
Chadwick (J.), elected, 95
Charlton (J.), elected, 251
Cheetham (A. E.), elected, 152
Cheyne (Dr. R.), elected, 95
Circulation of the atmosphere in the Southern hemisphere, 138
Circulation of the atmosphere, Vertical, 163
Circulation of water in the North Atlantic 234
Clark (J. E.), appointed scrutineer of ballot, 152
Climate and diseases of Northern Brazil, The, 288
Climate of the Valley of the Joux (Jura), 298
Climatic conditions necessary for the propagation and spread of plague, 37
Climatology of the Sonnblick group, 241
Cole (O. B.), elected, 154
Collenette (A.), elected, 152
Colvile (E. L. M.), elected, 154
Commemoration Dinner, April 4, 1900, 192
——— Medal, 184
——— Meeting, 174
Comparison by means of dots, 247
Congress, Paris, International meteorological, 96
Conversazione, 188
Correspondence and Notes, 96, 162, 252, 288
Council and Officers, 153
Council, Report of the, 203
Cullinan (Dr. N.), elected, 287
Curtis (R. H.), The diurnal variation of the barometer in the British Isles, 1

Dawson (A. M.), elected, 251
Death of Mr. G. J. Symons, F.R.S., 159, 251, 287
Delegates to Jubilee Celebration, 174
Denison (F. N.), elected, 152
Description of Halliwell's self-recording rain gauge, 281
Dines (W. H.), The ether sunshine recorder, 243

Dinner, Commemoration, April 4, 1900, 192
Diseases of Northern Brazil, The climate and, 288
Distribution of relative humidity, The geographical, 296
Diurnal variation of the barometer in the British Isles, 1
Dobie (Capt. W. A.), elected, 251
Donations, 221
Dots, Comparison by means of, 247
Druce (F.), appointed scrutineer of ballot, 152
Duncanson (T. J. G.), elected, 154
Dunn (J.), elected, 287
Dust haze at Teneriffe, Note of a remarkable, 33

Earth temperature observations, 27
East, Hurricanes of the Far, 165
Edinburgh, Royal Observatory, Report from, 232
Ether sunshine recorder, The, 243
Eunson (G. S.), elected, 152
Evans (A. J. L.), elected, 288
Exhibition of meteorological instruments, 189
Expedition to the Antarctic, "The Southern Cross," 292

Fiji and Hawaii, Weather conditions between, 235
Flagg (A. T.), elected, 251
Fog, Tule, 253
Free air, Temperature of the, 242

Galton (Sir D. S.), Obituary notice of, 215
Gaster (F.), appointed auditor, 95
Geographical distribution of relative humidity, 296
German Meteorological Society, Address from the, 186
Greenwich, A new reduction of the meteorological observations at, 101
——— Royal Observatory, Excursion to, 173
——— ———, Report from, 232
Guilbert (T. J.), elected, 251
Gunn (Dr. J. St. C.), elected, 288
Gunner (W. A.), elected, 251

Hall (D.), elected, 152
Hall (P. C.), elected, 251
Halliwell's self-recording rain gauge, 281
Halos, Solar, and mock suns, 97
Harrison (G. H.), elected, 251
Hawaii and Fiji, Weather conditions between, 235
Hawksley (C.) elected, 152
Haze, Dust, at Teneriffe, February 1898, 33
Heavy rainfall in local storms, 286
Henshall (E.), elected, 95
Hepworth (Capt. M. W. C.), Hurricane at Sombrero, September 1899, 25
——— ———, Hurricanes of the Far East, 165
——— ———, Remarks on the weather conditions of the steamship track between Fiji and Hawaii, 235
Heywood (H.), elected, 95
Hind (T. A.), elected, 287
Hodgson (J. S.), Obituary notice of, 216
Hooker (C. P.), elected, 251
Horner (D. W.), elected, 251
Humidity, Relative, Geographical distribution of, 296
Humidity, Vertical gradients of, 252
Hurricane at Sombrero, September 1899, 25
Hurricanes and birds, 154
Hurricanes of the Far East, 165

Inspection of stations, 210
International Meteorological Congress, Paris 1900, 96

Jackson (M.), appointed auditor, 95
Jones (Dr. A. B.), elected, 152
Joux, Climate of the Valley of the, 298
Jubilee Address, by G. J. Symons, 176
——— ———, by Dr. C. T. Williams, 181
Jubilee celebration, April 3-4, 1900, 173
Jura, Climate of the Valley of the, 298

Kew Observatory, Report from, 232
Kite and balloon station near Berlin, 163
Kite experiments at Blue Hill Meteorological Observatory, 252
Knobel (E. B.), Solar halos and mock suns, January 11, 1900, 97
Küchler (G. W.), elected, 152

Lancaster (A.), elected honorary member, 251
Lantern slides, 229
Lapage (Capt. W. P.), elected, 288
Latham (B.), The climatic conditions necessary for the propagation and spread of plague, 37
Leete (W. H.), elected, 152
Linnel (F. G.), elected, 152
Lipscomb (Dr. E. H), elected, 152
List of Presidents, 1850-1900, 202
Little (J.), elected, 288
Local storms, Heavy rainfall in, 286

M'Douall (D.), elected, 95
MacDowall (A. B.), Comparison by means of dots, 247
Macknight (W. A.), Solar halos and mock suns, January 11, 1900, 97
Mander (A.), elected, 95
Maples (C. E.), elected, 251
Marriott (W.), Inspection of stations, 210
———, Rainfall in the west and east of England in relation to altitude above sea-level, 273
Marsh (L. S. M.), elected, 152
Marshall (S. A.), elected, 154
Marston (A.), elected, 152
Maund (R. H.), elected, 287
Mauritius Meteorological Society, Letter from, on death of Mr. G. J. Symons, F.R.S., 287
Mawley (E.), Report on the phenological observations, 1899, 113

Medal, Commemoration, 184
Meetings of the Society, Proceedings at the, 95, 152, 174, 251, 287
Memorial to the late Mr. G. J. Symons, F.R.S., 272
Meteorological charts of the southern ocean between the Cape of Good Hope and New Zealand, 253
Meteorological Congress, International, Paris, 1900, 96
Meteorological observations at Greenwich, A new reduction of the, 101
Meteorological Office, Report from, 231
——————, Retirement of Dr. R. H. Scott, F.R.S., from the, 96
Meteorology, Atlas of, 112
Meteorology of Tropical Africa, 151
Millard (C. H.), elected, 95
Milner (W. E.), elected 152
Minimum temperatures on mountain peaks, 162
Mitchell (F. J.), elected, 251
Mock suns and solar halos, January 11, 1900, 97
Morris (Dr. H. C. L.), elected, 95
Mountain peaks, Minimum temperatures on, 162

Newman (T. P.), elected, 251
New reduction of meteorological observations at Greenwich, 101
New Zealand, Meteorological charts of the southern ocean between Cape of Good Hope and, 253
Noble (A.), elected, 154
North Atlantic, Circulation of water in the, 234
Northern Brazil, Climate and diseases of, 288
Note of a remarkable dust haze experienced at Teneriffe, Canary Islands, February 1898, 33
Notes and Correspondence, 96, 162, 252, 288
Notices, Obituary, 155, 214

Obituary Notices, 155, 214
Observatories, Reports from, 231, 291
Officers and Council, 153
Ormerod (Dr. A. L.), elected 152
Outram (F. D.), elected, 287
Oxley (E.), elected, 95

Palairet (H. H.), elected, 251
Peggs (J. W.), Obituary notice of, 218
Percolation experiments at Rothamsted, Results of, 139
Phenological observations, 1899, 113
Pigott (T. D.), Hurricanes and birds, 154
Plague, Climatic conditions necessary for the propagation and spread of, 37
Poyser (E. J.), elected, 152
President, Appointment of, 154
————, Resignation of, 154
Presidential Address, 101
Presidents, List of, 1850-1900, 202
Prigg (H. V.), elected, 95
Prince (C. L.), Bequest by, 230
——————, Obituary notice of, 218
Proceedings at the meetings of the Society, 95, 152, 174, 251, 287
Publications, Recent, 99, 169, 255, 299

Radcliffe Observatory, Oxford, 291
Rainfall, Heavy, in local storms, 286
Rainfall in the west and east of England in relation to altitude above sea-level, 273
Rainfall of the Central Rhine Provinces, 297
Rain gauge, Description of Halliwell's self-recording, 281
Rankin (Sir J.), elected, 251
Rao (M. B. Subha), elected, 251
Recent Publications, 99, 169, 255, 299
Reduction, New, of the Greenwich meteorological observations, 101
Relative humidity, Geographical distribution of, 296
Remarkable dust haze at Teneriffe, Note of, 33
Report of the Council, 203
Report on the phenological observations, 1899, 113
Reports of Observatories, 231
Resignation of President, 154
Results of percolation experiments at Rothamsted, Sept. 1870 to Aug. 1899, 139
Retirement of Dr. R. H. Scott, F.R.S., from the Meteorological Office, 96
Rhine Provinces, Rainfall of the Central, 297
Riviera in the last century, The, 234
Rofe (H.), elected, 251
Rofe (H. J.), elected, 251
Rothamsted, Percolation experiments at, 139
Royal Meteorological Society, Jubilee Celebration, April 3-4, 1900, 173
Rykatcheff (Gen. M. A.), elected honorary member, 251

Schaw (Maj.-Gen. H.), Circulation of the atmosphere in the southern hemisphere, 138
——————, Vertical circulation of the atmosphere, 163
Scott (R. H.), Note of a remarkable dust haze experienced at Teneriffe, Canary Islands, February 1898, 33
————, Results of percolation experiments at Rothamsted, Sept. 1870 to Aug. 1899, 139
————, Retirement of, from the Meteorological Office, 96
Scrutineers, 152
Self-recording rain gauge, Halliwell's, 281
Shaw (W. N.), elected, 154
Shepherd (J. W.), elected, 251
Simpson (E.), elected, 251
Slatter (Rev. J.), Bequest by, 230
——————, Obituary notice of, 219
Snowden (Rev. H. C. V.), elected, 287

Solar halos and mock suns, January 11, 1900, 97
Sombrero, Hurricane at, September 1899, 25
Sonnblick group, Climatology of the, 241
Southall (J. T.), elected, 251
"Southern Cross," Expedition to the Antarctic, 1898-1900, 292
Southern Hemisphere, Circulation of atmosphere in the, 138
Southern Ocean, Meteorological charts of the, 253
Sprot (Lt.-Gen. J.), elected, 95
Stations, Inspection of, 210
Steamship track between Fiji and Hawaii, Weather conditions of the, 235
Sunshine recorder, The ether, 243
Suns, Mock, 97
Symons (G. J.), A short note on earth temperature observations, 27
———, Bequest by, 287
———, Death of, 159, 251, 287
———, Jubilee Address, 176
———, Memorial to the late, 272
———, Obituary notice of, 155
———, Resignation of Presidency, 154
———, The Wiltshire whirlwind of October 1, 1899, 261

Taylor (F.), elected, 95
Temperature, Earth, 27
Temperature of the free air, 242
Temperature, Vertical gradients of, 252
Temperatures, Minimum, on mountain peaks, 162
Teneriffe, Remarkable dust haze at, 33
Thunderstorms, Air currents in, 32
Trebeck (P. C.), elected, 287
Trevaskis (W. J.), elected, 287
Tropical Africa, Meteorology of, 151
Tule fog, 253
Tween (C. N.), elected, 152

Valley of the Joux, Climate of the, 298
Vertical circulation of the atmosphere, 163
Vertical gradients of temperature, humidity, and wind direction, 252

Walker (Dr. G. C., Jr.), elected, 95
Water in the North Atlantic, The circulation of, 234
Weather conditions of the steamship track between Fiji and Hawaii, 235
Weller (G.), elected, 251
Whirlwind of October 1, 1899, The Wiltshire, 261
Wilkinson (W. K., Jr.), elected, 95
Williams (Dr. C. T.), appointed President, 154
———, Jubilee Address, 181
Wilmshurst (A. J.), elected, 251
Wilson (A.), elected, 95
Wilson (Capt. C. L. N.), elected, 95
Wiltshire whirlwind of October 1, 1899, 261
Wind direction, Vertical gradients of, 252
Wortham (H.), Obituary notice of, 220

Yool (G. A.), elected, 251

Zambra (M. W.), elected, 152

THE END OF VOLUME XXVI.

Printed by R. & R. Clark, Limited, *Edinburgh*

Lightning Source UK Ltd.
Milton Keynes UK
UKHW02f1251170918
329045UK00014B/1066/P